Religious Life and Thought
(11th-12th centuries)

Giles Constable

Religious Life and Thought
(11th-12th centuries)

VARIORUM REPRINTS
London 1979

British Library CIP data

Constable, Giles
  Religious life and thought (11th-12th centuries).
  — (Collected studies series; CS89).
  1. Christianity — Middle Ages, 600-1500
  I. Title   II. Series
  209'.021   BR270

  ISBN 0-86078-034-1

Published in Great Britain by   Variorum Reprints
                                   21a Pembridge Mews London W11 3EQ

Printed in Great Britain by   Kingprint Ltd
                                   Richmond Surrey TW9 4PD

VARIORUM REPRINT CS89

CONTENTS

This volume contains a total of 380 pages

INTRODUCTION

A concern with the practical application of Christianity runs through most of the articles collected in this volume, although they were written over a period of almost exactly twenty-five years. Ever since my interest in the crusades was aroused by a seminar under the direction of Professor Robert Wolff during my first year of graduate work at Harvard, I have been concerned with the question of how men and women in the Middle Ages interpreted the teachings of Christianity and attempted to put them into practice in their own lives. The articles, aside from three of a more general character (I, II, and XVI), fall roughly into three groups, corresponding to different aspects of my research over the past years.

The first group concentrates on pilgrimage and the crusades and grew out of the seminar paper on 'The Second Crusade as Seen by Contemporaries' (X), which was written in 1951 and published two years later, thanks to Professor Stephan Kuttner, in *Traditio*. The brief note on the route of the Anglo-Flemish crusaders (XI) and the report of a lost sermon by Bernard of Clairvaux on the failure of the crusade (XII) are in effect appendices to this article. Articles III and IV are more distantly connected, since in the course of my work on the Second Crusade I was impressed by the fact that many religious leaders expressed reservations about crusading and even about pilgrimage in general (cf. X 269–270). I therefore continued to gather material on this theme and eventually wrote the two articles on monasticism and pilgrimage and on opposition to pilgrimage (III and IV), both of which study the question of whether detachment from the world could better be achieved by travel or by stability. Since these articles were written for different audiences, the first as a lecture and the second as a contribution to a *Festschrift*, there is some overlap between them.

three general articles. Like article III, it was prepared as a lecture, and it draws on some of the material presented in article XVI. Finally, the article on the theme of *Reformatio* in the Middle Ages (II), which was a report on a seminar in the Roman Catholic-Protestant Colloquium held at Harvard in 1963, and the bibliographical survey of recent work in the history of medieval monasticism (I) deal with many of the themes that run through the other articles in this volume and have inspired my research and writing.

Among the scholars to whom I am particularly indebted, in addition to the teachers named above, I should pay tribute to Dom Jean Leclercq, who has been a friend and mentor since 1952 and who has done more than any other living writer to promote the study of religious life in the Middle Ages, and also to Dom Kassius Hallinger, whose pioneering work on monastic necrologies and customaries has opened the way toward a new understanding of the importance of monasticism in medieval society.

GILES CONSTABLE

Dumbarton Oaks,
Washington, D.C.
June 1978

ii

The second group of articles (VI–VIII) includes three out-growths from my work on monastic tithes, which appeared as a book in 1964 and was itself an outgrowth from my edition of the letters of Peter the Venerable, which I prepared as my doctoral dissertation under the direction of Professor Herbert Bloch and the Rev. Professor David Knowles. These letters open windows on almost every aspect of religious life in the twelfth century, including the questions of whether or not monks should engage in pastoral work and especially whether or not they were entitled to receive parochial revenues such as tithes. This research led me into some fascinating but little-studied aspects of the history of ecclesiastical finances and of the attitudes of those who both received and paid ecclesiastical revenues.

The work on Peter the Venerable also involved me in the study of manuscripts, which loosely link the third group of articles. The text *Hortatur nos* (IX) turned up in the course of my researches into the pastoral activities of monks. The article on the structure of society according to twelfth-century masters of letter-writing (XIII) arose from my interest in medieval *dictamen*, which grew out of my work on the letters of Peter the Venerable, and earlier on the letters of John of Salisbury, and which gave rise later to a booklet on medieval letters and letter-collections published in 1976 in the *Typologie des sources du Moyen Age latin*. The article on the text and manuscript of the *Liber memorialis* of Remiremont (V) started as a review of the new edition and facsimile of this work. The text concerning the relics of St Helen (XIV) was a more or less chance discovery in the second edition of Severt's history of the archbishops of Lyons. It illustrates my belief that there are still interesting new texts to be discovered in the books and papers of sixteenth- and seventeenth-century scholars. The fact that many important early texts are preserved in late medieval manuscripts is shown by the article on the popularity of twelfth-century spiritual writers in the late Middle Ages (XVI). My attention was first drawn to this by the number of fifteenth-century manuscripts of the works of Peter the Venerable.

Some possible reasons for this late medieval interest in twelfth-century spirituality are suggested in article XV, one of the

iii

three general articles. Like article III, it was prepared as a lecture, and it draws on some of the material presented in article XVI. Finally, the article on the theme of *Reformatio* in the Middle Ages (II), which was a report on a seminar in the Roman Catholic-Protestant Colloquium held at Harvard in 1963, and the bibliographical survey of recent work in the history of medieval monasticism (I) deal with many of the themes that run through the other articles in this volume and have inspired my research and writing.

Among the scholars to whom I am particularly indebted, in addition to the teachers named above, I should pay tribute to Dom Jean Leclercq, who has been a friend and mentor since 1952 and who has done more than any other living writer to promote the study of religious life in the Middle Ages, and also to Dom Kassius Hallinger, whose pioneering work on monastic necrologies and customaries has opened the way toward a new understanding of the importance of monasticism in medieval society.

GILES CONSTABLE

Dumbarton Oaks,
Washington, D.C.
June 1978

I

THE STUDY OF MONASTIC HISTORY
TODAY

The serious study of monastic history is now about a century old. With a few honourable exceptions in the seventeenth and eighteenth centuries—principally Dugdale and his collaborators in England, and D'Achéry, Mabillon, Martène, and their learned colleagues in the Congregation of St. Maur—historians before the middle of the nineteenth century considered monasticism to be of interest only to monks, antiquarians, and religious controversialists.[1]

There is no reference whatsoever in Gibbon's *Decline and Fall* either to St. Benedict or to Cluny, and St. Bernard of Clairvaux appears purely as a figure in the political history of the twelfth century. Gibbon's only account of monasticism is contained in a few pages at the beginning of chapter thirty-seven. It does not go beyond the fifth century and dwells heavily on the monks' superstition, slave-like obedience, and unnatural sufferings and devotions, which must have destroyed, Gibbon said, 'the sensibility both of the mind and the body'. 'A cruel unfeeling temper has distinguished the monks of every age and country,' he wrote, 'their stern indifference . . . is inflamed by religious hatred; and their merciless zeal has strenuously administered the holy office of the Inquisition.'[2]

These sentiments were characteristic of enlightened opinion, Catholic as well as

Protestant, in the eighteenth and early nineteenth centuries; and the historians of that age naturally saw no purpose in studying such a depraved and useless institution or in discussing its history in works which were designed to promote progress, tolerance, and liberty. According to the Englishman Samuel Maitland writing in about 1840, 'For centuries the general notion in this country has been that a monastery naturally, almost necessarily, is a place dedicated to idleness, gluttony, lewdness, hypocrisy, political intrigue, fraud, treachery, and blood.'[3]

Nor has this attitude entirely vanished even in the twentieth century. The eminent historian of monasticism G. G. Coulton was described by Dom David Knowles as having 'very deeply engrained, two atavistic prejudices which ever since the days of Wyclif have possessed a large section of his countrymen, the one a fear and distrust of ecclesiastical potentates in general and of Romans in particular, the other a conviction that monasticism is an unnatural institution which of itself always leads inevitably to disaster.'[4] Few educated people today would go as far as this, but many still feel that monasticism is intrinsically unsocial, anti-humanistic, and morally cowardly.[5] Milton expressed this attitude in a passage of the *Areopagitica* which is still often applied to monasticism: 'I cannot praise a fugitive and cloister'd vertue, unexercis'd and unbreath'd, that never sallies out and sees her adversary . . . .'[6] More prosaically, Dr. Johnson once said to an abbess, 'Madam, you are here, not for the love of virtue, but the fear of vice.'[7]

The reaction against this point of view came in the first half of the nineteenth century, partly as a result of the Romantic movement, which looked with favour upon all aspects of the Middle Ages, including the peculiarly medieval institution of monasticism. The first signs of this more sympathetic attitude can be seen in literature and the arts, but it soon touched historical scholarship. In England one of the first writers to defend monasticism was the Samuel Maitland whom I have already quoted and who was the grandfather of the great legal historian F. W. Maitland. In a series of articles that appeared in 1844 as a book entitled *The Dark Ages*, Maitland argued that the Middle Ages are called dark not because they were morally dark but because they are obscure and hard for us to understand. 'There is no subject in the history of mankind,' he declared, 'which appears to me more interesting, or more worthy of investigation, than the actual state of the Christian church during the dark ages.'[8] Most of the book is in fact an account, which can still be read with profit, of the social and cultural services of monks to Western civilization.

At the same time a new sympathy and concern for monasticism appeared on the continent. The first scholarly biography of St. Benedict was written by Peter Lechner in 1857.[9] The following year H. d'Arbois de Jubainville published his pioneering *Études sur l'état intérieur des abbayes cisterciennes*, which was largely based on documents from Clairvaux in the library at Troyes, where D'Arbois de Jubainville was archivist. Franz Winter's long and valuable studies on the Cistercians and Premonstratensians in northwest Germany first appeared between 1865 and 1871. The first critical edition of the Rule of St. Benedict was published in 1880. Meanwhile in Paris, in 1860, the liberal Catholic publicist and politician Montalembert published the first volumes of *Les moines d'Occident depuis saint Benôit jusqu'à saint Bernard,* of which the final volumes appeared posthumously in 1877. This is

The Study of Monastic History Today

overtly the work of an apologist. It is uncritical, unanalytical, and almost entirely dependent for factual material on the works of Mabillon. Montalembert was a leading Romantic author, however, and a member of the French Academy. His work is written in an exalted style and addressed to a wide audience. It was translated at the time it appeared into English and other European languages; and its highly sympathetic, not to say laudatory, tone both reflected and shaped the favourable attitude towards monasticism that increasingly existed in cultivated circles all over Europe in the middle and late nineteenth century.

Even the rationalist historian Lecky praised the ideal of renunciation and the civilizing and charitable work of the early monks in his influential *History of European Morals from Augustus to Charlemagne,* which came out in 1869, though he disliked their 'passive obedience' and 'servitude', which he considered incompatible with free political institutions. 'However advantageous the temporary preeminence of this moral type may have been,' he wrote, 'it was obviously unsuited for a later stage of civilization.'[10] The Protestant historians Harnack and Workman, whose works on monasticism are still widely read today, likewise recognized the intrinsic value of the monastic ideal as well as the importance of monks in the history of European civilization, although they were still inclined to condemn as basically unChristian its rejection of human nature and the world.

Scholarly work in the twentieth century has tended to divide along the line of what may be called the external and internal histories of monasticism. Secular scholars in particular have concentrated on the contribution of monks to social, economic, intellectual, literary, artistic, and architectural history.[11] An important group of German and Austrian historians working early in the century studied in detail the constitutional position of the monasteries in the Empire and their relations with the local ecclesiastical and secular authorities and with the pope and emperor.[12] The importance of monasteries in the development of territorial principalities in Germany, especially in the twelfth century, was emphasized by Hirsch and more recently by Theodor Mayer in his book entitled *Fürsten und Staat.*[13] Some modern constitutional and institutional historians have likewise stressed the interest of monasteries as selfgoverning communities and of the grouping of monasteries into selfregulating associations, in which power flowed from below as well as from above. These scholars have not for the most part, however, been interested in monasticism itself. There has indeed been a marked tendency to regard these external influences as incidental to the history of the monks themselves, who had no direct concern for the world outside their monasteries.[14]

The internal history of monasticism, which deals both with the organization of monastic life and with monastic spirituality, has not attracted the attention of many secular scholars. The authorities whose names come first to mind are all monks: Dom J.M. Besse, who founded in 1905 the *Archives de la France monastique* and reedited the great repertory of French monasteries compiled by Dom Beaunier in the eighteenth century; Dom Ursmer Berlière, whose *L'ordre monastique des origines au XIIe siècle* (first ed., 1912; third, 1924) is still the best brief history of Western monasticism; Dom Cuthbert Butler, whose *Benedictine Monachism* (first ed., 1919; second, 1924) has deeply influenced the interpretation of monastic history; Dom André Wilmart, the great textual scholar and student of monastic spirituality; and,

I

among contemporary scholars, Dom Philibert Schmitz, who completed his seven-
volume history of the Benedictine order a few years before his death in 1963; Dom
David Knowles, whose four-volume history of the monastic and religious orders
in England (1940–1959) is a monument of English historical scholarship; Dom
Jean Leclercq ('that indispensable "all-rounder"', as he was recently called by
Knowles),[15] whose researches during the past twenty years have thrown light on
almost every aspect of medieval monasticism and who is at present engaged in the
gigantic task—one at which even Mabillon produced less than his best work—of
preparing a new edition of the works of St. Bernard; and Dom Kassius Hallinger,
who in his *Gorze-Kluny* (1950) reinterpreted the history of monasticism in the tenth
and eleventh centuries and who is editing a much needed *Corpus* of Benedictine
customaries, of which the first two volumes appeared in 1963.

The principal periodicals on monastic history are likewise all edited by monks:
the *Revue bénédictine* of Maredsous; the *Revue Mabillon* of Ligugé; the *Studien und
Mitteilungen zur Geschichte des Benediktiner-Ordens und seiner Zweige* (St. Boniface's
abbey in Munich); *Benedictina* (St. Paul Outside the Walls, Rome); and the new
Studia monastica of Montserrat.[16] To these must be added the journals devoted to
the history of particular orders, such as the *Cistercienser-Chronik*, the *Collectanea
ordinis Cisterciensium reformatorum*, *Cîteaux in de Nederlanden* (now called simply
Cîteaux), and the *Analecta sacri ordinis Cisterciensis*, not to mention the numerous
journals concerned with the history of canons, such as the *Analecta Praemonstratensia*,
and of the Mendicant orders. Several of these periodicals date back to the end of the
nineteenth century, and all of them now publish serious and scholarly articles.
Their very existence is a sign, therefore, of the great interest in monastic history
today as well as of the predominant part in its study played by monks.

G. G. Coulton is almost the only outstanding secular Protestant historian of
monasticism in the twentieth century. He was in some ways, however, more of a
critic than an historian. His *Five Centuries of Religion,* although undoubtedly a work
of great learning, stresses almost exclusively the dark side of monastic decline in the
late Middle Ages. Coulton delighted in finding errors in the works of those whom
he regarded as uncritical apologists for monasticism, such as Montalembert and
especially F. A. (later Cardinal) Gasquet. Yet no avowed apologist could have
written warmer praise of St. Bernard and St. Francis than Coulton; and no reader
of his pages on these two saints can accuse him of being without sympathy for
medieval monasticism.[17] I believe that in fact Coulton had a deep admiration for
the ideal of monasticism but abhorred 'the spotted actuality'. He would indeed have
made a good monastic reformer himself, believing as he did, with puritanical zeal,
that no shame should be concealed and no crime unpunished.

Coulton is therefore no exception to the general rule that monasticism has been
principally studied by those who are personally involved in it and has been on the
whole neglected by disinterested secular historians. This situation has been accepted
and even applauded by scholars outside the field. Eileen Power, who herself wrote
a book on *Medieval English Nunneries* before turning to economic history, said in a
review of Knowles's *Monastic Order* that, 'It is completely objective, but gains
enormously from the fact that the author knows monasticism from the inside and
brings to his work a depth and delicacy of understanding that only such knowledge

can give.'[18] I do not dispute this judgment, but by using the word 'only' Miss Power suggested that monks alone are really suited for the study of monastic history. This is a limitation that she certainly would not have applied to other fields of history, and it implies a continuation of the point of view that sets monasticism aside from the rest of history and regards it as a special preserve of historians who are also monks.

Yet monks, who obey a written code and whose lives are oriented in terms of a fixed ideal, are not likely to be able to study impartially the origins and development of that code and ideal.[19] Even the Maurist historians, though always careful and sober in their judgments, were far from impartial in their attitude towards ancient and medieval monasticism. They were themselves dedicated to an ideal of monastic regularity with great emphasis on austerity and interior piety.[20] At least one recent historian has warned against the danger of seeing all monastic history through the ascetic spectacles of monastic purists such as D'Achéry, Mabillon, and Martène.[21]

The history of Benedictine monasticism during the past century has also heavily influenced the interpretation of its earlier history. This is not the place to study in detail the development of modern monasticism, but since the middle of the nineteenth century Benedictine monachism has made a recovery that historians in the future will doubtless regard as of major historical significance.[22] Most modern European states were founded on aggressively secular principles, and throughout the nineteenth century monks were systematically suppressed all over Europe. The last expulsion of monks from France took place in 1901. It is not therefore surprising that authors like Maitland, Lecky, Harnack, and Workman wrote of monasticism as almost entirely a thing of the past and as belonging to a previous stage of European history. In fact, however, the number of monks and monasteries all over the Christian world has multiplied many times over in the past hundred years. I have no exact figures, but the rate of increase may well be comparable with that in England during the century following the Norman Conquest, when the total number of monks, nuns, and regular canons is said to have grown from just over a thousand to somewhere between eleven and twelve-and-a-half thousand.[23] I cannot speculate here on the reasons for these phenomenal increases, either in the twelfth century or today; but they are clearly facts of prime importance in the history of monasticism.

Needless to say, this modern expansion met with heavy opposition, even in Catholic countries and within the Catholic hierarchy. Not all prelates, either in the past or today, are sympathetic to monasticism. At a time when there is a shortage of clergy for pastoral and missionary work, bishops are not always pleased to see dedicated young men disappear behind the walls of monasteries. Bishops and priests who themselves have no vocation for the monastic life, furthermore, often share with laymen the view that monks are anti-social and unwilling to face the problems of Christian life in the world. The leaders of the modern monastic revival have had therefore to justify themselves in the eyes of both the laity and the secular clergy. They have had to reconstruct from the history of monasticism a way of life that is at the same time basically and traditionally monastic and yet morally and socially acceptable in the modern world. It is no accident that so many modern monastic leaders have also been prominent scholars. One thinks of Guéranger (the founder and first abbot of Solesmes) in France, of Herwegen (the abbot of Maria Laach) in Germany, and of Gasquet, Butler, and Chapman (respectively prior, abbot, and abbot of Downside) in England. I do not wish to suggest that the works of these and other monastic historians are consciously tendentious. They are indeed often based on serious research. But their writers can hardly be expected to separate their own deepest spiritual and practical concerns from the subjects about which they are writing.

The influence of these concerns, and the consequent correlation of the results of research to the needs of monasticism, can be seen in both general attitudes and specific findings. Gasquet's emphasis upon the independence and seclusion of the individual Benedictine abbey, and on the complete absence of any direct social aim or action, was clearly influenced by the pressing need of monks in late nineteenth-century England for freedom from interference, either by bishops or by the abbot-president of the English Benedictine Congregation, and from the necessity of performing pastoral work.[24] Butler's emphasis on the moderation of Benedictine monasticism, and on its rejection of extreme austerity, served to allay the anti-monastic prejudices of many of his countrymen.[25]

Many issues of contemporary monastic life are deeply rooted in the past. The modern movement towards simplifying the liturgy is to a great extent a reaction against the ritualism of the liturgical movement inspired by Guéranger and other nineteenth-century Benedictines who were themselves reacting against the religious subjectivism of the early modern period.[26] The hostility of many modern historians to the elaborate liturgy at Cluny in the tenth and eleventh centuries is thus a reflection of their desire to simplify the liturgy today.[27] Guéranger himself, referring to the ninth-century liturgist Amalarius of Metz, complained of 'the incorrigible mania of the French for ceaselessly revising the liturgy'.[28] The issues of monastic priesthood and of monastic performance of pastoral work were no less hotly debated in the twelfth century than they are now.[29] The modern emphasis on the role of the laity in the Church has sharpened many of the problems associated with the history of lay-brothers (conversi) and the impact of laymen on monasticism from the tenth to the twelfth centuries.[30] A like effect is seen in works on monastic stability, manual labour by monks, abbatial elections, and other topics which are important not only in the history of monasticism but also in the life of monks today.

The study of monastic history has thus been shaped by a variety of factors that have tended to isolate it from the rest of history and to give it a distinctive character of its own. Some historians have even questioned whether a real history of monasticism is possible. As Newman said in his essay on 'The Mission of St. Benedict', written in 1858, 'Monachism was one and the same everywhere, because it was a reaction from that secular life, which has everywhere the same structure and the same characteristics.'[31] Harnack likewise asked, 'Of what variety are the ideals of poverty, chastity, and resolute flight from the world capable? . . . Is not the renun-ciation of the world essentially the abnegation of all development and of all history?'[32] And Knowles recently said that the principal difficulty of all historians of monasticism is 'to avoid confusing two processes which in the actual stream of

time are interwoven but not intermingled: the living, permanent, unchanging
spiritual idea or force . . . and the outward, historical shapes and forms which the
idea and the life take when working in a world which has its own myriad influences
of life and growth.'[33]

This concept of monasticism as an immutable ideal, itself without history but
with changing historical manifestations, raises fundamental questions about the
nature, origins, and development of monasticism—questions to which there are no
clear and generally accepted answers. Harnack, for instance, traced the spirit of self-
sacrifice and renunciation through the early monks, the Benedictines, the Mendicants, and finally the Jesuits, whom he considered to be, 'the last and authentic
word of Western monasticism.'[34] Workman went yet further and found the 'lineal
descendants' of monasticism in the Puritans and Methodists, who seemed to him
to share with the monks and friars of the Middle Ages the spirit of discipline, anti-
sacerdotalism, and service to God.[35] Other scholars have emphasized the element
of separation from the world as the essence of monasticism.[36] Yet it has recently been
suggested that the term *monachus* derives not from μόνος (*solitarius*), as has been
generally believed since the fourth century, but from μονάς (*singularis*) and that the
early monk was therefore characteristically not so much a solitary or hermit as a
one-of-a-kind ascetic.[37]

Many historians have tended to see monasticism in fundamentally negative
terms, as a reaction against secular society and the Church. Montalembert dwelt
heavily on the evils of the Church in the fourth century, and for Newman the 'one
idea' and 'one purpose' of monks was to be quit of secular life.[38] Ladner in his
recent book on *The Idea of Reform* stressed the importance of monks in 'the ever
repeated efforts by man to reassert and augment values pre-existent in the spiritual-
material compound of the world'.[39] Some Protestant writers have gone further and
seen monasticism not only as an effort to recover lost spiritual values but also as a
protest against the Church. Harnack and Workman thus saw monasticism as
something outside and sometimes opposed to the sacramental-sacerdotal Church, a
non-Christian, dualist child grafted onto the Church in the third and fourth
centuries.[40] This point of view was developed by Troeltsch and Von Martin into
the influential theory of monks as a revolutionary sect-type, world-denying in
contrast to the world-ruling Church.[41]

Historians who are themselves monks naturally tend to emphasize positive
factors in the monastic spirit and to see themselves not only as within the Church
but also as the highest expression of its ideal of Christian life. For them, the desire
to leave the world was a fulfilment of the commands of the Gospel rather than a
rejection of secular life. Needless to say, these commands were often crudely interpreted, but the fundamental motive was love of God, not hate of the world, fear,
penance, or prudence.[42] This ideal is in appearance highly individualistic, and
most monastic theorists, especially in the East, have stressed the search of monks to
achieve individual perfection. A number of theorists in the nineteenth and twentieth centuries, however, have developed an ecclesiological view of monasticism as
part of the Church and as the living expression of the presence and action of the
Holy Spirit in the Church.[43] Peter Damiani in the eleventh century saw the
individual monk as the *ecclesia minor*, the fulfilment of the mystic union of love.[44]

This view has been transferred to monasticism as a whole, which is seen not as a group of individual pneumatics but as the work of the Holy Spirit in the Church. According to Odo Casel, who together with Guéranger, Maur Wolter (the founder of Beuron), and Herwegen was one of the principal exponents of this view, 'It is the mission of Christian monasticism to maintain and safeguard the pneumatic aspect of the Church.'[45] This view naturally emphasizes the liturgical activity and redemptory expiation of the monk exercising himself in the Church through prayer and penance.[46]

These differing views of the nature of monasticism have influenced the interpretation of the origins of Christian monasticism. Abbot Herwegen, for example, 'considered the appearance of monasticism above all not as the result of certain historical conjunctures . . . but as a substantial part of the Church, as an essential manifestation of its body born of the Spirit of Christ.'[47] Blazovich looked upon monasticism as a special way of life within the Church resulting not from protest but from a process of differentiation based on the varieties of individual religious dispositions.[48] In contrast to the older views of monasticism as the result of pagan practices or examples and of secular influences on the Church,[49] modern research has stressed the great role played by the Bible, and especially by the example of the apostles, in the life and thought of the early monks.[50] 'At the beginning of monasticism,' wrote Steidle, 'stood the exemplar of the Old Testament "men of God", of the prophets, the exemplar of the apostles of Christ, of the martyrs, and of the angels.'[51]

Throughout their history monks have looked back for their origins and ideals to the Gospel and above all to the lost paradise of the life of the apostles in Jerusalem. There is a strong element in the monastic ideal of what Bainton has called 'Christian primitivism',[52] a wistful lookingback to a golden age of the early Church, 'poor, simple, and penitential', as it was described by McDonnell, 'with interests and activities restricted to the spiritual domain'.[53] Cassian, for instance, maintained that monastic life was born in the earliest days of the Church and prolonged the *vita apostolica* over the centuries.[54] According to this view, masses of nominal Christians joined the Church in the fourth century as a result of its worldly success. This view of monastic history has been supported ever since the days of the historian Eusebius by the references in the works of Philo to the obscure community of Jewish ascetics in Egypt known as Therapeutae; and recently it has been supported by references in the Dead Sea scrolls to ascetic groups of the New Testament period, who may be antecedents of Christian monks.[55] There is no positive evidence to confirm this view, however; and for the time being Christian monasticism must be viewed as having arisen in Egypt in the third and fourth centuries.

The development of monasticism has often been explained by metaphors. Individual monasteries in the Middle Ages were described as a ship, a city, Jerusalem, an earthly paradise, and by other images commonly applied to the Church as a whole.[56] Philip of Harvengt in the twelfth century compared the contemporary revival of monasticism, all in a single paragraph, to the coming of spring after winter, the fructification of a tree, the kindling of a furnace, the revival of a dead body, the stoking of a fire, and the manufacture of an artifact.[57] Newman compared the 'outward circumstances' of monasticism to 'some great natural growth' shaping itself to events 'from an irrepressible fulness of life within'; Workman saw it as a sea ebbing and flowing eternally around the unchanging rock of its ideals; and Butler at one point spoke of cycles within the growth of monasticism and of a smouldering old fire bursting into flame and reasserting itself within the soul of the monastic body corporate.[58] Almost all monastic historians make use of some mechanistic or naturalistic metaphors and of cycles of decline and reform.

Metaphors are doubtless useful in the writing of history, but they tend to short-cut, not to say short-circuit, the task of historical analysis. They are a kind of historical pathetic fallacy by which life, feeling, and behaviour are attributed to institutions that in fact have no life of their own. Monasticism is not a fire, a sea, a tree, or any kind of living body, nor is it a self-contained idea or entity that includes within itself its own development and means of change. A monastery has no life apart from the lives of its monks, and many monks, even in the Middle Ages, were raised in the secular world and turned to monasticism as a result of their experiences there. Monasteries are thus a part of, and essentially related to, the surrounding society, and the impetus to change comes from outside as well as inside their walls. I am therefore tempted to reverse the customary view that the ideals and motives of monks have remained one while their outer circumstances have changed, and to suggest instead that their inner life has changed while the institutional structure has remained remarkably stable. Benedict or Bernard, and perhaps also Pachomius and Basil, would recognize without too much difficulty the framework of monastic life today, but they would have very little in common with the monks. Indeed, the genius of Benedict's Rule seems to me to be precisely that its institutional frame has been able to contain the spiritual needs of very different periods.

Several scholars in recent years have stressed the need to study individuals as well as institutions in the history of monasticism;[59] and Paul Antin has coined the term 'monachology' to refer to the personal monastic view of individual monks as distinct from the institutional approach suggested by the term 'monachism'.[60] Monks make monasticism rather than monasticism making monks; and if the monastic institutions of a given period are not suited to the spirituality of that age, they will change, or even vanish, and new ones will be founded. There is an increasing willingness even in Benedictine circles to recognize what may be called the relativity of monasticism. According to Hilpisch, for instance, the balance of emphasis on renunciation (solitude), liturgy (prayer), and work (culture) in the history of Benedictine monasticism has varied and will continue to vary as a result of the influence of the 'Spirit of the Age' on the ideal of the Rule.[61] Leclercq in a recent article studied the 'elements of relativity' in the practice and theory of the Church, with particular regard to the priesthood of monks.[62] And the sociologist Blazovich asserted that, 'The distinction of what is essential and what is time-conditioned in the Rule is a task set to every generation, including today's.'[63]

Monasticism must therefore be studied from 'outside' as well as 'inside', and there is a real need for a sociological and comparative approach to its history. Some beginnings have been made towards the study of what may be called monastic ecology: the mutual relations between monasteries and their environment.[64] But this must be broadened into a consideration of the relation of monks to society not only in western Europe but in all countries where monastic institutions occur. Christian Courtois pointed out that the organization and success of monasticism in Gaul in the late fourth and early fifth centuries must be studied in social terms.[65] More generally, it is impossible to understand the different concepts and forms of monasticism in the Christian East and West without taking into consideration the differences in culture and society.

This broader and more personal approach to the history of monasticism has tended to break down the dichotomies of eremitism and cenobitism, action and contemplation, and wandering and stability, in terms of which the development of monastic institutions has often been explained. The strict distinction between eremitism and cenobitism, that is, of monks living in solitude from those in a community, and the accompanying view that cenobitism developed after and out of eremitism are important parts of the 'new look' of monasticism in the twentieth century, because almost all the extravagant features of monastic life and extreme examples of anti-social behaviour are associated with eremitism. The 'natural development' of monasticism has been depicted as from solitude to community life, where the monk, though cut off from the world, practises brotherly love within the monastery and thus sets before secular society an example of what Gasquet called 'Christian social sanctity'.[66] Almost all modern Benedictine commentators and historians, among whom Butler has been perhaps the most influential, have emphasized the community life and essential moderation of Benedictine monasticism in contrast to the earlier forms of monastic life. They have condemned eremitism, and the excesses believed to go with it, in terms worthy of an eighteenth-century rationalist and have branded as retrogressive any tendency for eremitism to emerge at the expense of the more advanced and socially acceptable form of cenobitism.[67]

The preference for cenobitism of many Western monastic historians is closely allied to their dislike of monasticism in the East, where monks have always tended to be more eremitical than in the West. Montalembert castigated the Eastern monks in a thoroughly unecumenical fashion for their decadence and lack of discipline. 'They ended up,' he wrote, 'like all the Eastern clergy, by becoming the slaves of Islam and accomplices in schism.'[68] Butler has almost nothing good to say about Eastern monks, and even Protestants like Harnack and Workman had no use for Orthodox monasticism. For Harnack, as for Butler, it remained in a stage of passive stagnation;[69] and Workman, while defending Eastern monks from the charge of extremism, none the less considered them 'amorphous' and 'prone to many of the diseases of hysterical subjectivism'.[70]

Recent research has shown that this view, even if not entirely without basis, needs to be greatly modified. Several scholars have demonstrated that the differences between the forms of monasticism in Egypt and the Near East in the fourth century were not of category but of degree. The great communities of Egyptian anchorites had some elements of common life, and there was no striking antagonism between adherents of the various forms of monastic life. Bacht has stressed the difficulty in finding any real line of demarcation between the ideals of Anthony and Pachomius, though he adheres to the view that cenobitism evolved out of eremitism.[71] Not all contemporaries welcomed this development, however, as

I

The Study of Monastic History Today

Vööbus has shown in his article on anti-cenobitic feeling among Syrian monks in the fourth and fifth centuries. 'The new forms were not satisfactory for the entire monastic movement,' he remarked.[72] There was thus a spectrum of forms of monastic life, ranging from complete solitude to strict common life, among which an individual could choose that which suited him best, rather than a rigid dichotomy between eremitism and cenobitism.

The study of both literary and archaeological sources in the past twenty years has also shown the importance of the co-existence of eremitism and cenobitism in the West and especially of an eremitical tradition *within* many cenobitic communities.[73] This usually took one of two forms: a monk might make long eremitical retreats between periods of life in a community or he might be a permanent recluse or anchorite and yet remain more or less attached to a monastery and under the control of its abbot. Scores of monasteries in the Middle Ages were surrounded by small hermitages whose inhabitants were associated with the community. There were of course many independent hermits, and not infrequently a group of hermits formed the historical basis for a cenobitical establishment. But it is clear that this was not part of an inevitable historical development from solitary to common life, since many monks left their monasteries, either temporarily or permanently, to live in solitude.

The situation in the West was not therefore entirely unlike that in the East. The difference again was of degree rather than of type. Jerome, Cassian, Benedict, Isidore of Seville, and other influential monastic theorists in the West were not opposed to hermits and anchorites.[74] St. Benedict's personal attitude towards eremitism is a matter of doubt, but the famous final chapter of the Rule suggests that he regarded cenobitical life as a preparation for a more perfect life in solitude.[75] Leclercq and others have emphasized that Benedict had no desire to break with the Eastern monastic tradition, and Rousseau referred to the Benedictine Rule as 'a Western adaptation of the old monasticism of the desert'.[76] In a recent article on *stabilitas loci* in Byzantine monasticism, Emil Herman has shown that in the East the technically illegal practice of monks leaving their monasteries without permission was sanctioned when their object was to live an eremitical life.[77] Thus the barriers between Eastern and Western monasticism are being broken down from both sides. No longer can the semi-eremitical and ascetic movements in Italy in the eleventh century—Camaldoli, Vallombrosa, Fonte Avellana—and north of the Alps at La Grande Chartreuse be regarded as reversions or the result of the re-introduction into the West of eremitical individualism and ascetic subjectivism from the East.[78] They re-emphasized elements that had always been present in the Western monastic tradition.

It is likewise a mistake to interpret monastic history in terms of a dichotomy between action and contemplation, either by identifying community life with action and solitude with contemplation or by presenting monasticism as essentially contemplative in contrast to the active life of men living in the world. In antiquity and the Middle Ages, action and contemplation were not divided in the way they often are today;[79] and the life of monks, though considered different from that of clerics and laymen, was not considered contemplative in the modern sense of the term.[80] Action and contemplation were considered complementary rather than

31

mutually exclusive, and an active life of ascetic discipline and manual labour (not, of course, of secular activities or even of pastoral work in the world) was believed to be not only the preparation but also the indispensable basis for contemplation by monks. Even Cassian, who was almost alone among the early monastic theorists in equating action with cenobitism and contemplation with eremitism, insisted, following Evagrius, that contemplation depended on an 'active' conquest of vices.[81] For Gregory the Great and later for St. Bernard, the perfect life was a wedding of action and contemplation.[82] Aelred of Rievaulx saw the *vita actualis* or *activa* as a life of effort to conquer self-will and evil; it went hand in hand with a life of prayer and contemplation.[83] 'Certainly St. Aelred's monks could, in his own termino-logy,' wrote Squire, 'be accurately described as leading both the active and the contemplative lives, and it would seem that his view that action and contemplation are two activities of a single life was common teaching for his period and later.' The distinction between action and contemplation as applied to monasticism generally or to entire monastic communities is comparatively recent.[84]

The third cliché of monastic history is the dichotomy of stability and wandering. Nearly all early monastic legislators expressed their disapproval of monks who refused to stay in one place or obey a recognized superior;[85] and for many modern historians and commentators stability is the essence of Benedictine monasticism.[86] The fact is, however, that in both East and West many monks who were admired in their own time neither preached nor practised stability in the sense of remaining until death in a single monastery. They moved for many reasons: to escape the crowds attracted by their sanctity, to undertake pilgrimages and special missions, above all to seek a more austere life, either in another monastery or in solitude.[87] Leclercq in particular has investigated the concept of monastic peregrination in the sense not of pilgrimage but of ascetic exile.[88] The so-called missionary monks of the early Middle Ages were probably monks of this sort, who left their families and native land in search of penance, prayer, and martyrdom, and who kept moving precisely in order to avoid contracting ties with any one group or place. By wandering they constantly renewed and restored their separation from the world and maintained a *stabilitas in peregrinatione*. By the twelfth century, most monastic theorists opposed monastic peregrination, and the idea of stability in peregrina-tion was replaced by that of an interior peregrination, in which the emphasis was on leaving oneself rather than on leaving one's country. The great issue in the twelfth century was that of *transitus* from one monastery to another.[89] St. Bernard actually encouraged such moves when the second monastery was stricter than the first. Scholars have thus replaced the idea of stability of place with the more subjective concept of stability of order or profession[90] and have recognized that in practice there was a wider variety of legitimate forms of monastic life than the old idea of stability implied.

Among the most interesting of these various forms of religious life in the Middle Ages was that of the regular canons, whose importance has been shown by the works of Dickinson and Dereine.[91] Nothing is more difficult to define than a canon. Fundamentally they were ordained clerics organized into groups for the performance of the holy offices in cathedrals and other large churches. They might live separately, dividing the revenues of the church into individual prebends (in which case they were later known as secular canons); or they might live communally and according to a rule, hence the name of regular canons, whose way of life and spiritual ideals often resembled those of monks. A great deal of work still needs to be done on the history of regular canons in the early Middle Ages. They are frequently thought to have been of comparatively small importance in the period between the Carolingian Renaissance, when the rules for canons of Chrodegang of Metz and of Aix-la-Chapelle were compiled, and the Investiture Controversy, when the reformed papacy tried to enforce individual poverty on canons and the so-called Augustinian Rule, in various forms, was adopted by many groups of canons. In a recent article on the ideal of the *vita apostolica* among canons in the ninth, tenth, and eleventh centuries, however, Dereine has argued that this opinion is based on the denigration of the canons by monastic reformers of the period and that the canons in fact shared many ideals with the monks.[92] This view is strongly supported by Siegwart in his book on canons in the German-speaking areas of Switzerland, where the regular canons maintained a higher level of regularity, reforming activity, and spirituality than the monks.[93] He particularly stresses the close relations between monastic, canonical, and eremitical circles at this time and the number of monastic reformers who were trained by canons.[94] The same was true at Tours, where the famous old abbey of St. Martin became a house of canons early in the ninth century. Some of the canons, however, although living separately and supported by prebends, led lives of great austerity. The Blessed Hervé of Tours, for instance, who died in 1022, led a solitary life of silence and bodily mortification, though he was in touch with many of the monastic reformers of the day. His life is an example of what has been called the conpenetration of strict canonical and monastic ideals, which existed not only at this time but also in the twelfth century.[95]

From this evidence it is clear that monks in monasteries were not the only ones who withdrew from the world in the Middle Ages and that hermits, recluses, canons, lay brothers and lay men and women leading penitential lives, and wandering penitents, preachers, and pilgrims must be taken into consideration in a broad view of monasticism.[96] There was considerable variation in how the monastic ideal was expressed and carried out,[97] and an individual might during the course of his lifetime spend time not only in a community but also in a hermitage or as a canon, pilgrim, or penitent.

At the same time as the general concept of monastic history has broadened, many specific problems have been critically examined. I should like now to discuss three of these and to show their significance for the history of monasticism in the West.

The first is the problem of the Rule of St. Benedict, the *Regula Magistri*, and Benedictinism'. The *Regula Magistri* or Rule of the Master (so-named because the anonymous author is referred to simply as the Master) was universally regarded until the late 1930's as an expansion of the Rule of St. Benedict, written probably in the seventh century. In 1940, however, the revolutionary idea was proposed, and has gradually make headway in spite of the bitter opposition of conservative scholars, that the Rule of St. Benedict was written after, and to a great extent derived from, the *Regula Magistri*. During the past twenty-five years every possible type of scholarly technique and evidence, some of it highly specialized, has been brought to bear on the problem, and a vast number of different theories have been put forward; but no definite solution has been—or perhaps ever will be—found.[98] The whole issue was recently reviewed by Knowles, who concluded that: 'The thesis of the Master's priority may never be proved to demonstration, but it is hard to see that its opponents can ever regain the ground that they have lost in the past twenty-five years, and, unless some wholly unforeseeable discovery is made, the hypothesis that St. Benedict made extensive use of the previously existing Rule of the Master must remain as one enjoying a very high degree of probability.'[99]

From the point of view of later history, it does not perhaps matter very much whether or not St. Benedict copied from the *Regula Magistri*. For most of the Middle Ages his Rule enjoyed an absolute priority among monastic legislation in the West; and it is fair to say that the credit for this fact still belongs to Benedict, since what he excluded from the *Regula Magistri* is almost as important as what he included. His changes and additions bear without question the stamp of administrative genius. His Rule thus preserves its unique constitutional importance for the history of Western monasticism.

In other respects, however, the controversy has broad implications for the study of monastic history. The distinctiveness of St. Benedict as a spiritual master will never be seen in the same light as before. His monastic doctrine now appears as more dependent on the work of earlier theorists, especially in the East, and as marking far less sharp a break in monastic theory than was previously believed. Another blow has thus been dealt at the radical differentiation of Eastern and Western monasticism, and the way to a more ecumenical approach to monastic history has been opened.

Scholars can no longer concentrate so narrowly on the special character of Benedictinism and the historical importance of literal observance of the Benedictine Rule. According to Mabillon, indeed, the very term *Benedictinus* was not used before the fifteenth or sixteenth centuries.[100] Since then, as might be expected, the estimates of essential Benedictinism have varied according to the spiritual temper and monastic needs of the times. In the nineteenth century the main emphasis was on moderation—the *discretio* praised by Gregory the Great—and on the good nineteenth-century virtues of family life, work, obedience, and stability. Guéranger, for instance, laid great stress on the position of the abbot as the representative of God and centre of unity in the abbey and on stability, which he considered to be 'the entire Benedictine institution . . . a revolution that saved the monastic order.'[101] The importance of the *opus Dei* in Benedict's Rule was also emphasized by the founders of the liturgical movement. More recently, Blazovich, following Gundlach, suggested that the essence of Benedictinism lay in its distinctive view of Christ;[102] and there has been a greater tendency to stress the subjective elements, such as solitude, in the Rule. As long as its origins and sources are a matter of doubt, however, it is hard to call any feature of the Rule uniquely Benedictine.

Almost since the day it was written, Benedict's Rule has required study and interpretation, owing both to obscurities and vaguenesses in its regulations and to changes in the meaning of terms. The term *conversatio morum*, for instance, is still the subject of dispute,[103] and the military expressions which have long given

Benedictine monasticism a somewhat martial tone probably in fact connoted service and obedience rather than warfare.[104] Yet more striking is the term *biblio-theca* in chapter forty-eight, which has been taken since at least the eighth century to mean 'library' but which very likely in fact meant the Bible: Benedict wanted his monks to read books from the Bible, not from the library, during Lent.[105] The age-old disputes over whether Benedictines were allowed to eat the flesh of birds were the result of obscurities in chapters thirty-six and thirty-nine of the Rule.[106] Other prescriptions were perhaps intentionally vague. The obligation of the abbot to consult with the entire community before doing *aliqua praecipua* (chapter three)[107] and the instructions for selecting a new abbot (chapter sixty-four) clearly required interpretation and adjustment in individual cases. Grundmann has recently pointed out the error of reading modern legal and political attitudes into chapter sixty-four and proposed that Benedict had in mind not a single legally binding electoral procedure but a variety of ways of discovering the will of God in the selection of an abbot.[108]

This need to interpret Benedict's Rule, and the consequent development of Benedictine monasticism, was the major reason for the second controversial issue I wish to discuss: the influence of Benedict of Aniane, the great Carolingian monastic legislator, and the character of reformed monasticism in the tenth and eleventh centuries. The role of the second Benedict is almost as disputed as that of the first. A few historians have regarded his work as a legitimate extension of the aim and spirit of Benedict of Nursia.[109] According to Hilpisch, for example, Benedict of Aniane was 'the first Benedictine'; he ended the period of mixed monastic rules and really put the Benedictine Rule into effect.[110] Many scholars and commentators, however, have deplored the narrow view of monastic life, the tendency towards uniformity and centralization, and the prolongation of the liturgy found in the monastic legislation inspired by Benedict of Aniane. Gasquet considered it a 'cast-iron system of uniformity . . . an idea wholly alien to the most elementary conception of Benedictine life.'[111] Dekkers said that Benedict 'resolutely took the road to ritualism'.[112] And Butler and Schmitz called his view of monasti-cism more oriental than Benedictine.[113] The critics of Benedict of Aniane admit that some of his reforms were necessary and that not all of his measures were without precedent;[114] but he summed up and centralized the features of Benedictine monasticism that had changed since the death of the founder and handed it on to the future in a new form.

The most impressive examples of this new form of Benedictinism were found in some of the reform movements of the tenth century and above all at Cluny, which is considered the culmination of Benedict of Aniane's influence. To his ideals of uniformity, centralization, and concentration on the liturgy, Cluny added exemp-tion from episcopal authority; and almost since the date of its foundation it has been criticized for its alleged independence, rigidity, and neglect of manual and intellectual activities. The role of Cluny in the monastic world of the tenth and eleventh centuries has been for a long time a subject of scholarly dispute and has often been exaggerated, owing in part to the late medieval usage of loosely referring to all black Benedictine monks as Cluniacs, whether or not they were officially affiliated with Cluny. The title of Ernst Sackur's influential book *Die*

Cluniacenser, which appeared in 1892–1894, has also been misinterpreted, although Sackur himself recognized the importance of other centres of monastic reform, particularly of Gorze in Lorraine and east of the Rhine. The belief in the preponderance of Cluny was fully overthrown only in 1950, however, with the appearance of Kassius Hallinger's *Gorze–Kluny*, which is probably the single most important work on medieval monasticism to come out since the Second World War. Not all of Hallinger's points are new, and some of his distinctions are too rigid, but he has established beyond doubt the variety of movements of monastic reform in the tenth and eleventh centuries.[115] He studied in great detail the differences in monastic attitudes and observances and showed in particular that the influence of Gorze was predominant in the Empire before the second half of the eleventh century. The 'problem of Cluny' has thus been reduced in scope but increased in complexity. In recent years it has been re-examined by a number of scholars, especially in Germany, who have studied not only Cluny itself and its monastic rivals in the tenth century but also, following in Hallinger's footsteps, the modified 'neo-Cluniac' movements in the Empire in the late eleventh and twelfth centuries.[116]

It is impossible to discuss in detail here the many questions that have been raised concerning the monastic reforms of the tenth century. Their organization, economy, and attitudes towards episcopal authority, secular powers, intellectual activity, and the liturgy have all been investigated with great care, even though the results have not always been conclusive. There has been a tendency to draw sharp distinctions between the various movements. Hallinger especially identifies Cluny with liturgy and the Lorraine centres with intellectual activity, a dichotomy characterized by Hilpisch as *Kultkloster* and *Kulturkloster*.[117] Leclercq, on the other hand, has defended Cluny against the charge of emphasizing ritual to the exclusion of learning and literary culture.[118] Some historians have stressed the feudal aspects of Cluniac organization,[119] while others have considered it un- or even anti-feudal.[120]

The most sharply disputed issue has been the attitude of Cluny towards the Investiture Controversy in the eleventh century and the efforts of the papacy to reform the Church and the world. The traditional view was that the Cluniacs, led by Gregory VII, inspired the reform movement and were the principal opponents of secular control over ecclesiastical affairs.[121] The reaction against this view started in the late nineteenth century with the works of Cauchie and Sackur and was summed up in the well-known book on the Investiture Controversy by Gerd Tellenbach, who maintained that Cluny was primarily concerned with the liturgy and with monastic reform and that it was essentially non-political, and certainly not anti-imperial, since it relied heavily on secular support for its program of strict monastic seclusion. The monks of Cluny, he insisted, were not interested in the reform either of the Church generally or of lay society.[122] The belief that Gregory VII was a Cluniac was described by Bennett in his translation of Tellenbach's book as an 'entirely discredited legend'.[123] This view was rapidly accepted by historians,[124] and the prevailing opinion today is that Cluny took a conservative stand in the Investiture Controversy and even favoured the imperialists, who were by no means as hostile to monastic reform as they were to the radical program of Gregory VII.[125] There are signs, however, of a return to a more moderate position.

Borino has shown, for instance, that Gregory VII almost certainly had some Cluniac experience;[126] and Hallinger and Lemarignier, and most recently Violante, Schieffer, and Hoffmann, have strongly argued that although Cluny may not itself have played a leading part in the Investiture Controversy it helped to lay the basis for the reform movement by its influence on lay piety, its promotion of the independence of monasteries and individual churches, and its support of papal power and ecclesiastical centralization.[127]

The question of medieval monastic reform has thus been expanded to include every feature of monastic life and to involve every aspect of the history of the age. Nowhere is this more true than in my third controversial problem: the origins and character of the Cistercian order and its relation on the one hand to Cluny and on the other to the new religious movements of the eleventh and twelfth centuries. This is a vast problem, and I can touch here only on some of the principal points.[128]

The differences between Cluny and Cîteaux have been very variously assessed by modern historians. Some have seen the controversy as a spiritual dichotomy: a contrast in the way of observing the Rule, either according to the letter or in the light of tradition, or a contrast of liberty and ritualism, asceticism and humanism, eremitism and cenobitism, or simply unworldliness and worldliness. For some the Cistercians restored the pure Benedictine ideal, while for others the Cluniacs lived more in accord with the spirit, if not the letter, of the Rule, whereas the Cistercians revived the harsher spirit of pre-Benedictine monasticism.[129] For Leclercq the crisis was primarily economic. 'The "crisis of cenobitism",' he wrote, 'was in reality a crisis of prosperity.'[130] Wealth did not necessarily bring laxity, but it brought involvement in worldly affairs, and the best antidotes were poverty and solitude. For Cantor, on the other hand, the Cistercian withdrawal from the world was the result of the failure of the Gregorians to reform secular society.[131] In contrast to these broad interpretations, several German historians have laid great stress on the specific differences in liturgy and monastic observances at Cluny and Cîteaux. These material differences, according to Hallinger, created the psychological tension between the two orders. It was a contrast of Old and New in which Cluny, which had been the 'New' of the tenth century, became the 'Old' of the twelfth.[132] Others have pointed out the differences in organization—the so-called feudalism of Cluny as contrasted with the federalism of Cîteaux—and in the position of abbot, who at Cluny was a king and at Cîteaux a father.[133] Ernst Werner saw the reform in Marxist terms as the expression of economic and social changes in the feudal order and of the hate of the lower classes for the aristocratic bishops and Cluniacs.[134] Grundmann long ago demonstrated that there is no evidence to support this view. The monks in the reformed monasteries were not drawn primarily from the lower classes, and they were certainly not inspired by a desire to break with the established social order.[135]

These differing interpretations clearly reflect some of the views of monastic history that I have already discussed, above all the concentration on the essence of Benedictinism and the dichotomy of eremitism (austerity) and cenobitism (moderation). These views have also influenced the study of early Cistercian history, and particularly the importance assigned to each of the first three abbots of Cîteaux, Robert, Alberic, and Stephen Harding. Angelo Manrique, the father of Cistercian historiography, compared the roles of these three to those of the Trinity: to Robert belonged the first creation, to Alberic the *passio,* and to Stephen Harding the great diffusion of the order.[136] For a long time the claims of Robert were neglected by scholars on account of his reputation for spiritual instability and eremitical subjectivism, but his role as true founder of the Cistercians has been strongly asserted by Lenssen and Lefèvre.[137] Müller and Ducourneau, on the other hand, maintained that Alberic was the guiding spirit and element of perseverance in the foundation.[138] More recently Duvernay has argued, from a careful comparison of the customs of Cîteaux with those of Vallombrosa, that Stephen Harding was the real organizer of Cistercian monasticism and brought it into the main stream of monastic development of the eleventh and twelfth centuries.[139] There is no final solution to these differences in interpretation, which depend largely upon the relative weight given to individualism and organization in the early years of Cîteaux.

A scholarly bombshell almost of the proportions of the *Regula Magistri* controversy was thrown into the camp of Cistercian research by the Belgian scholar J.-A. Lefèvre, who published between 1954 and 1959 a series of articles throwing serious doubt on the dating of the *Carta caritatis, Exordium parvum,* and other documents upon which the early history of Cîteaux was almost entirely based.[140] A few questions had already been raised in the 1930's and 1940's by the textual discoveries of Hümpfner and Turk, but the essential validity of these documents was as previously undoubted as that of the Rule of St. Benedict.[141] There was a sharp reaction in Cistercian circles to Lefèvre's challenge, and the fighting still continues. The details are too technical to examine here, and the solution of the main issues will have to await a complete study of the manuscripts and a systematic survey of the problem by an impartial scholar. As in the *Regula Magistri* controversy, however, it appears that the conservatives have had to give ground, even if the challengers have not proved all their points; and most serious scholars today accept that the early documents of Cistercian history—and the institutions they describe—developed over a considerable period of time and do not reflect the nature of the order at its beginnings.

These researches, while showing how little is really known about the origins of Cîteaux, suggest that it was less well organized and less distinctive than the Cistercians wished to believe later, following the phenomenal success of their order in the first half of the twelfth century. The relative positions of the mother-abbey and the chapter-general in the government of the order changed during its early years; and the order gradually achieved a degree of emancipation from the diocesan bishops, in spite of its early opposition to exemption.[142] Certain recent authors have pointed out the dependence of the Cistercian liturgy and observances on previous Benedictine usages,[143] while others (such as Duvernay in his study of Cîteaux and Vallombrosa) have shown its close resemblance, and possible debt, to other contemporary centres of monastic reform. Thus the study of early Cistercian history has moved towards a greater emphasis on development, continuity, and interrelationship. Presse, Ducourneau, and Lenssen were among the first to see that Cîteaux was not a negative but a positive movement, not a rejection of contemporary monasticism but a search for primitive purity and basic monastic values.[144]

They exaggerated the originality and uniqueness of Cîteaux, however, and Canivez, Lefèvre, Dimier, and Van Damme have all recently stressed that Cîteaux was part of a broad movement of return to the sources (*ressourcement*) and that the ideals of eremitical solitude and primitive monastic purity were not re-stricted to the Cistercians at this time.[145]

The Cistercian reform must therefore be studied in relation to the whole monastic movement, which was itself an aspect of the spiritual upheaval of the eleventh and twelfth centuries. It included not only the foundation of countless new monasteries and orders but also lay movements of spirituality and heresy of which the conse-quences for the medieval Church and society only later became clear. Grundmann in his important book on religious movements in the Middle Ages, which came out in 1935, and more recently Chenu and Delaruelle have emphasized the connections between the spiritual, monastic, and heretical movements of the twelfth century and their association with the Mendicants, who thus appear not as a radically new departure but as the culmination of a basic shift in medieval spirituality of which the first signs can be found in the eleventh century.[146] Person-ally I believe (though not all scholars would agree with me on this point) that the Cistercians were part of this movement and that in their origins they looked not only backwards to the Benedictine past but also forwards to the Franciscans and Dominicans, in whom the ideal of the *vita apostolica* ultimately emerged as a life combining evangelical poverty, charitable love, and wandering proselytism in the world.

The development of this apostolic ideal over the centuries, and particularly in the twelfth century, is the subject of a small book by Vicaire entitled *L'imitation des apôtres*.[147] I have already discussed the importance of this ideal among the early monks, for whom it meant a common life of personal poverty and prayer. Down until the twelfth century, indeed, the life of the apostles in Jerusalem was inter-preted in purely monastic terms, without any commitment to engage in prosely-tism.[148] It was then gradually reinterpreted, partly by the canons,[149] so as to include pastoral work, and finally emerged in the thirteenth century as the ideal of the Mendicants, who found in the apostolic life of the New Testament the example for their own communities of poor itinerant preachers.[150]

This was not a sudden transformation, and its history can be traced in the use of various monastic slogans: *ecclesiae primitivae forma*, which was first used in the middle of the eleventh century to mean a common life of personal poverty, like the *vita apostolica*, but was revised in the twelfth century to include preaching;[151] *pauperes Christi*, which was commonly applied to monks in the eleventh and twelfth centuries;[152] and *nudus nudum Christum sequi*, naked to follow the naked Christ, which was taken from Jerome and expressed the ideals of the twelfth-century reformers.[153] The use of these terms corresponded to changes in the spiri-tuality of the age, to a turning away from a purely ascetic ideal of Christian perfection,[154] and to the new devotion to the humanity of Christ. The ideal of im-itating the apostles and saints was replaced by the ideal of the imitation of Christ, which was epitomized by St. Francis and the early friars.

This is an ideal that both cut across and incorporated many of the traditional monastic values and combined, in a new synthesis, action and contemplation, stability and peregrination, eremitism (in a broad sense) and cenobitism—even, in a way, East and West: St. Francis is one of the few medieval Western saints who is honoured in the East. It thus developed into a new vision of a life which is in but not of this world and which is open to laymen as well as to clerics and monks.

The emergence of this new ideal marks the end of the period when monasticism was universally regarded as the highest ideal of Christian life. In the later Middle Ages, Benedictine monasticism lived on and still played an important historical role, but it lost its spiritual supremacy in the Christian world, and the monastic order gradually merged into the clerical order as its regular branch.[155] During the Benedictine centuries, however, monks were considered to be a separate and superior order of society, and their ideals and activities must be taken into consideration by any historian of the period.

Notes

The following abbreviations will be used in the notes: *Anal. SOC = Analecta sacri ordinis Cisterciensis* (now called *Analecta Cisterciensia*); *Coll. OCR = Collectanea ordinis Cisterciensium reformatorum; Rev. bén. = Revue bénédictine; Rev. d'hist. ecc. = Revue d'histoire ecclésiastique; Rev. Mab. = Revue Mabillon; SMGBOZ = Studien und Mitteilungen zur Geschichte des Benediktinerordens und seiner Zweige.*

1. On Dugdale and the beginnings of medieval historical scholarship in England, see David C. Douglas, *English Scholars, 1660–1730*, 2nd ed. (London, 1951). There are many works on the Maurists, none of them entirely satisfactory. The principal source is Edmond Martène, *Histoire de la Congrégation de Saint-Maur*, ed. G. Charvin (Archives de la France monastique, 31-35, 42-43, 46-48; Ligugé–Paris, 1928–54); see also the brief account by David Knowles, 'The Maurists' (1959), reprinted in *Great Historical Enterprises* (Edinburgh, 1963), pp. 33–62. Mabillon above all deserves to be known as the father of monastic history. His works constitute 'the most valuable contribution, beyond all comparison, ever made to monastic history', according to G. G. Coulton, *Five Centuries of Religion* (Cambridge, 1929 [2nd ed. of vol. 1]– 1950), 1: xxvi, who was not inclined to be over-indulgent to monastic authors. Jean Leclercq, 'Pour une histoire intégrale du monachisme', *Analecta monastica*, 6 (Studia Anselmiana, 50; Rome, 1962): 1-2, recently stressed again that almost all the primary sources for the study of Benedictine monasticism down to the twelfth century are contained in Mabillon's great collections.

2. Edward Gibbon, *History of the Decline and Fall of the Roman Empire*, ed. J. B. Bury (New York, 1914), 4: 80. On Gibbon and Eastern monasticism, see Deno J. Geanako-

plos, 'Edward Gibbon and Byzantine Ecclesiastical History', *Church History*, 35 (1966): 1–16, esp. 7 and 13–16.

3. S. R. Maitland, *The Dark Ages*, ed. Frederick Stokes (London, 1889), p. 7. Maitland had in mind particularly the works of Robertson, Milner, Warton, and lesser eighteenth-century writers. On literary attitudes towards monasticism, see Rudolf Schneider, *Der Mönch in der englischen Dichtung bis auf Lewis's 'Monk' 1795* (Palaestra, 155; Leipzig, 1928).

4. David Knowles, 'Cardinal Gasquet as an Historian' (1957), reprinted in *The Historian and Character and Other Essays* (Cambridge, 1963), p. 258.

5. On the difficulty of approaching monasticism without prejudice, especially for Protestants, see R. Newton Flew, *The Idea of Perfection in Christian Theology* (Oxford, 1934), p. 160; cf. also Owen Chadwick, *John Cassian* (Cambridge, 1950), p. 163, citing Luther's condemnation of Jerome and the apparent tendency of early monastic writers 'to push the Gospel aside'.

6. *The Works of John Milton* (New York, 1931–40), 4: 311.

7. James Boswell, *Life of Samuel Johnson*, ed. G. B. Hill (New York, 1891–1904), 2: 498.

8. S. R. Maitland, *Dark Ages*, p. 208.

9. See Stephan Hilpisch, 'St. Benedikt in der neueren Hagiographie', *SMGBOZ*, 61 (1947–48): 115, and 'Benediktinerhistoriker der neueren Zeit', *Beten und Arbeiten*, ed. Theodor Bogler (Liturgie und Mönchtum, 28; Maria Laach, 1961), pp. 16–17.

10. W. E. H. Lecky, *History of European Morals from Augustus to Charlemagne* (London, 1930), 2: 79.

11. Adolf Harnack, *Monasticism: Its Ideals and History and the Confessions of St. Augustine*, trans. E. E. Kellett and F. H. Marseille (London, 1901); Herbert Workman, *The Evolution of the Monastic Ideal* (London, 1913; reprinted with Introduction by David Knowles, Boston, 1962).

12. Georg Schreiber, *Kurie und Kloster im 12. Jahrhundert* (Kirchenrechtliche Abhandlungen, 65–68; Stuttgart, 1910); E. E. Stengel, *Die Immunität in Deutschland bis zum Ende des 11. Jahrhunderts*, vol. 1: *Diplomatik der deutschen Immunitäts-Privilegien vom 9. bis zum Ende des 11. Jahrhunderts* (Innsbruck, 1911); Albert Brackmann, *Die Kurie und die Salzburger Kirchenprovinz* (Studien und Vorarbeiten zur Germania Pontificia, 1; Berlin, 1912); Hans Hirsch, *Die Klosterimmunität seit dem Investiturstreit* (Weimar, 1913).

13. Hans Hirsch, *Die hohe Gerichtsbarkeit im deutschen Mittelalter* (Reichenberg, 1922; reprinted with Epilogue by Theodor Mayer, Graz–Cologne, 1958); Theodor Mayer, *Fürsten und Staat* (Weimar, 1950).

14. Cf. Gerd Tellenbach, *Church, State and Christian Society at the Time of the Investiture Contest*, trans. R. F. Bennett (Studies in Mediaeval History, 3; Oxford, 1940): p. 55; David Knowles, *The Monastic Order in England*, 2nd ed. (Cambridge, 1963), p. 4: 'No work done within it [the Benedictine abbey], whether manual, intellectual or charitable, is directed to an end outside its walls.'

15. David Knowles, in a short notice in *English Historical Review*, 79 (1964): 822.

16. Cf. Romuald Bauerreiss, 'Bibliographie der benediktinischen Zeitschriften und Schriftenreihen II (1949)', *SMGBOZ*, 62 (1950): 48–55.

17. They have been published separately under the title *Two Saints: St Bernard and St Francis* (The Cambridge Miscellany, 4; Cambridge, 1932).

18. In *The New Statesman and Nation* (Aug. 24, 1940), p. 190.

19. See the remarks on this topic (one of his favourites) by G. G. Coulton, *Five Centuries* (cited n. 1 above), 1: 2–3, 318, 439–41, etc.

20. Cf. René Hesbert in *Théologie de la vie monastique d'après quelques grands moines des*

époques *moderne et contemporaine* (Archives de la France monastique, 50 [= *Rev. Mab.*, 51: 2–3], Ligugé–Paris, 1961, cited hereafter as *Théologie*, II), pp. 109–56.

21. H. R. Philippeau, 'A propos du coutumier de Norwich', *Scriptorium*, 3 (1949): 295, who pointed out that the editors of many monastic customaries were inspired by ascetic rather than documentary purposes.

22. A good general account will be found in vol. 5 of Philibert Schmitz, *Histoire de l'Ordre de Saint Benoît* (Maredsous, 1948–56).

23. David Knowles and R. Neville Hadcock, *Medieval Religious Houses: England and Wales* (London–New York–Toronto, 1953), p. 364. This rate of increase of approximately tenfold has been accepted by subsequent scholars. Cf. also J. C. Russell, 'The Clerical Population of Medieval England', *Traditio*, 2 (1944): 177–212, who said that 'A wave of enthusiasm for monasticism followed the Conquest and set up a system which included probably twenty times as many members by 1300 as in 1066' (p. 212).

24. See in particular F. A. Gasquet's introduction to C. R. F. de Montalembert, *The Monks of the West from St. Benedict to St. Bernard* (London–New York, 1896), 1: xi–xiv. (This introduction, which is said to have been written for Gasquet by Edmund Bishop and Elphege Cody, had some influence on Leo XIII and others engaged in revising the English Benedictine constitutions: see Knowles, *Historian and Character*, p. 252.) Montalembert made the same point himself and stressed that the missionary and cultural work of monks was not part of their purpose or essence. Cf. *Moines d'Occident* (cited in text), 2: 70–71 and 6: 324.

25. Dom Cuthbert Butler, *Benedictine Monachism*, 2nd ed. (Cambridge, 1924), pp. 24–26.

26. Cf. the account and bibliography of the liturgical movement in F. L. Cross, ed., *The Oxford Dictionary of the Christian Church* (London–New York–Toronto, 1957) p. 815.

27. See Damasus Winzen, 'Guéranger and the Liturgical Movement—Comments on Bouyer's *Liturgical Piety*', *American Benedictine Review*, 6 (1955–56): 419–26. Eligius Dekkers, 'Were the Early Monks Liturgical?' *Coll. OCR*, 22 (1960): 120–37, argued that the early monks were not inclined towards the liturgy and showed 'no trace of that ritualistic mania which was so dear to certain monastic circles in the Middle Ages' (p. 137). In his article 'Moines et liturgie', *ibid.*, 329–40, Dekkers insisted that monastic liturgy should be sober, authentic, and 'interior'.

28. Prosper Guéranger, *Institutions liturgiques*, 2nd ed. (Paris–Brussels, 1878–85), 1: 246.

29. See Jacques Winandy, 'Les moines et le sacerdoce', *La vie spirituelle*, 80 (1949): 23–36; O. Rousseau, 'Sacerdoce et monachisme', *Études sur le sacrement de l'ordre* (Lex Orandi, 22; Paris, 1957), pp. 216–31; and Jean Leclercq, 'Le sacerdoce des moines', *Irénikon*, 36 (1963): 5–40, who urged that the priesthood of monks should be justified only by the liturgical needs of the community. These three articles, all by eminent scholars, are good examples of the different lessons for monks today found by different historians of monasticism. On monastic performance of pastoral work, see also Philip Hofmeister, 'Mönchtum und Seelsorge bis zum 13. Jahrhundert', *SMGBOZ*, 65 (1955): 209–73, and the short and sensible article of Marjorie Chibnall, 'Monks and Pastoral Work: A Problem in Anglo-Norman History', *Journal of Ecclesiastical History*, 18 (1967): 165–72.

30. See Kassius Hallinger, 'Ausdrucksformen des Umkehr-Gedankens: Zu den geistigen Grundlagen und den Entwicklungsphasen der Instituta Conversorum', *SMGBOZ*, 70 (1959): 169–81.

31. J. H. Newman, *Historical Sketches*, 2 (London, 1881): 373. Later in the essay he said that 'Its spirit indeed is ever one, but not its outward circumstances' (p. 388).

32. Harnack, *Monasticism*, p. 10.

33. Introduction of Workman, *Mon Ideal* (cited n. 11 above), p. 4.

34. Harnack, *Monasticism*, p. 110. See also David Knowles, *From Pachomius to Ignatius: A Study in the Constitutional History of the Religious Orders* (The Sarum Lectures, 1964–65; Oxford, 1966).

35. Workman, *Mon. Ideal*, p. 340.

36. See *La séparation du monde* (Paris, 1961), with essays on the subject by various authors.

37. Alfred Adam, 'Grundbegriffe des Mönchtums in sprachlicher Sicht', *Zeitschrift für Kirchengeschichte*, 65 (4th S., IV; 1953–54): 209–39; cf. also Jean Leclercq, *Études sur le vocabulaire monastique du moyen âge* (Studia Anselmiana, 48; Rome, 1961), pp. 7–38.

38. Newman, *Historical Sketches*, 2: 374.

39. Gerhart Ladner, *The Idea of Reform* (Cambridge, Mass., 1959), p. 35.

40. Harnack, *Monasticism*, pp. 45–46; Workman, *Mon. Ideal*, pp. 10–11, and 85, citing with approval the view of E. G. Smith, *Christian Monasticism* (London, 1892), p. 3, that monasticism was 'the inheritance of the Church, not its invention; not the offspring, but the adopted child'.

41. Cf. Augustin Blazovich, *Soziologie des Mönchtums und der Benediktinerregel* (Vienna, 1954), pp. 112–14.

42. See Jacques Winandy, 'L'idée de fuite du monde dans la tradition monastique', *Le message des moines à notre temps* (Paris, 1958), pp. 102–4, citing Pius XII's encyclical of 11 April 1958.

43. François Vandenbroucke, 'Théologie de la vie monastique: A propos d'une publication récente', *Studia monastica*, 4 (1962): 373–76.

44. Giovanni Miccoli, in *Théologie de la vie monastique* (Théologie: Études publiées sous la direction de la Faculté de Théologie S. J. de Lyon-Fourvière, 49; Paris, 1961, cited hereafter as *Théologie*, I), p. 466.

45. Cited by Burkhard Neunheuser in *Théologie*, II (cited n. 20 above), p. 258. On Casel's study of St. Benedict as a pneumatic, see Stephan Hilpisch, in *SMGBOZ*, 61: 125.

46. Vandenbroucke, in *Studia monastica*, 4: 384–85.

47. Emmanuel de Severus, in *Théologie*, II, p. 251.

48. Blazovich, *Soziologie*, p. 116.

49. Cf. Karl Heussi, *Der Ursprung des Mönchtums* (Tübingen, 1936), pp. 280–304.

50. See L. T. Lefort, reviewing Heussi, *Ursprung*, in *Rev. d'hist. ecc.*, 33 (1937): 345–46; Heinrich Bacht, in *Théologie*, I, pp. 42–43; and M.-H. Vicaire, *L'imitation des apôtres: Moines, chanoines, mendiants (IVe–XIIIe siècles)* (Paris, 1963), pp. 25–27. This view applies particularly to Pachomius and the early cenobites.

51. Basilius Steidle, '"Homo Dei Antonius": Zum Bild des "Mannes Gottes" im alten Mönchtum', *Antonius Magnus eremita, 356–1956* (Studia Anselmiana, 38; Rome, 1956), pp. 182–83. According to Steidle, Athanasius presented Anthony as an ideal monastic type, a 'man of God', of this sort.

52. Roland Bainton, 'Changing Ideas and Ideals in the Sixteenth Century' (1936), reprinted in his *Collected Papers in Church History*, I: *Early and Medieval Christianity* (Boston, 1962), p. 166. M.-H. Vicaire, *Imitation*, p. 23, called it 'a powerful nostalgia for the primitive Church'.

53. Ernest McDonnell, 'The *Vita Apostolica*: Diversity or Dissent', *Church History*, 24 (1955): 15; cf. Vicaire, *Imitation*, pp. 17–23.

54. Adalbert de Vogüé, in *Théologie*, I, pp. 220–21.

55. See Eusebius, *Ecclesiastical History*, ii, 17, for excerpts from Philo's writings on the Therapeutae, whom Eusebius regards as primitive Christian ascetics. On the Qumran

I

community as a precursor of Christian monasticism, cf. the remarks of Bo Reicke, 'Die Verfassung der Urgemeinde im Lichte jüdischer Dokumente', *Theologische Zeitschrift*, 10 (1954); 106–7.

56. Henri de Lubac, *Exégèse médiévale* (Théologie, 41; Paris, 1959), p. 576.

57. Cited by Coulton, *Five Centuries* (n. 1 above), 2: 509. Coulton used some good metaphors himself in 1: 315, and 2: 18.

58. Newman, *Historical Sketches*, 2: 388; Workman, *Mon. Ideal*, p. 224; Butler, *Ben. Monachism*, p. 214 (the whole page displays a remarkable luxuriance of metaphors).

59. Jean Leclercq, 'Pour une histoire humaine du monachisme au moyen âge', *Analecta monastica*, 4 (Studia Anselmiana, 41; Rome, 1957): 1–7, stressing the importance of the spirituality and psychology of individual monks.

60. Paul Antin, 'Une question de vocabulaire: monachisme, "monachologie"', *Rev. d'hist. ecc.*, 59 (1964): 89–90.

61. Stephan Hilpisch, 'Das benediktinisch-monastische Ideal im Wandel der Zeiten', *SMGBOZ*, 68 (1957): 73–85. St. Benedict intended such adjustments to the *Zeitideal*, according to Hilpisch (pp. 75–76), who considered that contemporary monasticism is oriented predominantly towards prayer but shows signs of an increasing emphasis on solitude.

62. Leclercq, in *Irénikon*, 36: 33.

63. Blazovich, *Soziologie* (cited n. 41 above), p. 48: 'Die Trennung des wesentlichen von dem Zeitbedingten in der Regel ist eine Aufgabe, die jeder Generation, also auch der heutigen, aufgegeben ist.'

64. See especially the works cited nn. 12–13 above.

65. Christian Courtois, 'L'évolution du monachisme en Gaule de St Martin à St Columban', *Il monachesimo nell'Alto Medioevo e la formazione della civiltà occidentale* (Settimane di studio del Centro italiano di studi sull'Alto Medioevo, 4; Spoleto, 1957), pp. 47–72. 'The epidemic of vocations' at this time, according to Courtois, was 'a social phenomenon' (p. 52). Cf. Friedrich Prinz, *Frühes Mönchtum im Frankenreich: Kultur und Gesellschaft in Gallien, den Rheinlanden und Bayern am Beispiel der monastischen Entwicklung (4. bis 8. Jahrhundert)* (Munich-Vienna, 1965).

66. F. A. Gasquet, Introduction to Montalembert, *Monks of the West*, 1: xiv.

67. Cf. Butler, *Ben. Monachism*, pp. 301–3.

68. Montalembert, *Moines d'Occident*, 1: 139.

69. Harnack, *Monasticism*, pp. 62 and 114–15.

70. Workman, *Mon. Ideal*, p. 134. The words quoted apply to early monasticism in the East and 'even in the West'.

71. Heinrich Bacht, 'Antonius und Pachomius: Von der Anachorese zum Cönobitentum', in *Antonius Magnus* (cited n. 51 above), pp. 66–107, esp. 100, 101 and 104 on Anthony and 106–7 on the debt of Pachomius to eremitism; cf. also S. G. A. Luff, 'Transition from Solitary to Cenobitic Life(c.250 to 400)', *The Irish Ecclesiastical Record*, 84 (1955): 164–84, who pointed out that even hermits recognized the dangers of complete solitude and that there was 'a frame of common life' at Nitria (p. 171).

72. Arthur Vööbus, 'Sur le développement de la phase cénobitique et la réaction dans l'ancien monachisme syriaque', *Recherches de science religieuse*, 47 (1959): 406.

73. See especially Jean Leclercq, 'Pierre le Vénérable et l'érémitisme clunisien', *Petrus Venerabilis, 1156–1956* (Studia Anselmiana, 40; Rome, 1956), pp. 99–120, and, more generally, *L'eremitismo in Occidente nei secoli XI e XII* (Pubblicazioni dell'Università cattolica del Sacro Cuore, 3rd S., 4; Milan, 1965).

74. Cf. Louis Gougaud, 'Les critiques formulées contre les premiers moines d'Occident', *Rev. Mab.*, 24 (1934): 151–52.

75. See Adrian Hastings, 'St. Benedict and the Eremitical Life', *Downside Review*, 68 (1950): 191–211, who concluded that, 'It appears plain that St Benedict recognized the superiority of the eremitical life, and most likely made provision at Monte Cassino for elder monks, suitably inclined, to become hermits near the oratory of St John' (p. 211). Cf. Adalbert de Vogüé, *La communauté et l'abbé dans la Règle de Saint Benoît* (Paris, 1961), pp. 47–77, and for other works on this subject, Gregorio Penco's references in C. Vagaggini, *Problemi e orientamenti di spiritualità monastica, biblica e liturgica* (Rome, 1961), p. 218.

76. Jean Leclercq, *L'amour des lettres et le désir de Dieu* (Paris, 1957), p. 87; Rousseau, in *Études* (cited n. 29 above), p. 218; De Vogüé, Cf. *Communauté*, passim.

77. Emil Herman, 'La "stabilitas loci" nel monachismo Bizantino', *Orientalia christiana periodica*, 21 (1955): 115–42.

78. Cf. Kassius Hallinger, 'Progressi e problemi della ricerca sulla riforma pregregoriana', in *Monachesimo* (cited n. 65 above), p. 263, who mentioned the reduced importance given to Eastern influences on these movements as a result of recent research.

79. See, among others Jean-Marie Leroux, in *Théologie*, I (cited n. 44 above), p. 183, who said of Chrysostom that 'La distinction entre action et contemplation lui est totalement étrangère.'

80. This difference can be clearly seen in the exegesis of Luke 10:38–42, which is today almost universally interpreted as indicating the superiority of contemplation over action. The Church Fathers, however, believed that the *optima pars* chosen by Mary rather than her busy sister Martha showed the superiority of theory to practice, of complete (pneumatic) Christians to simple (fleshly) Christians, or of the Church to the Synagogue: see D. A. Csányi, 'Optima pars: die Auslegungsgeschichte von Lk 10, 38–42 bei den Kirchenvätern der ersten vier Jahrhunderte', *Studia monastica*, 2 (1960): 75. For Theodore the Studite, according to Julien Leroy in *Théologie*, I, p. 425, 'le rôle de Marie n'est pas seulement d'écouter la parole de Dieu, c'est aussi et surtout la mettre en pratique, et chercher à "plaire à Dieu".'

81. M. Olphe-Galliard, 'Vie contemplative et vie active d'après Cassien', *Revue d'ascétique et de mystique*, 16 (1935): 252–88; Chadwick, *Cassian* (cited n. 5 above), p. 83; D. A. Csányi, in *Studia monastica*, 2: 77–78; Adalbert de Vogüé, in *Théologie*, I, 230: 'Vie "active" culminant dans une vie "contemplative", voilà donc ce qu'est la vie monastique. Est-il besoin de préciser que ces termes ont un sens fort différent de celui que nous leur donnons couramment? Dire que la vie monastique est "active", ce n'est pas la faire consister dans des œuvres de bienfaisance ou d'apostolat; c'est au contraire la définir comme une ascèse visant à la purification du sujet, en vue de la contemplation.'

82. See the chapters on these two saints in Cuthbert Butler, *Western Mysticism*, 2nd ed. (London, 1926).

83. Aelred Squire, 'Aelred of Rievaulx and the Monastic Tradition Concerning Action and Contemplation', *Downside Review*, 72 (1954): 297.

84. Ibid., 290.

85. Gougaud, in *Rev. Mab.*, 24: 151–52.

86. Cf. Guéranger, cited by Gabriel Le Maître in *Théologie*, II, p. 171; Butler, *Ben Monachism*, pp. 123–34; Philibert Schmitz, *Ordre* (cited n. 22 above), 1: 32.

87. Cf. Herman, in *Orientalia christ. period.*, 21: 127–38.

88. Jean Leclercq, 'Mönchtum und Peregrinatio im Frühmittelalter', *Römische Quartalschrift für christliche Altertumskunde und Kirchengeschichte*, 55 (1960): 212–25, and 'Monachisme et pérégrination du IXᵉ au XIIᵉ siècle', *Studia monastica*, 3 (1961): 33–52; see also his article in *Séparation* (cited n. 36 above), pp. 81–82. Cf. Hans von Campenhausen, *Die asketische Heimatlosigkeit im altkirchlichen und frühmittelalterlichen Mönchtum* (Sammlung gemeinverständlicher Vorträge und Schriften aus dem Gebiet der Theologie und Reli-

gionsgeschichte, 149; Tübingen, 1930) and Gerhart B. Ladner, 'Homo Viator: Medieval Ideas on Alienation and Order', *Speculum*, 42 (1967): 233–59.

89. See on this topic Kurt Fina, 'Anselm von Havelberg [II]', *Analecta Praemonstratensia*, 32 (1956): 208–26, and ' "Ovem suam requirere": Eine Studie zur Geschichte des Ordenswechsels im 12. Jahrhundert', *Augustiniana*, 7 (1957): 33–56.

90. Cf. Augustin Blazovich, *Soziologie* (cited n. 41 above), pp. 66–67, referring to the works of Brechter and Rothenhäusler. In a parallel fashion, monastic separation from the world has shifted from a physical to a spiritual concept, a separation of intention rather than one in the desert or the monastery: see Leclercq, in *Irénikon*, 36: 20.

91. J. C. Dickinson, *The Origins of the Austin Canons and their Introduction into England* (London, 1950); Charles Dereine, *Les chanoines réguliers au diocèse de Liège avant saint Norbert* (Académie royale de Belgique: Classe des lettres . . ., Mémoires in-8°, 47.1; Brussels, 1952), an article under 'Chanoines' in *Dictionnaire d'histoire et de géographie ecclésiastiques*, 12 (1953): cols. 353–405, and a number of important articles, of which the early ones are analysed by J.-F. Lemarignier, 'Spiritualité grégorienne et chanoines réguliers', *Revue de l'histoire de l'Église de France*, 35 (1949): 36–38.

92. Charles Dereine, 'La "vita apostolica" dans l'ordre canonial du IXᵉ au XIᵉ siècle', *Rev. Mab.*, 51 (1961): 47–53.

93. Josef Siegwart, *Die Chorherren und Chorfrauengemeinschaften in der deutschsprachigen Schweiz vom 6. Jahrhundert bis 1160* (Studia Friburgensia, N.F., 30; Fribourg, 1962), Chap. 4.

94. Ibid., pp. 159–60, 225.

95. Guy Oury, 'L'idéal monastique dans la vie canoniale: Le bienheureux Hervé de Tours († 1022)', *Rev. Mab.*, 52 (1962): 1–29.

96. The author of the twelfth-century *Liber de diversis ordinibus et professionibus quae sunt in ecclesia* (in *Patrologia cursus completus, series latina*, ed. J. P. Migne [Paris, 1844–64], 213: 814 and 830–31) distinguished three types each of monks and canons and stressed the similarities between the more austere types of both groups, who lived in solitude and worked with their hands; cf. on this treatise and generally on this subject, Dickinson, *Canons*, pp. 198–208, who emphasized that the differences between the regular and secular canons in the twelfth century were in many ways more striking than those between the regular canons and monks. Some of the monks maintained that the strict regular canons really were monks: see Fina, in *Anal. Praem.*, 32: 204–5.

97. This variation is clearly shown by the twenty-six chapters in *Théologie*, I (cited n. 44 above), in spite of the recurrent stress on the obvious monastic virtues of renunciation, humility, and poverty.

98. See the bibliography (down to 1957) of nine books and a hundred and thirteen articles, by a total of fifty-three authors, compiled by Odo Zimmermann, 'An Unsolved Problem: The Rule of Saint Benedict and the Rule of the Master', *American Benedictine Review*, 10 (1959): 86–106.

99. David Knowles, *Hist. Enterprises* (cited n. 1 above), p. 195 and cf. David Knowles, 'Some Recent Work on Early Benedictine History', *Studies in Church History*, 1 (1964): 35–46.

100. *Acta sanctorum O.S.B.* (Venice, 1738): 6: 150, cited by Robert Gillet in *Théologie*, 1, p. 323.

101. Cited by Gabriel Le Maître in *Théologie*, II, p.171. Work and obedience were the basic principles of Benedictinism for Guéranger's friend Montalembert, *Moines d'Occident*, 2: 49.

102. Blazovich, *Soziologie* (cited n. 41 above), pp. 108–9 (and 104–11 generally on the problem of the 'key' to Benedictinism).

103. Cf. the opposing views of Odon Lottin, 'Le vœu de "conversatio morum" dans la Règle de saint Benoît' (1957), reprinted with additions in his *Études de morale, histoire et doctrine* (Gembloux, 1961), pp. 309–28, and Jacques Winandy, 'Conversatio morum', *Coll. OCR*, 22 (1960): 378–86.

104. E. Manning, 'La signification de *militare-militia-miles* dans la Règle de saint Benoît', *Rev. bén.*, 72 (1962): 135–38.

105. Anscari Mundò,' "Bibliotheca": Bible et lecture du Carême d'après saint Benoît', *Rev. bén.*, 60 (1950): 65–92. This article has profound implications for the accepted view of Benedictine literary culture.

106. Cf. Paul Volk, 'Das Abstinenzindult von 1523 für die Benediktinerklöster der Mainz-Bamberger Provinz', *Rev. bén.*, 40 (1928): 334–36; Sister M. Alfred Schroll, *Benedictine Monasticism as Reflected in the Warnefrid-Hildemar Commentaries on the Rule* (New York, 1941), pp. 174–76; and Josef Semmler, ' "Volatilia": Zu den benediktinischen Consuetudines des 9. Jahrhunderts', *SMGBOZ*, 69 (1958): 163–76.

107. Stephan Hilpisch, 'Der Rat der Brüder in den Benediktinerklöstern des Mittel-alters', *SMGBOZ*, 67 (1956): 221–36, discusses the pre-Benedictine history of this regulation and its development in the later Middle Ages from a doctrine of counsel to one of consent.

108. Herbert Grundmann, 'Pars quamvis parva: Zur Abtwahl nach Benedikts Regel', *Festschrift Percy Ernst Schramm* (Wiesbaden, 1964), I, 237–51. Cf. the reply and counter-reply by Hallinger and Grundmann in *Zeitschrift für Kirchengeschichte*, 76 (1965): 233–45, and 77 (1966): 217–23.

109. See the examples cited by Philibert Schmitz, 'L'influence de saint Benoît d'Aniane dans l'histoire de l'ordre de saint-Benoît', in *Monachesimo* (cited n. 65 above), pp. 401–2. Cf. Kassius Hallinger, *Gorze-Kluny: Studien zu den monastischen Lebensformen und Gegen-sätzen im Hochmittelalter* (2 vols; Rome, 1950), pp. 803–18.

110. Hilpisch, in *SMGBOZ*, 68: 77.

111. Introduction to Montalembert, *Monks of the West*, I: xxv, xxvii; cf. Workman, *Mon. Ideal*, p. 227; Schmitz, in *Monachesimo*, pp. 408–9; Blazovich, *Soziologie*, p. 157.

112. Eligius Dekkers, in *Coll. OCR*, 22: 336 (Cf. also his other article, ibid., 137: see n. 27 above); cf. Butler, *Ben. Monachism*, pp. 295–96.

113. Ibid., p. 357 ('He had even a contempt of St Benedict's Rule as fit only for tiros and weaklings, and his desire was to revert to the severer rules of Basil and Pachomius.'); Shmitz, *Ordre* (cited n. 22 above), I: 108–9.

114. See Schroll, *Ben. Monasticism*, pp. 114–15, 118 and 156–57 (on liturgical additions), and Mundò's comments during discussion of Schmitz's paper (cited n. 109), in *Monachesimo*, pp. 543–46 (on the eating place of the abbot, monastic prisons, etc.).

115. See Hallinger's own résumé, seven years after the appearance of *Gorze-Kluny*, in *Monachesimo*, pp. 257–61. There are useful surveys of the issues raised by Hallinger, with some reservations, by Theodor Schieffer, 'Cluniazensische oder Gorzische Reformbewe-gung?' *Archiv für mittelrheinische Kirchengeschichte*, 4 (1952): 24–44, and by Hubert Dauphin, 'Monastic Reforms from the Tenth Century to the Twelfth', *Downside Review*, 70 (1952): 62–74. The sharpest disagreements with Hallinger have been expressed by Gerd Tellen-bach and his pupils in *Neue Forschungen über Cluny und die Cluniacenser* (Freiburg-im-Br., 1959). In the preface to this volume (p. 6) Tellenbach said, 'The question is whether the pendulum in the history of learning has not now swung too far and whether in place of too great unities, as previously, the divisions are being seen too sharply.'

116. See, for instance, the works of Schieffer's students: Josef Semmler, *Die Klosterreform von Siegburg* (Bonn, 1959), and Hermann Jakobs, *Die Hirsauer: ihre Ausbreitung und Rechtsstellung im Zeitalter des Investiturstreits* (Cologne, 1961).

117. Hilpisch, in *SMGBOZ*, 68: 83; cf. Kassius Hallinger, 'Le climat spirituel des premiers temps de Cluny', *Rev. Mab.*, 46 (1956): 117-40 (a revised version of part II of an article first published in the *Deutsches Archiv*, 10).

118. Jean Leclercq, 'Cluny fut-il ennemi de la culture?', *Rev. Mab.*, 47 (1957):172-82 and, most recently, 'Pour une histoire de la vie à Cluny', *Rev. d'hist. ecc.*, 57 (1962): 385-408.

119. Cf. Ursmer Berlière, *L'ordre monastique des origines au XIIe siècle*, 3rd ed. (Maredsous, 1924), p. 218 ('L' "ordre" clunisien offrait un reflect de la féodalité.'), Wollasch and Mager in *Neue Forschungen*, and Ernst Werner, *Die gesellschaftlichen Grundlagen der Klosterreform im 11. Jahrhundert* (Berlin, 1953), who stressed the alliance of Cluny with the feudal aristocracy and its opposition to the anti-feudal heresies of the eleventh century. (See also the refutation by Kassius Hallinger, and rebuttal by Ernst Werner, in *Monachesimo*, pp. 272-89 and 474-78.

120. In addition to Kassius Hallinger, who considered Cluniac exemption to be anti-feudal as well as anti-episcopal, see J.-F. Lemarignier, 'Hiérarchie monastique et hiérarchie féodale', *Revue historique de droit français et étranger*, 4th S., 31 (1953): 171-74 and 'Structures monastiques et structures politiques dans la France de la fin du Xe et des debuts du XIe siècle', in *Monachesimo*, pp. 357-400, esp. 393-94, where he argued that the monastic hierarchy had nothing to do with, and was indeed opposed to, the feudal hierarchy, and Hartmut Hoffman, 'Von Cluny zum Investiturstreit', *Archiv für Kulturgeschichte*, 45 (1963): 165-69.

121. This point of view is still held, for instance, by Eugen Rosenstock-Huessy, *The Driving Power of Western Civilization: The Christian Revolution of the Middle Ages* (Boston, 1950), pp. 64 ff.: 'The first revolution of the Christian era began in the loneliness of a monk's cell and a monk's heart . . . . Gregory fused the functions of Cluny and of the Apostolic Majesty . . . .' (p. 82).

122. Gerd Tellenbach, *Church* (cited n. 14 above), pp. 82-85 (and esp. R. F. Bennett's Appendix V on pp. 186-92) and 'Zum Wesen der Cluniacenser', *Saeculum*, 9 (1958): 370-78, where he summed up his previous points in the light of subsequent research.

123. Tellenbach, *Church*, p. 189.

124. Cf. Norman Cantor, 'The Crisis of Western Monasticism, 1050-1130', *American Historical Review*, 66 (1960): 47-67, who said that Cluny was 'inflexibly dedicated to the preservation of the prevailing system' (p. 57) and that 'the older view . . . that the Cluniac movement directly inspired the Gregorian reform was not only naïve but almost the complete opposite of the truth' (p. 61).

125. This important point was clearly made by Alfred Cauchie, *La querelle des investitures dans les diocèses de Liège et de Cambrai* (Louvain, 1890-91), 1: 18-62, and in several recent works (such as those of Josef Semmler), which show that many anti-Gregorians favoured monastic reform and that the attitude of an individual monastery in the Investiture Controversy often depended upon its relations with the local ecclesiastical and secular authorities.

126. The most recent discussion, citing Borino's articles, is by Alberic Stacpoole, 'Hildebrand, Cluny and the Papacy', *Downside Review*, 81 (1963): 142-64 and 254-72.

127. See the works cited n. 120 above, and Kassius Hallinger, *Gorze-Kluny*, pp. 582 and 584, where he said that Cluny's anti-feudal attitude (although essentially monastic in conception) helped prepare the way for Gregory VII; Cinzio Violante, 'Il monachesimo cluniacense di fronte al mondo politico ed ecclesiastico (Secoli X e XI)' *Spiritualità cluniacense* (Convegni del Centro di studi sulla spiritualità medievale, 3; Todi, 1960), pp. 155-242; Theodor Schieffer, in *Archiv f. mittelrheinische Kirchengeschichte*, 4: 35-38, and 'Cluny

et la querelle des Investitures', *Revue historique*, 225 (1961): 47–72; and Hartmut Hoffman, in *Archiv f. Kulturgeschichte*, 45: 165–209. Cf. also the interesting discussion of Lemari-gnier's article in *Monachesimo*, pp. 522–43, and Tellenbach, in *Saeculum*, 9: 370–78, and in *Neue Forschungen*, pp. 3–16 (esp. 14–16). Tellenbach argued that Cluny, though not perhaps opposed to ecclesiastical reform, followed the lead of the papacy in this respect in the eleventh century (cf. Mager's article in *Neue Forschungen*). But he admitted that Cluniac stress on the sacraments and well-organized Christian life may have helped prepare the way for the Investiture Controversy (*Saeculum*, 9: 376–77).

128. For two general studies, very different in point of view, of this crisis of cenobitism (a term which appears to have been used first by G. Morin, in *Rev. bén.*, 40 [1928]: 99–115), see Jean Leclercq, 'La crise du monachisme aux XIᵉ et XIIᵉ siècles', *Bulletino dell'Istituto storico italiano per il Medio Evo*, 70 (1958): 19–41, and the article by Cantor cited n. 124 above.

129. These interpretations, which all stress a difference in spirit between Cluny and Cîteaux, are found in the works of Berlière, Butler, Coulton, Schmitz, Bishop, Dekkers, and Knowles.

130. Leclercq, in *Bull. dell'Istituto storico it.*, 70: 24–25.

131. Cantor, in *American Hist. Rev.*, 66: 65.

132. Hallinger, *Gorze-Kluny*, pp. 419–22: 'Die oben gezeichneten "psychologischen" Widerstände gegen Kluny wollen letztlich als Ausdruck darunterliegender *sachlicher* Spannungen verstanden werden' (p. 422).

133. Suitbert Gammersbach, 'Das Abtsbild in Cluny und bei Bernhard von Clair-vaux', *Cîteaux in de Nederlanden*, 7 (1956): 85–101.

134. See n. 119 above.

135. Herbert Grundmann, *Religiöse Bewegungen im Mittelalter* (Historische Studien, 267; Berlin, 1935; new ed. with additions, Hildesheim, 1961), pp. 29–38, and 'Eresie e nuovi ordini religiosi nel secolo XII', *Relazioni del X Congresso internazionale di scienze storiche*, III: *Storia del Medioevo* (Bibliotheca storica Sansoni, N.S., 24; Florence, 1955), p. 396.

136. Cited by Alexis Presse, 'Saint Étienne Harding', *Coll. OCR*, 1 (1934–35): 27 and Séraphin Lenssen, 'Saint Robert: Fondateur de Cîteaux', *Coll. OCR*, 4 (1937–38): 170, n. 2, who also cited Henriquez's comparison of Robert to Abraham (faith), Alberic to Isaac (victim), and Stephen to Jacob (fecundity). An impartial account of the roles of these three is given by J.-M. Canivez, in *Dictionnaire d'histoire et de géographie ecclésiastiques*, 12 (1953), cols. 853–55.

137. Séraphin Lenssen, 'Saint Robert', *Coll. OCR*, 4: 2–16, 81–96, 161–77, 241–53 (also separately, Westmalle, 1937), and J.-A. Lefèvre, 'S. Robert de Molesme dans l'opinion monastique du XIIᵉ et du XIIIᵉ siècle', *Analecta Bollandiana*, 74 (1956): 50–83, who concluded that Robert was 'le vrai chef de la réforme spirituelle qui vient de se concréter dans la fondation de Cîteaux (p. 83).

138. See esp. J. Othon [Ducourneau], 'Les origines cisterciennes', *Rev. Mab.*, 23 (1933): 153–63, who called Alberic 'Le véritable fondateur de l'ordre cistercien' (p. 162). For Séraphin Lenssen, in *Coll. OCR*, 4: 95–96, Alberic contributed persévérance but not initiative.

139. Roger Duvernay, 'Cîteaux, Vallombreuse et Étienne Harding', *Anal. SOC*, 8 (1952): 379–495, who argued that Cîteaux was the end of a development which began at Vallombrosa and that Stephen Harding visited Vallombrosa on his trip to Rome in 1080/90. For other opinions of Stephen, see the article by Presse cited n. 136 above and J. B. Van Damme, 'Saint Étienne Harding mieux connu', *Cîteaux*, 14 (1963): 307–13. Ducourneau, in *Rev. Mab.*, 23 (1933): 163–69, believed that under Stephen Harding

Cîteaux became increasingly ascetic and rigorous. For many Cistercian historians Stephen played the role of Brother Elias in Franciscan history.

140. See the bibliography and most recent survey of the issue by Polykarp Zakar, 'Die Anfänge des Zisterzienserordens: Kurze Bemerkungen zu den Studien der letzten zehn Jahre', *Anal. SOC*, 20 (1964): 103–38 and the reply by J. B. Van Damme, 'Autour des origines cisterciennes: Quelques à-propos', *Anal. SOC*, 21 (1965): 128–37; also the account by David Knowles, 'The Primitive Cistercian Documents', in *Hist. Enterprises* (cited n. 1 above), pp. 197–222.

141. See the pre-Lefèvre survey, with references, by Ernst Werner, 'Neue Texte und Forschungen zur Charta Caritatis', *Forschungen und Fortschritte*, 29 (1955): 25–29, who stressed that the *Carta caritatis* is a document second only to the Rule of St. Benedict in importance in the history of Western monasticism.

142. See in particular Jean Lefèvre and Bernard Lucet, 'Les codifications cisterciennes aux XIIᵉ et XIIIᵉ siècles d'après les traditions manuscrits', *Anal. SOC*, 15 (1959): 3–22 and J. B. Van Damme, 'Formation de la constitution cistercienne', *Studia monastica*, 4 (1962): 111–37 and 'La constitution cistercienne de 1165', *Anal. SOC*, 19 (1963): 51–104. For later developments see the important work by Jean-Berthold Mahn, *L'ordre cistercien et son gouvernement des origines au milieu du XIIIᵉ siècle (1098–1265)* (Bibliothèque des Écoles françaises d'Athènes et de Rome, 161; Paris, 1945). Mahn's untimely death in 1944 was a great loss to the study of monastic history.

143. Bruno Griesser, 'Die "Ecclesiastica officia Cisterciensis ordinis" des cod. 1711 von Trient', *Anal. SOC*, 12 (1956): 153–288, who remarked in his commentary on the close resemblance to Cluniac customs (pp. 171, 174); Bruno Schneider, 'Cîteaux und die benediktinische Tradition', *Anal. SOC*, 16 (1960): 169–254 and 17 (1961): 73–114, who showed that the majority of Cistercian usages derived from Cluny (see esp. 17: 97–98).

144. See the works cited in nn. 136 and 138 above. For a characteristic statement of the earlier view, which saw Cîteaux as a reaction to Cluny and the lax standards of contemporary monasticism, see Ursmer Berlière, 'Les origines de Cîteaux et l'ordre bénédictine au XIIᵉ siècle', *Rev. d'hist. ecc.*, 2 (1901): 264, 267.

145. The attitudes of these writers are far from identical. For J.-M. Canivez see n. 136 above, and for J.-A. Lefèvre see the article cited n. 137 above and 'Que savons-nous du Cîteaux primitif?', *Rev. d'hist. ecc.*, 51 (1956): 5–41 (esp. 20, n. 1, on Ducourneau). M.-Anselme Dimier, 'Les concepts de moine et de vie monastique chez les premiers Cisterciens', *Studia monastica*, 1 (1959): 399–418, maintained that the Cistercians resembled other movements of monastic reform in their basic purpose, but not in their radical character or their later success. J. B. Van Damme, in *Studia monastica*, 4 (1962): 111–16 (see 116, n. 2, on Presse, Ducourneau, Laurent, and Lenssen), considered Cîteaux the natural outcome of the monastic work of Benedict of Aniane. Cf. Edith Pásztor, 'Le origini dell'crdine cisterciense e la riforma monastica', *Anal. SOC*, 21 (1965): 112–27.

146. For Herbert Grundmann, see n. 135 above; M.-D. Chenu, 'Moines, clercs, laïcs au carrefour de la vie évangélique', *Rev. d'hist. ecc.*, 49 (1954): 59–89, reprinted with other articles in *La théologie au douzième siècle* (Études de philosophie médiévale, 45; Paris, 1957); Étienne Delaruelle, 'La pietà popolare nel secolo XI', in *Relazioni* (cited n. 135 above), pp. 309–32 (and other articles by Delaruelle in the same volume).

147. See n. 50 above and the works by McDonnell, Dereine, Grundmann, and Chenu cited in nn. 53, 92, 135, and 146.

148. Historically, this view may not be altogether incorrect. See A. D. Nock, *Conversion* (Oxford, 1933), pp. 187–88: 'It is not likely that the Apostles in Jerusalem had a missionary aim in the full sense.' They were driven by opposition into a more active proselytizing role.

149. On the highly disputed question of the attitude of regular canons towards pastoral work, see my work *Monastic Tithes from their Origins to the Twelfth Century* (Cambridge Studies in Medieval Life and Thought, N.S., 10; Cambridge, 1964), pp. 154–57, with references to previous literature.

150. See M.-D. Chenu, in *Rev. d'hist. ecc.*, 49 (1954): 69–80, and M.-H. Vicaire, *Imitation*, pp. 59 ff., on this change in the ideal of the *vita apostolica*.

151. Giovanni Miccoli, 'Ecclesiae primitivae forma', *Studi medievali*, 3rd S., 1 (1960): 470–98, reprinted with additions in his *Chiesa Gregoriana* (Storici antichi e moderni, N.S., 17; Florence, 1966), pp. 225–99.

152. Ernst Werner, *Pauperes Christi* (Leipzig, 1956).

153. Matthäus Bernards, 'Nudus nudum Christum sequi', *Wissenschaft und Weisheit*, 14 (1951): 148–51, and Antin, in *Théologie*, I (cited n. 44 above), p. 195, n. 24.

154. On the beginnings of this shift, see Bernhard Schmeidler, 'Anti-asketische Äusser-ungen aus Deutschland im 11. und beginnenden 12. Jahrhundert', *Kultur und Universal-geschichte (Festschrift Walter Goetz)* (Leipzig–Berlin, 1927), pp. 35–52, who remarked on the great rarity in the eleventh century of any statement of the superiority of the secular clergy (bishops and priests) over monks (p. 49).

155. Cf. Philibert Schmitz, *Ordre* (cited n. 22 above), 3: 3–11.

II

REFORMATIO*

THE TITLE *Reformatio* was chosen for the third seminar in the Roman Catholic-Protestant Colloquium not, as might be thought, in order to emphasize the narrow and scholarly nature of the approach but rather to broaden the subject of the seminar so as to include not only the sixteenth-century Protestant Reformation, with which the English term "reform" is often associated, but also the whole background and tradition of reform in the medieval Church. The two papers presented to the seminar by Prof. Ladner and Prof. Schmidt, which are printed elsewhere in this volume, were concerned with the idea and reality of reform from the eleventh to the fifteenth century and showed clearly that medieval *reformatio* was important in its own right and not simply as the background of the Protestant Reformation. The discussion among the members of the seminar ranged yet more broadly. It concentrated in the period of the Middle Ages and Reformation, down to the Council of Trent, but it also touched on the issue of reform in the early and in the contemporary Church.

It is impossible to condense into a few pages all the points that were raised during the discussion, which lasted many hours during the three mornings of the Colloquium and included over a hundred contributions by almost thirty participants in the seminar. Even a simple transcript would

* This paper has been read by the Rt. Rev. J. Joseph Ryan, a Professor at St. John's Seminary, Brighton, Massachusetts, who made certain suggestions which were incorporated into the text but who otherwise stated that in his judgment the report is faithful to the spirit and tenor of the discussions, "as well as to the wide-ranging substance of its hundred-odd interventions." The Harvard graduate students who took notes on the proceedings to assist the writer were E. David Willis and David B. Evans. A special word of gratitude is due them for their assistance.

give a false tone of finality to opinions uttered in a spirit of give and take or of inquiry. Many remarks were made on the spur of the moment, without the opportunity to consult works of reference, and might have been corrected or revised after further investigation and consideration. In the following account, therefore, I have not tried to reproduce the discussion as it took place but to examine the methods by which the problem was studied and to summarize the principal points that emerged during the discussion. I cannot speak of any conclusions, because the seminar attempted only to discuss the issues arising from the papers and the general problem of *reformatio* and not to arrive at any definite agreement. The views expressed here of any general agreement are based upon my subjective impressions of the sense of the meeting; but I shall try not to overgeneralize and to indicate both individual opinions and areas of disagreement.

Three types or levels of approach to the problem of *reformatio* were apparent in the discussion. They often overlapped and were not always clearly formulated by the participants, but they represent three distinct aspects of the question, on different levels of abstraction and concreteness. The first, and most abstract, level was methodological and was concerned with the meaning of the term *reformatio* and the nature of reform. The second level was also theoretical, but more historical: the causes of the need for reform and the methods of reform, as seen by contemporaries. The third level was specifically historical and dealt with the history of reform: how the church and society have been reformed and who were the reformers. The distinction between these aspects is in some respects artificial, but they are a useful basis for studying and summarizing the discussion.

It was clear from the beginning that the term "reform" is used in very different meanings by theologians, ecclesiolo-

gists, historians, and laymen. Most simply, the difference
can be seen in the terms "reform" and "re-form," with a
hyphen, which are distinguished in the dictionaries and
carry very different implications. "Reform" may be said to
look backward to a perfect form or state that has been
changed or corrupted but may hopefully be restored. "Reform," on the other hand, is a forward-looking term and implies a change from one form into a new and different one.
"Reform" without the hyphen is thus associated with "restoration," "renewal," "rejuvenation," and "rebirth," whereas
"re-form" is more like "re-shape" and "innovate," which has
distinctly pejorative implications for many Roman Catholic, Orthodox, and Protestant Christians.

The distinction between backward-looking and forward-
looking reform was never clearly drawn in the discussion,
but it is very important in order to understand both the role
of *reformatio* in the history of the Church and some of the
differences between the members of the seminar. The backward-looking reform is associated with the incarnational
view of the institutional Church as the body of Christ. It is
an ideal form, and any change or falling away, in the Augustinian sense, is evil. Reform is thus the work of recovering
and restoring the perfect form that has been lost. Forward-
looking reform is entirely different. It is associated with an
eschatological view of the Church, which stresses its final
end rather than its original form and looks to the future
rather than to the past. This type of reform accepts the
necessity and desirability of change and even of innovation
and resembles in many respects the modern concepts of
development and adjustment. Both of these views of *reformatio* are strongly historical, but in different ways. One
stresses a point in the past, where the Church should strive
to remain or to return to; the other stresses changing circumstances in the present and the future, in accordance
with which the Church must change.

The importance of this changing historical background was frequently emphasized during the discussion, but its importance was variously assessed by members of the seminar. For those who assumed that reform looks backward, the historical change involved the loss of the original perfection, and they searched both for the causes of corruption and the ways of restoration. This view of reform often makes use of the naturalistic and biological metaphors of decay and old-age. Reform is then seen as a sort of rejuvenation. The corruption may also be seen as the result of specific human weaknesses, above all of pride, concupiscence, and ignorance. In either case it involves a definite break with the past. For other members of the seminar it was clear that *reformatio* need not involve the decay or corruption of an originally perfect form. At most, they accepted the inevitable imperfection of all human institutions, which men must strive at all times to improve. Reform for them was a process of adjustment to changing conditions, looking toward the final end. They emphasized that the Word of God is active in the Church, not only in the past but also in the present, re-forming in the true sense of the term. Thus, eschatology, as one member put it, transmutes the idea of reform as restoration into the idea of reform as innovation.

Besides this distinction of looking backward or forward, there are methodological distinctions in the views of the nature and the object of reform. Philosophically and theologically, "form" is unchanging, the inner determining principle of a thing, as distinct from its externals and accidents; and in this sense to reform means to change fundamentally the nature of a thing. For backward-looking reformers, this form is the ideal state in which the Church and Christian society were created, the Platonic idea, which they must try to recover. For eschatological, forward-looking reformers, although the innermost form is unchanging, it is linked to potentiality, in Aristotelian terms, and there is constant development and change. Both types of reformer have to distinguish, although not always consciously, between the substance and the accidents, the internals and the externals, of the object of reform. They must determine the nature of the form, the unchanging inner substance which they seek to restore or to uncover; and in practical terms they must decide what can and what cannot be reformed.

The nature of any reform will therefore depend both on its direction and on its object. Dogmas, institutions, and individual persons can all be the object of reform, but in different ways, and historians must distinguish between dogmatic, institutional, and, in individuals, moral and intellectual reforms. There was some lively discussion in the seminar over the possibility of dogmatic reform; and the distinction between essentials and externals, especially wording, was sharply drawn. Reformulation was here used in a new sense, suggesting a change in the wording but not in the essence of a dogma. There was agreement among the Roman Catholic members of the seminar that the inner truth of a dogma cannot be changed, but some were of the opinion that its verbal expression, as Cardinal Bea suggested in his third lecture, might be reformulated. The dogma might thus be set, according to one theologian, in a broader doctrinal context, and its inner truth more clearly brought out.

There was more general agreement on the possibility of institutional reform, but not on its scope. Change in the Church, one participant maintained, must involve change in the world, and true reform must be of the kingdom of God. Here again the distinction between the inner form and the outer accidents of both ecclesiastical and secular institutions is essential. One member of the seminar suggested that reform in the Church is basically a manifestation of its deepest nature, as if it were (the simile is mine, not his) an onion, off of which the reformers peeled the outer layers as they became outmoded, eventually to reveal its inner heart. The form may thus appear to change, but it has always been there. Most institutional reform, however, is concerned not with internals but with externals, above all with the correction of abuses.

Unlike dogmatic and much institutional reform, personal reform, both moral and intellectual, must be concerned with essentials. The Christian in baptism becomes a new man in the deepest sense of the term and is re-formed in Christ, although his external appearance may remain unchanged.

It was clear from the discussion in the seminar that these methodological distinctions were necessary in order to understand the significance of *reformatio*, both in the past and in the present, because it means different things and works in different ways. It can be directed backward or forward, be concerned with essentials or externals, and have as its object dogmas, institutions, or persons. The confusion of these various directions and types of reform—so as to maintain that a dogma can be reformed in the same way as an individual—can lead only to misunderstanding.

The theory of reform, historically considered, has tended to concentrate on the problems of how the ideal form of the early Church has been changed and corrupted and on how it should be reformed. This question was studied by Dr. Schmidt in his paper "Who Reforms the Church?"; he was concerned with the answers given to this question by Occam, Wyclif, Hus, and other theorists, and by men of action in the late Middle Ages and Reformation period. The discussion, in particular, brought out the connection of medieval nominalism with ideas on the nature of the Church and reform and how the pressing problems of the Church at that time stimulated reforming theory.

Most members of the seminar clearly thought of reform as the recovery of an ideal form, and various ways were

II

336

suggested in which this form had been lost. Some saw it, as mentioned above, as a natural process of aging and decay; others, as the result of human weaknesses, above all of pride, which is at the same time the principal cause of corruption and the principal obstacle to reform. To counteract this continual process of falling away, one member suggested, the Church has ordinary as well as extraordinary methods of reform. The sacramental system, for instance, is a constant reform which sustains individual Christians and repairs their corruption. The diocesan bishop is likewise responsible for the constant institutional reform of his diocese. More general and deep-seated troubles, however, must be the object of occasional and extraordinary *reformatio.*

The author of all reform, theologically speaking, is God himself, and it is often said that the Church, as a divine institution, reforms itself. The triune nature of God is here associated with some of the methodological distinctions mentioned above, since as three Persons God is active in the Church in different ways. The idea of the creation of the Church in the image of Christ naturally stresses the backward-looking type of reform, seeking to restore the lost ideal. As the Holy Spirit, however, God is active in the Church and the world today, and eschatological reformers rely heavily on the doctrine of the Holy Spirit and of his reforming activity in individuals and institutions.

God as a reformer acts through as well as in created institutions and individuals, and there was considerable discussion in the seminar over the *locus* of reforming activity in the Christian community. The relative importance of *charisma* and *auctoritas* came up on each day of the seminar, and there was a strong tendency to contrast reform and authority and to assume that reform always starts with charismatic individuals outside the hierarchy, although it may be approved and supported by the ecclesiastical authorities. One member of the seminar mentioned, however, that the reforming role of the small group, both within and outside the Church, should not be lost sight of in this polarization of charismatic individuals and the authoritative hierarchy.

Individual reformers might be either members of the lower clergy, laymen, or even schismatics and heretics who are outside the official Church. Their prime characteristic is that they are unofficial and unexpected, and the character of their reforms cannot be predicted. The roles of teachers, lawyers, and laymen were especially discussed. One member of the seminar stressed that reform must start with education and that in the late Middle Ages, especially in the conciliar period, the universities and professors took a prominent part in the movements for reform. Another discussed the canon lawyers, who were often pictured as obstacles to reform but who in fact played an important part in the development of institutions and the application of the working of Christ in the Church. Particular interest was shown in the distinction and respective roles of the clerical and lay elements in the Church. Up until the eleventh and twelfth centuries, for instance, monks were usually regarded as neither clerics nor laymen but as a distinctive third order of society, and the strict modern distinction of clerical and lay is a product of the Investiture Contest. A member of the seminar pointed out that in the early Church the laity participated in what would now be considered clerical decisions and that the spiritual authority of inspired laymen only gradually became institutionalized in the office of the bishop and, finally, in the pope. The reforming activity of nonclerical monks and laymen, and of schismatics and heretics, is thus itself part of the historical development of the Church.

The question of the motives of these individual, or unofficial, reformers was also raised, but it was not discussed at length. Schismatics and heretics are obviously moved by some deep spiritual discontent to seek a reformation of both institutions and individuals, and sometimes also of dogmas. One speaker mentioned the possibility of exterior pressures and subconscious motivations. A fundamentally orthodox reformer, whose motives are primarily moral, may be driven into an extreme position by official opposition and even seek refuge in more basic reforms, affecting the substance of existing institutions, than he originally had in mind. Power factors may also play a part, and it was pointed out that shifts in the *locus* of power (as from the lay rulers to the hierarchy, and from the bishops to the pope in the eleventh century) may affect the movements of reform. Other members of the seminar disagreed. They accepted that the element of power could not be disregarded in either secular or ecclesiastical institutions, and the desire for power might be in some cases legitimate, but they felt that movements of reform were motivated basically by moral rather than by power factors.

The role of the hierarchy in reform, though generally considered less important than that of charismatic individuals and groups, was not entirely neglected. Authority rarely initiates reform, but it must judge the validity of individual reformers and movements of reform. The Roman Catholic members of the seminar in particular agreed that the Church must decide the nature of legitimate reform and that, for instance, in order to be legitimate, any institutional reformer must accept the validity of visible ecclesiastical institutions.

This point raised the important question of the nature and *locus* of final authority within the Church, which was called by one participant the principal area of disagreement between Roman Catholic, Orthodox, and Protestant Christians. During the conciliar period, as Dr. Schmidt brought out in his paper, even some Roman Catholics opposed papal absolutism and sought a broader basis for final authority in the Church in the totality of believers expressed through a council. They emphasized the role of the pope as the servant of the servants of God, which, though nothing new, had been in abeyance during the twelfth and thirteenth centuries, and they returned to the ministrative rather than dominative aspects of the papal position. Besides the papal and conciliar theories, the spiritual authority of pious monks and laymen, particularly of secular rulers, was recognized in various Christian traditions, and the *locus* of authority to validate reform is not therefore as clear as it might be. Institutional reform is obviously the particular province of the hierarchy; dogmatic reform (or reformulation), of the theologians; moral reform, of the ministers and preachers; and intellectual reform, of the teachers. These differing roles and authorities have been recognized to some extent in certain Protestant churches, but they have never been clearly distinguished in theory or in practice and have contributed to the confusion of many reforming movements.

The discussion of the theory of reform thus overlapped and interlocked with the study of specific reformers and movements of reform from the eleventh to the sixteenth centuries. In the first paper presented to the seminar Dr. Gerhart Ladner examined the reforms associated with the names of Pope Gregory VII (Hildebrand) and Francis of Assisi. He emphasized that the Gregorian reform, of which the Investiture Controversy was a central aspect, was the first general institutional reform, "in head and members," as it was later called, in the history of the Western Church. He associated it with the monastic and evangelical movements of the eleventh and twelfth centuries, out of which the Franciscan reform grew during the pontificate of Innocent III. Both from his paper and from the discussion it was clear that Gregory and Francis are central and characteristic figures, although in different ways, in the *reformatio* of the Middle Ages.

Gregory emerged primarily as an institutional reformer, in the methodological terms outlined above, but it is not certain whether he was principally concerned with the reform of externals and the correction of abuses or with a real change in the structure of the Church, above all by the exclusion of lay elements. According to some members of the seminar, Gregory's reform marked the first emergence of a real ecclesiastical party and a split of the Church into two branches, one clerical, which now included the monks, and the other lay, the *congregatio fidelium*. This view was apparently too extreme for other participants, who argued that Gregory was not trying to exclude all lay participation in ecclesiastical affairs but only the quasi-clerical functions of secular rulers, especially their control over ecclesiastical appointments. They pointed out that Gregory regarded himself not as an innovator but as a restorer and renewer and that he had a deep respect for canon law. Whatever his view of himself, however, it was pointed out that in practical terms Gregory introduced some fundamental changes into the structure of the Church and laid the basis for later medieval hierarchism.

In one area at least it was agreed that Gregory was an innovator. That was his relations with and concern for the East, which was discussed by several participants. Gregory's letters to the eastern emperors were said to have prefigured the crusades. At the same time his reforms in the West initiated a new period of Greek-Latin relations. They were misunderstood by the Greeks, it was said, whose image of the Latin Church was dominated by the corruption of the ninth and tenth centuries and for whom the Gregorian reform led the Latin Church further from, rather than nearer to, reunion. The Greek sense of continuity contributed to their view of the reforms as innovations, or changes away from the ancient forms, and they distrusted the tendency toward papal absolutism. The Latin theologians at the same time were suspicious of the Greek theological traditions.

Francis of Assisi was a different type of reformer from Gregory VII. He summed up the strivings toward repentance and poverty of the spiritual movements of the twelfth century, which sometimes led into heresy, and emerged with the most powerful and attractive movement of personal moral reform of the entire Middle Ages. His predominantly moral rather than institutional concern may account, according to one participant, for the fact that Francis is one of the very few Western medieval saints who is honored in the East. For the student of medieval *reformatio*, Francis is the supreme example of the charismatic individual reformer whose reform springs from outside the hierarchy, and almost from outside the institutional Church. Yet the history of his reform is the best corrective for too sharp a separation of *auctoritas* and *charisma*, because Francis himself, unlike many contemporary reformers, always respected authority and the hierarchy, above all in the person of Innocent III, who approved and supported the Franciscan reform. The institutional Church of the thirteenth century, thus, came to include, though admittedly in a modified form, many of the spiritual ideals which in the twelfth century tended to develop outside the Church. Many of the most effective movements of reform, indeed, have depended on the cooperation of the authoritative and charismatic factors and cannot be described as coming exclusively either from inside or from outside the hierarchy.

One of the central topics on this level of historical discussion was Luther and the Protestant reformers and their relation to the medieval tradition of *reformatio*. There were, of course, considerable differences of opinion among the members of the seminar, but it was clear that Luther marked a new departure in several respects. In at least one, his rejection of hierarchism, he actually reacted against one of the principal objects of some earlier reformers. Above all, however, several participants emphasized that Luther was concerned less with institutional and moral reform, as were the medieval reformers, some of whom had also rejected hierarchism, than with doctrinal reform. In itself, it was said, Luther's desire for reform was medieval, but his type and methods of reform were far from traditional. The distinction between the Gospel and the law, and between faith and morals, underlay his entire reform, and although this in itself was not new, it acquired in his teachings a new dynamic force which emphasized the helplessness of the individual before the Divine. The result was a reformation that affected the very essence of the Church and its teachings.

The seminar did not continue its discussions into the problems of contemporary *reformatio*, but a few points were made which may be summarized here by way of conclusion. The problem of reform is at the heart of the ecumenical movement, and many of the remarks made in the seminar have a direct bearing on the contemporary Christian dilemma. Above all, Christians, today, must distinguish clearly between essentials and externals and decide what can and what cannot be changed in existing institutions and dogmas. To this extent, the problem of reformers in the Middle Ages is the problem of reformers today. We too must decide whether to look backward or forward for the essential nature of the Church, and we must learn from the study of the history of reform that reform may come from both outside and inside not only the hierarchy but also the official Church—from unexpected as well as from expected reformers. Thus for many contemporaries Pope John XXIII was seen as embodying the perfect combination of *charisma* and *auctoritas*, who brought to the highest position of ecclesiastical authority a personal zeal and individual vision. A true contemporary reformation cannot be concerned simply with the abolition of abuses. It must indeed distinguish and preserve the essential truths of the Christian revelation and tradition, but on this basis it must be ready to face with new answers the present problems of Christendom. It must take account, as one speaker emphasized, of both old and new elements and face firmly, for instance, the continued separation from the Jewish people, who were first elected by God and from whom he has never withdrawn his electing grace. *Reformatio* today is not simply an undoing of the past, a tearing down of the barriers that have grown up within God's community, essential as this is, but also a creative realization of God's will for his community in the future.

Harvard University

III

Monachisme et pèlerinage au Moyen Age

Le monachisme et le pèlerinage sont deux institutions parmi les plus familières du Moyen Age, et deux des plus incompatibles en apparence puisque l'une insiste sur l'obligation de demeurer au même endroit et que l'autre implique mouvement et voyage[1]. Toutefois elles ont de nombreux points de contact et quelques points communs. De nombreux monastères étaient centres de pèlerinage, ou se développaient autour des tombeaux des saints et le long des routes de pèlerinage. Leurs membres se consacraient à des saints particuliers, développaient leur culte, aidaient les pèlerins et vivaient de leurs dons. Beaucoup de moines et de moniales, malgré leur profession de stabilité et d'obédience, abandonnaient leur monastère pour errer comme des exilés sans demeure, pour visiter les Lieux saints associés à la vie du Christ et des saints, ou pour échapper à la routine et à la discipline de la vie monastique dans leur cloître ; d'autres, même, étaient envoyés en pèlerinage par leurs supérieurs, soit pour expier leurs péchés, soit pour débarrasser le monastère de leur présence. L'objet de cet article sera d'étudier les idéaux opposés du monachisme et du pèlerinage et de voir comment la tension entre eux fut résolue, en théorie et en pratique, aux différentes époques du Moyen Age, en tenant compte de l'aspect changeant des institutions monastiques aussi bien que de la pratique du pèlerinage. Individuellement, des personnalités religieuses n'ont pas répondu de la même façon aux différents idéaux offerts par les institutions de la société dans laquelle elles vivaient, et de nombreux compromis personnels furent possibles, de telle façon qu'il y eut toujours une certaine reconnaissance en pratique, et aussi,

---

1. Cf. Georg SCHREIBER, Mönchtum und Wallfahrt in ihren Beziehungen zur mittelalterlichen Einheitskultur, *Historisches Jahrbuch*, 1935, LV, p. 160-181, qui les considère indépendamment comme éléments unificateurs de la culture médiévale, et aussi Jean LECLERCQ, Mönchtum und Peregrinatio im Frühmittelalter, *Römische Quartalschrift für christliche Altertumskunde und Kirchengeschichte*, 1960, LV, p. 212-225, et Monachisme et pérégrination du ixᵉ au xiiᵉ siècle, *Studia monastica*, 1961, III, p. 33-52, ces deux articles réimprimés, le premier révisé et doté d'une nouvelle introduction, dans *Aux sources de la spiritualité occidentale*, Paris, 1964, p. 40-90 ; nos citations renvoient à cet ouvrage. Sur le pèlerinage en général, voir le livre récent de Jonathan SUMPTION, *Pilgrimage : An Image of Mediaeval Religion*, Londres, 1975.

dans une certaine mesure, en théorie, des caractères complémentaires autant que contradictoires du monachisme et du pèlerinage.

Un moine ou une moniale, vivant seul ou en communauté, était en principe coupé du monde et devait, même en voyage (comme le dit Venantius Fortunatus de l'évêque Albinus d'Angers au vie siècle), être « enfermé pour toujours dans la prison de son propre cœur »[1]. Plus tard dans le Moyen Age, et surtout après l'acceptation générale de la règle bénédictine aux viiie et ixe siècles, cette clôture devait normalement prendre la forme des murs d'un monastère que les religieux n'étaient autorisés à quitter que pour des raisons pressantes et avec la permission de leur supérieur. La règle a des mots sévères au sujet des moines qui vivent dans leur propre bercail, sans supérieur, plutôt que dans celui du Seigneur, et des mots encore plus sévères au sujet des gyrovagues qui sont « toujours errants et jamais stables ». La stabilité en effet était l'un des caractères de base de la vie bénédictine (la vie régulière, comme on l'appelait alors) et quoique les commentateurs aient discuté de sa signification précise, on admettait qu'elle signifiait qu'un moine devait rester toute sa vie au même endroit comme membre de la communauté dans laquelle il avait fait sa profession[2].

Le pèlerinage impliquait aussi un état séparé du monde[3]. Le terme latin *pereger* dont dérive *peregrinatio* vient de *per ager* et se rapporte au voyageur qui va à travers le pays, et par extension à tout étranger voyageant loin de son pays. Il reçut dès les premiers temps une signification spirituelle ; il désigna le pèlerinage ascétique loin du pays *(ex patria)*, que certains Savants appelaient pérégrination ou expatriation, et aussi la pratique plus familière du voyage vers certains lieux saints *(ad loca sancta)*, qui eut plus tard, presque exclusivement, droit au nom de pèlerinage. On concevait souvent la vie humaine comme un pèlerinage à la fois loin de notre séjour éternel et vers lui, et comme un voyage à travers la mer : le monastère passait parfois pour un port ou un refuge contre ses dangers. Saint Augustin et d'autres théologiens appliquaient le concept de pérégrination à la communauté de la foi tout entière progressant dans ce monde vers l'autre monde[4]. Cette conception du chrétien

1. Venantius FORTUNATUS, Vita sancti Albini, 6 (14), in *Opera pedestria*, éd. Bruno KRUSCH, Berlin, 1885, p. 29 (« Monumenta Germaniae historica : Auctores antiquissimi », 4, 2).
2. Voir l'article récent d'Ambrose WATHEN, *Conversatio* and Stability in the Rule of Benedict, *Monastic Studies*, Advent, 1975, XI, p. 1-44, et not. p. 31-32 et 37, où est recensée la récente littérature sur ce sujet.
3. Baudouin de GAIFFIER, Pellegrinaggi e culto dei santi : Réflexions sur le thème du Congrès, *Pellegrinaggi e culto dei santi in Europa fino alla Iª Crociata*, Todi, 1963, p. 12-14 (« Convegni del Centro di studi sulla spiritualità medievale », 4).
4. Sur cette image de la vie comme pèlerinage dans l'Eglise ancienne, voir Bernhard KÖTTING, *Peregrinatio religiosa. Wallfahrten in der Antike und das Pilgerwesen in der alten Kirche*, Münster W., 1950, p. 302-307 (« Forschungen zur Volkskunde », 33-35),

Monachisme et pèlerinage au Moyen Age

comme un voyageur et un étranger était figurée dans l'Ancien Testament
par Abraham, qui avait reçu du Seigneur l'ordre de quitter son pays,
ses parents, la maison de son père et d'aller dans le pays que le Seigneur
lui indiquerait (Genèse 12, 1), et dont saint Paul dit qu'il partit « ne
sachant pas où il allait » et qu'il vécut par la fci « dans la terre promise
comme dans une contrée étrangère » (Hébreux 11, 8.9). Les termes de
peregrinus, advena et *colonus* reviennent fréquemment dans l'Ancien
Testament et ils servirent à la fois à saint Paul et à saint Pierre qui,
dans la première épître, exhorte ses lecteurs à s'abstenir « comme des
étrangers et des pèlerins » des actes charnels (Pierre 1, 2.11). Jésus
lui-même promit semblablement la vie éternelle à ceux qui quitteraient
leur famille et leur pays pour l'amour de Lui (Matthieu 19, 29).

La haute valeur spirituelle attachée à l'état de sans-foyer et d'exilé était
en partie inspirée par un désir primitif de détachement vis-à-vis du
monde et de simplicité, et en partie par une association plus profonde,
que ceux qui font l'étude comparée des religions ont soulignée, entre
le voyage et la conversion religieuse. Ce n'est pas un hasard si tant de
conversions spectaculaires (dont le prototype pour les chrétiens est celle
de saint Paul sur le chemin de Damas) étaient associées à des voyages
au loin qui aidaient à préparer la voie vers un nouveau système de croyance
et vers la voie du salut, grâce à ce que Victor Monod appelait « un appau-
vrissement de la personnalité normale, une moindre résistance de l'organisation psychique »[1].

Pour les Musulmans, le pèlerinage est une aspiration et exprime selon
Burton « le sentiment ressenti par l'homme de n'être qu'un passager sur
la terre, errant vers un monde différent et plus noble »[2]. Par conséquent,
le voyage physique, à la fois *ex patria* et *ad loca sancta*, est plus qu'un
simple acte de piété et de dévotion. Il peut marquer une étape décisive
dans la vie religieuse et le développement d'un individu, comportant en
même temps le renoncement aux soins individuels, un sens du contact
avec des personnes et des événements éloignés et une ouverture à une

et Roland M. Smith, Three Obscure English Proverbs, *Modern Language Notes*, 1950,
LXV, p. 441-447, qui cite des exemples du iiie au xviie siècle ; sur l'image d'un voyage
maritime, voir Hugo Rahner, *Greek Myths and Christian Mystery*, trad. Brian
Battershaw, Londres, 1963, p. 84-86 et 341-353 ; sur l'*ecclesia peregrinans*, voir
Robert T. Marshall, *Studies in the Political and Socio-Religious Terminology of the
De Civitate Dei*, Washington, 1952, p. 27 (« Catholic University of America Patristic
Studies », 86), et Yves-Marie-Joseph Congar, Eglise et Cité de Dieu chez quelques
auteurs cisterciens à l'époque des croisades, en particulier dans le *De peregrinante
civitate Dei* d'Henri d'Albano, *Mélanges offerts à Etienne Gilson*, Toronto-Paris, 1959,
p. 192-194.

1. Victor Monod, Le voyage, le déracinement de l'individu hors du milieu natal
constituent-ils un des éléments déterminants de la conversion religieuse ?, *Revue
d'histoire et de philosophie religieuses*, 1936, XVI, p. 392.

2. Richard Burton, *Personal Narrative of a Pilgrimage to Al Madinah and Meccah*,
Londres, 1924, II, p. 279.

vie nouvelle. Dans beaucoup de religions et de littératures, la voie et le voyage sont les symboles de la vie humaine et de la recherche de Dieu, enseignant à la fois l'insignifiance de l'individu et la possibilité de son accomplissement par la foi et par le travail[1].

En ce sens, l'idéal du pèlerinage n'est pas très différent de celui du monachisme, qui implique aussi une nouvelle vie religieuse, coupée des valeurs et des chemins du siècle[2]. Les premiers moines chrétiens attachaient une grande importance à l'idée — et à la pratique — de l'exil volontaire, ou *xeniteia*, comme on disait en grec. « Quitter son pays, écrit M. Guillaumont dans un article sur le dépaysement comme forme d'ascèse dans le monachisme ancien, est donc la voie d'accès à une vie nouvelle, spirituellement plus haute, embrassée par fidélité à un appel, à une vocation »[3]. La *xeniteia* était associée à l'*hesycheia*, le sens de la quiétude du corps et de l'esprit, considérée comme essentielle à l'état monastique : on ne pouvait y atteindre qu'à une certaine distance de sa propre famille et de ses amis. Par conséquent, beaucoup de moines se déplaçaient plus d'une fois dans leur vie et certains, surtout en Syrie et en Mésopotamie, adoptaient une vie d'errance perpétuelle, souvent critiquée (comme dans la règle bénédictine) pour ses abus, mais qui représentait dans son essence un idéal monastique reconnu, porté à son terme logique. La *xeniteia* était rangée, avec l'humilité, la pauvreté et le silence, parmi les vertus monastiques, surtout lorsqu'elle était recherchée d'une façon intérieure et spiritualisée, au sein d'une communauté et sans mouvement physique ; le terme était parfois employé comme synonyme de la cellule monastique[4].

Aussi longtemps que le monachisme fut compris comme une forme de séparation ou de fuite hors du monde, il eut de nombreux points

---

1. Cf. Antoine GUILLAUMONT, Le dépaysement comme forme d'ascèse, dans le monachisme ancien, *Ecole pratique des Hautes Etudes, V*e *section, Sciences religieuses : Annuaire*, 1968-1969, LXXVI, p. 31-58, not. p. 31 ; Léon ZANDER, Le pèlerinage, *1054-1954. L'Eglise et les églises. Etudes et travaux sur l'unité chrétienne offerts à Dom Lambert Beauduin*, Chevetogne, 1954-1955, II, p. 474-478 (coll. « Irénikon »), qui associe, au plan métaphysique, le pèlerinage à l'état bergsonien d'anamnèse. Voir aussi Victor TURNER, Passages, Margins, and Poverty : Religious Symbols of Communitas, *Worship*, 1972, XLVI, p. 399-400, qui compare les pèlerinages aux périodes de réclusion, pendant lesquelles tous les jours se valent et ont valeur d'éternité, comme moyen de transmettre modèles et valeurs de la société.
2. LECLERCQ, *Sources*, p. 35-40.
3. GUILLAUMONT, *loc. cit.*, in *Annuaire*, LXXVI, p. 34.
4. Hans von CAMPENHAUSEN, *Die asketische Heimatlosigkeit im altkirchlichen und frühmittelalterlichen Mönchtum*, Tübingen, 1930, p. 9-10 (« Sammlung gemeinverständlicher Vorträge und Schriften aus dem Gebiet der Theologie und Religionsgeschichte », 149), GUILLAUMONT, *loc. cit.*, in *Annuaire*, LXXVI, p. 55 ; Peter NAGEL, *Die Motivierung der Askese in der alten Kirche und der Ursprung des Mönchtums*, Berlin, 1966, p. 90-96 (« Texte und Untersuchungen zur Geschichte der altchristlichen Literatur », 95) ; cf. Emil HERMAN, La « stabilitas loci » nel monachismo bizantino, *Orientalia christiana periodica*, 1955, XXI, p. 115-142.

Monachisme et pèlerinage au Moyen Age

communs avec le pèlerinage. Non seulement le moine était un pèlerin, à la fois dans un sens spirituel et aussi, parfois, dans un sens physique, mais le pèlerin était une sorte de moine, du moins un individu consacré qui s'était séparé — temporairement ou pour toujours — de la vie du siècle[1]. « Le pèlerin avance par la voie royale, ne tournant ni à droite ni à gauche... », dit Bernard de Clairvaux, faisant un commentaire sur les étrangers et les pèlerins mentionnés dans la première épître de saint Pierre (2.11). « Il désire ardemment son pays, il lutte pour aller vers son pays »[2]. Bien que Bernard en vienne à ranger le pèlerin à la fois en dessous de l'homme mort et du crucifié qui sont encore plus séparés du monde que lui, il les considère tous trois comme inspirés par un idéal commun. On croyait que la sagesse, de même que la sainteté, s'acquerrait mieux loin du foyer, et Hugues de Saint-Victor, dans le *Didascalicon*, range ces philosophes « pour qui le monde entier est un exil » haut sur l'échelle de la perfection humaine, au-dessus de ceux à qui leur foyer est doux et de ceux pour qui le monde entier est un foyer[3]. Il n'est donc pas surprenant que beaucoup de moines et de moniales se soient trouvés parmi les innombrables pèlerins qui partaient à la fois *ex patria* et *ad loca sancta* pendant le haut Moyen Age. La moniale Egeria — l'exposé qu'elle fit de son voyage vers l'Orient, probablement à la fin du IVe ou au début du Ve siècle, fut l'un des premiers travaux sur le pèlerinage chrétien — faisait de nombreuses références à des moines pèlerins, incluant la foule des moines ou des *aputactitae* de diverses provinces qui venaient à Jérusalem pour la fête de l'Invention de la Croix[4]. En plus de ces pèlerins volontaires, il y en avait d'involontaires, dont les moines et les moniales à qui des pèlerinages pénitentiels étaient imposés en punition de leurs péchés[5]. En pratique, ces divers types de

1. Le pèlerinage était associé à la pauvreté (et *peregrini* aux *pauperes*) dans diverses sources anciennes comme ANTONIN DE PLAISANCE : *Itinerarium*, 27 ; *Versum de Mediolano civitate*, 16 ; cf. *Itineraria et alia geographica*, Turnhout, 1965, p. 143 et 375 (« Corpus Christianorum : Series latina », CLXXV). Sur le concept de monachisme comme séparation du monde, voir Jacques WINANDY, L'idée de fuite du monde dans la tradition monastique, *Le message des moines à notre temps*, Paris, 1958, p. 95-104 ; Jean LECLERCQ, La séparation du monde dans le monachisme au Moyen Age, *La séparation du monde*, Paris, 1971, p. 75-94 ; Gregorio PENCO, Forme ascetiche e pratiche penitenziali nella tradizione monastica, *Bollettino della Deputazione di storia patria per l'Umbria*, 1967, LXIV, 2, p. 342-343.
2. BERNARD DE CLAIRVAUX, In Quadragesima sermo 6 (De peregrino, mortuo et crucifixo), dans *S. Bernardi opera*, éd. J. LECLERCQ et H. ROCHAIS, Rome, 1966, V, p. 377-380.
3. Hugh de SAINT-VICTOR, *Didascalicon*, III, 19, éd. Charles H. BUTTIMER, Washington, 1939, p. 69 (« Catholic University of America Studies in Medieval and Renaissance Latin », 10) ; cf. III, 12, éd. cit., p. 61. Sur la nécessité d'étudier à l'étranger, voir Philippe DELHAYE, L'organisation scolaire au XIIe siècle, *Traditio*, 1947, V, p. 240, qui cite Jean de Salisbury et Pierre Comestor.
4. Itinerarium Egeriae, 49, dans *Itineraria*, p. 90.
5. Cf. Ursmer BERLIÈRE, Les pèlerinages judiciaires au Moyen Age, *Revue bénédictine*, 1890, VII, p. 520-526 ; Etienne VAN CAUWENBERGH, Les pèlerinages expiatoires

III

pèlerinage se recouvraient, sans doute, partiellement, puisque tous les pèlerinages, et non pas seulement ceux qu'entreprenaient les criminels, présentaient un caractère expiatoire ; et beaucoup de ceux qui s'expatriaient par ascèse visitaient les Lieux saints au cours de leur errance dans l'espoir de recevoir le même bénéfice spirituel que les pèlerins qui projetaient de rentrer dans leur foyer. Mais il y avait en principe une distinction importante entre les pèlerins faisant le voyage des Lieux saints, ceux qui expiaient leurs péchés et ceux qui passaient en exil leur vie entière.

Les pèlerinages ascétiques *ex patria* étaient particulièrement populaires chez les moines irlandais et anglo-saxons aux vi[e], viie et viiie siècles[1]. Les *vitae* des saints insulaires font de nombreuses allusions à leur désir de quitter le pays et de pérégriner pour l'amour du Christ. « Que le Seigneur soit notre secours et le pilote de notre navire », déclara saint Brendan à ses compagnons quand le vent se calma, et un moine du nom de Cormac, qu'Adomnan décrit comme un *miles Christi*, partit trois fois à la recherche « d'un ermitage sur l'océan » et « d'un désert parmi les flots »[2]. Certains de ces voyageurs erraient continuellement, d'autres s'installaient, comme Colomban qui se mit en route, d'Irlande vers l'Angleterre, à quarante-deux ans, selon Adomnan, « désireux de pérégriner pour le Christ », et qui vécut pendant plusieurs années en pèlerin dans l'île de Iona où d'autres exilés volontaires s'assemblaient autour de lui. Parmi eux, il y avait à la fois des moines et des laïcs, mais Colomban refusa, un jour, de recevoir deux laïcs qui désiraient faire avec lui un pèlerinage d'un an

et judiciaires dans le droit communal de la Belgique au Moyen Age, Louvain, 1922 (Université de Louvain, « Recueil de travaux publiés par les membres des conférences d'histoire et de philologie », 48) ; Cyrille VOGEL, Le pèlerinage pénitentiel, *Revue des sciences religieuses*, 1964, XXXVIII, p. 113-153 ; Walter DELIUS, *Geschichte der irischen Kirche von ihren Anfängen bis zum 12. Jahrhundert*, Munich-Bâle, 1954, p. 100 : « Die Peregrinatio war nicht nur freiwillige Leistung, sondern ein Mittel der Klosterzucht, eine Form der Busse, die von dem Abt einem Mönch auferlegt wurde, der gegen die Regel verstossen hatte. »

1. DELIUS, *Geschichte*, p. 100-124 ; Kathleen HUGHES, The Changing Theory and Practice of Irish Pilgrimage, *Journal of Ecclesiastical History*, 1960, XI, p. 143-151 ; Karl HAUCK, Von einer spätantiken Randkultur zum karolingischen Europa, *Frühmittelalterliche Studien*, 1967, I, p. 57-68 ; Arnold ANGENENDT, *Monachi peregrini. Studien zu Pirmin und den monastischen Vorstellungen des frühen Mittelalters*, Munich, 1972 (« Münstersche Mittelalter-Schriften », 6), qui montre que saint Firmin venait d'un milieu monastique franco-irlandais.

2. Vita prima Sancti Brendani, 16, in *Vitae Sanctorum Hiberniae*, éd. Charles PLUMMER, Oxford, 1910, I, p. 108, et *Adomnan's Life of Columba*, 1, 6 et 2, 42, éd. A. O. et M. O. ANDERSON, Londres-Edimbourg, 1961, p. 222-224 et 440 ; cf. BÈDE, *Historia ecclesiastica*, éd. Charles PLUMMER, Oxford, 1896, II, p. 170-171, où Plummer dit que ce « trait saillant dans le caractère ascétique très marqué de l'Eglise irlandaise » dura du vi[e] au ixe siècle ; souvent, « les saints irlandais se risquaient sur mer dans une barque étroite, sans rames ni gréement, et confiaient leur destin et la direction de leur voyage aux vents et aux eaux ».

Monachisme et pèlerinage au Moyen Age

mais sans devenir moines[1]. Les œuvres de Bède font de nombreuses références aux pèlerinages entrepris par les moines, à la fois *ex patria* et vers les Lieux saints, tels que les visites de Rome par Benoît Biscop qui, en quittant son pays, dit Bède, mérita la récompense promise par le Christ[2]. Saint Fursa vint en Angleterre « désireux de mener la vie d'un pèlerin *(peregrina vita)* pour l'amour du Seigneur, quel que soit le lieu où il en trouverait l'occasion », et saint Egbert, qui avait fait le vœu, quand il pensait qu'il allait mourir, de ne jamais revenir en Angleterre vint en revanche en Irlande et y vécut en pèlerin « afin de gagner sa place dans le ciel »[3].

Bien que le nombre des insulaires expatriés ait décliné après le VIIIe siècle, quand les conditions eurent changé sur le continent comme chez eux et quand la stabilité fut de plus en plus reconnue comme la norme de la vie monastique[4], la pratique continua. Walafrid Strabon dans sa *vita* de saint Gall disait que chez les Irlandais « l'habitude de partir en pèlerinage était presque devenue une nature » ; on trouve un écho à ces mots au Xe siècle dans la *vita* de saint Dunstan par Osborn, qui, après avoir décrit les pèlerins irlandais à Glastonbury, disait que « cette habitude demeurait toujours vivace chez beaucoup d'Irlandais, parce que, ce que chez les autres la bonne volonté a transformé en coutume, chez eux la coutume l'a transformée en nature »[5]. Que la pratique de la pérégrination ait aussi été connue des moines du continent, cela est montré par une page de la *vita* de saint Anskar par Rimbert ; saint Anskar était moine à Corbie avant de partir en « apôtre du Nord »,

---

1. ADOMNAN, Préface, 1, 13, et 3, 22 (sur Columban) et 1, 32 (sur les deux laïcs) (éd. cit., p. 186, 234, 514 et 270-272), cf. 2, 39 (éd. cit., p. 420-424) pour un exemple de *penitens peregrinus*, qui vint à Columban *ad delenda in perigrinatione peccamina* et qui fut chargé d'une pénitence de sept ans.
2. BÈDE, Homilia in natale Benedicti episcopi, dans *Patrologia latina*, XCIV, p. 224-228 ; cf. *Bede's Ecclesiastical History of the English People*, 1, 23 et 5, 7, éd. B. COLGRAVE et R. A. B. MYNORS, Oxford, 1969, p. 68 et 472 (« Oxford Medieval Texts »), concernant la mission de saint Augustin de Canterbury, considérée comme *peregrinatio*, et les pèlerinages, *ad limina beatorum apostolorum* des rois Caedwalla et Ine, qui voulaient « passer une partie de leur temps sur terre comme des pèlerins dans le voisinage des Lieux saints, en sorte qu'ils puissent être dignes d'un meilleur accueil de la part des saints du Ciel ».
3. BÈDE, *Hist. eccl.*, 3, 19, 3, 27 et 5, 9, éd. COLGRAVE et MYNORS, p. 268, 314 et 474-476.
4. HUGUES, dans *J. Eccl. hist.*, XI, p. 146 ; cf. LECLERCQ, *Sources*, p. 61-64.
5. Walafrid STRABO, Vita Galli, 2, 46, dans *Monumenta Germaniæ historica : Scriptores rerum Merovingicarum*, Hanovre, 1902, IV, p. 336, et OSBORN, Vita sancti Dunstani, 6, dans William STUBBS, *Memorials of Saint Dunstan*, Londres, 1874, p. 74 (« Rolls Series », 63) ; cf. la référence, à l'année 891 dans *The Anglo-Saxon Chronicle*, tr. D. WHITELOCK, D. DOUGLAS, et S. TUCKER, Londres, 1961, p. 53, aux trois Irlandais qui vinrent au roi Alfred « dans un bateau sans rames, depuis l'Irlande, qu'ils avaient quittée secrètement, parce qu'ils souhaitaient être en terre étrangère pour l'amour de Dieu, se souciant peu en quel pays ».

comme on l'appela plus tard, au Danemark et en Suède et il mourut
en 865, bien après l'acceptation quasiment universelle de la règle bénédictine. Rimbert se sentait visiblement obligé de donner une explication
de l'infraction à la stabilité et à l'obédience que commettait son héros
en quittant Corbie, ce qu'il attribua à la nécessité, « de peur que
quelqu'un n'attribue à la légèreté ce que l'homme de Dieu concevait
poussé par la componction et par amour de la pérégrination pour le
salut des âmes »[1]. Cette référence à la notion de *peregrinationis amor
pro salute animarum* pose la question, qui a longtemps intéressé les
savants, des relations entre ces pèlerinages et l'œuvre missionnaire de
conversion. Les moines irlandais et anglo-saxons, dont les errances
couvrirent l'Europe pendant le haut Moyen Age, ont traditionnellement
été considérés, avant tout, comme des missionnaires, mais depuis la
publication du bref mais important ouvrage de von Campenhausen sur
l'exil ascétique dans le monachisme de l'Antiquité et du haut Moyen
Age, leurs voyages — du moins ceux des moines irlandais — ont été
perçus comme d'un caractère essentiellement monastique, et leur œuvre
missionnaire comme un effet plus ou moins accidentel, plutôt que comme
le résultat d'un dessein conscient de convertir les païens. « Le moine
irlandais quittait sa patrie comme un *peregrinus*, disait Delius, non
comme un réfugié, un aventurier ou un pèlerin ; il cherchait plutôt une
nouvelle patrie au gré de son âme. L'intention missionnaire ne prenait
pas de part dans la *peregrinatio* irlandaise, au contraire de l'anglo-
saxonne »[2]. Prêcher la parole de Dieu était un objectif plus important
pour les *peregrini* anglo-saxons tels que Egbert, Willibrord et surtout
Boniface, chez qui les motifs de pérégrination et d'évangélisation sem-
blent avoir été mélés, comme ils l'étaient chez saint Anskar ; Bède insis-
tait sur les nombreux résultats positifs des voyages de Benoît Biscop à
travers la mer[3]. Des savants ont récemment prétendu que l'idéal de
l'œuvre missionnaire n'était pas étranger aux moines irlandais eux-
mêmes[4]. Par conséquent, la question de la part respective exacte des
motifs reste en suspens, et le restera probablement puisque cela reflète

1. RIMBERT, *Vita Anskarii*, 6, éd. Georg WAITZ, Hanovre, 1884, p. 26 (« Scriptores
rerum Germanicarum in usum scholarum », 55).
2. DELIUS, *Geschichte*, p. 100 et 111 ; voir sur Columban, Theodor SCHIEFFER,
Winfrid-Bonifatius und die christliche Grundlegung Europas, Fribourg-en-Br., 1954,
p. 86, et Pierre RICHÉ, *Education et culture dans l'Occident barbare (VIe-VIIIe siècles)*,
Paris, 1962, p. 375 (« Patristica Sorbonensia », 4).
3. BÈDE, *Hist. eccl.*, 5, 10 (éd. COLGRAVE et MYNORS, p. 480), sur Egbert, et Homilia,
dans *Patr. lat.*, XCIV, 226 C - 228 B sur Benoît. Voir, sur Boniface, Stephan HILPISCH,
Bonifatius als Mönch und Missionar, *Sankt Bonifatius. Gedenkgabe zum zwölfhun-
dertsten Todestag*, 2e éd., Fulda, 1954, p. 3-21, not. p. 19-20.
4. HAUCK, dans *Frühmitt. Studien*, I, p. 61-62 ; cf. ANGENENDT, *Monachi*, p. 162-
164.

Monachisme et pèlerinage au Moyen Age

le mélange des motifs individuels conscients ou inconscients, qui continuaient tout au long du Moyen Age de tenter les moines et les moniales pour qu'ils quittent leur pays et leur monastère.

La pérégrination ascétique des moines continua même aux Xe et XIe siècles, bien que la règle bénédictine ait insisté sur la stabilité et qu'elle ait condamné l'errance ; on la trouve particulièrement au XIIe siècle, quand l'appel de l'individualisme spirituel fut fortement ressenti dans les monastères de l'Europe occidentale. La pratique en était encouragée par l'exemple des moines grecs et arméniens, qui venaient en Europe occidentale au cours de leurs errances ascétiques et dont un certain nombre s'établirent aussi bien au nord qu'au sud des Alpes, excitant l'admiration tout autour d'eux par leur humilité, leur austérité, leur pratique du travail manuel et leur ardeur à la prière[1]. L'ermite Engilmar, l'un des fondateurs de ce qui allait devenir l'abbaye de Windberg, était un disciple de saint Grégoire ; il vint d'Arménie dans la région de Passau, cherchant « une pauvreté volontaire dans la pérégrination, avec un espoir accru de la récompense dans le ciel », et il mourut en 1093[2]. L'exemple des *peregrini* irlandais était aussi fécond, spécialement en Allemagne où ils apportèrent d'importantes contributions à la vie religieuse et intellectuelle, du Xe au XIIe siècle[3]. Saint Cadroe, le second abbé de Waulsort, qui mourut en 975, quitta l'Irlande jeune homme afin d'entrer « dans la voie de la pérégrination, de l'abandon de tout » ; il vint aux Pays-Bas par Cumbria, Londres, la France et Fleury[4]. On pense que l'écrivain Honorius Augustodunensis, qui passa la plus grande part de sa vie dans la solitude en Allemagne du Sud, était un moine irlandais qui demeura un certain temps à Canterbury avant de venir sur le continent[5]. En 1117, Reimbaud de Liège écrivit une lettre pour un pèlerin irlandais du nom de Dermot, qui se désignait lui-même comme un exilé pour l'amour de Dieu, portant sur lui la croix du Christ, comme il la portait sur son vête-

1. Patricia McNulty et Bernard Hamilton, Orientale lumen et magistra Latinitas : Greek Influences on Western Monasticism (900-1100), *Le millénaire du mont Athos (963-1963)*, Chevetogne, 1963, I, p. 197-204.
2. Historiae et annales Windbergenses, 3, dans *Monumenta Germaniae historica : Scriptores*, XVII, p. 561-562.
3. Cf. cependant, Hugues, dans *J. Eccl. Hist.*, XI, p. 197-198, sur le déclin du prestige du pèlerinage en Irlande aux VIIIe et IXe siècles, et sur la tendance à remplacer l'errance, comme idéal ascétique, par la solitude. Sur les anachorètes irlandais en Islande et autres îles de l'Atlantique-Nord au IXe siècle, voir Dag Strömbäck, *The Conversion of Iceland*, tr. Peter Foote (Londres, 1975), p. 60-63.
4. Vita sancti Cadroe, 2, 14, 20, et 21, dans *Acta sanctorum*, 6 mars, 3e éd., Paris, 1863-1870, I, p. 475-477.
5. Voir Hubert Dauphin, L'érémitisme en Angleterre aux XIe et XIIe siècles, dans *L'eremitismo in Occidente nei secoli XI e XII*, Milan, 1965, p. 307-309 (« Pubblicazioni dell'Università cattolica del Sacro Cuore : Contributi, Varia », 4) ; et Roger E. Reynolds, Further Evidence for the Irish Origin of Honorius Augustodunensis, *Vivarium*, 1969, VII, p. 1-7.

ment, et marchant « vers Dieu non pas seulement à Jérusalem mais partout, puisqu'Il est partout »[1].

De semblables motifs inspiraient de nombreux moines sur le continent. Au xie siècle, Pierre Damien divise les ermites entre ceux qui vivaient en cellule et ceux qu'il appelle anachorètes — il les approuve clairement, malgré ses principes bénédictins — et qui « dédaignent d'avoir fixé leur foyer et errent au hasard à travers le désert de leur ermitage »[2]. Le thème de l'exil volontaire et de l'errance ascétique apparaît dans le *Vitae* de nombreux saints moines et chanoines des xie et xiie siècles, mais c'était plus qu'un type, et cela reflétait certainement une réalité autant qu'un idéal. On rapporte ainsi que Richard de Saint-Vanne avait cherché, jeune homme, à imiter la nudité et la pauvreté du Christ et à exécuter l'ordre, donné à Abraham, de quitter son pays et sa famille ; Adalelmus de La Chaise-Dieu « quitta secrètement sa terre natale pour devenir un pèlerin » et passa deux ans à voyager en mendiant, pieds nus, « exilé, pèlerin et étranger »[3]. Robert d'Arbrissel « quitta la terre de son père comme un exilé et un fugitif » et Norbert de Xanten entreprit, après le concile de Fritzlar, « un pèlerinage volontaire » avec deux compagnons « suivant nus le Christ nu », voyageant pieds nus, sans toit ni domicile assuré et « avec le Christ seul pour guide »[4]. Gaucherius, le fondateur d'Aureil, « quitta sa mère et son père, ses pieuses relations et sa douce patrie » et Etienne d'Obazine (le premier livre de sa *Vita* fut écrit vers 1166) quitta sa terre natale en secret, « avec les pieds nus, comme un exilé », après avoir décidé de suivre le Christ et d'entrer dans « la voie du salut d'un pas libre et sans entraves »[5].

1. REIMBAUD DE LIÈGE, *Opera omnia*, éd. C. de CLERCQ, Turnhout, 1966, p. 4 (« Corpus Christianorum : Continuatio Mediaeualis », 4).
2. PIERRE DAMIEN, Op. XV de suae congregationis institutis, 3, in *Patr. lat.*, CXLV, 338 B. Les mots *per eremi deserta* sont difficiles à traduire.
3. HUGUES DE FLAVIGNY, Chronicon (Vita Richardi), 2, 3, dans *Monumenta Germaniae historica : Scriptores*, VIII, p. 370, et *Patr. lat.*, CLIV, 201 B ; cf. Hubert DAUPHIN, *Le bienheureux Richard, abbé de Saint-Vanne de Verdun* († *1046*), Louvain-Paris, 1946, p. 62 (« Bibliothèque de la Revue d'histoire ecclésiastique », 24), sur l'influence irlandaise à Saint-Vanne au début du xie siècle ; Vita sancti Adelelmi, 3-5, dans *España sagrada*, XXVII, Madrid, 1772, p. 834-835 ; cf. Pierre-Roger GAUSSIN, *L'abbaye de la Chaise-Dieu (1043-1518)*, Paris, 1962, p. 126-128.
4. BAUDRI DE DOL, Vita beati Roberti, 1 (7), dans *Patr. lat.*, CLXII, 1047 A ; Vita [B] sancti Norberti, 4 (22), dans *Patr. lat.*, CLXX, 1272 B.
5. Vita beati Gaucherii, dans *Nova bibliotheca manuscriptorum librorum*, éd. P. LABBÉ, Paris, 1657, II, p. 561 ; Vita beati Stephani, 1, 2-3, dans Etienne BALUZE, *Miscellanea*, éd. J.-D. MANSI, Lucca, 1761-1764, I, p. 150-151 ; cf. *Vie de saint Etienne d'Obazine*, éd. et tr. Michel AUBRUN, Clermont-Ferrand, 1970, p. 8 (« Faculté des Lettres et Sciences humaines de l'Université de Clermont-Ferrand : Publications de l'Institut d'Etudes du Massif central », 6), sur la date du livre I. On trouvera d'autres exemples dans les *Annales Rodenses*, éd. P.-C. BOEREN et G. W. A. PANHUYSEN, Assen, 1968, p. 24 ; la *Vita* de Henry de Coquet-Island, 1, 1, dans *Acta sanctorum*, 16 janvier (éd. cit., II, 424) ; la *Vita* de Drogo de Salzbourg, 1, 3, dans *Acta sanctorum*, 16 avril (éd. cit., II, 439).

Monachisme et pèlerinage au Moyen Age

Les exilés volontaires visitaient souvent des Lieux saints aux cours de leurs pérégrinations et la distinction entre pèlerinages *ex patria* et *ad loca sancta* n'était pas clairement établie aux xiᵉ et xiiᵉ siècles. Richard de Saint-Vanne mena, en 1026 et 1027, une expédition fameuse vers Jérusalem et, selon McNulty et Hamilton, « les pèlerinages du xiᵉ siècle étaient pour une bonne part organisés par les abbés des maisons monastiques réformées en Lorraine, en Bourgogne, en Flandre et en Normandie et patronnés par les évêques et les barons qui favorisaient le renouvellement de l'Eglise »[1]. Guillaume Firmat, qui mourut vers 1090, alla à Jérusalem parce qu'il avait médité sur les souffrances du Seigneur et qu'il désirait porter sa croix et marcher sur ses traces ; Géraud de La Sauve Majeure, qui mourut en 1095, alla, alors qu'il était encore oblat à Corbie, en pèlerinage dans le sud de l'Italie et plus tard à Jérusalem, malgré la crainte qu'avait son abbé de le voir « rester quelque part dans son voyage, soit comme reclus, soit comme ermite »[2]. La combinaison des motifs d'expatriation et de pèlerinage est aussi visible chez le cistercien Christian de l'Aumône qui fut, jeune homme, un ermite et un ascète et qui « pensa à s'imposer à lui-même une tâche telle que, en s'exilant pour toujours parmi les Lieux saints, il passerait sa vie tout entière en pèlerin »[3].

La pérégrination ascétique était presque aussi importante dans le programme de réforme monastique des xiᵉ et xiiᵉ siècles que la pauvreté et l'érémitisme[4] et en harmonie avec une large tendance de la culture de l'époque. « Dans l'ordre monastique, écrit Ladner, un passage de l'*habitus* sédentaire à celui du voyageur et du missionnaire se répète sur une vaste échelle entre le xiᵉ et le xiiiᵉ siècle, augmentant et remplaçant en partie la *stabilitas* bénédictine par diverses formes de *peregrinatio* ascétiques et apostoliques »[5]. Le changement est évident dans la littérature : le titre de W. P. Ker, *Epic and Romance*, était appliqué à l'histoire de la spiritualité dans R. W. Southern, *The Making of the Middle Ages*, dont le dernier chapitre est intitulé « From Epic to Romance » et montre comment, au xiiᵉ siècle, on conçoit de plus en plus la vie comme une recherche

---

1. McNulty et Hamilton, dans *Millénaire du mont Athos*, p. 194 ; cf. Dauphin, *Richard*, p. 273-308, sur le pèlerinage de Richard de Saint-Vanne, qui passa ensuite cinq ans comme ermite.
2. Vita sancti Guillelmi Firmati, 1, dans E.-A. Pigeon, *Vies des saints du diocèse de Coutances et Avranches*, Avranches, 1898, II, p. 402 ; Vita de Geraud de La Sauve-Majeure, 17, dans *Patr. lat.*, CXLVII, 1034 C.
3. Bruno Griesser, Christian von L'Aumône, eine neue, vollständigere Handschrift seiner Vita, *Cistercienser-Chronik*, 1950, LXII, p. 25 ; cf. Jean Leclercq, Le texte complet de la vie de Christian de L'Aumône, *Analecta Bollandiana*, 1953, LXXI, p. 21-52.
4. Jean Becquet, L'érémitisme clérical et laïc dans l'ouest de la France, dans *Eremitismo*, p. 190, souligne l'association du pèlerinage et du mouvement d'érémitisme en France et la difficulté qu'il y a à distinguer pèlerins et ermites.
5. Gerhart B. Ladner, Homo Viator : Mediaeval Ideas on Alienation and Order, *Speculum*, 1967, XLII, p. 245.

ou un voyage, et les hommes comme des pèlerins et des chercheurs. « Bien sûr, l'idée de pèlerinage a tenu longtemps une place importante dans la vie chrétienne... », écrit-il, citant les missionnaires irlandais et anglais, « mais leur idéal n'était pas tant le mouvement que l'exil : un changement d'amis et de pays, plutôt qu'une recherche d'expériences nouvelles et de nouvelles aventures. Ce n'est pas avant le xiie siècle que l'imagerie du voyage devint une expression populaire de la quête spirituelle »[1].

La puissance de l'idéal de la recherche et du mouvement, ressenti d'un bout à l'autre de la société, fut un facteur important qui aida à introduire la grande période du pèlerinage médiéval, depuis la première croisade jusqu'aux *Canterbury Tales*, qui montrent des hommes et des femmes de tous milieux s'unissant dans le pèlerinage au tombeau de saint Thomas Becket[2]. A cette époque, les réalités du pèlerinage avaient changé à de nombreux égards depuis le haut Moyen Age. Déjà au xie siècle, les pèlerins avaient tendance à voyager en groupe plutôt qu'isolés et leur statut, en tant qu'ordre dans la société, l'*ordo peregrinorum*, fut reconnu comme une loi spéciale qui réglait leurs privilèges et leur façon de vivre[3]. Les moines et les moniales continuaient de prendre part aux pèlerinages et les monastères jouaient un rôle important, qui n'a pas encore été étudié par les historiens, en promouvant et en finançant ce mouvement, et surtout les croisades[4]. On retrouve l'influence du pèlerinage monastique sur la liturgie monastique en Angleterre dans l'addition, au calendrier bénédictin, de plusieurs saints associés aux centres de pèlerinage du continent[5].

Malgré la popularité du pèlerinage et l'influence de l'idéal de quête et de voyage, de nombreux et importants chefs religieux prirent toutefois, à la même époque, une conscience croissante de ce que la véritable

---

1. R. W. SOUTHERN, *The Making of the Middle Ages*, New Haven, 1953, p. 222.
2. Voir en particulier, sur les xie et xiie siècles, les deux articles de Edmond-René LABANDE, Recherches sur les pèlerins dans l'Europe des xie et xiie siècles, *Cahiers de civilisation médiévale*, 1958, I, p. 159-169 et 339-347 ; et *Ad limina* : le pèlerin médiéval au terme de sa démarche, *Mélanges offerts à René Crozet*, éd. Pierre GALLAIS et Yves-Jean RIOU, Poitiers, 1966, I, p. 283-291.
3. Cf. Romuald BAUERREISS, *Kirchengeschichte Bayerns*, II, St-Ottilien, 1950, p. 117-121, et Colette BLANC, Les pratiques de piété des laïcs dans les pays du Bas-Rhône aux xie et xiie siècles, *Annales du Midi*, 1960, LXXII, p. 141-143, sur les changements dans la pratique du pèlerinage, et F. GARRISSON, A propos des pèlerins et de leur condition juridique, *Etudes d'histoire du droit canonique dédiées à Gabriel Le Bras*, Paris, 1965, II, p. 1165-1189, sur le statut légal des pèlerins.
4. Cf. Bernard BLIGNY, *L'Eglise et les ordres religieux dans le royaume de Bourgogne aux XIe et XIIe siècles*, Paris, 1960, p. 182-189 (« Collection des Cahiers d'histoire publiée par les Universités de Clermont, Lyon, Grenoble », 4), et, sur les cisterciens, p. 381-385.
5. H. MAYR-HARTING, Functions of a Twelfth-Century Recluse, *History*, 1975, LX, p. 345-346.

Monachisme et pèlerinage au Moyen Age

recherche se trouvait, pour l'homme, en lui-même, non dans le monde extérieur, et que, dans nombre de cas, le pèlerinage causait plutôt un dommage spirituel qu'un bien[1]. Déjà au ive et au ve siècle, quand la pratique du pèlerinage commençait de se développer, les Pères de l'Eglise exprimaient des doutes quant à l'idée que certains endroits fussent plus saints que d'autres et qu'ils dussent, pour cela, être visités par les croyants. Plus tard, ceux qui critiquaient le pèlerinage citaient en particulier la célèbre parole de saint Jérôme : « *Non Hierosolymis fuisse, sed Hierosolymis bene vixisse laudandum est* », parole dont le sens précis est ambigu mais dont on admettait universellement qu'elle signifiait qu'un homme devait plutôt aspirer à la Jérusalem céleste que se contenter de visiter celle qui est sur terre[2]. Quoique ces réserves aient eu, apparemment, peu d'effet sur la pratique réelle du pèlerinage dans le haut Moyen Age, elles représentent une attitude critique que l'on n'oublia jamais complètement et qui s'appliquait particulièrement aux moines et aux moniales, lesquels devaient rester dans la Jérusalem de leur monastère plutôt que de visiter les Lieux saints sur terre[3]. En 451, le concile de Chalcédoine spécifia que les moines devaient « aimer la quiétude et être ardents au jeûne et à la prière, en restant dans les lieux où ils avaient renoncé au monde »[4].

Le concile insista également sur l'importance de l'obédience qui, dans le haut Moyen Age, était peut-être un frein encore plus sévère que la stabilité au pèlerinage monastique. Presque toutes les sources sur la pérégrination ascétique en Irlande mentionnent la nécessité de la permission du supérieur ecclésiastique pour le moine qui voulait partir en pèlerinage ; cette permission n'était pas toujours accordée[5]. Columban prédit

---

1. Voir mon article, Opposition to Pilgrimage in the Middle Ages, paru dans les *Mélanges Gérard Fransen*. On y trouvera plusieurs références sur la critique du pèlerinage par les Pères et sur l'opposition au pèlerinage laïc et clérical.
2. JÉROME, *Epistulae*, 58, 2, éd. Isidor HILBERG, Vienne-Leipzig, 1910, I, p. 529 (« Corpus scriptorum ecclesiasticorum latinorum », 54). La formulation est reprise de CICÉRON, *Pro Murena*, 6, 12 : « *Non Asiam nunquam uidisse sed in Asia continenter uixisse laudandum est.* » Jérôme en vint à dire que la cité que l'on devait chercher n'était pas celle qui avait tué les prophètes et répandu le sang du Christ mais celle qui, d'après la Bible, est emplie de joie par le cours du fleuve, qui ne peut être cachée, qui est la mère des saints et en qui un homme peut se réjouir avec les justes.
3. Sur l'idée que le monastère est une Jérusalem, voir Robert KONRAD, *Das himmlische und das irdische Jerusalem im mittelalterlichen Denken*, *Speculum Historiale*, éd. Clemens BAUER, Laetitia BOEHM, et Max MÜLLER, Fribourg-in-Br - Munich, 1965, p. 523-540 et not. p. 533-540 (« Festschrift Johannes Spörl ») ; cf. Adriaan BREDERO, *Jérusalem dans l'Occident médiéval*, dans *Mélanges Crozet*, I, p. 259-271, et la lettre de Bernard de Clairvaux citée ci-dessous à la n. 1.
4. Concile de Chalcédoine (451), canon 4, dans *Conciliorum oecumenicorum decreta*, éd. J. ALBERIGO, 3e éd., Bologne, 1973, p. 89 ; cf. la version dans GRATIEN, *Decretum*, C. XVI, q. 1, c. 12, éd. Emil RICHTER et Emil FRIEDBERG, *Corpus iuris canonici*, Leipzig, 1879, I, p. 764.
5. Cf. *Vitae*, éd. PLUMMER (citée n. 2), I, CXXIII.

l'échec d'une expédition à laquelle participait un moine qui était parti sans le consentement de son abbé, et dans la *Vita sancti Berachi*, un vœu de pèlerinage sans permission est accompli en rêve, avec l'aide d'un ange, sans quitter vraiment le monastère[1]. Le désir de voyager fut parfois décrit comme une inspiration du diable ; des moines qui voulaient partir en furent dissuadés par l'intervention du Ciel. Saint Comgall expulsa le démon qui habitait dans la chaussure de Mochuda et l'empêchait de passer plus de deux nuits dans un même endroit ; c'est un ange qui persuada l'évêque Lugidus de rester en Irlande, et saint Coemgen fut dissuadé par deux fois de partir en pèlerinage, la première fois par saint Munna et la seconde fois par l'ermite Garbanus, qui dit que « mieux vaut maintenant rester à la place fixée par le Christ que d'errer de place en place en la vieillesse ». Un démon avoua qu'il essayait de pousser Coemgen à partir en pèlerinage « et à quitter sa place, ce qui est le mal sous la forme du bien »[2]. Au cours du viiie siècle, l'attitude à l'égard de la pérégrination commença de changer en Irlande, comme Hughes l'a montré, et le principe de « non-désertion du monastère » apparut dans beaucoup de règles monastiques irlandaises. Saint Samthann « enseignait à ses disciples que Dieu est aussi proche de l'Irlande que de Rome ou de n'importe où, et que la route du Royaume des Cieux est à la même distance de tous les pays : il n'est donc pas besoin de traverser les mers »[3].

En Angleterre et sur le continent, cette tendance à désapprouver les pèlerinages entrepris par des moines et des moniales fut renforcée aux viiie et ixe siècles par l'acceptation croissante des normes de la règle bénédictine et par la mauvaise conduite de nombreux pèlerins, particulièrement de ceux à qui les pèlerinages avaient été imposés en pénitence[4]. Bède et Boniface mettaient en doute la valeur des pèlerinages, qu'ils fussent entrepris par des laïques ou par des moines et des moniales[5]. Le concile de Ver en 755 décréta que « les moines qui vivent véritablement d'après la règle *(regulariter)* ne seraient pas autorisés à entreprendre de pèlerinage à Rome ou ailleurs s'ils n'avaient un ordre écrit de leur

---

1. ADOMNAN, 1, 6 (éd. cit., p. 224), et *Vitae*, éd. PLUMMER, I, p. 85-86 ; cf. *Vita sancti Fintani*, 12, *ibid.*, II, p. 100.
2. The Expulsion of Mochuda from Rahen, 36, dans *Bethada Náem nErenn : Lives of the Irish Saints*, éd. Charles PLUMMER, Oxford, 1922, II, p. 301-302 ; Vita sancti Coemgeni, 12, 21 et 29-30, dans *Vitae*, éd. PLUMMER, I, p. 240, 245, et 249-250 ; cf. Vita sancti Comgalli, 13, *ibid.*, II, p. 7.
3. HUGHES, dans *J. Eccl. hist.*, XI, p. 147 ; cf. le poème attribué à Sedulius SCOTUS, dans *Thesaurus Palaeohibernicus*, éd. Whitley STOKES et John STRACHAN, Cambridge, 1901-1903, II, p. 296 ; voir à ce sujet Hermann FREDE, *Altlateinische Paulus-Handschriften*, Fribourg-en-Br., 1964, p. 50-79, et not. p. 67 (« Vetus latina : Aus der Geschichte der lateinischen Bibel », 4).
4. VOGEL, dans *Rev. des sciences rel.*, XXXVIII, p. 136-140, et SUMPTION, *Pilgrimage*, p. 112.
5. Wilhelm LEVISON, *England and the Continent in the Eighth Century*, Oxford, 1946, p. 38-39 (« Ford Lectures », 1943).

Monachisme et pèlerinage au Moyen Ag

abbé » ; le concile de Frioul en 796 ou 797 décréta que l' « on ne donnerait jamais, à aucune abbesse ni à aucune moniale, la permission de se rendre à Rome et de visiter d'autres lieux vénérables, quand Satan, ayant pris l'aspect d'un ange de Lumière, leur suggérait cela comme pour le bien de la prière ». En 850, le concile de Pavie décida que les clercs et les moines qui pérégrinaient à travers des provinces et des villes diverses, colportant des erreurs et troublant les esprits simples, seraient surveillés, et, au besoin, disciplinés[1].

L'idée que le véritable pèlerinage se trouvait, pour les moines et les moniales, chez eux et non dans le voyage se retrouve aussi dans les écrits spirituels des xe et xie siècles. L'abbé du Mont-Cassin dit à Gaudentius, en route pour Jérusalem en 990 : « La voie que vous avez choisie pour acquérir la béatitude est éloignée de la vraie, de celle qui mène à la Vie. C'est, bien sûr, le fait d'une grande âme de fuir les compromissions avec le monde passager, mais il est moins louable de bouger chaque jour vers d'autres lieux. » Par conséquent, il conseille à Gaudentius « de demeurer en un endroit et d'y jouir là plus librement d'une vie céleste ». Saint Nilus lui conseille, de même, de retourner chez lui et de rejoindre un monastère à Rome[2].

La conception spirituelle de la vie monastique comme un pèlerinage se retrouve dans la mention d'obit de l'abbé Arbodus de Saint-Rémi de Reims, mort en 1005 ; il y est dit que tous les hommes entrent et sortent de « la captivité de ce pèlerinage » nus ; ils sont à la fois captifs et pèlerins. « Nous sommes venus au monde nus, nous mourrons en pèlerins. Car nous devons savoir que notre vie présente est une route et non pas un foyer »[3]. Même Pierre Damien, malgré sa sympathie à l'égard des anachorètes errants et son approbation du pèlerinage des laïques et des clercs, écrivait que « ceux qui vivent selon la règle et qui observent comme une loi les préceptes de la vie monastique ou de la religion canonique » devraient rester « dans la vocation où ils sont établis »[4]. Et saint Anselme, dans une lettre écrite alors qu'il était encore abbé du Bec exhortait un jeune homme qui projetait de faire un pèlerinage avant de devenir moine à ne pas différer son entrée dans « la meilleure des voies », à « se détourner de la Jérusalem, qui est, maintenant, non pas une vision de paix mais d'épreuves,

1. Concile de Ver (755), canon 10, dans *Capitularia regum Francorum*, éd. A. BORE-TIUS et V. KRAUSE, Hanovre, 1883-1897, I, p. 35 (« Monumenta Germaniae historica : Leges », 2) ; Concile de Frioul (796-797), canon 12, dans *Concilia aevi Karolini*, éd. A. WERMINGHOFF Hanovre, 1906-1908, p. 194 (« Monumenta Germaniae historica : Leges », 3, 2) ; Concile de Pavie (850), canon 21, dans *Capitularia*, II, p. 122.
2. Jean CANAPARIUS, Vita sancti Adalberti, 14-15, dans *Monumenta Germaniae historica : Scriptores*, IV, p. 587-588.
3. Léopold DELISLE, *Rouleaux des morts du IXe au XVe siècle*, Paris, 1866, p. 37-38 (« Société de l'histoire de France » [11]).
4. Pierre DAMIEN, Ep. 7, 17 au marquis Rainier de Toscane, dans *Patr. lat.*, CXLIV, 456 AB. Cette lettre a probablement été écrite dans les années 1030.

et des trésors de Constantinople et de Babylone que gardent des mains souillées de sang, et de prendre le chemin de la Jérusalem céleste qui est la vision de paix où se trouvent les trésors que seuls reçoivent ceux qui méprisent les autres trésors »[1].

Les sources officielles, au xie siècle, désapprouvent également l'errance des moines que l'on assimilait souvent au pèlerinage. Un décret du pape Alexandre II, souvent inclus par la suite dans de nombreux recueils de lois canoniques, ordonnait aux moines bénédictins de garder le cloître « conformément aux décisions du très excellent concile de Chalcédoine » et leur interdisait de pérégriner *(peragrare)* à travers villages, châteaux ou villes[2]. Yves de Chartres, dans sa lettre aux moines de Coulombs, condamnait violemment les moines qui erraient comme des vagabonds en proclamant qu'ils constituaient à eux seuls l'Eglise de Dieu, quoiqu'il ne désapprouvât pas les anachorètes « qui se retirent dans un ermitage en suivant une règle après avoir été instruits dans les monastères des disciplines régulières »[3].

La question prit une importance nouvelle à la fin du xie siècle, avec la question de la participation des moines à la croisade[4]. Le pape Urbain II, lui-même moine et ancien prieur de Cluny, interdit aux clercs et aux moines, dans ses lettres aux gens de Bologne et à la communauté de Vallombrosa (1096), de se rendre à Jérusalem sans la permission de leurs supérieurs, disant que cette expédition était celle de soldats armés pour combattre les Sarrasins, non celle de « ceux qui ont quitté le monde et se sont consacrés aux combats spirituels ». Quoique les moines ne fussent pas spécifiquement désignés dans le rapport que fit Robert le Moine de l'appel à la croisade prononcé par Urbain à Clermont, ils étaient sans doute englobés dans l'interdiction générale faite aux prêtres et aux clercs « de tous ordres » de partir sans la permission de leur évêque[5].

---

1. Anselme, Ep. 117, dans *Opera omnia*, éd. F. S. Schmitt, Edimbourg, 1946-1961, III, 254, écrite probablement en 1086 ; cf. sur l'attitude d'Anselme à l'égard des pèlerinages et de la croisade, H. de Sainte-Marie, Les lettres de saint Anselme de Cantorbéry et la règle bénédictine, *Mélanges bénédictins publiés à l'occasion du XIVe centenaire de la mort de saint Benoît*, Abbaye Saint-Wandrille, 1947, p. 279-281 ; Southern, *Making*, p. 50, et *Saint Anselm and his Biographer*, Cambridge, 1963, p. 122-123. Le fondateur de Monte Vergine, Guillaume de Vercelli (1085-1142), fut exhorté par Jean de Mathera de ne pas aller à Jérusalem, mais à demeurer chez lui *ad fidelium salutem* ; Vita sancti Guillelmi, 2 (7), dans *Acta sanctorum*, 25 janvier (éd. cit., VII, p. 101).

2. Gratien, *Decretum*, C. XVI, q. 1, c. 11 (éd. cit., p. 763) ; cf. James Brundage *Medieval Canon Law and the Crusader*, Madison-Milwaukee-Londres, 1969, p. 16.

3. Yves de Chartres, Ep. 192, dans *Patr. lat.*, CLXII, 201 C.

4. Cf. James Brundage, A Transformed Angel (X, 3.31.18) : The Problem of the Crusading Monk, *Studies in Medieval Cistercian History Presented to Jeremiah F. O'Sullivan*, Spencer, 1971, p. 55-62, et not. p. 56-57 sur le xiie siècle (« Cistercian Studies Series », 13).

5. *Patr. lat.*, CLI, 483 CD, et Wilhelm Wiederhold, Papsturkunden in Florenz, *Nachrichten von der königl. Gesellschaft der Wissenschaften zu Göttingen, Phil.-Hist. Kl.*,

Monachisme et pèlerinage au Moyen Age

On retrouve des références à ces déclarations papales, ou à de semblables, dans de nombreuses sources de l'époque, notamment dans une lettre d'Anselme à un moine dont, disait-il, le désir de visiter Jérusalem était contraire à sa profession de stabilité et à l'obédience due à la fois au pape et à son abbé[1], et dans une lettre de Geoffroi de Vendôme à l'abbé de Marmoutier : « De même que le Siège apostolique l'a ordonné aux laïques, il a interdit aux moines de se rendre à Jérusalem, ce que je sais par moi-même puisque mes oreilles étaient toutes proches de la bouche du pape Urbain lorsqu'il ordonna aux laïques de devenir pèlerins en se rendant à Jérusalem et qu'il interdit le même pèlerinage aux moines. » Les moines, continuait-il, ne devraient pas aller à Jérusalem, de peur que, à la recherche d'une béatitude illusoire, ils ne trouvent une réelle misère du corps et de l'âme[2]. Dans une autre lettre, à Hildebert du Mans, Geoffroi écrivait, faisant écho à saint Jérôme, qu'un moine qui s'est rendu à Jérusalem aurait mieux fait de vivre une bonne vie dans son monastère. « Ce sont les hommes qui se sont bien comportés, non tous ceux qui ont vu la Jérusalem terrestre, qui méritent de recevoir la Jérusalem des Cieux »[3].

On trouve une opposition semblable entre les vertus du monachisme et celles du pèlerinage dans une page du récit de la fondation de Mortemer relatant l'histoire d'un chevalier qui, souhaitant suivre le Christ et voir son tombeau, « avait agrafé la croix du Seigneur à ses épaules » et se trouvait sur le point de partir. « Mais l'abbé, voyant un homme qui était à la fois suffisamment pieux et inspiré par Dieu, commença de le sermonner et de lui montrer la voie qui mène à la Jérusalem céleste ». Il le persuada ainsi de se mettre lui-même en croix, plutôt que de mettre une croix sur ses vêtements, et de suivre l'exemple d'Abraham en devenant moine[4]. Pierre le Vénérable écrivit également à un chevalier qui avait décidé d'aller à Jérusalem après avoir promis de devenir moine à Cluny : « On peut abandonner de petits biens pour des biens plus grands, non des plus grands pour des plus petits, ou des biens égaux pour des

---

1901, p. 313-314, n. 6 ; cf. *Italia pontificia*, éd. Paul KEHR, Berlin, 1906-1962, V, p. 248, n. 14, et III, p. 89, n. 8 ; ROBERT LE MOINE, Historia Iherosolimitana, 1, 2. dans *Recueil des historiens des croisades : historiens occidentaux*, III, Paris, 1866, p. 729.

1. ANSELME, Ep. 410 (éd. cit., V, p. 355) ; cf. Ep. 195 (éd. cit., IV, p. 85-86), écrivant à l'évêque de Salisbury, probablement en 1095, pour interdire aux moines de son diocèse d'aller à Jérusalem.

2. GEOFFROI DE VENDÔME, Ep. 4, 21, dans *Patr. lat.*, CLVII, 162 BC ; cf. L. COMPAIN, *Etude sur Geoffroi de Vendôme*, Paris, 1891, p. 67-68 (« Bibliothèque de l'Ecole des Hautes Etudes », 86).

3. GEOFFROI DE VENDÔME, Ep. 3, 24, dans *Patr. lat.*, CLVII, 127 BC ; cf. Peter von MOOS, *Hildebert von Lavardin, 1056-1133*, Stuttgart, 1965, p. 144-145 (« Pariser historische Studien », 3) ; Ep. 3, 29-30, dans *Patr. lat.*, CLVII, 131-132.

4. J. BOUVET, Le récit de la fondation de Mortemer, *Collectanea ordinis Cisterciensium reformatorum*, 1960, XXII, p. 152.

biens égaux. Servir Dieu perpétuellement dans l'humilité et la pauvreté est plus grand que d'aller à Jérusalem avec orgueil et luxe. Donc, quoi-qu'il soit bien de visiter Jérusalem, où se posèrent les pieds du Seigneur, il est bien meilleur de regarder le Ciel où l'on contemple Sa face. Celui qui a promis ce qui est le meilleur ne peut par conséquent remplacer cela par quelque chose de moins bon »[1].

Ces textes soulèvent la question des vœux contradictoires, puisque dans les deux cas les chevaliers avaient fait le vœu d'être pèlerin, le premier après et l'autre avant de devenir moine. Ils reflètent la conception qui prévaut : dans ces circonstances, le vœu le plus important, devenir moine, qu'il soit antérieur ou postérieur, l'emporte sur le vœu moindre de pèlerinage. Selon une sentence attribuée à Anselme ou à Hugues de Cluny, le vœu de visiter Jérusalem, Rome ou le tombeau d'un saint, était accompli si l'on devenait moine, parce que : « Ceux qui, après s'être partiellement voués à Dieu, se sont plus tard entièrement donnés à Lui n'ont pas ensuite à accomplir ce qui n'était qu'une partie du tout »[2]. Anselme cite cette phrase dans une lettre où il démontre que des vœux prononcés « sans promesse de foi et sacrement » (par quoi il entend proba-blement ce que l'on appelait plus tard les vœux privés, en opposition avec les vœux solennels) étaient accomplis par un vœu monastique « par lequel un homme s'offre entièrement à Dieu, lui-même et tout ce qui lui appartient » ; et il écrivit à un moine qui était troublé par un vœu de pèlerinage prononcé avant de devenir moine : « Vous pouvez être sûr que, quand vous vous êtes voué et offert vous-même entièrement à Dieu par la profession monastique, vous remplissez tous les vœux moindres, de toute sorte, que vous aviez prononcés sans serment ni engagement sur la foi »[3].

Bernard de Clairvaux pense de même, dans une lettre à l'évêque Geoffroi de Chartres au sujet du conflit entre le vœu de vivre en ermite et celui d'aller à Jérusalem : « Je ne pense pas que des vœux moindres doivent mettre obstacle à des vœux plus étendus, ou que Dieu exige quelque chose qui lui a été promis si on lui offre quelque chose de plus

1. PIERRE LE VÉNÉRABLE, Ep. 51, dans The Letters of Peter the Venerable, éd. Giles CONSTABLE, Cambridge, Mass., 1967, I, p. 152 (« Harvard Historical Series », 78).
2. Jean LECLERCQ, La lettre de Gilbert Crispin sur la vie monastique, Analecta monastica, II, Rome, 1953, p. 119 et 123 (« Studia Anselmiana », 31). Gilbert Crispin étant mort en 1119, l'abbé de Cluny en question était probablement Hugues. Sur la question des vœux, en général, voir James BRUNDAGE, The Votive Obligations of Crusaders : The Development of a Canonistic Doctrine, Traditio, 1968, XXIV, p. 77-118, not. p. 78-81 sur la première moitié du XIIe siècle, et Medieval Canon Law, p. 30-65 (« The Crusade Vow to the Early Thirteenth Century »).
3. ANSELME, Ep. 188 et 468 (éd. cit., IV, p. 73-74, et V, p. 417) ; cf. Ep. 95 (éd. cit., III, p. 221-222), qui comprend, en quelques manuscrits, un abrégé de la sentence, non attribué à l'abbé de Cluny. Sur la distinction entre vœux privés et vœux solennels, voir BRUNDAGE, Medieval Canon Law, p. 45-50 et passim.

Monachisme et pèlerinage au Moyen Age

beau »[1]. Ecrivant à l'évêque Alexandre de Lincoln, Bernard expliquait de quelle façon un clerc qui se rendait à Jérusalem avait décidé de devenir moine à Clairvaux, et avait trouvé un raccourci pour se rendre là où il le souhaitait : « Il a traversé rapidement cette mer grande et spacieuse, et, naviguant avec succès, il a déjà atteint le rivage souhaité et est finalement arrivé dans le port du Salut. » Il était devenu, selon Bernard, un citoyen, non de la Jérusalem terrestre et servile, mais de la cité, céleste et libre, de Clairvaux. « C'est là Jérusalem, liée à la [Jérusalem] céleste dans sa dévotion complète d'esprit, l'imitation de son mode de vie et une certaine parenté spirituelle »[2]. Bernard mêle ici deux images, unies dans son cœur : celle de la vie comme *peregrinatio* vers la cité céleste dont tous les hommes aspirent à être citoyens, et celle du monastère, spécialement de Clairvaux, comme la cité céleste sur la terre, la seule où l'on pouvait trouver le vrai repos et la vraie paix. A peu près à la même époque, il écrivit à l'abbé de Saint-Michel-en-Thiérache, dont il avait persuadé un moine de revenir de pèlerinage : « Le but des moines est de rechercher non la Jérusalem terrestre mais la céleste, et cela non pas en avançant avec leurs pieds mais en progressant avec leur cœur »[3].

D'autres maîtres du monachisme partageaient, au XIIe siècle, cette conception de la vie comme un pèlerinage que l'on menait mieux à terme à l'intérieur d'un cloître. Guillaume de Saint-Thierry, dans sa *Lettre d'or* aux chartreux de Mont-Dieu, fait allusion à la *peregrinatio huius seculi* et à la préparation constante de l'homme à émigrer « vers notre pays et notre cité, dans la maison de notre éternité »[4]. Le but du *De Mira-*

1. BERNARD, Ep. 57, dans *Opera omnia*, éd. Jean MABILLON, Paris, 1839, I, 202 CD, daté par Mabillon de 1128 environ et de 1127 environ par E. VACANDARD, *Vie de saint Bernard*, Paris, 1895, I, p. 136.
2. BERNARD, Ep. 64 (éd. cit., I, 208 A - 209 B), daté de 1129 environ par Mabillon et par David KNOWLES, *The Monastic Order in England*, 2e éd., Cambridge, 1963, p. 222, qui commente l'éloquence de cette lettre ; cf. CONGAR, dans *Mélanges... Etienne Gilson*, p. 194 et LECLERCQ, *Sources*, p. 82-84, sur le thème de la pérégrination dans les sermons de saint Bernard.
3. BERNARD, Ep. 399 (éd. cit., I, 717 C), daté d'avant 1130 par VACANDARD, *Saint Bernard*, I, 182. Quelque temps auparavant, Bernard avait écrit au pape, au nom du monastère de Clairvaux, pour l'exhorter à empêcher l'abbé Arnaud de Morimond et quelques-uns de ses moines de se rendre à Jérusalem, insistant, comme l'avait fait Urbain II, sur le fait que des soldats en armes étaient préférables à des moines qui gémissent et qui chantent : Ep. 359 (éd. cit., I, 656 AB), datée de 1143 par Mabillon mais de 1124 par VACANDARD, *Saint Bernard*, I, 162, n. 4, et de 1124-1125 par BREDERO, dans *Mélanges René Crozet*, I, p. 270. En 1147 Bernard écrivit à tous les abbés cisterciens pour interdire à tous les moines et les frères laïcs de se joindre à la deuxième croisade : Leopold GRILL, *Ein unbekannter Brief Bernhards von Clairvaux*, *Mitteilungen des Instituts für österreichische Geschichtsforschung*, 1953, LXI, p. 384. Bernard lui-même a toujours rappelé qu'il avait assumé la charge de prêcher la croisade à la demande insistante du pape : Giles CONSTABLE, *The Second Crusade as Seen by Contemporaries*, *Traditio*, 1953, IX, p. 276-278.
4. Guillaume de SAINT-THIERRY, *Epistola ad fratres de Monte Dei*, 65, éd. M. M. DAVY, Paris, 1940, p. 114 (« Etudes de philosophie médiévale », 29, 1).

culis de Pierre le Vénérable était d'informer les hommes « sur le pays dont ils sont exilés au cours de ce pèlerinage et vers lequel ils aspirent constamment » ; bon nombre des histoires rapportées reflètent la réaction de Pierre contre la matérialisation croissante du pèlerinage à son époque, et son idée que le pèlerinage ne pouvait pas, par lui-même, sauver un pécheur[1]. Pierre lui-même refusa de visiter la Terre sainte et demanda au patriarche de Jérusalem d'agir à sa place « parce que l'ordre monastique nous interdit de voir ces lieux, que je disais super-célestes, de notre rédemption, de verser physiquement nos larmes, et de prier sur les Lieux où se posèrent les pieds du Seigneur »[2].

Ce ton plein d'émotion reflète l'enthousiasme de la dévotion que Pierre porte aux Lieux saints associés à la vie du Christ, lieux que, seul, son statut de moine l'empêche de visiter. Tous ses contemporains n'étaient pas aussi scrupuleux et beaucoup succombaient, comme on l'a vu, à la tentation du pèlerinage ascétique et au désir de visiter les tombeaux des saints. Le moine Martinien, écrivant à la fin du XIe siècle ou au début du XIIe, considérait toutes les conversations sur le voyage à Jérusalem comme l'œuvre du diable « par lequel de nombreux moines, dans beaucoup de monastères, sont méchamment importunés et troublés, et non seulement eux-mêmes, mais aussi, hélas, de plus simples qu'eux »[3].

Il semble que l'exemple de saint Bernard prêchant la deuxième croisade ait été particulièrement troublant pour les cisterciens à qui l'on racontait beaucoup de contes moraux au sujet de la stabilité, de l'obédience, et de la supériorité de la vie monastique sur le pèlerinage. Selon Caesarius de Heisterbach, par exemple, un chanoine de Liège (probablement l'archidiacre Philippe, plus tard prieur de Clairvaux) prit la croix à la demande de Bernard, mais non la croix « des expéditions à travers les mers, mais celle de l'ordre, trouvant meilleur pour le salut d'imprimer une grande croix dans son esprit que de coudre, pour un temps, une petite croix sur son vêtement ». Après avoir cité le privilège octroyé par le pape, qui permet à un pèlerin de devenir moine mais interdit à un moine d'être pèlerin, Caesarius concluait que le pape jugeait meilleur pour l'âme « de combattre intérieurement, de façon constante, contre l'aiguillon des vices » que

---

1. Pierre le Vénérable, De miraculis, 1, 9, dans *Bibliotheca Cluniacensis*, éd. M. Marrier et A. Duchesne, Paris, 1614, 1265 A ; voir aussi Ep. 20 (éd. cit., I, p. 30), lettre à l'ermite Gilbert, où Pierre dit que la *longinqua transmigratio* et les autres pratiques ascétiques ne servaient à rien sans le mur élevé par le Christ autour de l'homme ; Ep. 80 (éd. cit., I, p. 216) aux moines du mont Thabor, soulignant le pouvoir rédempteur des bonnes œuvres plutôt que des lieux saints ; cf. Paolo Lamma, *Momenti di storiografia cluniacense*, Rome, 1961, p. 140-144 (« Istituto storico italiano per il Medio Evo : Studi storici », 42-44), et Labande, dans *Cahiers de civ. méd.*, I, p. 345-346.
2. Pierre le Vénérable, Ep. 83 (éd. cit., I, p. 220).
3. H. Roux, L'écrit spirituel du moine Martinien, dans *Mélanges bénédictins*, p. 340.

Monachisme et pèlerinage au Moyen Age

« de combattre extérieurement, et de façon temporaire, contre l'épée des Sarrasins »[1]. C'est peut-être en relation avec la deuxième croisade que le maître Isembold de Saint-Paul d'Halberstadt écrivait au moine Elvingus de Corbie, qui avait cité les exemples d'Abraham et de Lazare pour appuyer son désir de visiter Jérusalem : il disait à Elvingus qu'il avait déjà quitté son pays, sa famille et la maison de son père quand il était devenu moine, il l'exhortait à aspirer et à se hâter « vers la Jérusalem céleste qui est en haut, qui est notre mère », et à renoncer à la cité terrestre dont la vue en elle-même n'apporte aucun profit[2].

Les sources législatives nous montrent une semblable conception, quoiqu'une exception ait été d'habitude faite pour les pèlerinages accomplis avec la permission du supérieur, ce qui peut expliquer le nombre des abbés croisés au XIIe siècle[3]. Gratien traite la question avant tout comme une question d'obédience, remarquant avec insistance qu'aucun vœu fait par un moine, vœu d'abstinence et de rigueur spéciales inclus, n'est valable sans le consentement de l'abbé, et en donnant pour raison que « ceux qui cherchent à s'échapper de la discipline régulière prononceraient pour eux-mêmes des vœux de pèlerinage, ce qui n'est permis ni à un moine ni à un clerc, de peur que, par cette voie, il ne retourne vers un mode de vie séculier »[4]. Le pape Innocent III atténua la ligne de conduite officielle au regard des moines croisés, mais la majorité des canonistes continua de dénier aux moines le droit de prononcer des vœux sans la permission de leurs supérieurs. Le grand Hostiensis attribuait à Satan, travesti en ange, le désir, ressenti par un moine, de faire un vœu de pèlerinage, et lui interdisait de le faire « de crainte qu'il ne scandalise ses frères auxquels il doit se conformer et que l'occasion de partir en errant ne se présente à lui »[5]. En 1134, le chapitre général cistercien interdit à tous les membres de l'ordre de se rendre à Rome, « sauf avec un évêque de l'ordre ». En 1157, il ajouta une exception pour les cas de soudaine

---

1. Caesarius de Heisterbach, *Dialogus miraculorum*, 1, 6, éd. Joseph Strange, Cologne-Bonn-Bruxelles, 1851, I, p. 12-13. Sur les cisterciens, voir Giles Constable, The Vision of Gunthelm and Other *Visiones* Attributed to Peter the Venerable, *Revue bénédictine*, 1956, LXVI, p. 106 ; Herbert de Clairvaux, De miraculis, 1, 25, dans *Patr. lat.*, CLXXXV, 1300 A ; British Museum, Harley 2851, fol. 85ro.
2. *Monumenta Germaniae historica : Scriptores*, III, p. 13-14.
3. Cf. l'exemple des abbés de Marmoutier, Morimond, et Odenheim, que nous avons cité. Quand l'abbé de Saint-Colomban de Sens demanda à Pierre le Vénérable de lui donner quelque encouragement pour son voyage à Jérusalem, Pierre répondit qu'il ne voyait pas de meilleur encouragement que « le témoignage de votre propre conscience », et la pensée que ce pèlerinage avait aux yeux de Dieu la même valeur que la visite des trois Maries et des disciples au tombeau du Christ : Ep. 144 (éd. cit., I, p. 358-359).
4. Gratien, *Decretum*, C. XX, q. 4, d. p. c. 3 (éd. cit., p. 852) ; cf. Brundage, dans *Traditio*, XXIV, p. 80 ; *Medieval Canon Law*, p. 43-44 ; *Studies in Cistercian History*, p. 57.
5. Brundage, *Medieval Canon Law*, p. 101 et n. 118 ; *Studies in Cistercian History*, p. 57-60.

III

nécessité, mais décréta également que quiconque était allé en pèlerinage à Jérusalem ou ailleurs serait transféré de sa propre abbaye vers une autre, sans espoir de retour[1]. D'autres règles étaient moins sévères, mais, comme l'observance de Barnwell, qui date probablement du xiiie siècle, elles tendaient à accentuer la distinction entre les voies qui mènent vers la Jérusalem céleste et la Jérusalem terrestre[2].

De nombreux réformateurs monastiques partageaient ces conceptions au xiie siècle, et, parmi eux, certains avaient ressenti par eux-mêmes — en y succombant parfois — ce désir pressant d'accomplir un pèlerinage à un moment de leur vie. « Que les autres aillent à Jérusalem, disait Guigue de La Chartreuse, vous, allez vers l'humilité et la patience. Ainsi, vous sortirez du monde, ils y resteront »[3]. Elizabeth de Schönau exhorta l'abbé d'Odenheim et l'un de ses moines à ne pas se rendre à Jérusalem, comme les criminels, mais à rechercher comme des « enfants de lumière » le Christ dans leur cœur, à faire leur devoir chez eux et à suivre « le chemin de la contemplation »[4]. Etienne de Grandmont interdit formellement, aussi bien à un supérieur qu'à un disciple, de se rendre à Jérusalem ou sur le tombeau d'un saint « pour le bien de la prière » et il interdit, plus loin, de pardonner à qui que ce soit qui désobéirait à cette règle. Agir ainsi serait oublier la raison pour laquelle ils entrèrent au monastère : comment, demandait Etienne, celui qui s'est coupé les jambes pourrait-il se rendre à Rome[5] ?

On ne doit déduire de ces exemples de voix influentes qui s'élevèrent contre les pèlerinages monastiques, ni que de nombreux moines aient été détournés du départ en pèlerinage, ni que ces maîtres du monachisme, en protestant si fortement, aient montré leur incapacité à retenir les moines dans leur monastère. Ces critiques montrent plutôt, si l'on prend en considération les preuves, présentées plus haut, de la popularité du pèlerinage et de la pérégrination ascétique auprès des moines au xie et au xiie siècle, que cette question de savoir si un moine devait ou non aller en pèlerinage présentait deux aspects. Les sources reflètent parfois l'hésitation et les doutes d'individus incertains de ce qu'ils devaient faire,

1. *Statuta capitulorum generalium ordinis Cisterciensis*, éd. J.-M. Canivez, I, Louvain, 1933, p. 30 (1134, cap. 74) et 65-66 (1157, cap. 43 et 53) (« Bibliothèque de la Revue d'histoire ecclésiastique », 9).
2. *The Observances in Use at the Augustinian Priory of S. Giles and S. Andrew at Barnwell, Cambridgeshire*, éd. J. W. Clark, Cambridge, 1897, p. 30-35 (cap. 2-3).
3. *Le recueil des pensées du B. Guigue*, éd. et tr. André Wilmart, Paris, 1936, p. 111 et p. 232 (« Etudes de philosophie médiévale », 22).
4. *Die Visionen der hl. Elisabeth und die Schriften der Aebte Ekbert und Emecho von Schönau*, éd. F. W. E. Roth, Brünn, 1884, p. 142-143 ; cf. Hildegard de Bingen, Ep. 158, dans *Analecta sanctae Hildegardis*, éd. J. B. Pitra, Monte Cassino, 1882, p. 573 (« Analecta sacra », 8), demandant à l'évêque Eberhard de Bamberg de se garder de la *peregrina filia G.*, dont l'esprit était oppressé par une « grande anxiété ».
5. Etienne de Grandmont, Liber sententiarum, 70, 1-3, in *Patr. lat.*, CCIV, 1114 CD ; cf. Jean Becquet, Bibliothèque des écrivains de l'ordre de Grandmont, *Revue Mabillon*, 1963, LIII, p. 62, sur la date et l'auteur de l'œuvre.

Monachisme et pèlerinage au Moyen Age

et mettent ainsi en lumière les motivations du pèlerinage. Que la cause des errances de Mochuda, par exemple, fût qu'il se soit rendu coupable d'une infraction à la discipline monastique, cela est montré par l'amusant petit discours du démon que l'on expulsa de sa chaussure et qui déclara : « C'est une chance pour vous d'avoir rencontré Comgall, ô Mochuda, car je ne vous aurais pas permis de rester deux nuits au même endroit, à cause de l'avantage injuste que vous donniez à vos propres souliers, par rapport aux souliers du couvent, en en frottant vos mains sur eux [*sans doute afin de les graisser*] quand vous découpiez la viande des repas ; je n'ai pas trouvé d'autre moyen de vous atteindre »[1]. On trouve un autre type de conflit intérieur dans le cas de Geoffroi de Chalard, dont le désir de se joindre à la première croisade alarmait gravement ses compagnons, et qui fut dissuadé de partir, selon son biographe, par une vision, que le Christ lui envoya, d'un abbé qui lui prédit les maux qui surviendraient à son église s'il la quittait, et le convainquit de ne pas entreprendre son voyage. De même Christian de l'Aumône ne put abandonner son désir d'être pèlerin et exilé, et ne décida de demeurer ermite qu'après avoir pris conscience de ce que son envie de s'en aller lui était inspirée par le diable[2].

La source de cette tension ne résidait pas seulement dans le conflit entre les valeurs traditionnelles du pèlerinage *ex patria* et *ad loca sancta* d'un côté, et celles de la stabilité et de l'obédience monastiques de l'autre, mais aussi dans le changement de caractère du pèlerinage et, plus profondément, dans l'importance de plus en plus grande prêtée au pèlerinage intérieur et à l'intériorité dans la spiritualité en général à la fin du Moyen Age. « Le pèlerinage du chrétien, écrivait Delaruelle dans un essai sur le pèlerinage intérieur au XVe siècle, est essentiellement une marche intérieure en la grâce de Dieu, à la fois terme et moyen »[3]. Alphandéry faisait des observations sur la tendance, dans la spiritualité de la croisade, au XIIe siècle déjà, à ce que « le centre animateur de la geste de Croisade — la Terre sainte — devienne un symbole, et à ce que la croisade prenne la forme d'un combat intérieur. « Nous sommes plus près, disait-il, du *Pilgrim's Progress* que de Pierre l'Ermite »[4]. De nombreux savants ont montré, dans les écrits du bas Moyen Age, la prédominance du thème du pèlerinage intérieur et des formules de désir et de souhait ardent qui l'accompagnent. « La quête est le pendant littéraire, selon Bloomfield,

---

1. Voir Bethada Náem nErenn, II, p. 301-302.
2. Vita beati Gaufredi, 6, éd. A. Bosvieux, dans *Mémoires de la Société des Sciences naturelles et archéologiques de la Creuze*, 1862, III, p. 93-95 ; voir ci-dessus sur Chrétien.
3. Etienne Delaruelle, Le pèlerinage intérieur au XVe siècle, *Eléona*, 1962, XLII, p. 6-12, cité ici d'après *La piété populaire au Moyen Age*, Turin, 1975, p. 559.
4. Paul Alphandéry, *La chrétienté et l'idée de croisade* ; II. *Recommencements nécessaires (XIIe-XIIIe siècles)*, éd. Alphonse Dupront, Paris, 1959, p. 109-110.

de l'attitude innée du xiie siècle, nouvelle ou ressuscitée, à l'égard de la vie ; de l'image de la vie — générale chez les chrétiens — conçue comme un pèlerinage ou comme un véritable voyage, image affermie comme résultat des croisades et de l'opulence plus importante ; et enfin de ce que l'on pourrait appeler l'idée de croisade elle-même, qui s'empara de toute l'Europe »[1].

Cette accentuation de l'idéal du pèlerinage intérieur impliquait aussi une nouvelle évaluation du pèlerinage actif, déjà remis en question en raison des accusations portées contre son caractère séculier et matériel, et aussi de la peur, grandissante à la fin du Moyen Age, du vagabondage, qui tendait à creuser le fossé dans la pratique populaire entre l'errance ascétique et solitaire et les expéditions organisées pour visiter les tombeaux[2]. De nombreuses voix s'élevèrent, à partir du xiie siècle, mettant en cause les motifs des pèlerins et des croisés, et insistant sur le besoin de bonnes intentions aussi bien que d'une bonne conduite dans la pratique du pèlerinage. D'autres insistèrent sur les responsabilités au foyer de ceux qui voudraient être pèlerins : vis-à-vis de leur famille, de leurs dépendants et, dans le cas des prêtres, de leurs congrégations. Certains suggérèrent même que l'argent dépensé en pèlerinage pourrait être mieux utilisé à des fins charitables[3]. « Ceux qui font beaucoup de pèlerinages, écrivait l'auteur de l'*Imitation* (1, 23, 2), sont rarement sauvés. »

Quoique ces avertissements aient été principalement adressés à des laïques et à des clercs séculiers, ils s'appliquaient encore plus particulièrement aux moines et aux moniales dont on pensait qu'ils visaient plutôt la Jérusalem céleste que la Jérusalem terrestre, que leur exil était plutôt dans un monastère qu'en pays étranger et leur combat plutôt contre leurs propres vices que contre les païens. Enfin, leur pèlerinage, comme le disait Bernard, s'accomplissait avec les sentiments plutôt qu'avec les

---

1. Morton W. Bloomfield, *Piers Plowman as a Fourteenth-century Apocalypse*, Nouveau-Brunswick, [1962], 8-9, cf. p. 59 ; voir aussi Hugues, dans *J. Eccl. hist.*, XI, p. 148-151, sur la survie de l'idéal d'errance dans la littérature irlandaise, et F. C. Gardiner, *The Pilgrimage of Desire : A Study of Theme and Genre in Medieval Literature*, Leiden, 1971, qui dégage le thème du pèlerinage intérieur, *human and destinal* et ses formulations.

2. Cf. Alexandre Vexliard, *Introduction à la sociologie du vagabondage*, Paris, 1956, qui souligne l'apparition du vagabondage comme résultat de pressions économiques à la fin du Moyen Age, et sa répression en France et en Angleterre à partir du milieu du xive siècle.

3. Outre les sources citées dans mon article (cf. ci-dessus), voir Jean Chatillon, *Galandi Regniacensis Libellus Proverbiorum. Le recueil de proverbes glosés du cistercien Galland de Rigny*, *Revue du Moyen Age latin*, 1953, IX ; Jacques de Vitry, Historia Hierosolimitana, 82, dans *Gesta Dei per Francos*, éd. Jacques Bongars, Hanovre, 1611, I, p. 1096-1097 ; et les sermons de Berthold de Regensburg, éd. Franz Pfeiffer et Joseph Strobe, Vienne, 1862-1880, I, p. 442-461 (Serm. 28), de Giordano da Rivalto, éd. Enrico Narducci, Bologne, 1867, p. 109 (Serm. 20), et les autres sources citées par Sumption, *Pilgrimage*, p. 289-290 et 351.

Monachisme et pèlerinage au Moyen Age

pieds. « L'important n'était plus tellement de sortir de son pays, mais de sortir de soi..., le monastère pouvait être pour tous un désert où l'on reste stable avec un esprit d'exilé. On avait jadis pratiqué une *stabilitas in peregrinatione*; on découvrait maintenant une *peregrinatio in stabilitate* »[1]. Les deux idéaux restèrent vivants tout au long du Moyen Age, l'un attirant l'attention des moines et des moniales sur le besoin constant de renoncer au monde et d'être des exilés volontaires, l'autre insistant sur la nature essentiellement intérieure de leur vocation et sur l'importance qu'il y avait à rester à l'intérieur de leur monastère. Rien ne montre plus clairement l'intensité de ce conflit que l'engagement des forces surnaturelles de chaque côté. Pour chaque vision ou chaque miracle appuyant l'idéal de l'obéissance, il y en avait d'autres qui appuyaient celui du pèlerinage. Le fait que l'on ait, durant tout le Moyen Age, considéré le désir de partir en pèlerinage ressenti par les moines et les moniales comme une inspiration du diable sous l'aspect d'un ange — le mal sous la forme du bien, comme disait l'auteur de la *Vita* de saint Coemgen — montre à quel point les contemporains étaient conscients des exigences opposées du monachisme et du pèlerinage, et combien le besoin d'un guide était vif chez nombre d'individus déchirés entre les deux idéaux.

De semblables hésitations ont été ressenties par des personnalités religieuses perspicaces de tous les temps. Elles ne sont pas inconnues de nos jours. On peut les retrouver par exemple, quoique sous une apparence séculière, dans la publicité d'une compagnie aérienne pour un programme de vacances : « Vos vacances devraient être aussi uniques que votre personnalité. Pendant des années, les hommes ont cherché dans toute la terre pour trouver les vacances parfaites. Mais ils ont regardé dans la mauvaise direction. Ils auraient dû chercher en eux-mêmes. » Ces mots auraient pu être écrits, avec très peu de modifications, par un réformateur monastique au Moyen Age. *Vacatio* était un terme très usité dans la spiritualité monastique, et impliquait un idéal de liberté, de paix et de détachement vis-à-vis du monde[2]. Où pouvait-on trouver, en effet, les vacances parfaites ? Près des Lieux saints ? Dans un état d'errance perpétuelle ou d'exil spirituel ? Entre les murs d'un monastère ? Ou bien, seulement, à l'intérieur de son propre cœur ? Telles sont les questions auxquelles s'intéressaient les moines et les moniales au Moyen Age, et auxquelles, pas plus que les hommes d'aujourd'hui, ils ne trouvèrent jamais de réponse pleinement satisfaisante.

---

1. LECLERCQ, dans *Sources*, p. 86-87.
2. Jean LECLERCQ, *Otia monastica. Etudes sur le vocabulaire de la contemplation au Moyen Age*, Rome, 1963, p. 42-49 (« Studia Anselmiana », 51).

IV

OPPOSITION TO PILGRIMAGE IN THE MIDDLE AGES

The practice of pilgrimage in the Middle Ages was so popular, and generally regarded as so praiseworthy, that the reservations voiced by serious churchmen are easily overlooked (1). When the practice first spread, in the fourth and fifth centuries, long–distance pilgrimages in particular were criticized on the grounds

---

(1) The article is concerned primarily with the eleventh and twelfth centuries, the period when *peregrinatio* was the ruling social concept, according to GERHART B. LADNER, *Homo Viator: Mediaeval Ideas on Alienation and Order*, in *Speculum* 42 (1967) 233-59. There is still no good general book on pilgrimage in the Middle Ages: for the ancient church, see BERN-HARD KÖTTING, *Peregrinatio religiosa. Wallfahrten in der Antike und das Pilgerwesen in der alten Kirche (Forschungen zur Volkskunde* 33-5; Münster in W. 1950) and, for the later period, the collected essays, especially those by BAUDOUIN DE GAIFFIER and EDMOND-RENÉ LA-BANDE, in *Pellegrinaggi e culto dei santi in Europa fino alla I Crociata (Convegni del Centro di studi sulla spiritualità medievale* 4; Todi 1963), to which should be added two further ar-ticles by LABANDE, *Recherches sur les pèlerins dans l'Europe des XIe et XIIe siècles*, in *Cahiers de Civilisation médiévale* 1 (1958) 159-69 and 339-47 and *Ad limina: le pèlerin médiéval au terme de sa démarche*, in *Mélanges offerts à René Crozet*, ed. PIERRE GALLAIS and YVES-JEAN RIOU, 1 (Poitiers 1966) 283-91. On the legal status of pilgrims, which was formulated be-tween the eighth and eleventh centuries, see F. GARRISSON, *A propos des pèlerins et de leur condition juridique*, in *Études d'histoire du droit canonique dédiées à Gabriel Le Bras*, 2 (Paris 1965) 1165-89; and on the relation of monasticism to the concept of peregrination, see the two articles by JEAN LECLERCQ, *Mönchtum und Peregrinatio im Frühmittelalter*, in *Römische Quartalschrift für christliche Altertumskunde und Kirchengeschichte* 55 (1960) 212-25 and *Mo-nachisme et pérégrination du IXe au XIIe siècle*, in *Studia monastica* 3 (1961) 33-52, which were reprinted (and the former one translated and revised) in *Aux sources de la spiritualité occidentale* (Paris 1964) 40-90. Several of these works touch on the question of opposition to pilgrimage, but so far as I know there is no single study of this subject. The book by JO-NATHAN SUMPTION, *Pilgrimage: An Image of Mediaeval Religion* (London, 1975) appeared too late for consideration in this article.

that they detracted from the honor paid to local shrines, implied that some places were more holy than others, and exposed the pilgrims to physical and moral risks (2). Even St Jerome, who was a notable pilgrim himself, warned in a passage from Letter 58 which was often cited by later critics of pilgrimages that, 'It is praiseworthy not to have been in Jerusalem but to have lived well for Jerusalem' (3). St Augustine stressed in the *Contra Faustum* that, 'God is in all places and... is not contained or enclosed in any one place', though in the same work he defended the practice of dedicating altars to the memory of saints and martyrs and in Letter 78 asserted the special power of such holy places (4). At about the same time in the East, Gregory of Nyssa said that travel cannot bring a man closer to God and that the Holy Spirit does not dwell more in Jerusalem than in any other town (5).

These expressions of doubt by the Fathers apparently did little to stem the growing tide of pilgrimage in the early Middle Ages, when many pilgrims set forth in both East and West, and especially from Ireland and England, on pilgrimages *ad loca sancta* and, as a form of ascetic devotion, *ex patria*, wandering from place to place in a state of permanent physical and spiritual

---

(2) Kötting, *Peregrinatio* 421-6, who further pointed out that there is no known patristic homily or exhortation in favor of pilgrimage, though various works praising individual saints and martyrs may have had the same effect. Cf. also Steven Runciman, *A History of the Crusades*, 1: *The First Crusade and the Foundation of the Kingdom of Jerusalem* (Cambridge 1951) 39-40. Martin Bechthum, *Beweggründe und Bedeutung des Vagantentums in der lateinischen Kirche des Mittelalters* (*Beiträge zur mittelalterlichen, neueren und allgemeinen Geschichte* 14; Jena 1941) 23-30 and De Gaiffier, in *Pellegrinaggi* 30-1 both cite examples of opposition to wandering monks and clerics.

(3) *Sancti Eusebii Hieronymi Epistulae*, ed. Isidor Hilberg, 1 (*Corpus scriptorum ecclesiasticorum latinorum* 54; Vienna/Leipzig 1910) 529: ‹ Non Hierosolymis fuisse, sed Hierosolymis bene uixisse laudandum est ›. The second *Hierosolymis* should perhaps literally be translated "in Jerusalem", but the context (especially the following contrast between the two cities which killed the prophets and spilled the blood of Christ and which was made joyful by the stream of the river [*Ps.* 45.5] and was called the mother of saints by St Paul [*Gal.* 4.26]) shows that Jerome had in mind the earthly and heavenly Jerusalems, and the dictum was always subsequently interpreted in this way.

(4) *Contra Faustum* 20.21 in *Patrologia latina* (=*PL*) 42, 384-6 and *S. Aurelii Augustini Hipponiensis episcopi epistulae*, ed. A. Goldbacher, 2 (*Corpus scriptorum ecclesiasticorum latinorum* 34; Prague/Vienna/Leipzig 1898) 335.

(5) Kötting, *Peregrinatio* 423, with references to other Greek Fathers.

exile. The motives of these pilgrims were not always above suspicion, however, as some contemporaries noted. A formula from Merovingian Gaul, for instance, referred to a pilgrimage to Rome made not, as was the custom with many, for the sake of idleness but on account of the name of the Lord (6). Bede's remarks that Benedict Biscop never returned 'empty and useless' from his many trips across the sea, as is the custom with some', and that Oftfor's decision to visit Rome 'was at that time considered of great merit' shows that he questioned whether all pilgrimages were of value (7). St Boniface was disturbed by the misbehavior of many pilgrims and in 747 urged the archbishop of Canterbury to prohibit pilgrimages to Rome by women, many of whom became prostitutes in the towns of Italy and France (8).

These doubts concerning voluntary pilgrims were reinforced by the abuses of penitential pilgrimages which were imposed upon criminals by ecclesiastical (and later also by civil) courts as a form of punishment (9). The *Admonitio generalis* of 789 prohibited wandering penitents along with other vagabonds and decreed that criminals of this sort should stay in one place while

---

(6) Marculf, *Formula* 2.49, ed. KARL ZEUMER, *Formulae Merowingici et Karolini Aevi* (*Monumenta Germaniae historica* [=*MGH*], *Leges* 5; Hanover 1886) 104. On this collection, which is dated ca. 650 by some scholars and 721/35 by others, see RUDOLF BUCHNER, *Die Rechtsquellen* (WATTENBACH-LEVISON, *Deutschlands Geschichtsquellen im Mittelalter. Vorzeit und Karolinger*, Beiheft; Weimar 1953) 51-2. The term *vacandi*, which I have here translated as 'idleness', is given as *vagandi* by BECHTHUM, *Vagantentum* 33, which fits the sense but has no manuscript authority. The context clearly shows that a pejorative implication was intended.

(7) Bede, *Homilia in natale Benedicti episcopi*, in *PL*, 94, 228A and *Historia ecclesiastica gentis Anglorum* 4.23, ed. BERTRAM COLGRAVE and R.A.B. MYNORS (*Oxford Medieval Texts*; Oxford 1969) 408. Cf. WILHELM LEVISON, *England and the Continent in the Eighth Century* (*Ford Lectures 1943*; Oxford 1946) 38-9.

(8) Boniface, Letter 78, ed. ERNST DÜMMLER, *Epistolae Merowingici et Karolini aevi* 1 (*MGH, Epistolae* 3; Berlin 1892) 354-5. Cf. LEVISON, *England* 39; BECHTHUM, *Vagantentum* 34-5; KÖTTING, *Peregrinatio* 425; and CYRILLE VOGEL, *Le pèlerinage pénitentiel*, in *Pellegrinaggi* 70 and 75 and in *Revue des sciences religieuses* 38 (1964) 136 and 140, citing this letter and others by Boniface and his followers.

(9) See ÉTIENNE VAN CAUWENBERGH, *Les pèlerinages expiatoires et judiciaires dans le droit communal de la Belgique au moyen âge* (Université de Louvain: *Recueil de travaux publiés par les membres des conférences d'histoire et de philologie* 48; Louvain 1922) esp. 8-16; BECHTHUM, *Vagantentum* 32-7; the article cited above by VOGEL, in *Pellegrinaggi* 69-76 and *Rev. des sc. rel.* 38, 136-8 (where many of the sources cited here are considered under the heading 'Les abus dans la *peregrinatio* pénitentielle'); and GARRISSON, in *Études Le Bras* 2, 1174-5.

performing the penance imposed upon them (10). The council of Chalon in 813 warned against injudicious pilgrimages to Rome, Tours, and other places and specifically forbade pilgrimages by priests without permission from their bishops and urged the emperor to take steps against various types of illegitimate pilgrims.

> There are priests, deacons, and other clerics who live negligently thinking that they can free themselves from sin and perform their ministry by going to these places. There are laymen who think they either sin or have sinned with impunity because they visit these places for prayer. There are powerful men who have enriched themselves by obtaining rents under the pretext of visiting Rome or Tours, have oppressed many poor men, and pretend that what they do only from cupidity is done for the sake of prayer and visiting holy places. There are poor men who do the same in order to have better means of begging. Among these are vagabonds who lie that they are going to a particular place and who, being so foolish as to think that they can be freed from sin simply by the sight of holy places, disregard the words of St Jerome that, 'It is praiseworthy not to have been in Jerusalem but to have lived well for Jerusalem'.

Only after these warnings did the council grudgingly recognize that there were also legitimate pilgrims who visited Rome and other holy places after confessing their sins and accepting penance at home from their parish priests (11). Also in the early ninth century Bishop Haito of Basel, besides prohibiting priests to leave their churches to visit Rome 'for the sake of prayer', required laymen who wished to do the same to leave only after confessing their sins at home, 'since they should be bound or

---

(10) *Admonitio generalis* 79, in *Capitularia regum Francorum*, ed. ALFRED BORETIUS and VICTOR KRAUSE (*MGH, Leges* 2; Hanover 1883-1897) 1, 60-1. Cf. *Capitulare missorum item speciale* 45, *ibid.* 1, 104, which was dated 802? by BORETIUS and 806? by F.L. GANSHOF, *Recherches sur les capitulaires* (Paris 1958) 68.

(11) Council of Chalon (813) 44-5, in *Concilia aevi Karolini* 1, ed. A. WERMINGHOFF (*MGH, Leges* 3.2; Hanover/Leipzig 1906-1908) 282-3.

loosed by their own bishop or priest, not by an outsider' (12). Paricides in particular were required by the council of Mainz in 847 to perform penance in one place rather than by wandering around (13). This decree was cited by Rabanus Maurus and later by Regino of Prüm and Burchard of Worms (14). The continued interest in this issue is also shown by later conciliar legislation requiring penitents not to wander around but to stay where their own priest could keep an eye on them (15).

Reformers in the Carolingian period were concerned for the general spiritual welfare of pilgrims as well as for the good order of society and the church. In a little poem entitled 'God should not be sought in a place but cherished with piety', Theodulph of Orléans said that the way to the stars was through good behavior rather than through Rome (16). The acerbic critic of popular religion Claudius of Turin wrote in about 825 concerning pilgrimages to Rome that, 'I neither approve nor disapprove of that journey, since I know that it is neither of disadvantage nor of advantage to everyone, nor does it hurt or help everyone' (17). A mid–ninth century Irish poem ran: 'To go to Rome, much labor, little profit: you will not find the King whom you seek here unless you bring Him with you' (18). This emphasis

---

(12) Haito of Basel, *Capitularia ecclesiastica* 18, in *Capitularia* 1, 365, where it is dated 807/23. Cf. C. DE CLERCQ, *La législation religieuse franque de Clovis à Charlemagne* (Université de Louvain: *Recueil de travaux publiés par les membres des conférences d'histoire et de philologie* 2.38; Louvain/Paris 1936) 282-4, suggesting 806/13.

(13) Council of Mainz (847) 20, in *Capitularia* 2, 181.

(14) Rabanus Maurus, *Poenitentiarum liber* 11, in *PL*, 112, 1410C; Regino of Prüm, *De ecclesiasticis disciplinis* 2.28, in *PL*, 132, 291AB; Burchard of Worms, *Decretorum libri XX* 6.35, in *PL*, 140, 773AB.

(15) Cf. Council of Seligenstadt (1022) 19, in *Sacrorum conciliorum nova et amplissima collectio*, ed. G.D. MANSI (Florence/Venice 1759-1798) 19, 399AB.

(16) Theodulph of Orléans, *Carmina minora* 67, ed. ERNST DÜMMLER, *Poetae latini aevi Carolini* 1 (*MGH, Antiquitates* 1; Berlin 1881) 557.

(17) *Epistolae Karolini aevi* 2, 612. Cf. REGINALD L. POOLE, *Illustrations of the History of Medieval Thought and Learning*, 2nd ed. (London/New York 1920) 30-1 and (on the somewhat weak reply by Jonas of Orléans) VOGEL, in *Rev. des sc. rel.* 38, 137-8.

(18) WHITLEY STOKES and JOHN STRACHAN, *Thesaurus Palaeohibernicus* (Cambridge 1901-1903) 2, 296, with a revised translation of the second quatrain (not cited here) in WHITLEY STOKES, *A Supplement to Thesaurus Palaeohibernicus* (Halle a.S. 1910) 78. The editors (p. xxxiv) cite the opinion of LUDWIG TRAUBE, *O Roma nobilis*, in *Abhandlungen der bayerischen Akademie der Wissenschaften, Phil.-hist. Kl.* 19 (1891) 349 that the manuscript from

on the spiritual attitude of the pilgrim is found in the early tenth
century in the *Life* of Gerald of Aurillac by Abbot Odo of Cluny,
who was generally favorable to pilgrimage but said of Gerald's
many visits to Rome that, 'Since he was a spiritual man, he strove
to look spiritually at those two lights of the world, Peter and
Paul' (19).

What was true for the laity and clergy obviously applied
even more to monks and nuns, who were by their profession
supposed to be cut off from the world. Venantius Fortunatus
said of Bishop Albinus of Angers that even when travelling outside the cloister he remained 'forever enclosed within the prison
of his own heart' (20). The ascetic peregrination *ex patria* was
also seen as a means of escaping ties with family and the world.
In fact, however, pilgrimages were often a source of worldly contacts and presented a serious threat to the monastic vocation,
especially after the spread of the Benedictine Rule, with its stress
on obedience and stability and its strong condemnation of *gyro-
vagi* who spent their entire lives wandering from place to place
following their own wills. The council of Ver in 755 forbade
monks 'who live according to a rule *(regulariter)*' to go to Rome
or to wander about unless they were carrying out the orders
of their abbot (21). A century later the biographer of St Anskar,
who was a monk at Corbie before he set forth as 'Apostle of the
North', felt it necessary to explain his hero's breach of stability
and obedience as the result, he said, not of levity but of divine

which this poem comes (Codex Boernerianus: Dresden A. 145b) — and hence the poem itself — was written by Sedulius Scotus; but this has been denied by H. FREDE, *Altlateinische
Paulus-Handschriften* (*Vetus latina* 4; Freiburg im B. 1964) 50-79, esp. 67, who attributed
the manuscript to St Gall. It was considered a forerunner of the Goliardic poems by BORIS
I. JARCHO, *Die Vorläufer des Golias*, in *Speculum* 3 (1928) 558 but seems to belong in the
context of contemporary criticism of pilgrimages to Rome.

(19) Odo of Cluny, *Vita sancti Geraldi* 2.17, in *Bibliotheca Cluniacensis*, ed. MARTIN
MARRIER and ANDRÉ DUCHESNE (Paris 1614) 95C. Cf. his *Collationes* 2.26, *ibid.* 206A, on
the uselessness of a pilgrimage to obtain impunity for a crime of which the sinner does not
repent in his heart.

(20) Venantius Fortunatus, *Vita sancti Albini* 6 (14), in *Opera pedestria*, ed. BRUNO
KRUSCH (*MGH, Auctores antiquissimi* 4.2; Berlin 1885) 29. Cf. EDMOND MARTÈNE, *De antiquis monachorum ritibus libri quinque* 5.17.21, in *De antiquis ecclesiae ritibus* (Antwerp 1736-
1738) 4, 825.

(21) Council of Ver (755) 10, in *Capitularia* 1, 35. Cf. DE CLERCQ, *Législation* 136.

inspiration and 'love of pilgrimage for the salvation of souls' (22). Even the highly individualistic Irish monks were expected to seek the permission of their superiors before setting out as *peregrini*. There are many stories in the *Lives* of the Irish saints about would-be pilgrims who were dissuaded from leaving by holy men or angelic visitations and about devils who sought to persuade monks to leave their monasteries. A devil who inhabited the shoe of Mochuda, for instance, and kept him from spending more than two nights in any one place, was expelled by St Comgall, who then told Mochuda to go home and attend to his hours (23). And St Coemgen abandoned his solitary pilgrimage at the behest of the hermit Gorbannus, who said that, 'It is better at this time to remain in Christ fixed in one place than in old age to wander about from place to place' (24).

With regard to nuns, the council of Friuli in 796/7 decreed that permission should never be given to an abbess or nun to visit Rome or 'other venerable places' and attributed this desire to the inspiration of Satan in the form of an angel (25). Half a century later the council of Pavia expressed concern at the dissemination of errors by clerics and monks peregrinating through various provinces and cities and deceiving the hearts of the simple (26). These legislative sources have to be interpreted with a grain of salt, since they probably reflect a growth in the practices they were designed to suppress; but they show that the tradition of opposition to pilgrimage persisted even during its period of greatest growth and popularity and with regard to monks was strengthened in the Carolingian period by the new regard for the Benedictine Rule.

The distinction between the legitimacy of pilgrimages by monks, on one side, and by clerics and laymen, on the other,

---

(22) Rimbert, *Vita Anskarii* 6, ed. Georg Waitz (*MGH, Scriptores rerum germanicarum in usum scholarum* 55; Hanover 1884) 26.

(23) Charles Plummer, *Bethada Náem Nérenn. Lives of the Irish Saints* 2 (Oxford 1922) 301-2.

(24) *Vita sancti Coemgeni* 29, in Charles Plummer, *Vitae sanctorum Hiberniae* (Oxford 1910) 1, 249; cf. 240, 245, 250 (*Vita sancti Coemgeni* 2, 21, 30) 2, 7 (*Vita sancti Comgalli* 13) and 1, cxxii-cxxiii for other examples.

(25) Council of Friuli (796/7) 12, in *Concilia* 194. Cf. De Clercq, *Législation* 251.

(26) Council of Pavia (850) 21, in *Capitularia* 2, 122.

is brought out in an interesting letter written by Peter Damiani,
probably in the early 1030s, to Marquis Rainier of Tuscany,
who had failed to perform a pilgrimage imposed upon him as
a penance for his sins. Such penances, Peter wrote, were not
lightly or universally imposed.

> For we urge those who live according to a rule (*regulariter*) and who lawfully observe the precepts of either
> the monastic or the canonical religion to remain in the
> vocation in which they are established and not to omit
> those things which are necessary for the sake of things
> which lie within human discretion. ...But we urge those
> who either serve the world as soldiers or who prefer
> the spiritual army but do not observe the institute of
> its profession to take the journey of spiritual exile and
> to give satisfaction in foreign parts to the fearful judge
> whose laws and mandates they neglect among the cares
> of the court of their lord. Thus by wandering they can
> gain peace [and] by pilgrimage, a home in the father-
> land (27).

Here, therefore, one of the strictest ascetics of the eleventh century, and one of the leaders of the new monastic movement,
while praising the practice of peregrination (the *spiritualis exsilii
iter*, as he calls it) for laymen and clerics, clearly laid down that
monks and canons should not leave their monasteries.

The incompatibility of monasticism and pilgrimage was the
subject of a letter written probably in 1086 by St Anselm, while
he was still abbot of Bec, to a young man whom he urged to become a monk rather than go to Jerusalem.

> Be not ashamed to call yourself a poor man of Christ,
> for yours will be the kingdom of heaven. Fear not to
> make yourself the soldier of such a king, since this king
> will be with you in every danger. Do not wait in this

---

(27) Peter Damiani, Letter 7.17, in *PL*, 144, 456AB. I am not certain that the two
groups described by Peter as 'vel paludati mundo deserviunt vel spiritualis quidem praefe-
runt militiae titulum sed professionis suae non custodiunt institutum' were laymen and clerics,
but this seems to make sense. Cf. JEAN LECLERCQ, *Saint Pierre Damien ermite et homme
d'église* (*Uomini e dottrine* 8; Rome 1960) 89.

life to begin the better way upon which you have decided, lest by chance you put off receiving the blessed crown in the next life. I advise, counsel, pray, beseech, command, as to one I love greatly, that you put aside the Jerusalem which is now the vision not of peace but of tribulation and the treasures of Constantinople and Babylon which are to be seized with bloodstained hands and begin the way to the heavenly Jerusalem which is the vision of peace, where you will find treasures which can be received only by those scorning the other ones (28).

The same point was made by Pope Urban II, who was himself a monk and former prior of Cluny, with regard to the First Crusade. In his letter of 19 September 1096 to the people of Bologna, promising remission from punishment for confessed sins to anyone who went to Jerusalem for the sake of his soul and to free the church, he forbade clerics and monks to go without permission from their bishop or abbot (29). Three weeks later, on 9 October, he specifically forbade the monks and *conversi* of Vallombrosa to join the soldiers going to Jerusalem, saying that the expedition was for soldiers armed to fight the Saracens and not for 'those who have left the world and enrolled in the spiritual army'. Then he repeated his prohibition for clerics and monks to go without permission from their superiors (30).

---

(28) Anselm, Letter 117, in *Opera omnia*, ed. F.S. SCHMITT (Edinburgh 1946-1961) 3, 254. Cf. RICHARD SOUTHERN, *The Making of the Middle Ages* (New Haven 1953) 50 n. 1, dating it probably 1086.

(29) *PL*, 151, 483CD. Cf. *Italia pontificia*, ed. PAUL KEHR (Berlin 1906-1962) 5, 248 no. 14 for other editions.

(30) WILHELM WIEDERHOLD, *Papsturkunden in Florenz*, in *Nachrichten der Gesellschaft der Wissenschaften zu Göttingen, Phil.-hist. Kl.* 1901, 313-4 no. 6. Cf. *Italia pont.* 3, 89 no. 8 (correcting the date from 7 to 9 October) and GIOVANNI MICCOLI, *Aspetti del monachesimo toscano nel secolo XI*, in *Chiesa gregoriana (Storici antichi e moderni*, N.S. 17; Florence 1966) 72. On crusading by monks, cf. J.A. BRUNDAGE, *A Transformed Angel (X.3.31.18): The Problem of the Crusading Monk*, in *Studies in Cistercian History Presented to Jeremiah F. O'Sullivan (Cistercian Studies Series* 13; Spencer, Mass. 1971) 55-62, esp. 56-7 on the eleventh and twelfth centuries. On the question of the actual involvement of monks and hermits in the crusades, see PAUL ALPHANDÉRY and ALPHONSE DUPRONT, *La chrétienté et l'idée de croisade* 1: *Les premières croisades (Évolution de l'humanité* 38.1; Paris 1954) 50-6, who bring out the relation of eremitism and eschatology to the mass movement, and BERNARD BLIGNY, *L'église et les ordres religieux dans le royaume de Bourgogne aux XIᵉ et XIIᵉ siècles (Collection de Cahiers d'histoire publiée par les Universités de Clermont, Lyon, Grenoble* 4; Paris 1960) 182-9,

134

There are references in contemporary sources to these pronouncements or others of the same sort. St Anselm, who was by this time archbishop of Canterbury, wrote to a monk of St Martin at Séez that his desire to visit Jerusalem was contrary to his spiritual welfare, his stability, and his obedience both to his abbot and to the pope, 'who ordered with his great authority that monks should not undertake this journey except for a religious person who may be useful in ruling the church of God or instructing the people, and this only with the advice of and in obedience to his superior' (31). Within his own province, Anselm refused to give such permission, instructing the bishop of Salisbury to stop the abbot and monks of Cerne from going to Jerusalem and to forbid under pain of anathema any monks in his diocese from joining the expedition (32). Geoffrey of Vendôme also referred to the pope's ruling in a letter to the abbot of Marmoutier who was planning to visit Jerusalem for the second time. 'For going to Jerusalem is indicated for laymen but interdicted for monks by the apostolic see. I know this myself from the mouth of the lord Pope Urban when he ordered laymen to make a pilgrimage by going to Jerusalem and forbade the same pilgrimage to monks.' After referring to St Benedict's views on peregrinating monks who made no vow of stability, Geoffrey said that monks who carry the cross of Christ and follow Him in their own monasteries have no need to seek a pilgrim's tomb. 'Therefore we should not stray from the journey of our profession in order to make a journey to Jerusalem, lest by seeking a false blessedness we should find a true misery in both body and soul' (33). 'Men who have behaved well,' Geoffrey wrote in

stressing the economic support given to the crusades by monasteries. According to SOUTHERN, *Making* 50, however, 'The monastic ideals of the eleventh century were in the main hostile to the idea of the Crusade'.

(31) Anselm, Letter 410, *ed. cit.* 5, 355. On Anselm's attitude towards the crusade, see H. DE SAINTE-MARIE, *Les lettres de saint Anselme de Cantorbéry et la Règle bénédictine*, in *Mélanges bénédictins publiés à l'occasion du XIVᵉ centenaire de la mort de saint Benoît par les moines de l'abbaye de Saint-Jérôme de Rome* (Abbaye S. Wandrille 1947) 279-81; NORMAN F. CANTOR, *Church, Kingship, and Lay Investiture in England, 1089-1135* (*Princeton Studies in History* 10; Princeton 1958) 105; and RICHARD W. SOUTHERN, *Saint Anselm and his Biographer* (Cambridge 1963) 122-3.

(32) Anselm, Letter 195, *ed. cit.* 4, 85-6.

(33) Geoffrey of Vendôme, Letter 4.21, in *PL*, 157, 162BC. Cf. L. COMPAIN, *Étude sur Geoffroi de Vendôme* (*Bibliothèque de l'École des Hautes Études* 86; Paris 1891) 67-8.

another letter, 'not all those who have seen the earthly Jerusalem, deserve to receive the Jerusalem that is in heaven' (34).
Pilgrimages by monks raised questions not only concerning
their monastic vocation and responsibilities but also about the
nature of vows, of which a clear doctrine was now for the first
time worked out in connection with the crusades (35). What
happened, in particular, if some one made a vow to go on a pilgrimage or crusade after becoming, or promising to become, a
monk? There was general agreement that under these circumstances the greater vow, to become a monk, whether antecedent
or subsequent, superseded the lesser vow of pilgrimage. According to a sentence which was variously attributed to Anselm
and the abbot of Cluny, a vow to go to Jerusalem or Rome was
fulfilled by joining a monastery because 'those who surrender
themselves to God partially may later surrender themselves to
God totally [and] do not subsequently have to render the part
in the whole' (36). This sentence was cited by Anselm in Letter 468, where he argued that the monastic vow, 'by which a
man offers himself and whatever pertains to him totally to God,'
fulfilled lesser vows, 'which are made without promise of faith
or sacrament' (37). In Letter 188 Anselm told a monk who before making his profession had vowed to visit Saint-Gilles that
he should give up his pilgrimage and strive to be obedient, penitent, and well-behaved in his monastery. 'For you may be sure
that when you vowed and totally surrendered yourself to God
by the monastic profession, you fulfilled all previous minor vows
made without an oath and binding of faith' (38). I am uncertain

---

(34) Geoffrey of Vendôme, Letter 3.24, in *PL*, 157, 127BC: to Hildebert of Le Mans,
saying that a monk who had gone to Jerusalem would have done better to have stayed in
his monastery. See on this monk, Letters 3.29-30, *ibid.* 131-2, and PETER VON Moos, *Hildebert von Lavardin, 1056-1133* (*Pariser historische Studien* 3; Stuttgart 1965) 144-5.

(35) See JAMES A. BRUNDAGE, *The Votive Obligations of Crusaders: The Development
of a Canonistic Doctrine*, in *Traditio* 24 (1968) 77-118, esp. 77-8 and *Medieval Canon Law and
the Crusader* (Madison/Milwaukee/London 1969) 30-65.

(36) JEAN LECLERCQ, *La lettre de Gilbert Crispin sur la vie monastique*, in *Analecta monastica*, 2 (*Studia Anselmiana* 31; Rome 1953) 123; cf. 119 n. 3 for other appearances of
this sentence.

(37) *Opera omnia* 5, 417. Anselm here attributed the sentence to the abbot of Cluny,
but it is found appended to Letter 95 as if it were by himself, *ibid.* 3, 221-2.

(38) Anselm, Letter 188, *ibid.* 4, 73-4.

exactly what restrictions Anselm had in mind by oaths taken without binding of faith and an oath or sacrament. Perhaps he was thinking of marriage, which could not be set aside by a subsequent vow even for a greater good. But he clearly held that monastic vows superseded any vow of pilgrimage.

This view of the superiority of monastic to other obligations was shared by Peter the Venerable and Bernard of Clairvaux. Peter wrote to a knight who decided to make a pilgrimage to Jerusalem after promising to become a monk at Cluny that

> Lesser goods can be put aside for greater, but not greater for lesser or equal for equal. Serving God perpetually in humility and poverty is greater than making a journey to Jerusalem with pride and luxury. While therefore to visit Jerusalem where the Lord's feet stood is good, to look towards the heavens where He is seen face to face is far better. He who has promised the better cannot replace it by the worse (39).

Bernard wrote almost the same in a letter concerning the conflicting claims of vows to live as a hermit and to make a crusade. 'I do not think that minor vows should impede greater ones or that God demands any good thing which has been promised if something better is given in its place' (40). He made the same point in a different way in a letter to the bishop of Lincoln explaining how a cleric had decided to become a monk at Clairvaux rather than go to Jerusalem. 'Your Philip, wishing to go to Jerusalem, found a short cut and swiftly arrived where he wished to go. He speedily crossed this great and spacious sea and successfully navigating has already reached the hoped-for shore and landed at the port of salvation', that is, at Clairvaux, which is associated with the free and heavenly city of Jerusalem by its devotion of mind, way of life, and spiritual kinship (41).

---

(39) *The Letters of Peter the Venerable*, ed. GILES CONSTABLE 1 (*Harvard Historical Studies* 78; Cambridge, Mass. 1967) 152.

(40) Bernard, Letter 57, in *Opera omnia*, ed. JEAN MABILLON 1 (Paris 1839) 202CD.

(41) Bernard, Letter 64, *ibid.* 1, 209AB, where it is dated ca. 1129. Cf. DAVID KNOWLES, *The Monastic Order in England*, 2nd ed. (Cambridge 1963) 222 and LECLERCQ, *Sources* 82-4 on Bernard's concept of the monastic life as a *peregrinatio* in which the monk travelled with his heart while remaining stable with his body.

Both Peter and Bernard encouraged the crusades and supported pilgrimages by laymen (42), but they were resolutely opposed to pilgrimages by monks or abbots. 'The monastic order prohibits us,' wrote Peter to the patriarch of Jerusalem, explaining his own inability to visit the Holy Land, 'to see those, those I say supercelestial places of our redemption, to pour out our tears physically, and to adore in the place where our Lord's feet stood' (43). When he was asked to write some encouraging words to an abbot who was going to Jerusalem, Peter could only cite the testimony of the abbot's own conscience, emphasizing the essentially spiritual and interior nature of the undertaking (44). Monks are saved by holy works rather than by holy places, he wrote to the monks of Mt Thabor; and to the hermit Gilbert he said that ascetic practices such as reclusion, mortification, and expatriation (*longinqua transmigratio*) were useless unless the monk was surrounded by the wall set around him by Christ (45). Bernard at about the same time, or a few years earlier, wrote to the abbot of St Michael in Thiérache that a monk should do penance within his monastery rather than by pilgrimage. 'For the object of monks is to seek out not the earthly but the heavenly Jerusalem, and this not by proceeding with [their] feet but by progressing with [their] feelings' (46). Gratian concurred with

---

(42) See in particular VIRGINIA BERRY, *Peter the Venerable and the Crusades*, in *Petrus Venerabilis 1156-1956. Studies and Texts Commemorating the Eighth Centenary of his Death*, ed. GILES CONSTABLE and JAMES KRITZECK (*Studia Anselmiana* 40; Rome 1956) 141-62, who said 'that Peter the Venerable was consistently sympathetic to the crusade throughout his life' (141). In his sermon in praise of the Holy Sepulchre, which though addressed to monks was designed to arouse enthusiasm for the Holy Land, Peter addressed the crusaders as 'o salvatae gentes' and promised that God would appear as Truth and Everlasting Life to those 'in hac peregrinatione... ad patriam tendentes': *Petri Venerabilis sermones tres*, ed. GILES CONSTABLE, in *Revue bénédictine* 64 (1954) 232-54, cf. 228-9. For a somewhat different view, emphasizing Peter's concern with peace and difference from Bernard with regard to the crusade, see PAOLO LAMMA, *Momenti di storiografia cluniacense* (Istituto storico italiano per il Medio Evo: *Studi storici* 42-4; Rome 1961) 140-4.

(43) Peter the Venerable, Letter 83, *ed. cit.* 1, 220.

(44) Peter the Venerable, Letter 144, *ed. cit.* 1, 358. He went on to warn against the dangers of the undertaking. Cf. LABANDE, in *Cahiers de civ. méd.* 1, 346, citing the *De miraculis* as evidence of Peter's resistance to the excessive materialization of pilgrimages, which in themselves could not win salvation for a sinner.

(45) Peter the Venerable, Letters 80 and 20, *ed. cit.* 1, 216 and 30.

(46) Bernard, Letter 399, *ed. cit.* 1, 717AC. Cf. E. VACANDARD, *Vie de saint Bernard*

this view in his *Decretum*, where he gave as the reason for abbatial control over vows of special abstinence or strictness that monks and clerics 'avoiding regular discipline' were not permitted to take vows of pilgrimage lest in this way they returned to a secular way of life (47).

The question of participation in the crusades was especially difficult for the Cistercians owing to Bernard's role in the preaching of the Second Crusade, although he himself always asserted that he was a man under authority who preached only at the command of the pope (48). The chapter–general prohibited Cistercians to go to Rome except with a bishop of the order in 1134 and again in 1157, when it added that a monk who went to Jerusalem or on another pilgrimage was to leave his own house and be sent to another without hope of return (49). Bernard wrote to the pope in 1124/5 to head off Abbot Arnold of Morimond and some of his monks who were going to Jerusalem. 'Soldiers who fight rather than monks who sing and weep are needed there,' he wrote, adding that they should be stopped even if they were planning to establish a Cistercian abbey in the Holy Land, since it might serve as an excuse for monks wishing to wander to visit a house of their own observance (50). At the time of the Second Crusade Bernard wrote to all Cistercian abbots forbidding in the name of the pope and under pain of excommunication any monk or lay–brother to join the expedition (51).

---

1 (Paris 1895) 182 on the date and recipient of this letter. It was sent with a monk whom Bernard had turned back from a pilgrimage undertaken with the permission of his abbot.

(47) Gratian, *Decretum*, C.20 q.4 d.p. c.3, ed. EMIL FRIEDBERG, *Corpus iuris canonici* 1 (Leipzig 1879) 852. Cf. BRUNDAGE, in *Traditio* 24, 80.

(48) Cf. Appendix A (*St. Bernard's Preaching of the Second Crusade*) to my article on *The Second Crusade as Seen by Contemporaries* in *Traditio* 9 (1953) 276-8.

(49) J.-M. CANIVEZ, *Statuta capitulorum generalium ordinis Cisterciensis* 1 (*Bibliothèque de la Revue d'histoire ecclésiastique* 9; Louvain 1933) 30 (1134 cap. 74) and 65-6 (1157 cap. 43 and 53).

(50) Bernard, Letter 359, *ed. cit.* 1, 656AB, where it is dated 1143. It was redated 1124 by VACANDARD, *Bernard* 1, 162 n. 4 and 1124/5 by ADRIAAN BREDERO, *Jérusalem dans l'Occident médiéval*, in *Mélanges Crozet* (cited n. 1 above) 1, 270. Bernard was apparently afraid that by going to another Cistercian abbey a monk could claim not to have violated his profession.

(51) LEOPOLD GRILL, *Ein unbekannter Brief Bernhards von Clairvaux*, in *Mitteilungen des Instituts für österreichische Geschichtsforschung* 61 (1953) 384.

There are many Cistercian sources from the twelfth and early thirteenth centuries emphasizing the importance of stability and discouraging peregrination. Such is the story, of which one version is attributed to Peter the Venerable, about the vision of a Cistercian novice who was tempted to visit Jerusalem and who promised the Virgin, who appeared to him, that he would continue to serve her in the house of his profession (52). The founder of Mortemer, William of Le Pin, persuaded a knight who wished to visit the Holy Sepulchre to become a monk, urging him to crucify himself for God rather than to carry a cross on his clothing (53). Caesarius of Heisterbach told a story about a canon of Liège (probably the Archdeacon Philip, later prior of Clairvaux) who was inspired by Bernard's preaching of the Second Crusade to take the cross of the order rather than of the overseas expedition, 'judging it better for his soul to have a long cross imprinted on his mind than a short sign sewn temporarily on his clothing'. Caesarius cited in support of this the version in Luke 9, 25 of Christ's command to 'take up his cross daily and follow me', explaining that the word daily (which appears in this version only) referred to monastic life, which crucifies monks in all their members, rather than to pilgrimage, which lasts for only a year or two and from which many people return more sinful than before. Caesarius then cited the papal privilege allowing some one who had taken a vow of pilgrimage or crusading to become a monk, which showed the superiority of the Cistercian order to pilgrimage because a monk who takes the cross, with or without the permission of his superior, is considered 'not a pilgrim of Christ but an apostate'. 'The continual interior fight against the pricks of vice is much better for the soul than the temporary exterior fight against the swords of the Saracens' (54).

It may also have been in association with the Second Cru-

(52) GILES CONSTABLE, *The Vision of Gunthelm and other 'Visiones' Attributed to Peter the Venerable*, in *Revue bénédictine* 66 (1956) 106; cf. 102-3.

(53) J. BOUVET, *Le récit de la fondation de Mortemer*, in *Collectanea ordinis Cisterciensium reformatorum* 22 (1960) 152.

(54) Caesarius of Heisterbach, *Dialogus miraculorum* 1.6, ed. JOSEPH STRANGE 1 (Cologne/Bonn/Brussels 1851) 12-3; cf. the translation by H. VON E. SCOTT and C.C. SWINTON BLAND 1 (Broadway Medieval Library; London 1929) 12-3. On Philip, who took the cross at Liège, see the note in *Letters of Peter the Venerable* 2, 200.

sade that Master Isenbold of St Paul at Halberstadt wrote to
the monk Elvingus of Corbie praising the motives for his desire
to visit Jerusalem but urging caution. Elvingus had cited as
exemplars the exile of Abraham and the poverty of Lazarus;
but Isenbold replied that these could be found better at home
than by a pilgrimage, since a monk leaves his country, kindred,
and father's house when he renounces his property, vices, and
first father, the Devil. 'A change of places may not only not
improve your conduct but may sometimes also make it worse,'
Isenbold warned, citing the line from the *Epistles* of Horace that,
'Those who run across the sea change the climate not the soul'.
He therefore urged Elvingus to aspire and hasten to the heavenly
rather than the earthly Jerusalem, of which the sight is not necessarily a source of blessing (55).

These sentiments were echoed by many monastic leaders in
the twelfth century. 'Let others go to Jerusalem,' said Guigo
of La Chartreuse; 'you, to humility and patience. For you thus
go outside the world, he within [it]' (56). Elizabeth of Schönau,
in a letter urging the abbot of Odenheim not to go to Jerusalem
with one of his monks, wrote that unlike the criminals going
to Jerusalem to do penance and to seek the advice of the patriarch, they were 'the children of light', who should seek Christ
in their hearts, do their duty at home, and walk 'on the way
of contemplation' (57). Hildegard of Bingen expressed her concern for a pilgrim nun in a letter to Bishop Eberhard of Bamberg (58). And Stephen of Grandmont in Sentence 70 categorically forbade his monks to go to Jerusalem or anywhere else
'for the sake of prayer', even with the permission of the superior and community, which share in his sin if they thus encourage

---

(55) This letter is found inserted at the year 1146 in the manuscript of the Annals of
Corbie, in *MGH, Scriptores* in-fol. 3, 13-4. Cf. BREDERO, in *Mélanges Crozet* 1, 271.

(56) Guigo, *Meditatio* 262, ed. ANDRÉ WILMART, *Le recueil des pensées du B. Guigue*
(*Études de philosophie médiévale* 22; Paris 1936) 111 and 232.

(57) *Die Visionen der hl. Elisabeth und die Schriften der Aebte Ekbert und Emecho von
Schönau*, ed. F.W.E. ROTH (Brünn 1884) 142-3.

(58) Hildegard, Letter 158, asking the bishop to care for *peregrina filia G.* who 'gave
everything she had and bought a pearl [by becoming a nun] and whose mind is now suffo-
cated in great anxiety, like a grape in a wine-press', in *Analecta sanctae Hildegardis*, ed. J.B.
PITRA (*Analecta sacra* 8; Monte Cassino 1882) 573; cf. *Liber vitae meritorum* 5.5, *ibid.* 186 for
the reply of Tranquillity to Wandering, urging the virtues of stability.

him on his way to hell. How can a man who has cut off his feet make a journey? To do so is to renounce his life and to ignore the good for which he came to the monastery. 'If the superior goes somewhere for the sake of prayer, he irreparably wounds the monastery internally, indicating to all others that they may do likewise' (59).

Many small communities clearly suffered from the departure of their superiors and members as pilgrims and crusaders; and while some abbots, like those of Marmoutiers, Cerne, Morimond, and Odenheim mentioned above, appear to have regarded pilgrimages to the Holy Land as legitimate and laudable, others hesitated and even refused to go. The followers of Geoffrey of Chalard were greatly alarmed by his desire to join the First Crusade, and according to his biographer he decided not to go only after seeing a vision sent by Christ, 'Who did not wish him to leave this region', of an abbot who foretold the evils which would befall his church if he left and who instructed him to put off his journey (60). Christian of L'Aumône was also long afflicted by a wish to exile himself among the holy places and to spend his whole life as a pilgrim and decided to remain stable in his hermitage only after he recognized that the desire to leave was inspired by the Devil (61). In another case, two followers of Geoffrey of Fontaines-les-Blanches were allowed to go to Jerusalem, but the historian of the community took care to emphasize both that they obtained permission from Geoffrey (and in one case also from the bishop of Tours) and that the community benefitted from these pilgrimages, since the first pilgrim was said to have become patriarch of Jerusalem and to have given to the second one priceless relics which he brought back to Fontaines-les-Blanches (62).

(59) Stephen of Grandmont, *Sententia* 70, in *PL*, 204, 1114CD. On the *Liber sententiarum*, which was compiled either by Peter of Limoges, prior of Grandmont from 1124 to 1137, or by Hugh of Lacerta (d. 1157), see JEAN BECQUET, *Bibliothèque des écrivains de l'ordre de Grandmont*, in *Revue Mabillon* 53 (1963) 62.

(60) *Vita beati Gaufredi* 6, ed. J. BOSVIEUX, in *Mémoires de la Société des sciences naturelles et archéologiques de la Creuse* 3 (1862) 95.

(61) BRUNO GRIESSER, *Christian von L'Aumône, eine neue vollständigere Handschrift seiner Vita*, in *Cistercienser-Chronik* 57 (1950) 25-6; Cf. JEAN LECLERCQ, *Le texte complet de la Vie de Christian de L'Aumône*, in *Analecta Bollandiana* 71 (1953) 21-52.

(62) *Historia monasterii beatae Mariae de Fontanis Albis* 1.4-5, ed. ANDRÉ SALMON, *Recueil de chroniques de Touraine* (Tours 1854) 260-1.

These accounts reflect not only a view of monasticism which put a greater stress on stability and obedience than in the early Middle Ages but also the shift in moral teaching, which was characteristic of the twelfth century, from exterior behavior to interior attitudes. The true pilgrimage for the monk, therefore, as Bernard put it, was with the feelings (*affectus*) rather than the feet and had as its object the heavenly rather than the earthly Jerusalem. 'The important thing was no longer to leave one's country but to leave oneself. ...', Leclercq said. 'The monastery could be a desert where everyone would remain stable with the spirit of exile. Previously they practiced a *stabilitas in peregrinatione*; now they discovered a *peregrinatio in stabilitate*' (63).

This emphasis on intention and interiority also influenced attitudes towards pilgrimages by laymen and clerics. 'You decided correctly that you would prefer to follow the buried Christ rather than the burial-place of Christ,' wrote Hildebert of Le Mans to Agnes, the daughter of Duke William of Aquitaine (64). The spiritual effect of pilgrimage was stressed in a passage, attributed to Abelard, in the so-called Cambridge Commentary on the Epistles of Paul, which compared a visit to Jerusalem with the reception of the Eucharist, emphasizing the compunction and fervor for God inspired by the site and relics of Christ's passion in those who travelled to Jerusalem (65). But even this was useless without prior internal reform, said Maurice of Sully (who was bishop of Paris from 1160 to 1196) in one of his vernacular homilies. 'God has no regard for the works of a bad Christian, for neither he nor his works please Him. ...What profit can it be to him to go on pilgrimage and travel far from his village if he does not travel far from his sin and vice?' (66)

Many writers in the twelfth and thirteenth centuries also stressed the responsibilities at home of laymen and clerics who

(63) Leclercq, in *Studia monastica*, 3, 50-1.

(64) Hildebert, Letter 1.5, in *PL*, 171, 149A. Cf. Von Moos, *Hildebert* 146.

(65) *Commentarius Cantabrigiensis in epistolas Pauli e schola Petri Abaelardi in epistolam ad Hebraeos*, ed. Artur Landgraf (*Publications in Mediaeval Studies* 2.4; Notre Dame 1945) 747.

(66) Cited from C.A. Robson, *Maurice de Sully and the Medieval Vernacular Homily* 108-9 (which I have not seen) in C.R. Cheney, *From Becket to Langton* (*Ford Lectures* 1955; Manchester 1956) 163.

wanted to go on pilgrimages. Ivo of Chartres cited the obligations of marriage in a letter to the count of Troyes, advising him not to go to Jerusalem and join the army of Christ without obtaining the voluntary consent of his wife (67). Hildebert of Le Mans emphasized the public duties of the count of Anjou, who was planning to visit Compostela, saying that he was needed at home to care for the weak and poor. 'I recognize that you have bound yourself by a vow, o prince', Hildebert wrote, 'but God [has bound] you to an office. You [bound yourself] to a journey in which you will see the memorial of the saints, but God [bound you] to obedience, by which you will provide for the saints' memories [of yourself]' (68). Somewhat later Adam of Perseigne wrote a letter to the bishop of Le Mans in which he strongly attacked priests and clerics who deserted their congregations in order to go on crusades, hastening 'at the instigation of a whim to work which God does not impose upon them', and who for this purpose sheared their flocks rather than tended them. 'Christ gave the price of His blood not to acquire the land of Jerusalem but rather to acquire and save souls,' Adam said. 'Wherefore it seems to me that those who strive to acquire that land and therefore neglect the salvation of souls disguise with an appearance of piety the business of [their own] damnation' (69).

Adam's reference to the shearing of flocks shows that the costs of pilgrimages were also used as an argument against them.

---

(67) Ivo of Chartres, Letter 245, in *PL*, 162, 251-2. Cf. James A. Brundage, *The Crusader's Wife: A Canonistic Quandary* and *The Crusader's Wife Revisited*, in *Studia Gratiana* 12 (*Collectanea Stephan Kuttner* 2) 425-42 (430-1 on this letter) and *Studia Gratiana* 14 (*Collectanea Stephan Kuttner* 4) 241-52, who studies the general problem of the relation of marital obligations to crusading. Ivo clearly regarded the count's crusading vow as illegitimate insofar as it conflicted with his legitimate vow of marriage. Cf. also Rolf Sprandel, *Ivo von Chartres und seine Stellung in der Kirchengeschichte* (*Pariser historische Studien* 1; Stuttgart 1962) 140-1, who argued (against Erdmann) that Ivo took a very cautious line with regard to the crusades.

(68) Hildebert, Letter 1.15, in *PL*, 171, 181D-183B. The ellipsis and play of words is hard to translate exactly, but I think I have preserved Hildebert's sense. Cf. Von Moos, *Hildebert* 144-5.

(69) Adam of Perseigne, Letter 6, ed. J. Bouvet, *Lettres d'Adam de Perseigne à ses correspondants du Maine* [fin], in *La Province du Maine*, N.S. 32 (1952) 13.

Stephen of Grandmont (70) said that the money used by a monk
for a pilgrimage was stolen, and Honorius *Augustodunensis* condemned pilgrimages inspired by curiosity or desire for praise
and paid for with money from profits, fraud, rapine, or oppression. He admitted that a pilgrimage undertaken for the love
of God and confession of sins and paid for with honestly–acquired
money was praiseworthy but argued that money was better used
for the poor than for a visit to Jerusalem and other sacred places (71). An even stronger note of social concern was sounded
by Lambert le Bègue in the apology he addressed to the anti-
pope Calixtus III in 1175/7. While denying the accusation that
he wanted to abolish overseas pilgrimages, Lambert admitted
that he had seen many people attempting pilgrimages unwisely
and uselessly and had often advised them 'to carry it out more
carefully and with regard for the health of the soul or indeed
to change it for something better'. The money spent on pilgrimages could be better used for redeeming captives, helping strangers, nourishing the hungry and thirsty, clothing the naked, con-
soling widows, and defending orphans. 'Is there a region or
province on earth,' Lambert asked, 'where numerous and varied
needs are not·to be found?' (72).

As so often in the Middle Ages, the views of the future were
voiced by heretics. As time went on, pilgrimage sank lower and
lower on the scale of Christian good works, below not only monasticism but also pastoral duties, charity, and the obligations of
public office and even marriage. It still had prestige and was
immensely popular with all classes of society, but serious folk
were more inclined to stress the dangers and difficulties than
the benefits of pilgrimage. Petrarch in his *Secretum* put into
the mouth of St Augustine the view that a change of location
only adds to the labor of some one who is already burdened with
evil, citing the Socratic maxim that, 'You peregrinate with your-

---

(70) See n. 59 above.

(71) Honorius *Augustodunensis*, *Elucidarium* 2.23, in *PL*, 172, 1152B and, better, re-
numbered 2.77, in YVES LEFÈVRE, *L'Elucidarium et les lucidaires* (*Bibliothèque des Écoles
françaises d'Athènes et de Rome* 180; Paris 1954) 434-5.

(72) PAUL FRÉDÉRICQ, *Note complémentaire sur les documents de Glascow concernant
Lambert le Bègue*, in *Bulletins de l'Académie royale des sciences, lettres et des beaux-arts de Belgique* 3.29 (1895) 999-1000 and, with a commentary in Dutch, *Corpus documentorum haere-
ticae pravitatis Neerlandicae* (Ghent/The Hague 1889-1906) 2, 28.

self' (73). In a more popular vein, more like that of Chaucer in *The Canterbury Tales*, Thomas à Kempis said that, 'Those who make many pilgrimages rarely find salvation' (74).·

A would-be pilgrim in the late Middle Ages might therefore have to overcome many objections. Some of these went back to the Fathers, stressing that the true Christian acquires eternal life by living well rather than by visiting holy places, that God is not to be found in some places more than in others, and that pilgrims are exposed to many dangers of body and soul (75). Others derived from the circumstances of the Middle Ages, such as the nature of vows and penance and the differing status of individual pilgrims. Thus a monk or nun was considered bound to be stable and obedient and therefore to walk a path of patience, humility, and contemplation within the cloister. A layman or cleric might be held at home by public or private responsibilities, or be asked to consider whether the money to be used for the pilgrimage was honestly acquired or might be put to a better use. All pilgrims were reminded that in itself a pilgrimage cannot secure remission from the penalty of sin and that real forgiveness depends on interior attitudes rather than exterior actions.

It is doubtful whether many pilgrims or crusaders were in fact persuaded to stay at home by these arguments, but they show that the decision may not always have been an easy one. Sensitive religious personalities were doubtless torn between these arguments in favor of stability and others, equally valid in their eyes, in favor of peregrination, including not only the specific spiritual benefits promised to pilgrims *ad loca sancta* but also the older values attached to physical and spiritual exile and the association, found in many religious traditions, of conversion from former evils with a state of homelessness and travel (76).

---

(73) Francesco Petrarca, *Prose* (*La letteratura italiana* 7; Milan/Naples 1955) 164-6.

(74) Thomas à Kempis, *Imitatio Christi* 1.23.2. Cf. also the Lollard Conclusions of 1394, c. 8, in *Fasciculi zizaniorum*, ed. WALTER SHIRLEY (*Rolls Series* 5; London 1858) 364 and references in KÖTTING, *Peregrinatio* 426.

(75) I have found no sign in the Middle Ages of the Patristic argument that long-distance pilgrimages detracted from local shrines.

(76) See most recently, with references to previous literature, ANTOINE GUILLAUMONT, *Le dépaysement comme forme d'ascèse dans le monachisme ancien*, in *École pratique des Hautes Études. Ve Section: Sciences religieuses. Annuaire* 76 (1968-1969) 31-58.

This dilemma is perhaps most clearly illustrated in the sources used here by the enlistment of supernatural forces on both sides. For every miracle and vision supporting a decision to stay at home there were others encouraging pilgrims on their way. Together they emphasize the ambiguity of medieval attitudes towards this characteristic activity.

V

THE *LIBER MEMORIALIS* OF REMIREMONT*

"It is the teaching of the Church," wrote Pope Gregory III in about 732, replying to an inquiry from St Boniface, "that everyone should offer oblations for his dead who were truly Christians and that the priest should make a commemoration of them. And although we are all subject to sin, it is fitting that the priest should make a commemoration and intercede for dead catholics."[1] This practice of liturgical commemoration and intercession was widespread in the early and mediaeval Church[2] and was usually performed either annually, on the death-days of those whose names were entered on a calendar called a necrology or obituary, or daily, for those whose names were inscribed on the diptychs or other tablets, listing both dead and living, out of which developed the long lists of names known as *libri vitae* and *libri memoriales*.[3] Until recently the historical value of these works has not been highly esteemed, though they were occasionally used by palaeographers, philologists, genealogists, and historians, who found in necrologies the death-days of many prominent figures.[4] In the past few years, however, as the techniques of prosopographical research have developed and historians have concentrated on the political, sociological, and familial groupings of men in the early Middle Ages, these works have been seriously studied, especially by the group of scholars trained at Freiburg-im-Breisgau under Professor Gerd Tellenbach.[5] Their research has shown, what has also proved true in other fields, that for the progress of mediaeval studies the discovery of previously unknown sources

---

* Eduard Hlawitschka, Karl Schmid, and Gerd Tellenbach, edd., *Liber memorialis von Remiremont.* (Monumenta Germaniae historica: Libri memoriales, 1.) Dublin/Zürich: Weidmann, 1970. i (text): Pp. xxxv, 288; ii (plates): 116 plates. (Cited henceforth in the notes as *Lib. mem.*) This article is intended primarily as a discussion of the historical importance and value of the *Lib. mem.*, not as a contribution to the history of Remiremont, which was an ancient foundation — first a double monastery, then an abbey of Benedictine nuns, and finally a chapter of canonesses — in the Vosges, in the diocese of Toul.

[1] *Die Briefe des heiligen Bonifatius und Lullus*, ed. Michael Tangl (Mon. Germ. hist.: Epistolae selectae, 1; Berlin 1916), pp. 50–51, ep. 28: "Sancta sic tenet ecclesia, ut quisque pro suis mortuis vere christianis offerat oblationes atque presbiter eorum faciat memoriam. Et quamvis omnes peccatis subiaceamus, congruit, ut sacerdos pro mortuis catholicis memoriam faciat et intercedat." Cf. trans. in C. H. Talbot, *The Anglo-Saxon Missionaries in Germany* (New York, 1954), p. 86.

[2] Cf. Gregory Dix, *The Shape of the Liturgy* (2nd ed., London, 1945), pp. 498–511; Archdale King, *The Liturgies of the Past* (London, 1959), pp. 168–170.

[3] As the lists became longer, it was naturally impossible to read each name individually, and Charlemagne in the *Admonitio generalis*, cap. 54, forbade the public recitation of names: *Capitularia regum Francorum*, edd. A. Boretius and V. Krause (Mon. Germ. hist.: Leges, ii; Hanover, 1883–97), i, 57.

[4] Cf. the remarks on the value of the two types of work in Edmund Bishop, "Some Ancient Benedictine Confraternity Books" (1885), *Liturgica historica* (Oxford, 1918), p. 349.

[5] See in particular Gerd Tellenbach, "Liturgische Gedenkbücher als historische Quellen," *Mélanges Eugène Tisserant*, v (Studi e Testi, 235; Vatican City, 1964), 389–399.

is often less important than the exploitation of material long known but regarded as useless or intractable.

Thus it is that the *Liber memorialis* of Remiremont, which has been called by Tellenbach "uno dei piu singolari libri del mondo,"[6] was described by Molinier as late as 1890 as "sans grande importance"[7] and is the last of the seven surviving commemoration-books from before the year 1000 to be published in its entirety,[8] although it has been known to scholars since the eighteenth century.[9] This delay is not without advantage, however, since it now appears in a form which marks a notable advance, both substantively and methodologically, over all previous editions of such works. For although the *Liber memorialis* is not the largest known commemoration-book (containing 11,500 names in comparison with 40,000 in that of Reichenau), it is one of the most difficult to edit, since its history stretches over almost four centuries (820-ca. 1200) and involves the work of some 160 scribes. In addition to several liturgical texts, it incorporates four theoretically-distinct types of work: (1) a commemoration-book proper, containing about 1000 entries ranging in length from one to 400 names;[10] (2) three full necrologies;[11] (3) a *Traditionscodex* or chartulary containing scattered copies of about 750 short grants to the abbey; and (4) a rent-book on ff. 65–69 listing both rents owing to

[6] *Lib. mem.*, p. 215.

[7] Auguste Molinier, *Les obituaires français au Moyen Âge* (Paris, 1890), p. 219, citing some printed extracts from the *Lib. mem.*

[8] The six others are from Durham (published by J. Stevenson in 1841 and in facsimile in 1923), Brescia (A. Valentini in 1887), Salzburg (S. Herzberg-Fränkel in 1904), St Gall, Reichenau, and Pfäfers (P. Piper in 1884).

[9] The first known scholar to use the *Lib. mem.* was Giuseppe Garampi, who published some excerpts in his *De nummo argenteo Benedicti III* (Rome, 1749) and announced his intention to publish the whole work (p. 38: "quod annuentibus clarissimis hujus Monasterii Sanctimonialibus mea opera fortasse vulgabitur"). When and where Garampi saw it, however, and how it reached its present home in the Bibliotheca Angelica at Rome, are not known. The editors suggest that by 1749 it was either already in the Angelica or perhaps in the Augustinian library at Aquila-Amiterno (where it was seen by G. C. Amaduzzi before 1767) or the collection of Cardinal Passionei, whose books were acquired by the Angelica in 1762 (pp. xiv–xv). This overlooks the force of Garampi's intention to publish the work with the aid of the nuns "of this monastery," which in the context can only mean Remiremont and suggests that he saw it there, or at least was in communication with the abbey, though he is not known to have visited Remiremont before 1749. In the nineteenth century the *Lib. mem.* was consulted by various scholars, including F. Blume, J. Fr. Boehmer, L. Bethmann, and especially A. Ebner, who published substantial excerpts in the *Neues Archiv* in 1894.

[10] The importance of the difference between the short entries (mostly groups of individuals present at the time of the entry) and the long entries (mostly lists of members of monastic houses) will be discussed later. Long lists of monks and nuns were exchanged between monasteries as a result of the system of ecclesiastical association or confraternity which is said to have originated in England and spread from there to the continent: see Wilhelm Levison, *England and the Continent in the Eighth Century* (Ford Lectures, 1943; Oxford, 1946), pp. 101–103; cf. also Joseph Duhr, "La confrérie dans la vie de l'Église," *Revue d'histoire ecclésiastique*, xxxv (1939), 437–478, and Karl Schmid and Joachim Wollasch, "Die Gemeinschaft der Lebenden und Verstorbenen in Zeugnissen des Mittelalters," *Frühmittelalterliche Studien*, i (1967), 370–372.

[11] The first begins at Christmas, the other two on 1 January, which may reflect a change in style of dating at Remiremont.

the abbey and 52 additional grants.[12] Aside from the liturgical texts, rent-book, and a few folios containing only charters, these different types of work are all mixed together, and the scribes entered both lists of names and records of grants wherever they could, tucking them when necessary into any available blank space, between lines, in the margins, and over erasures.[13] This fact raises some important questions about the character and purpose of the work, and about commemoration-books in general, since it can hardly have served as a practical record of individual names and donations. The inclusion of three distinct necrologies further calls into question the nature of necrologies as usually defined, which was to gather under each day of the year all the names to be commemorated on that day. A necrology was kept in the chapter-house, according to most scholars, and a commemoration-book in the church. At Durham, as A. Hamilton Thompson said,

> It [the *liber vitae*] lay upon the altar, in sight of the congregation and ready to the celebrant's hand. Although the long and ever-growing list of names it contained could not be read publicly, . . . it was a silent reminder to the priest and to the assembled convent of the living and departed, whose prayers were joined with their own, and of the duty of remembering collectively at the most solemn moment of the service those whose individual names were written in its pages.[14]

At Remiremont this must have applied to both the necrologies and to the donation-records, and the fundamental purpose of the *Liber memorialis* therefore seems to have been to insure the liturgical commemoration of all the names entered on its pages.

It is introduced by a liturgical text, written probably in 862/3, declaring the intention of the abbey to celebrate mass daily for all those

> who have for the love of God enriched this place with their property for the use of the nuns, have bestowed alms on us or on our predecessors, or have commended themselves to our or to their prayers, for both the living and the dead; wherefore we have written below the names of those who lived at the time of our predecessors and have always

---

[12] The technical character of this rent-book is disputed by scholars. It is called a *polyptychon* in the *Lib. mem.*, pp. xi and xxix, and a *censier* by Ch.-Edmond Perrin, *Recherches sur la seigneurie rurale en Lorraine d'après les plus anciens censiers (IX*ᵉ*-XII*ᵉ* siècle)* (Publications de la Faculté des Lettres de l'Université de Strasbourg, 71; Paris, 1935), pp. 141–169 and 693–703, editing the part of it on ff. 65–67. On the distinction between these two types of work, see Émile Lesne, *Histoire de la propriété ecclésiastique en France*, III: *L'inventaire de la propriété* (Mémoires et travaux publiés par des professeurs des Facultés catholiques de Lille, 44; Lille, 1936), pp. 79–80, who said that a polyptych as distinct from a *liber censualis* included not only the revenues but also a description of the property itself, though he admitted elsewhere that in practice the distinction was not always clear. By this standard, the rent-book in the *Lib. mem.* is closer to a *censier* than a polyptych.

[13] These erasures (of which there are a considerable number) constitute a methodological problem. Was a name erased from a commemoration-book on account of a misdeed forfeiting the right of the individual to liturgical commemoration? Or with the passage of time did some names become so indistinct that later scribes wrote over them, without in principle excluding them from the book of life?

[14] *Liber vitae ecclesiae Dunelmensis* (Surtees Society, 136; Durham, 1923), p. xv; cf. the introduction to the *Liber vitae: Register and Martyrology of New Minster and Hyde Abbey, Winchester*, ed. Walter De Gray Birch (Hampshire Record Society [5]; London/Winchester, 1892), p. 12, and the article by Schmid and Wollasch in *Frühmit. Studien*, I, 368.

taken care to record in this commemoration-book the men and women who lived in our times. We urge the nuns who succeed us under the holy rule of our father Benedict always to write the names of their friends in this commemoration-book and to have a mass specially celebrated daily, as written above, for all the aforementioned.[15]

In particular, the text continued, prayers should be offered "for all the living and the dead of both sexes, whose number and names You know, O Lord," who have given property or alms to the nuns or commended themselves to their prayers "or whose names are seen below written in this breviary. Grant graciously that this holy offering may win forgiveness for the dead and serve as a remedy for the living. . . ."[16] This suggests that at Remiremont no effort was made to recite individually the names in the *Liber memorialis* or to draw any distinctions between the various categories of names. There is no sign of the development, such as Hamilton Thompson found at Durham, from "a *Liber vitae* pure and simple," with lists of names of people for whom the monks felt bound to pray but with whom they had no special agreements, to a *liber confraternitatum*, as lists from other monasteries were added and as the contractual obligation for intercession became specific, and finally into "a receptacle of the names of any who had qualified for remembrance by the convent."[17] It seems that from the beginning at Remiremont (as at St Gall, according to Bishop[18]) all whose names were entered in the *Liber memorialis* received the same spiritual benefits. One of the striking

---

[15] *Lib. mem.*, f. 1ᵛ (p. 1): ". . . pro omnibus his utriusque sexus missam cotidie caelebrari. qui hunc locum pro amore dei ad usus monacharum de rebus suis ditauerunt uel suas nobis seu antecessarum nostrarum largiti sunt ęlemosinas siue qui se in nostris uel illarum se commendauerunt orationibus. tam pro uiuis quam et pro defunctis. unde et eorum nomina qui in tempore antecessarum nostrarum fuerunt subter scripsimus. illorum uero seu illarum qui in tempóribus nostris extiterunt in hoc semper curauimus scribere memoriali. Hoc nostras ammonentes successores sub sancta patris nostri Benedicti regula militaturas. ut nomina amicorum seu amicarum suarum semper in hoc scribant memoriali et pro omnibus praedictis. specialiter missa cotidie quae super scripta est cęlebrętur." The printed text slightly changes the punctuation and sentence structure of the original, especially by placing a semi-colon after "defunctis" and a period after "scripsimus" (thus separating the related phrases beginning "eorum nomina" and "illorum uero") and by not beginning a new sentence at "Hoc nostras," which is clearly marked in the manuscript.

[16] *Lib. mem.*, f. 2ʳ (pp. 1–2): "pro omnibus his tam uiuis quam defunctis utriusque sexus, quorum numerum et nomina tu scis domine . . . seu quorum nomina subter in hoc breuiario scripta adesse uidentur. concede propitius ut hęc sacra oblatio defunctatis prosit ad ueniam et uiuis proficiat ad medellam. . ." Cf. f. 3ʳ, for another form of this prayer. There are also references to the names written "in this breviary" and "in this commemoration-book" in the mass to be said at the cemetary on ff. 19ᵛ–20ʳ. These texts closely resemble those in use at Brescia and elsewhere in north Italy (see pp. xxxii–xxxv). On the variation in liturgical texts for commemoration, which was probably the result both of the antiquity of the practice and of the lack of definitive formulas in the oldest Roman liturgical books, see Claude Gay, "Comment enricher le repertoire des pièces chantées aux Messes pour les défunts," *Ephemerides liturgicae*, LXX (1956), 344, and Hieronymus Frank, "Der älteste erhaltene *Ordo defunctorum* der römischen Liturgie und sein Fortleben in Totenagenden des frühen Mittelalters," *Archiv für Liturgiewissenschaft*, VII.2 (1962), 360–415. According to Jean Mabillon, *Vetera analecta* (2nd ed., Paris, 1723), pp. 160–161, commemoration for the dead in the early Middle Ages included masses, vigils or *agendae*, reciting the Lord's prayer or some psalms, and distributions to the poor either every day for 30 days or on certain days for a year.

[17] *Lib. vit. Dunelmensis*, p. xxvi, cf. xiii–xvi.

[18] *Liturgica historica*, p. 354.

V

The Liber Memorialis *of Remiremont*   265

features of the *Liber memorialis*, indeed, as the editors point out, is the high
proportion of short commemoration-entries, many of them probably made in the
presence of the individuals named, in relation to long classified lists, which pre-
dominate in some commemoration-books and may have received distinctive
liturgical treatment.[19]
    The recognition of the importance of individual entries marks the most signifi-
cant methodological advance of this over previous editions of such works, in
which scripts were distinguished either in the footnotes or by varied fonts of type.
No effort is made here to reproduce in print the appearance or arrangement of
the manuscript, which can be studied in the facsimile. Each entry, whether
unified or scattered on the page, is printed as a unit and numbered either with an
Arabic numeral, for commemoration-entries, or with a Roman numeral, for
donation-entries. The necrology-entries are identified simply by date. In addition,
there is an indication of the location of the entry on the page, to facilitate finding
it in the facsimile, and of the script when identifiable. Thus a commemoration-
entry like the "royal entry" on f. 43ʳ, which will be discussed below, is numbered
1 and printed as a unit, although it consists of four scattered groups of names,
located A1, A3, B1, and B3 according to indications in the margin of the facsimile.
The scribe is identified as "5." On the same page there are 32 other commemoration-entries, some unified and some scattered, written both by "5" and other
scribes. On the following page, f. 43ᵛ, in addition to two months of a necrology,
with 32 names in various scripts, there are 17 commemoration-entries and seven
donation-entries.
    The advantage of this method of presentation is not only that it reflects the
actual process of formation of the *Liber memorialis* but also that it makes pos
sible, by a comparison of the contents and scripts of individual entries, and of
their position on the page, a tentative reconstruction of the chronological order of
the entries. Working from the known to the unknown — that is, from identifiable
scripts, from references to known historical persons, and from the order of entries
on a page, as when one entry is written over or around another — , the editors
have been able, by their own account, to date to a quarter-century over ninety
per cent of the total number of names in the book. The sheer amount of hard work
and technical expertise required for this achievement must command the respect
and gratitude of all scholars, even though the method is not equally reliable at
every stage and some of the conclusions are debatable. The stage of transcription

[19] Cf. *Lib. mem.*, pp. xxx–xxxi. No general term is used in the *Lib. mem.* to describe the status of
those whose names appear there; but the reference to a priest as *confrater* in the mid-eleventh century
(32ʳ IV) shows that this term, which was used elsewhere, was known at Remiremont. The *Lib. mem.*
includes lists of monks and nuns from Annegray, Gregorienmünster, Lobbes, Murbach, Prüm,
Reichenau, St Germain (Paris?), St Léger-lès-Pontailler, St Médard (Soissons), Säckingen, Schienen,
and Stavelot-Malmédy, in addition to Remiremont itself, but these account for only a small per-
centage of the total number of names. On the value of these lists, see Franz Beyerle, "Eine Reiche-
nauer Konventsliste aus der Zeit Abt Ruodmans (972–985)," *Zeitschrift für die Geschichte des Oberrheins*, LXXXI (N.F. XLII, 1929), 382–399, who draws some interesting demographic conclusions from
a comparison of this with other lists of monks at Reichenau, and Schmid and Wollasch, in *Frühmit.
Studien*, I, 365–405, esp. 373–388 on the Reichenau lists.

and identification of the entries appears almost flawless. I found only one small mistake in the text;[20] and the only editorial policy to which exception can be taken is on punctuation, which is occasionally misleading. The first legible words of entry XIV on f. 58^r, for instance, are "comito Odolrici," which are printed here in that way, thus suggesting that Odolricus was a count (and he is identified as such in the index). In another publication, however, Hlawitschka plausibly suggested that "comito" in fact belongs with the lost name at the beginning of the entry, which was probably Regimbald, and should therefore be separated by a comma (of which there are signs in the manuscript) from "Odolrici," which refers to a well-known archbishop of Rheims and commendatory abbot of Remiremont.[21] The punctuation of the liturgical texts has also been unnecessarily revised in places, and there are a few inconsistencies in the expansion of abbreviations,[22] but these are minor matters and easily rectified by comparison with the facsimile. The stages of identification of scripts and classification of entries, however, are clearly more problematical and may give rise to some disagreement, although it is not always easy to judge on such matters from the facsimile.[23] The main elements of the reconstruction offered here, however, are sure to stand.

This clear presentation and classification of entries has made available to historians a body of hitherto unused material for the study of early mediaeval social history. Oskar Mitis, in a methodological article published over 20 years ago, criticized the existing editions of commemoration-books precisely because they failed to identify the individual entries, of which he stressed the importance. "Independently entered groups, including only a few names," he said, "are the most valuable content of confraternity-books."[24] Such groups, based either on kinship or community, are at the basis of early mediaeval social structure. Kinship is sometimes indicated in the entries by specific references (*pater, mater, filius,* etc.), but more frequently it has to be deduced from internal evidence, such as the repetition of the same name within a single group, which might include several generations and even dead ancestors, or from comparison with other entries in either the same or other commemoration-books. In this way, according to Mitis, the historian can construct kinship charts (as distinct from genealogical trees)

---

[20] "Gerardus" for "Geradus" in 14^v 1 (cf. index, p. 243, where it appears correctly).

[21] Eduard Hlawitschka, *Studien zur Äbtissinnenreihe von Remiremont (7.–13. Jh.)* (Veröffentlichungen des Instituts für Landeskunde des Saarlandes, 9; Saarbrücken, 1963), p. 46, citing this text with a comma between "comito" and "Odolrici" (spelled "Odelrici").

[22] See nn. 15 above and 27 below.

[23] The omission, furthermore, of 14 folios in the facsimile (ff. 27–31, 37, 44, 51–52, and 65–69) makes it impossible to reach an independent judgment on the identity and dating of certain scripts, such as "55", which will be discussed below. These folios were presumably omitted because they contain only copies of donations and the rent-book and therefore present no problems of transcription. Perrin, *Recherches*, pp. 156–164, however, stresses the palaeographical complexity of some of these folios and in the notes to his edition of ff. 65–67, on pp. 693–703, he indicates a number of interlinear additions, some in a second hand, which are not referred to in the apparatus here.

[24] Oskar Mitis, "Bemerkungen zu den Verbrüderungsbüchern und über deren genealogischen Wert," *Zeitschrift für Schweizerische Kirchengeschichte*, XLIII (1949), 28–42.

showing the links between influential families and individuals over wide areas and considerable lengths of time.[25] The historical value of several entries in the *Liber memorialis* has already been demonstrated by the editors in some independently-published works. Schmid, for example, has studied the "royal entry" mentioned above, which consists of four groups of names: (1) five kings whom he identifies as Lothar II, Louis the German, his sons Louis the Young and Charles III, and Lothar's brother Charles of Provence; (2) eight members of the royal family, seven female and one male, including Louis the German's wife Emma, Lothar II's morganatic wife Waldrada, and her son Hugo; and (3–4) two groups of respectively 43 and seven nobles and royal officials, of whom sub-groups appear in other entries in the *Liber memorialis* and in the commemoration-books of St Gall and Reichenau and among whom are a few identifiable figures like Lothar II's *domesticus a secretis* and *fidelis ministerialis* Walter. On the basis of the known activities and relationships of these people, Schmid shows that this "royal entry" includes the names of those present at a meeting of the kings at Remiremont, probably at Christmas, 861.[26]

A simpler example, illustrating family relationships, is found in two entries concerning Dado, bishop of Verdun from 880 to 923: "Domini Dadoni episcopi cum genitore Radaldo et matri Rotrude sororibusque Uuilburh et Lansint cum fratre Adelberto et filiis suis . . ." and "Dadoni episcopi benefactorem loci huius, Berhardi episcopi atque Attonis, Rodoldi, Rutrude, Uuilburdis, Lansendis, Humberti et omni grege predicti episcopi Uirdunensium Dadoni cum omnibus consanguineis illius."[27] Since it is known from other sources that Dado's predecessor Berhard and successor Bernuin were respectively his maternal uncle and nephew and also that Bernuin may have been a son of Count Matfrid (IV) of Metz and brother of Count Adalbert,[28] an interesting picture of the episcopal dynasty at Verdun emerges:

[25] Cf. Karl Schmid, "Zur Problematik von Familie, Sippe und Geschlecht, Haus und Dynastie beim mittelalterlichen Adel: Vorfragen zum Thema 'Adel und Herrschaft im Mittelalter,' " *Zeitschrift für die Geschichte des Oberrheins*, CV (1957), 1–62, and "Über das Verhältnis von Person und Gemeinschaft im früheren Mittelalter," *Frühmittelalterliche Studien*, I (1967), 225–249, stressing the growing emphasis on family rather than office or estate in the arrangement of names in commemoration-books in the ninth and tenth centuries.

[26] Karl Schmid, "Ein karolingischer Königseintrag im Gedenkbuch von Remiremont," *Frühmittelalterliche Studien*, II (1968), 96–134.

[27] 4ʳ 16 (910/30) and 53ᵛ 1 (ca. 900), previously published by Ebner in *Neues Archiv*, XIX, 59 and 77. (The dates of entries given here and below, except when specifically excepted, are based on the editorial dating of the scripts.) In the printed text, "episcopi" is used in the former entry and "ep." ("ęp.") in the latter, although in the manuscript the abbreviation "epi." ("ępi.") is used in both and has been expanded here uniformly to "episcopi" ("ępiscopi"). Dado also appears in 4ᵛ 7, 23ʳ 3, and in the necrology (7 Oct.) on 34ʳ.

[28] Mon. Germ. hist., *Scriptores* in fol. (Hanover/Leipzig, 1826–1934), IV, 37 (a fragment by Dado referring to Berhard as "avunculus noster"), 38 (a fragment of a polyptych from Verdun calling Bernuin Dado's "nepos"), and 347 (*Vita Iohannis Gorziensis*, cap. 38); cf. Robert Parisot, *Le royaume de Lorraine sous les Carolingiens (843–923)* (Paris, 1898), pp. 451, n. 1, and 501, n. 4. The relationship between Bernuin and Counts Matfrid and Adalbert is uncertain. All three appear elsewhere in the

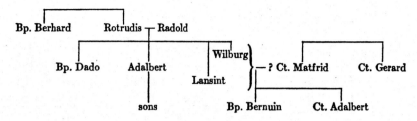

Further research might identify the other members of the family mentioned in the two entries in the *Liber memorialis*. An "Umbertus" appears with "Dado episcopus" in the late ninth century (f. 23ʳ 3); and the conjunction of the names Umbertus, Lansint (twice), Adalbert, and Rotrudis in the mid-tenth century (f. 53ʳ 6) and of Rotrudis (twice) and Lansint about the year 1000 (f. Cᵛ I) may indicate descendants.

The names of over fifty bishops in all, mostly of the ninth and tenth centuries,[29] are found in the *Liber memorialis*, bearing witness to the widespread influence of Remiremont at that time.[30] Many of these are identified in the section of notes on individual entries,[31] but a look through Duchesne's *Fastes épiscopaux* adds Folco and Hunfridus of Thérouanne and Hildoardus and Halitgarius of Cambrai — two dioceses otherwise unrepresented — to the list of probable identifications. May not, also, "Oto ep." (f. 6ᵛ 1) be Adon of Vienne? When the identifications are doubtful, dioceses close to Remiremont, or with which it is known to have had an association, should be preferred.[32] Among those represented with a fair degree of certainty are sixteen contiguous dioceses around the abbey[33] and five outlying

---

Lib. mem. with no suggestion of kinship aside from the common use of the name Adalbert. Indeed, the bishop in question may be Bernuin of Vienne (ca. 886–899), though the proximity of Verdun to Remiremont and the known relationship of Dado's family to the abbey makes Bernuin of Verdun the more likely candidate.

[29] Though broad, this range was not as great as those of houses like St Gall and Reichenau, which stretched all over Europe. It should be remembered, however, that some names may have been entered in commemoration-books without a personal visit to the abbey: cf. Mitis, in *Zs. f. Schweizerische Kirchengeschichte*, XLIII, 32–33.

[30] The earliest identifiable bishop seems to be Hildoardus of Cambrai (d. 816/25) and the latest either Odelricus of Rheims (d. 969) or Guichard of Besançon, whose dates are uncertain but was bishop probably in the time of Otto III.

[31] *Lib. mem.*, pp. 177–209, which is in several respects the least satisfactory part of the work. Many references are omitted even about individuals identified by the editors in their other works; and the notes provided are often inadequate and sometimes inaccurate. Bishop Dado of Verdun is dated from 880 (pp. 179, 188, and 205), 881 (pp. 165 and 192), and 891 (p. 161); Ruotbert of Metz is dated to 916 (p. 178) and 917 (p. 191); 983 appears for 893 (p. 181); Rodes for Rodez (p. 203); 59ʳ IV (which does not exist) for 59ʳ III (p. 207). There are also several small slips in the bibliography (pp. 213–215), which, like the notes, includes a confusing number of references to unpublished and forthcoming works by the editors.

[32] Aglimarus of Vienne (841–859) thus seems a better candidate for Bishop Allimaro (49ʳ 3) than either Agilmar of Auvergne or Aimar of Rodez, who are proposed in the notes; and John of Cambrai (d. after 878) for Bishop John (24ᵛ 5), who is identified in the notes (pp. 160 and 189) as John of Rouen (876–888).

[33] Trier, Metz, Toul, Verdun (in the province of Trier); Rheims, Châlons, Cambrai, Thérouanne (province of Rheims); Liège (province of Cologne); Strasbourg, Worms (province of Mainz); Be-

dioceses: Bourges to the west, Avignon and Die to the south (though these are among the less certain identifications), and Vercelli and Brescia in the southeast, of which the appearance is accounted for by the religious and political ties between north Italy and Lorraine at that time.[34] There is also an elusive Bishop William of Ravenna (f. 4ʳ 8), who is found on no known list of the patriarchs of Ravenna in the ninth and tenth centuries. The number of bishops still remaining unidentified is eloquent proof of the incompleteness of the episcopal *fasti* of early mediaeval Europe.[35]

Both the historical value of the donation-entries, and the difficulty of their dating, are illustrated by the grants of the nun Geza,[36] of which one in particular (9ʳ I), which was issued in the time of King Henry, the advocate Gerard, and Abbess Gisla and with the consent of Geza's brother Gerard and his sons, was used by Hlawitschka in his discussion of the advocacy of Remiremont.[37] He identified the advocate Gerard with Duke Gerard (I) of Upper Lorraine (1048–1070)[38] and therefore dated the beginning of the abbacy of Gisla (II) before 1070. He further identified the "Ierardus inuasselatus," who appears with Abbess Willeburgis in 41ᵛ VI, with Count Gerard of Metz, the grand-father or grand-

sançon, Basel (province of Besançon); Troyes (province of Sens); Langres and Chalon-sur-Saône (province of Vienne).

[34] Cf. Nicolas Huyghebaert, "Moines et clercs italiens en Lotharingie (VIIIᵉ–XIIᵉ siècle)," *Miscellanea Tornacensia* (XXXIIIᵉ Congrès de la Fédération archéologique et historique de Belgique; Brussels, 1951), I, 95–111. This may also explain the similarity between the liturgical texts at Remiremont and Brescia.

[35] Collectus (59ʳ 1), Eberardus (6ᵛ 1) — possibly bishop of Sion ca. 1000, who appears in the commemoration-book of Reichenau 165.15: Mon. Germ. hist., *Libri confraternitatum* (Berlin, 1884), p. 207 —, Eldigarius (11ᵛ 2) — perhaps Hildegarius of Cologne (d. 753) or Halitgarius of Cambrai —, Huono (H 2), Itmarus (24ᵛ 5), and Pascasicius (53ᵛ 10).

[36] Geza made four separate grants of serfs to the abbey: 9ʳ I (discussed in the text), 17ʳ VII (at the request of her paternal aunt Alda), 36ʳ I, and 37ʳ III. The second and third of these entries are attributed by the editors to scribe "55." For the first and fourth, no scribe is given. In the notes, however, 9ʳ I is said to be only a little earlier than 59ʳ III (which is independently assigned to "55" and dated 1070/1114 from references to Duke Theoderic and Abbess Gisla) and is further compared to 32ʳ IV, though whether on the basis of script or content is uncertain. Likewise in the notes, 36ʳ I is compared to 44ᵛ XIII (which is assigned to "55" and explicitly dated 1065) and 37ʳ III is assigned to scribe "51a" and dated in the mid-eleventh century, before scribe "55". In the section on scribes, all these entries except 9ʳ I, 32ʳ IV, and 37ʳ III, are attributed to "55", who is dated in the last quarter of the eleventh century, primarily of the basis of 59ʳ III. Five other entries on ff. 37 and 44 are also attributed to "55" in this section (p. 175). These conclusions cannot be checked, however, owing to the omission in the facsimile of these folios, on which the essential entries for dating this script occur. Entry 36ᵛ I, which begins "ipsa etiam Geza dedit sancto petro aliam ancillam" and is written in a box close to the inner margin, is probably related to 37ʳ III, though they are attributed to different scribes. Cf. Hlawitschka, *Äbtissinnenreihe*, p. 74, n. 257, who cited these four references to Geza and identified the scribe of 17ʳ VII and 36ᵛ I with that of 44ᵛ XIII, which is here dated 1065, although in the *Lib. mem.*, p. 175, it is called a later copy, presumably to fit in with dating "55" in the last quarter of the eleventh century.

[37] Hlawitschka, *Äbtissinnenreihe*, pp. 73–75, also citing 59ʳ III (here dated 1070/84), where Abbess Gisla and Duke Theoderic, Gerard's successor, appear together.

[38] Cf. Robert Parisot, *Les origines de la Haute-Lorraine et sa première maison ducale (959–1033)* (Paris, 1909), p. 11, on the confusion of his genealogy and history resulting from the efforts of sixteenth-century forgers to link the house of Lorraine to the family of Charlemagne.

uncle of Duke Gerard, calling him also advocate of Remiremont[39] and thus showing that already in the early eleventh century the advocacy of the abbey was
hereditary in the family of the counts of Metz, later dukes of Upper Lorraine.
There is no explicit evidence for this, however, in any source of the eleventh
century. In the *Liber memorialis* the term *advocatus* first appears in the second
half of the tenth century, when it was applied to five different individuals, none of
them of more than local importance.[40] The only other use of the term is in reference to Gerard in 9[r] I and to "Girardus aduocatus Uosagi" in 29[r] LXXIV, which
probably dates from early in the abbacy of Judith (1114–1161/4).[41] To these can
be added another reference to an advocate Gerard in a document of uncertain
date published by Hlawitschka.[42] No one of these three Gerards, nor the "Ierardus inuasselatus" in 41[v] VI, can be identified with certainty; and the date of 9[r] I,
therefore, which depends upon identifying the advocate Gerard with Duke Gerard, may in fact be later than 1070, since Abbess Gisla II lived until 1114 and
kings named Henry ruled from 1039 until 1125. Thus Gisla's abbacy may have
started later than Hlawitschka suggests, the nun Geza may have lived at the end
of the eleventh and beginning of the twelfth century,[43] and the advocate Gerard
in 9[r] I may have been the same as the Gerard advocate of the Vosges in 29[r]
LXXIV.[44] For while the importance of advocates certainly grew during the eleventh century,[45] it is improbable that the advocacy of Remiremont passed in
only a generation from the hands of local monastic officials into those of the
counts of Metz, the ancestors of the dukes of Upper Lorraine, and later evidence
confirms that in the twelfth century the advocates in the area of Remiremont
were regional officials with considerable powers (which they often abused) but
were clearly subordinates of the duke, who at most exercised an over-advocacy
for the abbey.[46]

[39] Hlawitschka, *Äbtissinnenreihe*, pp. 52 (n. 164), 59–60, cf. 65–66. He dates Willeburgis in the
first two decades of the eleventh century. According to Parisot, *Origines*, p. 531, n. 3, Count Gerard
(III) was great-uncle to Duke Gerard I; but he is shown as grandson on the genealogical chart between pp. 514–515.

[40] Rauengerus (58[r] XIV and 69[r]: before 962), Lizerus (19[r] I: 970/80), Benno (41[v] IV; ca. 970/5),
Eltramnus (68[r] I; ca. 965), and Arbertus (68[r]: before 965), to whom can be added Imbert in a document of 960/90 published by Hlawitschka, *Äbtissinnenreihe*, p. 141, no. 87, who discusses these references (pp. 45–51, 53, and 127) and tentatively identifies Arbertus with the Albertus and Arbertus
in 58[r] XIII–XIV and Rauengerus with the *maior* Rangerus who appears in the rent-book.

[41] He is third among the witnesses to a grant to Remiremont by Albert of Darney, on whose dealings with Abbess Judith in 1121/4 see Hlawitschka, *Äbtissinnenreihe*, pp. 86–87.

[42] *Ibid.*, p. 144. This document survives only in a late copy, and its evidence (while seeming to
identify this Gerard with the count of Saargau) is ambiguous.

[43] Rather than the mid-eleventh century: cf. Hlawitschka, *Äbtissinnenreihe*, p. 74, n. 257.

[44] It is tempting to speculate that he may have been Count Gerard of Vaudemont, father of Abbess
Judith (cf. 28[v] LXVI and 29[r] LXXVI; Hlawitschka, *Äbtissinnenreihe*, p. 92) or even the nun Geza's
brother Gerard, who appears with his sons on 9[r] I. Geza's aunt Alda is also unknown. The name occurs only four times in the *Lib. mem.*, once in conjunction with Gerart (39[r] I).

[45] In addition to the standard works on advocates by Senn and Pergameni, see Perrin, *Recherches*,
pp. 671–677, who associated the increase in their powers (and ecclesiastical efforts to limit them) to
the increasing use by landlords of the ban to exact revenues to make up for losses resulting from the
break-down of the domainal régime.

[46] An imperial diploma for Remiremont of Henry V in 1113, confirmed by Conrad III in 1141,

Investigations of this sort in the *Liber memorialis* are greatly facilitated by the index of persons, which marks a second important methodological advance in this over previous editions of such works. A straight alphabetical index, as Mitis pointed out, is almost useless in a work in which the same name may be spelled in many different ways,[47] and the index here is therefore arranged under the roots from which the names are derived (211 in all), thus bringing together even widely divergent forms of the same name. The result is not always easy to use for some one who is unfamiliar with the roots of personal names, and who is not always sufficiently guided by the cross-references. Thus the names Adulfus, Alulf, Hadulfus, Haldulfus, and Haluf are found under five different roots (Ad-, Adel-, Hadu-, Ald-, and Al-); Altramnus and Eltramnus appear respectively under Ald- and Hildi-; and several names which might strike the unwary as forms of Hato or of Herbert are found under a variety of roots.[48] Even philologists may disagree over the roots of certain names, and occasionally the index falls into demonstrable error. Thus Bishop Dado's father, whose name is spelled both Radaldo and Rodaldi, appears under Rad- and Hrod- without any cross-reference, and two pairs of names identified by Hlawitschka (Rauengerus/Rangerus and Albertus/Arbertus) are found under different roots (Hraban-/Ragan- and Adel-/Ar-).[49] These examples illustrate the fallibility of philologists rather than a fault in the method, however, and the index here is on the whole much more useful than those in other editions of commemoration-books. It is also a mine of information in itself, showing both the extraordinary variety of Germanic personal

---

mentioned the depredations of the advocates and forbade any advocate, forester, or minister in the Vosges except "de familia ecclesiae": Léopold Duhamel, "Des relations des empereurs et des ducs de Lorraine avec l'abbaye de Remiremont, VIIᵉ–XIIIᵉ siècle," *Annales de la Société d'émulation du départment des Vosges*, XII.2 (1865), 251 (Stumpf 3039a=3103) and 258 (Stumpf 3426; Mon. Germ. hist.: *Diplomata*, IX [Vienna/Cologne/Graz, 1969], 103, no. 58). In 1147/51 the abbess and the duke made an agreement (Hlawitschka, *Äbtissinnenreihe*, pp. 146–148), confirmed by Archbishop Hillinus of Trier in 1152 (*Gallia christiana*, XIII, instr., 507–509; *Ann. de la Soc. . . . des Vosges*, XII.2, 267–271), referring to the duke and "his advocates" and to the subprovosts and subadvocates "qui a duce et ab aduocatis iniuste substituebantur" and regulating their powers. Cf. also the references to "Guezo advocatus Vosagi" in a bull of Calixtus II in 1121/4 (Ulysse Robert, *Bullaire du pape Calixte II, 1119–1124* [Paris, 1891], II, 271–272, no. 459) and to two advocates, Gerard and Albert, who are tentatively identified as respectively of Metz and Remiremont, in a document of Conrad III in 1141/2 concerning the dispute between the abbey and the duke (Mon. Germ. hist., *Diplomata*, IX, 132–134, no. 75). In spite of these efforts at mediation, the dispute continued for many years. On the advocacy of Remiremont generally, see Duhamel, in *Ann. de la Soc. . . . des Vosges*, XII.2, 218–219, and Jacques Choux, *Recherches sur le diocèse de Toul au temps de la réforme grégorienne: L'épiscopat de Pibon (1069–1107)* (Nancy, 1952), pp. 131–133.

[47] Cf. Mitis, in *Zs. f. Schweizerische Kirchengeschichte*, XLIII, 36, n. 1, who pointed out that the name Dietburg is spelled 81 different ways in the index to the printed edition of the commemoration-books of St. Gall, Reichenau, and Pfäfers.

[48] Ado, Ato, and Atto are under Ad-; Hado, Hato, and Hatto under Hadu-; and Heddo and Heito under Haid-. Arbert(us) is under Ar-; Erbert(us) under Era-; Hartbertus, Hartpertus, and Artpertus under Hard-; and Harbert(us), Harpert(us), Herbert(us) and Herpert(us) under Hari-. Though Arpert is only under Ar-, Arpertus appears under both Ar- and Hard-. These names are also found in many other forms.

[49] Idricus is found, without any cross-references, both under Hildi- (p. 253) and under Id- (p. 257), and the reference "29ʳ LXXIV" under Hugo belongs with Hugo (forestarius) 12 lines below.

names used at that time (including such gems as Gopo, Hacheeu, Helbonc, Saradoms, Scroht, Sogintinso, and Zuzulinus)[50] and the comparatively small number of Christian names.[51] Scholars in the future, with more sophisticated philological and prosopographical techniques, may also draw from these lists conclusions concerning the tribal origins and social structure of the group.

The only serious weakness in the index is the omission of many references to positions and titles, which is reinforced by the absence of an *index rerum et verborum*. Of the seven advocates mentioned above, for instance, all of whom are called *advocatus* in the text, only four are identified as such in the index. Even great positions like count and bishop are not always indicated, and references to minor offices like *hebdomadarii, cancellarii, prepositi, villici, maiores, decani,* and *scabini* have to be dug out of the text by the individual reader.[52] The same is true of more unusual ranks and positions, such as the group of *franci fideiussores* in 44[r] III and the isolated references to *iudex, forestarius, legis doctor, culterus, uenator, celerarius,* and hermit. Only one person seems to have been a *magister* as well as an *hebdomadarius*, and two are referred to as monk and priest. Just one person is described as *liber*, and only five as *miles*, which was clearly not an established status in the area of Remiremont at that time. These indications, though only approximate, are not without interest for the administrative organization and the religious and social life of the region, and it is regrettable that they cannot be found more completely and quickly.

Most of this incidental information is found in the donation-entries, of which the *Liber memorialis* was not the only repository, since 105 more, including a few repeats and some apparently written by the same scribes, are found in an Evangeliary from Remiremont now at Epinal.[53] Of the 800 odd donation-entries in the *Liber memorialis* all but 47 are grants of serfs to the abbey.[54] The donors ranged all the way from counts and bishops to small proprietors, including not only laymen and women but also priests, monks, nuns (such as Geza, mentioned above), and at least one *conversa*. Sometimes they joined together, presumably as family groups disposing of common property, as when 11 people gave a single man (67[v]). Sometimes, though rarely, they specified that the grant was made at the point of death or at the request of a third party, either a relation or lord. Nearly

---

[50] Marc Bloch, *La société féodale* (L'évolution de l'humanité, 34; Paris, 1939–40), I, 214, cited an example from the polyptych of Irminon where a couple named Teud-ricus and Ermen-berta named their children Teut-hardus, Erment-arius, and Teut-bertus.

[51] Thus there are 14 references (some to the same person) to Andrew, 16 to Peter, 5 to Mark, 24 to Mary, 10 to Martin, etc.

[52] The *hebdomadarii* were the priests who celebrated the religious offices at Remiremont and also acted as secular officials for the abbey: cf. Perrin, *Recherches*, p. 141, n. 1, and Choux, *Pibon*, pp. 130–131, who discusses other monastic officials (whom he tends to equate except for the provosts, who controlled the other ministerials) on pp. 134–135.

[53] The entries from this volume (Épinal, Bibl. pub., *Ms* 105), which has been known for many years, are published as a group in Hlawitschka, *Äbtissinnenreihe*, pp. 129–143, and are cited here by his numbering.

[54] About three-quarters of the remainder are grants of land and one-quarter grants of rents and other types of property (houses, mills, granaries, springs, etc.).

all the grants were made directly to St Peter, the patron saint of the abbey, and gave as their purpose the *remedium anime* of the donors and their families.

The serfs who were thus given to St Peter were usually called *servus* or *ancilla*, but also, more rarely, *mancipium, mancipia, abra*, and, at least once, *vernaculus* or simply *nomen*, suggesting that they had little individuality beyond a name. Certainly their status was not much above that of slaves,[55] since they were regarded as the property of their donors, who gave, bought, and sold their rights in them at will.[56] Once given to St Peter, however, their status was clearly privileged, and they were referred to (though no general term is commonly used) either as *servientes* or, more rarely, as *censuales* or *cerarii*, from the rent (*census*) they paid in money or wax (*cera*).[57] They were described in one grant as having been given liberty and as having cast off the yoke of servitude (15ʳ III). They are to hold "the firmness of perfect liberty" (18ᵛ III) or "the firm firmness of liberty all the days of their lives" (17ᵛ I). Even if one of them failed to pay his rent to the abbey for a year, he need only pay the arrears "and he will not lose his liberty" (A 1ᵛ[a] I).[58] Henceforth they were free from other powers and owed no service to their former lords; they were in the *familia* and under the protection (*mundiburone*) of St Peter (55ᵛ I and 34ʳ II) and must not be taken from "the liberty of the church" (29ʳ LXX and LXXI). Even in comparison with the abbey's other dependents they enjoyed a privileged status. Thus a family of six in the midtenth century declared that, "They were *franci* and refused to render service to St Peter at the festival" (63ᵛ I); and in 1052 three serfs were given "belonging to the administrative region (*potestas*) of Crévic and having henceforth the better law of that region" (44ʳ III).

Not all the donors were lords, and there are examples of people giving themselves (auto-donation), parents their children, husbands their wives, and families their relations.[59] In the last quarter of the tenth century, a priest named Siricius gave his wife, whom he had acquired from Woluinus, and her children.[60] About the middle of the eleventh century, Mainerus, who had married a serf belonging to Girbertus, bought her and her children, present and future, and gave them to St Peter (15ʳ VII). And toward the end of the century Count Rainardus and his wife gave a little girl named Lanzinda "at the request and service of her father and mother and owing to an infirmity in her lower leg" (51ᵛ V). In these cases

[55] *Abra* is defined by Niermeyer, *Mediae latinitatis lexicon minus*, as a female slave.

[56] See 14ᵛ II, 15ʳ VII, 26ᵛ I (a father redeems his son and gives him to St Peter), and Hlawitschka, no. 73 ("ancilla suę proprietatis").

[57] Cf. Perrin, *Recherches*, pp. 150–151, who equated them with the south German *censuales* or *tributarii*, the Belgian "sainteurs," and the later *mundiliones* in Lorraine and stressed the scholarly disputes over their precise juridical status.

[58] Conversely, Hlawitschka, no. 6 refers to 13 dependents of the abbey whom an unspecified individual sought to hold unjustly "in seruitium."

[59] For auto-donations, see 44ʳ XII, 53ʳ I, 55ᵛ II, 57ᵛ III, 71ʳ IV; for a father giving a son, 26ᵛ I; etc.

[60] 6ʳ II and 7ʳ II. Other examples of married priests are found in 37ʳ V, 44ʳ VII, 44ᵛ IV and XI: cf. Choux, *Pibon*, p. 106.

some sort of payment was rendered to the lord, and this was probably customary, though not always mentioned, on account of the lord's loss of service and dues.

In return for, and perhaps as a sign of, the protection of the abbey and the freedom from former obligations, these *servientes* paid to St Peter a fixed annual rent, usually defined in money or in wax. The amount as a rule varied between two to five pennies for men and one to three pennies for women, with men always paying more than women.[61] A grant in the last quarter of the tenth century specified that the men should pay twelve pennies and the women no *census* at all (63ʳ III). Sometimes the rent was set in so many pennies or units (*pensa*) of wax, and it is probable that the two methods of payment were in practice interchangeable.[62] That real payments in kind were not unknown, however, is shown by a grant in the mid-eleventh century of an *abra* for a rent of five eggs and a hen (44ᵛ I). The payments in wax, as some scholars have suggested, may have been used for making the candles on the altar of the patron saint to whom the rent was paid.[63]

A few entries show that the abbey took seriously its responsibility to protect its dependents. On one occasion in the mid-eleventh century it threatened with interdict and excommunication a certain Count Warno who claimed in servitude the children of an *ancilla* of St Peter who had married a serf of Saint-Etienne (17ᵛ V). In the last quarter of the tenth century it established that "no *villicus* or *decanus* should exact a *census* or any service" from the sons of a serf of St Peter at Hennecourt "whose father took a free wife named Waldrada . . . because they pertain to (*respicientes ad*) the treasury of St Peter" (10ᵛ IV). These documents also show that status derived from the mother. A noble woman who married a serf likewise seems to have maintained her right to own property and to act as a free woman (51ʳ VI; cr. 51ʳ I). Whether or not the *censuales* enjoyed freedom in this sense is open to doubt. They were considered to hold liberty and to be within the liberty of the church, but they were not referred to as *liberi*, let alone as *nobiles*, and the reference in 27ʳ I to two *censuales* marrying wives "sibi pares uel liberas" suggests (unless this is a tautology and the *vel* means "and") that they were considered less than fully free. Their status was certainly privileged in comparison with serfdom, however, and hereditary at least in the female line.

Much work remains to be done on these donation-entries, such as statistical studies on the proportions of men and women, but in themselves they leave un-

---

[61] Cf. B. Guérard, *Polyptyche de l'abbé Irminon* (Paris, 1844), I, 428, and Perrin, *Recherches*, p. 150, n. 1. The reasons for these differential payments, both between individual grants and between the sexes, are unclear and probably depended on particular circumstances, including age and marital status. In 27ʳ I (first half of the twelfth century), for instance, two brothers were to pay two pennies "as long as they lacked wives . . . but four if they married wives equal to themselves or free" and their sisters were to pay one penny "when they are adult." The rate for men may have included their wives and children as well as themselves. The average *census* does not seem to have increased with time, and examples of two pennies for men and one for women still occur in grants of the late eleventh and early twelfth century (27ʳ XIV and Hlawitschka, no. 49).

[62] Cf. 39ʳ II ("II den. uel in cera") and 57ᵛ II and III. In two versions of the same grant (10ᵛ XII and 27ʳ XVIII; Hlawitschka, no. 56), the rent is set once as "singulos denarios" and once as "singulas cęrę obboletas."

[63] Guérard, *Polyptyche*, I, 368 and 428–429, equating the *cerarii* and *luminarii* at St Bertin.

answered almost as many questions as they answer. Who precisely were the *censuales?* Did they include former freemen as well as serfs? Why did men pay a higher rent than women? Was this rent symbolic or economic? Did the continuing grants of *censuales* reflect improving or deteriorating social and economic conditions? Demographic growth or the reducing estates of landlords, who gave away laborers whom they could no longer use on their own demesne lands? Did the *censuales* remain on their previous holdings or move onto the abbey's lands? Why were the donations recorded in the *Liber memorialis?* Perrin in his book on the rural seigneurie in Lorraine associates the high proportion of non-free among the *censuales* at Remiremont, as contrasted with south Germany, with the progressive reduction of the *indominicatum* of the landlords.[64] But there is no evidence that the *censuales* moved when they were given to St Peter, and the imperial charters of the first half of the twelfth century suggest that the abbey's own holdings were as seriously reduced as those of lay landlords[65] and that it could not therefore have used on its own lands workers unwanted elsewhere.[66] It may therefore be necessary to look beyond purely social and economic factors — important though these were — in seeking an explanation for the phenomenon of the *censuales,* and here the character of the *Liber memorialis* provides a clue.

It cannot have been, as Perrin believes, primarily a utilitarian record of dues owing to the sacristan.[67] Though it may be true in a general way, as Perrin says, that "the inscription of a tradition-notice in a *Liber vitae* was considered as confering a supplementary guarantee to a juridical act," it was not designed for routine consultation. Perrin himself admitted at the end of his chapter on the *censier* of Remiremont that, "It is hard to see how collections as incoherent in their composition as the *Libri traditionum* can, in practice, have been an effective aid in the administration of the lands of religious establishments."[68] He also recognized the difficulty posed for his view by the absence of witness lists in most of the donation-entries.[69] This difficulty disappears, however, if they are seen not as legal records (though they may have served this purpose in an ancillary way) but as memorials of the good deeds of the donors, entitling them to special liturgical commemoration. For whatever the broader socio-economic significance of the grants of *censuales,* they were essentially benefactions to the abbey, in return for which the donors expected spiritual compensation. This view is con-

---

[64] Perrin, *Recherches,* pp. 152-153; cf. 634 ff. on the breakdown of the domainal régime in Lorraine, owing in part to reduction of reserve land.

[65] See the documents cited n. 46 above, referring to the abbey's original endowment of 1400 *mansi* and the subsequent negligence of the abbesses and depredations of the advocates; cf. Choux, *Pibon,* p. 135, and Hlawitschka, *Äbtissinnenreihe,* pp. 144 and 147, docs. III and VI, showing the reduction of the *potestates* belonging to the abbey. Perrin, *Recherches,* pp. 652-653, however, argues that on ecclesiastical estates the reserve suffered less than on lay estates.

[66] A detailed study is needed to determine the rate of grants of *censuales* to the abbey, which should (if Perrin is correct) have increased as the reserve land on lay estates reduced.

[67] Perrin, *Recherches,* pp. 147-149 and 168.

[68] *Ibid.,* p. 169.

[69] *Ibid.,* p. 147, n. 2: "L'absence de la liste des témoins dans la plupart des notices pose des problèmes délicats, qu'il n'y a pas lieu d'aborder dans le présent ouvrage."

firmed by the appearance of similar grants (and some of the same ones) in the
Evangeliary which probably lay, like the *Liber memorialis,* on the altar at Remiremont.[70] All those whose names appeared in either book expected commemoration, and to distinguish the intentions, as apart from the forms, of the different
types of entries is to do violence to this essential unity of purpose.[71]

This lack of historiographical bias is the prime source of the value to historians
of the *Liber memorialis.*[72] It was never intended to serve either worldly pride or
legal ends, nor, indeed, in all probability, to be seen by any eyes other than those
of God. The historical light it sheds is therefore entirely incidental. The only
great events of history recorded in its pages are in a few passing references —
all the more moving for that — to the Magyar incursions, such as a list, written
about the middle of the tenth century, of "the names of those who died for the
faith of Christ, killed by the pagans" (f. 57v) and two donations of women, later
in the century, of whom one had been taken by the Huns and later returned and
the other, apparently a relation or neighbor (*proxima*) of the donors, had been
redeemed by them from the Huns and given to St Peter (32v II and 33v V). In
the Evangeliary, also, there is a well-known entry, dated by Hlawitschka about
970/90, recording the halving of the service owing from the demesne *mansi*
in the *potestas* of Liézey (or Lezey) as an act of mercy after the slaughter by the
pagans.[73] There are occasional references to great economic movements, too, such
as land-clearance, as when Abbess Gisla I in 980/90 allowed the men of Dainviller
(or Deinvillers) to hold without service and as their own property (*proprie*) the
lands which they had cleared and cultivated from the forests of St Peter.[74] But
such entries are exceptional, and even these, though perhaps serving in part as
evidence for the future, are primarily records of meritorious concessions by the
donors.

There is likewise no evidence in the *Liber memorialis* even of spiritual movements, and at times it is hard for the reader to remember that Remiremont was
located in an area full of religious activity. In the tenth century, the wave of
monastic reform centered at Gorze came within a few miles of Remiremont at
Senones, Moyenmoutier, and St Die, yet had no apparent effect there.[75] About
1040, the reformer Richard of St Vanne spent two years as a hermit on the

---

[70] This view is also supported by the fact that no apparent effort was made to enter names from
the donation-entries in the necrologies or commemoration-entries, although the names of various
prominent benefactors are found in more than one type of entry. Mitis, in *Zs. f. Schweizerische
Kirchengeschichte,* XLIII, 31, discusses the practice of "double entry" in both *Traditionscodex* and
Liber vitae.

[71] That there are some entries still with witness lists and other marks of legal records is not surprising, showing that in their original form the documents served a double purpose. As entries in the
Lib. mem., however, they primarily record benefactions.

[72] *Lib. mem.,* intro., p. xi.

[73] This entry has been published by various scholars since the eighteenth century, most recently
by Hlawitschka, no. 94 (cf. p. 52, n. 166). The commemoration-book of St Gall 390.10 includes a
recluse named Wiberat "killed by the pagans"; Mon. Germ. hist., *Libri confraternitatum,* p. 126.

[74] 19r I; cf. Hlawitschka, *Äbtissinnenreihe,* pp. 52–53.

[75] See the map in Kassius Hallinger, *Gorze-Kluny* (Studia Anselmiana, 22–25; Rome, 1950–51),
I, 50.

mountain above Remiremont, on or near the site of its original location,[76] but there is no reference to him in the *Liber memorialis*, nor to Pope Leo IX and Cardinal Humbert, both of whom came from the diocese of Toul, or Bishop Pibo, a reformer against whom the abbey fought a vigorous battle to preserve its privileges.[77] Later in the century, Remiremont was surrounded by centers of canonical reform. Hérival was only three kilometers away, and Seher of Chaumouzey lived on the mountain above the abbey until he left on account, perhaps, of the hostility of the nuns.[78] Not even the change of Remiremont itself from an abbey into a chapter of canonesses, which marked the end of regular religious life there,[79] left any mark in the *Liber memorialis*, in which the entries continued until they petered out, and the book apparently fell into desuetude, in the later twelfth century.

The *Liber memorialis* represented an older and less personal current of spirituality, in which groups of men and women bound by ties of kinship and community stood together in the battle against oblivion, confident that their memory, enshrined in the prayers and masses of the nuns, would find them favor in the eyes of the Almighty.[80] They desired not to struggle for the perfection of Christian life as described in the Gospels, of which the individualistic message had still hardly touched them, but rather to associate themselves with the endless work of praising God, which was the major task of monastic communities.[81] The *Liber memorialis* thus in its very essence, as well as in its incidentals, opens paths towards an understanding of an age and a people about whose inner life and aspirations almost nothing is otherwise known.

HARVARD UNIVERSITY

[76] See the accounts of Richard's life in Jean Mabillon, ed., *Acta sanctorum ordinis sancti Benedicti* (Venice, 1733–40), vi.1, 463 and 471; cf. Hubert Dauphin, *Le bienheureux Richard, Abbé de Saint-Vanne de Verdun, +1046* (Bibliothèque de la Revue d'histoire ecclésiastique, 24; Louvain/Paris, 1946), pp. 300–305.

[77] In addition to Choux, *Pibon*, who argues that in spite of this quarrel Remiremont favored the Gregorian side in the Investiture Contest (pp. 146–147), see Léopold Duhamel, "Le Palefroi du chapitre de Remiremont (1099–1681)," *Bibliothèque de l'École des Chartes*, xxxiii (5 S., VI; 1869), 639–640.

[78] Dauphin, *Richard*, p. 303, n. 4, and Choux, *Pibon*, pp. 152–153 and 156–160 (and 123 and 177–178 on the later conflict between Remiremont and Chaumouzey).

[79] This change probably occurred in the second half of the eleventh century, but the exact date is disputed: cf. Perrin, *Recherches*, p. 141, n. 1; Choux, *Pibon*, p. 143, and *Lib. mem.*, intro., p. x.

[80] Cf. Schmid, in *Frühmit. Studien*, i, 248: "Klostergemeinschaften und Adelssippen bildeten die Kerne im frühmittelalterlichen Sozialgefüge."

[81] On the *laus perennis* at Remiremont and other monasteries, see C. Gindele, "Die gallikanischen 'Laus Perennis'-Klöster und ihr 'Ordo Officii,' " *Revue Bénédictine*, lxix (1959), 32–48.

VI

NONA ET DECIMA
An Aspect of Carolingian Economy

HISTORIANS of feudalism have long been interested in the recompense given to churches and monasteries in return for grants of ecclesiastical lands made by Carolingian rulers to their vassals and *fideles*.[1] The legal basis of such grants is clear. "With respect to the Church," according to Marc Bloch, "the property was therefore, juridically, a *precarium*. From the king the man held it 'in benefice.'"[2] In the sources they are usually referred to as ecclesiastical benefices or as benefices from the property of such and such a bishopric or monastery. Charles the Bald carefully defined the division of rights in a charter for the archbishop of Lyons in 871: the church of St Stephen at Lyons has permanent possession "jure proprio et more ecclesiastico" of a certain estate which is held temporarily "jure beneficiario et usufructuario" by the king's *fidelis* Lambert.[3] Thus the tenant had beneficiary and usufructuary rights, while the estate remained the church's property. Such grants were generally recognized as a necessary means for the king to support his followers; but they were regarded as in theory temporary and abusive, and the proprietary rights of the church were always protected. In recognition of these rights, and as a measure of recompense to the church for the loss of the use of its lands, the holder of the benefice was required to pay a rent amounting to one-fifth of the produce, usually defined as "ninths and tenths," *nonae et decimae*, or a double tenth.[4] Thus in the charter cited above Lambert was

---

[1] On the meaning of these disputed terms, which together include all those owing fealty to the king, see C. E. Odegaard, *Vassi and Fideles in the Carolingian Empire*, Harvard Historical Monographs, XIX (Cambridge, Mass., 1945) and J.-F. Lemarignier, "Les Fidèles du roi de France (936–987)," *Recueil de travaux offert à M. Clovis Brunel*, Mémoires et documents publiés par la Société de l'Ecole des Chartes, XII (Paris, 1955), II, 138–162, with references to recent literature. I am very grateful to my friend Mr. Walter Goffart, of Harvard University, for reading this paper and making several valuable suggestions.

[2] Marc Bloch, *La Société féodale: La formation des liens de dépendance*, L'Evolution de l'humanité, XXXIV (Paris, 1939), p. 254; cf. Heinrich Brunner, *Deutsche Rechtsgeschichte*, II, ed. C. von Schwerin (Munich-Leipzig, 1928), 337, and F.-L. Ganshof, *Feudalism*, trans. Philip Grierson (London-New York-Toronto, 1952), pp. 17–18.

[3] *Recueil des actes de Charles II le Chauve*, ed. A. Giry, M. Prou, F. Lot, and G. Tessier, Chartes et diplômes relatifs à l'histoire de France (=CDRHF) (Paris, 1943–1955), II, 290.

[4] Louis Halphen, *Charlemagne et l'empire carolingien*, L'Évolution de l'humanité, XXXIII (Paris, 1947), p. 178, n. 2, was of the opinion that the second tithe (*nona*) was levied after the first tithe had been deducted and therefore amounted to 9% of the original total. Many sources show, however, that two-tenths of the original total were intended (i.e., one-ninth of the total after the first tenth had been taken): cf. C. J. Hefele, *Histoire des conciles*, ed. and trans. Henri Leclercq (Paris, 1907 ff.), III-2, 979, n. 2, and Brunner, *Rechtsgeschichte*, II, 338, n. 35. Occasionally the *nona et decima* were referred to together as a fifth: see the councils of Langres and Savonnières cited n. 67 below. Émile Lesne maintained that the ninth and tenth was due only from the *indominicatum* of the holder of the benefice, that is, from the lands cultivated for the lord's own use as contrasted with the *precaria* and benefices granted to tenants: see "La dîme des biens ecclésiastiques aux IXe et Xe siècles [IV]," *Revue d'histoire ecclésiastique*, XIV (1913), 494–496 and, on the meaning *indominicatum*, "L'Indominicatum dans la propriété foncière des églises à l'époque carolingienne,'" *Rev. d'hist. ecc.*, XXVII (1931), 74–85, esp.

obliged to pay each year to the church of St Stephen a ninth and a tenth from his benefice "on account of his possession," either until he died, when the estate was to return into the direct possession of the church, or until the king gave him another grant of land.[5]

The origin of the *nona et decima* is a subject of dispute. Roth and Waitz maintained that they were introduced by Charlemagne and that references before his time were forgeries or later interpolations.[6] More recent scholars have tended to believe that they began during the reign of Pepin.[7] Most recently, Ganshof ap-

---

79–80. This conclusion has been accepted by recent scholars, including Catherine Boyd, *Tithes and Parishes in Medieval Italy* (Ithaca, 1952), pp. 38–39, and H. F. Schmid, "Byzantinisches Zehntwesen," *Jahrbuch der österreichischen byzantinischen Gesellschaft*, VI (1957), 99, n. 327. Lesne's argument rests, however, on an analogy with the practice (which will be discussed later) of reserving for charitable purposes the tithes from the demesne lands of churches and monasteries, which has nothing to do with the system of *nonae et decimae*; and there is no reference in the legislative sources to such a restriction on the *nona et decima*. Tenure *ad nonas et decimas* was a privileged, not a peasant or servile, tenure: cf. Paul Roth, *Geschichte des Beneficialwesens von den ältesten Zeiten bis ins zehnte Jahrhundert* (Erlangen, 1850), pp. 365–366, and Alfons Dopsch, *Die Wirtschaftsentwicklung der Karolingerzeit*, 2nd ed. (Weimar, 1921–1922), II, 24–25; but grants of this sort were at least originally planned to support just one *fidelis* and apparently averaged in size between twenty and fifty households, though some were probably larger. The tenant was clearly expected to pay one-fifth from the produce of the entire benefice to the church or monastery owning the land and certainly could not escape payment by sub-infeudating part of the benefice and then paying only from his own demesne lands. In the case of large grants, the rent of one-fifth was presumably low enough to permit sub-infeudation at an advantageous rate (i.e., *ad medietatem*: see n. 58 below), but the landlord or the tenant would still have to pay the *nona et decima*. The degree of Louis the Pious in 829 (see n. 33 below) seems to show not that *nonae et decimae* were due only from demesne lands but that holders of grants *ad nonas et decimas* were trying to escape payment by not cultivating the land over which they had direct control.

[5] *Actes de Charles II*, II, 290.

[6] Roth, *Beneficialwesen*, p. 364; Georg Waitz, *Deutsche Verfassungsgeschichte*, III, 2nd ed. (Kiel, 1883), 38, n. 2, and IV, 2nd ed. (Berlin, 1885), 193: "Dass der doppelte Zehnte jetzt [in 779] zuerst eingeführt ist, nicht bereits von Pippin, kann nicht bezweifelt werden." The reference to Pepin in connection with ninths and tenths in a charter of Louis the Pious for Rheims in 816–825, in *Recueil des historiens des Gaules et de la France* (=RHGF) (Paris, 1738–1904), VI, 510, was considered an interpolation by Waitz, Simson, and Mühlbacher; see J. F. Böhmer, *Regista Imperii*, I: *Die Regesten des Kaiserreichs unter den Karolingern 751–918*, ed. E. Mühlbacher and J. Lechner, 2nd ed. (= Mühlbacher²) (Innsbruck, 1899–1908), no. 801. Albert Hauck, *Kirchengeschichte Deutschlands*, 8th ed. (Berlin, 1954), II, 234, n. 5, also said it was "nicht wahrscheinlich" that Pepin issued a general decree on *nona et decima*.

[7] Ulrich Stutz, "Das karolingische Zehntgebot," *Zeitschrift der Savigny-Stiftung für Rechtsgeschichte*, XLII: *Germanistische Abteilung*, XXIX (1908), 180–224; Ernst Perels, "Die Ursprünge des karolingischen Zehntrechts," *Archiv für Urkundenforschung*, III (1911), 233–250; Émile Lesne, in *Rev. d'hist. ecc.*, XIV, 494–496, and *Histoire de la propriété ecclésiastique en France*, II: *La propriété ecclésiastique et les droits régaliens à l'époque carolingienne*, 1: *Les étapes de la sécularisation des biens d'église du VIIIe au Xe siècle*, Mémoires et Travaux des Facultés Catholiques de Lille, XIX (Lille, 1922), p. 101; Brunner, *Rechtsgeschichte*, II, 338, n. 34 (who said it was "nicht unwahrscheinlich" that *nona et decima* began under Pepin); Charles de Clercq, *La législation religieuse franque de Clovis à Charlemagne*, Université de Louvain: Recueil de Travaux publiés par les membres des Conférences d'Histoire et de Philologie, II, 38 (Louvain-Paris, 1936), p. 159, who wrote that the second tithe found in the capitulary of Heristal "fut sans doute imposée par Pépin, en même temps que la première;" André Déléage, *La vie rurale en Bourgogne jusqu'au début du onzième siècle* (Mâcon, 1941), I, 610; Boyd, *Tithes*, p. 38.

pears to have returned to the view that they originated with Charlemagne.[8] Pepin in his capitulary of Aquitaine in 768 decreed, "That both bishops and abbots, or those laymen who hold a benefice from their lands, should restore those churches which are deserted" and "That all laymen and seculars who hold ecclesiastical property should take it as a *precarium*."[9] In view, therefore, of his concern for the responsibilities of laymen holding church lands,[10] it is not improbable that Pepin also instituted *nonae et decimae*, at least on a local level.[11] Be this as it may, the system was made general by Charlemagne in his capitulary of Heristal in 779.[12] Here he decreed:

Concerning church lands for which a rent (*census*) is now paid, a tenth and a ninth should be paid in addition to the rent; and from those for which no rents have hitherto been paid, a ninth and a tenth should also be given, and a shilling for fifty houses, half a shilling for thirty houses, and a third for twenty houses. And where there are now *precaria*, they should be renewed; and where there are none, they should be written down. And *precaria* made at our order should be distinguished from *precaria* made from the lands of churches by their own free will.[13]

<hr/>

[8] F.-L. Ganshof, *Recherches sur les capitulaires* (Paris, 1958), p. 80 and p. 82, n. 336, where he refers to Charlemagne's initiating a new régime governing ecclesiastical estates held as benefices by royal vassals.

[9] *Monumenta Germaniae Historica* (=MGH), *Leges*, ii: *Capitularia regum Francorum*, ed. A. Boretius and V. Krause (Hanover, 1883–1897), i, nos. 18.1 and 11, pp. 42–43, cf. De Clercq, *Législation*, pp. 145–146.

[10] On the general question of the responsibility of the holders of ecclesiastical benefices to maintain and repair churches, see Roth, *Beneficialwesen*, p. 366; Waitz, *Verfassungsgeschichte*, iv, 197; and Brunner, *Rechtsgeschichte*, ii, 338 and n. 39. It is not clear whether this obligation of maintenance and repair applied to the churches which owned the land or to the churches on the lands held by the tenant: cf. the sources cited in nn. 9, 19, 22, 24, etc.

[11] Cf. pp. 236–237 and nn. 64–65 and 74 below.

[12] The authenticity of this and several other capitularies edited by Boretius has been denied by Simon Stein, "Étude critique des capitulaires francs," *Le Moyen Age*, XLI (3rd Series, XII, 1940), 1–75, who later also attempted to prove that the *Lex Salica* was forged in the ninth century: "Lex Salica [I and II]," SPECULUM, XXII (1947), 113–134 and 395–418. While the inadequacy of Boretius' edition is generally admitted (cf. Ganshof, *Recherches*, pp. 8–9 and 37–39), most scholars have rejected Stein's ideas: see Halphen, *Charlemagne*, p. 511; Auguste Dumas, "La parole et l'écriture dans les capitulaires carolingiens," *Mélanges . . . Louis Halphen* (Paris, 1951), p. 208, n. 1, where he calls Stein's points "fort aventeureuses"; Rudolf Buchner, "Kleine Untersuchungen zu den fränkischen Stammesrechten, I," *Deutsches Archiv für Erforschung des Mittelalters*, ix (1951), 59–102, where he calls Stein's wholesale attack on German scholarship an example of "war psychosis," and Wattenbach-Levison, *Deutschlands Geschichtsquellen im Mittelalter*, Beiheft: R. Buchner, *Die Rechtsquellen* (Weimar, 1953), p. 44; and most recently and authoritatively, various works by Ganshof, esp. *Recherches*, pp. 37 ff. and nn. 5, 27, and 294, who wrote that, "Les conclusions de Stein procèdent d'erreurs manifestes et de raisonnements absurdes: il n'y a pas lieu de leur accorder la moindre importance."

[13] *Capitularia*, i, no. 20.13, p. 50. This common form of the text should be compared with the Lombard form, which represents, according to Boyd, *Tithes*, p. 40, "the glosses of Lombard judges, made sometime between the promulgation of the capitulary and the close of the eighth century," but is called by Ganshof, *Recherches*, p. 17, an Italian version of the capitulary and attributed to the last thirty years of the ninth century; cf. also De Clercq, *Législation*, p. 162. The Lombard form is printed in parallel columns with the common form: "Concerning church lands which until now laymen have held in benefice by order of the king, that they should hold them thus in the same way as before

Charlemagne thus required all holders of ecclesiastical benefices to pay a *nona et decima* in addition to either the previous rent or a rent now established on a scale according to the size of the grant.[14] Presumably this requirement applied particularly to involuntary *precaria* made *de verbo regis*,[15] since grants made voluntarily by prelates might be on different terms and be recovered into the direct possession of the church.

From this time on, references to *nonae et decimae* are frequent in both royal and ecclesiastical legislation. In a letter to his civil officials in Italy, written (according to De Clercq, who is followed by Ganshof[16]) between 779 and 781, Charlemagne complained at the diversion of "ninths and tenths or rents . . . from the churches from which they are held in benefice" and at the failure to accept *precaria* from their lands.[17] In 789, echoing his father's capitulary of 768, he told his *missi* in Aquitaine to inquire into the repair of churches by those who

---

unless they are restored to the churches by order of the king. And if previously a tenth and ninth was paid from these lands to the church, it should be done now as before; and in addition he should pay to those churches a shilling for fifty houses, half a shilling for thirty, and a third for twenty; and whoever previously paid another rent should do now as he did before. And a rent should be paid for church land for which until now no rent has been given, and where they are not [church lands], they should be written down. And *precaria* made by order of the king should be distinguished from *precaria* made by bishops, abbots, and abbesses at their own desire and on their own terms, in order that as they wish they may recover for the possession of their church lands which were granted in benefice and make every man serve faithfully and constantly for the sake of God and His honor." Cf. also MGH, *Leges* in fol., IV: *Leges Langobardorum* (Hanover, 1868), Charlemagne no. 60, p. 499.

[14] On the nature of this *census* and its earlier history, see Waitz, *Verfassungsgeschichte*, III, 38, no. 2; Stutz, in *Savigny Zeitschrift*, XLII, 203 ff.; Dopsch, *Wirtschaftsentwicklung*, II, 24; Brunner, *Rechtsgeschichte*, II, 337–338 and the long n. 36; and Heinrich Mitteis, *Lehnrecht und Staatsgewalt* (Weimar, 1933), p. 122. These authors agree in calling it essentially a "Rekognitionszins" or, according to Mitteis, "Anerkennungszins," paid in recognition of proprietary rights rather than as an economic rent. Dopsch pointed out that it "betrug für eine Haushaltung (casata) jetzt nur mehr 1/5 Denar" (p. 24). Later it seems to have disappeared in many cases and to have been replaced by the *nona et decima* as the "Rekognitionszins" in proof of proprietary rights: cf. *Actes de Charles II*, II, 329–331 (charter of 874).

[15] This is not the place to enter at length into the vexed issue of the *precaria verbo regis*, which Charlemagne here apparently put on a semi-permanent basis and distinguished clearly from benefices granted voluntarily from church lands. A. Bondroit, "Les 'Precariae verbo regis' avant le concile de Leptines (a. 743)," *Rev. d'hist. ecc.*, I (1900), 41–60, 249–266, and 430–447, concluded that it is "très douteuse" whether they existed before 743 (p. 430) and that, "Le précaire *verbo regis*, s'il existait alors, n'était donc qu'un abus" (p. 443). He is cited with approval by Brunner, *Rechtsgeschichte*, II, 340. Hauck, *Kirchengeschichte*, I, 386, n. 1, on the other hand, maintained that they originated much earlier: "man kann höchstens bezweifeln, ob die Formel precariae verbo regis vor dem achten Jahrhundert vorhanden war, dass die Sache vorhanden war, liegt, wie mich dünkt, in den Stellen." Hauck was strongly supported in this view, as might be expected, by Alfons Dopsch, *Wirtschaftliche und soziale Grundlagen der europäischen Kulturentwicklung*, 2nd ed. (Vienna, 1923–1924), II, 314–316. Cf. Mitteis, *Lehnrecht*, pp. 117–122, who concluded that *precariae verbo regis* were "zum ersten Male gesetzgeberisch erfasst" in 743, but certainly existed before this legal formulation, and Halphen, *Charlemagne*, pp. 204–205. There is in any case no question of their difference from the freely-granted and retractable *precaria*.

[16] De Clercq, *Législation*, pp. 161–162, and "Capitulaires francs en Italie à l'époque de Charlemagne," *Hommage à Dom Ursmer Berlière* (Brussels, 1931), p. 254; cf. Ganshof, *Recherches*, p. 17.

[17] *Capitularia*, I, no. 97, p. 203.

have held their property for the past twenty years.[18] And in the capitulary issued
at the synod of Frankfurt in 794 he decreed both "that, in accordance with the
previous royal capitularies, all those who hold ecclesiastical benefices and lands
should pay tenths and ninths or all rents, and everyone should bring the legitimate tithe from his own property to the church," and "that the buildings and
roofs of churches should be improved and repaired by those who hold benefices
from their lands."[19] In the *capitularia missorum specialia* of 802, which are known
in slightly different forms for at least six *missi*, Charlemagne instructed, "Concerning tenths and ninths and the repair of the churches of God, they should
take care to give and to improve."[20] And again in the so-called *capitulare missorum item speciale*, which is in fact probably a collection of extracts compiled in
806, there is an article, "That those who hold ecclesiastical lands by benefice of
the emperor should take care to give the ninth and tenth and to repair the
churches."[21] Charlemagne's son Pepin, in a capitulary for Italy issued during the
first decade of the ninth century, required the holders of ecclesiastical benefices
both to pay the *nona et decima* in full and to assist as much as possible in the upkeep of churches on their lands.[22] At the same time the bishops concerned themselves with *nonae et decimae* in conciliar legislation. At least two of the five regional councils which met at the emperor's order in 813 passed decrees on this
subject. Canon forty-two of the council of Mainz repeated that holders of ecclesiastical benefices must help repair the churches and pay ninths and tenths.[23]
And the council at Tours decreed concerning the upkeep of churches on ecclesiastical lands held by laymen and complained at the frequent diversion of the *nona
et decima*, "which those who hold church lands are required to pay to the rectors
of the churches for lighting and the support of the clergy."[24]

This policy with regard to *nonae et decimae* was maintained and defined by
Louis the Pious.[25] A diplomatic formula dating from about 814 confirmed the

---

[18] *Capitularia*, I, no. 24.2, p. 65; cf. De Clercq, *Législation*, p. 178.

[19] *Capitularia*, I, no. 28.25–26, p. 76; cf. Hefele-Leclercq, *Conciles*, III-2, 1045–1060; De Clercq,
Législation, pp. 183–191; and F.-L. Ganshof, "Observations sur le Synode de Francfort de 794,"
Miscellanea historica in honorem Alberti de Meyer, Université de Louvain: Recueil de Travaux d'Histoire et de Philologie, 3rd Series, XXII–XXIII (Louvain-Brussels, 1946), I, 306–318, who said of canon 26:
"Répétition plus explicite, plus formelle et peut-être généralisation d'une disposition dont il avait
déjà été fait application en faveur des églises d'Aquitaine en 789 . . . et sans doute dès 768 . . . "
(p. 314, n. 2).

[20] W. A. Eckhardt, "Die Capitularia missorum specialia von 802," *Deutsches Archiv*, XII (1956),
503, cf. also 507.

[21] *Capitularia*, I, no. 35.56, p. 104; cf. Ganshof, *Recherches*, p. 68, who bases himself on the research
of Eckhardt. Cf. also no. 84.12, p. 183, dated 802–813 by De Clercq, *Législation*, p. 381.

[22] *Capitularia*, I, no. 102.6, p. 210; cf. De Clercq, *Législation*, pp. 218–219 and 381.

[23] MGH, *Leges*, III-2: *Concilia aevi Karolini*, I, ed. A. Werminghoff (Hanover-Leipzig, 1906–1908),
271; cf. the council of Arles in 813, canon 25, *ibid.*, p. 253.

[24] *Ibid.*, pp. 292–293.

[25] On the religious legislation of Louis the Pious, see the series of articles, continuing his earlier book,
by Charles de Clercq, "La législation religieuse franque depuis l'avènement de Louis le Pieux jusqu'aux Fausses Décrétales," *Revue de droit canonique*, IV (1954), 371–404, V (1955), 5–55, 269–306,
390–429, VI (1956), 145–162 and 263–289. These are continued in turn by a series of articles in the
same periodical entitled, "La législation religieuse franque depuis les Fausses Décrétales jusqu'à la

rights of a bishop or abbot to the ninths and tenths which had been granted, according to Louis, by his father "in order that any of his *fideles* who held benefices from such and such a bishopric or monastery should not neglect to give to the church or monastery every year ninths and tenths or a rent from these benefices and to assist as much as possible in repairing the buildings of the church."[26] In another formula, of about 817, Louis again required the payment of *nonae et decimae* from villas "which our vassals hold from the property of such and such a church as a benefice of our generosity and from all of which they derive sufficient support for their needs."[27] In his capitularies of 818/19 Louis further defined the *nona et decima* and the obligation to maintain ecclesiastical buildings and established for the first time a penalty for non-payment. Ninths and tenths were to be paid "from the produce of the land and the fodder of animals."[28] Failure to pay was to be punished by a fine and payment of arrears and, if repeated, by loss of the benefice.[29] In his *Admonitio ad omnes regni ordines* of 823-25 Louis decreed that *nonae et decimae* must be fully and faithfully paid "from all produce and from wine and from hay" and he added the important proviso that, "if some bishop wishes to receive money in place of this, he may do so on terms suitable to himself and him who has to pay this."[30] There were also important decrees on *nonae et decimae* in the capitulary of Worms in 829, which was issued, according to Amann, in accordance with the desires of the clergy and as a result of "un vaste examen de conscience" at a series of councils in 828.[31] In article 5 Louis repeated

fin du IXe siècle." These articles have since been gathered into a book, which came into my hands too late for use in this article.

[26] MGH, *Leges*, v: *Formulae merovingici et karolini aevi*, ed. K. Zeumer (Hanover, 1882-1886), pp. 301-302.

[27] *Ibid.*, p. 304.

[28] "Fodder of animals" here probably means the same as "animals," i.e., the increase of herds and flocks, although Georg Schreiber, *Kurie und Kloster im 12. Jahrhundert*, Kirchenrechtliche Abhandlungen, LXV-LXVI (Stuttgart, 1910), I, 291, argued that in the twelfth century "nutrimen animalium" referred literally to food for animals and not to the animals themselves; cf. Paul Viard, *Histoire de la dîme ecclésiastique principalement en France jusqu'au Décret de Gratien* (Dijon, 1909), pp. 102 and 152.

[29] *Capitularia*, I, no. 140.5, pp. 287-288, =*Ansegisi abbatis capitularium collectio*, IV, 38, *ibid.*, p. 442, =*Leges Langobardorum*, Louis the Pious no. 31, ed. cit., p. 536. Cf. *Capitularia*, I, no. 138.14, pp. 277-278: "De ecclesiis sane destructis vel de nonis et decimis sive de claustris canonicorum, qualiter constitui et ordinari nobis placuerit, aliis capitulis subter adnotavimus"; and also no. 141.6, p. 289; see F.-L. Ganshof, "Note sur la date de deux documents administratifs émanant de Louis le Pieux," *Recueil* . . . *Clovis Brunel*, i, 517, and *Recherches*, pp. 84-85; and De Clercq, in *Rev. de droit can.*, IV, 401-402.

[30] *Capitularia*, I, no. 150.23, p. 307, =*Ansegisi collectio*, II, 21, *ibid.*, p. 418. De Clercq, in *Rev. de droit can.*, V, 8, interpreted the passage in this capitulary that, "de nutrimine vero pro decima, sicut hactenus consuetudo fuit, ab omnibus observetur," as a modification of earlier legislation, in particular of no. 140.5 (n. 29 above), and a restriction of the *nona et decima* from animals to a tithe only; but the exact meaning is not clear. Dopsch, *Wirtschaftsentwicklung*, II, 270, saw in the last part of this decree evidence of the "Tendenz der Umwandlung von Natural- in Geldzinse." On the date, see Ganshof, *Recherches*, p. 53, n. 212.

[31] Émile Amann, *L'Époque carolingienne*, Histoire de l'Église, ed. A. Fliche and V. Martin, VI (Paris, 1947), 216-217. De Clercq, in *Rev. de droit can.*, V, 32-34, studied the three series of instructions to *missi* issued after the councils (nos. 191-193) and showed that they corresponded to the reform program of 829. On the diet and council of Worms generally, see Hefele-Leclercq, *Conciles*, IV-1, 76-78.

his legislation of 818/19 and instructed his *missi* to force those who failed to pay *nonae et decimae* not only to make restitution for a year but also to pay a fine and the royal ban, with a warning that repetition of the offence would entail loss of the benefice.[32] And in article 10 he decreed: "Concerning a man who has neglected to cultivate his demesne lands (*agros dominicatos*) in order to avoid paying the ninth and tenth from them and has for this reason accepted lands belonging to another (*alienas terras*) to cultivate, we decree that he should pay the ninth and tenth for three years together with his fine. . . . "[33] By the end of Louis' reign, therefore, the legal theory of *nonae et decimae* was fully established. Benedictus Levita included in his collection of capitularies, compiled between 845 and 855 as a continuation to the collection of Ansegisis,[34] an alleged decree, "Concerning those who hold ecclesiastical lands by order of the lord king. That those men who hold ecclesiastical lands by order of the lord king are required to repair the churches from which they are held or the buildings of the bishopric or monastery to which they are known to belong, . . . and to pay in full the rents or the tenths and ninths in those places, as we ordered them at Vernum. And he who fails to do so will lose the lands."[35] And all the canons concerning the *nona et decima* included by Regino of Prüm in his *Libri duo de synodalibus causis et disciplinis ecclesiasticis*, which was compiled about 906, date from before 850.[36] Subsequent capitularies occasionally told the *missi* to check up on the payment of *nonae et decimae*;[37] popes and bishops attempted to enforce their payment; and

[32] *Capitularia*, II, no. 191.5, p. 13; cf. art. 9 on the repair of church buildings.

[33] *Capitularia*, II, no. 191.10, p. 14. This statute has been variously interpreted. Viard, *Dîme*, p. 144, argued from it that the *seniores* who had received church lands had made grants to tenants, who tried to avoid paying the *nona et decima*; but it seems equally probable that the *seniores* themselves tried to avoid payment. In opposition to the interpretation of K. von Inama-Sternegg, *Deutsche Wirthschaftsgeschichte*, I (Leipzig, 1879), 252, Dopsch, *Wirtschaftsentwicklung*, II, 26–27, emphasized that his decree applied not to "Königsland" but to "herrschaftliches Land" and "kirchliches Benefizialland"; but his suggestion that new lands were being opened ("excolore") from which no tithes were owed is not probable. The implications of the decree are not entirely clear, but it seems that as a result of acquiring other lands, certain holders of *precaria verbo regis* were cultivating for their own use, as their demesne, land which was not part of their ecclesiastical benefice, which thus lay fallow, and avoided paying *nonae et decimae* from the produce.

[34] Schafer Williams, "The Pseudo-Isidorian Problem Today," SPECULUM, XXIX (1954), 704; Ganshof, *Recherches*, p. 71, basing himself largely on earlier authorities, dated the collection between 847 and 852.

[35] MGH, *Leges* in fol., II (Hanover 1837), *Capitularia spuria*, I, 13, p. 47. The authenticity of this capitulary has been the subject of a lively debate: see Emil Seckel, "Studien zu Benedictus Levita, VI," *Neues Archiv der Gesellschaft für ältere deutsche Geschichtskunde*, XXXI (1905–1906), 65–67, where he concluded that it is a genuine capitulary of Pepin into which the words "vel illas decimas et nonas" and the final sentence had been interpolated, either by Benedict himself or by an earlier forger. It was certainly accepted as genuine at the time and was probably used by Hincmar: see E. Mühlbacher, "Ein angebliches Capitulare Karls des Grossen," *Mittheilungen des Instituts für oesterreichische Geschichtsforschung*, I (1880), 609–610. Cf. also Brunner, *Rechtsgeschichte*, II, 338, nn. 36 and 39.

[36] Ed. F. G. A. Wasserschleben (Leipzig, 1840), pp. 45–47, Book I, canons 44 (n. 56 below), 46 (n. 30 above), 47 (n. 32 above), 50 (n. 33 above), and 51 (n. 60 below). On the date, see Paul Fournier and Gabriel Le Bras, *Histoire des collections canoniques en Occident* (Paris, 1931–1932), I, 245.

[37] *Capitularia*, II, p. 268 (853, art. 6), 292 (857, art. 1), 331 (865, art. 10).

ecclesiastical councils passed decrees on the subject. But these on the whole repeated and enforced earlier legislation.

The purpose of this article, however, is not to write a complete history of *nonae et decimae*,[38] but rather to determine their nature and in particular to study their relation to the normal ecclesiastical (later known as sacramental) tithe, which every Christian was obliged to pay from his annual revenue. The point is more important than may appear at first sight, since it affects not only the *nona et decima* but also the whole history of tithes. Certain historians have used evidence concerning the *nona et decima* to prove that the normal tithe was a secular rent;[39] and others have completely confused the two sorts of tithe.[40] Most scholars, however, have tended to identify the *decima* with the normal ecclesiastical tithe and to treat the *nona* as a secular rent. As early as the seventeenth century, Du Cange in his *Glossarium* remarked that the *nonae* were paid "jure colonario" and the *decimae* "jure Ecclesiastico."[41] Benjamin Guérard, in the introduction to his edition of the polyptych of Irminon, wrote that "the holders of ecclesiastical benefices were obliged to pay both ninths and tenths, *nonae et decimae*, the former as users or farmers, the latter as Christians."[42] This view was emphasized by the great pioneer of the legal and economic history of the Church, Ulrich Stutz, who vigorously attacked those who held that *nonae et decimae*, when paid in recognition of a benefice (*Leihengelt*), were "non-ecclesiastical, purely secular tithes, based as far as they could be on private law" and maintained on the contrary that the *nona et decima* combined elements from both public and private law and "was the general ecclesiastical tithe, simply increased by the addition of a rent (*Leihezuschlag*)," that is, it was the normal tithe doubled.[43] This view has been generally accepted since the appearance of Stutz's work.[44]

[38] The most satisfactory account may be found scattered in the second and third parts of Vol. II of Lesne, *Propriété ecclésiastique*.

[39] This point of view still has defenders in Italy, where under the law of 1887, which abolished "sacramental" tithes, so-called dominical or secular tithes "should be commuted into fixed money rents or redeemed by the payment of a capital sum" (Boyd, *Tithes*, p. 10). It is therefore in the interests of the former owners of tithes, and especially of the clergy, to prove the secular origins of tithes. Almost all historians today agree that the normal tithe, as it prevailed in Europe throughout the Middle Ages, was essentially sacramental: cf. Boyd, *Tithes*, pp. 241–249. H. F. Schmid, in the *Jahrbuch der öst. byz. Gesellschaft*, VI, 98–99, etc., however, still maintained that, "the most powerful roots of the western ecclesiastical law of tithing" lay in the secular agricultural tithes of the Roman Empire; but there is no evidence for the continuity of such dues.

[40] See, among others, Von Inama-Sternegg, *Wirthschaftsgeschichte*, I, 252, and Henri Sée, *Les classes rurales et le régime domanial en France au Moyen Age* (Paris, 1901), p. 114.

[41] *Glossarium mediae et infimae latinitatis*, s.v. "nona," ed. Léopold Favre (Niort, 1883–1887), V, 605. The same distinction, probably taken from Du Cange, is found in M.-C. Ragut, *Cartulaire de Saint-Vincent de Mâcon*, (Mâcon, 1864), p. lxxxiv.

[42] *Polyptyche de l'abbé Irminon* (Paris, 1844), I-2, 560–561.

[43] Stutz, in *Savigny Zeitschrift*, XLII, 202, n. 1. In support of this view he cited only two sources: the council of Frankfurt in 794 (n. 19 above) and the council of Toul [Savonnières] in 859, which will be discussed later.

[44] The only recent authority whom I have found who opposes this view, aside from those who maintain that all the tithes are secular (see n. 39 above), is E. W. Watson, "The Development of Ecclesiastical Organisation and its Financial Basis," *Cambridge Medieval History*, VI (Cambridge, 1929),

Viard, although he criticized Stutz for not properly distinguishing the *nona* from the *decima*, held the same opinion of the nature of the two dues. "Beneficiaries [from church lands]," he wrote, "paid the tithe like all inhabitants of the realm, a rent (*cens*), and the none."[45] "The tithe is a tax," he explained later, "the none, an agricultural rent."[46] According to Ernst Perels, "While everyone else had to pay to the Church the simple ecclesiastical tithe, the holder of an ecclesiastical benefice was burdened with a double tithe, the so-called ninths and tenths." He went on to say that the simple or general church tithe had nothing to do with ecclesiastical benefices: "The distinction between the general tax and the rent for church benefices is clearly expressed in many capitularies and synods. . . ."[47] This rent was the ninth which was added (Stutz's *Leihezuschlag*) to the ordinary tithe and which replaced the old *census* previously paid by holders of church lands. Friedrich Philippi also accepted the distinction between the two dues but argued, somewhat perversely, that the ninth was the ecclesiastical tithe and the tenth, a civil rent. "It is clear," he concluded, "that in this way the name *decima* marked the tenurial rent (*Pachtabgabe*) originally based on private law, whereas the ecclesiastical tithes were called *nonae*."[48] Emile Lesne supported Stutz's view, both in his series of articles on the tithing of ecclesiastical property in the ninth and tenth centuries and in his *Histoire de la propriété ecclésiastique*. "These tithes," he wrote, referring to the *nona et decima*, "were distinguished from ordinary tithes only because, in view of the condition of the lands which bore the charge, the tariff was double and sometimes the receiver of the tithes was a different person. Apart from that, the order requiring the holders of benefices to pay tithes and nones was only a special article of the general law which required everyone to pay tithes."[49] Later scholars have either followed this lead or taken refuge in ambiguity on the subject of *nonae et decimae*. Brunner, for instance, speaks of the double tithe "in which the general church tithe was included";[50] and Dopsch, citing Stutz, also says: "Besides the general church tithe, the nona, that is a double tithe, was also raised from ecclesiastical lands granted as benefices."[51] De Clercq in his commentary on article 25 of the capitulary of Frankfurt adheres strictly to the interpretation of Stutz and Lesne: "All the

---

534, who said that the *nona et decima* "was a purely secular arrangement" and suggested that it originated in the Roman land tax and rent of a tenth.

[45] Viard, *Dîme*, p. 82.

[46] *Ibid.*, p. 142, citing Imbart de la Tour and Werminghoff in support of his opinion.

[47] Perels, in *Archiv. f. Urkundenforschung*, III, 236, and 242, n. 4.

[48] Friedrich Philippi, "Zehnten und Zehntstreitigkeiten," *Mitteilungen des Instituts für österreichische Geschichtsforschung*, XXXIII (1912), 396.

[49] Lesne, *Propriété ecclésiastique*, II-1, 107, citing Stutz and the two sources cited by Stutz.

[50] Brunner, *Rechtsgeschichte*, II, 337–338.

[51] Dopsch, *Wirtschaftsentwicklung*, II, 24. Hans von Schubert, *Geschichte der christlichen Kirche im Frühmittelalter* (Tübingen, 1917–1921), p. 552, remarked, after discussing the normal tithe, that tenants of *precaria verbo regis* owed "in addition to the tithe also a ninth, thus a second tithe from the remainder, in total a double tithe."

faithful must pay tithes; those who hold church lands give in addition the rent and the ninth part of the revenue of the lands."[52] This also is the view of Jesús San Martín, Louis Halphen, F.-L. Ganshof, H. F. Schmid, and Catherine Boyd, who frankly asserts that, "Ulrich Stutz cleared up the perplexities of earlier writers by showing that the *decima et nona* was merely the ordinary tithe doubled."[53] Other historians have avoided the problem of the exact nature of the *nona et decima* by speaking simply of a double tithe,[54] which strongly suggests, however, a connection with the single or normal tithe and in effect subscribes to the position of Stutz and Lesne.

An examination of the legislative, conciliar, and documentary sources, however, does not support the view that the *nona et decima* was "merely the ordinary tithe doubled." The confusion seems to have arisen from the assumption that the term *decima* must always have the same meaning and refer to the same type of payment. The authors against whom Stutz and his followers argued held that since they found references to the *nona et decima* as a secular land rent, the ordinary *decima* must also be secular. Stutz, on the contrary, insisted on the sacramental character of the normal tithe and assumed that half of the *nona et decima* was sacramental and only the *nona* was secular. He therefore drew the important distinction between the two halves, one ecclesiastical and based on public law, the other secular and based on private law. Both these views, however, fail to draw a sufficient distinction between the single ecclesiastical *decima*, of which the origins and nature were certainly sacramental, and the combined *nona et decima*.

All the early legislative texts separate the ordinary tithe from the ninth and tenth. In the capitulary of Heristal, article 7 was concerned with the ordinary tithe, of which the payment was for the first time made universal and compulsory, and article 13 dealt with the ninth and tenth, which was owed only by holders of ecclesiastical benefices. The same distinction appeared in article 25 of the capitulary of Frankfurt, which both Stutz and Lesne cited in support of their argument. Here all holders of church lands and benefices were required to pay *nonae et decimae* and all men must pay "ex sua proprietate legitimam decimam." Thus only the former had to pay one-fifth of the produce from their benefices to the church which owned the land, whereas all men had to pay the "legitimate" or normal tithe, a tenth of their annual revenue, to the church where they received the sacraments. The so-called *capitula ecclesiastica* of 810–13?, which probably was in fact a purely ecclesiastical text, either a diocesan statute or a synodal

---

[52] De Clercq, *Législation*, p. 187.

[53] Jesús San Martín, *El diezmo eclesiástico en España hasta el siglo XII* (Palencia, 1940), p. 34; Halphen, *Charlemagne*, p. 178, n. 2; Ganshof, *Feudalism*, p. 35 ("ninth (nona), a second tithe in addition to the tithe due to the Church which since the reign of Pepin III had been paid by every type of land") and *Recherches*, p. 82, n. 336; Schmid, in *Jahrbuch der öst. byz. Gesellschaft*, VI, 99; Boyd, *Tithes*, p. 38, n. 41.

[54] Hefele-Leclercq, *Conciles*, III-2, 947, n. 2; Hauck, *Kirchengeschichte*, II, 234; Mitteis, *Lehnrecht*, pp. 122–123; Déléage, *Bourgogne*, II, 1376, defined the *nona et decima* as "double tithe paid to a church by a royal vassal with a fief on the lands of that church."

decree,[55] is more ambiguous: "That those who hold benefices from churches should give a ninth and a tenth from them to the church which owns the land. *Et qui tale beneficium habent, ut ad medietatem laborent, ut de eorum portione proprio presbytero decimas donent.*"[56] The second part of this decree has been variously interpreted, but it seems to mean: "Those who hold such a benefice by métayage should give tithes from their portion to their own [parish] priest."[57] The decree as a whole, therefore, refers to two ways of holding ecclesiastical lands: one *ad nonas et decimas*, by which one-fifth of the produce was paid as rent, and the other *ad medietatem*, by which one-half the produce was paid as rent;[58] and it stipulated that tenants *ad medietatem* should give tithes to their parish priest from their own portion, that is, after the half which they owed as rent was paid. Boretius and Brunner confused the two tenures and the two tithes and thought that the purpose of the decree was to free tenants *ad medietatem* from paying ninths as well as tithes.[59] But the tenures were in fact distinct and the tithes different: one tithe, together with the ninth, was paid to the church which owned the benefice; the other, the normal ecclesiastical tithe, was paid to the parish priest of the tenant. The statute probably, therefore, arose out of complaints from churches and monasteries that tenants on their lands were not paying the proper rents and from parish priests that tenants *ad medietatem* were not paying

---

[55] See De Clercq, *Législation*, p. 291; P. W. Finsterwalder, "Quellenkritische Untersuchungen zu den Capitularien Karls des Grossen," *Historisches Jahrbuch*, LVIII (1938), 425; Ganshof, *Recherches*, p. 12, n. 33.

[56] *Capitularia*, I, no. 81.18, p. 179, =*Ansegisi collectio*, I, 157, *ibid.*, 413, =Regino of Prum, I, 44, ed. cit., p. 45. Not all the manuscripts include the two troublesome *ut*'s in the section cited in Latin. Some omit the first *ut* or have *et*, *unde*, or *quod* in its place; some also omit the second *ut* or have *et* in its place. It is clear, therefore, that the phrase "ut ad medietatem laborent" refers back to "tale beneficium": "such a benefice as they work at métayage."

[57] Viard, *Dîme*, p. 144, n. 2, interpreted the statute to mean that tenants holding by métayage need pay *nonae et decimae* only from their own part of the harvest. Hefele-Leclercq, *Conciles*, III-2, 1131, translated it as, "Celui qui a un fief, de quelque nature qu'il soit, doit le cultiver, percevoir le moitié des revenus, et donner sur sa part le dîme au prêtre." Cf. also the paraphrase by De Clercq, *Législation*, p. 291.

[58] Tenure *ad medietatem*, or métayage, was not uncommon in the Carolingian Empire: see Brunner, *Rechtsgeschichte*, I, 2nd ed. (Leipzig, 1906), 289, and n. 40, citing this statute, and Dopsch, *Wirtschaftsentwicklung*, I, 277.

[59] Boretius, in his note to this statute, interpreted the second part to mean that tenants at métayage need pay "decimas tantum, non nonas et decimas, cum pro nonis laborent"; and Brunner, *Rechtsgeschichte*, II, 338, n. 35, wrote that, "He who held an ecclesiastical benefice at métayage (*auf Halbteilung der Früchte*) was freed from paying ninths." Hauck, *Kirchengeschichte*, II, 235, n. 1, agreed with this: "He who was burdened with forced labor (*Fronarbeit*) was freed from paying the ninths," although he apparently confused *Fronarbeit* with métayage. It would be odd, however, to free from paying a ninth a tenant who has already to pay half his annual produce as rent; and Dopsch, *Wirtschaftsentwicklung*, II, 26, n. 5, called Boretius' interpretation "far from decisive," though he gave no reason against it. Dopsch himself thought the statute meant "that from the part of the profits which came to the peasant householder, only the tenth, not however, as from the other half which fell to the landlord, the tenth and ninth, had to be paid." He therefore also confused the two tithes and apparently thought that the peasants paid only one tithe from their portion while the lord paid a double tithe from his and that the purpose of the statute was to distinguish the tithe-obligations of the peasants and the landlords.

normal tithes from their own half of the produce. There is no reference to the payment of normal tithes by tenants *ad nonas et decimas*, but it is improbable that tenants at a low rent would have been free from an obligation which tenants at a high rent had to pay. By comparison with métayage, tenure at one-fifth was far from burdensome; and although tenants *ad nonas et decimas* were originally held responsible for a *census* and for the upkeep of church buildings in addition to the rent, it was probably a privileged tenure reserved for benefices *de verbo regis*, which in the capitulary of Heristal were carefully distinguished from benefices granted by the bishop or abbot himself, who might be expected to make an arrangement more advantageous to his church. But tenants by both tenures were presumably expected to pay normal tithes to their own priests.

Nonae et decimae were also distinguished from normal tithes in royal and ecclesiastical legislation after Charlemagne. The decrees of Louis the Pious punishing non-payment of ninths and tenths (818/19 and 829) and allowing their commutation into a money rent by agreement between the bishop and the tenant (823–25) clearly treated the *nona et decima* as a secular rent distinct from the ecclesiastical tithe, which in the ninth century could not properly be commuted. The council of Meaux-Paris in 845–46 decided that a tenant who failed to pay ninths and tenths "from ecclesiastical property" and to repair church buildings would lose his benefice, "in accordance with the legal and ancient dictum 'qui neglegit censum, perdat agrum'."[60] The council of Soissons in 853 urged, "That from property which by sure proof is shown to belong to the church and which cannot be fully restored [to it] on account of various necessities, ninths and tenths at least should be paid";[61] and the king issued corresponding instructions to his *missi*.[62] In 855 bishops from the provinces of Lyons, Vienne, and Arles gathered at Valence, and

it pleased them to ordain that from estates and farms which are known formerly to have been given to the church by faithful Christians and now to be subject to the power of laymen, ninths and tenths should be faithfully paid to those churches from which the lands were taken, as was ordered in the decrees of the rulers; those who keep them [i.e. refuse to pay ninths and tenths], should know that they will be driven from the boundaries of the church as sacrilegious men. But also (*Sed et*) all the faithful should promptly offer to God their tithes from everything that they possess and should not dare by any opposition to change what has been decreed, lest we be forced to bind them by ecclesiastical punishment.[63]

Here, as in the decree of 853, the abusive character of tenure *ad nonas et decimas*

---

[60] *Capitularia*, II, no. 293.62, p. 413, =Regino of Prüm, I, 51, *ed. cit.*, pp. 47–48; cf. Hefele-Leclercq, *Conciles*, IV-1, 120–127, and De Clercq, in *Rev. de droit can.*, V, 294–301. On the "ancient dictum," cf. Brunner, *Rechtsgeschichte*, I, 305.

[61] *Capitularia*, II, no. 258.8 (Codex B), p. 266; cf. Hefele-Leclercq, *Conciles*, IV-1, 192–196. De Clercq, in *Rev. de droit can.*, VI, 350, n. 9, suggested that this is not part of the authentic acts of the council but simply a résumé of the orders to the *missi* cited in the following note.

[62] *Capitularia*, II, no. 259.6, p. 268; see Ganshof, *Recherches*, p. 41, n. 156, and p. 56, n. 224, on the relation of the royal capitulary to the conciliar decrees.

[63] J. D. Mansi, *Sacrorum conciliorum nova et amplissima collectio*, XV (Venice, 1770), 9 AB; cf. Hefele-Leclercq, *Conciles*, IV-1, 204–210, and De Clercq, in *Rev. de droit can.*, VI, 355–357.

was emphasized, and the ninths and tenths paid as a rent for church lands were treated as different from the *decimas suas* paid by everybody. Three years later the same points emerge from a letter probably written by Archbishop Hincmar of Rheims and sent by the synod of Quierzy to Louis the German: "And since he [the king] could not restore all the lands to the churches from which they had been taken, on account of his controversy with Waïfer, duke of Aquitaine, he asked that *precaria* be made by the bishops out of these lands and ordered that ninths and tenths for the repair of roofs and twelve pennies from each household should be paid to the church from whose lands the benefice was granted, as is found in the book of royal capitularies, until the land is restored to the church."[64] Since Duke Waïfer died in 768,[65] the king concerned must have been Pepin; and the passage therefore throws light on the origins of the system of *nonae et decimae*, which as late as the middle of the ninth century was apparently still regarded as an essentially temporary recompense to the church until its lands could be restored.

A yet more important conciliar text concerning *nonae et decimae* is canon 13 of the council of Langres in 859, which was attended by a group of bishops from Provence led by their king Charles. They were on their way to Savonnières, near Toul, where they met again later in the same year, together with two other kings and a host of ecclesiastical dignitaries, and where the canons of the council of Langres were read and approved.[66] These two councils agreed

That ninths and tenths at least should be paid faithfully from lands consecrated to God by those who hold the lands to the churches to which they are justly owed. For if tithes should be offered to God ex voto from one's own property, by a much more divine legal precept, after the oblation of giving back (*redhibitionis oblationem*, i.e. the normal tithe), a fifth part over and above (*insuper*) should rightly be offered to His ministers. Whoever scorns this precept will suffer the curse of the law in these matters. And we humbly request as a group that from now on nothing will be taken from churches but that in these modern times that which has been taken away may be returned to God.[67]

Both Stutz and Lesne cited this canon, but it lends no support to their argument that the *nona et decima* was simply the normal tithe doubled. On the contrary, the second sentence leaves no doubt that the ninths and tenths were to be given in addition to the normal tithe, which simply returned to God what every Christian owed Him. Archbishop Vulfadus of Bourges (866–76), a famous opponent of Hincmar,[68] advised the laymen in his diocese by a pastoral letter: "Those who possess ecclesiastical land by right of a benefice should pay ninths and tenths to the churches to which the lands are known to belong, and in addition they should

---

[64] *Capitularia*, II, no. 297, p. 433; cf. Hefele-Leclercq, *Conciles*, IV-1, 214–215, and IV-2, 1335; Walter Mohr, "Die Krise des kirchlichen Einheitsprogrammes im Jahre 858," *Archivum Latinitatis Medii Aevi (Bulletin Du Cange)*, XXV (1955), 204–207; and De Clercq, in *Rev. de droit can.*, VI, 363–365.

[65] Léonce Auzias, *L'Aquitaine carolingienne (778–987)*, Bibliothèque méridionale, II, 28 (Toulouse-Paris, 1937), p. 7; Halphen, *Charlemagne*, p. 52.

[66] Hefele-Leclercq, *Conciles*, IV-1, 217–220 and IV-2, 1338–1342, and De Clercq, in *Rev. de droit can.*, VI, 365–372.

[67] Mansi, *Conciliorum . . . collectio*, XV, 539–540.

[68] Louis Duchesne, *Fastes épiscopaux de l'ancienne Gaule*, 2nd ed. (Paris, 1907–1915), II, 31.

by no means keep them lest they incur the sin of sacrilege."[69] Here as in the other sources, payment of the *nona et decima* was directly dependent upon the holding of ecclesiastical lands and ended when the lands were restored to the church. The normal tithes, on the other hand, continued to be paid to the local church. This distinction is entirely in accord with the theory of ecclesiastical tithing which prevailed in the eighth and ninth centuries.[70] Numerous Carolingian capitularies emphasized that the normal tithe, whatever its ultimate destination, must be paid to the priest of the church where the payer received the sacraments. The bishop then supervised their distribution and use, but he was not himself the proper recipient of tithes; and under no circumstances should they be paid to a monastery.[71] *Nonae et decimae*, however, were never paid to a parish priest and normally went to the bishopric or monastery from whose lands the benefice *de verbo regis* had been granted.[72] Doubtless there were exceptions to both these rules, even as early as the ninth century; but the fact that the *decima* of the *nona et decima* was properly paid to a bishop or abbot strongly militates against identifying it with the normal tithe and against the view that the *nona et decima* was simply the normal tithe doubled.[73]

Evidence of actual practice drawn from charters fully confirms the distinction between the ninth and tenth and the normal tithe. There are no known authentic references to *nonae et decimae* in royal charters before the reign of Louis the Pious. A memorandum in the chartulary of St Vincent at Mâcon, however, records Pepin's guarantee that, "concerning the farms and abbacies, whoever held them in benefices should each year pay ninths and tenths from whatever they produced there to the bishop or his agents."[74] Hincmar's letter for the synod of Quierzy referred to the establishment in Aquitaine before 768 of *precaria verbo regis ad nonas et decimas*. In 874 Hincmar mentioned in a letter to Louis the German that Charlemagne had obtained the villa of Douzy from Archbishop Tilpin of Rheims "on condition that the bishop of Rheims would keep the chapels

---

[69] MGH, *Epistolae*, vi: *Epistolae karolini aevi*, iv, ed. E. Dümmler and E. Perels (Berlin, 1925), 191.
[70] This subject will be discussed at length in my work, which is in preparation, on monastic tithes.
[71] Cf. Amann, *L'Époque carolingienne*, p. 92.
[72] Cf. *Capitularia*, ii, no. 275.12, p. 336 (capitulary of Pîtres in 869), which guaranteed the payment of *nonae et decimae* to the bishop.
[73] Lesne, *Propriété ecclésiastique*, ii-1, 107, recognized that the difference between the *nona et decima* and the normal *decima* was not only that the charge was doubled but also "que parfois la personne du décimateur est différente," and later he again stressed that the system of *nona et decima* substituted for the canonical receiver of the normal tithe the owner of the *precaria verbo regis*. He apparently missed the basic objection put by this discrepancy in the way of his argument that the *nona et decima* was the normal tithe doubled.
[74] Ragut, *Cart. de St Vincent*, pp. 54–55, dated this document 751–768. Being an unauthenticated memorandum, it is not included in Mühlbacher or in Vol. i of the MGH, *Diplomata Karolinorum*. Waitz, *Verfassungsgeschichte*, iii, 38, n. 2, called it "verwirrt und aus späterer Zeit," apparently on account of the reference to *nona et decima*, which he thought originated under Charlemagne (see n. 6 above); and Viard, *Dîme*, 70, considered its documentary value "plus que douteuse." On the other hand, Lesne, *Propriété ecclésiastique*, ii-1, 101, and Déléage, *Bourgogne*, i, 414–415 and 494, n. 2, accepted it as authentic.

belonging to it together with the ninths and tenths and that the king would give twelve pounds of silver for the lights of the church. . . . "[75] And in his memorandum *De villa Novilliaco* Hincmar described how the villa of Neuilly-Saint-Front, which Carloman had given to the church of Rheims in 771, was granted as a benefice in 794 to one Anscherus, who paid *nonae et decimae* to the church of Rheims until his death.[76] Finally, a phrase in a grant by Bishop Betto of Langres to the abbey of St Stephen at Dijon in 793 mentions certain villas "where the men ought to pay the ninths and tenths of the Lord."[77] Individually these references are not particularly impressive or reliable, and Hincmar especially may in his own interests have read back conditions of the ninth century into the eighth, but together they suggest that the system of *nonae et decimae* was not only known but functioning during the reign of Charlemagne.

In charters of the ninth century references to *nonae et decimae* are very numerous. Their history can be clearly followed, for instance, in the charters of the cathedral of St Vincent at Mâcon. At the request of Bishop Hildebald, in 816, Louis the Pious ordered "that whoever out of our generosity holds benefices from the lands of this church, should not neglect to give ninths and tenths every year, without any opposition or delay, to the said Bishop Hildebald and his successors."[78] Over the years, however, payments tended to lapse, and the cathedral thus lost not only an important source of revenue but also proof of its possession of the lands. Take, for example, the history of its distant estate at Saint Hymetière (Jura, co. Arinthod),[79] which was held for many years by one Raginardus, after those death it passed to his brother Raculfus. Raculfus told Charles the Bald that the land was part of the royal domain ("ex nostre proprietatis fisco") and thus fraudulently received a royal grant of the land. The bishop of Mâcon, Braindingus,[80] however, claimed that "this cell had been taken from the lands of his church on account of the carelessness of the rectors and the violence of evil men and in the times of his predecessors had paid ninths and tenths to St Vincent"; and on this basis he secured a charter of confirmation from Charles the Bald in 861.[81] By the middle of the tenth century, however, matters were in a bad way; and Bishop Maimbod, Duke Hugh, and Count Leotald, the advocate of the cathedral, decided to take joint action to relieve the poverty of the canons. Together, therefore, they issued a document in which Leotald agreed to restore to St Vincent "the ninths and tenths from the estates in the region of Mâcon and in other regions lying all around."[82] In a separate document Leotald, acting

---

[75] Flodoard, *Historia Remensis ecclesiae*, III, 20, in MGH, *Scriptores rerum germanicarum*, XIII, 513. The authenticity of the documents used by Hincmar is not above reproach: cf. nn. 6 and 35 above.

[76] MGH, *Scriptores*, XV-2, 1168.

[77] J. Courtois, *Chartes de l'abbaye de Saint-Étienne de Dijon [des origines à 1100]*, Collection de textes relatifs au droit et aux institutions de la Bourgogne (Paris-Dijon, 1908), no. 1, pp. 7–8. The text of the charter is not entirely clear.

[78] *Cart. de St Vincent*, p. 45; Mühlbacher[2] no. 609.

[79] Cf. Déléage, *Bourgogne*, II, 1219–1224.

[80] Duchesne, *Fastes*, II, 198.

[81] *Cart. de St Vincent*, p. 84, and *Actes de Charles II*, II, 22.

[82] *Cart. de St Vincent*, p. 58.

as advocate, agreed that "the ninths and tenths from estates in the region of
Mâcon, which the canons of that place had formerly possessed, had unjustly
been taken from them" and "he restored to them the ninths and tenths from all
their estates situated in various regions, whatever their officials (*ministeriales*)
were able to discover."[83] Duke Hugh and Leotald jointly restored "the church of
St Romanus at Chanillon [?] with all its possessions and the ninths and tenths
from that estate which had previously been taken by them. . . . And from all
the estates lying everywhere around, which had formerly belonged to St Vincent,
they gave back the ninths and tenths."[84] They then secured confirmations of
these restitutions both from King Louis IV, in a charter dated 948,[85] and from
Pope Agapitus II.[86] In all these transactions there is no suggestion that half of
the *nona et decima* represented the normal ecclesiastical tithe, to which the
cathedral of St Vincent would probably not have been entitled at this early date.
Without exception the ninth and tenth was treated as a purely secular rent in
return for ecclesiastical lands.

This impression is borne out by other documents from the reign of Louis the
Pious, who repeatedly confirmed the possession of *nonae et decimae* for cathedrals
and monasteries which had no right to receive normal tithes. In 816, for instance,
he ordered in a charter for the abbey of St Michael at Verdun that "any of our
counts or vassals holding benefices by our generosity from the lands of this
monastery" should pay ninths and tenths every year "to the said venerable abbot
Smaragdus and his successors or to the agents (*missi*) of the monastery."[87] In
827 Louis made a grant to St Maxentius in Poitou, which was confirmed the following year by his son Pepin I, king of Aquitaine: "Concerning those lands of
this monastery which are known to be up until now in the power of various men
as benefices, we order . . . that they should pay ninths and tenths and maintenance (*opera*) in full to the said monastery of St Maxentius and its rectors, until
either we ourselves or our sons or our successors have the said lands returned
and restored in full and intact to the said venerable monastery, to which they
justly belong."[88] *Nonae et decimae* were by this time clearly an important source
of revenue for many churches. The inventory of the property of the abbey of St
Riquier in Picardy, which was drawn up under Abbot Hericus (d. before 822),
mentions after describing the cell at Encre (now Albert, Somme, arr. Péronne)

---

[83] *Ibid.*, pp. 107–108; cf. Déléage, *Bourgogne*, I, 524, n. 6.

[84] *Cart. de St Vincent*, p. 79.

[85] *Ibid.*, pp. 74–75, and *Recueil des actes de Louis IV roi de France (936–954)*, ed. P. Lauer, CDRHF
(Paris, 1914), p. 76.

[86] *Cart. de St Vincent*, p. 56; Philip Jaffé, *Regesta pontificum romanorum*, 2nd ed. (Leipzig, 1885–
1888), no. 3657, dated 946–954.

[87] RHGF, VI, 493; Mühlbacher² no. 621.

[88] *Chartes et documents pour servir à l'histoire de l'abbaye de Saint-Maixent*, I, ed. Alfred Richard,
Archives historiques du Poitou, XVI (Poitiers, 1886), p. 7; *Recueil des actes de Pépin Ier et de Pépin
II rois d'Aquitaine (814–848)*, ed. Léon Levillain, CDRHF (Paris, 1926), p. 30, confirmed by Pepin
II in 848, *ibid.*, p. 264. The version of Pepin differs slightly from that of his father. Levillain trans-
lated the term *opera* as "corvées," but it probably refers here to the responsibility for upkeep of
church buildings.

that, "There are twelve canons there, who live off (*habent ad victum*) the tenth and the ninth and one mill."[89]

The enforcement of the obligation to pay *nonae et decimae* and to repair ecclesiastical buildings was a constant source of trouble. In a charter issued early in his reign for St Benignus, at Dijon, Louis the Pious told his vassals not only to pay ninths and tenths but also to help repair the building "because you hold benefices from the land of that church."[90] In 838 Pepin of Aquitaine restored the *nona et decima* to St Maurice at Angers and decreed that "from all the lands which are known to have been secured by you as benefices from St Maurice . . . no one should henceforth presume to keep the ninth and tenth for himself."[91] It may have been in order to ease the problem of collection that Louis the Pious allowed *nonae et decimae* to be commuted into money rents; and various churches seem to have taken advantage of this permission. In the diocese of Le Mans, for instance, benefices *de verbo regis* were regularly held on a lifetime tenure either for a fixed money rent or for ninths and tenths "from all the produce," apparently as suited the tenant.[92] Here, therefore, the *nona et decima* was treated as fully equivalent to a money rent. The bishops of Le Mans seem to have been particularly plagued with difficulties of collection, and in about 835–40 (or perhaps rather later) they resorted to forging a charter alleged to be by Charlemagne and a confirmation by Louis the Pious. In this document the bishop complained to the emperor "that our *fideles* who held the lands of St Gervase as benefices either paid negligently or failed to pay at all the ninths and tenths from which they ought to have the customary charges" and received from Charlemagne a confirmation of his rights to the *nona et decima*.[93] St Martin at Tours had similar difficulties, and in 878 Pope John VIII instructed the bishops in whose dioceses the lands of the abbey lay to order its tenants to pay the *nona et decima* to those "to whom they should give, in accordance with ancient custom."[94]

In spite of these troubles, however, the *nona et decima* was fully established both in theory and in fact by the middle of the ninth century and was treated as a regular charge upon certain lands. When in 845 Charles the Bald granted some lands previously held by his *fidelis* Itharius to the abbey of Glanfeuil, he stipulated "that the ministers and rectors of that place should not neglect to pay ninths and tenths every year to the holy churches to which those lands are known legally

---

[89] Hariulf, *Chronique de l'abbaye de Saint-Riquier*, ed. Ferdinand Lot, Collection de textes pour servir à l'étude et à l'enseignement de l'histoire, xvii (Paris 1894), p. 96; cf. p. 84, n. 1, on the date of Hericus.

[90] RHGF, vi, 557; Mühlbacher[2] no. 800.

[91] *Actes de Pépin Ier*, p. 113. Levillain's identification of the *nonae et decimae* as "grosses, menues, et vertes dîmes" (p. 112) is based on a confusion between the *nona et decima* and the normal tithe.

[92] *Gesta domni Aldrici Cenomannicae urbis episcopi*, ed. R. Charles and L. Froger (Mamers, 1889), pp. 174–175, 179–181, 191–192, etc. The authenticity of many of these documents is doubtful, but they probably reflect accurately conditions in the middle of the ninth century.

[93] MGH, *Diplomata Karolinorum*, i: *Die Urkunden Pippins, Karlmanns, und Karls des Grossen*, ed. A. Dopsch, J. Lechner, M. Tangl, and E. Mühlbacher (Hanover, 1906), p. 386; cf. the "confirmation," also partly forged, by Louis the Pious in 832, in *Gesta Aldrici*, pp. 34–44, Mühlbacher[2] no. 912.

[94] MGH, *Epistolae*, vii: *Epistolae karolini aevi*, v (Berlin, 1928), p. 88; Jaffé, *Regesta*, no. 3145.

and properly to belong."[95] In 854 he gave some estates to St Philibert on condition that the monks should pay ninths and tenths "to the rectors and ministers of the church to which it [the land] is known to belong."[96] And in a charter for the cathedral of Rheims in 847 Charles confirmed that *nonae et decimae* must be paid from all lands "which had been taken from that holy church either by the gift of the kings or ancestors or ourselves or by the imprudence or grant of the rectors of the church or by the trick of evil men."[97] Thus the *nona et decima* tended to lose its original character as a special charge on *precaria* granted by the king to his *fideles* for their lifetimes, and it increasingly became a standing rent from lands which were recognized as belonging to a church but had been granted for one reason or another to a family of laymen or to another ecclesiastical institution on a long-term basis.[98] Thus almost a century later, in 934, Count Gislebert of Autun gave to his *fidelis* Guitbaldus "a *mansus* and a half from the land of St Stephen [at Dijon] which is part of the adjacent villa Blasiacum, with the consent of the archdeacon Ratherius and his canons, and the said church should receive ninths and tenths, as is established, for all time."[99]

This development, by which the *nona et decima* tended to become a generally recognized and normal type of tenure, raises the problem of the permanence of the grants of land for which they were paid. The French historian Guizot, writing in the early nineteenth century, said: "It is probable that few of these lands were restored to the churches and that the majority of the temporary benefices which had originated in these concessions *in precario* . . . became, like the others, the hereditary property of the holders."[100] Most historians have shared this opinion. Brunner maintained that the *precaria verbo regis* were in effect permanent alienations of ecclesiastical lands and that the system of *nonae et decimae* was instituted with this in mind. "In any case," he wrote, "the Carolingian legislation concerning the doubled tithe is connected with the fact that the land which had been taken from the Church could no longer be given back." Later he again remarked with regard to the Lombard form of the capitulary of Heristal: "The restitution [of lands] appears here as an exception . . . the granting of church lands amounted to secularisation."[101] Ganshof also wrote, in his well-known book on feudalism, that, "Benefices granted in early times by the crown out of church

[95] *Actes de Charles II*, I, 222.
[96] *Ibid.*, I, 419. Again in 874 he granted certain lands to Montiéramey on condition that the monks pay ninths and tenths to the church of Troyes, *ibid.*, II, 321–322.
[97] *Ibid.*, I, 264.
[98] Rents may have declined in the first half of the ninth century; and the *nona et decima*, which was probably a low rent in the eighth century, may therefore have become a more suitable rent for all ecclesiastical lands held by laymen or other churches. In the diocese of Lucca, in the middle of the ninth century, lands were granted by the bishop for a rent of one-quarter of the produce: *Memorie e documenti per servire all'istoria del ducato di Lucca*, v-2 (Lucca, 1837), no. 586, pp. 350–351. This argument is speculative, however, and the development was certainly the result more of custom than of falling rents.
[99] *Chartes de St Étienne*, no. 38, p. 59.
[100] F. Guizot, "De l'état social et des institutions politiques en France, du cinquième au dixième siècle," *Essais sur l'histoire de France* (Paris, 1823), p. 139.
[101] Brunner, *Rechtsgeschichte*, II, 338, n. 34, and 339, n. 40.

property were usually converted either into benefices held purely and simply of the king or into benefices or precariae held of the churches themselves. This at least is true of those benefices which had not been usurped by the vassals, as must frequently have happened."[102] And in a recent article on the return of proprietary churches in France from the ninth to the eleventh century, Mollat remarked that, "In spite of the prudent complaints of the episcopate, the Carolingians made only a mockery or show of restoring the ecclesiastical property which they or their predecessors had unjustly seized."[103] This position may be right in its broad lines, but it takes too little account of the facts that there were in reality a substantial number of restitutions and that references to *nonae et decimae*, especially in the second half of the ninth century, were much more frequent in charters of restitution than in new grants or confirmations. Over a century ago Roth made this point against Guizot: "One finds such restitutions very frequently";[104] and recent publications of charters have confirmed his remark. During the reign of Louis the Pious, in spite of his threats of confiscation if the ninths and tenths were not paid and his promises (as in the charter for St Maxentius cited above) to restore the lands to the churches to which they belonged, I have found no authentic restitutions of *precaria verbo regis*, aside from a dubious series for the cathedral of Le Mans in 838 and 839.[105] Later in the ninth century, however, they become frequent. In 843 Emperor Lothar restored a villa to the church of Vienne.[106] In 845 Charles the Bald gave back to the church of Rheims, at the request of Archbishop Hincmar, "the lands of the bishopric of Rheims which, [when we were] in great necessity and compelled by all circumstances, . . . we for a period commended to our *fideles* from which they might derive some worldly comfort in our service."[107] In 855/60 Charles of Provence, who had attended the councils of Langres and Savonnières where the bishops had requested

---

[102] Ganshof, *Feudalism*, p. 35.

[103] Guillaume Mollat, "La restitution des églises privées au patrimoine ecclésiastique en France du IXe au XIe siècle," *Revue historique de droit français et étranger*, 4th series, xxvii (1949), 408.

[104] Roth, *Beneficialwesen*, p. 363, n. 178.

[105] In 831, Louis returned to the church of Vienne a village which had been held *beneficiario munere ex nostra largitione* by count Abbo of Vienne but there is no reference to *precaria* or to *nona et decima*: Migne, *Patrologia Latina*, civ, 1203–1204; Mühlbacher² no. 885. The Le Mans documents are found in the *Gesta Aldrici*, pp. 119–121, 197–200, 175–177, and 192–194; Mühlbacher² nos. 972–974 and 999. In each charter Louis the Pious returned to Le Mans an estate which had been held *ad nonas et decimas*, in addition to a rent, by a prominent layman who feared it was sinful to keep the land. These documents were accepted as authentic by Sickel and Mühlbacher; by Julien Havet, "Les actes des évêques du Mans," *Oeuvres de Julien Havet (1853–1893)*, i: *Questions mérovingiennes* (Paris, 1896), pp. 295–317, who concluded after a careful examination that, "toutes les chartes rapportées dans les *Gesta Aldrici* sont authentiques"; and by Ferdinand Lot, "Textes manceaux et Fausses Décrétales, I," *Bibliothèque de l'École des Chartes*, ci (1940), 15. It seems curious, however, that four different tenants in the same diocese and at the same time felt the same scruples, and that the diocese was Le Mans, which was a center of forgery at this time: cf. Mühlbacher² nos. 976, 980, and 982.

[106] RHGF, viii, 379; Mühlbacher² no. 1112; cf. Viard, *Dîme*, p. 148, who remarked that Lothar "fit d'ailleurs restituer souvent ces biens ainsi secularisés."

[107] *Actes de Charles II*, i, 212.

the return of lands taken from the Church, restored to Archbishop Agilmar of Vienne, at the request of Count Gerard and Archbishop Remigius of Lyons, various lands which Louis the Pious had granted to Count Gerard.[108] In 867 Charles the Bald made a restoration, of great historical interest, to the church of Paris of the island of Notre Dame, "which was previously held, except for the ninth and the tenth, for the uses and in the demesne of the count of that city and region."[109] And Hincmar in his memorandum on Neuilly-Saint-Front described how this villa, after almost a century of adventures in secular hands, was finally restored to the cathedral of Rheims in 877.[110] In such restitutions the life interest of the tenant was sometimes protected. Thus, in one of the three restorations made to the church of Lyons in 852,[111] Lothar I specified: "In those above-mentioned lands which our *fidelis* Adalard holds, we wish that he will be lord by usufructuary right only for his lifetime, on condition, however, that he pay annually ninths and tenths from them to that church. . . ."[112] Charles the Bald made a similar stipulation in the charter quoted in the first paragraph of this article, by which he returned to the church of Lyons a villa which "that church might forever hold and possess like its other possessions by proprietary right and ecclesiastical custom, in such a way and manner that our *fidelis* Lambert may meanwhile hold it for his lifetime by beneficiary and usufructuary right in return for paying, on account of his possession, ninths and tenths from the villa each year to the church of St Stephen, up until either we grant him a replacement or he himself dies, when the land will return into the direct possession of the church."[113] Here the act of restitution was used, therefore, to reassert the primitive character of the *precaria verbo regis* as a temporary tenure *ad nonas et decimas*, with protection for the proprietary rights of the church. Elsewhere restorations were made frankly in order to guarantee to a church lands and rents it was in danger of losing. Carloman in 881 gave back to the church of Orléans various villas "which are known to have previously been taken from that church through carelessness or the violence of evil men. On account of this restitution, however, since by divine inspiration [these lands] have been restored in our times, the said holy mother church may always have possession of the ninths and tenths without loss or disturbance from anyone."[114] Many acts of restitution, such as this and the charter of Charles the Bald for Rheims in 845, included a recognition that the original alienation was unjust and even illegal. Louis (II)

---

[108] *Recueil des actes des rois de Provence (855–928)*, ed. René Poupardin, CDRHF (Paris, 1920), pp. 10–12.

[109] *Actes de Charles II*, II, 155.

[110] MGH, *Scriptores*, xv-2, 1167–1169. I do not agree with Ganshof, *Feudalism*, p. 36, n. 1, that this document shows three successive methods of holding church lands. The grants were always at least in theory *precaria verbo regis* and liable to the payment of *nonae et decimae*, as in the original grant of 794. The benefice never became hereditary and was always regranted by the king, once to a monastery and once to the son of the previous holder, until it was eventually restored to Rheims.

[111] RHGF, VIII, 389–391; Mühlbacher² nos. 1156–1158.

[112] *Ibid.*, VIII, 390.

[113] *Actes de Charles II*, II, 290.

[114] *Cartulaire de Sainte-Croix d'Orléans*, ed. Joseph Thillier and Eugène Jarry (Orléans, 1906), p. 73.

the Stammerer admitted the same in 879, when he restored to the church of
Autun a villa "which had previously been taken from the bishopric and associated with the county, with ninths and tenths paid to it from the said church."[115]
These acts of restitution were particularly frequent in the half century following the death of Louis the Pious and may have been a result of the influence
and initiative of the Church at this time. Benedictus Levita inserted in his collection of capitularies a royal order, almost certainly forged, "that anyone who
has hitherto held any ecclesiastical property by our grant and who wishes to hold
it in the future must go to the proper bishops and try to procure the properties,
in whatever way he justly can, from them or from the provosts of the churches to
which they belong, and he should not seek, desire, or accept anything from them
in any other way, lest by coveting holy things these people should be burned to
ashes." The purpose of this forgery is not entirely clear, but the reference to
property held "ex iure ecclesiastico . . . nostra largitate" suggests that Benedict
may have had in mind *precaria verbo regis* held *ad nonas et decimas*; and according to Emil Seckel, "Benedict is striving for a general restitution of alienated
ecclesiastical property . . . but holds out the prospect of regranting by the
Church on terms acceptable to the ecclesiastical institutions. The forger therefore wants to deprive the king of the right of granting [church property]."[116]
In the sixth decade of the ninth century, the councils of Soissons, Valence,
Quierzy, Langres, and Savonnières, all urged the payment of *nonae et decimae*
and the return to the church, if possible, of the lands from which they were owed.
Towards the end of the ninth century, however, with the further breakdown of
the Carolingian Empire, such restitutions became rarer. Still, in 924 King
Rudolph restored to the abbey of St Symphorien in Autun the villa of Auxey,
which had long been held as a benefice by certain soldiers and from which the
nona et decima was listed as part of the conventual *mensa* in the polyptych of St
Symphorien compiled between 866 and 924.[117] Over the years, therefore, a considerable number of *precaria verbo regis* came back into the direct possession of
the churches from which they had been taken.

References to *nonae et decimae* were increasingly rare in the tenth century,
although they appear in charters of confirmation for various churches.[118] This

---

[115] RHGF, IX, 415; J. F. Böhmer, *Regesta chronologico-diplomatica Karolorum* (Frankfurt, 1833,
=Böhmer), no. 1848.

[116] MGH, *Leges* in fol., II-2, *Capitularia spuria*, III, 261, p. 119; Seckel, in *Neues Archiv*, XL
(1916), 33.

[117] *Recueil des actes du prieuré de Saint-Symphorien d'Autun de 696 à 1300*, ed. André Déléage
(Autun, 1936), no. 5, pp. 16–18, and no. 4, p. 16.

[118] MGH, *Diplomata regum Germaniae ex stirpe Karolinorum*, II: *Die Urkunden Karls III*, ed. Paul
Kehr (Berlin, 1937), no. 185, pp. 309–311 (a forged confirmation, of uncertain date, by Charles
III in 885); *Receuil des actes de Charles III le Simple*, ed. F. Lot and P. Lauer, CDRHF (Paris,
1940–1949), I, 67–68 (for St Martin of Autun in 900). Viard, *Dîme*, p. 236, said that the none was
no longer collected by the end of the tenth century and remarked that "la disparition de la none est
aussi difficilement explicable qu'aisément constatée." In a recent article, however, "La none dans le
Namurois du XIe au XIIIe siècle," *Revue historique de droit français et étranger*, 4th series, XXIX
(1951), 584–586, Emile Brouette takes issue with Viard and cites six examples of ninths alone and

gradual disappearance may be attributed not only to the restitution of *precaria verbo regis*, and even more to their secularization, but also to the exchange and commutation of ninths and tenths into more practical forms of revenue. Like the normal ecclesiastical tithe, the ninth and tenth was difficult to collect in kind, particularly from distant estates and during the troubles of the late ninth and early tenth centuries; and there must always have been a tendency among proprietors to find an easier way in which to collect their rents. At some time between 965 and 980, for instance, the abbot of St Symphorien at Autun accepted an annual rent from the canons of the cathedral of St Cyr at Nevers in return for the *nona et decima* from three villas in the county of Nevers.[119] The origins of such a transaction could easily be forgotten; and the abbey, even while receiving a regular rent from the canons, could have lost its proprietary claim to the lands from which the *nona et decima* was now paid to the cathedral of St Cyr. Thus, either in error or by fraud, Raculfus claimed that certain lands belonging to St Vincent at Mâcon came from the royal domain and on this basis secured a charter of confirmation from the king.[120] To avoid confusions of this sort, King Rudolph added at the end of his confirmation of the possessions of his *fidelis* Adelard in 933: "If these afore-mentioned lands were taken from the bishopric, they should pay ninths and tenths, as is the custom of churches, without any opposition."[121] Thus the proprietary claims of the original owners tended to become lost, and the *nona et decima* was either forgotten, exchanged, or absorbed into simple ground rents.

During the ninth and tenth centuries, therefore, the system of *nonae et decimae* became more and more complicated, and their history is further obscured by at least four specific sources of confusion. The first of these was the possibility of dividing the *nona et decima*. Bishop Inchadus of Paris,[122] for example, in 829 made provision for his canons by dividing the property of the see between the bishop and the chapter: "and we also grant to them half of the ninths which are paid to our church from its lands by those who use them."[123] This arrangement seems at first sight to apply only to the *nonae*, but that it applied to both the ninths and the tenths emerges from the confirmation granted by Charles the Bald in 851 at the request of Ercanradus, who succeeded Inchadus as bishop of

---

of ninths and tenths (two of which, nos. 3 and 6, are the same) in the region of Namur dating from 1026 to 1289. These certainly show the survival of the terms *nona et decima* and *noene et dime*, either in one of the senses which will be discussed below or as a customary due remotely derived from the Carolingian payment; but they do not refer to the special rent paid by tenants of *precaria verbo regis*, and in this technical sense *nona et decima* seem to have died out in the tenth century.

[119] *Actes de St-Symphorien*, no. 13, pp. 33–34.

[120] See p. 238 and nn. 79–81 above, and Hincmar, *De villa Novilliaco*, in MGH, *Scriptores*, xv-2, 1167–1169, where doubt arose over whether the land belonged to the church or to the king.

[121] Estienne Pérard, *Recueil de plusieurs pièces curieuses servant à l'histoire de Bourgogne* (Paris, 1664), p. 163; Böhmer no. 1993.

[122] Duchesne, *Fastes*, ii, 474.

[123] *Cartulaire général de Paris*, ed. Robert de Lasteyrie, Histoire générale de Paris (Paris, 1887), no. 35, p. 50.

Paris:[124] "half of the ninth and tenth which is customarily paid from the lands of that church by those who use them."[125] From this time on, therefore, the *nona* or *decima* alone was paid to the bishop or canons; and the *decima*, although originally half of the *nona et decima*, could easily be mistaken for the normal ecclesiastical tithe, to which neither the bishop nor the chapter was entitled.[126]

The addition of a *nona* to a single *decima*, which originated as a normal ecclesiastical tithe, created a second source of confusion. St Landoalius, who lived in the seventh century, was said by his tenth-century biographer to have given a *nona* to one church because the *decima* already belonged to another.[127] And St Anskar in the ninth century occasionally gave a second tithe as charity in addition to the first.[128] Louis the Pious in 822 granted to the monks of St Amand "the ninth part from all the goods of the church throughout all the property and estates of the rector of the monastery"; and Charles the Bald in 847 confirmed "what our most serene and august father decreed before us, that a ninth part from all the goods from the demesne villas should be given to the monks," and in addition he granted the tithe to the gate and hospice of the abbey.[129] Such a second tithe, or ninth, usually had a charitable purpose. St Gerald of Aurillac, who died in 909, "was not unmindful that the justice of Christians ought to surpass the justice of the Pharisees and ordered that after all his produce had been strictly tithed ninths should be set aside for the various needs of the poor."[130] This practice was particularly common on ecclesiastical estates, from which a ninth as well as a tenth, the normal tithe, was often devoted to a specific charity.[131] Paul the Deacon in the late eighth century explained in his commentary on the

---

[124] Duchesne, *Fastes*, II, 475.

[125] *Actes de Charles II*, I, 364–365.

[126] Viard, *Dîme*, pp. 144–145, for instance, who did not know the charter of 851, had trouble in explaining the act of 829.

[127] Heriger, *Vita S. Landoaldi*, III, in *Patrologia Latina*, CXXXIX, 1119 C: "Licet enim tot antea fusis nequaquam profecisset orationibus, tunc omni virtutis conamine praecordialia accumulans vota, plurimaque spondens obsequia, delegavit ad ipsam quietis eorum basilicam, nonam frugum suarum portionem, quia decimam alterius constaret esse ecclesiae." On the author and date, see Wilhelm Wattenbach, *Deutschlands Geschichtsquellen im Mittelalter: Deutsche Kaiserzeit*, ed. Robert Holtzmann, I-1 (Tübingen, 1948), 142.

[128] Rimbert, *Vita S. Anskarii*, XXXV, in MGH, *Scriptores*, II, 719. The second tithe was not called a ninth here.

[129] RHGF, VI, 530–531 (Mühlbacher² no. 757) and *Actes de Charles II*, I, 250.

[130] Odo of Cluny, *Vita S. Geraldi*, I, 28, in *Bibliotheca Cluniacensis*, ed. M. Marrier and A. Duchesne (Paris, 1614), p. 80; cf. also I, 14, *ed. cit.*, p. 75: "In order that in accordance with the Lord's command he should surpass the justice of the Pharisees, he had put aside from the produce of his fields a ninth part, from which the poor were fed in certain of his houses, and clothes and shoes were bought for them."

[131] The standard treatment of this topic is in the series of articles by Lesne, *Rev. d'hist. ecc.*, XIII–XIV, cited in n. 4 above. With regard to the normal tithe paid by cathedrals and monasteries, he concluded that, "à l'exemption de l'*indominicatum* des cathédrales et des monastères vis-à-vis des églises paroissiales correspond de dîmage opéré dans cette portion du domaine ecclésiastique en faveur de l'hôtellerie ou de la mense. Cette dîme n'est pas étrangère à la loi générale. Elle n'est qu'une part de la dîme ecclésiastique ordinaire, part reservée, qui a été refusée à l'église paroissiale et affectée à une autre destination, eu égard à la qualité ecclésiastique de la personne dont les revenus sont dîmés" (XIV, 494).

Rule of St Benedict that a monastery should devote its tithes entirely to the support of the poor,

> But since the Lord says in the Gospel *that unless your justice abound more than that of the scribes and Pharisees, you shall not enter into the kingdom of Heaven*, the justice of the scribes is to give tithes from all things; for we should give two tithes in order that we may enter the kingdom of Heaven; . . . that is, when we give tithes, we will then give a ninth part. For we should give this ninth part to the hospice for the wealthy, whatever it will be, and from this we should cater to the needs of the wealthy.[132]

The application of this doctrine, and the resulting confusion with *nonae et decimae*, may be followed in the charters of St Martin at Tours. In 862 Charles the Bald issued an important charter settling the constitution of the canons' *mensa* and established, among other things, that "a ninth part of all the produce and wine both from demesne estates, even if they are held in benefice or will be so granted in the future, and also from those which are assigned to the monks, that is, from all lands which were devoted to the use of the abbot and monks in the time of our said lord and father, should be entirely devoted to the hospice of the nobles. The hospice of the poor, on the other hand, should keep to the old establishment."[133] Louis the Stammerer confirmed this arrangement in 878: "We wish and decree that, as is contained in the command of our lord and father, the tenths and ninths from the demesne lands, that is, both from demesne estates and from estates granted in benefice, should be devoted to the hospice of the nobles and the poor."[134] This charter was in turn confirmed in almost identical terms by Charles (III) the Fat.[135] Had the charter of 862 been lost, it would be very hard to determine the true nature of the *nona et decima* referred to in the charters of Louis the Stammerer and Charles the Fat. In fact, the normal tithe from the demesne lands of the monks was originally devoted to the hospice for the poor; Charles the Bald then provided that a second tithe should be paid to the hospice for the nobles; and his successors duly confirmed that the *nona et decima* should be paid to the hospice of the poor and the nobles. A similar arrangement existed at the abbey of St Médard at Soissons, where it is recorded in the division of property between the monks and abbot made in 866/70: "The chamber of the monks' clothing should have three estates . . . and the hospice of the nobles, receiving in accordance with ancient custom the ninth part from the estates of the abbey, should have Choisy-au-Bac together with the woods of Pinon, and the hospice of the pilgrims, receiving the tithe, should have Hattencourt."[136] Marquis Adalbert I of Tuscany apparently made a somewhat similar division in the foundation charter (884) of the abbey of St Caprasius at Aulla in

[132] Paul the Deacon, *In sanctam regulam commentarium* (Monte Cassino, 1880), pp. 418–419.

[133] *Actes de Charles II*, II, 39; see on this charter, Georges Tessier, "Les diplômes carolingiens du chartrier de Saint-Martin de Tours," *Mélanges . . . Louis Halphen*, p. 688.

[134] *Veterum scriptorum . . . amplissima collectio*, ed. E. Martène and U. Durand, I (Paris, 1724), 209; Böhmer no. 1838.

[135] *Urkunden Karls III*, no. 139, p. 225; cf. *Actes de Charles III*, pp. 102 (903), 143 (910/11), and 239 (919).

[136] *Actes de Charles II*, II, 253. This grant was confirmed by the council of Douzy in 871: Michel Germain, *Histoire de l'abbaye royale de Notre-Dame de Soissons* (Paris, 1675), p. 432; cf. Hefele-Leclercq, *Conciles*, IV-2, 619–635.

the diocese of Luni, granting some of the ninths and tenths from his demesne estates to the monastery and others to the hospice.[137]

The *nonae et decimae* referred to in these documents have nothing to do with the ninths and tenths paid by the holders of *precaria verbo regis*. But they are not always easily distinguished, and it was probably a confusion of this sort that led Lesne to believe that the secular *nona et decima* was paid only from the demesne estates of the tenant.[138] On occasion, however, the practice of adding a charitable ninth to the normal tithe paid by a cathedral or monastery from its demesne lands seems to have influenced the use to which the secular ninths and tenths were put. Thus Charles the Simple, in his charter of 900 restoring the villa of Cravant on the Yonne to St Stephen at Auxerre, explained that "this estate was previously taken from the mother church and on account of its possession was known to pay ninths and tenths each year to the hospice of the church."[139]

A third source of confusion arose from the fact noted above that already in the first half of the ninth century the *nona et decima* lost its special character as a charge on *precaria verbo regis* and was apparently recognized as a suitable rent for any tenant of church lands. Charles the Bald in his confirmation for Rheims in 847 required the payment of ninths and tenths from any land granted either by a king or bishop or simply usurped by a layman.[140] In 899 one Aymo and his wife Maimbourg gave a vineyard to the abbey of Savigny "on condition that we may have the use and produce while we live, and we shall give to that house of God ninths and tenths from the produce which the Lord may grant as increase, and after the death of both of us, it will come into the possession of the said house of God."[141] In 947(?) one Arlaboldus and his family gave some land to Savigny "on condition that each year we shall pay ninths and tenths from the produce which the Lord will give as increase and after our death the land will come improved to the monastery."[142] At least in the Lyonnais, therefore, the *nona et decima* was used as a rent to be paid to a church by anyone who used its lands.[143]

---

[137] L. A. Muratori, *Delle antichità Estensi ed Italiane* (Modena, 1717), I, 211; cf. *Regesta pontificum romanorum: Italia pontificia*, ed. P. F. Kehr, VI-2 (Berlin, 1914), 385. The text may be corrupt and is far from clear. The relevant section reads: "Me (*pro* De?) autem vero omnibus nutriminibus meis majoris vel minoris domnicatis, quantas in finibus Romae de finibus Chiviae habuimus, et decimas, et nonas in ipsa ecclesia sanctae Mariae [i.e. S. Caprasii] in ipso castello venient, decimas ab ipso abbate et monacis, qui in ipsa ecclesia deserviant. Nonae vero exinde ad hospitale nostrum illic de ipso Castello venient, pro animae nostrae remedio pauperes reficiens, excepto de illis nutriminibus majoris vel minoris, quanti ubique in quolibet locis nos cum aliis hominibus in societate habemus vel habuimus, unde minime ad ipsa ecclesia de ipso Castello venient. Nonae vero de illis Curtis nostris domnicatis, ubi ecclesiae nostrae constructae sint omnibus exinde ibi sint datae decimae."

[138] See n. 4 above.

[139] *Actes de Charles III*, I, 66.

[140] See p. 241 and n. 97 above.

[141] *Cartulaire de l'abbaye de Savigny*, ed. A. Bernard, Collection de documents inédits sur l'histoire de France (Paris, 1853), I, 28.

[142] *Ibid.*, I, 39.

[143] Such rents naturally varied from time to time and place to place. Prior Robert and dean Hugh of Cluny in 993/1048 granted a small *precarium* to one Adalbert in return for a quarter and a tenth: *Recueil des chartes de l'abbaye de Cluny*, ed. A. Bernard and A. Bruel, Collection de documents in-

This practice, although the *nonae et decimae* were no longer associated exclusively with *precaria verbo regis*, preserved the original character of the system as a lifetime charge from a temporary grant of land. After the death of the tenant, the rent ceased and the land returned into the direct possession of the church. There is no suggestion, furthermore, that the tenth in these cases was the same as the normal ecclesiastical tithe, which the tenant was still required to pay to the church where he received the sacraments.

The fourth difficulty in the history of *nonae et decimae* is the appearance in charters of these terms in their root meanings of ninth and tenth parts, referring neither to the ecclesiastical tithe nor to a ground rent. A tenth part was often given as a bequest or charity; and references to *nona* alone, meaning a ninth part, though less common, were also not unusual in the ninth century.[144] In 839 Louis the Pious granted to Reichenau "a certain part of the rent or tribute which is paid to us annually from Alamannia." This included the tenth part (*decima*) of certain revenues and the ninth part (*nona*) of others. Louis stipulated in addition "that the ninths and tenths (*nonae atque decimae*) which we have granted to the monastery for our charity should be paid to the agents of the monastery first, before the total of the rents and tributes is dispersed, and the division of the parts which belong to us and our counts should be made afterwards."[145] The context makes it clear that the *nona et decima* here can refer only to the ninth and tenth parts mentioned earlier in the charter. This document serves as a reminder that these terms were used in their literal meanings not only separately but joined and did not necessarily have any technical meanings in the Carolingian period.[146]

The conclusion of this study is therefore a warning against confusing the terms *nona* and *decima* as they were used in the eighth, ninth, and tenth centuries. *Nona et decima* in its technical sense referred to the system devised to compensate the church for losing the use of lands granted as *precaria verbo regis*. It was recognized as an essentially temporary measure and, although universally valid on account of its inclusion in the capitularies, was principally used in the older regions of

---

édits sur l'histoire de France (Paris, 1876 ff.), III, no. 2217, p. 360. Or a church itself might pay a rent in tenths. Thus in a grant of 840, copied under the seal of the bishop of Barcelona in 924, one Reybulfus and his wife granted their lands in the region of Arles to the abbey of Lérins in return for an annual rent of a tenth of the produce: *Cartulaire de l'abbaye de Lérins*, ed. H. Moris and E. Blanc, Société des Lettres, Sciences, et Arts des Alpes-Maritimes (Saint-Honorat de Lérins-Paris, 1883–1905), I, 264.

[144] See *Cart. de Savigny*, I, 19 (825?), 23 (858), 6 (883), 7 (889?); Heriger, *Vita S. Landoaldi*, III; cf. Waitz, *Verfassungsgeschichte*, IV, 122–123.

[145] *Wirtembergisches Urkundenbuch*, I (Stuttgart, 1849), 117; Mühlbacher² no. 994; cf. Waitz, *Verfassungsgeschichte*, IV, 117–118. The document survives in the original and is of indubitable authenticity, although the reference to *nonae et decimae* is unusual. The "confirmation" by Charles III, however, wás forged in the tenth century: *Urkunden Karls III*, no. 189, p. 319.

[146] As late as the eleventh century, in 1096/99, King Peter I of Aragon mentioned a *novena* to be paid to the king in addition to a *decima* for the Church: *España sagrada*, XLVIII (Madrid, 1862), App. I, 213; cf. San Martín, *Diezmo*, p. 103.

Carolingian authority.[147] In the ninth and tenth centuries it tended to die out for
a number of reasons, including the restoration of the lands to their original owners,
the secularization of the grants, and the transference of the *nona et decima* into
a ground rent paid either in kind or in money. At the same time, however, the
terms *nona* and *decima* were used, both separately and together, in a variety of
meanings other than the special rent from *precaria verbo regis*. Above all, the
normal ecclesiastical tithe, and the supererogatory second tithe occasionally
added to it, had nothing to do with the technical *nona et decima*. It therefore
seems wise to translate the *nona et decima* not as nones and tithes or as the
doubled tithe, which suggests an association with the single tithe, but literally as
the ninth and tenth or as the double tenth. This distinction also emphasizes that
evidence concerning *nonae et decimae* cannot be used to prove the secular origins
or nature of the normal tithe. The single tithe was sacramental in origin and
nature and prevailed universally throughout the Middle Ages. The *nona et decima*
was essentially a secular rent, of limited application both in time and in space,
and a distinctive feature of the close interaction of political, ecclesiastical, and
economic factors in the Carolingian Empire.

HARVARD UNIVERSITY

[147] I have found no authentic examples of *precaria verbo regis ad nonas et decimas* either east of the
Rhine or south of the Alps or Pyrenees. Erica Widera, "Der Kirchenzehnt in Deutschland zur Zeit
der sächsischen Herrscher," *Archiv für katholisches Kirchenrecht*, CX (1930), 51, remarked on the fact
that there are no references to *nonae et decimae* in charters of the Saxon kings and emperors and attributed their disappearance to the proprietary church system. In fact, tenure *ad nonas et decimas*
seems never to have been introduced into the Eastern Kingdom. San Martín, *Diezmo*, makes no
reference to the *nona et decima* in Spain. In Italy, grants were made from the lands of the bishopric
of Lucca to the French and German followers of Lothar I; but they were held at various rents and
not *ad nonas et decimas*: see Robert Endres, "Das Kirchengut im Bistum Lucca vom 8. bis. 10.
Jahrhundert," *Vierteljahrschrift für Sozial- und Wirtschaftsgeschichte*, XIV (1916–1917), 240–292,
esp. 273–279 and 281, n. 130, where he wrote that, "Es ist wohl kein Zweifel, dass diese Franken,
Baiern u. Alemanen Gefolgsleute Lothars I. sind, die mit Kirchengut ausgestattet wurden."

VII

Resistance to Tithes in the Middle Ages

I

The system of compulsory tithes in the Middle Ages has long been used by protestant and liberal historians as a stick with which to beat the medieval Church. 'This most harassing and oppressive form of taxation', wrote H. C. Lea in his well-known *History of the Inquisition*, 'had long been the cause of incurable trouble, aggravated by the rapacity with which it was enforced, even to the pitiful collections of the gleaner'.[1] Von Inama-Sternegg remarked on the growing hatred of tithes in the tenth, eleventh, and twelfth centuries, especially among the small free land-holders, 'upon whom the burden of tithes must have fallen most heavily'.[2] Gioacchino Volpe said that tithes were 'the more hated because they oppressed the rich less than the poor, the dependents on seigneurial estates less than the small free proprietors to whose ruin they contributed. . . . At that time tithes were both an ecclesiastical and secular oppression, a double offence against religious sentiment and popular misery'.[3] G. G. Coulton, writing before the introduction in England of an income tax at a rate of over ten per cent., proclaimed that before the Reformation tithes 'constituted a land tax, income tax and death duty far more onerous than any known to modern times, and proportionately unpopular'.[4]

The influential American medievalist J. W. Thompson repeatedly used tithes as an example of the tyranny and rapacity of the medieval clergy and particularly emphasised the economic motives of the Christian mission-aries in eastern Germany. 'The missionary propaganda of the German Church in the Middle Ages was largely a money-making proposition', he wrote in his *Feudal Germany*; 'Christians had to pay tithes, so the "saving of souls" became a lucrative commercial interest'.[5] He repeated this

[1] Henry C. Lea, *A History of the Inquisition of the Middle Ages*, New York 1887–8, i. 26; iii. 183.

[2] K. T. von Inama-Sternegg, *Deutsche Wirtschaftsgeschichte*, Leipzig 1879–1901, ii. 42.

[3] Gioacchino Volpe, 'Eretici e moti ereticali dal XI al XIV secolo nei loro motivi e riferimenti sociali', *Il Rinnovamento*, i (1907), 649–50, reprinted in his *Movimenti religiosi e sette ereticali nella società medievale italiana*, Florence 1922, 16.

[4] G. G. Coulton, 'Priests and People before the Reformation', (1907) reprinted in his *Ten Medieval Studies*, Cambridge 1930, 124; cf. *The Medieval Village*, Cambridge 1925, 290–306 ('Tithes and Friction') and *Five Centuries of Religion*, Cambridge 1923–50, iii. 150–1 and 224–5, where he said that in order to understand the system of tithes we must realise 'how these contributions were dragged, as it were, from the entrails of the peasantry'.

[5] James W. Thompson, *Feudal Germany*, Chicago 1928, 394; cf. 133 ff.

RESISTANCE TO TITHES IN THE MIDDLE AGES

opinion in his text-books on medieval social and economic history and *An Introduction to Medieval Europe*, where he cited Coulton's description of tithes as 'a land tax, an income tax, and a death duty of no mean weight' and mentioned both the popular resistance to tithes and the clerical pressure to enforce payment.[1] Thompson's works were recently cited by H. C. Krueger to support his statement, in a symposium on the twelfth century, that, 'Tithe-collecting rather than soul-saving was the reason for the conquest and conversion of the Slavs'.[2]

This view of tithes is found in many recent works, even by authors who are sympathetic to the medieval Church. E. S. Davison, for instance, said that 'tithes were most difficult to collect and were evaded in every way known to man mediaeval or modern'.[3] H. S. Bennett and George Homans referred to the difficulties of collecting tithes in their studies on English rural life.[4] C. R. Cheney, quoting the remark of W. A. Pantin that, 'It must have required the tact of a saint to make the system run smoothly', added that, 'The difficulty of determining the obligation must have given rise constantly to evasion and dispute and ill-feeling'.[5] In a recent study on the oppression of peasants in Germany in the high Middle Ages, Siegfried Epperlein said that the conciliar and legislative sources clearly show 'that considerable opposition by the peasants had to be overcome and that tithes were among the dues that peasants paid only unwillingly'.[6] In text-books and popularisations this opinion has become so universal that Tenant de La Tour sarcastically described the tithe as 'an infamous word, an ever-shameful symbol of the moral and material oppression of the "little men" in former times, a disgrace to the Middle Ages, the most flagrant of its social iniquities, in the opinion of its detractors'.[7] On account of this feeling, when a priest in New Jersey recently 'instituted' a tithe in his parish, the vicar-general of the diocese felt obliged to refute the charge of 'totalitarianism' by explaining that the tithe was not compulsory.[8]

All these writers, whatever their disagreements on other points,

---

[1] James W. Thompson, *An Economic and Social History of the Middle Ages*, New York–London 1928, 651–2 and 693; James W. Thompson and Edgar Johnson, *An Introduction to Medieval Europe*, New York 1937, 670.

[2] Hilmar C. Krueger, 'Economic Aspects of Expanding Europe', in *Twelfth-Century Europe and the Foundations of Modern Society*, ed. Marshall Clagett, Gaines Post, and Robert Reynolds, Madison 1961, 64.

[3] Ellen S. Davison, *Forerunners of Saint Francis*, London 1928, 351.

[4] H. S. Bennett, *Life on the English Manor*, Cambridge 1937, 331 (citing G. G. Coulton); George C. Homans, *English Villagers in the Thirteenth Century*, Cambridge (Mass.) 1943, 393.

[5] W. A. Pantin, *The English Church in the Fourteenth Century* (Birkbeck Lectures, 1948) Cambridge 1955, 204; Christopher R. Cheney, *From Becket to Langton* (Ford Lectures, 1955), Manchester 1956, 162.

[6] Siegfried Epperlein, *Bauernbedrückung und Bauernwiderstand im hohen Mittelalter* (Forschungen zur mittelalterlichen Geschichte, 6), Berlin 1960, 82–3.

[7] Geoffroi Tenant de La Tour, *L'Homme et la terre de Charlemagne à saint Louis*, Paris 1943, 539.

[8] *The New York Times*, 28 December 1960.

VII

share a common dislike of the clerical taxation and fear of clerical rule,[1] and their attitude towards tithes in the Middle Ages is based more on this contemporary prejudice than on medieval evidence. They appeal more frequently to human nature, as they see it, and to logic—the verb 'must' occurs frequently in their discussions of tithes—than to documents and chronicles. The sources which they cite are mostly conciliar decrees and manuals for parish priests, which, though very valuable for the history of law and ethics, are unreliable guides, as Arquillière pointed out, to the actual extent of the abuses which they opposed.[2] Thompson, it is true, cited a number of documents, but he was forced to equate tithes with *labores* and with the *census* and *tributum* in order to prove his case of widespread popular opposition.[3]

Writers who have studied the history of tithes, on the other hand, are agreed, when they mention the matter at all, that open resistance to tithes was comparatively rare in the Middle Ages. The principal specialist, Paul Viard, wrote in his book on tithes in France up to the middle of the twelfth century that, 'One encounters very few complaints concerning the ill-will of the people', although in his volume on the later period he mentioned the growth of popular opposition to tithes in the thirteenth century.[4] Hauck, in his discussion of Carolingian enforcement of tithes in Germany, also said that in spite of some resistance, 'It is none the less certain that the majority of people really paid tithes and that thereby the revenue of the Church was very significantly increased'.[5] These general conclusions are confirmed by regional studies. The rarity of resistance to tithes is mentioned by Bruhat in his book on monasticism in the Saintonge and the Aunis, which devotes considerable attention to tithes, and by Tremel in his article on tithing in Styria and Carinthia;[6] and the

[1] The attitudes of Lea, Coulton, and Thompson are well-known to medievalists. On Volpe, who was a politician as well as an historian, see the *Enciclopedia Italiana*, xxxv. 563; and on the involvement of tithes with politics in contemporary Italy, see Catherine E. Boyd, *Tithes and Parishes in Medieval Italy*, Ithaca 1952, 1–25.

[2] Review by H.-X. Arquillière of A. Luchaire, *La société française au temps de Philippe-Auguste*, cited by H. Netzer, in *Mélanges . . . Ferdinand Lot*, Paris 1925, 601. Even more dangerous are arguments based on an absence of conciliar legislation on tithes: cf. Gonzalo Martínez Diez, 'El patrimonio eclesiástico en la España Visigoda', *Miscelanea Comillas*, xxxii (1959), 24, who wrote that, 'El valor de este silencio, particularmente si se tiene en cuenta la natural resistencia humana ante cualquier impuesto o prestación obligatoria, se pondera por sí mismo'.

[3] Thompson, *Feudal Germany*, 395, n.1, and 584, n.3.

[4] Paul Viard, *Histoire de la dîme ecclésiastique principalement en France jusqu'au Décret de Gratien*, Dijon 1909, 92–3 and 228–9, and *Histoire de la dîme ecclésiastique dans le royaume de France aux XIIe et XIIIe siècles*, Paris 1912, 71–2.

[5] Albert Hauck, *Kirchengeschichte Deutschlands*, 8th (unchanged) ed., Berlin 1954, ii. 232. On p. 729 he said that, 'Die rücksichtslose Eintreibung der Zehnten machte da und dort böses Blut'.

[6] L. Bruhat, *Le monachisme en Saintonge et en Aunis (XIe et XIIe siècles)*, La Rochelle 1907, 214–15; Ferdinand Tremel, 'Das Zehentwesen in Steiermark und Kärnten von den Anfängen bis ins 15. Jahrhundert', *Zeitschrift des historischen Vereines für Steiermark*, xxxiii (1939), 13.

RESISTANCE TO TITHES IN THE MIDDLE AGES

authors of a recent book on tithes in the Forez twice remarked that, 'We do not see open resistance, revolt against the tithe . . .' and that, 'We see few refusals of the tithe, certainly no more than of other seigneurial rights'.[1] My own research on monastic tithes up to the end of the twelfth century has also yielded no sign of extensive opposition.[2]

Even a strictly *a priori* consideration of the question suggests that refusal to pay tithes was probably less easy and natural than many modern writers assume. It may be true that the small tithes, from vegetables, poultry, and the like, were hard to assess and collect, but in view of the organisation of the manor and the publicity of most agricultural operations in the Middle Ages, evasion of the tithes from the principal crops was certainly not easy. When it occurred and was discovered, records would have been kept in order to enforce payment in the future. Unlike any other specific and regular charge in the Middle Ages, tithes rested directly upon divine precept and were mentioned many times in the Bible. In theory they were paid not to the Church but to God Himself through his ministers. Refusal to pay was an act of ingratitude and contempt towards God and endangered the eternal salvation of the culprit.[3] The attitude of peasants in the Middle Ages was therefore probably more like that of peasants in Turkey in the nineteenth century, among whom it was a common saying that, 'If only Allah gives us a good harvest, we are quite willing to pay the Pad[i]shah his tenth',[4] than that of modern historians, who dislike any ecclesiastical tax. The majority of men in the Middle Ages, as Hauck said, paid tithes from agricultural and other types of income—even the North Sea pirates paid tithes from their spoils to the hermits living on Heligoland[5]—and to assume that tithes were commonly opposed and even refused is to misinterpret both the attitudes of men and the economic realities of the Middle Ages.

II

The purpose of this article is not to argue that tithes were always paid fully and cheerfully, which is certainly far from the truth, but to study the evidence for resistance to tithes, especially in the documents

---

[1] *Chartes du Forez*, xv: *Les Dîmes en Forez*, Mâcon 1957, 207, 210.

[2] To appear under the title *Monastic Tithes from their Origins to the Twelfth Century* (Cambridge University Press).

[3] Cf. ibid., ch. i, sect. 1. Medieval penitentials, which are a safer guide to actual practice than conciliar and episcopal decrees, contain comparatively few references to evasion of tithes.

[4] E. J. Davis, *Anatolica*, London 1874, 331, who discussed the tithes ('Ushr' or 'Ushoori') paid in Turkey. Tithing was known in several religious systems, but its comparative history has not yet been seriously studied: cf. H. F. Schmid, 'Byzantinisches Zehntwesen', *Jahrbuch der österreichischen byzantinischen Gesellschaft*, vi (1957), 68.

[5] Adam of Bremen, *Gesta Hammaburgensis ecclesiae pontificum*, ed. B. Schmeidler (Scriptores rerum Germanicarum in usum scholarum), Hanover–Leipzig 1917, 231. On the payment of personal tithes in the later Middle Ages, see A. G. Little, 'Personal Tithes', *English Historical Review*, lx (1945), 67–88.

and chronicles of the eleventh and twelfth centuries, and to show (without, it is hoped, underestimating the importance either of the legislative sources or of the natural desire of men to avoid financial obligations) that most known instances of refusal to pay tithes were caused by specific conditions or circumstances rather than by any objection to tithes in theory. Many reasons other than sheer avarice or ill-will can account for resistance to paying tithes.

The imposition of tithes on recent converts, on Christians who had previously paid no tithes, or on goods from which no tithes had been exacted was a frequent source of trouble, especially in Germany. It is impossible to discuss fully here the payment of tithes by conquered and converted peoples. It is known that the obligation to pay tithes was a hindrance to conversion in certain regions, such as Saxony in the Carolingian period and Denmark, according to Adam of Bremen, in the eleventh century.[1] Elsewhere in Germany, however, in spite of the alleged rapacity of the missionaries, substantial concessions appear to have been made with regard to tithes. A special system of tithing prevailed in Thuringia; the *Acta Murensia* distinguished between the 'given' and the 'constituted' tithes in Switzerland in the first half of the eleventh century; and a charter from Carinthia in the middle of the eleventh century referred to tithing 'according to the custom of the Slavs', who apparently paid a fixed amount, less than a tenth, in lieu of tithes.[2]

When, in the eleventh and twelfth centuries, the Church attempted to impose the regular system of tithing in these areas, it often encountered violent opposition. In 1123 the archbishop of Mainz, when he tried to collect tithes in the march of Duderstadt, on the borders of Thuringia, was resisted by the inhabitants, 'some of whom were killed by the bishop's men, others were maimed, and many were taken captive'.[3] The archbishops of Salzburg tried to impose normal tithes on the Slavs in their diocese in the eleventh century;[4] and a charter from the diocese of Halberstadt in 1145 mentioned the Slavs on an estate named Mose who paid no tithes (*decimam non solventes*) unless they were compelled to by the soldiers of duke Albert the Bear of Saxony.[5] Most celebrated, perhaps, was the resistance of the Stedinger, who lived on drained lands in the lower Weser

---

[1] Hauck, *Kirchengeschichte*, ii. 412; Adam of Bremen, *Gesta*, 264.

[2] H. F. Schmid, 'Der Gegenstand des Zehntstreites zwischen Mainz und den Thüringern im 11. Jahrhundert und die Anfänge der decima constituta in ihrer kolonisationsgeschichtlichen Bedeutung', *Zeitschrift der Savigny-Stiftung für Rechtsgeschichte*, Germ. Abt., xliii (1922), 267–300; *Die ältesten Urkunden von Allerheiligen in Schaffhausen, Rheinau und Muri* (Quellen zur Schweizer Geschichte, 3), Basel 1883, pt. 3, 21–2; *Salzburger Urkundenbuch*, ed. W. Hauthaler and F. Martin, Salzburg 1910 ff., i. 236. Further references may be found in the notes to chap. ii of my *Monastic Tithes*.

[3] *Chronica S. Petri Erfordensis moderna*, s.a. 1123, in *Monumenta Erphesfurtensia*, ed. O. Holder-Egger (Scriptores rerum Germanicarum in usum scholarum), Hanover–Leipzig 1899, 164. On the 'tithe-war' in Thuringia, see Hauck, *Kirchengeschichte*, iii. 731 ff.

[4] Tremel, in *Zs. d. hist. Vereines f. Steiermark*, xxxiii. 14–18.

[5] *Urkundenbuch des Klosters Unser Lieben Frauen zu Magdeburg*, ed. G. Hertel, Halle 1878, 16, 17, 27–9.

valley, to the demands for tithes from the archbishops of Bremen in the late twelfth and early thirteenth centuries. They were eventually declared heretics, and their resistance was overcome by a series of 'crusades'. In this case, political as well as economic factors apparently fostered the resistance to the archbishop, but modern scholars are agreed that there was no element of heresy in the refusal to pay tithes.[1]

Political conflict between the clergy and the laity might easily lead to difficulty in collecting tithes. The townsmen of Vézelay, for instance, who were excommunicated by abbot Pontius of Vézelay because they resisted his authority, said that, 'Since you excommunicate us undeservedly, we shall openly behave as excommunicates. We shall no longer pay you any tithes, *census*, or other customary dues'.[2] The refusal to pay tithes here was clearly an act of political retaliation and not of resistance to tithes as such.

The collection of non-agricultural tithes posed a special problem throughout the Middle Ages, since the obligation to pay tithes from all types of income was easily forgotten in an age when agriculture was the predominant method of production. Thus the decree of the synod of Trosly in 909, which has been cited by some historians as evidence of general resistance to tithes, was concerned only with those who claimed that they owed no tithes 'from military activity, trade, crafts, the shearing of wool, and other trades given them by God'; and it cited a battery of Biblical and patristic texts to prove that tithes must be paid from every kind of product, revenue, and skill.[3] The bishop of Arezzo in 1033 reminded the merchants in his diocese 'how grave a sin it is not to give tithes to God (which the poorest peasants never dare withhold from the just labour of their hands) from the profits of your trade . . .'.[4] As custom hardened into law, however, non-agricultural revenues often came to be regarded as free from tithes, and a number of documents and decrees in the eleventh and twelfth centuries are concerned with this point.

The diocese of Milan seems to have been a centre of such difficulties in the twelfth century. In 1145 pope Eugene III wrote to the archbishop of Milan that he had heard (probably from the monks of Crescenzago, who had repeatedly complained that they were forced to pay tithes from goods produced by themselves and for their own use), 'that a so-called

---

[1] H. A. Schumacher, *Die Stedinger*, Bremen 1865, 72–3, 82, and 223–31 (on their 'heresy'); Lea, *Inquisition*, iii. 182–9; A. P. Evans, 'Social Aspects of Medieval Heresy', *Persecution and Liberty: Essays in Honor of George Lincoln Burr*, New York 1931, 98.

[2] Hugh of Poitiers, *Historia Vizeliacensis*, iii, in Migne, P.L., cxciv. 1611 C; cf. Rose Graham, *An Abbot of Vézelay*, London 1918, 56. There is no evidence that these townsmen were associated with the heretics at Vézelay mentioned below.

[3] J. D. Mansi, *Sacrorum conciliorum nova et amplissima collectio*, Florence–Venice 1759 ff., xviii. 281–3.

[4] Jean Mabillon, *Annales ordinis s. Benedicti*, Lucca 1739–45, iv. 357–8. A somewhat different version of this charter is found in *Documenti per la storia della città di Arezzo nel medio evo*, ed. Ubaldo Pasqui, i (Documenti di storia italiana pubblicati a cura della regia deputazione toscana, 11), Florence 1899, 220–1.

priest named John, seduced by a diabolic belief, openly preaches that
tithes need not be paid by laymen and that no amendment need be made
for unpaid tithes and maintains that laymen may justly possess tithes'.
Eugene instructed the archbishop to investigate the matter and, if necessary, to excommunicate John 'as a perverter and teacher and author of
evil doctrine'.[1] A few months later he wrote again to the archbishop,
apparently with reference to this affair, saying that, 'We have prohibited
them in our letters from that evil preaching about which you wrote
to us, although they completely denied it in our presence'.[2] This suggests
that no heresy was involved, or denial of the theoretical obligation of
laymen to pay tithes. The priest John probably taught that tithes need
not be paid from all types of revenue. Thus Eugene wrote, also in 1145,
to a doctor B., probably in the diocese of Milan, saying that he endangered
his eternal salvation by paying no tithes from his earnings and by lending
money at interest.[3] A letter of pope Hadrian IV shows that the peasants
in the area between the Adda and Ticino rivers in Lombardy were
accustomed to subtract the seed and all expenses from their crops before
paying tithes and that their lords gave no tithes from revenues which
their dependents paid in kind.[4] An interesting poem from the diocese
of Milan also shows that at a relatively early date tithes in Lombardy
were regulated by custom and were not paid from certain revenues and
products.[5]

Changes of this sort in the system of tithing often led to misunderstand-
ings and sometimes to refusal to pay tithes. The commutation of tithes
to a fixed charge in either kind or money might cause trouble, especially
if the yield increased or the crops were changed. Peasants who were used
to paying a set measure of grain might object to giving a tenth of some

[1] *Acta pontificum Romanorum inedita*, ed. J. von Pflugk-Harttung, Tübingen–Stuttgart
1880–8, ii. 342; Philip Jaffé, *Regesta Pontificum Romanorum*, 2nd ed., Leipzig 1885–8
(=JL), no. 8774. The identity of the priest John is uncertain, but he may have been the
same John who wrote a letter to provost Martin of Sant'Ambrogio in Milan excusing
himself from a visit because he was having a book of the Digest made: J. von Pflugk-
Harttung, *Iter Italicum*, Stuttgart 1883, 480, who remarked that 'Das Studium des
römischen Rechtes wird ihn auf solche Gedanken [rejection of tithes] gebracht haben'.
But he adds that John was a common name in Milan at this time.
[2] *Acta*, ii. 343; JL 8814.   [3] *Acta*, ii. 344; JL 8784.
[4] *Acta*, iii. 198; JL 10447 (1154/9). Hadrian ordered the archbishop to compel 'the
lords to pay tithes from their revenues and the peasants from all the fruits of their
labours'. Innnocent III in a letter to the bishop of Ely, however, allowed that, 'in the
case of articles which have been purchased or manufactured we believe that expenses
should be deducted from the sum which is tithed when they are sold, and that tithes
should be paid on the residue as being the profit': *Selected Letters of Pope Innocent III
Concerning England*, ed. C. R. Cheney and W. H. Semple (Nelson's Medieval Texts),
Edinburgh 1953, 76; Gregory IX, *Decretals*, iii. 30, 28.
[5] *Liber consuetudinum Mediolani anni MCCXVI*, ed. Francisco Berlan, Milan 1866,
57–61, esp. 60, n.1; cf. Alfredo Bosisio, *Origini del comune di Milano*, Messina–Milan
1933, 22–3, who dated this poem in the eleventh century, although its contents suggest
a considerably later date. It was cited by Schmid, in *Jb. d. öst. byz. Ges.*, vi. 106, n.360,
as evidence of the agricultural origin of tithes, but it probably shows on the contrary
the progressive customary restriction of the revenues from which tithes were paid.

other crop and forget that both were tithes. The archbishop of Mainz in 1127 required some peasants on land belonging to the abbey of Disiboden-berg, who were accustomed to render a set measure after the crops were collected and stored, to pay their tithes 'in the places where the crops grow' and 'in accordance with the fecundity or sterility of the year and the harvest.'[1] The settlement of a tithe-dispute between Marienfeld and Kappel in 1258, however, arranged that the peasants were to be forced, 'by ecclesiastical censure' if necessary, to pay a set measure in place of tithes.[2]

Another potential source of confusion was the occasional freedom from tithes of noval lands, since in certain regions the opening of new lands was encouraged by allowing the cultivators to pay no tithes. An elaborate enquiry in 1217 into the tithes paid from the lands at Steinberg, in the Rhineland, ascertained that no tithes were paid from certain new vineyards at Eltville; and, when one of the priests was asked why the peasants refused to pay tithes, he replied 'on account of the privilege of noval lands'.[3] Elsewhere, however, noval tithes were a valuable potential source of revenue. The archbishop of Trier in 1140 required the peasants at Bullingen to pay tithes from lands which they had opened, and from which they had at first paid no tithes, to the abbey of Stavelot, which owned the noval tithes in this area.[4] There is no evidence in this case that the failure to pay tithes continued after the obligation was made clear.

The system of tithing at Brildel, where the tithes belonged to the abbey of St. Trond, was described in an interesting charter of the archbishop of Trier in 1154:

'When the grapes had been harvested at the villa of Brildel, it was customary for the priest, together with the manager and his assistants, to collect from each house the tithe which the parishioners owed. Some paid their tithes joyfully and reverently, as suited the blessing they had received; others gave hardly anything, holding back and arguing; worse were those who blasphemed and gave nothing. Some men who lived outside the parish bought the vineyards of the poor parishioners and trust-ing in their strength gave abuse rather than tithes. We discussed these troubles of the church first with our equals and then with the parishioners and decided at their request that each man must pay what he owes in his own vineyard at the time of the harvest.'

The trouble here may in part have been caused by the fact that the parishioners had to pay two tithes, for the charter continued: 'There is

[1] *Urkundenbuch zur Geschichte der . . . mittelrheinischen Territorien*, i, ed. Heinrich Beyer, Coblenz 1860, 514–15; cf. Epperlein, *Bauernbedrückung*, 45–6.
[2] *Westfälisches Urkunden-Buch*, iii, Munster 1859, 338.
[3] *Urkundenbuch der Abtei Eberbach im Rheingau*, ed. K. Rossel, Wiesbaden 1862–70, i. 180–8 (quoted passage on p. 183).
[4] *Quellen zur Geschichte der Stadt Köln*, i, ed. Leonard Ennen, Cologne 1860, 511.

on this estate a second tithe after the better one, which was established at one time for ordering and furnishing the church and which the abbot and church of St. Trond gave to the pastor of that church on condition that all the church's needs both inside and outside, in ornamentation, in books and binding, and in enclosing the atrium should be met from this tithe and that they [the monks] should be free from all these things'.[1] It is not surprising that the peasants here were ready to listen to voices encouraging them to pay no tithes.

This, therefore, is an instance of genuine resistance to paying tithes by Christians whose obligation was clear. Another example is found in a charter of St. Jean d'Angély in about 1084: 'Rainald Forgiunclus refused to pay tithes from his allod, but he was subdued by a judgment that he should pay, and he paid. Herbert of Néré paid no tithe from his carrucate, but he was subdued by a judgment that he should pay, and he also paid before the lord Odo'.[2] Further evidence of such negligence and ill-will can naturally be found in *exempla* and moral tales, some of which may reflect actual situations. Walter Map tells of an excommunicate who appeared after his death seeking absolution and said to the priest, 'I am that miserable man whom you once excommunicated, unnamed, with others in a crowd, on account of unjustly retaining tithes . . .'.[3] And in the chronicle attributed to John Brompton there is a story of how the former lord of Compton in Oxfordshire rose from his grave and told St. Augustine of Canterbury that he had been excommunicated and had suffered in hell for not paying tithes and how the present lord, who had previously maintained that he was entitled to a full return from his crops, was thus induced to pay tithes.[4] Such tales and visions certainly confirm that the clergy had some difficulty in collecting tithes; but their number is less than has been suggested by some historians, and they cannot be used as evidence for widespread resistance to tithes.

III

The attitude of heretics towards tithes is a special aspect of the general question under discussion in this article. Most authorities on heresy, if they mention tithes at all, have agreed that the heretics rejected

---

[1] *Ub. z. Gesch. d. . . . . mittelrhein. Terr.*, i. 641.

[2] *Cartulaire de Saint-Jean d'Angély* (Archives historiques de la Saintonge et de l'Aunis, 30, 33), Paris–Saintes 1901–4, i. 202–3.

[3] Walter Map, *De nugis curialium*, ii. 30, ed. M. R. James (Anecdota Oxoniensia, iv. 14), Oxford 1914, 101–2.

[4] *Chronicon Johannis Bromton*, in *Historiae Anglicanae scriptores X*, ed. Roger Twysden, London 1652, 736–7. Other versions of this tale are found in the *Acta Sanctorum*, May, vi. 396–7, and the *Nova legenda Anglie*, ed. Carl Horstman, Oxford 1901, i. 100. On the chronicle attributed to John Brompton, who was abbot of Jervaulx in 1437, see Thomas Wright, *Biographia Britannica literaria: Anglo-Norman Period*, London 1846, 412–13, who attributed it to the late twelfth century, and Charles Gross, *The Sources and Literature of English History*, 2nd ed., London 1915, 347, who said it was made up of earlier sources.

tithes. The Cathars, according to Ernst Troeltsch, abrogated ecclesiastical duties and tithes, and E. S. Davison said that the Waldensians 'rejected the theory of tithes, alms, parishes, and all forms of benefices . . .'.[1] The question deserves to be studied by a specialist on heretics in the light of their theological and economic doctrines, but a few observations may be made here.

A number of heretics in the eleventh, twelfth, and thirteenth centuries are known to have rejected tithes. Most celebrated, perhaps, was the heretic Leutard, who lived in the diocese of Châlons-sur-Marne at the beginning of the eleventh century and who maintained, according to Rodulf Glaber, that 'to give tithes . . . is completely superfluous and stupid'.[2] He was apparently considered mad by his contemporaries, including the diocesan bishop, and his views are not known to have had any immediate influence. In the early twelfth century, however, Tanchelin (or Tanchelm) of Antwerp had a number of followers, whom he urged to reject the Eucharist and forbade 'to pay tithes to the ministers of the Church'.[3] Henry of Lausanne, the follower of Peter of Bruys, denied oblations, first-fruits, and tithes, according to the author of the *Actus pontificum Cenomannis*.[4] Some heretics called *Telonarii* or *Poplicani* at Vézelay in the middle of the twelfth century were said to reject all the sacraments, including 'the remedies of tithes and oblations'.[5] Ébrard of Béthune in his *Liber antihaeresis*, which was written about 1210/12, accused the Waldensians of refusing to pay tithes, oblations, and first-fruits;[6] and in the *Contra Waldenses* attributed to Rainerius Sacconi, but really by an anonymous inquisitor in the diocese of Passau about 1260, the Waldensians

[1] Ernst Troeltsch, *The Social Teaching of the Christian Churches*, tr. Olive Wyon, London–New York 1931, i. 351; Davison, *Forerunners*, 261–2.

[2] Raoul Glaber, *Les cinq livres de ses Histoires (900–1044)*, ed. M. Prou (Collection de textes pour servir à l'étude et à l'enseignement de l'histoire, 1), Paris 1886, 49; cf. Ilarino da Milano, 'Le eresie popolari del secolo XI nell'Europa occidentale', *Studi Gregoriani*, ii (1947), 46–7, and Arno Borst, *Die Katharer* (Schriften der Monumenta Germaniae Historica, 12), Stuttgart 1953, 73. Volpe's small diatribe against tithes formed part of his discussion of Leutard.

[3] *Monumenta Bambergensia*, ed. P. Jaffé (Bibliotheca Rerum Germanicarum, 5), Berlin 1869, 297 (a letter from the canons of Utrecht to the archbishop of Cologne in 1112/14). No reference to his resistance to tithes is found in the other contemporary sources on Tanchelin: Monumenta Germaniae Historica, *Scriptores*, vi. 449 and 459 (continuations of the chronicle of Sigebert of Gembloux) and xii. 690–1 (life of St. Norbert). On Tanchelin, see Lea, *Inquisition*, i. 64–5; Hauck, *Kirchengeschichte*, iv. 96 ff.; and esp. Henri Pirenne, 'Tanchelin et le projet de démembrement du diocèse d'Utrecht vers 1100', *Académie royale de Belgique: Bulletin de la Classe des Lettres*, 5th Series, xiii (1927), 112–13.

[4] *Actus pontificum Cenomannis in urbe degentium*, ed. G. Busson and A. Ledru (Archives historiques du Maine 2), Le Mans 1902, 437–8.

[5] Hugh of Poitiers, *Historia Vizeliacensis*, iv, in Migne, P.L., cxciv, 1682; cf. Borst, *Katharer*, 247–8, on the Popelicani.

[6] Ébrard of Béthune, *Liber antihaeresis*, x, in *Trias scriptorum adversus Waldensium sectam*, ed. J. Gretser, Ingolstadt 1614, pt. i. 116–18; cf. *Enchiridion fontium Valdesium*, ed. G. Gonnet, i, Torre Pellici 1958, 143–4 on the title and date.

are said to have maintained, 'That tithes need not be given, because first-fruits will not be given to the Church'.[1]

Several works written against the heretics insisted upon the necessity of paying tithes and oblations. Bernard of Fontcaude, in his *Adversus Waldensium sectam*, written about 1190/2, said that oblations must be given to the clergy 'as a sign of devotion and humility'.[2] The Waldensians Durand of Huesca and Bernard Prim specified in their confessions of faith when they rejoined the Church, in 1208 and 1210 respectively, that, 'We believe that tithes, first-fruits, and oblations must be paid to the clergy by order of the Lord'. And in a letter sending the confession of Durand of Huesca to the archbishop of Tarragona, Innocent III specifically remarked on this recognition of the obligation to pay tithes.[3]

Various sources suggest that the primary objection of these heretics was to the misuse of tithes and above all their payment to corrupt and worldly clerics. Arnold of Brescia held that tithes and first-fruits must be used for 'the chaste uses of the body' and not for luxury;[4] yet he damned laymen who refused to pay tithes, according to the anonymous Bergamasque poet, and ranked tithes with oblations and first-fruits as the proper means to support the clergy.[5] According to an anonymous anti-heretical *Manifestatio* in an early thirteenth century manuscript at Rheims, the Waldensians held that oblations should be given to the poor rather than to the priest or at the altar.[6] Arno Borst remarks at one point that the Cathars gathered tithes with the rapacity of a modern bourgeois.[7]

[1] *Maxima bibliotheca veterum patrum*, Lyon 1677, xxv. 265; cf. *Un traité néo-manichéen du XIIIe siècle: Le Liber de duobus principiis*, ed. A. Dondaine, Rome 1939, intro., p. 61; Mario Esposito, 'Sur quelques écrits concernant les hérésies et les hérétiques aux XIIe et XIIIe siècles', *Revue d'histoire ecclésiastique*, xxxvi (1940), 155–6; and Ilarino da Milano, *L'eresia di Ugo Speroni nella confutazione del Maestro Vacario* (Studi e Testi, 115), Vatican City 1945, 458, n.2.
[2] Bernard of Fontcaude, *Adversus Waldensium sectam*, ii, in *Trias scriptorum*, pt. ii, 13, and *Enchiridion*, 68.
[3] *Enchiridion*, 132, 134, and 139, cited from Migne, P.L., ccxv. 1510–13, and ccxvi. 290–3.
[4] Gunther 'Ligurinus', *De rebus gestis imp. caes. Friderici I*, iii. 279–82, in Migne, P.L., ccxii. 370: 'Illis primitias, et quae devotio plebis/Offerat, et decimas castos in corporis usus/Non ad luxuriam, sive oblectamina carnis/Concedens . . .'. Cf. Arsenio Frugoni, *Arnaldo da Brescia nelle fonti del secolo XII* (Istituto storico Italiano per il medio evo: Studi storici, 8–9), Rome 1954, 100.
[5] *Gesta di Federico I in Italia*, ed. Ernesto Monaci (Fonti per la storia d'Italia, 1), Rome 1887, 32, l. 774: 'Pro decimis laicos dampnabat quippe retentis . . .'. Cf. Frugoni, *Arnaldo*, 79–95, and G. W. Greenaway, *Arnold of Brescia*, Cambridge 1931, 167, n.3, who pointed out that this passage was ambiguous and might refer either to lay refusal to pay tithes or to lay possession of tithes, but the use of *retinere* with reference to tithes in Gratian, *Decretum*, c. xvi, q. ii, c. 5 ('Nam qui Deo non vult reddere decimas, quas retinuit . . .'), in the chronicle of John Brompton cited above ('decimarum retentor'), and in the chronicle of Henry Knighton cited below suggests that it meant 'withhold' or 'not to pay'.
[6] Antoine Dondaine, 'Durand de Huesca et la .polémique anti-cathare', *Archivum fratrum praedicatorum*, xxix (1959), 271.
[7] Borst, *Katharer*, 228. In the dioceses of Béziers and Arles, about 1200, Cathar nobles apparently collected and kept tithes owed to the Church: Jean Guiraud, *Histoire de l'Inquisition au Moyen Âge*, Paris 1935–8, i. 328.

RESISTANCE TO TITHES IN THE MIDDLE AGES

It seems probable from this evidence that tithes were not a central point in the teaching of most heretics at this time. Their opposition to tithes was part of their desire to purify the Church and the clergy, who should lead, they believed, simple lives and own neither money nor honours.[1] Many orthodox reformers attacked the misuse of tithes in terms no less strong, and sometimes stronger, than the heretics, and for the same motives.[2] Recent research has confirmed that the early Waldensians concentrated their attention on the issues of clerical corruption, poverty, and lay preaching; and it may be significant that there is no reference to tithes in the confession of faith, very like those of Durand of Huesca and Bernard Prim, made by Peter Valdes himself in 1179/80.[3] The denial of ecclesiastical doctrines and the other more extreme elements in Waldensian teaching came as a result of official opposition and persecution.[4] The Cathars, on the other hand, who denied the validity of the orthodox clergy, naturally refused to pay them tithes, but they apparently had no objection to paying tithes to their own leaders.

The attitudes of these heretics towards tithes may also have been influenced by their differing attitudes towards the Bible, and especially the Old Testament, where the principal references to tithes occur. Several early heretics, including Leutard and Peter of Bruys, denied the authority of certain books of the Old Testament,[5] and various heretics rejected the entire Old Testament. According to Ralph Ardens, the Cathars at Agen in the early twelfth century 'damned the Old Testament; but of the New [Testament] they accepted some parts and not others.'[6] The 'Boni homines' at the council of Lombars in 1165 admitted that they rejected the law of Moses, the prophets, psalms, and Old Testament and accepted only the Gospels, the letters of St. Paul, the seven canonical epistles, the Acts of the Apostles, and the Apocalypse.[7] The heretic Balazinansa of Verona, held 'that Abraham, Isaac, Jacob, Moses, and all the ancient fathers and John the Baptist were the enemies of God and the

---

[1] Cf. the short treatise written about 1133/5 and published by Raoul Manselli, 'Il monaco Enrico e la sua eresia', *Bullettino dell'Istituto storico italiano per il medio evo*, lxv (1953), 60–1.

[2] Cf. the twelfth-century poem published by Jean Leclercq, 'Un débat sur le sacerdoce des moines au XIIe siècle', *Analecta monastica*, iv (Studia Anselmiana, 41), Rome 1957, 103–8.

[3] *Enchiridion*, 32–6.

[4] Cf. Gottfried Koch, 'Neue Quellen und Forschungen über die Anfänge der Waldenser', *Forschungen und Fortschritte*, xxxii (1958), 141–9.

[5] Glaber, *Histoires*, 49; Peter the Venerable, *Contra Petrobrusianos*, in *Bibliotheca Cluniacensis*, ed. M. Marrier and A. Duchesne, Paris 1614, 1135–43. Gerbert in his so-called Profession of Faith swore that he believed in 'one and the same author, both Lord and God, of the New and Old Testament', which implies that certain heretics in the late tenth century held that parts of the Bible were written by the Devil: *Lettres de Gerbert (983–997)*, ed. Julien Havet (Collection de textes pour servir à l'étude et à l'enseignement de l'histoire, 6), Paris 1889, 162. Cf. also Charles Schmidt, *Histoire et doctrine de la secte des Cathares ou Albigeois*, Paris–Geneva 1849, ii. 273, and Steven Runciman, *The Medieval Manichee*, Cambridge 1947, 150–1.

[6] Ralph Ardens, *Homiliae*, ii. 19, in Migne, P.L., clv. 2011.

[7] Mansi, *Collectio*, xxii. 159.

VII

ministers of the devil'; and the Cathars of Concorrezo rejected 'the entire Old Testament, believing that the devil was its author, excepting only those words which are introduced into the New Testament by Christ and the Apostles . . .'.[1] The converted Waldensian Durand of Huesca specifically defended the Mosaic law against the attacks of the Cathars.[2] The so-called mitigated Cathars, however, recognised the divine mission of all the prophets and patriarchs and accepted the validity of the entire Bible;[3] and at least one sect, the Pasagini, insisted upon the literal observance of all the precepts in the Old Testament.[4] These heretics cannot entirely have rejected the principle of tithing.

Even in the late Middle Ages, with which this article is not really concerned, many reformers and heretics seem to have opposed the misuse more than the theory of tithes. The followers of Wyclif taught 'that parishioners need not give their tithes and oblations to their curates who do not live chastely' or who were absentees or even spent their revenues outside the parish. 'Likewise if they are insufficient in learning or difficult in speech, so that they could not preach or competently instruct the parishioners, then the parishioners might withhold their tithes and give them to whomsoever they wished'.[5] In 1424 the Franciscan William Russell was officially condemned for teaching, 'that personal tithes need not be paid to the parson of the parish but might be allocated *in pios usus pauperum* at the will of the tithe-payer'.[6] Even the peasants who refused to pay various tithes in the German revolution in 1524–5 objected less to the tithes themselves than to their misappropriation.[7]

The conclusion of this article is therefore a warning against the assumption that tithes were universally opposed and a source of trouble between the clergy and the laity and, more generally, against reading back into the Middle Ages the attitudes of modern times.[8] Resistance to tithes seems in fact to have been comparatively rare, at least before the thirteenth century, and the majority of men paid their tithes, in accord with local custom, without recorded complaints. Most specific instances of refusal to pay, furthermore, can be explained by special circumstances. Rival claims to ownership were, indeed, far more frequently an obstacle

---

[1] Alan of Lille, *Contra hereticos*, i. 37, in Migne, P.L., ccx. 341; Rainerius Sacconi, *Summa de catharis*, in *Liber de duobus principiis*, ed. Dondaine, 71 and 76.
[2] Christine Thouzellier, 'Controverses vaudoises-cathares à la fin du XIIe siècle', *Archives d'histoire doctrinale et littéraire du Moyen Âge*, 1960, 175–94.
[3] *Liber de duobus principiis*, ed. Dondaine, 19.
[4] *The Summa contra haereticos Ascribed to Praepositinus of Cremona*, ed. J. N. Garvin and J. A. Corbett (Publications in Mediaeval Studies, 15), Notre Dame 1958, 92–104, cf. intro. p. xxxv.
[5] Henry Knighton, *Chronicon*, v, in Twysden, *Scriptores X*, 2667.
[6] Little, in *Eng. Hist. Rev.*, lx. 67.
[7] B. J. Kidd, *Documents Illustrative of the Continental Reformation*, Oxford 1911, 175–6; cf. Hans Nabholz, in *The Cambridge Economic History of Europe*, Cambridge 1942 ff., i. 560–1, who suggested that the peasants opposed the small tithe 'because—unlike the great tithe—there was no Biblical authority for it'.
[8] It is concerned with actual evidence for resistance to tithes, not with the question of whether tithes were justified or oppressive.

RESISTANCE TO TITHES IN THE MIDDLE AGES

to peaceful collection of tithes than refusal to pay.[1] Open resistance appears to have increased in the fourteenth and fifteenth centuries, on account both of the growing hostility to the Church and the general movement towards freedom from traditional dues.[2] But too great an emphasis on resistance to tithes at any time in the Middle Ages tends to obscure their real importance in the ecclesiastical, economic, and social history of Europe.

[1] The vast majority of medieval litigation over tithes, to which Coulton refers in *Five Centuries*, iii. 225, dealt with the possession rather than the payment of tithes.
[2] Papal levies of a tenth, which were often resisted even by local ecclesiastical authorities, may have been confused with tithes: cf. Lea, *Inquisition*, ii. 137, 433, and William E. Lunt, 'Clerical Tenths Levied in England by Papal Authority during the Reign of Edward II', *Anniversary Essays in Mediaeval History by Students of Charles Homer Haskins*, Boston–New York, 1929, 157–82, esp. 165–6 on opposition.

VIII

MONASTIC POSSESSION OF CHURCHES
AND « SPIRITUALIA » IN THE AGE OF REFORM

Monastic finances in the eleventh century presented the reformers of the Church with a typical problem of confusion between spiritual and secular concerns. Most monks made no distinction between their various revenues. Tithes, oblations, and other *spiritualia*, which had often become separated from the church to which they belonged and divided among different owners, were generally treated in the same way as secular revenues.

This was one of the principal abuses against which the reformers drew their weapons of *ordo, veritas,* and *iustitia.* Their object was to restore good order in the world and to define clearly the functions of the various social orders. As Gregory VII wrote in 1079: « The dispensation of divine providence ordained that there should be distinct grades and orders, so that when reverence is shown by the lesser for the greater and love by the greater for the lesser, then a single concord may be made out of diversity and a harmony and proper administration of individual offices may arise. For the *universitas* could not exist without the support of the great order of this *diversitas* » [1].

This theme of social harmony is found in many works of the period. The Church according to Otloh of St Emmeram should be like the household of a good prince or a harmonious orchestra, of which some members play the high notes of contemplation and others the low

---

The following abbreviations will be used: JL = Philip Jaffé, *Regesta pontificum Romanorum,* 2nd ed. (Leipzig 1885-1888); Mansi = *Sacrorum conciliorum nova et amplissima collectio,* ed. J.D. Mansi (Firenze - Venezia 1759 ff.); *M.G.H.* = *Monumenta Germaniae historica;* P.L. = *Patrologia latina.*

[1] *Das Register Gregors VII.,* ed. E. Caspar (*M.G.H., Epistolae selectae,* 2), Berlin 1920-1923, p. 450, no. VI, 35; cf. *The Correspondence of Pope Gregory VII,* tr. E. Emerton (Columbia Records of Civilization), New York 1932, p. 142.

notes of action [2]. « The whole world will be entirely corrupted », he said, « when the clerical office seeks the work of the laity and when laymen are established in the order of the clergy » [3]. The proper functioning of society depends upon the *consonantia* of all orders.

One of the most important aspects of this harmony was the proper distribution of the economic functions of society. Monks should remember, Otloh warns, that they depend upon laymen for their food, clothing, and shelter [4]. And Wolferad of Constance said more simply that God created the left hand to deal with material affairs and the right hand to deal with eternal affairs [5]. This economic side of reform ideology in the eleventh century has been less studied by historians than the moral, legal, and political aspects, but it followed naturally from the reformers' insistence upon a clear distinction of sacred and secular matters. Religious movements, as Marc Bloch emphasized, often have unconscious economic results which are more important than conscious economic motives [6]. And the campaign against simony, the emphasis on common life and poverty, the desire of the new monastic orders for solitude and manual labor all had religious motives, but they also had far-reaching economic effects.

The radical nature of these ideals was reflected in some of their results, and together they threatened (as the proposals of Paschal II clearly showed) to revolutionize the finances of the Church. Even high-minded churchmen in the ninth and tenth centuries had considered simony only a disciplinary abuse, not a heresy, as it was now declared [7]. And they had not regarded monastic poverty and common life as essential for a high level of religious life. On the contrary, as recent research has shown, many monastic reformers and spiritual leaders in the tenth century were trained in houses of secular canons possessing individual prebends [8], and wealth was considered indispensable

---

[2]   Otloh of St. Emmeram, *In ps. LII comm.*, in *P.L.*, 93, 1107 C-D and 1110 A; see on Otloh generally, H. SCHAUWECKER, *Otloh von St. Emmeram*, Munich 1964.

[3]   OTLOH OF ST. EMMERAM, *De doctrina spirituali*, in *Thesaurus anecdotorum novissimus*, ed. B. PEZ, Augsburg-Graz 1721-1729, III.2, 449 B.

[4]   OTLOH OF ST. EMMERAM, *Dialogus de tribus quaestionibus*, XLIV, in *Thesaurus*, ed. PEZ, III.2, 229 A-B; cf. SCHAUWECKER, *Otloh*, p. 152.

[5]   J. AUTENRIETH, *Die Domschule von Konstanz zur Zeit des Investiturstreits*, (Forschungen zur Kirchen - und Geistesgeschichte, N.F. 3), Stuttgart 1956, p. 164.

[6]   M. BLOCH, reviewing J. W. THOMPSON, *An Economic and Social History of the Middle Ages*, in « Annales d'histoire économique et sociale », I (1929), 258.

[7]   J. LECLERCQ, « *Simoniaca heresis* », « Studi Gregoriani », I (1947), 523-530.

[8]   Cf. J. SIEGWART, *Die Chorherren - und Chorfrauengemeinschaften in der deutschsprachigen Schweiz von 6. Jahrhundert bis 1160*, Studia Friburgensia, (N.F. 30), Fribourg 1962, ch. IV, esp.

to a strict monastic and liturgical discipline. Monastic fervor and economic prosperity went together for Richard of St Vanne, as Dauphin remarked [9]; and spiritual and material decay were often linked in Cluniac documents. Abbot Odo of St Jean d'Angély wrote in a charter of 1090 that he had enlarged and reformed the *camera* of his abbey in order that material need might not cool the spiritual ardor of the monks [10]. At this very time, however, reformers were beginning to preach the opposite: that wealth was fatal to monastic virtue and that monks must support themselves by the labor of their own hands [11]. They therefore objected strongly to the possession by monks of churches and spiritual revenues which properly belonged to the secular clergy.

The precise definition of these *spiritualia* was not altogether clear, however, and even contemporaries often had difficulty in distinguishing between the various revenues, in both money and produce, that made up the income of most monasteries in the middle of the eleventh century. « Ce qui frappe... quand on examine la série des chartes des XIe et XIIe siècles », said Ferdinand Lot in his book on St Wandrille, « c'est que la fortune de l'établissement ne consiste que rarement en domains entiers, comme aux VIIIe et IXe siècles; elle se compose de dîmes, de fractions de dîmes, de cens, etc., à percevoir sur des domaines où d'autres seigneurs, laïques ou ecclésiastiques, possèdent des droits au moins égaux à ceux du monastère » [12]. This process of fragmentation was hastened by the growing number of revenues paid in money rather than produce. The rate of transfer naturally varied from region to region depending upon the extent of commercial activity [13]. At St Martin of Tours all rents were paid in

pp. 159-161; and G. OURY, *L'idéal monastique dans la vie canoniale: Le bienheureux Hervé de Tours* († 1022), « Revue Mabillon », LII (1962), 1-29.

[9] H. DAUPHIN, *Le bienheureux Richard abbé de Saint-Vanne de Verdun*, † 1046 (Bibliothèque de la Revue d'histoire ecclésiastique, 24), Louvain-Paris 1946, p. 174 (with other references on this point).

[10] *Cartulaire de Saint-Jean d'Angély*, ed. G. MUSSET (Archives historiques de la Saintonge et de l'Aunis, 30), Paris 1901-1903, I, p. 46, no. 20.

[11] Cf. for instance, *Narratio de fundatione Fontanis monasterii*, 8, in *Memorials of the Abbey of St. Mary of Fountains*, ed. J. R. WALBRAN, I (Surtees Society, 42), Durham-London-Edinburgh 1863, p. 11.

[12] F. LOT, *Études critiques sur l'abbaye de Saint-Wandrille* (Bibliothèque de l'École des Hautes Études, 204), Paris 1913, p. CXI; cf. also L. GENICOT, *L'évolution des dons aux abbayes dans le comté de Namur du Xe au XIVe siècle*, XXXe Congrès de la Fédération archéologique et historique de Belgique: *Annales*, Bruxelles 1936, pp. 139-142, and F.L. GANSHOF, in *The Cambridge Economic History of Europe*, I, Cambridge 1941, p. 287.

[13] Cf. J. A. RAFTIS, *Western Monasticism and Economic Organization*, « Comparative Studies in Society and History », III (1961), 463.

money in the tenth century [14], whereas at Cluny the period of transfer was between 1080 and 1120. Within a generation, as Duby said, a money economy replaced a domainal economy at Cluny [15]. This led to a reorganization of Cluniac finances (which may in turn have influenced the reorganization of papal finances under Urban II [16]) and involved both expanding the functions of the chamberlain [17] and arranging the revenues into a carefully organized budget [18].

Under these circumstances, revenues from different sources tended to lose their distinctive characters. Tithes and oblations in particular were freely received as gifts, bought, sold, exchanged, and usurped by monks [19]. According to Imbart de La Tour, indeed, tithes in the tenth century became in effect a seigneurial due and a rent on land [20], and Thomas even said (though this seems to me an exaggeration) that the idea that tithes were a spiritual right appeared only in the twelfth century [21]. The entire property of a church became fused in the *res ecclesiae*, the complex of lands and revenues over which it exercised *dominium* and from which sections were granted to monks and laymen [22]. Several Cluniac charters of this period began with the assertion that « Custom is law, although unwritten, and it is now established as law by common usage that any ecclesiastical property may be

---

[14] P. GASNAULT, *Les actes privés de l'abbaye de Saint-Martin de Tours du VIIIe au XIIe siècle*, « Bibliothèque de l'École des Chartes », CXII (1954), 47.

[15] G. DUBY, *Économie domaniale et économie monétaire: Le budget de l'abbaye de Cluny entre 1080 et 1155*, « Annales », VII (1952), 160-164; cf. N. HUNT, *Cluny under Saint Hugh, 1049-1109*, London 1967, p. 75.

[16] See in particular J. SYDOW, *Cluny und die Anfänge der apostolischen Kammer*, « Studien und Mitteilungen zur Geschichte des Benediktiner-Ordens und seiner Zweige », LXIII (1951), 45-66, citing in particular the work of Karl Jordan; and HUNT, *Cluny*, pp. 60, 76.

[17] SYDOW, in « Stud. und Mitt. », LXIII, 50; HUNT, *Cluny*, p. 58.

[18] See, in addition to the article cited in n. 15 above, G. DUBY, « Un inventaire des profits de la seigneurie clunisienne à la mort de Pierre le Vénérable », *Petrus Venerabilis, 1156-1956: Studies and Texts Commemorating the Eighth Centenary of his Death*, ed. G. CONSTABLE and J. KRITZECK (*Studia Anselmiana*, 40), Roma 1956, pp. 129-140.

[19] Cf. G. CONSTABLE, *Monastic Tithes from their Origins to the Twelfth Century* (Cambridge Studies in Medieval Life and Thought, N.S. 10), Cambridge 1964, pp. 63-64.

[20] P. IMBART DE LA TOUR, *Les paroisses rurales dans l'ancienne France, II: L'organisation de la paroisse à l'époque carolingienne*, « Revue historique », LXIII (1897), 30; cf. R. A. R. HARTRIDGE, *A History of Vicarages in the Middle Ages* (Cambridge Studies in Medieval Life and Thought), Cambridge 1930, pp. 3-5.

[21] P. THOMAS, *Le droit de propriété des laïques sur les églises et le patronage laïque au moyen âge* (Bibliothèque de l'École des Hautes Études: Sciences religieuses, 19), Paris 1906, p. 88.

[22] Cf. A. DUMAS, *La notion de la propriété ecclésiastique du IXe au XIe siècle*, « Revue d'histoire de l'église de France », XXVI (1940), 14-34.

granted to anyone, even a layman, by the authority of a charter » [23]. The original character of such grants was easily forgotten, and in the eleventh and twelfth centuries even the courts had difficulties in establishing the difference between spiritualities and temporalities [24]. « Each word had a variety of meanings », wrote Lunt, « and an attempt to define all their usages would lead far afield and end probably in an inextricable labyrinth » [25]. The term *regalia* was also unclear. It was first defined in the Investiture Controversy as rights held from the crown, in return for which homage and service were given [26]. But the type and extent of the rights and services varied from region to region [27].

In spite of these practical difficulties, which complicated the task of reformers, the term *spiritualia* in the eleventh century usually referred to any payment specifically associated with a sacerdotal function. They were thus comparable to the *altaria,* of which the distinction from the *ecclesia* (meaning the church buildings and landed property) dated back to the late tenth century [28]. A monastery might own both the *ecclesia* and the *altaria* or just the spiritual revenues alone, which might have become separated from the church, sometimes centuries before, and subsequently commuted and divided among several owners. The exact types of *spiritualia* held by a monastery thus depended upon the legal position of the church in terms both of proprietary rights and the jurisdiction it exercised either as a parish church or a subordinate chapel [29]. A further distinction in the rights of the monastery depended on whether the divine services were performed by the monks themselves or by secular priests.

[23] *Recueil des chartes de l'abbaye de Cluny,* ed. A. BERNARD and A. BRUEL (Collection de documents inédits sur l'histoire de France), Paris 1876-1903, I, 126, no. 112; II, 181, no. 1088; III, 360, no. 2217.

[24] Cf. F. POLLOCK and F. W. MAITLAND, *The History of English Law Before the Time of Edward I,* 2nd ed., Cambridge 1898, I, p. 127, and N. ADAMS, *The Judicial Conflict over Tithes,* « English Historical Review », LII (1937), 1-22.

[25] W. E. LUNT, *The Valuation of Norwich,* Oxford 1926, p. 75.

[26] Cf. I. OTT, *Der Regalienbegriff im 12. Jahrhundert,* « Zeitschrift der Savigny-Stiftung für Rechtsgeschichte: Kanonistische Abteilung », XXXV (1948), 234-245, and R. BENSON, *The Obligations of Bishops with « Regalia »,* in *Proceedings of the Second International Congress of Medieval Canon Law* (Monumenta iuris canonici, C: Subsidia, 1), Città del Vaticano 1965, pp. 123-127.

[27] OTT, in « Sav. Zs.: Kan. Abt. », XXXV, 272-297.

[28] THOMAS, *Droit de propriété,* pp. 76-78; HARTRIDGE, *Vicarages,* p. 12; and J. CHOUX, *Recherches sur le diocèse de Toul au temps de la réforme grégorienne: L'épiscopat de Pibon (1069-1107)* (Recueil de documents sur l'histoire de Lorraine), Nancy 1952, pp. 66-67.

[29] Cf. G. SCHREIBER, *Kurie und Kloster im 12. Jahrhundert* (Kirchenrechtliche Abhandlungen, 65-68), Stuttgart 1910, II, pp. 19-40.

The question of the amount of pastoral work performed by monks in the Middle Ages has been much disputed, and in recent years there has been a tendency to revise upwards the somewhat conservative estimates of earlier scholars [30], some of whom (being monks themselves) were personally involved in the problem [31]. It is very difficult, however, to distinguish in the sources between real parochial work and chaplain and other altar service which was certainly performed by monks [32]. There is evidence for the twelfth century that attitudes were changing and that a certain amount of pastoral work, especially in the Empire, was being done by monks [33], even though (as Schreiber and Berlière pointed out) the papacy never specifically authorized Benedictine monks to administer parishes before the end of the twelfth century [34]. In these churches, the monks had a legitimate claim to the *spiritualia*.

In a majority of churches owned by monasteries, however, it is probable that the services were performed by priests or vicars appointed by the monks and supported by a fixed stipend or a share of the revenues of the church. These arrangements for the division of ecclesiastical revenues are a valuable source of information about monastic possession of *spiritualia*, and parochial revenues generally, in the eleventh and twelfth centuries. In an agreement made in 1050/70 between the monks of La Trinité at Vendôme and the priest of Mazé, the landed revenues were distinguished from those from religious functions and the priest was alloted a fixed quantity of grain in addition to half the common oblations in bread and pennies and all the other oblations, including those for baptisms, marriages, ordeals, and pilgrimages. The remaining revenues belonged to the monastery [35]. In 1146 the monks of Baigne and the chap-

---

[30] Cf. CHOUX, *Pibon de Toul*, p. 75, who said that « Dans l'ensemble il est difficile de dire quelles paroisses sont desservies par des moines; il n'est pas impossible que le cas soit assez fréquent », and D. J. A. MATTHEW, *The Norman Monasteries and their English Possessions* (Oxford Historical Series), Oxford 1962, pp. 59-61.

[31] See my forthcoming paper on *The Study of Monastic History Today.*

[32] This point is clearly made by M. CHIBNALL, *Monks and Pastoral Work: A Problem in Anglo-Norman History*, « Journal of Ecclesiastical History », XVIII· (1967), 166-168.

[33] See SCHREIBER, *Kurie*, II, pp. 40-49; Ph. HOFMEISTER, *Mönchtum und Seelsorge bis zum 13. Jahrhundert*, « Studien und Mitteilungen zur Geschichte des Benediktiner-Ordens und seiner Zweige », LXV (1955), 254-262; and W. SCHLESINGER, *Kirchengeschichte Sachsens im Mittelalter* (Mitteldeutsche Forschungen, 27), Cologne-Graz 1962, II, pp. 430-431.

[34] SCHREIBER, *Kurie*, II, p. 41, and U. BERLIÈRE, *L'exercice du ministère paroissial par les moines du XIIe au XVIIe siècle*, « Revue bénédictine », XXXIX (1927), 351.

[35] C. VAN DE KIEFT, *Une église privée de l'abbaye de la Trinité de Vendôme au XIe siècle*, « Le Moyen Âge », LXIX (4th S., XVIII, 1963), 157-168, who studies charter no. 80 in the

lain of Pavancelles agreed that if only a single penny was offered
in a day the chaplain would receive half and if more than a penny
was offered he would receive a third, so long as he received at least
one penny from the total oblations on Sunday and Monday. He was
also to receive all the oblations for visiting the sick, half the oblations
for marriages, and a third of the oblations after births and for baptisms and confessions and of any alms given either to the prior or to
himself or his vicar [36]. Another charter from Baigne, showing the
growing importance of money, replaced a division of the revenues at
Alas-Champagne by a flat rent to be paid by the priest to the
monks [37]. Similar divisions between monks and other proprietors
(including laymen) were made when a monastery owned only part
of a church [38].

The historical significance of monastic control over churches in
the tenth and eleventh centuries is another subject of dispute among
scholars. Schreiber in particular argued that the possession of churches by Cluny prepared the way for the reform of the Church in the
eleventh century by freeing many churches from lay control,
improving their material circumstances, and raising the moral
level of the clergy [39]. This view has been accepted by some
historians [40] but rejected by others, who have maintained that Cluny
had no systematic policy of acquiring churches and freeing them from
lay proprietary rights [41]. In a question of this sort, however, it is essential to distinguish clearly between motives and effects. Many churches
were given to monasteries, especially after the invasions of the ninth

Cartulaire de l'abbaye cardinale de la Trinité de Vendôme, ed. C. MÉTAIS (Société archéologique
du Vendômois), Paris-Vendôme 1893-1897, I, pp. 150-151.

[36] *Cartulaire de l'abbaye de Saint-Étienne de Baigne*, ed. P.-F.-E. CHOLET, Niort 1868,
pp. 220-221, no. 528. The charter also specifies that the expenses of the parish, such as the
synodal dues, should be divided two-thirds/one-third between the prior and chaplain.

[37] *Ibid.*, p. 33, no. 52.

[38] *Cart. de St-Jean d'Angély* (cited n. 10 above), I, pp. 45-46, no. 19.

[39] G. SCHREIBER, *Cluny und die Eigenkirche* (1942), reprinted in his *Gemeinschaften des
Mittelalters*, Münster 1948, pp. 130-132.

[40] Cf. J.-F. LEMARIGNIER, *Étude sur les privilèges d'exemption et de juridiction ecclésiastique des abbayes normandes depuis les origines jusqu'en 1140* (Archives de la France monastique, 44), Paris 1937, p. 43; K. HALLINGER, *Gorze-Kluny* (Studia Anselmiana, 22-25), Roma
1950-1951, pp. 757-760; C. VIOLANTE, *Il monachesimo cluniacense di fronte al mondo politico
ed ecclesiastico (secoli X e XI)*, in *Spiritualità cluniacense* (Convegni del Centro di studi sulla
spiritualità medievale, 2), Todi 1960, p. 218, n. 95.

[41] See in particular H.-E. MAGER, *Studien über das Verhältnis der Cluniacenser zum Eigen-
kirchenwesen*, in *Neue Forschungen über Cluny und die Cluniacenser*, ed. G. TELLENBACH,
Freiburg 1959, p. 207; also G. TELLENBACH, *Zum Wesen der Cluniacenser*, « Saeculum », IX
(1958), 375.

and tenth centuries, in order to assure their physical upkeep and the performance of divine services [42]. And it is probable that most monasteries maintained their churches and supervised the clergy more effectively than other proprietors. In the agreement between La Trinité of Vendôme and the priest of Mazé, for instance, the priest was required to live chastely and according to the clerical order [43]. And the cellarer of St. Florence at Saumur in about 1120 forced the negligent priests at Pons to perform their pastoral duties [44]. The effect of monastic possession of churches may, therefore, often have been to the advantage of the Church.

The motives of the monks in acquiring churches, however, were primarily economic. Thus the price of peace given by the clergy of Pons to the abbey of St. Florence was the surrender of the oblations for masses, visiting the sick, marriages, and births [45]. Proprietary churches were a valuable source of revenue for monasteries, and the donors of churches to Cluny, for instance, as countless charters show, hoped to assure their own spiritual welfare by promoting the material welfare of the monks [46]. These rights over churches developed in the twelfth and thirteenth centuries into the legal relationship known as incorporation, which was defined by Stutz as « systematically built-up proprietary church law » and of which the principal significance, as Pöschl emphasized, lay in the area of economics [47].

Most monasteries also owned *spiritualia* which had become separated from the *ecclesia* to which they belonged. The most important of these was tithes, of which a great number were either usurped, received as gifts, or bought by monks in the ninth and tenth centu-

---

[42] Cf. F. GOSSO, *Vita economica delle Abbazie Piemontesi (secc. X-XIV)* (*Analecta gregoriana*, 22), Roma 1940, p. 189, and SCHLESINGER, *Kirchengeschichte*, II, pp. 428-429, both of whom stressed the combined religious and economic motives for grants; on rebuilding and restoration by monks, see L. BRUHAT, *Le monachisme en Saintonge et en Aunis (XIe et XIIe siècles)*, La Rochelle 1907, pp. 200-202.

[43] VAN DE KIEFT, in « Le Moyen-Âge », LXIX, 166-167.

[44] *Chartes saintongeaises de l'abbaye de Saint-Florent près de Saumur*, ed. P. MARCHEGAY, « Archives historiques de la Saintonge et de l'Aunis », IV (1877), 43-46, no. 1.

[45] *Ibid.*

[46] W. JORDEN, *Das cluniazensische Totengedächtniswesen vornehmlich unter den drei ersten Äbten Berno, Odo und Aymard (910-954)* (Münsterische Beiträge zur Theologie, 15), Münster 1930, pp. 47-69.

[47] SCHREIBER, *Kurie*, II, p. 17 (citing Stutz), and A. PÖSCHL, *Die Inkorporation und ihre geschichtlichen Grundlagen*, « Archiv für katholisches Kirchenrecht », CVII (1927), 48-49 (where he defines incorporation as « Abhängigkeitsverhältnisse kirchlicher Anstalten untereinander » and CVIII (1928), 59 (« Die Hauptbedeutung des Rechtsinstitutes der Inkorporationlag auf wirtschaftlichen Gebiete ».

ries [48]. Monastic possession of tithes was technically uncanonical, and from time to time it aroused the opposition of the episcopate, as in Germany at the beginning of the ninth century [49] and in France in 993, when several bishops at the council of St. Denis vigorously protested against the number of tithes owned by monasteries [50]. The monks justified their holdings on the basis of long possession and of grants and confirmations, which they forged when necessary or inter-polated into historical and hagiographical texts. In Abbo of Fleury, furthermore, they found a champion who not only replied to the bishops at the council of St. Denis but also formulated for almost the first time a theoretical argument for the possession of tithes by monks [51]. By the middle of the eleventh century, tithes were in fact an established part of monastic revenues all over Europe.

Oblations were less frequently separated from churches than tithes because they were closely associated with liturgical ceremonies. For this reason, though they have been less studied by historians, obla-tions were for many churches economically even more important than tithes [52]. Their principal form was the so-called « common » oblations in bread and wine (and later also in money) given *ad altare* for the celebration of the Eucharist [53], but offerings of some sort were expected to be given *ad manus presbyteri* on almost every ceremonial occasion in the ecclesiastical calendar and in the life of the individual Christian [54]. Some of these have already been seen in the divisions of parochial revenues cited above, including oblations for births, baptism, confession, marriage, visiting the sick, burial,

---

[48] On this, see CONSTABLE, *Mon. Tithes* (cited n. 19 above), pp. 57-83, from which much of the following material is drawn.

[49] See the councils at Tegernsee (804), Salzburg (807), and Chalon-sur-Saône (813) in *M. G. H., Leges*, III:*Concilia*, ed. F. MAASSEN and A. WERMINGHOFF, Hannover 1893-1924, II, pp. 231-233, 234, 277.

[50] On this council, see CONSTABLE, *Mon. Tithes*, pp. 79-80.

[51] AIMOIN OF FLEURY, *Vita s. Abbonis*, IX, in *P.L.*, 139, 396; also Abbo's own *Apology* and letter to G., *ibid.*, 463-465 and 441.

[52] G. SCHREIBER, *Untersuchungen zum Sprachgebrauch des mittelalterlichen Oblationen-wesens*, Wörishofen 1913, pp. 17-19 (stressing the compulsory and personal nature of oblations), and *Kirchliches Abgabenwesen an französischen Eigenkirchen aus Anlass von Ordalien* (1915), reprinted in *Gemeinschaften*, pp. 153-154.

[53] See L. THOMASSIN, *Ancienne et nouvelle discipline de l'église*, III, I, 12-15, ed. M. ANDRÉ, Bar-le-Duc 1864-1867, VI, pp. 71-91; F. DE BERLENDIS, *De oblationibus ad altare commu-nibus et peculiaribus*, 3rd (1st Latin) ed., Venezia 1743; and SCHREIBER, *Abgabenwesen*, in *Gemeinschaften*, pp. 156-164, and *Gregor VII., Cluny, Citeaux, Prémontré zu Eigenkirche, Parochie, Seelsorge, ibid.*, pp. 306-318.

[54] Cf. DE BERLENDIS, *De oblat.*, p. 275.

pilgrimages, and ordeals [55]. Schreiber has particularly emphasized the importance of oblations associated with the blessings of persons as well as of objects [56], and has also studied the divisions of oblations in the twelfth century.

In addition to receiving parts of oblations from their proprietary churches, monks also owned various oblations paid directly to their monasteries. These included, among others, oblations for pilgrimages, burials, and private masses, each of which I shall discuss briefly. Pilgrims were an important source of revenue for religious houses. The priory of Bussy-Albieux, a dependency of Savigny-sur-Bresse, was given in 1046 « the oblations of pilgrims and those on their way to Rome and strangers travelling to some saint, both Our Lady, St. Peter, St. James, and St. Giles » and also « whatever may be offered at that church on the feasts of Our Lady and on the feast of St. Baldomer (the patron saint) by strangers and neighbours and the oblations and tithes of its men living in the vicinity and belonging to that church ». The donors further specified that « if the monks living there celebrate another mass after the public mass, we grant them everything that is offered there » [57]. The oblations at St. Jean d'Angély on the feast of its patron saint were stolen from the altar by Duke William X of Aquitaine, who in 1131 gave handsome compensation and performed penance for this act of sacrilege [58]. And the biographer of Abbot Berthold of Garsten, who died in 1142, referred as a matter of course to the people of the neighbouring parishes visiting the monastery of Garsten and honoring Berthold's body « with oblations and votive offerings » [59].

The oblations of pilgrims, and the relics that attracted them, were often the object of quarrels between monasteries [60]. Late in the twelfth century a Cluniac house in Spain accused a neighbouring priory of

[55] SCHREIBER, *Abgabenwesen*, in *Gemeinschaften*, pp. 198-212, especially studies the oblations associated with ordeals.

[56] SCHREIBER, *Abgabenwesen*, in *Gemeinschaften*, pp. 162-164, and *Mittelalterliche Segnungen und Abgaben* (1943), ibid., pp. 221-229.

[57] *Cartulaire de l'abbaye de Savigny*, ed. A. BERNARD (Collection de documents inédits sur l'histoire de France), Paris 1853, I, p. 378, no. 731.

[58] *Cart. de St-Jean d'Angély* (cited n. 10 above), I, pp. 270-272, no. 217; cf. BRUHAT, *Monachisme*, pp. 13-14, 216, 289-290.

[59] J. LENZENWEGER, *Berthold, Abt von Garsten († 1142)* (Forschungen zur Geschichte Oberösterreichs, 5), Graz-Köln 1958, p. 249.

[60] E. LESNE, *Histoire de la propriété ecclésiastique en France*, III: *L'inventaire de la propriété, églises et trésors des églises du VIIIe à la fin du XIe siècle* (Mémoires et travaux publiés par des professeurs des facultés catholiques de Lille, 44), Lille 1936, pp. 139-140.

usurping its rights « both in its parishioners and in pilgrims » [61]. And the body of St. Stephen of Aubazine was jealously guarded while being brought to Aubazine after his death in 1159. At the abbey of Tulle, said his biographer, « There was no order, discipline, or moderation among the monks, who fell upon [the body of] the saint with not only their hands but also their teeth and uncontrollably bit him in the manner of wild beasts ». The monks of Aubazine refused to let the body rest at all in a church belonging to the countess of Comborn, for fear she would keep it not only out of piety but also, doubtless, as a source of revenue [62].

The right of burial was another frequent source of controversy among monks and between monks and clerics, for although the ceremony of burial was technically free, the officiating priests were allowed to receive oblations (not to mention legacies), and already in the ninth century burial dues are mentioned as a valuable revenue for churches and monasteries [63]. Efforts were occasionally made to restrict the right of monasteries to bury others than their own members. The burial rights of the parish church were protected in the foundation charter of Bénévent-l'Abbaye in the diocese of Limoges [64], and Bishop Pibo of Toul forbade the monks of Châtenois, which had been newly raised from a priory to an abbey, from burying any of the parishioners « without the permission and the presence of the priest » [65]. Such restrictions were as a rule in vain, however, and by the late eleventh century, as Choux said, « On voit que le droit exclusif des églises-mères d'avoir un cimitière était plutôt théorique et qu'en fait des abbayes avaient également des nécropoles qui n'étaient pas pour leur seul usage privé » [66].

The right to be buried where one wished was generally recognized in the Middle Ages [67], and many clerics and laymen chose to be buried in monastic cemeteries. The *ius sepeliendi* for monasteries was confirmed by the papacy in the tenth century [68], and in the

[61] *Chartes de Cluny* (cited n. 23 above), V, pp. 679-680, no. 4326.
[62] *Vita b. Stephani abbatis monasterii Obazinensis*, III, 5-7, in E. BALUZE, *Miscellanea*, ed. J. D. MANSI, Lucca 1761-1764, I, pp. 174-175.
[63] LESNE, *Prop. ecc.*, III, pp. 123-135, and (on the later Middle Ages particularly) G. G. COULTON, *Five Centuries of Religion* (Cambridge Studies in Medieval Life and Thought), Cambridge 1929-1950, III, pp. 41-64, esp. 51-57 on burial by monks.
[64] *Gallia christiana*, Paris 1715 ff., II, instr. p. 199 (ca. 1073).
[65] CHOUX, *Pibon de Toul* (cited n. 28 above), pp. 56, n. 1 and 244, no. 117.
[66] *Ibid.*, p. 57.
[67] SCHREIBER, *Kurie*, II, p. 105.
[68] C. DEVIC and J. VAISSETE, *Histoire générale de Languedoc*, Paris 1730-1745, II, preuves 156; JL 3898.

1090's Urban II declared in his privileges for Sauxillanges and Con-
ques-en-Rouergue that « the burial-right of this place shall be entirely
free, so that no one shall oppose the devotion and last wish of those
who decide to be buried there, unless they are excommunicated » [69].
A substantially similar formula was used in many twelfth-century
monastic privileges, in spite of scattered efforts to protect previously
established burial rights [70].

A third form of oblations given directly to monks was in return for
private and commemorative masses. In the charter of 1046 cited
above, for instance, the monks of Bussy-Albieux were given the oblations from a mass which they might celebrate after the public mass [71].
And the archbishop of Sens arranged in the early twelfth century
that the monks at the priory of St. Aigulf near Provins should receive
half the oblations when the priest celebrated mass for the dead or
at burials and all the oblations (in the words of the charter) « if a
monk celebrates mass when the body is present... and also on Mon-
days and Wednesdays when a monk celebrates mass for the dead » [72].
The practice of celebrating anniversary masses was of increasing
importance for monks in the eleventh century — the earliest reference at Cluny was in 1062 [73] —, and its influence on the history of
monasticism has been emphasized by several scholars. De Berlendis
in his book on oblations, which appeared in the eighteenth century,
noted the association between the growing numbers of monks in holy
orders, the replacement of « common » by « peculiar » oblations,
and the practice of private and commemorative masses by monks [74].
More recently, Nussbaum has shown how the desire for *oblationes
cottidianae* or *gratuitae* added numerous private masses to the monastic liturgy [75].

---

[69] *Cartulaire de Sauxillanges*, ed. H. DONIOL (Académie des sciences, belles-lettres et arts de
Clermont-Ferrand), Clermont-Ferrand-Paris 1864, p. 358, no. 472, and *Cartulaire de l'abbaye
de Conques en Rouergue*, ed. G. DESJARDINS (Documents historiques publiés par la Société
de l'École des Chartes), Paris 1879, p. 399, no. 570; JL 5604 and 5802. The earliest use of
this formula cited by SCHREIBER, *Kurie*, II, p. 106, n. 2, is by Paschal II for Beaulieu in 1103:
Cartulaire de l'abbaye de Beaulieu (en Limousin), ed. M. DELOCHE (Collection de documents
inédits sur l'histoire de France), Paris 1859, p. 9, no. 2; JL 5918.

[70] Cf. SCHREIBER, *Kurie*, II, pp. 105-137.

[71] See n. 57 above.

[72] *Collection des principaux cartulaires du diocèse de Troyes*, ed. CH. LALORE, VI: *Cartulaire
de Montier-la-Celle*, Paris-Troyes 1882, p. 255, no. 216.

[73] JORDEN, *Totengedächtniswesen* (cited n. 46 above), p. 108.

[74] DE BERLENDIS, *De oblat:*, pp. 312-361, esp. 334-339; cf. also SCHREIBER, *Abgabenwesen*,
in *Gemeinschaften*, pp. 172-178.

[75] O. NUSSBAUM, *Kloster, Priestermönch und Privatmesse* (Theophania, 14), Bonn 1961,
pp. 171-173 (with further references).

Many contemporaries were aware of the dangers of these developments, especially of the endless search and rivalry for oblations. The prolongation of the liturgy owing to the multiplication of masses was a particular cause of concern to many monastic reformers [76], and already in the eleventh century several monasteries took steps to reduce the number of commemorative masses [77]. More generally, the reformers saw that the possession of churches and *spiritualia* tended inevitably to involve monks in secular affairs. The very machinery for collecting, transporting, and storing the *spiritualia* of a parish, as Bishop emphasized in his article on monastic granges in Yorkshire, promoted the acquisition of temporal property [78]. In Norman England, tithe-collectors were often given to monasteries together with gifts of tithes [79]. And in the 1130's a lay-brother of the abbey of Byland had to travel everywhere with Roger of Mowbray in order to collect, and when necessary to sell, the tithe of the food of Roger's household, which he had given to the monks [80].

Worse than these problems of collecting *spiritualia* were the innumerable disputes and law-suits which fill the monastic annals and charters of the eleventh and twelfth centuries. The records of such controversies, which often dragged on for years and involved appeals to both popes and kings, are of great value to historians, but they filled the hearts of the reformers with alarm. When the archbishop of Salzburg gave some tithes to Admont in 1074/89, he specified that the third part owing to the parish priests was to be paid from other tithes belonging to himself, not from the portion of the monks, « lest as often happens jealousy and controversy should develop between the parish priests and the monks of the monastery out of the division of the tithes » [81]. All property was a source of conflict in the Middle

---

[76] DE BERLENDIS, *De oblat.*, pp. 374-389, who attributed the trouble in part to the growing number of priests who were not ordained to specific churches and supported themselves by celebrating private masses (pp. 377-379); cf. also COULTON, *Five Centuries*, I, pp. 130-131, and III, pp. 65-86.

[77] DE BERLENDIS, *De oblat.*, pp. 388-389.

[78] T. A. M. BISHOP, *Monastic Granges in Yorkshire*, « English Historical Review », LI (1936), 206.

[79] R. LENNARD, *Peasant Tithe-Collectors in Norman England*, « English Historical Review », LXIX (1954), 580-596.

[80] W. DUGDALE, *Monasticon anglicanum*, ed. J. CALEY, H. ELLIS and B. BANDINEL, London 1817-1830, V, p. 350; cf. F. STENTON, *The First Century of English Feudalism, 1066-1166*, 2nd ed. (Ford Lectures, 1929), Oxford 1961, p. 74.

[81] *Urkundenbuch des Herzogthums Steiermark*, ed. J. ZAHN, I, Graz 1875, p. 93, no. 77; cf. J. WICHNER, *Geschichte des Benediktiner-Stiftes Admont*, Graz 1874-1880, I, p. 37.

Ages [82]. Only a naked man, as the chronicler of Morigny remarked, cannot be robbed [83].

Finally, the possession of churches and *spiritualia* aroused the pride and avarice of monks and led them to usurp the functions of the clerical order. The anonymous author of the early twelfth century treatise *De professione monachorum* from Bec particularly stressed this danger for monks who had had no property in the world and who after they became monks (as he put it) « become proud from the benefices and oblations of the faithful and grow rich and promote themselves by this to so great a pride in thought and in action that it is marvellous not only to say but even to consider » [84].

II - THE REFORMERS

To remedy this situation, and to restore the proper order both to monastic finances and to the economic functioning of society as a whole, the reformers proposed three parallel but independent lines of action. They tried in the first place, and most generally, to recover all ecclesiastical property and revenues from lay control. Second, they undertook to restore the authority of the bishops over the property of the Church. And third, some of the more radical reformers sought to separate the types of revenues owned by the various orders of society. The first of these policies did nothing but benefit the finances of monasteries; but the other two threatened to restrict in important ways both the methods of acquiring property and the types of possessions held by monks [85].

The effort to recover churches, tithes, and other ecclesiastical property from the hands of laymen had been going on since the ninth century on a local basis, owing to the initiative of individual bishops. In France, as Mollat has shown, there was a movement of restoration of private churches to the ecclesiastical patrimony from the ninth to the eleventh centuries [86]; and decrees against lay possession of tithes

[82]   COULTON, *Five Centuries*, III, p. 507.
[83]   *La Chronique de Morigny (1095-1152)*, ed. L. MIROT, 2nd ed. (Collection de textes pour servir à l'étude et à l'enseignement de l'histoire, 41), Paris 1912, p. 30.
[84]   E. MARTÈNE, *De antiquis ecclesiae ritibus*, II, 2, Antwerp 1736-1738, II, col. 488 B.
[85]   SCHREIBER, *Kurie*, II, p. 17, remarked on the contradictory effects for monasteries of the pressure to recover ecclesiastical property from laymen.
[86]   G. MOLLAT, *La restitution des églises privées au patrimoine ecclésiastique en France du IXe au XIe siècle*, « Revue historique de droit français et étranger », 4th S., XXVII (1949), 399-423.

and other spiritual revenues were issued from time to time by local councils throughout this period [87]. The majority of such restitutions, however, as Dumas and Mollat emphasized, were made not to the canonical owners but to religious houses favored by the previous holders of the property. « Les monastères de moines ou de chanoines », Dumas said, « furent les principaux bénéficiaires de leurs bonnes résolutions » [88].

This program to redeem the property of the Church was taken over and intensified by the Papacy in the middle of the eleventh century [89]. The Gregorian reformers were particularly alarmed by the sales and purchases of *spiritualia* owing to the dangers of simony, which they regarded as a form of heresy [90]. One of their first objects, therefore, was to define and assert the sacred character of spiritual revenues and to forbid their possession by laymen or sale in any form. Tithes are like deadly poison for a layman, said Peter Damiani [91]. For Gregory VII lay possession of tithes was an act of sacrilege incurring the danger of damnation [92]. And Paschal II said that « To give *altaria* or tithes for money and to sell the Holy Spirit is the heresy of simony » [93]. A series of papal decrees in the second half of the eleventh century put this policy into effect and declared that all Christians must pay their tithes and oblations exclusively to the Church. And a vigorous campaign to this effect was waged by papal legates, councils, and reforming bishops all over Europe [94].

---

[87] THOMASSIN, *Discipline*, III, I, 11.1-9, ed. cit. (n. 53 above) VI, 54-60, cites a series of conciliar decrees prohibiting lay possession tithes and other *spiritualia* from the late tenth to the twelfth centuries.

[88] E. AMANN and A. DUMAS, *L'église au pouvoir des laïques (888-1057)* (*Histoire de l'église*, ed. AUGUSTIN FLICHE and VICTOR MARTIN, 7), Paris 1940, p. 286.

[89] See, among recent works with references to earlier literature, C. BOYD, *Tithes and Parishes in Medieval Italy*, Ithaca 1952, pp. 103-128; B. BLIGNY, *L'église et les ordres religieux dans le royaume de Bourgogne aux XIe et XIIe siècles* (Collection des cahiers d'histoire publiée par les Universités de Clermont, Lyon, Grenoble, 4), Paris 1960, pp. 64-65 and 88; CONSTABLE, *Mon. Tithes*, pp. 83-89; and G. MICCOLI, *Chiesa gregoriana* (Storici antichi e moderni, N.S. 17), Firenze 1966, p. 28, who said that the preservation and stabilization of the ecclesiastical patrimony was one of the central issues of the Reform on both a theoretical and a practical level.

[90] See n. 7 above and, on the practice of simony in the eleventh century, A. DRESDNER, *Kultur- und Sittengeschichte der italienischen Geistlichkeit im 10. und 11. Jahrhundert*, Breslau 1890, pp. 80 ff.

[91] PETER DAMIANI, *Ep.* IV, 12, in *P.L.*, 144, 324.

[92] *Register Gregors VII.* (cited n. 1 above), p. 404, no. VI, 5b, can. 7 (16).

[93] Fragments of two letters of uncertain date by Paschal II are preserved in several canonical collections and printed in *P.L.*, 163, 436-437; JL 6598 and 6607.

[94] Cf. E. DE MOREAU, *Histoire de l'église en Belgique*, III: *L'église féodale, 1122-1378* (Museum Lessianum: Section historique, 3), Bruxelles 1945, pp. 390-384, who concluded on

It is hard to judge the success of these efforts, but in many regions there seems to have been a definite reduction in the number of churches and *spiritualia* held by laymen in the late eleventh and twelfth centuries [95]. Many of these renunciations were doubtless sales as well as gifts, and their motives are often unclear. But occasional references in both charters and chronicles show that the moral persuasion of the reformers' campaign was not without effect. In the early twelfth century, some laymen in the diocese of Mâcon gave up out of fear for the decree of the council of Clermont and consideration for the safety of their souls a church which they had long held (as the charter puts it) « by the tenure of tyrannical power » [96]. In this case, the renunciation was to the bishop, but as in the ninth and tenth centuries, religious houses rather than bishops or parish priests were frequently the beneficiaries of such restitutions. The reformers at this time were principally concerned with the recovery of ecclesiastical property, not with its ultimate destination. On the whole, furthermore, they were well-disposed towards monks and canons and believed (though mistakenly) that religious houses might with episcopal permission legitimately hold any part of the *spiritualia* except the fraction (usually a third or a quarter) belonging to the parish priests. In this respect, as Catherine Boyd said, « both the theory and the practice of the Gregorian reformers present themselves as strange anomalies, aberrations from canon law » [97].

This situation therefore promoted the second aspect of reforming policy with regard to *spiritualia*: the assertion of episcopal control over ecclesiastical property and of the canonical rules for dividing spiritual revenues [98]. Already in the 1050's these principles were raised in certain quarters on account of the increasing monastic possession of churches and *spiritualia*, and in the last quarter of the century they became a major theme in papal and conciliar legislation. Gregory VII at the Roman synod of 1078 decreed not only

p. 384 that « Nous croyons donc pouvoir conclure qu'il a existé aux XIIe et XIIIe siècles, de la part des évêques, des abbayes et des chapitres, une véritable politique ayant pour but d'obtenir des laïques l'abandon des églises et des biens qui en dépendaient, notamment des dîmes ».

[95] Cf. BRUHAT, *Monachisme* (cited n. 42 above), p. 182, on the proportions of seigneurial and monastic proprietary churches in western France.

[96] *Cartulaire de Saint-Vincent de Mâcon*, ed. M.-C. RAGUT, Mâcon 1864, p. 314, no. 536.

[97] BOYD, *Tithes*, p. 119.

[98] Cf. THOMASSIN, *Discipline*, III, I, 10, ed. cit. (n. 53 above) VI, 46-53; VIOLANTE, in *Spiritualità clun.* (cited n. 40 above), pp. 198 ff.; and CONSTABLE, *Mon. Tithes*, pp. 89-98, upon which the following is based.

that no layman should possess tithes but also that « No abbot should hold tithes, firstfruits, or other revenues which canonically belong to the bishops without the authority of the pope or the consent of the bishop in whose diocese he lives » [99]. A similar decree was issued by the council of Poitiers in the same year [100]. Urban II confirmed this policy at the council of Melfi in 1089 by prohibiting any layman to give « his tithes, church, or any ecclesiastical property to a monastery or house of canons without the consent of the bishop or of the pope ». This alternative of papal permission was important, because some bishops seem to have abused their rights and to have forced monasteries to buy back their churches and tithes whenever the priests died or changed. Urban therefore added to the decree of Melfi that « If on account of dishonesty or avarice the bishop should withhold his consent, the pope should be informed and the grant made by his permission » [101]. These decrees were repeated with minor modifications by later popes and councils and were included in several canonical collections [102]. In the twelfth century, both Gratian and Alexander III supported the doctrine that churches and tithes might be given to religious houses only with the consent of the diocesan bishop [103].

This policy naturally created some alarm in monastic circles. As early as 1070, the abbess of Göss in Styria, probably on account of the efforts of Archbishop Gebhard of Salzburg to establish control over the tithes in his diocese, surrendered to him all the tithes from her abbey's lands and other property and then received them back [104]. In 1120/1 the abbot of Morigny likewise surrendered his abbey's churches and tithes, which it had acquired by purchase as well as

---

[99] Register Gregors VII. (cited n. 1 above), p. 450, no. VI, 5b, can. 9 (25).
[100] MANSI, XX, 498 D.
[101] Ibid., 723; cf. CONSTABLE, Mon. Tithes, pp. 91-92 on the abuses of episcopal power.
[102] See the councils of Poitiers (1100), London (1102), Toulouse (1119), London (1125), Westminster (1127), and Rouen (1128) in, respectively, MANSI, XX, 1123 (can. 9); D. WILKINS, Concilia Magnae Britanniae et Hiberniae (London 1737), I, p. 383 (can. 22); PIERRE DE MARCA, De concordia sacerdotii et imperii, 4th ed., Frankfurt 1708, pp. 1183-1184 (can. 7); The Chronicle of John of Worcester, 1118-1140, ed. J. R. H. WEAVER (Anecdota Oxoniensia, IV, 13), Oxford 1908, pp. 20 (can. 4) and 25 (can. 10); and ORDERICUS VITALIS, Historia ecclesiastica, XII, 48, ed. A. LE PRÉVOST and L. DELISLE (Société de l'histoire de France), Paris 1838-1855, IV, pp. 496-497. On canonical collections, see Register Gregors VII., p. 405, n. 3.
[103] CONSTABLE, Mon. Tithes, pp. 92-93.
[104] Urkundenbuch ... Steiermark (cited n. 81 above) I, pp. 80-81, no. 69.

by gift, into the hands of the Cardinal-legate Cuno of Palestrina, and received them back again [105].

From an economic point of view, however, the acquisition of churches and *spiritualia* by monks and canons was not as a rule seriously hindered by bishops. In spite of their decrees, the reforming popes of the eleventh and twelfth centuries in fact encouraged the monastic possession of *spiritualia* and regularly confirmed them in monastic privileges. Calixtus II in particular supported the monks on two important occasions: first, at the council of Lyons in 1119, when the archbishop of Lyons and his suffragans objected to the number of tithes held by Cluny [106], and again at the Lateran Council of 1123, when the bishops renewed their attacks on monastic possession of « churches, villas, castles, tithes, and the oblations of the living and of the dead » [107]. At both councils the pope categorically confirmed the rights of the monks, and it is clear that by this time, as the evidence presented in the first part of this paper shows, there were no effective barriers to the possession by monks of the economic rights from churches and altars.

From an institutional point of view, on the other hand, the assertion of episcopal control by the reformers contributed to reestablishing the diocesan authority of the bishop, since the monasteries were allowed to exercise only economic control over their churches and chapels. The founder of the Cluniac priory of Bertrée, in the 1120's, made this distinction when he specified that the prior would own the prebend of the parish church and would present it to a suitable priest but « that the priest will be responsible to his archdeacon for the investiture of the altar and for the cure of souls and for his own sins » [108]. Through the archdeacon, therefore, the bishop had complete authority over the parish priest and the *cura animarum* [109]. As Violante put it, « si tende a liberare dal controllo — diretto o indiretto — dei monasteri il normale reggimento spirituale dei fedeli e la struttura in cui esso è inquadrato » [110]. A measure of in-

---

[105] *Chronique de Morigny* (cited n. 83 above), p. 42.

[106] HESSO SCHOLASTICUS, *Relatio de concilio Remensi*, in *M.G.H., Libelli de lite*, Hanover 1891-1897, III, pp. 27-28.

[107] PETER THE DEACON, *Chronicon Casinensis*, IV, 78, in *M.G.H., SS.*, Hanover 1826-1934, VII, 802-803.

[108] *Chartes de Cluny* (cited n. 23 above) V, p. 336, no. 3976; cf. J. STIENNON, *Cluny et Saint-Trond au XIIe siècle*, « Anciens pays et assemblées d'états », VIII (1955), 72-73.

[109] Cf. SCHREIBER, *Kurie*, II, pp. 49-75, on the relation of bishops to the priests of proprietary churches in the twelfth century.

[110] VIOLANTE, in *Spiritualità clun.* (cited n. 40 above), p. 214.

stitutional as well as of economic stability was thus established in the twelfth century in the relations between bishops and monasteries with regard to control over churches [111].

A more radical effort in the same direction was made by the reformers who wanted to separate the types of revenues owned by members of different orders of society and who thus undertook the almost impossible task of untangling the monastic, clerical, and lay finances of the day. This attempt was part of their broad effort to restore good order in society and was related to the changing ideas about the structure of society in the eleventh century, when the old view of the three orders of clerics, monks, and laymen was increasingly replaced by the new tripartite division into *oratores*, *bellatores*, and *laboratores* and by the bipartite division simply into clergy and laity. In these two schemas, monks were regarded as part of the clerical order, whereas according to the older view, to which many of the reformers in the eleventh and twelfth centuries sub-scribed, the monastic order was distinct in both nature and functions [112].

The proponents of this view included, paradoxically, both re-formers and enemies of monasticism. They argued that monks should not concern themselves with worldly affairs but should live in solitude and poverty and support themselves by their own labor [113]. Under no circumstances should they perform pastoral work or possess churches or *spiritualia*, which properly belonged to the secular clergy. A strongly worded statement of this position was given by Theobald of Etampes, one of the first known masters at Oxford, in a letter in 1124/33. « A church is one thing and a monastery another », he wrote, « for a church is the convocation of the faithful but a monastery is the home and prison of the damned, that is, of monks, who have damned themselves in the hope of avoiding eternal damnation... ». In Theobald's view, monks were inferior to priests and might not rule churches or exercise sacramental offices. Tithes, he said, belong to priests and not to monks and must be paid rather than received by monks. « No tithes or churches properly belong to them », he concluded, « and there should be

---

[111] *Ibid.*, p. 227.
[112] On this problem, see CONSTABLE, *Mon. Tithes*, pp. 145-165.
[113] The relation between eremitism and manual labor in the eleventh and twelfth centuries needs further study: cf. *Vita s. Bernardi Tironiensis*, III (19), in *P.L.*, 172, 1380 B. among other sources.

none of the strict collections which many monks use to extort money;
but like the early monks, they should live from the labor of their
hands and from the common lot, which is God »[114].

The secular clergy, according to this view, should live off the
spiritualia. In the *Regula clericorum* compiled at Ravenna in about
1116, the clergy were compared to the Levites, who had no land
or inheritance and lived off tithes, and to the Apostles, who had
no private property. Possessions and land were forbidden to the
Levites and Apostles, and also to the clergy. « To keep this rule
forever », the *Regula* said, « God ordained that the price of sins,
the pledges and oblations of the faithful, [and] the first-fruits and
tithes of things should be given to His churches, so that those who
have been freed for holy worship and deprived of personal property
should have permanently established revenues off which they can
live » and fulfill their sacramental and charitable duties. The *Regula*
then cited many Biblical passages showing « that clerics serving
Christ are forbidden to hold land, to claim the property of the
Church (*res ecclesiae*), to have a worldly patrimony, and to receive
a share of the churches »[115].

This section of the *Regula clericorum* was cited by Gerhoh of
Reichersberg[116], and a very similar passage is found in the unpublished *Meditationes* of Godwin of Salisbury[117]. More important,
the entire *Regula* was confirmed by Paschal II in 1116[118]; and
some scholars have said, owing to an ambiguity of wording, that
the section quoted by Gerhoh was part of a lost treatise by Paschal
himself[119]. Though this is untrue, the *Regula* may nevertheless

[114] This letter, which was addressed to Archbishop Thurstan of York, has been printed
twice: by T. E. HOLLAND, *The University of Oxford in the Twelfth Century*, in *Oxford Historical Society: Collectanea*, II, Oxford 1890, pp. 153-156 and by R. FOREVILLE and J. LECLERCQ,
Un débat sur le sacerdoce des moines au XIIe siècle, in *Analecta monastica*, IV (Studia Anselmiana, 41), Roma 1957, pp. 52-53, where a full discussion of Theobald will also be found.
[115] PETER DE HONESTIS, *Regula clericorum*, I, 1, in *P.L.*, 163, 705 B-D. On this rule,
which is almost certainly not by Peter de Honestis, see *Regesta pontificum Romanorum:
Italia pontificia*, ed. P. KEHR, Berlin 1906 ff., V, pp. 94-97, and J. DICKINSON, *The Origins of
the Austin Canons and Their Introduction into England*, London 1950, pp. 44 and 165.
[116] GERHOH OF REICHERSBERG, *Commentarius in psalmum LXIV*, in *M.G.H., Libelli de lite*,
III, pp. 475-477. The first version of this work is dated 1151 by P. CLASSEN, *Gerhoch von
Reichersberg*, Wiesbaden 1960, p. 419.
[117] Oxford, Bodleian Library, MS Digby 96, ff. 21ʳ-22ʳ.
[118] *P.L.*, 163, 414; JL 6533; *Italia pont.*, V, pp. 96-97, no. 2.
[119] MANSI, XX, 1087-1091 (entitled *Fragmentum Tractatus Paschalis II*); cf. H. WHITE,
Pontius of Cluny, the Curia Romana and the End of Gregorianism in Rome, « Church History », XXVII (1958), 215, n. 24, and ID., *The Gregorian Ideal and Saint Bernard of
Clairvaux*, « Journal of the History of Ideas », XXI (1960), 332, n. 31.

reflect Paschal's ideas on the subject of clerical finances and therefore throw light on his celebrated agreement with Henry V in 1111. Several' recent scholars have seen in Paschal's concessions a sincere expression of his desire to restore the primitive, apostolic poverty of the Church [120]. As don Zerbi put it, « La decisione di Pasquale II fu un atto di coerenza impeccabile, perfetta, paragonabile a quello compiuto da Gregorio VII quando, trentasei anni prima, aveva proibito ogni investitura laica » [121]. But it has not been fully studied, I believe, in the light of the view that *spiritualia* were the proper support of the clergy, manual labor of monks, and feudal property of the laity.

Some of the most eminent supporters of this view, and most vigorous critics of monks, came from the ranks of the regular canons, many of whom were anxious to defend the distinctive prerogatives of their own clerical order, whether or not they personally exercised the *cura animarum* and received spiritual revenues. In various works written about the middle of the twelfth century by Gerhoh of Reichersberg, Philip of Harvengt, and Anselm of Havelberg, the monks found serious and reasoned arguments against their performance of pastoral work and possession of churches and *spiritualia* [122].

At the same time a number of influential writers rose to defend the rights of the monks [123]. Their arguments followed several lines. One, more moderate, tried to establish a limited right of monks to perform pastoral work to receive the revenues of churches they served themselves. This was the position of Rupert of Deutz, Honorius *Augustodunensis*, and Bernard of Tiron — and also, with greater emphasis on episcopal control, of Gratian and his followers. Even some of the opponents of monastic possession of *spiritualia*, such as Gerhoh and the Cistercian critics of Cluny, directed their attacks primarily against unearned tithes and oblations and implied that monks who performed pastoral work were entitled to receive clerical

---

[120] W. KRATZ, Der Armutsgedanke im Entäusserungsplan des Papstes Paschalis II. (Diss. Freiburg), Fulda 1933, p. 3 (citing earlier works); WHITE, in « Church History », XXVII, 188, and in « J. Hist. Ideas », XXI, 332-333; N. CANTOR, The Crisis of Western Monasticism, 1050-1130, « American Historical Review », LXVI (1960) 56; P. ZERBI, Pasquale II e l'ideale della povertà della Chiesa, in Annuario dell'Università Cattolica del Sacro Cuore, 1964-1965, Milano 1966, pp. 215-217 and 226-227 in particular; and G. MICCOLI, « Ecclesiae primitivae forma » (1960), reprinted in his Chiesa greg. (cited n. 89 above), pp. 276-285.

[121] ZERBI, in Annuario, 1964-65, p. 216.

[122] See CONSTABLE, Mon. Tithes, pp. 158-165.

[123] Ibid., pp. 165-185, from which the material in this and the next paragraph is largely drawn.

revenues. This moderate position, whether of approval or of opposition, was based historically on the greater number of monks who
were ordained and might exercise sacerdotal functions and on the
progressive merging, which was referred to above, of the clerical and
monastic orders.

The extremists at both ends argued along different lines. The
strongest opponents asserted that under no circumstances could a
monk properly exercise the *cura animarum* or receive clerical revenues. The extreme defenders, on the contrary, tried to establish a
general right of monks to own *spiritualia,* whether or not they performed pastoral work. Their reasons fell, broadly speaking, into
three categories. One argument claimed that monks were *ipso facto*
clerics and therefore entitled to clerical rights and revenues [124]. Another was that monks had as good a right as clerics to *spiritualia* on
account of their services to the Church and the superior purity of
their lives. A third and historically more interesting argument was
that monks were the *pauperes Christi,* the true poor, to whom tithes
really belonged [125], or the real heirs of the Levites, to whom the Lord
said that tithes should be paid [126].

The Cluniac Abbot Hugh of Reading, who was later archbishop of
Rouen, combined these arguments in a chapter of his *Dialogues,* of
which the first version was written before 1126. All monks are
clerics, Hugh said, and are superior to clerics who are not monks.
They are therefore ideally suited, he continued, « by virtue of their
more perfect lives... to preach the kingdom of God to the people, to
reprove sinners, and to receive, loose, and bind penitents. They
should serve altars diligently and live off oblations and tithes. Tithes
indeed belong to the poor, but the true poor are those who in
accordance with the Gospel are poor in spirit, because they are those
who give up not only their possessions but also their wills to their
fathers. Cenobites do this by their public profession. By virtue of
their true poverty, therefore, and by their rejection of property, the
true poor of Christ should live off oblations and tithes » [127].

[124] See, for example, the arguments of the monks who replied to ROBERT OF MOLESME
(see p. 323 below) in ORDERICUS VITALIS, *Hist. ecc.,* VIII, 26, ed. cit. (n. 102 above), III, p. 441.
[125] IVO OF CHARTRES, *Ep.* 192, in *P.L.,* 162, 199-200, was one of the first to use this
argument: cf. CONSTABLE, *Mon. Tithes,* pp. 169-170, esp. n. 1 on p. 170.
[126] This point was made by, among others, Peter the Venerable in his ep. 28 to Bernard
of Clairvaux, where he defended Cluniac possession of churches, first-fruits, and tithes: *The
Letters of Peter the Venerable,* ed. G. CONSTABLE (Harvard Historical Studies, 78), Cambridge
(Mass.) 1967, I, p. 81.
[127] HUGH OF ROUEN, *Dialogorum ... libri VII,* VI, in *Thesaurus novus anecdotorum,* ed.

Hugh was an important spokesman for the old monasticism against the attacks of the reformers, who both criticized the Cluniacs for possessing churches and *spiritualia* and refused themselves to perform pastoral work or accept clerical revenues [128]. Already in the first half of the eleventh century, the Vallombrosians were unwilling to accept churches to be served by themselves [129]. A good general statement of this policy is found in the *Narratio restaurationis abbatiae sancti Martini Tornacensis* by Herman of Tournai, who wrote that the reforming Abbot Odo at the end of the eleventh century « was determined to accept neither *altaria* nor churches or tithes but to live solely from the labor of his hands, from the land cultivated by his teams, and from the nourishment of his herds, [and] he refused to have any ecclesiastical revenues which they [clerics joining the abbey] had held and said that such revenues should be owned only by clerics, not by monks. And his determination in this respect conformed to the life and practices of the monks of old » [130]. Odo likewise insisted, when he undertook to restore the abbey of St. Martin, that no laymen should be buried there [131].

At about the same time, probably in 1095, according to Ordericus Vitalis, Robert of Molesme complained to his monks that « We have an abundance of food and clothing from the tithes and oblations of churches, and by skill or violence we appropriate what belongs to the priests. Thus surely we feed upon the blood of men and share in their sins ». He therefore urged his monks to adhere strictly to the rule of St. Benedict. « Let us procure our food and clothing by the labor of our own hands... Let us give up tithes and oblations to the clergy who serve the diocese. Thus let us zealously strive to follow Christ in the footsteps of the Fathers » [132]. These sentiments apparently roused little enthusiasm among the monks at Molesme, but they were embodied in Robert's new foundation of Cîteaux and in the earliest Cistercian legislation. One of the canons probably presented to Calixtus II in 1119 established that « The ordinance of our name and order prohibits [the possession of] churches, *altaria,*

E. MARTÈNE and U. DURAND, Paris 1717, V, pp. 972-973. On the date of this work, see D. VAN DEN EYNDE, *Nouvelles précisions chronologiques sur quelques oeuvres théologiques du XIIe siècle*, « Franciscan Studies », XIII (1953), 74-77.

[128] The following section is substantially similar, with a few additions, to CONSTABLE, *Mon. Tithes*, pp. 137-144.

[129] ANDREW OF STRUMI, *Vita s. Iohannis Gualberti*, XIX, in *M.G.H., SS.*, XXX, 1085.

[130] HERMAN OF TOURNAI, *Narratio*, LXVIII, in *M.G.H., SS.*, XIV, 306.

[131] HERMAN OF TOURNAI, *Narratio*, XI, *ibid.*, 279.

[132] ORDERICUS VITALIS, *Hist. ecc.*, VIII, 26, ed. cit. (n. 102 above) III, p. 436.

burial rights, the tithes from the work and nourishment of other men, manors, dependent laborers, land rents, revenues from ovens and mills, and similar [property] which is not in accord with monastic purity » [133].

Other reformed monks were no less strict in their determination to own no churches or *spiritualia*. The first Carthusian *Consuetudines*, drawn up probably in 1116, forbade the possession of fields, vineyards, gardens, churches, cemetaries, oblations, and tithes « outside the boundaries of their hermitage » [134]. The rule of Fontevrault declared « That they would not receive parish churches or their tithes » [135]. And the Grandmontines, who were perhaps the strictest of all in this respect, relied completely on divine providence for their material support, rejected all possessions outside the boundaries of their own houses, and refused to keep the tithes even of their own labor [136].

The influence of these principles was felt throughout the monastic world of the twelfth century. Some preachers even urged monks to leave any monastery where the abbot had acquired tithes [137]. One of the founders of Fountains Abbey, Prior Richard of St. Mary's at York, said that the revenues of churches and tithes « should be held by the legitimate and canonical determination of the bishop and be spent only for the uses of the poor, pilgrims, and guests » [138]. And the Premonstratensian Philip of Harvengt, speaking of the revival of monasticism in his own times, especially praised the example and desire for poverty of the Cistercian, who, he said, « did not seek the tithes of the people but with eager vigor stretched out his hands to work, so that by striving to gain his humble food and clothing in this way he showed that never forgot his original purpose » [139].

---

[133]   J.-A. LEFÈVRE, *La véritable constitution cistercienne de 1119*, « Collectanea ordinis cisterciensium reformatorum », XVI (1954), 104 (dating this statute 1119) and J.-B. VAN DAMME, *Documenta pro Cisterciensis ordinis historiae ac juris studio*, Westmalle 1959, p. 28 (dating it 1123/4).

[134]   *Consuetudines*, XLI, 1, in *P.L.*, 153, 719-720.

[135]   JOHANNES VON WALTER, *Die ersten Wanderprediger Frankreichs*, I: *Robert von Arbrissel* (Studien zur Geschichte der Theologie und der Kirche, IX, 3), Leipzig, 1903, p. 194.

[136]   *Regula s. Stephani Grandimontensis*, IV, V, XXXII, in *P.L.*, 204, 1140-1142 and 1150; cf. *Liber sententiarum seu rationum s. Stephani Grandimontensis*, L, 1, *ibid.*, 1108 D, on burials. On the Grandmontine rule, which was largely based on the teachings of Stephen though drawn up in the late twelfth century, see J. BECQUET, *La règle de Grandmont*, « Bulletin de la Société archéologique et historique du Limousin », LXXXVII (1958), 9-36.

[137]   IVO OF CHARTRES, *Ep.* 192, in *P.L.*, 162, 199.

[138]   *Memorials of Fountains* (cited n. 11 above), p. 21.

[139]   PHILIP OF HARVENGT, *De institutione clericorum*, IV, 125, in *P.L.*, 203, 836.

These texts show that the refusal to own churches and spiritual revenues was an important part in the program for monastic reform and the ideal of the apostolic life in the eleventh and twelfth centuries [140]. In the first place, it fitted with the desire of the reformers to be poor both communally and individually and to support themselves by their own labor. Second, it was in accord with their wish to return to the purity of the primitive church and early monasticism. Lastly and in practice perhaps most important, it saved them from involvement in worldly affairs and especially from litigation.

Several of the early reformers suffered personally from the claims of other monks and of parish priests to *spiritualia* [141]. Bernard of Tiron had to move twice, the second time owing to the claims to tithes and burial dues of the monks of Nogent-le-Rotrou; and the followers of Stephen of Muret, after his death in 1124, were forced to move to Grandmont by the abbey of St. Augustine at Limoges [142]. The complaints against the new monks were not always unjustified. The biographer of Geoffrey of Chalard said with pride that the neighbours flocked to hear him preach and bring him gifts, and it is not therefore surprising that he was resented by the archdeacon and parish priest, who accused him of illegitimately building a church, celebrating public masses, and receiving oblations [143]. Such experiences naturally persuaded the reformers to look for places to live where there were no established claimants to these revenues. Their choice of a deserted site was thus often in order to avoid not only contacts with other people but also controversies over *spiritualia*.

Churches and their incomes, whether they were owned by clerics, monks, or laymen, were a valuable form of property and an inevitable source of disputes. St. Norbert told the pope in 1119 that his aim was to lead an evangelical and apostolic life, « not to seek what belongs to others, never to claim by legal pleadings or secular judges what has been taken [from us], not to bind by anathema anyone on

---

[140] See in particular the stimulating article by M.-D. CHENU, *Moines, clercs, laïcs au carrefour de la vie évangélique*, « Revue d'histoire ecclésiastique », XLIX (1954), 59-89, esp. 62-66, reprinted in his *La Théologie au douzième siècle* (Études de philosophie médiévale, 45), Paris 1957, pp. 225-251.

[141] Cf. SCHREIBER, *Kurie*, II, pp. 48-49, on complaints against monastic usurpation of pastoral rights and functions.

[142] *Vita s. Bernardi Tironiensis*, IX (77-78), in *P.L.*, 172, 1412-1414, and *Vita s. Stephani Grandimontensis*, XLVII, in *P.L.*, 204, 1028.

[143] *Vita b. Gaufredi Castaliensis*, I, 4, ed. A. BOSVIEUX, « Mémories de la Société des sciences naturelles et archéologiques de la Creuze », III (1862), 86-88.

account of any injuries or damages done to us » [144]. Abelard in one of his sermons sharply criticized monks for usurping « clerical property and parochial revenues, both tithes and oblations. ... On this account », he continued, « we are often drawn to synods and councils and go daily to public lawsuits, and at great expense we bribe judges and lawyers to overlook our unjust actions » [145]. And Bernard of Clairvaux, in a letter written jointly with Hugh of Pontigny to the abbot of Marmoutier, expressed amazement that some monks seemed to prefer « the poor revenues of a single altar to the glory of the world » and said that « It is for the clergy to serve the altar and to live from the altar. Our profession and the example of the monks of old prescribe that we should live from our own labors and not from the sanctuary of God » [146].

From a theoretical point of view, these arguments against monastic possession of churches and tithes were certainly strong. There can be no question that early monks in the West owned no *spiritualia*, that canon law before Gratian recognized no right of monks to such revenues, and that in practice their possession involved monasteries in secular affairs. The arguments for the defence, on the other hand, were relatively weak. The claim that monks as *ipso facto* clerics or as parish priests were entitled to tithes and oblations was weak because most monasteries claimed more than the quarter or third canonically assigned to priests exercising the *cura animarum*. The argument that monks were the poor of Christ was weak because most of the monks who owned *spiritualia*, though individually poor, were collectively rich and because many really poor monks refused to own tithes and oblations. The canonical texts upon which the defenders relied were mostly forgeries or of doubtful authenticity [147]. Even their strongest arguments — long possession and papal and episcopal grants — were weak in theory.

In practice, however, the refusal of the reformers to accept any *spiritualia* was unrealistic and radical in the strict sense of the term. Their economic principles were aimed, as Hoffmann said of the Cistercians, not towards the future but towards a golden vision of the past [148], on which they hoped to base a new and reformed monastic

[144] *Vita Norberti*, IX, in *M.G.H., SS.*, XII, 678.
[145] ABELARD, serm. XXXIII, in *P.L.*, 178, 588.
[146] BERNARD, Ep. 397, in *Sancti Bernardi ... opera omnia*, Paris 1839, I, p. 712.
[147] Cf. CONSTABLE, *Mon. Tithes*, pp. 166, n. 3, 183, n. 2, and 304-306.
[148] E. HOFFMANN, *Die Entwicklung der Wirtschaftsprinzipien im Cisterzienserorden während des 12. und 13. Jahrhunderts*, « Historisches Jahrbuch », XXXI (1910), 702.

life. Their hopes to support their monasteries purely by manual labor had no greater chance of practical success than the proposal of Paschal II to finance the Church exclusively by ecclesiastical revenues. Within a comparatively short time, certainly not over half a century, almost all the reformers in fact accepted types of property and revenues which they had originally rejected.

The history of this failure mostly lies outside the scope of this paper [149], but it began already in the eleventh century, when Odo of St. Martin of Tournai (whose original refusal to own *altaria* was mentioned above) was persuaded, as Herman wrote, « that like other religious abbots he should not refuse to accept them if someone for the sake of his soul wished without simony to give *altaria* to our church » [150]. By 1145 St. Martin possessed thirty-seven altars worth about six pounds *per annum* each [151]. By this time, indeed, the Cistercians, Carthusians, Premonstratensians, Templars, and probably also the Grandmontines had all accepted *spiritualia* of one sort or another. The Savigniacs not only kept all their churches, *altaria*, and tithes after they joined the Cistercians in 1147 but even continued to acquire them [152]. After 1150, there are many examples of Cistercian burials [153], commemorative masses [154], and *spiritualia*, particularly in England [155].

It is difficult to discover the reason for these developments. Contemporaries, especially in the second half of the twelfth century, were inclined to see them as a sign of avarice and moral degeneration among the new orders. Recent historians, however, have seen the change as the result of economic factors. Hoffmann, for instance, stressed the difficulty of maintaining a small natural economy based on manual labor in an expanding money economy [156]. Other scholars have pointed out the practical impossibility of avoiding possession of all the forbidden revenues, the inclusion in the new orders of

---

[149] See CONSTABLE, *Mon. Tithes*, pp. 187-197.

[150] HERMAN OF TOURNAI, *Narratio*, LXXIV, in *M.G.H., SS.*, XIV, 309.

[151] A. D'HAENENS, *Moines et clercs à Tournai au début du XIIe siècle*, in *La vita comune del clero nei secoli XI e XII*, Pubblicazioni dell'Università Cattolica del Sacro Cuore, III, Scienze storiche, 2-3, Milano, 1962, II, pp. 95-96.

[152] J. BUHOT, *L'abbaye normande de Savigny, chef d'ordre et fille de Cîteaux*, « Le Moyen Âge », XLVI (3rd S., VII, 1936), 115, 121, 178-190, and 255-260.

[153] CHOUX, *Pibon de Toul* (cited n. 28 above), p. 57.

[154] See the statute of the Cistercian Chapter-General in 1192, in *Statuta capitulorum generalium ordinis Cisterciensis*, ed. J. M. CANIVEZ, I (Bibliothèque de la Revue d'histoire ecclésiastique, 9), Louvain 1933, p. 147, no. 3.

[155] CONSTABLE, *Mon. Tithes*, pp. 192-193.

[156] HOFFMANN, in « Hist. Jahrbuch », XXXI, 708 and 726.

monasteries already owning churches and *spiritualia*, and the acquisition of lands already cultivated by peasants paying regular dues, which were often indistinguishable from clerical revenues [157].

The acceptance of these revenues may also have been influenced by the shift in ideals of the reformers themselves during the first half of the twelfth century. Like all reform programs, theirs was made up of old and new elements, and as time went on many reformers no longer sought their fulfillment within the traditional monastic framework, with its ideal of separation from the world. They increasingly sought to lead an evangelical life based on communal poverty and on proselytism, pastoral work, and service to others « in the world » [158]. At the same time, the more conservative reformers returned to the ideals of the strict black monks who emphasized regularity of monastic observance and accepted spiritual revenues while refusing to perform any pastoral work which would disturb their *clausura*. The economic organization of monasticism was thus influenced by its inner spiritual developments, which help to explain both the changing attitudes towards the possession of various types of property and the fact that by the end of the twelfth century almost all monasteries freely owned churches and *spiritualia* to which their right was so strongly challenged during the age of reform.

---

[157] Cf. SCHREIBER, *Kurie*, I, p. 257, n. 3; BUHOT, in « Le Moyen Âge », XLVI, 260 and 268-269; and GANSHOF, in *Cambridge Econ. Hist.* (cited nn. 12 above), I, p. 315.
[158] Cf. CHENU, in « Rev. d'hist. ecc. », XLIX, 69-80.

IX

The Treatise "Hortatur nos" and Accompanying Canonical Texts on the Performance of Pastoral Work by Monks

This brief and hitherto unpublished treatise was apparently written by an anonymous monk in southern Germany about the middle of the twelfth century[1]. It is found in Clm 27129, which formerly belonged to the Benedictine abbey of Ottobeuren[2]. This is a composite manuscript, of which the first nine and the final signatures (ff. 1–75 and 122–33) date from the tenth century and the other six (ff.76–121) from the twelfth. The last of these twelfth-century signatures (ff.114–21) forms an independent unit containing four texts: 1) the treatise and texts printed and discussed below (ff. 114r–116v); 2) the account by Rupert of Deutz of his debate on the topic of whether monks might preach, here entitled *Conflictus Ruodperti Coloniensis abbatis ... cum Noperto clerico* (ff. 116v–118v)[3]; 3) an extract from the so-called *Recognitiones* of Clement (ff. 118v–120v)[4]; and 4) in a smaller an different hand, an incomplete copy of Peter the Venerable's letter VI, 4 to Bernard of Clairvaux (ff. 120v–121v)[5].

In the treatise *Hortatur nos* and in selecting the accompanying texts the author took a strong stand on the questions, hotly debated in the twelfth century, of whether monks were permitted to perform pastoral work and to possess tithes and other parochial revenues. He answered both these questions in the affirmative. He argued in particular that there was no strict separation between the contemplative and active lives, which he compared to the two loves of God and one's neighbor, both of which are essential for salvation. He cited examples of hermits and monks in the Bible and among the Fathers who were also priests and performed sacerdotal duties. A priest may be equivalent to an angel, he said, since he is sent by the Lord to preach; but a priest who is also a monk, and therefore distinguished by the purity of his life, is an archangel. Having given up worldly things, monks are closer to God than other men and therefore particularly suited to perform the divine offices of preaching, baptizing, and administering penance. Finally, he argued that this work was not, as the enemies of monks claimed, forbidden by St Benedict. On the

---

[1] The claim that a text is unpublished must always be accompanied by "to the best of my knowledge". It appears in none of the standard catalogues of incipits and is not cited by the principal authorities on the subject. It deserves to be better known, therefore, even if it has been printed before.

[2] See Catalogus codicum latinorum bibliothecae regiae Monacensis, II.4 (Catalogus codicum manu scriptorum bibliothecae regiae Monacensis, IV.4; Munich, 1881) pp. 246–7.

[3] Patrologia latina, ed. J.-P. M i g n e (Paris, 1844–64; = PL) CLXX, 537–42; cf. G i l e s C o n s t a b l e, Monastic Tithes from their Origins to the Twelfth Century (Cambridge Studies in Medieval Thought and Life, N.S. 10; Cambridge, 1964) pp. 173–4.

[4] Inc.: Montes excelsi. I am indebted for the identification of this text to Professor Lynn Thorndike of Columbia University, who informs me that this is the only manuscript of this extract known to him.

[5] Bibliotheca Cluniacensis, ed. M a r t i n M a r r i e r and A n d r é D u c h e s n e (Paris, 1614) coll. 897–901. This text will be discussed in my forthcoming edition of the letters of Peter the Venerable.

contrary, in accord with the divine precept to visit the sick, it was specifically approved in the Rule.

In addition to the Bible and the Rule of St Benedict, the author cited in the text of his treatise passages from Gregory the Great, Augustine, and Jerome to prove, respectively, the superiority of monastic life, the interdependence of the contemplative and active lives, and the obligation of clerics as well as monks to avoid worldly entanglements. He also appended to the treatise six papal decrees[6], which will be discussed below, authorizing the performance of pastoral work by monks, prohibiting the exaction of tithes and first-fruits from them, and protecting their property.

It is impossible to discuss fully here the position of these ideas in the debate over monastic cure of souls and freedom from tithes[7]. The author clearly agreed with Rupert of Deutz (with whose work his treatise was copied), Honorius "Augustodunensis", Idungus of Regensburg, and other conservative monastic authors who defended the right of ordained monks to serve in churches and to receive parochial revenues[8]. They denied that there was any theoretical distinction of function between a monk and a cleric and maintained that sacerdotal ordination entitled a monk to perform all the duties of a priest. They thus recognized that the status of a monk might be combined with the status, or at least the functions, of a cleric or priest.

This position depended historically on the growing number of monks who were ordained and performed pastoral work, on the new importance of the sacraments, especially of the mass, and on the consequent merging of the clerical and monastic orders. The opponents of monastic performance of pastoral work, on the other hand, based their case on the earlier distinction between the nature, finances, and function of the two orders and maintained that a monk could under no circumstances properly exercise the *cura animarum* or receive clerical revenues. This was theoretically a strong argument, since according to early canon law and theology monks were considered distinct from priests and were not entitled to perform pastoral work.

The weakness of the legal position favoring monastic performance of pastoral work is shown by the fact that out of the six canonical texts appended to *Hortatur nos* no less than five were forged, interpolated, or attributed to false authorities. There is no evidence that the author invented them himself. He doubtless sincerely believed that they were written by Gregory the Great and Boniface IV. But the

---

[6] They may have been appended to it by some one else, but the fact that several of the ideas in the treatise seem to derive from the decrees suggests that they were selected by the author.

[7] See in particular Ursmer Berlière, L'exercice du ministère paroissial par les moines dans le haut moyen âge, in: Revue bénédictine, XXXIX (1927) 227–50; Charles Dereine, Le problème de la cura animarum chez Gratien, in: Studia Gratiana, II (1954) 309–18; M. Peuchmaurd, Le prêtre ministre de la parole dans la théologie du XIIe siècle, in: Recherches de théologie ancienne et médiévale, XXIX (1962) 52–76; and Constable, Monastic Tithes, pp. 136–97, esp. 184–6, on which most of the following two paragraphs are based.

[8] The author may have been one of these men, although none of them use exactly the same arguments and texts. The contents of the work, as well as the provenance of the manuscript, indicate that he was a Benedictine monk in a South German monastery, writing about the middle of the twelfth century. The *terminus post quem* is apparently established by the canonical texts numbered four and five (see pp. 571 below).

fact that all but one were composed not more than a century before the time he was writing, and two probably only very shortly before, shows the difficulty encountered by those who agreed with his position in establishing a legal basis for their claims.

The first two texts, *Sunt nonnulli stulti* and *Episcopus debet missam*, attributed to Boniface IV and Gregory I respectively, are now generally considered by scholars to be forgeries composed in Italy about the middle of the eleventh century, probably soon before 1060[9]. They won rapid acceptance, however, and played an important part in establishing the legal right of monks to perform sacerdotal offices. Together or singly they were cited by Peter Damiani, Ivo of Chartres, Honorius "Augustodunensis", and many less well-known writers, and they occur in at least two dozen manuscripts, from all over Europe, listed by Leclercq, Dereine, and Ryan. They were used as the textual basis for the second and third canons of the council of Nîmes in 1096 and were later incorporated into the permanent law of the Church as part of the *Decretum* of Gratian.

The decree attributed to Boniface exists in two distinct forms, of which there are several subforms[10]. Form A, which begins *Sunt nonnulli nullo dogmate fulti*, was used by Peter Damiani, Ivo of Chartres, and Gratian and seems to have been the more usual form in Italy and France[11]. Form B, which was first published by Labbe from a manuscript at St Symphorien at Metz[12], begins *Sunt nonnulli stulti dogmatis* and was used as the second canon of the council of Nîmes[13]. This is the form that was used by Rupert of Deutz in his *De trinitate*[14] and is printed here from Clm 27129, with variants (aside from five differences in word order) from the Metz (= M 1) and Angers (= M 2) manuscripts as printed in Mansi.

The decree attributed to Gregory the Great also exists in several forms, of which the longest and best-known was first published in its entirety by Frank in 1937 from Ms Châlons-sur-Marne 32, with variants from seven other manuscripts and partial printed versions[15]. Substantial portions of this text were used as the third

---

[9] Berlière, in Rev. bén., XXXIX, 233–4; Hieronymus Frank, Zwei Fälschungen auf den Namen Gregors d. Gr. und Bonifatius IV., in: Studien und Mitteilungen zur Geschichte des Benediktiner-Ordens und seiner Zweige, LV (1937) 19–47, esp. 46–7; Jean Leclercq, Analecta monastica, II (Studia Anselmiana, 31; Rome, 1953) pp. 137–8; Dereine, in Studia Gratiana, II, 309–18, esp. 317; J. J. Ryan, Saint Peter Damiani and his Canonical Sources (Pontifical Institute of Mediaeval Studies: Studies and Texts, 2; Toronto, 1956) pp. 56–8; Constable, Monastic Tithes, pp. 166, 168, 175, 183.

[10] Cf. Philip Jaffé, Regesta pontificum Romanorum, ed. S. Löwenfeld, F. Kaltenbrunner, and P. Ewald (Leipzig, 1885–8; = JL, JK, JE) no. 1996 and Dereine, in Studia Gratiana, II, 309.

[11] Damiani, Apologeticus monachorum adversus canonicos, in PL, CXLV, 515–16 (cf. Ryan, Damiani, pp. 56–7); Ivo, Decretum, VII, 22, in PL, CLXI, 549–50 (cf. Frank, in Studien u. Mitt. OSB, LV, 28–32); Gratian, Decretum, C. XVI, q. 1, c. 25, ed. Emil Richter and Emil Friedberg, Corpus iuris canonici, I (Leipzig, 1879) col. 767 and notes. On its later importance and use by Thomas Aquinas, see Leclercq, Anal. mon., II, 138.

[12] Sacrorum conciliorum nova et amplissima collectio, ed. J. D. Mansi (Florence and Venice, 1759 ff.) X, 506–8 (reprinted in PL, LXXX, 104–6).

[13] Mansi, Collectio, XX, 934 (from a manuscript at St Aubin at Angers).

[14] Rupert of Deutz, De trinitate, VIII, 8, in PL, CLXVII, 1791: Credimus a sacerdotibus ... certissime conficitur. This passage agrees with M1 on readings o, s, t, and u and has four readings of its own.

[15] Frank, in Studien u. Mitt. OSB, LV, 25–6. This form is classified B by Dereine, in Studia Gratiana, II, 309.

canon of the council of Nîmes[16], as part of an *ordo ad faciendum monachum* in Ms Einsiedeln 112[17], in the *De trinitate* of Rupert of Deutz[18], and as an independent text on monastic profession in Ms Vatican Reg. lat. 173[19]. It was cited by Peter Damiani[20], perhaps by Ivo of Chartres[21], and in a fragmentary form by Gratian[22]. The Ottobeuren text printed here from Clm 27129 differs considerably from the Châlons-sur-Marne version printed by Frank, which includes a number of additions, particularly two citations from Acts and Matthew. The Ottobeuren version agrees on the whole, however, with those classified by Frank as D (Ms Vat. lat. 1358), E (Ms Einsiedeln 112), F (Rupert of Deutz, *De trinitate*), and with the version in Ms Vatican Reg. lat. 173[23]. The text printed here, however, includes an interesting passage (Sicut enim ... in terris.), comparing monks to angels, which is found in no printed version of this text and is published here for the first time.

The problems associated with these two decrees are still far from fully solved. The inclusion of variant readings here is an indication of the different forms in which they are found, not that this is a full critical edition. A definitive study will have to depend upon a complete survey of the manuscripts.

The third text begins with two extracts from the first part of the famous *Libellus responsionum* sent by Gregory the Great to Augustine of Canterbury[24], which was universally regarded as authentic throughout the Middle Ages, although some doubts have been caste upon it in recent years[25]. These two extracts were used as

---

[16] Mansi, Collectio, XX, 934–5: = Unde oportet ... penitentes soluere. This canon is cited by Peuchmaurd, in Recherches de théol., XXIX, 68–9, without indicating its origin.
[17] Odilo Ringholz, Wernher II, Abt und Dekan von Einsiedeln, seine "Constitutiones" und "Ordo ad faciendum Monachum", in: Studien und Mittheilungen aus dem Benedictiner- und dem Cistercienser-Orden, VI. 1 (1885) pp. 333–4; also cited by Frank, in Studien u. Mitt. OSB, LV, 20–1: abbas ... ab omnibus peccatis.
[18] PL, CLXVII, 1791: Episcopus ... ab omnibus peccatis. and Tribus diebus ... auferat.
[19] Leclercq, Anal. mon., II, 137: Episcopus ... peccata [ab]soluere. and Tribus diebus ... residebant. Leclercq, while citing Frank's work, does not mention his publication of this text in a more complete form. Cf. André Wilmart, Codices reginenses latini, I (Bibliothecae apostolicae Vaticanae codices manu scripti recensiti; Vatican City, 1937) p. 408.
[20] Ryan, Damiani, pp. 57–8.
[21] Two of the manuscripts cited by Frank (Vat. lat. 1357 and 1358) are of Ivo's Decretum and Panormia (see Frank, in Studien u. Mitt. OSB, LV, 29–36); but this canon does not appear in the printed versions of these works and may have been, as Frank believed, interpolated into these manuscripts.
[22] C. XVI, q. 1, c. 24, in ed. cit., col. 767.
[23] All of these contain only parts of the text. Frank's list of variants is incomplete, but a comparison with the printed versions shows that the Einsiedeln text agrees with Clm 27129 on all variants except f, h, and i; Rupert's text agrees with all but i and three independent readings; Reg. lat. 173 agrees with all but f, h, i, p, and r and has seven readings of its own.
[24] Bede, Historia ecclesiastica, I, 27, ed. Charles Plummer (Oxford, 1896) I, 48–9, and Gregory I, Registrum epistolarum, ed. P. Ewald and L. M. Hartmann (Monumenta Germaniae historica: Epistolae, 1; Berlin, 1887–99) II, 333–4: Mos apostolicae sedis ... reparandis. and Si quando sunt ... sunt vobis.
[25] Suso Brechter, Die Quellen zur Angelsachsenmission Gregors des Großen (Beiträge zur Geschichte des alten Mönchtums und des Benediktinerordens, 22; Münster in Westf., 1941); Margaret Deanesly and Paul Grosjean, The Canterbury Edition of the Answers of Pope Gregory I to St. Augustine, in: Journal of Ecclesiastical History, X (1959) 1–49; Paul Meyvaert, Les "Responsiones" de S. Grégoire le Grand à S. Augustin de Cantorbéry, in: Revue d'histoire ecclésiastique, LIV (1959) 879–94; and Margaret

separate decretals by Gratian and other canonists[26]; but here they are run together and followed, with no indication that the source has changed, by an additional passage (Neque enim . . . distribuunt.) that is certainly not by Gregory. It resembles most closely certain passages relating to monastic freedom from tithes in various bulls issued by Pope Paschal II at the beginning of the twelfth century[27]. The first sentence (Neque . . . debeant.) expresses a similar idea to the famous decretal *Novum genus*[28], and the final sentence (Etenim . . . distribuunt.) is almost identical to one in the privilege granted by Paschal to St Vanne in 1114[29]. Paschal appears to have been the first authority, furthermore, to apply Gregory's *Libellus* to the subject of monastic payment of tithes and cited it in several bulls as evidence that those living a common life and giving all they can spare to charity should not be required to pay tithes[30]. The text in Clm 27129 was therefore almost certainly composed after 1100. It may have been pieced together out of fragments. I am inclined to believe, however, that it was taken *en bloc* from a lost bull by Paschal, or perhaps by a later pope, and was then presented as a decree entirely by Gregory the Great.

The two decrees numbered four and five are found under the names of various authorities, often with a third similar decree, in several canonical collections of the second half of the twelfth century. They appear under the names of Gregory and John respectively, for instance, in the influential *Breviarium extravagantium* (the so-called First Compilation) composed by Bernard of Pavia between 1188 and 1192[31]. They probably originated during the pontificates of Hadrian IV or Alexander III and were designed to defend the claims of monks to receive but not to pay

---

Deanesly, The Capitular Text of the Responsiones of Pope Gregory I to St. Augustine, in: Journal of Ecclesiastical History, XII (1961) 231–4. To summarize very briefly their conclusions, B r e c h t e r maintained that the Libellus was a forgery composed in 731; D e a n e s l y and G r o s j e a n argued that it was a composite document with some Gregorian and some later elements; M e y v a e r t stressed that a great deal of work needs to be done on the history of the text before the question of its authenticity can be settled. These scholars are agreed that it was composed before it was used by Bede. From the point of view of a writer in the twelfth century, therefore, it was an authentically ancient document. Specifically on Responsio I, from which the texts in Clm 27129 were taken, see B r e c h t e r, Quellen, pp. 65–8, and D e a n e s l y and G r o s j e a n, in Journal of Ecc. Hist., X, 39–40, who defended its Gregorian character.

[26] 1) Mos . . . reparandis = I v o, Panormia, II, 8, in PL, CLXI, 1084–5, and G r a t i a n, Decretum, C. XII, q. 2, c. 30, in ed. cit., col. 697 (and after n. 378 for other canonical collections containing this canon); 2) Si . . . uobis = part of G r a t i a n, Decretum, C. XII, q. 1, c. 8, in ed. cit., col. 679 (and after n. 95 for another collection).

[27] See C o n s t a b l e, Monastic Tithes, pp. 229–33.

[28] JL 6605 (with references to its use in canonical collections); PL, CLXIII, 437.

[29] Acta pontificum Romanorum inedita, ed. J. v o n P f l u g k - H a r t t u n g (Tübingen-Stuttgart, 1880–8) I, 108, no. 123: Nec enim ratio exigit, nec sanctorum canonum auctoritas sanxit, ut ab eis decimae vel primitiae exigantur, qui in piis operibus universa distribuunt.

[30] See the privilege for Montmajour in Epistolae pontificum Romanorum ineditae, ed. S. L ö w e n f e l d (Leipzig, 1885) pp. 75–6, no. 152, from which was taken the famous decretal Decimas a populo (JL 6443; PL, CLXIII, 437), and the letter to the bishop of Noyon-Tournai in Acta pont. Rom. inedita, I, 101, no. 113. Cf. C o n s t a b l e, Monastic Tithes, p. 231.

[31] Comp. I, III, 26, 14 and 21, in Quinque compilationes antiquae, ed. E m i l F r i e d - b e r g (Leipzig, 1882) pp. 36–7. Cf. C o n s t a b l e, Monastic Tithes, pp. 304–5, where the origins of these canons and the collections in which they are found are briefly discussed.

tithes. The presence.in the version printed here of the final sentence of the fourth decree (Unde . . . patiuntur.), which does not appear in the printed text of the First Compilation, suggests that it may have been taken from an authentic papal letter to a bishop, possibly by Eugene III, under whose name it is sometimes found. It may therefore be that only the attributions of these decrees are forged.

The sixth decree is the only one of which both the text and the attribution are reasonably certain. It is derived from Gregory the Great's letter to Patriarch Marinianus of Ravenna[32], which was apparently adapted at a relatively early date from a specific injunction into a decree of general application. It is found in this form, with minor differences, in the collections of Ivo of Chartres, Gratian, and other canonists[33]. Of the six decrees cited in Clm 27129, however, this is the least applicable to the subject of monastic performance of pastoral work and possession of clerical revenues. The fact therefore remains that the five relevant decrees, although attributed to early popes, were all not much more than a century old at the time *Hortatur nos* was written.

The treatise and canonical texts are printed here exactly as they appear in Clm 27129, ff. 114r–116v, except for 1) the expansion of abbreviations, including numerals, 2) the capitalization of proper names, and 3) the substitution of commas, semi-colons, colons, and periods for the punctuation (. and :) of the manuscript. Peculiarities of spelling have been preserved, including the use of h after z and of c for t, occasional doubling of letters, unassimilated prefixes (especially con-), and the division of a few words that in classical usage are normally written as one (et si, nec non, etc.)[34].

[114 r] *Ratio quod liceat monachis predicare, baptizhare,*
et penitentiam iniungere.

Hortatur nos beatus Petrus apostolus, *paratos nos esse semper ad satisfactionem omni poscenti nos rationem de ea spe quae in nobis est, ut hi qui detrahunt nobis confundantur*[1]. Apostolico igitur exemplo atque precepto, his qui uitam nomenque monachorum non simplici oculo aspiciunt[2], eosque sacerdotalis officii indignos dicunt, eo quod mundo mortui sunt et deo uiuunt, pro posse nostro satisfacere litterulis nostris parati sumus, rationeque atque exemplis et dictis sanctorum patrum speramus affirmare, nulli magis dictum, *quae habitas in ortis amici ausculta, fac me audire uocem tuam*[3], et qui audit dicat ueni, quam illi qui mundo mortuus est, idem ᵃ seculi actibus, a uitiis scilicet et concupiscentiis remotus ᵇ, cum Maria sedens secus pedes domini, sedulo uerbum illius audit. Omnis igitur lex diuina, omnis religio christiana, constat aut precepto, aut consilio. Precepto, ut est illud: *Non concupisces, non occides*[4]. Consilio, ut illud: *Si uis perfectus esse, uade et uende omnia que habes*, et caetera[5]. Precepta nobis sunt in necessitudine, consilia in deliberatione. Si deliberamus, si subire proponimus, ipsa deliberatio uertitur nobis in necessitudinem. Nullus excipitur; omnibus dicitur: *Si uis ad uitam ingredi, serua mandata*[6]. Et si uouemus, reddere debemus[7]. Sunt etiam quedam bona ob humanae uitae gratiam concessa. Concessa dico, non precepta. Ex his

---

[32] Gregory, Ep. VIII, 17, in ed. cit., II, 19; JE 1504.

[33] Ivo, Decretum, VII, 11, in PL, CLXI, 547, and Gratian, Decretum, C. XVIII, q. 2, c. 5, in ed. cit., col. 830.

[34] I am indebted to my friend and student Mrs Eleanor Commo McLaughlin for verifying the text, which was prepared from photostats, from the manuscript.

a. a *add.* MS   b. remotos MS

[1] I Peter 3.15–16   [2] Matt. 6.22; Luc. 11.34   [3] Cant. 8.13
[4] Exod. 20.17,13   [5] Matt. 19.21   [6] Matt. 19.17   [7] Deut. 23,21

quedam quibusdam licent, quibusdam non licent. Licent enim laicis, quae non licent clericis. Et licent clericis, quae non licent monachis. Sed hoc de concessis bonis, uel etiam consultis dicimus, non de preceptis bonis. Omni enim sexui, omni professioni dicitur: Serva mandata. Verbi gratia: Licet laicis legittimum conubium, clericis et laicis non licet. Et hoc est laicis concessum, non preceptum. Item licet clericis rebus familiaribus uti, carnibus uesci, monachis uero interdum non licet, quia ut beatus Gregorius in libro pastorali ait, qui *maius bonum subire proposuit, minus bonum* sibi *illicitum fecit*[8]. Sed et hoc de concessis bonis est dictum. In toto ueteri nouoque testamento duas uitas tantummodo inuenimus, Liam et Rachel, Martham et Mariam, idem actiuam et contemplatiuam. Actiuam perfecte habere possumus, et debemus, contemplatiuam uero uix, *nunc per speculum et in enigmatae* uidemus[9], et si multum conamur, quasi raptim furtimque ad momentum uix attingere quid interdum ex minima eius parte ualemus. De actiua redire non licet, de contemplatiua licet, teste propheta qui de quatuor animalibus loquens dicit: *Non reuertebantur cum* [114 v] *incederent, et animalia ibant et reuertebantur*[10]. Hae duae uitae uno precepto implentur. *Plenitudo* enim *legis est dilectio*[11]. Haec diuiditur in duo: in dei scilicet dilectionem et proximi. Has dilectiones quidam sapiens duas pennas uocat, quibus quisque fidelis ad caelum est uolaturus, et qui una harum carebit, in terra pro ludibrio demonum remanebit[12]. Haec proposuimus contra eos ut diximus, qui non sincere monachorum uitam emulantes dicunt ipsos ab omni actione remotos solae contemplationi debere semper esse intentos, et ob hoc sacerdotalis officii indignos. His igitur quid conuenientius obicimus, quam illud dominicum de Phariseis dictum, *alligant onera grauia et importabilia, digito autem suo nolunt ea mouere?*[13] Nam si saltem digito tetigissent, nulli tam graue onus imposuissent. Patet ergo ipsos uim contemplationis prorsus ignorare. Legant igitur moralia, legant omelias super Ezhechielem, et quod in factis suis non agnoscunt, in dictis beati Gregorii agnoscant[14], nec quidem posse una hora integrum esse, quod ipsi astruunt debere semper esse. A secularibus negotiis fatemur monachum debere esse remotum, quod certissime scimus etiam debere et clericum. Dicit enim beatus Iheronimus in quedam aepistola: Clericum negotiis secularibus deditum, fuge quasi uenenum[15]. Et si monachi sacerdotalis officii sunt indigni, abiciendi sunt Iheronimus, Martinus, Hylarius, Gregorius, Augustinus doctor Anglorum aliique quam plurimi doctores sanctissimi. Monachos dicitis debere heremitas esse. Fatemur. Scimus Helyam fuisse heremitam. Si heremita Helyas, utique monachus Helyas. Helyas igitur heremita, Helyas monachus, predicabat, reges arguebat, prophetas Balaam interficiebat. Iohannem baptistam, quis negat fuisse heremitam? Si heremita, utique monachus Iohannes. Iohannes igitur monachus predicauit, baptizhauit, penitentiam dedit. Dicitis uero: Clericorum istud est officium. Verum hoc esse fatemur. Sed omnis sacerdos est clericus, et si non omnis clericus sacerdos. Quid enim sunt monachi, si non sunt de sorte domini? Sed dicitis: Quomodo predicabunt nisi mittantur? Verum dicitis. Sed omnis sacerdos est missus. *Labia enim sacerdotis custodiunt scientiam, et legem requirunt ex ore eius, quia angelus domini exercituum est*[16]. Si angelus, utique est missus. Mittitur igitur sacerdos dum unguitur, mittitur dum ordinatur. *Spiritus domini super me eo quod unxerit me*[17], ad *euangelizhandum pauperibus misit me*[18]. Igitur si omnis sacerdos angelus, monachus sacerdos utique archangelus. Nullus excipitur; omnibus quibus homo nobilis pecuniam suam commisit imperatur: *Negotiamini dum uenio*[19]. Et qui audit

---

[8] G r e g o r y, Reg. past., III, 27 (Sancti Gregorii...opera omnia [Paris, 1705] II, 81 D). This was a favorite text among monastic reformers in the twelfth century: cf. B e r n a r d o f C l a i r v a u x, ep. 94 (Sancti Bernardi ... opera omnia [Paris, 1839] I. 1, 268).
[9] I C o r. 13. 12   [10] E z e c. 1. 9, 14   [11] R o m. 13. 10
[12] Cf. A u g u s t i n e, Enar. in psal. CIII, I, 13 (S. Aur. Augustini ... opera omnia [Paris, 1836-8] IV, 1625 CD): "Quisquis dilexerit Deum et proximum, animam habet pennatam, liberis alis, sancto amore volantem ad Dominum." There are also other Augustinian elements in this text. See, for instance, De civ. Dei, XVIII, 18 (ed. cit., VII, 799) on the "ludificatio daemonum".   [13] M a t t. 23. 4
[14] Cf. G r e g o r y, Moralia, X, 31 (ed. cit., I, 353 DE), commenting on Ezec. 1. 9 and 14.
[15] J e r o m e, ep. LII, 5 (ed. I. Hilberg, in Corpus scriptorum ecc. lat., LIV, 422): "Negotiatorem clericum et ex inope divitem et ex ignobili gloriosum quasi quandam pestem fuge."
[16] Mal. 2. 7   [17] Isai. 61. 1   [18] L u c. 4. 18   [19] L u c. 19. 13

dicat ueni. Sacerdotes igitur monachos qui amore dei a bonis concessis et licitis se abstinent, [115 r] ut tanto facilius prohibita et illicita deuitare possint, manifestum est deo esse tanto uiciniores quanto a mundialibus illecebris sunt remotiores, et quantum deo uiciniores, intantum omnis diuini officii esse digniores. Predicare, baptizhare, penitentiam dare, quis negat diuinum esse officium ac spiritalem? Si ipsi qui *in caelum posuerunt*[c] *os suum et* quorum *linguâ transiuit in terra*[20] ex inferis redissent, numquam ausi essent dicere, spiritalia spiritalibus non licere. *Si uiuimus* inquit apostolus *spiritu, spiritu et ambulemus*[21]. Quid est spiritu ambulemus, nisi spiritalia opera agamus? Item apostolus: *spiritalis diiudicat omnia, ipse autem a nemine iudicatur*[22]. Audiuimus etiam aliquos dixisse: Grandis preuaricatio est regulae Benedicti, quod monachi soluunt silentium in nocte, causa uisitationis infirmorum, uel baptismi. Item aliqui: Inconueniens est monachum uisitare infirmum, et omnino contra illius propositum. Pro dolor, regulam proponit, qui nec regulam legit, nec forsitan uidit. Verum quidem fatebimur esse uirtutem silentii Benedictum nobis commendasse omni tempore maxime in nocte. Sed uir sanctus matris uirtutum plenus[23], ubi precipit *ut post completorium nemo loquatur,* dat licentiam loquendi causa hospitum et si cui *abbas aliquid iusserit*[24]. Ergo non est preuaricatio regulae, si cum precepto monachus per ministerium baptismi, seu per inpositionem penitentiae etiam in nocte animam aufert diabolo, et conmendat deo. Dicant precor, quomodo inconueniens sit preceptis dei obedire. *Visitare infirmum*[25], dei esse preceptum. Si preceptum est, utique omnibus preceptum est. Sed si inconueniens est, erubescendum est. Si erubescendum est, ubi queso illud est, *qui me erubuerit et meos sermones*[26], et cetera? Quiquis menbrum Christi est, contrarium Christo non est. Benedictus menbrum Christi est, consentiens ipsi est, non contrarius. In primordio institutionum suarum dilectionem dei et proximi nobis commendat, de inde per ordinem precepta ueteris ac nouae legis inculcat, inter quae iubet monachum mortuos sepelire, infirmos uisitare, et in omnibus preceptis dei obedire[27]. Desinant igitur desinant regulam proponere qui secundum regulam nolunt uiuere, desistant talia monachis obicere quae certissime constant non esse uerba religionis, sed uerba tenebrosae cupidinis, quia ab initio processere magis ardore cumulandorum manipulorum ac nummorum, quam amore lucrandarum animarum. Haec et talia dicta contra monachos iam uenisse ex inuidia testantur subscripta sanctorum patrum decreta.

[1] *Ex decreto beati Bonifacii papae.*

Sunt non nulli stulti dogmatis, magis zhelo amaritudinis quam dilectionis inflammati, asserentes monachos, [115 v] quia[a] mundo mortui sunt et deo uiuunt, sacerdotali officio indignos, neque penitentiam, aut christianitatem, seu absolutionem, largiri posse per sacerdotalis officii iniunctam gratiam, sed omnino falluntur. Nam si ex hac causa ueteres emuli uera predicarent, apostolicae sedis compar beatus Gregorius monachico cultu[b] pollens, ad summum apicem nullatenus conscenderet[c], cui soluendi ligandique potestas concessa est. Augustinus quoque eiusdem[d] Gregorii discipulus, Anglorum predicator egregius, et Pannoniensis Martinus aliique quam plurimi uiri sanctissimi preciosorum[e] monachorum habitu fulgentes, nequaquam anulo pontificali subarrarentur[f]. Neque enim Benedictus monachorum

---

          u
  c. posuerint MS
[20] Ps. 72. 9   [21] Galat. 5. 25   [22] I Cor. 2. 15
[23] Cf. Gregory, Dial., II, 8 (ed. U. Moricca, in Fonti per la storia d'Italia, LVII, 93).
[24] Benedict, Reg., XLII
[25] Ecli. 7. 39   [26] Luc. 9. 26   [27] Benedict. Reg., IV
  [Ad decretum 1: M1 = Mansi, Concilia, X, 506–8; M2 = Mansi, Concilia, XX, 934]
  a. qui M2
  b. habitu M2   e. pretioso M2
  c. conscenderent MS; conscenderit M1   f. subtraherentur M1,
  d. sanctissimi *add.* M1 M2   subarrharentur M2

preceptor ᵍ, huius rei aliquando ʰ fuit interdictor, sed eos secularium negotiorum dixit experces esse debere. Quod idem ⁱ apostolicis documentis a ʲ sanctorum patrum ᵏ institutis non solum monachis ˡ, uerum etiam ᵐ canonicis summopere imperatur. Vtrisque enim perspicatibus sanctorum patrum exemplis, ut mundo mortui sint precipitur. Credimus igitur a sacerdotibus monachis ligandi soluendique officium ⁿ digne ᵒ contigerit eos hoc ministerio sublimari. Quod euidenter affirmat, quisquis statum monachorum et habitum considerat. Angelus enim grece, latinae nuntius dicitur. Sacerdotes igitur monachi atque canonici, qui dei precepta annuntiant, angeli uocantur. Sed unusquisque angelicus ordo, quanto uicinius deum ᵖ contemplatur ᑫ, tanto sublimius dignitate firmatur ʳ. Numquid ut cherubim non monachi, sex alis uelantur? Due in capitio quo caput tegitur, ueris assertionibus demonstrat ˢ. Illud uero quod brachiis extenditur, alas duas esse dicimus ᵗ; illud quo corpus absconditur ᵘ, alas duas. Sic sex alarum numerus certissimae conficitur. Decertantes igitur contra monachos in hac re sacerdotalis potentiae arcere ᵛ precipimus officio, ut ab huiuscemodi nefandis ausibus in posterum reprimantur, quia quanto quisque excelsior, tanto potentior.

[2] *Ex decreto* ᵃ *beati Gregorii papae.*

Episcopus debet missam celebrare in ordinatione presbiteri ᵇ, et abbas in consecratione ᶜ monachi et quatuor orationes ᵈ super caput eius dicere, ut, sicut per quatuor euangelia docetur, ita per quatuor orationes consecretur, et ita usque in tercium diem uelatum habeat caput ᵉ cum summo silentio et debita ᶠ reuerentia, figuram gerens ᵍ dominicae passionis. Die tercia ʰ tollat ⁱ capicium de capite eius, ut deposita tristicia ueteris peccati ʲ, reuelata facie gloriam domini speculetur ᵏ. Secundo ergo ˡ baptizhatus est, et emundatus ab omnibus peccatis ᵐ. Vnde oportet eum habere maiorem sollicitudinem, et ⁿ pro peccatis hominum orare, et plus ualere eorum peccata soluere quam presbiteri seculares, quia hi secundum regulam apostolorum uiuunt et eorum sequentes uestigia, [116r] conmunem uitam ducunt ᵒ. Ideo nobis uidetur his qui sua pro deo relinquunt, et a passione et morte eius sumunt exordia ᵖ conuersationis ᑫ, dignius liceat baptizhare, communionem dare, confessionem audire ʳ, penitentiam imponere ˢ, peccata soluere. Sicut enim martyres laudant dominum purae in regione uiuorum,

g. sanctissimus *add.* M2
h. aliquo modo *pro* aliquando M1 M2
i. quidem M1 M2
j. et M1 M2
k. patrum *om.* M2
l. uniuersis M1
m. etiam *om.* M2
n. potestatem M2
o. administrari, si tamen digne *add.* M1 M2
p. Dominum M1
q. contemplantur M1
r. firmantur M1
s. demonstrantur M1 M2
t. et *add.* M1 M2
u. conditur M1, tegitur M2
v. arceri M2
[Ad decretum 2: variants from Châlons-sur-Marne 32 as printed in Studien u. Mitt. OSB, LV, 25–6]
a. decretis
b. similiter *add.*
c. ordinatione
d. iuxta numerum quattuor evangeliorum *add.*

e. caput velatum debet habere *pro* velatum ... caput
f. Deo *add.*
g. gestans dierum *pro* gerens
h. tertio
i. abbas *add.*
j. quasi resuscitatus iuxta apostolum *add.*
k. et quasi diem resurrectionis agens *add.*
l. ergo *om.*
m. a cunctis prioris vitae peccatis emundatus iuxta sententiam sanctorum patrum *pro* emundatus ... peccatis
n. et *om.*
o. iuxta quod in actibus apostolorum eorumdem scriptum est: Erat illis cor unum et anima una et erant illis omnia communia et.diuidebatur singulis prout cuique opus erat *add.*
p. mutatae *add.*
q. ut conresuscitati cum illo *add.*
r. confessionem audire *om.*
s. necnon et *add.*

ita et monachi qui die ac nocte psallunt deo debent eandem puritatem habere martyrum. Si quidem ipsi martyres sunt. Quod enim faciunt angeli in caelis, hoc monachi faciunt in terris t. Tribus diebus sunt u in silentio v iuxta apostolos, qui ob metum Iudeorum w in conclaui residebant, usque dum tercio die dominus resurgens dixit x illis: Pax uobis y. Sic abbas pacem det z monacho aa, et capitium bb de capite eius auferat cc. Censemus igitur dd monachum ee, baptizhare, predicare, communionem dare, penitentes soluere ff, iuxta constituta gg .ccc.xviii.hh patrum.

[3] *Gregorius papa Augustino Cantuariensi episcopo.*

Mos apostolicae sedis est ordinatis episcopis precepta tradere, quia de stipendiis uel de his quae fidelium oblationibus accedunt altario, quatuor debent fieri portiones, inde una horum episcopo et familiae, propter hospitalitatem atque susceptionem, alia clero, tercia pauperibus, quarta aecclesiis reparandis. Si quando sunt clerici extra sacros ordines constituti, qui se continere non possunt, sortiri uxores debent, et stipendia sua exterius accipere, qui etiam sub aecclesiastica regula sunt tenendi, bonis operibus uiuant, et canendis psalmis inuigilent, et ab omnibus illicitis abstineant, suamque linguam et corpus deo adiutore conseruent. Communi autem uita uiuentibus iam de faciendis portionibus, et exhibenda hospitalitate, et adimplenda misericordia, nobis quid erit loquendum, cum omne quod superest in causis piis ac religiosis erogandum est, domino magistro omnium docente, *quod superest date elemosinam, et omnia munda sunt uobis*[1]. Neque enim ipsi ab aliis sacramenta aecclesiastica suscipiunt, quibus laborum suorum mercedem rependere debeant. Indignum quippe est, rationi iusticiae contrarium, ut ab eis decimae exigantur, quorum totus labor et tota substantia, et aecclesiae prouectio et pauperum sustentatio est. Etenim nec ratio exigit, nec sanctorum canonum auctoritas sanxit, ut ab eis decimae uel primiciae exigantur, qui piis operibus uniuersa distribuunt.

[4] *Decretum beati Bonifacii papae, ne a monachis decimae exigantur.*

Statuimus secundum priorum diffinitionem, ut monasteria nullomodo ex suis prediis cogantur ab episcopis decimas dare, quia si legitimae dandae non sunt nisi orphanis et peregrinis, indignum ualde est ut ab eis exigantur, qui propter eum cuius decimae sunt pauperes efficiuntur. Nam si pauperes sunt domini hereditas, eius hereditas pauperibus est [116 v] eroganda, et illis uidelicet qui pro eius amore cuncta quae possidere poterant amittunt, eumque nudi sequentes potestati alterius se in monasterio subdunt. Vnde ammonere te uolumus, ut nullam molestiam a te frater karissime patiantur.

---

t. Unde considerare nos oportet quantae virtutis apud Deum sint qui saeculum relinquentes Domini praecepto obediunt dicentis: Relinque omnia quae habes et veni, sequere me. Et *pro* Sicut...terris.
u. sit (ŝt MS)
v. in initio ordinationis suae *add.*
w. post passionem Domini *add*
x. diceret
y. Et *add.*
z. debet dare *pro* det
aa. et communicare *add.*
bb. quod verecundiam significat vel metum penitentiae *add.*
cc. auferre. Unde *pro* auferat
dd. igitur *om.*
ee. eos qui apostolorum figuram tenent *pro* monachum
ff. suscipere
gg. constitutum
hh. trecentorum decem et octo

[1] Luc. 11. 41

The Treatise "Hortatur nos"

[5] De eodem.

Certam habemus predecessorum nostrorum constitutionem et regulam, nichil in hoc mundo habentibus decimas et oblationes mortuorum et uiuorum conuenire, qui spontaneam paupertatem eligentes, nichil in hoc mundo habere uolunt in quibus Christus alitur, uestitur, et pascitur.

[6] Item: Ne liceat episcopis res monasteriorum minuere uel auferre.

Priuilegium monasteriorum regularium a sancto papa Gregorio urbis Romae in generali synodo dictatum, nec non sub anathematis interpositione perpetualiter firmatum.

Quam sit necessarium monasteriorum quieti prospicere, et de eorum perpetua securitate tractare, ante actum nos officium quod in regimine cenobii exhibuimus informat. Et ideo quia in plurimis monasteriis multa a presulibus preiudicia atque grauamina ᵃ pertulisse cognouimus, oportet ut nostrae fraternitatis prouisio de futura eorum quiete salubri disponat ordinatione quatenus conuersantes in illis in dei seruitio gratia ipsius suffragante mente libera perseuerent. Sed ne ex ea que magis emendanda est consuetudine quisquam monachis molestiae presumat inferre, necesse est ut haec quae inferius enumerare curauimus, ita studio fraternitatis episcoporum debeant custodiri, ut ex eis non possit ulterius inferendo inquietudinis occasio reperiri. Interdicimus igitur in nomine domini nostri Ihesu Christi, et ex auctoritate beati Petri apostolorum principis prohibemus, cuius uice huic sanctae aecclesiae Romane presidemus auctore deo, ut nullus episcoporum ultra presumat de reditibus, rebus, uel cartis monasteriorum, uel de cellis, uel uillis, quae ad ea pertinent, quocumque modo, qualibet exquisitione, minuere, uel inmissiones aliquas facere, sed si qua causa forte inter terram uenientem ad partem suarum aecclesiarum et monasteriorum euenerit, et pacifice non potuerit ordinari apud electos abbates, et suos patres timentes deum sine uoluntaria dilatione mediis sacrosanctis euangeliis finiantur.

---

a. grauaminᵉ MS

X

THE SECOND CRUSADE AS SEEN BY CONTEMPORARIES

I. Introduction[1]

The years between 1146 and 1148 were signalized in the annals and chronicles of Medieval Europe by Christian campaigns on all fronts against the surrounding pagans and Moslems.[2] The most important of these was directed towards the Holy Land, against the Moslems, who had recently seized Edessa. It consisted of no less than five expeditions. The two largest armies, commanded by the Emperor[3] Conrad III and King Louis VII of France, followed the same route overland across the Balkans to Constantinople; both met with crushing defeats in Asia Minor and finally reached the Holy Land, as best they could, by land and sea. A third force, under Amadeus III of Savoy, moved down Italy, crossed from Brindisi to Durazzo, and joined the army

---

[1] A bibliography of the Second Crusade will appear as a part of the chapter by Virginia Berry in the forthcoming co-operative History of the Crusades. In spite of its age, the most complete account is still that of Bernhard Kugler, *Studien zur Geschichte des zweiten Kreuzzuges* (Stuttgart 1866); but for the German aspects of the crusade, that of Wilhelm Bernhardi, *Konrad III.* (Jahrbücher der deutschen Geschichte; 2 vols. paged consecutively, Leipzig 1883) 512-684, is fuller and more accurate. The best narrative in English is that of Steven Runciman in the second volume of his *A History of the Crusades* (Cambridge 1952) 247-88. In addition to the abbreviations listed at the front of this volume, the following will be used: Ann. for *Annales*; Bern. for *Sancti Bernardi ... Opera Omnia* I (PL 182; Paris 1859); Chron. for *Chronicon* or *Chronica*; MGH SS for *Monumenta Germaniae Historica, Scriptores (rerum Germanicarum)* (Hannover 1826ff.); MGH SS. r. G. for *Scriptores rerum Germanicarum in usum scholarum ex Monumentis Germaniae historicis separatim editi* (Hannover 1840ff.); PU for the *Papsturkunden* volumes in the series published by the 'Gesellschaft der Wissenschaften zu Göttingen'; RHGF for the *Recueil des Historiens des Gaules et de la France* (ed. Martin Bouquet; new. ed. by Léopold Delisle; Paris 1869ff.). For his encouragement and assistance in the preparation of this article I am especially grateful to Professor Robert L. Wolff of Harvard University. I am also indebted for many valuable suggestions to Mrs. Virginia Berry, of Winnipeg, and to Professors Helen M. Cam and Herbert Bloch of Harvard.

[2] For all references on the campaigns mentioned in this introduction, see individual discussions below. The twelfth-century sources draw no clear line between the Moslems and the heathens: they were both *pagani*. The heathen Slavs were even, on occasion, referred to as *Saraceni*, see PL 180.1385 (JL 9325) and Vincent of Prague, *Ann. seu Chron. Boemorum*, MGH SS 17.664.

[3] Conrad III is known only by courtesy as Holy Roman Emperor, since he was never crowned as such. The Popes always referred to him as 'King.' Alfonso VII of Castile (see below) was both crowned and recognized by the Papacy as King of Kings and was commonly called 'Emperor' by contemporaries: on the imperial title in Spain, see Percy Schramm, 'Das kastilische Königtum und Kaisertum während der Reconquista,' *Festschrift für Gerhard Ritter* (Tübingen 1950) 90f.

of Louis at Constantinople late in 1147. In August of the same year a naval expedition led by Alfonso of Toulouse left the South of France and arrived in Palestine probably in the spring of 1148. At the same time, a joint Anglo-Flemish naval force sailed along the north coast of Europe, assisted the King of Portugal in the capture of Lisbon, proceeded around the peninsula early in 1148, attacked Faro, and presumably reached the Holy Land later that year. Meanwhile, in the northeast, four armies co-operated in a campaign against the pagan Wends across the river Elbe: a Danish army joined the Saxons under Henry the Lion and Archbishop Adalbero of Bremen in an attack on Dubin; another, larger, army led by Albert the Bear of Brandenburg and many other temporal and spiritual lords advanced against Demmin and Stettin; a fourth expedition, finally, under a brother of the Duke of Poland attacked from the southeast. In 1148, on the south shore of the Mediterranean, a powerful fleet under George of Antioch extended the control of Roger II of Sicily over the entire littoral from Tripoli to Tunis. In the West, four campaigns were directed against the crumbling power of the Almoravides. The Genoese in 1146 sacked Minorca and besieged Almeria. During the following year, the Emperor Alfonso VII of Castile advanced south through Andalusia and captured Almeria with the aid of a strong Genoese fleet, which in 1148 sailed north and joined the Count of Barcelona in his campaign against Tortosa. In the previous year, Alfonso Henriques of Portugal had captured Santarem and secured the assistance of the Anglo-Flemish fleet for an attack on Lisbon, which fell late in 1147.

The magnitude and scope of these campaigns was without precedent in the early Middle Ages. Their permanent result was, however, inconsiderable. Ten years later, only Lisbon and Tortosa remained in Christian hands as the substantial gains of those tremendous efforts, which elsewhere met with miserable defeat or but ephemeral success. They raise, nevertheless, many interesting problems for the historian of the Middle Ages and of the crusades in particular. Were these campaigns interrelated? By what were they moved and how were they organized? Such questions provoke an inquiry into the attitude of contemporaries towards the expeditions and the reaction to, and explanation of, the incredible lack of Christian success. Finally, the whole subject has a bearing on the definition and development of crusading theory.

The answers to these problems must be sought in the contemporary western sources: contemporary, because later writers saw and interpreted the events in a different light; western, because these alone reveal the Latin point of view.[4] The evidence found in such material, however, leaves much to be

---

[4] I shall not consider here either William of Tyre, who was thoroughly non-Western in his attitude and also not fully contemporary, or the Greek historians Cinnamus and Nicetas, on whom see Kugler (n. 1 above) 36-43; id., *Neue Analekten zur Geschichte des*

desired. It would be hopeless to expect that in the twelfth, any more than in the twentieth, century contemporary writers could express completely the motives of the men whose actions they describe. Many factors other than those they mention must have played an essential part in the genesis and development of the campaigns of 1146-8. Moreover, like all medieval sources, these must be studied in the light both of the information available to the writer and of 'the sense of responsibility' with which he approached his task.[5]

In neither of these respects are the sources considered in this paper fully satisfactory. The defect is not in their numbers, for the contemporary sources in print must alone add up to well over a hundred. But the events which they record occurred thousands of miles apart, on the outermost edges of Christendom, and it is therefore not surprising that no one writer mentions all these expeditions. Each source was limited by its environment, both in space and in time; their writers could record only what came to their attention and this depended on where and when they lived and wrote and whom and what they saw and heard. They included, moreover, in their works only what they considered worthy or significant; and many, seeing the sad defeats of these Christian armies, agreed with Robert of Torigny that 'almost nothing successful and nothing worthy of mention was done on that expedition.'[6] Many jotted down merely the most outstanding facts, or copied them from a neighbor, with the result that several accounts of the events are virtually identical.[7] Here a seeming relation between the recorded events is evidence not of any connection in the mind of the author but merely of his adherence to strict chronology. Many writers did more than this, however, and their accounts suggest certain answers to the problems raised by a consideration of the campaigns of 1146-8. In accordance with their knowledge and position, from the humblest annalist to the Pope and Emperor, most of these writers found some connecting features in these expeditions. In their attitudes towards the events themselves, their genesis and their failure, may be found some idea of the medieval concept of crusade.[8]

---

zweiten Kreuzzuges (Tübingen 1883) 29-50; and Runciman (n. 1 above) II 475-7. The Gesta Ludovici VII is now believed to have been written after 1274: see Bernhard Kugler, Analecten (sic) zur Geschichte des zweiten Kreuzzuges (Tübingen 1878) 1-13, and Auguste Molinier, Les sources de l'histoire de France II: Époque féodale, les Capétiens jusqu'en 1180 (Paris 1902) 300-1.

[5] V. H. Galbraith, Historical Research in Medieval England (The Creighton Lecture in History, 1949; London 1951) 3-4.

[6] Robert of Torigny (Robertus de Monte), Chronica, in Chronicles of the Reigns of Stephen, etc. IV, ed. Richard Howlett (Rolls Series 82; London 1890) 154.

[7] Bernhardi, op. cit. (n. 1 above) 560 n. 61: 'Es scheint, dass derselbe Bericht über den Kreuzzug an mehrere Klöster versendet wurde.'

[8] In certain respects the approach of this article is paralleled for the First Crusade by

II. Military Scope and Popular Motives

It has long been customary for historians of the Second Crusade to deal with only two expeditions, those headed by Conrad III and Louis VII. Occasionally, also, they devote some attention to the capture of Lisbon and to the campaign across the Elbe. They almost universally omit any mention of the concurrent expeditions to the East of Amadeus of Savoy and Alfonso of Toulouse. Yet both of these involved considerable armies led by powerful princes, were directed towards the Holy Land, and should therefore be considered parts of the Second Crusade in its most restricted definition.[9] The reason for this narrowness in the prevalent modern view of the crusade is easily found in the original sources, where these omissions are no less striking

---

Paul Rousset in *Les origines et les caractères de la première Croisade* (Neuchâtel 1945). In his review of this work in *Speculum* 23 (1948) 328-31, John LaMonte accused Rousset of 'an infatuation with words' (329) and of trying 'to reestablish the old thesis of the crusade as essentially a religious movement, away from which recent research has been steadily moving' (331). 'To assume…,' LaMonte said, 'that because one finds repeated affirmations of the religious motive in contemporary literature religion was the essential cause of the crusade seems to be a rather naïve deduction' (329). While I agree with LaMonte that Rousset tends to neglect political, social, and military factors in the motivation of the crusade, I believe that it is misleading to speak of 'propaganda value' and of 'official clerical accounts' (329) in the Middle Ages, and that to call the early twelfth century 'a period when religiosity was at a premium' and to compare St. Bernard to *Pravda* (329-30) is carrying cynicism too far.

[9] On the expedition of Alfonso of Toulouse, see the *Continuatio Premonstratensis* (Sigeberti), MGH SS 6.454; *Chron. de Nîmes*, in Claude DeVic and Joseph Vaissete, *Histoire générale de Languedoc* (new ed. Toulouse 1872-92) V: Chroniques 5.27-31; Richard of Poitiers, *Chron.* RHGF 12.416: Geoffrey of Vigeois, *Chron.* in Philip Labbé, *Nova Bibliotheca* II (Paris 1657) 306; *Anonymous Chron. ad annum 1160*, RHGF 12.120; Henry of Huntingdon, *Historia Anglorum*, ed. Thomas Arnold (Rolls Series 74: London 1879) 279; *Chron. Turonense*, RHGF 12.473; and among more recent works see Reinhold Röhricht, *Beiträge zur Geschichte der Kreuzzüge* II (Berlin 1878) 94; P. Boissonade, 'Les personnages et les événements de l'histoire d'Allemagne, de France, et d'Espagne dans l'œuvre de Marcabru (1129-50),' *Romania* 48 (1922) 228-9 Runciman II 280; and especially DeVic and Vaissete III 752f. and IV 223-4. On the expedition of Amadeus of Savoy, see Odo of Deuil, *De profectione Ludovici VII in Orientem*, ed. and tr. Virginia Berry (Columbia Records of Civilization 42; New York 1948) 24, 66-8; *Anonymous Chron. ad annum 1160*, RHGF 12.120; *Ann. Mediolanenses minores*, MGH SS 18.393 and among more recent works see Carlo Guarmani, *Gl'Italiani in Terra Santa* (Bologna 1872) 169; C. W. Previté Orton, *The Early History of the House of Savoy* (Cambridge 1912) 309-13. Odo of Deuil refers to Amadeus as the Count of Maurienne, an alternative title of the Counts of Savoy that appears frequently in contemporary sources. *L'art de vérifier des dates* (3rd ed. Paris 1783-7) III 614, and Auguste Molinier, *Vie de Louis le Gros par Suger* (Collection de Textes pour servir à l'étude et à l'enseignement de l'Histoire; Paris 1887) 159 n. 20, err in calling him Amadeus II of Savoy, as do Mrs. Berry, in Odo of Deuil, *op. cit.* 78 n. 37, and Henri Waquet, in Odo of Deuil, *La Croisade de Louis VII, Roi de France* (Documents relatifs à l'histoire des Croisades 3; Paris 1949, 51 n. 1, in calling him Amadeus II of Maurienne.

than in more recent works. The authors of the most widely-known contemporary accounts accompanied in person the French or German armies and therefore concentrated their attention on these.

It is at once the great advantage and the great danger of an eye-witness source that it records certain events very fully. The author knows his facts, but he seldom knows all the facts, and his point of view is consequently often more limited than that of someone viewing the events from a distance. This applies preeminently to the writers on the Second Crusade. The *De profectione Ludovici VII in Orientem*, by Odo of Deuil,[10] is without question the most important single work on this campaign and at the same time a remarkable historical document. It is an authoritative account of the adventures of the troops under Louis VII until they reached Antioch early in 1148. Odo was an educated and observant author, who, as chaplain to the King, was in an excellent position to gather accurate information. It is, nevertheless, regrettable that he never continued the work beyond the Spring of 1148, and, above all, that he approached his subject from a very narrow viewpoint. Far from being 'an ecclesiastic of real stature,' as he has recently been called,[11] there is no evidence that he was outstanding either for his intellect or for his practical ability. His account of the Second Crusade is frankly devoted to the two aims of praising the King of France and of serving as a guide for future crusaders.[12] He is therefore at all times prone to exculpate the King and to dwell upon the difficulties besetting his soldiers. Odo blamed the failure of the expedition largely on the Greeks and their Emperor Manuel, whose alleged perfidy is almost a secondary theme of this work.[13] He eagerly hoped for revenge and in no way condemned the devastating attacks of the Sicilian fleet in 1147-8 on the Byzantine Empire at Corfu and on the Greek mainland.[14] He does not mention any of the other contemporaneous Christian campaigns.[15] Even the army of Conrad III, which preceded the French

---

[10] There have recently appeared two editions of this work, by Virginia Berry and by Henri Waquet (cited in n. 9 above); these were reviewed in *Speculum*, respectively, by John LaMonte, 23 (1948) 502-4, and Peter Topping, 26 (1951) 385-7.

[11] Topping 386; cf. Waquet (n. 9 above), introduction. It is, on the contrary, perhaps surprising that later, as Abbot of St. Denis, Odo did not play a more prominent part in the political and intellectual life of his time, cf. Berry (n. 9 above), intro. p. xvi.

[12] *Ibid.* xvii.

[13] With unblushing prejudice, Odo even attributes the aid given by the Greeks at Constantinople to their desire to lull the French into a sense of security in order to deceive them later: *ibid.* 68; cf. Richard Hirsch, *Studien zur Geschichte König Ludwigs VII von Frankreich* (Leipzig 1892) 55-6.

[14] Odo of Deuil, ed. Berry 98; cf. 58 and 82.

[15] One cryptic passage says that 'parant naves maritimi cum rege navigio processuri,' *ibid.* 12; but it is not clear whether this refers to the Anglo-Flemish crusaders (as Charles David assumes: *De expugnatione Lyxbonensi* [Columbia Records of Civilization 24; New York 1936] 12), or to the fleet of Alfonso of Toulouse, or to the ships that carried the soldiers of the Count of Savoy from Brindisi to Durazzo.

across the Balkans by a few months, is only casually mentioned, and then, as a rule, in a strongly anti-German tone.

Odo, to do him justice, was not altogether unaware of his own narrow attitude and of the gaps in his information. In several places he makes an effort to present a point of view different from his own; and once, with exceptional perspicuity, he remarks that, 'He who knows a matter partially, judges partially; but he who knows not a case as a whole in unable to make a correct judgment.' [16] It is therefore particularly unfortunate that in spite of its expressly limited purpose Odo's account has been pressed into service by modern writers as if it embraced the history of the entire Second Crusade.[17]

A useful corrective to Odo's attitude in the *De profectione* can be found in the letters of his royal master, Louis VII.[18] The most important of these are three in number, written respectively 'at the Gates of Hungary,' at Constantinople, and at Antioch; and they are all addressed to the Abbot Suger, the king's trusted adviser and regent, to whom he could express himself with complete frankness. Since Suger was critical of the entire undertaking,[19] Louis might have been expected to conceal some of his troubles, though his chronic lack of funds, for which he urgently asks in each letter, might on the other hand have led him to exaggerate his difficulties. His account is in fact remarkably moderate. In spite, he says, of 'many dangers and almost unbearable labors,' [20] he arrived safely at Constantinople, where he was well received by the Emperor Manuel[21] and everything was 'joyful and prosperous with us.' [22] In Asia Minor, however, 'both on account of the fraud of the Emperor and on account of our own guilt, we suffered many hardships.' [23] He tells of the raids of brigands, the difficulties of the terrain, the attacks of the Turks, and the lack of food. But throughout his account of the eventual arrival at Attalia on the south coast of Asia Minor and of the embarkation for Antioch, Louis makes no reference to the Greeks, whereas Odo of Deuil throughout blames the crusaders' misfortunes on the treachery of Manuel. Louis' account, moreover, though very brief, is accurate and specific, and its viewpoint, though limited, is sane and unprejudiced.[24]

---

[16] Odo of Deuil, ed. Berry 72.

[17] Runciman II 478, says, for instance, that 'The history of the Second Crusade is fully treated in the *De Ludovici VII profectione in Orientum* (sic) of Odo de Deuil...'

[18] RHGF 15.487, 488, 495-6; cf. Achille Luchaire, *Études sur les actes de Louis VII* (Paris 1885) nos. 224, 225, 229 (pp. 171-3). It should be remembered that as the King's chaplain, Odo may have seen and even have written Louis' letters.

[19] Bernhardi (n. 1 above) 518.

[20] RHGF 15.488.

[21] *Ibid.* 495-6.

[22] *Ibid.* 488.

[23] *Ibid.* 495-6.

[24] Writing to Manuel in the 1160's, Louis mentioned that 'honor quem nobis in Domino

The same can be said of the three letters written by the Emperor Conrad III to his regent and adviser, Abbot Wibald of Stavelot.[25] The first announces his safe arrival in the lands of the Byzantine Emperor, about July, 1147. The second was written early in 1148 from Constantinople, where Conrad had returned after his disastrous defeat near Dorylaeum in central Anatolia. Of the Emperor Manuel, he says that 'he showed us such honor as, we have heard, was never shown to any of our ancestors.'[26] Soon afterwards Conrad and part of his army went by sea to Palestine, whence he wrote again to Wibald to say that he planned to return in September, 1148, 'when all has been done in that region that God desires or the inhabitants permit.'[27] For, he goes on to explain, the siege of Damascus by the combined French, German, and Jerusalemite armies failed on account of the treason 'of those whom we least feared,' and the crusaders were forced to return 'equally in anger and in grief.' The Germans then proceeded to Ascalon, where, Conrad says, they were 'again cheated by those men.'[28] Just who these traitors were is not clear. Both the Templars and the King of Jerusalem were prominently mentioned.[29] But Conrad certainly attributed the crusaders' failure in Palestine to treachery, and his crushing defeat in Asia Minor to adverse circumstances and the attacks of the Turks, rather than to the hostility of the Greeks.

More important than these letters, both for its factual content and for its concept of the plan and failure of the crusade, is the report given by Bishop Otto of Freising in his *Chronica* and in his *Gesta Friderici primi*.[30] Otto was a personage of high importance, both secular and ecclesiastical: a half-brother of Conrad III and uncle of Frederick Barbarossa, a member of the Cistercian order and a scholar and thinker of exceptional learning, intellectual power, and piety. He was in addition among the leaders of the German army on the Second Crusade[31] and had therefore access to all sorts of in-

peregrinantibus apud vos exhibuistis, Deo auctore, a memoria nostra nunquam excidet,' *Lettres de rois, reines, et autres personnages ... tirées des Archives de Londres par Bréquigny* I, ed. J. J. Champollion-Figeac (Collection de documents inédits sur l'histoire de France; Paris 1839) 1.

[25] *Monumenta Corbeiensia*, ed. Philipp Jaffé (Bibliotheca Rerum Germanicarum 1; Berlin 1864) nos. 48 (p. 126), 78 (p. 152-3), and 144 (p. 225-6).

[26] *Ibid.* 153.

[27] *Ibid.* 225-6.

[28] *Ibid.* 225-6.

[29] See below, 273-4.

[30] Otto of Freising, *Chronica sive historia de duabus civitatibus*, ed. Adolf Hofmeister (MGH SS.r.G; Hannover-Leipzig 1912) and *Gesta Friderici primi imperatoris*, edd. Waitz and von Simson (MGH SS.r.G; 1912). On Otto, see Kugler (n. 1 above) 7-10; Max Manitius, *Geschichte der lateinischen Literatur des Mittelalters* III (ed. P. Lehmann; Munich 1931) 376-88; and Charles Mierow, introduction to Otto of Freising, *The Two Cities* (Records of Civilization 9: New York 1928).

[31] On Otto's part in the crusade, see Kugler (n. 1. above) 158-60, and Eberhard Pfeiffer, 'Die Cistercienser und der zweite Kreuzzug,' *Cistercienser-Chronik* 47 (1935) 107f.

X

formation. But Otto was one of those writers whose high hopes in the crusade
were sadly dashed by its failure, and he could never bring himself to write
a connected account of its disasters.[32] Only in isolated passages does he refer
to the crusade and display his powerful and original point of view.[33] His
first-hand knowledge was indeed no less restricted than that of Odo of Deuil
and concerned primarily the preaching of the crusade by St. Bernard, its
origins in Germany, and the movements of the German army. His *Gesta
Friderici*, moreover, was certainly written for the specific purpose of eulo-
gizing Frederick Barbarossa. But Otto had a broader approach than Odo
and in his works included references to the contemporary expeditions against
the Wends and against Lisbon and Almeria. Above all, he viewed his material
with a breadth of human experience and an integrated point of view altogether at variance with the petty reporting and ready prejudices of Odo
of Deuil.

In Otto's works can be seen something of a wider conception behind the
crusade, of a plan which included not only the expeditions to the Levant,
but also the campaign against the heathen Slavs[34] and perhaps also the expedition which captured Lisbon — which was, he says, 'recently seized
from the Saracens by our men.'[35] This broad concept of the crusade as a
whole required a broad explanation for the failure of the major armies. Otto
does not dwell on the treachery of the Greeks, the hardships of the route,
or the enemy attacks. On the contrary, he integrates this disaster into his
belief in human sinfulness and his attitude of Christian resignation combined
with optimistic trust in God, Whose ways are hidden, but Whose purpose
is always good. Otto never doubts that there is a valid reason for the failure
of this enterprise. 'If our expedition,' he says, 'was not good for the extension
of boundaries or the comfort of our bodies, it was good, however, for the
salvation of many souls.'[36]

---

[32] 'Verum quia peccatis nostris exigentibus, quem finem predicta expeditio sortita
fuerit, omnibus notum est, nos, qui non hac vice tragediam, sed iocundam scribere proposuimus hystoriam, aliis vel alias hoc dicendum relinquimus,' Otto of Freising, *Gesta*, p. 65.

[33] Principally in the *Chronica*, 1.26 (p. 59); 4.18 (p. 207); 5.18 (p. 247); cf. introduction,
xiii; and in the *Gesta*, 1.35-47 (pp. 54-67); 1.62-6 (pp. 88-95); and 2.16 (p. 119).

[34] 'Saxones vero, quia quasdam gentes spurciciis idolorum deditas vicinas habent, ad
orientem proficisci abnuentes cruces itidem easdem gentes bello attemptaturi assumpserunt
a nostris in hoc distantes, quod non simpliciter vestibus assutae, sed a rota subterposita
in altum protendebantur,' *Gesta* p. 61.

[35] '... a nostris nuper Sarracenis ablata est,' *Chronica* 1.26, p. 59. Since these crusaders
were mostly Flemings and Englishmen, and therefore not subjects of Conrad III, the *nostri*
presumably refers to them as brother-crusaders.

[36] *Gesta* 1.65, pp. 91-4. Later in this chapter, he says: 'Quamvis, si dicamus sanctum
illum abbatem (Bernardum) spiritu Dei ad excitandos nos afflatum fuisse, sed nos ob
superbiam lasciviamque nostram salubria mandata non observantes merito rerum perso-

X

The exploits and outcome of the naval expedition that assisted King Alfonso of Portugal at the siege of Lisbon are described by at least two eyewitnesses. Of these the more important is the anonymous author of the *De expugnatione Lyxbonensi*, a crusader, perhaps an Anglo-Norman priest, who wrote probably at Lisbon during the winter of 1147-8.[37] His remarkable and vivid narrative is perhaps the most detailed surviving record of any military expedition in the twelfth century.[38] Although few personal opinions are expressed, it is an entertaining and valuable description of the attitude of a simple crusader. There are in addition three letters written by participants in this expedition, which may be grouped together as the 'Teutonic Source,' since they present the German and Flemish as against the more English viewpoint of the author of the *De expugnatione*.[39] These two accounts show on the whole a remarkable agreement. Neither, however, clearly states what were the origins of the expedition or whether it was inspired by the preaching of the Second Crusade. Charles David has shown that among these crusaders the motive of personal profit was not unconsidered and that theirs was one of a series of semi-piratical Anglo-Flemish expeditions along the coast of Spain.[40] It appears, furthermore, in the *Annales Elmarenses* that these sailors pillaged the coastal towns and shipping in much the same way as the crusading armies pillaged the countryside.[41] On the other hand, the sources reveal that their aims were not entirely selfish and that this expedition should also be regarded as part of the broader crusading effort. When before the siege the Christians urged the Moslems to give up Lisbon in peace, a spokesman for the city replied that, 'Verily, it is not the want of possessions but ambition of the mind which drives you on... By calling

narumve dispendium reportasse, non sit a rationibus vel antiquis exemplis dissonum..,' *ibid.* 93.

[37] *De exp. Lyx.* (cited n. 15 above). On this crusade, besides the works of Cosack, Röhricht, Bernhardi, Kurth, Herculano, and De Castilho cited by David in his introduction, see H. A. R. Gibb, 'English Crusaders in Portugal,' *Chapters in Anglo-Portuguese Relations*, ed. Edgar Prestage (Watford 1935) 9-16; Alexander Cartellieri, *Der Vorrang des Papsttums zur Zeit der ersten Kreuzzüge 1095-1150* (Weltgeschichte als Machtgeschichte; Munich and Berlin 1941) 370-3; H. V. Livermore, *A History of Portugal* (Cambridge 1947) 74-80; and my own 'Note on the Route of the Anglo-Flemish Crusaders,' *Speculum* 28 (1953) 525-6. I have been unable to locate a copy of the study by A. A. L. Pimenta, *A conquista de Lisboa em 1147* (Lisbon 1937).

[38] Cf. Paul Riant, *Expéditions et pèlerinages des Scandinaves en Terre Sainte* I (Paris 1865) 223, who here also overthrows the old idea that Scandinavians took part in this expedition.

[39] *De exp. Lyx.* intro. p. 49.

[40] *Ibid.* 12-26; Gibb (n. 37 above) 8-9 and 16.

[41] *Ann. Elmarenses*, in *Les Annales de Saint-Pierre de Gand et de Saint-Amand*, ed. Philip Grierson (Commission Royale d'Histoire; Brussels 1937, pp. 74-115) 111.

your ambition zeal for righteousness, you misrepresent vices as virtues.[42] These men felt strongly that the hand of God was with them in their attack on Lisbon. Those who were killed were regarded as miracle-working martyrs.[43] The harangue to the troops, just before the final assault, was made by one of their priests and is an early example of a crusading sermon.[44] The stringent oath that was taken by everyone to preserve the peace and regularly to attend divine service shows the influence of St. Bernard and of the rule written by him for the Templars.[45] This oath, and the establishment of elected officials ('who were called judges and coniurati') to enforce its provisions, mark an important step in the organization of crusading armies.[46] Even more important is the fact that this oath included a vow of pilgrimage to the Holy Land, for, after the crusaders had wintered at Lisbon, Duodechin says, 'then they sailed through many perils and arrived, just as they had sworn, at the sepulchre of the Lord.'[47] On their way they attacked Faro, and some may have joined the siege of Tortosa,[48] but in any case these crusaders regarded their campaigns in Portugal as only a contribution to, or rather a stage in, the fulfilment of their vow against the enemies of Christendom.[49]

[42] 'Non enim vos rerum inopia, sed mentis cogit ambitio ... ambitionem vestram rectitudinis zelum dicentes, pro virtutibus vitia mentimini,' De exp. Lyx. 120-1.

[43] Letter of Duodechin of Lahnstein, MGH SS 17.28. See also the contemporary Indiculum fundationis monasterii sancti Vincentii Ulixbone, in Portugaliae Monumenta Historica, Scriptores I 91-3, whose author, perhaps an eye-witness, says: 'Contemplor barones istos fortissimos de terris suis ad hoc egressos fuisse, et ad hoc venisse ut hic moriantur pro Christo, eius bella bellando, et contra hostes fidei dimicando viriliter.' The church of the cemetery where the English dead were buried was known as Santa Maria dos Mártiros. Many miracles were performed at their tombs. See De exp. Lyx. 132-4 and 134 n. 1; see below, 237-40.

[44] De exp. Lyx. 146-58; see below, 239 and 241. The preacher may himself have been the author of the De exp. Lyx.; see 146 n. 3, and Valmar Cramer, 'Kreuzpredigt und Kreuzzugsgedanke von Bernhard von Clairvaux bis Humbert von Romans,' Das Heilige Land in Vergangenheit und Gegenwart (Palästinahefte des deutschen Vereins vom heiligen Lande, 17-20; ed. V. Cramer and G. Meinertz; Cologne 1939) 60-2.

[45] See Hermann Conrad, 'Gottesfrieden und Heeresverfassung in der Zeit der Kreuzzüge,' Zeitschrift der Savigny-Stiftung für Rechtsgeschichte, Germanistische Abteilung 61 (1941) 98-9, and Peter Rassow, 'Die Kanzlei St. Bernhards von Clairvaux,' Studien und Mitteilungen zur Geschichte des Benediktinerordens und seiner Zweige, Neue Folge 3 (1913) 270.

[46] De exp. Lyx. 56. David suggests (p. 57 n. 5) a possible connection between this oath and the leges pacis in certain municipal charters in Flanders. Cf. Conrad 90-1, 98-9, and 115.

[47] MGH SS 17.28.

[48] See my 'Note' (n. 37 above).

[49] Cf. the same point of view from the Portuguese side in the speech of the Bishop of Porto, De exp. Lyx. 68-84; see below, 246-7 and n. 178, and Cramer (n. 44 above) 55-60. See also the Translatio sancti Vincentii, in Analecta Bollandiana 1 (1882) 270-8, whose author says, '... visum est illis non contra Saracenos Syriae progrediendum, cum illi in Hispania sibi essent in offendiculum,' 273. I can find no justification for Erdmann's

X

This same attitude of participation in a larger undertaking is found in the references of many annalists and chroniclers not only to this expedition against Lisbon but also to many of the other campaigns of 1147-8. Most of these writers were not present at the events they describe, although they may frequently have had access to eye-witness material. Their accounts are seldom factually correct or complete and therefore have been perhaps unduly neglected by some historians. They often consider their subject, however, from a broader point of view and a wider scope of knowledge than do the eye-witnesses.

One of the most interesting of these secondary original sources is the *Chronica Slavorum*, written about 1167/8 in Schleswig-Holstein, by Helmold of Bosau, an important authority on the early history of the Slavs.[50] Helmold discusses the origins of the Second Crusade at some length. 'To the initiators of the expedition, however,' he remarks, 'it seemed (advisable) that one part of the army be devoted to the Eastern regions, another to Spain, and a third against the Slavs who live next to us.'[51] And in the following pages he devotes a chapter to each of these campaigns. Of the capture of Lisbon he says that, 'This alone was successful of the entire work which the pilgrim army achieved.'[52]

It is worth remarking that Helmold speaks here of the 'entire work' and the 'pilgrim army' both in the singular: each of these three campaigns was to him part of a universal enterprise undertaken by a single Christian army.[53]

---

sceptical view of the Portuguese crusades as purely economic and political enterprises into which the natives, in order to further their own selfish ends, tried to draw crusaders destined for the Holy Land: Carl Erdmann, 'Der Kreuzzugsgedanke in Portugal,' *Historische Zeitschrift* 141 (1929-30) 23-53. Cramer 56 n. 21 points out that, 'Erdmann spricht zu Unrecht davon, dass ‹ die Predigt des Bischofs (von Porto) gerade eine Rede zur Abhaltung vom Kreuzzug › sei.' The English, German, and Portuguese sources show that on neither side was the campaign in Portugal ever considered more than a temporary break in the achievement of the ultimate purpose of the crusaders in the Holy Land, although the Bishop emphasized that it is sinful for a Christian to neglect an opportunity to assist a brother and that the campaign in Portugal is in itself a righteous war. As Cramer says, 59: 'Wenn Bischof Peter alsdann den Kampf gegen die Mauren als gleichwertig mit der Jerusalemfahrt hinstellt, so befindet er sich keineswegs im Gegensatz zu den Urhebern der Kreuzzüge.' See below, 258f.

[50] Helmold of Bosau, *Chron. Slavorum*, edd. Lappenberg and Schmeidler (MGH SS.r.G; Hannover-Leipzig 1909). On Helmold and his work, see Manitius, *op. cit.* (n. 30 above) 493-8.

[51] Helmold, *op. cit.* 115.

[52] 'Hoc solum prospere cessit de universo opere, quod peregrinus patrarat exercitus,' *ibid.* 118. Of the Wendish Crusade he says: 'Statim enim postmodum in deterius coaluerunt; nam neque baptisma servaverunt nec cohibuerunt manus a depredatione Danorum,' 123.

[53] This point should be emphasized in opposition to those who consider each of these campaigns as a separate crusade, such as Riant (n. 38 above) 225 n. 1, and A. A. Vasiliev, *History of the Byzantine Empire* (2nd English edition, Madison 1952) 419.

224

This point of view was not uncommon among the German annalists and chroniclers. The Teutonic source on the capture of Lisbon seems to have circulated widely and to have been incorporated, to a greater or lesser degree, into the accounts of the more widely-known expeditions to the Holy Land and against the Slavs. This three-fold concept of the crusade is found in several German chronicles[54] and also, it will be remembered, in the works of Otto of Freising, who had certainly not seen the letters relating to the capture of Lisbon.[55]

Several other writers, who do not mention Lisbon, linked together the Eastern and the so-called Wendish Crusades. Among these is Vincent of Prague, who wrote his important annals not long after 1167.[56] He tells how the crusade was preached in Bohemia and how the members of the ruling family there took the cross with the intention of going to the Holy Land and only at the last minute decided to direct their crusading energies against the Wends.[57] Saxo Grammaticus in his *Gesta Danorum* gives a long description of the campaign of the Danish armies inspired by the crusading bull and sermons.[58] And an anonymous continuator of Sigebert's chronicle records that 'the Dacians, Westphalians, and leaders of the Saxons agreed that, while the others were going to Jerusalem against the Saracens, they would either altogether exterminate the neighboring people of the Slavs or would force them to become Christian.'[59]

This passage emphasizes not only the connection between these campaigns but also the savage spirit that inspired the expeditions against the Wends.[60]

---

[54] *Chron. Montis Sereni*, MGH SS 23.147; *Ann. Palidenses*, MGH SS 16.82-3 (cf. Wilhelm Wattenbach, *Deutschlands Geschichtsquellen im Mittelalter*, 6th ed. Berlin 1893-4; II 435-8); *Ann. Magdeburgenses*, MGH SS 16.188-90 (cf. Wattenbach II 438-9); *Continuatio Gemblacensis* (Sigeberti), MGH SS 6.389-90 (cf. Wattenbach II 162); *Chron. Regia Coloniensis*, ed. Georg Waitz (MGH SS.r.G.; Hannover 1880) 82-6.

[55] See above, 221.

[56] MGH SS 17.654-710; of him Wattenbach II 320 says, 'eine unserer wichtigsten Quellen.'

[57] MGH SS 17.663. The three leading Bohemians in the crusade were Prince Otto of Olmütz and his brothers Svatopluk and Wratislaw, see Bernhardi 569.

[58] Saxo Grammaticus, *Gesta Danorum*, edd. J. Olrik and H. Raeder (Copenhagen 1931) 14.3.5, pp. 376ff.

[59] MGH SS 6.392; cf. the same idea in the *Casus monasterii Petrishusensis*, MGH SS 20.674-5 (composed in 1156: Wattenbach II 391).

[60] On this campaign see Bernhardi 563-78; *Regesten der Markgrafen von Brandenburg* ed. Hermann Krabbo I (Veröffentlichungen des Vereins für Geschichte der Mark Brandenburg; Leipzig 1910) 28-9; George Artler, 'Die Zusammensetzung der deutschen Streitkräfte in den Kämpfen mit den Slaven von Heinrich I. bis auf Friedrich I.,' *Zeitschrift des Vereins für Thüringische Geschichte und Altertumskunde* 29 (Neue Folge 21; 1913) 313-319; Austin Lane Poole, 'Germany, 1125-52,' CMH 5 (Cambridge 1926) 354-6; Margret Bündung, *Das Imperium Christianum und die deutschen Ostkriege vom zehnten bis zum zwölften Jahrhundert* (Historische Studien, ed. E. Ebering 366; Berlin 1940) 35-50; and Cartellieri (n. 37 above) 374-6.

Certain recent historians have maintained that this spirit was altogether secular. They point out that this was but one of about a hundred and seventy-five campaigns conducted by the Germans against their neighbors in the East between 789 and 1157[61] and that it was part only of the political and economic 'Drang nach Osten' of the Germans throughout the early Middle Ages.[62] They imply that this campaign of 1147 should not be linked with that against the Moslems in the Near East. Such a view is in no way supported by the sources. Economic and political ambitions played an important, and for many individuals perhaps a decisive, part in the genesis and outcome of this campaign against the Wends.[63] But the dichotomy between temporal and spiritual motives and between the interests of the secular and ecclesiastical leaders should not be overemphasized.[64] The sources show that this campaign was almost universally regarded as a pilgrimage and its army as a *peregrinus exercitus*. 'A religious motive,' Tancred Borenius once said, 'provided the whole conscious basis of the idea of Pilgrimage,' of which the cross worn by these soldiers, like the later pilgrims' badges, was the outward sign.[65] Of these crusaders more than others perhaps, the real motives were mixed and secular interests played a dominant part. Nevertheless, the fact that some appear to have joined this campaign because it seemed less arduous than the crusade to the East;[66] the connection, how-

---

[61] Konrad Schünemann, 'Ostpolitik und Kriegführung im deutschen Mittelalter,' *Ungarische Jahrbücher* 17 (1937) 32-3.

[62] See, for instance, Bündung, *op. cit.* 50: 'Der Wendenzug ist im ganzen gesehen weniger ein ritterlicher Kreuzzug als ein Eroberungskrieg der deutschen Grenzfürsten geworden, der nur noch sehr beiläufig Spuren der Kreuzzugsidee zeigt.' Cf. Cartellieri 376, and James W. Thompson, 'The German Church and the Conversion of the Baltic Slavs,' *American Journal of Theology* 20 (1916) 205-30 and 372-89, who called the crusade a 'sinister mixture of bigotry and lust for land,' 381.

[63] Vincent of Prague, for instance, says: 'Saxones potius pro auferenda eis terra, quam pro fide Christiana confirmanda tantam moverant militiam,' MGH SS 17.663. But Vincent was a Bohemian and not unprejudiced.

[64] Karl Jordan, 'Heinrich der Löwe und die ostdeutsche Kolonisation,' *Deutsches Archiv für Landes- und Volksforschung* 2 (1938) 789: 'Das Unternehmen war vor allem an der Diskrepanz gescheitert, welche sich zwischen den Forderungen der Kirche und den politischen Zielen der sächsischen Fürsten im Wendenland auftat.' Carl Erdmann, on the contrary, emphasizes in his *Die Entstehung des Kreuzzugsgedankens* (Forschungen zur Kirchen- und Geistesgeschichte 6; Stuttgart 1935) 91-7, that the early campaigns against the Slavs in the East were marked by 'das Zusammentreffen von Heidenkrieg und Heidenmission,' 95.

[65] Tancred Borenius, *Mediaeval Pilgrims' Badges* (Opuscula of Ye Sette of Odd Volumes 90; London 1930) 7-8; Otto of Freising, *Gesta* (cited n. 30 above) 61. Theodor Mayer, in 'Das Kaisertum und der Osten im Mittelalter,' *Deutsche Ostforschungen*, edd. H. Aubin, O. Brunner, W. Kohte, and J. Papritz, I (Deutschland und der Osten 20; Leipzig 1942) 291-309, says with respect to the eastern policy of the Empire: 'Ideell deckten sich also die Absichten und Ziele des Kaisertums und des Papsttums völlig,' 295.

[66] *Casus monasterii Petrishusensis*, MGH SS 20.674.

ever obscure, of its origins with the diet called at Frankfurt to consider the crusade of Conrad III; the letters of Pope Eugene III and of Bernard of Clairvaux;[67] and above all the almost unanimous agreement of the sources leave no doubt that in fact as well as in the minds of contemporaries the crusade against the Wends was closely connected with the campaign to protect the Holy Land.[68]

The French and English annalists and chroniclers had on the whole only slight information about expeditions other than the principal crusade to the East. Often, however, they knew more than the Germans about events in Spain; and this is not surprising in view of their geographical proximity and especially of the popularity at this time of the pilgrimage route to Compostella.[69] At least four contemporary English writers, including the historian of Melrose in Scotland, and many of the minor French writers mention the attacks on Lisbon, Almeria and Tortosa.[70] Most of these were simple annalists, who merely listed events as they came to their attention. Their entries, however, are occasionally joined by some simple connective, such as 'meanwhile' or 'moreover,' in which can be seen the germ of a more fully related view of the crusade. More elaborate is the account of five of the campaigns given in the *Continuatio Premonstratensis* of Sigebert's chronicle,[71] where the references to the four less important expeditions are woven into the more complete description of the crusades of Conrad and Louis. This construction makes it clear that in the author's mind, although he nowhere says so, these campaigns were connected and directed towards one purpose.[72]

---

[67] See below, 245-6 and 255-7.

[68] Otto Volk, *Die abendländisch-hierarchische Kreuzzugsidee* (Halle a.S. 1911) 41: 'Der Slavenkreuzzug von 1147 ist aber unmittelbar mit dem zweiten orientalischen in Zusammenhang zu bringen...' See Mayer (n. 65 above) *passim*; Bündung (n. 60 above) 41; Michel Villey, *La Croisade: Essai sur la formation d'une théorie juridique* (L'Église et l'État au Moyen Age 6; Paris 1942) 210-12.

[69] Marcelin Defourneaux, *Les Français en Espagne aux XIᵉ et XIIᵉ siècles* (Paris 1949) *passim*; esp. 69: 'La grande époque du pèlerinage, l'« âge d'or » de Saint-Jacques de Compostelle, ne commencèrent cependant qu'avec les premières années du XIIᵉ siècle.' Cf. Borenius (n. 65 above) 10 and 18-9.

[70] Alexandre Herculano, *Historia de Portugal* I (4th ed. Lisbon 1875) 528-30, mentions in all fifteen contemporary and later sources on the fall of Lisbon. To these may be added Gervase of Canterbury, *Chronica de tempore regum Angliae Stephani, Henrici II, et Ricardi I*, ed. Wm. Stubbs in *The Historical Works of Gervase of Canterbury* I (Rolls Series 73; London 1879) 137-8; *The Chronicle of Melrose*, edd. Alan and Marjorie Anderson (Studies in Economics and Political Science 100; London 1936) 34; and several French chronicles, such as the *Chron. Sancti Victoris Massiliensis*, RHGF 12.349.

[71] MGH SS 6.454. It was composed, up to 1155, by an anonymous Premonstratensian monk in the diocese of Rheims or Lyons.

[72] Robert of Torigny, who as Abbot of St.-Michel-du-Mont had exceptional sources of information in an endless supply of pilgrims' tales, mentions all but two (the Wendish

The most important narrative of the capture of Almeria and Tortosa is that written by the Genoese historian Caffaro di Caschifellone in his *Ystoria captionis Almarie et Turtuose*.[73] Caffaro, who died in 1166, played a prominent part in public life in Genoa,[74] and this account, though probably not that of an eye-witness, was certainly based on first-hand reports[75] and rivals in vividness and wealth of detail even the longer *De expugnatione Lyxbonensi*. The Genoese fleet left in 1147, and co-operated with Alfonso VII of Castile, under the terms of a treaty concluded in 1146, in the siege and capture of Almeria. The Genoese then sailed to Barcelona, where they spent the Winter before assisting Count Ramon Berenger IV in his attack on Tortosa.

Crusade and the Genoese expedition of 1146) of the many Christian campaigns of these years: *Chron.* (n. 6 above) 152-5. But his notices are on the whole annalistic and unconnected.

[73] Caffaro, *Ystoria Captionis Almarie et Turtuose*, in *Annali Genovesi* I, ed. L. T. Belgrano (Fonti per la Storia d'Italia 11; Genoa 1890) 79-89. On this campaign see F. W. Schirrmacher, *Geschichte von Spanien* IV (Gotha 1881) 143f.; Otto Langer, *Politische Geschichte Genuas und Pisas im 12. Jahrhundert* (Historische Studien, ed. W. Arndt 7; Leipzig 1882) 23-35; C. Manfroni, *Storia della Marina Italiana (400-1261)* (Leghorn 1899) 207-15; Adolf Schaube, *Handelsgeschichte der Romanischen Völker des Mittelmeergebiets bis zum Ende der Kreuzzüge* (Handbuch der mittelalterlichen und neueren Geschichte, edd. Below and Meinecke, Abt. III; Munich-Berlin 1906) 317-19; Cartellieri (n. 37 above) 420-2. The principal objection to Caffaro's excellent account of the capture of Almeria and Tortosa is the impression it gives that this was one campaign, whereas it was in fact two campaigns, in both of which the Genoese cooperated. This is clearly seen in the treaties preserved in the *Liber iuris* and printed in the *Codice diplomatico della Repubblica di Genova*, ed. Cesare Imperiale di Sant'Angelo (Fonti per la Storia d'Italia 77, 79, 89; Rome 1936-42). Here are found the agreements, made in September, 1146, in which the Genoese promised to assist the Emperor of Spain in an attack on Almeria in May of the following year and in which the Emperor, in return, undertook to attack also and promised certain rights to the Genoese in the city if it fell (I nos. 166-7, pp. 204-9). The Genoese stipulated that they were bound to join in no enterprise other than that against Almeria, in case they wished to ally with the Count of Barcelona. This they did by a treaty, concluded in 1146, in which the Genoese agreed to assist, after the capture of Almeria, in an attack on Tortosa; the Count on his side granted to the Genoese property and privileges in Tortosa should the city be captured (I nos. 168-9, pp. 210-17). These treaties were quite separate and indicate that each of these campaigns was a distinct undertaking. The later dealings of the Genoese with Alfonso and Ramon Berenger confirm this impression: see in the *Codice dipl.* I nos. 182-3 (pp. 228-30), 190-1 (pp. 236-40), 214-6 and 243-4 (pp. 265-7 and 291-5), and III nos. 52-3 (pp. 137-40). On the other hand, it must be remembered that these campaigns were both part of the wider effort of the Spanish Reconquest; and no doubt Alfonso's summons to join the campaign against Almeria stimulated in Ramon Berenger a desire to recapture Tortosa.

[74] On Caffaro, see Cesare Imperiale di Sant'Angelo, *Caffaro e i suoi tempi* (Turin and Rome 1894).

[75] The *Ann. Ianuenses*, in *Annali Genovesi* (n. 73 above) 1-75, apparently referring to the *Ystoria*, say that it was made 'a sapientibus …, qui viderunt et interfuerunt,' 35. Belgrano, *Ann. Ianuenses*, intro. p. xc-xci, and Imperiale, *op. cit.* 210-1, however, both believe that Caffaro did not accompany the expedition in 1147-8. In this case, the passage in the *Ann.* may mean that Caffaro wrote his work from eye-witness reports.

Economic and political interests certainly played a large part in the origins of this expedition. Both Almeria and Tortosa were centres of Moorish pirates who preyed on Italian and other Christian shipping,[76] and both were wealthy cities: facts which weighed heavily with the hard-headed Genoese,[77] who had probably planned an expedition against Almeria before the Second Crusade was even thought of.[78] They had, however, a tradition of co-operation with the crusaders against the Moslems in both the East and the West;[79] and in 1147 the preaching of the crusade and a papal summons did not leave them unmoved, for Caffaro says that 'the Genoese (were) instructed and summoned by God through the Apostolic See (and) made an oath to raise an army against the Saracens of Almeria.'[80]

This combination of spiritual and temporal motives, which characterized many of the campaigns of the Spanish Reconquest, is strongly marked in the other sources. The Spanish sources in particular show more clearly than

---

[76] The anonymous chronicler of Alfonso VII says of the pirates at Almeria: 'qui circuentes diversa maria, nunc subito egressi terra Barensi, et terra Ascalonis, et Regionis Constantinopolitarum, et Siciliae, et Barcinonensis, et nunc Genuae, nunc Pisae, et Francorum, aut Portugaliae, et Galleciae, vel Asturianorum praedas captivos Christianos navibus adversantes fugiebant...,' *Chronica Adefonsi Imperatoris*, ed. H. Florez, *España Sagrada* 21.398.

[77] See the account of the capture of Almeria, under the year 1154, in the *Notae Pisanae*, MGH SS 19.266, which are called 'sehr merkwürdig und lehrreich' by Wattenbach (n. 54 above) II 326. Schaube (n. 73 above) emphasizes the economic aspects of this expedition, the expense of which produced a financial collapse in Genoa: see Imperiale (n. 73 above) 226f. and Hilmar C. Krueger, 'Post-War Collapse and Rehabilitation in Genoa, 1149-62,' *Studi in onore di Gino Luzzatto* (Milan 1949) I 117-28. Economic considerations always influenced the policy of the Genoese, who in 1137/8 had even allied with the King of Morocco: Manfroni (n. 73 above) 195.

[78] See below, 235.

[79] They had attacked Tortosa in 1093: see the *De liberatione civitatum Orientis*, in Annali Genovesi I 97-124; *Chron. Adefonsi Imperatoris*, ed. L. T. Belgrano, 'Frammento di poemmetto sincrono su la Conquista di Almeria nel MCXLVII,' *Atti della Società Ligure di Storia Patria* 19 (1887) 400. They had played an important part in the First Crusade: see Manfroni 136-65, and Runciman I 112 and 219.

[80] Caffaro, *Ystoria* 79; cf. Jacobus de Voragine: 'ad preces summi pontificis,' *Iacopo da Varagine e la sua Cronaca di Genova*, ed. Giovanni Monleone (Fonti per la Storia d'Italia 84-6; Rome 1941) II 336; Carlo Sigonio, *De Regno Italiae*, in *Opera Omnia*, ed. Ludovico Muratori (Milan 1732) II 698; and Angelo Manrique, *Cisterciensium ... Annalium Tomus Secundus* (Lyons 1642) under 1146, vi (pp. 35-6) and 1147, i 11-12 (pp. 55-7). On the crusading vow, see below, 240. The Genoese appear to have taken oaths in connection with this expedition on at least three other occasions: before leaving Genoa, the consuls 'omnibus discordantibus pacem iurare preceperunt' (Caffaro, *Ystoria* 80, line 6, cf. lines 12-4); then twice before the walls of Tortosa, the Genoese swore not to join battle without the common counsel and permission of the consuls (*ibid.* 86) and not to leave Tortosa before the city fell (*ibid.* 87). To capture Tortosa, 'pro honore Dei et civitatis Ianuensis' (*ibid.* 85), they wintered at Barcelona.

Caffaro's *Ystoria* that the attacks on Almeria and Tortosa were not one campaign, but two separate expeditions, in both of which the Genoese co-operated.[81] ·

There is an exceptionally complete account of the campaign against Almeria in the *Chronica Adefonsi Imperatoris*,[82] whose author may well have seen the events he records. The greater part of the description of the expedition — 'the celebrated deeds of the sainted men '[83] — is in heavy leonine hexameters, but a short introduction in prose tells of the alliance between Genoa and the Emperor Alfonso,[84] who then sent as an envoy the Bishop of Astorga to summon the Counts of Barcelona and Montpellier to join this army 'for the redemption of their souls.'[85] Within Alfonso's own territories, the Bishops of Toledo and Leon summoned the faithful to battle: 'They absolve crimes; they raise their voices to the heavens; they promise to everyone the reward of both lives; they promise gifts of silver and (heavenly?) crowns; they promise also whatever gold the Moors have.'[86] So, the author says, 'the trumpets of salvation sound throughout the regions of the world,'[87] and with pompous elaboration and eulogy he describes the gathering of the Spanish and French soldiers[88] under the Emperor Alfonso, the new Charlemagne.[89]

This reference to Charlemagne is interesting in view of the popular concept of the great Carolingian as the Christian champion against the Moslems and

---

[81] See above, n. 73.

[82] For the two editions cited, see above nn. 76 (Florez) and 79 (Belgrano). There is another edition in *Las Crónicas Latinas de la Reconquista*, ed. A. Huici (Valencia 1913) II 170-439. For the prose I use that of Florez, for the verse, that of Belgrano. The poem is incomplete, breaking off at verse 387.

[83] *Chron. Ad. Imp.* ed. Belgrano, verse 4.

[84] See above, n. 73.

[85] *Chron. Ad. Imp.* ed. Florez 398. On Bishop Arnold of Astorga, 'cuius micat inclytus ensis' in this campaign (*Chron. Ad. Imp.* ed. Belgrano v. 376), see Belgrano pp. 404 and 422 n. 2; and *España Sagrada* 16.207, where in 1150 Alfonso makes him a grant 'por el servicio que le hicieron en la guerra contra los Saracenos.'

[86] *Chron. Ad. Imp.* ed. Belgrano vv. 44-7: 'Crimina persolvunt, voces ad sydera tollunt, Mercedem vite spondent cunctis utriusque, Argenti dona promittunt cumque corona, Quidquid habent Mauri rursus promittunt auri,' as had Urban II in the First Crusade. On the celebrated Archbishop Raymond of Toledo, see Charles H. Haskins, *The Renaissance of the Twelfth Century* (Cambridge, Mass. 1927) 52 and 286.

[87] *Chron. Ad. Imp.* ed. Belgrano v. 55.

[88] *Ibid.* vv. 50f.; for the most complete description of the Spanish forces listed in this poem, see Prudencio de Sandoval, *Chronica del Inclito Imperador ... Alonso VII* (Madrid, 1600) 138-40; also Schirrmacher (n. 73 above) 147. The troops included men from Leon, Asturia, Castile, and Toledo; the Count of Zamora and Salamanca, the Count of Urgel, the King of Navarre, and many others.

[89] *Chron. Ad. Imp.* ed. Belgrano vv. 20-1; see Ramon Menendez Pidal, *El Imperio Hispanico y los Cinco Reinos* (Madrid 1950) 167.

of his war in Spain as a crusade.[90] These ideas were especially current towards the middle of the twelfth century, when the *Pèlerinage de Charlemagne* was composed in France and when the cult of Charlemagne was at its height in Germany and was soon to culminate in his 'canonisation' (1165).[91] Alfonso VII was, moreover, in his own right a celebrated crusader. In 1136 he had re-established the Confradía de Belchite 'in order to defend the Christians and to oppress the Saracens and to free the Holy Church.'[92] His crusading activity was extolled by the Provençal troubadour Alegret[93] and by Marcabru, who in his 'Emperaire, per mi mezeis,' written probably in 1138,[94] called for a general crusade against the Almoravides and condemned the inactivity of Louis VII:

> Mas Franssa Peitau e Beiriu
> Aclina un sol seignoriu,
> Venga sai Dieu son fieu servir!
> Qu'ieu non sai per que princes viu
> S'a Dieu no vai son fieu servir![95]

In this poem Marcabru adumbrated the plan of a joint crusade by the combined forces of Castile, Navarre, and Barcelona together with troops from across the Pyrenees. This idea was realized on a yet larger scale in the campaign of 1147. But since the *Chronica Adefonsi Imperatoris* breaks off sharply when the army was still at Baeza,[96] it throws no new light on

---

[90] On the development of the medieval legend of Charlemagne see Paul Lehmann, *Das literarische Bild Karls des Grossen* (*Sitzungsberichte der Bayerischen Akademie der Wissenschaften*, Philosophisch-historische Abteilung, 1934, IX): 'Unter dem Einfluss der religiösen Erregung ... hatte sich immer mehr das fromm-heroische Bild von Karl als dem Bekämpfer und Besieger der Ungläubigen in den Vordergrund gedrängt,' 34; and Robert Folz, *Le souvenir et la légende de Charlemagne dans l'Empire germanique médiéval* (Publications de l'Université de Dijon 7; Paris 1950), especially, with respect to the theme of Charlemagne as a crusader, 137-8 and 166-7; more generally, 159-237.

[91] On the pseudo-Turpin, composed 1147/68, see Lehmann 30, and Folz 223-5 and 235-7; on the *Vita sancti Karoli*, composed 1170/80, see Lehmann 33 and Folz 214-21; on the *Pèlerinage de Charlemagne* and its connection with the Second Crusade, see Alfred Adler, 'The *Pèlerinage de Charlemagne* in New Light on Saint-Denis,' *Speculum* 22 (1947) 550-61.

[92] See Schramm (n. 3 above) 110-1; and Peter Rassow, 'La Confradía de Belchite,' *Anuario de Historia del Derecho Español* 3 (1926) 220-6.

[93] In his 'Ara pareisson l'aubre sec': see Boissonade (n. 9 above) 237-8 and 239 n. 3, and Schramm 113.

[94] The date of this famous poem is much disputed: see *Poésies complètes du Troubadour Marcabru*, ed. J.-M.-L. Dejeanne (Bibliothèque Méridionale, 1ʳᵉ Série, 12; Toulouse 1909) 229, where Diez, Suchier, and Lewent are cited in favor of 1146-7 and Meyer, in favor of anterior to 1147. Boissonade 222 and 233-7 examines the poem in great detail with a view to dating it in 1138 or 1138-45 at the outside.

[95] *Poésies complètes* no. 22 (pp. 107-10) strophes 10-11; see Schramm 113.

[96] This army first moved on Calatrava, which fell in January, 1147 (Sandoval [n. 88 above] 123-4 and 126; Schirrmacher [n. 73 above] 147 n. 2) and was granted first to the

the capture of Almeria itself. Its account of the origins of the expedition is, nevertheless, of great value. The character of the arguments in the speeches of the Bishops of Toledo and Leon, the references to the redemption of souls and to *tuba salutaris*, the comparison of Alfonso VII with Charlemagne, and the characterization of the soldiers as 'sainted men' are all unmistakable signs of the crusading nature of this campaign. On the other hand, in case these spiritual blessings were insufficient inducement, the bishops also offered Moorish gold to participants in this enterprise. For there is a large measure of truth in Dozy's remark that 'a Spanish Knight of the Middle Ages fought neither for his country nor for his religion; he fought, like the Cid, to get something to eat.'[97]

No such complete description exists of the capture of Tortosa, Lerida, and Fraga by the Count of Barcelona and his allies in 1148-9.[98] An idea, however, of the character of this campaign may be gained from the records of Alfonso I of Aragon and of Ramon Berenger IV relating to these cities and to the Catalonian and Aragonese Reconquest in general.[99] Most im-

---

Templars and later was defended by the Cistercians of the Abbey of Fitero in Navarre. So was established the Order of the Knights of Calatrava, which Alexander III approved in 1164: A. H. Thompson, 'The Monastic Orders,' CMH 5.682. Alfonso's army then took Anjudar and Baños before setting siege to Baeza: *Chron. Ad. Imp.* ed. Belgrano v. 298 and pp. 420 n. 3, 421 n. 1. (On Anjudar: Schirrmacher 149; on Baeza: Sandoval 124-5; *España Sagrada* 16.483, 22.272, 36. cxciv [see n. 229 below]; Schirrmacher 149.) Here they encountered strong opposition, and many troops had already gone home (*Chron. Ad. Imp.* ed. Belgrano vv. 334-7) by the time when, during the summer, envoys arrived at Baeza from the Catalonian, French, and Genoese forces that had meanwhile gathered at Almeria (*ibid.* vv. 340f.). The Bishop of Astorga, however, rallied the remaining Spanish troops to go on to Almeria. The poem breaks off in the middle of his speech.

[97] Dozy, *Recherches sur les Musulmans d'Espagne* II 203 and 233, quoted by Roger Merriman, *The Rise of the Spanish Empire* I: *The Middle Ages* (New York 1918) 88; cf. Schramm 113.

[98] Excluding, that is, the very brief *Ann. Barcinonenses*, MGH SS 19.501, written in a twelfth-century hand on the last leaf of a manuscript of Visigothic laws. Later Spanish chronicles, of which there are several, naturally viewed this campaign in a different light from contemporaries.

[99] *Colección de documentos inéditos del Archivo General de la Corona de Aragon*, ed. D. Próspero de Bofarull y Mascaró, IV (Barcelona 1849) nos. 51 (pp. 113-23), 54 (126-9), 56 (130-5), 58 (136-40), 61 (144-68), 70 (193-6), 139 (328), and 147 (347-55). In 1131, Alfonso of Aragon willed that '... si Deus dederit michi Tortosam tota sit ospitalis ihierosolomitani,' *ibid.* no. 2, p. 11. Ramon Berenger in 1136, however, granted the entire city and diocese of Tortosa to William VI of Montpellier (*ibid.* no. 22, pp. 53-4, in a mutilated form; and *Liber Instrumentorum memorialium: Cartulaire des Guillems de Montpellier*, ed. A. Germain [Montpellier 1884-6] no. CLII, pp. 284-5), who in his will in 1146 bequeathed the city to his younger son William (Luc d'Achery, *Spicilegium*, edd. Baluze and Martène [Paris 1723] III 498-500; and *Liber Instr. mem.* no. xcv, pp. 177-83). Several of the charters listed above concern the problem of the division of Tortosa after the conquest. In' spite of the grants to the Hospitallers and to William of Montpellier, one third of the city seems

portant among these is Ramon Berenger's huge grant in 1143 to the Knights of the Temple in Jerusalem. The purpose of this great charter is explicit: 'for the crushing, conquest, and expulsion of the Moors, for the exaltation of the faith and religion of sacred Christianity, ... for the exercise of the office of a military order in the region of Spain against the Saracens, for the remission of my sins, for the honor of God, Who honors those honoring Him, (and) for the salvation of the soul of my father.'[100] This statement of a conscious religious motive could hardly be clearer, and its form here is certainly not purely conventional.[101] No less specific, although perhaps not disinterested, was Marcabru, who in his 'Pax in nomine Domini' contrasted the zeal against the Moslems of Ramon Berenger and the Templars with the inertia of the Christians living north of the Pyrenees.[102] It has been said that Alfonso I of Aragon 'placed the idea of reconquest before his successors as a feasible policy. In his hands this policy assumes a definitely religious character.'[103] Both of these tendencies lived on in the policy of Ramon Berenger, to whom the recovery of Tortosa, Lerida, and Fraga was a source of both temporal and spiritual satisfaction. So, after these victories, in a charter of 1149, he thanks God, 'Who in His love, after the space of so many years, has deigned to restore in our times the church of Lerida, (which was) subjected to the perfidy of the pagans, to its former state of the Christian religion.'[104]

The presence on the campaigns both against Almeria and against Tortosa of other than Spanish troops is not without importance. It has already

---

to have been given to William of Moncada and another to the Genoese (see n. 73 above) and yet another portion to the Templars (presumably under Ramon Berenger's grant of 1143: see n. 100 below). However, William, the son of William VI of Montpellier, still called himself 'William of Tortosa' as late as 1157 (D'Achéry III 526). The whole problem is confused, and the explanations advanced by DeVic and Vaissete, *op. cit.* (n. 9 above) III 739-40, and by Defourneaux, *op. cit.* (n. 69 above) 177, are not altogether satisfactory.

[100] *Colección* no. 63, pp. 93-9; also Pierre de Marca. *Marca Hispanica*, ed. E. Baluze (Paris 1688) 1291-4; *España Sagrada* 43.241-5 and 484-8 (Fifth Council of Gerona, 1143).

[101] It is too specific for a conventional arenga and was clearly composed for this charter.

[102]   En Espagna, sai, lo Marques
        E cill del temple Salamo
           Sofron lo pes
        E·l fais de l'orguoill paganor...

Poésies complètes no. 35 (pp. 169-71) strophe 7. The date of this poem is no less disputed than that of the 'Emperaire': see *ibid.* 235. Milà and Suchier date it 1146/7; Meyer argues from the reference to the death of the Count of Poitou (1137) 'que le *vers del Lavador* n'est pas de beaucoup postérieur à cet événement'; Crescini and Lewent follow Meyer, as does Boissonade (n. 9 above) 231. While 1138 is not impossible, the reference to the Templars appears to suggest a date posterior to the great privilege of 1143.

[103] H. J. Chaytor, *A History of Aragon and Catalonia* (London 1933) 55.

[104] *España Sagrada* 47.255.

been seen that the Genoese fleet co-operated in both these attacks. So, also, did the Templars and Count William VI of Montpellier, who was summoned to assist 'for the salvation of his soul' by Alfonso VII and who came with two of his sons and probably a considerable force of men.[105] This William was a remarkable man; among other things he was a friend of St. Bernard and after his return from Spain, before July 1149, he became a Cistercian monk at the abbey of Grandeselve near Toulouse.[106] Soldiers not only from all Christian Spain, therefore, with the exception of Portugal,[107] but also from France joined the army gathered against Almeria.[108] Campaigning with the Count of Barcelona, moreover, were both French and English soldiers, probably some of the Anglo-Flemish crusaders on their way to the Holy Land, as well as other foreigners.[109] The Viscount of Béarn, Peter of

---

[105] Caffaro, *Ysloria* 86; *Codice diplomatico ... di Genova* I 236-8; *Chron. Ad. Imp.* ed. Belgrano v. 348: 'in ordine magnus.' It is not impossible that William came with the Genoese, as DeVic and Vaissete (n. 9 above) III 738-9, suggest, although Caffaro does not mention this. The Counts of Montpellier had a tradition of co-operation with the Genoese, who with the Pope had assisted William VI to reestablish his power in Montpellier in 1143: A. Germain, *Histoire de la Commune de Montpellier* I (Montpellier 1851) 19-21: *Liber Instr.* (n. 99 above) xi; Manfroni (n. 73 above) 195; Archibald R. Lewis, 'Seigneurial Administration in Twelfth Century Montpellier,' *Speculum* 22 (1947) 568. 'Remarquons ... l'intervention génoise dans ces affaires Montpelliéraines et Aragonaises...,' says Germain, *Liber Instr.* xii; 'Guillem VI attacha une si haute valeur à cette intervention, que, pour en reconnaître le bienfait, il concéda aux Génois une maison à Montpellier, où ils eurent dès lors un centre commercial.'

[106] The new Abbot of Grandeselve, in 1149, was Alexander of Cologne, who had been converted to the monastic life by St. Bernard during his preaching of the crusade in the Rhineland, 1146-7: Joseph Greven, 'Die Kölnfahrt Bernhards von Clairvaux,' *Annalen des historischen Vereins für den Niederrhein* 120 (1932) 10-12. On William of Montpellier, see Manrique, *Cist. Ann.* II (n. 80 above) under 1149, III 5 (pp. 130-1); *Histoire littéraire de la France... par les religieux Bénédictins ... de Saint Maur*, 13.324f.; DeVic and Vaissete III 737f., 778, 820, and IV 182-3 (note 37, VIII); and the *Liber Instr.* vi-xii. The Counts of Montpellier were vassals for part of their lands both of the King of Castile and of the Counts of Barcelona and therefore had close relations with Spain in the twelfth century. William VI took a special interest in Catalonia, and as a monk he was present at the foundation of the Abbey of Vaullure (Santa-Cruz) by William of Moncada: DeVic and Vaissete III 820; Defourneaux (n. 69 above) 177. See also his interesting will, cited n. 99 above.

[107] Schirrmacher (n. 73 above) 147: '... man vereinigte sich zum erstenmal zu einer gemeinsamen kriegerischen Aktion.' See, also, Modesto Lafuente, *Historia General de España* V (Madrid 1851) 68-9; Defourneaux 175-6; Menendez Pidal (n. 89 above) 166-7.

[108] Menendez Pidal 166-7; DeVic and Vaissete III 737: 'La guerre qu'Alphonse VII, Roi de Castile, avoit entreprise alors contre les infidèles d'Espagne, partagea la noblesse de la Province entre cette expédition et celle de la Terre Sainte.'

[109] See my 'Note on the Route of the Anglo-Flemish Crusaders,' *Speculum* 28 (1953) 526. On the vexed problem of the participation of Pisans in the campaign, I do not agree with Belgrano in his belief (*Chron. Ad. Imp.* p. 398) that they were present: Caffaro and the *Notae Pisanae* make no mention of them, nor the letter from the Pisans to Ramon Berenger in *Colección* (n. 99 above) no. 154, pp. 371-2, nor a charter of Alfonso which mentions

Gabarret, assisted at the capture of Lerida and Fraga.[110] Nicholas, Abbot of St. Rufus, near Avignon, was with these troops at least some of the time.[111] Also present were Ermengarde, Viscountess of Narbonne, her uncle Berenger, Abbot of La Grasse, and the consuls of Narbonne, all of whom are mentioned in a charter dated during the siege, in September, 1148. By this Ramon Berenger granted a market place and exemptions to the Narbonnais 'in gratitude for what the inhabitants of Narbonne have expended of their goods and of their lives for the defense of the faith against the infidels.' [112]

The third campaign against the Moors in 1147-8 was in Portugal, and was led by King Alfonso Henriques, whom an anonymous contemporary called 'the wonder-making destroyer of the enemies of the cross of Christ'[113] and to whom Marcabru addressed a poem praising his victories over the Moors.[114] This campaign was by no means restricted to the attack on Lisbon, for which he secured the assistance of the Anglo-Flemish fleet. It opened in March, 1147, with the capture of Santarem, of which there is an excellent account in the anonymous *De expugnatione Scalabis*,[115] perhaps the work of an eye-witness. Though its main concern is a detailed description of the

---

Genoese aid: Peter Rassow, 'Die Urkunden Kaiser Alfons VII. von Spanien,' *Archiv für Urkundenforschung* 10 (1928) 444 and 11 (1929) 99-100. The two sources where they are mentioned — Robert of Torigny, *Chron.* (n. 6 above) 155 and *Chron. Ad. Imp.* ed. Belgrano v. 347 — are not reliable. The confusion may have arisen, as Langer (n. 73 above) 31 n. 2 suggests, out of the undoubted Pisan participation in the attack on Majorca in 1114-5: Chaytor (n. 103 above) 57; Defourneaux 155; or, I think, perhaps more likely, out of the fact that one of the Genoese leaders was named Ansaldo Pizo: Caffaro (n. 73) *passim*; *Ann. Ianuenses* (n. 75) 35; or possibly out of the presence at the siege of Lisbon of a Pisan engineer, who may have gone on to Tortosa: *De exp. Lyx.* 142 and 162; letter of Duodechin, MGH SS 17.28. Pisa was in any case throughout this period occupied by a war with Lucca. In point of fact, she objected to the Genoese attack in 1146 on Minorca, over which the Pisans asserted a claim on the grounds of their earlier expedition: Manfroni (n. 73 above) 208. Of the presence, however (which appears to have hitherto escaped notice), of Ventimiglians on this expedition, there can be no doubt: *Codice diplomatico* (n. 73 above) I no. 194, pp. 242-3.

[110] Defourneaux 177-8.

[111] See below, 262.

[112] Archives, Hôtel de Ville, Narbonne, caisson 5: cited in French translation by DeVic and Vaissete III 739. More generally on French participation in the Reconquista, see Defourneaux *passim* and E. Benito Ruana, 'España y las Cruzadas', *Anales de Historia antigua y medieval* (1951-2) 103-11.

[113] *Indiculum ... sancti Vincentii* (n. 43 above) 91: 'inimicorum crucis Christi mirificus extirpator.'

[114] Boissonade (n. 9 above) 229-30.

[115] In *Portugaliae Monumenta Historica, Scriptores* I 94-5. On this capture, see Herculano (n. 70 above) 360f. and n. xxi, 526-8; Luiz Gonzaga de Azevado, *História de Portugal*, ed. Domingos Maurício Gomes dos Santos, IV (Lisbon 1941) 46-55; Antonio Brandão, *Crónica de D. Afonso Henriques*, ed. A. de Magalhães Basto (Lisbon 1945) 99-111; Livermore (n. 37 above) 73-4.

attack on the formidable stronghold on the river Tagus, the introduction is a paean in praise of the victory. 'Gather all the people for the praise of Christ,' the author says, 'clap your hands, sing well to Him in acclamation, and say: Hear, O ye Kings, give ear, O ye princes of all the earth! The Lord has chosen new wars in our days ... God through our king has captured Santarem, the mightiest of all the cities of Spain.' [116] On this expedition Alfonso was accompanied by the Knights of the Temple, to whom all the ecclesiastical property in the city was granted after its capture.[117] Only then did the King proceed, presumably with the Templars, to the attack on Lisbon. After the fall of that city, he completed his campaign of 1147 by the capture of several strongholds near Lisbon: Cintra, Almada, and Palmela.[118]

There remain to consider only two expeditions against the Moslems in the years 1146-8. To one of these, the Genoese attack on Minorca and Almeria in 1146, reference seems to be made only in the *Annales Ianuenses* of Caffaro.[119] Here, in contrast with his account of the campaign in the following year, he makes no mention of a religious motive. Its purpose seems to have been largely strategic and economic, that is, piratical. The failure to take Almeria at this time led to the alliance of the Genoese with Alfonso VII.[120] But apart from this it is impossible to connect this expedition with the Second Crusade.

The same can be said of the attack on North Africa by Roger of Sicily in 1148.[121] Of the contemporary western writers consulted for this paper, three only refer to this campaign. Two of these, Robert of Torigny and the Premonstratensian continuator of Sigebert's chronicle, have already been mentioned. Both associate it with the Second Crusade and seem to have

---

[116] *De exp. Scal.* (n. 115 above) 33-5. Cf. Psalm 46; Jud. 5.3, 8.

[117] Grant of April, 1147: *Documentos da Chancelaria de Afonso Henriques*, ed. Abiah E. Reuter (Chancelarias Medievais Portuguesas 1; Coimbra 1938) no. 145, pp. 209-10. See Herculano 366 n. 1 and 367 n. 1; Brandão 109 and 110 (a document of 1154, showing that the Templars got the property). On the part played by the Templars in the Portuguese Reconquest, see Livermore 80-1.

[118] *De exp. Lyx.* 178; *Chron. Conimbricense*, in *Portugaliae Monumenta Historica, Scriptores* I 2; *Chron. Lamecense, ibid.* 19-20; Herculano I 404-6; Azevado 90-1; Gibb (n. 37 above) 16.

[119] *Ann. Ianuenses* 33-5.

[120] Langer (n. 73 above) 25.

[121] On this expedition see Michele Amari, *Storia dei Musulmani di Sicilia*, ed. Carlo Nallino (Catania 1933-9) III 421 and 441; Manfroni (n. 73 above) 198-201; Erich Caspar, *Roger II. und die Gründung der Normannisch-Sicilischen Monarchie* (Innsbruck 1904) 419-21; Ferdinand Chalandon, *Histoire de la domination normande en Italie et en Sicile* (Paris 1907) II 162-5; Edmund Curtis, *Roger of Sicily* (New York and London 1912) 251-4; Francesco Cerone, *L'opera politica e militare di Ruggiero II in Africa ed in Oriente* (Catania 1913) 63f.

regarded it as at least partly religious in purpose.[122] The third, Abbot Peter the Venerable of Cluny, is more specific. His letter to Roger, written probably in 1148, urged him to make his peace with Conrad III and to ally with him against the enemies of the Church. 'For as we have often heard,' he says, 'many gains for the Church of God have come from the lands of the enemies of God, that is, of the Saracens, through your military valor.'[123] Peter, however, had an axe to grind: he wanted to promote a Catholic alliance against the Byzantine empire; and his evidence for the religious motive of Roger's campaign is not altogether convincing.

The facts can hardly bear the interpretation that the expedition was a part of the Second Crusade, or a crusade in itself. The conquest of North Africa was a well-established political ambition of the Norman-Sicilian kings,[124] whose interest in the spread of Christianity was secondary to the extension of their own power. This is clearly shown by the fact that Roger's first reaction to the crusade in 1147 was to take advantage of the Byzantine Emperor's preoccupation with the crusaders at Constantinople to attack Greece,[125] in return for which Manuel called him 'the common foe of all Christians.'[126] Cerone has clearly shown that Roger's attack on Africa in 1148 was the result of an appeal for help from the rebel Jusûf at Gabes. Unable to maintain two naval campaigns at once, and at the same time unwilling to forego this opportunity to realize his ambitions on the south shore of the Mediterranean, Roger 'preferred the capture of Africa to that of Greece.'[127] He may indeed have also fostered the spread of Christianity there, but only in so far as this reinforced and established his political power.[128]

---

[122] Robert of Torigny, Chron. 153. The continuator of Sigebert, MGH SS 6.454, devotes five lines to this campaign and mentions that Roger restored the Archbishop of Africa (Al Mahdia) to his see: cf. J. Mesnage, Le Christianisme en Afrique: Déclin et extinction (Algiers and Paris 1915) 219-20 and 225. The fact that the Bishops of Al Mahdia seem to have resided at Palermo (Mesnage 219-20) suggests that Roger II may have used them as instruments of his dynastic policy.

[123] Peter the Venerable, Epistolae, in Bibliotheca Cluniacensis, ed. Martin Marrier (Paris 1614) ep. 6.16, col. 915. Peter here offers his sympathy to Roger on the death of his son, Roger, Duke of Apulia (May 2, 1148): Caspar 428: Curtis 294 and 239-40.

[124] See Caspar 397f.; Chalandon 157-62; Curtis 242-63; Cerone passim.

[125] Caspar 377-84; Chalandon 135-7; Curtis 227f.; Cerone 58-63; Cartellieri (n. 37 above) 367-9; Konrad Heilig, 'Ostrom und das Deutsche Reich um die Mitte des 12. Jahrhunderts,' Kaisertum und Herzogsgewalt im Zeitalter Friedrichs I. (Schriften des Reichsinstituts für ältere deutsche Geschichtskunde 9; Leipzig 1944) 161-2: '... zweifellos hat er (Roger) damit auch dem Kreuzzugsunternehmen schwer geschadet.'

[126] Cerone 68.

[127] Ibid. 63-4.

[128] Amari (the only scholar whom I have found who discusses this aspect of Roger's campaign) thought otherwise: 'Assaltando l'Affrica dunque nella state del 1148, il re de Sicilia comparia per la prima volta nel grande accordo cattolico,' op. cit. (n. 121 above) III 421. He, however, does not appear to have realized fully the connection of this cam-

This judgment on Roger II may be unjust or merely the result of a paucity of Christian sources. Decisions on mixed motives are always open to discussion. Certaihly the other campaigns of 1146-8 were also inspired by a variety of interests, but none the less these differed from Roger's undertaking. John LaMonte recently defined a crusade as 'a war against the enemies of the Church, conducted under the auspices of the Church for ecclesiastical purposes, with spiritual privileges specially assured to participants.'[129] If allowance is made for other than ecclesiastical causes and leadership, this definition may fairly be applied to most of the campaigns of 1146-8. But it certainly does not fit the expedition to North Africa.

The campaigns against the Moslems in the East and in Spain and against the Wends were marked by a specifically religious character which distinguishes them from the normal dynastic warfare of the Middle Ages: the character of pilgrimage. The participants in these expeditions all expected to enjoy the benefits accruing to pilgrims, that is, entire remission of their repented sins or at least of the penance imposed therefor. In nearly all the sources these expeditions have a marked salvatory or penitential character. It is a significant fact that contemporaries most frequently referred to these expeditions by the name of *peregrinatio* and to the participants as *peregrini* or *peregrinantes*, who were therefore only by context distinguished from the thousands of pilgrims who annually visited the Holy Land and other sacred places.[130] Several sources attributed a double purpose to the campaign: 'for

---

paign with Roger's withdrawal from Greece; but he realized Roger's aim, for he says of of the crusade that Roger 'ne usava gli avvantaggi,' *ibid.*

[129] John LaMonte, 'La Papauté et les Croisades,' *Renaissance* 2-3 (1944-5) 155.

[130] Other common names for the crusade include *iter, expeditio,* and *profectio,* sometimes with *Dei* or *Ierosolymitana,* and occasionally with some such phrase as *ad debellandos paganos* to indicate its military character. In no contemporary source is it called a crusade; the nearest equivalent is in the *Ann. sancti Iacobi Leodiensis,* MGH SS 16.641, where the soldiers are referred to as 'crucizatur.' Among the sources using the terms 'pilgrimage' and 'pilgrims,' see: *Ann. Herbipolenses,* MGH SS 16.3; *Ann. sancti Dionysii,* MGH SS 13.720; *Continuatio Praemonstratensis,* MGH SS 6.453; *Continuatio Claustroneoburgensis II,* MGH SS 9.614; Helmold of Bosau, *Chron. Slavorum* (n. 50 above) 115f.; Hildegard of Bingen, who referred to the Pope as 'pater peregrinorum': J. M. Watterich, *Pontificum Romanorum ... Vitae ab aequalibus conscriptae* (Leipzig 1862) II 302; William of Saint-Denis, in both the *Vita Sugeri* (in *Oeuvres complètes de Suger,* ed. Lecoy de la Marche [Société de l'Histoire de France; Paris 1867] 394-5) and 'Le dialogue apologétique du moine Guillaume, biographe de Suger,' ed. A. Wilmart, *Revue Mabillon* (1942) 103 and 109. Pfeiffer (n. 31 above) 8-9 has drawn attention to the fact that in the Middle Ages *peregrinatio* was a general term embracing the modern concepts of pilgrimage and crusade; but he maintains that medieval men in fact made this distinction. The sources on the Second Crusade do not support this view: they draw no clear line between a crusade and a pilgrimage. The crusaders were quite as much pilgrims as they were fighters: see Romuald of Salerno, *Chron.* ed. C. A. Garufi, RIS² 7. 1 229; Richard of Poitiers, *Chron.* RHGF 12.416, who says that King Louis '... in urbe Sancta, causa orationis, ut peregrinus re-

pilgrimage and for the avenging of Christianity,' says the author of the Gesta Abbatum Lobbiensium.[131] Others seem even to have considered that pilgrimage was the primary purpose of these expeditions.[132] Cardinal Boso, the papal biographer, refers to the Second Crusade merely as 'a very great expedition from the Western regions,'[133] which distinguishes it in no way in character from smaller pilgrimages.

Like their predecessors half a century earlier, and as befitted the members of 'the army of the living God,'[134] summoned by 'the edict of the true King,'[135] the participants in these expeditions marched or sailed under His banner, the *Vexillum crucis*, and all bore the mark of a cross.[136] A bull of

---

mansit'; Odo of Deuil, *De prof. Ludov.* ed. Berry (n. 9 above) 2; *Monumenta Boica* 12.329; *De glorioso rege Ludovico,* in *Vie de Louis le Gros par Suger* (n. 9 above) 160-1; and nn. 131 and 132 below. In their original forms, Erdmann has shown (*op. cit.* n. 64 above, 281-3), there was no popular association of the ideas of pilgrimage and of war against the heathen. By 1150, however, they were fully equated. This important development was principally the result of the fact that, through the exercise of the ecclesiastical power of remission of sins, a military expedition against non-Christians was put on an equal spiritual basis and rewarded with the same spiritual benefits as a pilgrimage: *ibid.* 306-7 and 319. There was as yet, however, little consciousness of the crusade as an institution or of the Second Crusade as a successor to the First. Very few sources refer to it as a *second* crusade at all; see *Chron. Regia Coloniensis,* rec. II (n. 54 above) 82; Bern. ep. 363, col. 568 (reference to Peter the Hermit); Henry of Huntingdon, *Hist. Angl.* (n. 9 above) 281; letters of the Emperor Manuel, RHGF 15.440-1 and 16.9-10. Louis VII was conscious of following a precedent: Odo of Deuil, ed. Berry 58 and 130; and Odo himself may have consulted an account of the First Crusade: William of Saint-Denis, 'Dialogue' 103. Important evidence of the survival at St. Denis of the tradition of the First Crusade is the window given by Suger, which is now lost but was reproduced by Montfaucon in his *Les Monuments de la Monarchie Françoise* I (Paris 1729) plates L-LIV (389f.): cf. F. de Mély, 'La Croix des premiers Croisés,' in vol. III of Paul Riant, *Exuviae sacrae Constantinopolitanae* (Paris 1904) 2-11.

[131] MGH SS 21.329. The *Chron. Regia Coloniensis* 82-3 says, '... mota sunt omnia regna Occidentis et accensa desiderio eundi in Ierusalem et visitare sepulchrum Domini ac dimicare contra gentes quae ignorant Deum et dilatare terminos christiani imperii in Oriente.'

[132] This is the case, for instance, with two crusaders who were not of very high rank. So Lambert of Ardres says that his father joined the crusade 'ut dominicum venerari et ... sepulchrum videre mereretur,' *Historia Comitum Ghisnenium et Ardensium,* MGH SS 24.633. Abbot Hermann of St. Martin of Tournai went '... gloriosum Domini Jesu Christi sepulchrum invisere multo ardore sitiens...,' D'Achéry, *Spicilegium* II 926. Cf. *Ann. Ratisponenses,* MGH SS 17.586.

[133] *Liber Pontificalis,* ed. Louis Duchesne II (Paris 1892) 387.

[134] Peter the Venerable (n. 123 above) ep. 6.16, col. 915.

[135] Charter of Henry of Prunnen, in Joseph von Hormayr, *Die Bayern im Morgenlande* (Munich 1832) 43.

[136] *De exp. Lyx.* 156. On the use of the cross and the cross-banner in the First Crusade and earlier, see Erdmann (n. 64 above) 30f. and 318-9. For an interesting archaeological study of the crusaders' cross, see F. de Mély (n. 130 above) 1-21; cf. the crosses worn by the crusaders illustrated on plate I in Runciman vol. II (fresco at Cressac, Charente)

Calixtus II refers to the soldiers of the Spanish Reconquest as those 'who have placed the sign of the cross on their clothes.'[137] Holding up the cross, and speaking in· words strongly reminiscent of the motto of Constantine, a priest cried 'In hoc vexillo ... vincetis'[138] to the Anglo-Flemish sailors and signed them with a cross.[139] Otto of Freising records that the crusaders against the Wends wore a cross with a circle underneath, a *globus cruciger*, to distinguish it from the simple cross of the crusaders in the Holy Land.[140] Those gathered at the great Council of Vézelay, in 1146, an anonymous chronicler says, 'received from Bernard (of Clairvaux) the sign of pilgrimage, as is the custom, that is, the cross.'[141] There is no reason to believe that this cross was restricted to the fighting members of these armies; it was the usual pilgrims' badge.[142] Here then is further evidence that the special religious

---

and Peter the Venerable, *Sermo de laude dominici sepulchri*, in Edmond Martène and Ursin Durand, *Thèsaurus Novus Anecdotorum* V (Paris 1717) 1439 B.

[137] JL 7116: Edmond Martène and Ursin Durand, *Veterum Scriptorum ... Amplissima Collectio* I (Paris 1724) 650-1, and *Bullaire du Pape Calixte II*, ed. Ulysse Robert (Paris 1891) II no. 454, pp. 266-7. See also the canons of the Ninth Ecumenical Council: Charles-Joseph Hefele, *Histoire des Conciles*, ed. and tr. H. Leclercq, V 1 (Paris 1912) 635.

[138] *De exp. Lyx.* 156 and n. 1.

[139] See above, 222, and n. 44.

[140] Otto of Freising, *Gesta* (n. 30 above) 61; cf. Bern. ep. 457, col. 652. As a Christian symbol, the *globus cruciger* dates back to late Antiquity. On the Ticinum silver festival issue of 315, Constantine 'bears on his shoulder the Cross of Christ with the globe on top': Andreas Alföldi, *The Conversion of Constantine and Pagan Rome*, tr. Harold Mattingly (Oxford 1948) 43 and 129 n. 14, cf. 131 n. 21. 'Die christlichen Kaiser führen als Bekrönung des Globus zunächst das Christusmonogramm, dann das Kreuz... Die Bedeutung des Kreuzes haben schon Prokop und Suidas richtig gewürdigt; es ist ein bildlicher Ausdruck für unsere Bezeichnung ‹ von Gottes Gnaden ›': Alois Schlachter, *Der Globus, seine Entstehung und Verwendung in der Antike* (*ΣΤΟΙΧΕΙΑ*, Studien zur Geschichte des antiken Weltbildes und der griechischen Wissenschaft 8; Leipzig-Berlin 1927) 69; cf. Alföldi, 'Eine spätrömische Helmform und ihre Schicksale im Germanisch-Romanischen Mittelalter,' *Acta Archaeologica* 5 (1934) 141-2. It persisted throughout the Middle Ages, in both Byzantine and Western art as a symbol of divine majesty and as an emblem of Christian temporal power: see Didron, *Iconographie Chrétienne* (Paris 1843) 597; Schlachter 105; Alföldi, 'Helmform' 143-4; André Grabar, *L'Empereur dans l'Art byzantin* (Publications de la Faculté des Lettres de l'Université de Strasbourg 75; Paris 1936), plates v, xxiv fig. 1, and xxx fig. 21; Percy Schramm, 'Das Herrscherbild in der Kunst des frühen Mittelalters,' *Vorträge der Bibliothek Warburg* 2 (1922-3) part I, 158 and plates vii-viii, figs. 13-17. It appeared frequently on medieval coins and seals: Gustave Schlumberger, Ferdinand Chalandon, and Adrien Blanchet, *Sigillographie de l'Orient Latin* (Haut Commissariat de l'État Français en Syrie et au Liban, Service des Antiquités: Bibliothèque archéologique et historique 37; Paris 1943), plates i (1,2,3,4), v (1), vi (1,2,3), vii (1,2,3, 5,6,9), etc.; and Florence Harmer, 'The English Contribution to the Epistolary Usages of the Early Scandinavian Kings,' *Saga-Book* of the Viking Society 13 (1949-50) part III, 137, 140-1 and figs. 3 and 4.

[141] RHGF 12.120.

[142] See above, 225, and n. 65; and Étienne van Cauwenbergh, *Les pèlerinages expiatoires*

nature of these crusaders, in the root meaning of the term, was that of pilgrimage.

The crusaders' cross had, by the middle of the twelfth century, advanced a long way from its early medieval significance as a battle standard against the pagans. But this character was not altogether lost.[143] It still had a significance for the organization of the crusading armies, as did various oaths taken by the soldiers. The military regulations established by the Anglo-Flemish crusaders, and accepted by them in a stringent oath, to preserve order, obey the leaders, and attend regular religious service, have already been noted.[144] Odo of Deuil says that for the French army at Metz, Louis 'established laws necessary for (the preservation of) the peace and for the other requirements on the way, which the leaders confirmed by (their) oaths and faith.'[145] The Genoese took vows to obey their leaders and to carry out the purpose of their expedition.[146] The reference of the Magdeburg chronicler to the army gathered against the Wends as a 'societas' implies that it was bound by some kind of common oath.[147] With justice, therefore, a charter of Duke Welf characterized the year 1147 as the time 'when the entire Roman world swore together ... for the expeditions to Jerusalem.'[148]

The nature of these oaths was related, however, not only to the military organization of the crusaders but also to their religious character as pilgrims. The vow of pilgrimage was, of course, a familiar concept in the Middle Ages; and to it now was linked the idea of the crusaders' cross, found in the chronicle previously quoted, as a badge of pilgrims, the external sign and reminder of their vow. The Genoese swore to remain at Tortosa until the city fell; the English and Flemings had sworn to reach Jerusalem, as had countless other soldiers in the eastward-bound armies: the oath was not taken simply to preserve order, but to attain a specific object and to reach a specific place. In this it closely resembled or was perhaps identical with the vow of pilgrimage.

This resemblance was naturally the closer in that both the pilgrimage and the crusade were undertaken in order to secure specific spiritual benefits for the participants. Unlike the pilgrimage, however, the crusade, in the view of many contemporaries, went beyond this highly personal religious relation. It had a marked spirit of self-sacrifice. 'To lay down their lives

---

et judiciaires dans le droit communal de la Belgique au Moyen Age (Université de Louvain: Recueil de Travaux publiés par les Membres des Conférences d'Histoire et de Philologie 48; 1922) 22-3.

[143] Erdmann (n. 64 above) 318 suggests that in this cross may be seen the first intimation of the modern uniform.

[144] See above, 222.

[145] Odo of Deuil, ed. Berry 20.

[146] See above, n. 80.

[147] *Ann. Magdeburgenses*, MGH SS 16.188.

[148] *Monumenta Boica* 7.348.

for their brethren and to free the Christian people from the sword of the pagans' were the aims of the crusaders according to an anonymous Bohemian monk.[149] The Anglo-Flemish priest compared them to the apostles: ' You, most dearly beloved brothers, (have) followed Christ as voluntary exiles who have willingly accepted poverty...'[150] Gerhoh of Reichersberg, in many respects the most bitter critic of the crusaders, nevertheless regarded their purpose as pious and indeed compared their sacrifice to that of Christ Himself: 'Since indulgence from sins was promised by the Apostolic See to fighters and penitents,' in this crusade, he explained, and 'most greatly to those who died in such holy strife, requiting their Savior, Who had died for them.'[151] The crusade had therefore a salvatory and penitential value far beyond the interests of the individual crusader; he who died on crusade was a martyr and a saint, who stored up merit in heaven for his brethren.[152] It was the concern therefore not only of the participants themselves but of the entire Christian community. So before the assault on Santarem, Alfonso of Portugal encouraged his troops with the news that 'today ... general prayer is offered for us both by the Canons of Santa Croce, to whom I announced this matter and in whom I trust, and by the other clergy together with the entire people.'[153] Likewise Conrad III, in a letter to Wibald in 1147, wrote that, 'As the progress of our journey is aimed at the welfare of the whole Church and the honor of our realm, we hope and request to be assisted greatly by your prayers.'[154] It is not suggested here that any strict uniformity of crusading theory can be found in the sources. In particular the idea of vicarious satisfaction went considerably beyond the more narrowly personal interpretation of the crusade found in the theories of Eugene III and St. Bernard, who were themselves, as will be seen, not in complete agreement over this problem.

Many of the more popular ideas are illustrated in the charters issued by

---

[149] *Monachi Sazavensis Continuatio* (Cosmae Chronicarum Bohemorum), MGH SS 9.159; cf. 1 John 3.16.

[150] *De exp. Lyx.* 152.

[151] Gerhoh of Reichersberg, *Commentarius aureus in Psalmos*, ed. Bernhard Pez in *Thesaurus Anecdotorum novissimus* V (Augsburg 1728) 794 (also in MGH, *Libelli de Lite* III [Hannover 1897] 437): '...reddentes vicem salvatori suo, qui pro eis mortuus est.' Cf. Lamentations 3.64 and 1 Timothy 5.4.

[152] See *Chron. Ad. Imp.* ed. Belgrano v. 4, and above p. 222 and n. 43. For references in the AS to miracles performed by participants in the Second Crusade, see Ch. Kohler, 'Rerum et personarum quae in Actis Sanctorum Bollandistis ... ad Orientem latinum spectant Index analyticus,' *Mélanges pour servir à l'histoire de l'Orient latin et des Croisades* I (Paris 1906) 104-212, to whose list may be added St. Ernest, AS 7 November, III 608-17.

[153] *De exp. Scal.* (n. 115 above) 95.

[154] *Monumenta Corbeiensia* (n. 25 above) ep. 48, p. 126.

crusaders. These have been collected for the region of Bavaria by Hormayr,[155] and others can be found in local cartularies and collections. Many gifts to ecclesiastical houses resembled that of Herant the Old of Falkenstein to Antwart, made 'at the time when the said Lord Herant desired to go to Jerusalem in order to visit the sepulchre of the Lord.'[156] Some grants were made on condition that the property was to be restored to the donor if he returned;[157] others specified that the gift was to be made only if the donor did not return.[158] Many crusaders were forced to sell their property in order to meet the heavy expenses of the journey. To raise money for this purpose and 'in remission of my sins,' Theoderic of Flanders sold some property to the monks of Clairvaux.[159] Others made grants to religious houses in return for protection for their wives and families.[160] These are but a few examples from many.[161] While it must be borne in mind that apparent gifts

---

[155] Hormayr (n. 135 above) 43-6, whose examples are mostly taken from the *Monumenta Boica*. His citations are occasionally erroneous, but there is no evidence that these documents are forgeries, like those in some of Hormayr's works: see Friedrich Bock, 'Fälschungen des Freiherrn von Hormayr,' *Neues Archiv* 47 (1928) 225-43.

[156] Hormayr 43.

[157] See, for instance, the *Monumenta Boica* 3.84 (Hormayr 43); *Urkundenbuch des Herzogthums Steiermark*, ed. J. Zahn I (Graz 1875) no. 270, p. 281, and no. 266, p. 279. Reginher of Tovernich made his grant to Admont whether he returned or not: *ibid.* no. 271, p. 282.

[158] *Ibid.* no. 294, p. 302 (cf. Jakob Wichner, *Geschichte des Benediktiner-Stiftes Admont von den ältesten Zeiten bis zum Jahre 1177* [Graz 1874] 100 and n. 2); *Codex traditionum ecclesiae collegiatae Claustroneoburgensis*, ed. Maximilian Fischer (Fontes Rerum Austriacarum, Abt. II, vol. 4; Vienna 1851) no. 396, p. 85 (cf. Fischer, *Merkwürdigere Schicksale des Stiftes und der Stadt Klosterneuburg* II [Vienna 1815] no. 87, p. 51).

[159] PL 185 ii. 1824. Likewise Conrad of Peilstein sold various lands 'pro remedio anime sue et pro precio sexaginta quinque librarum': *Urkundenbuch ... Steiermark* no. 265, p. 278 (Wichner 102-3; Albert von Muchar, *Geschichte des Herzogthums Steiermark* III [Graz 1846] 347).

[160] *Urkundenbuch ... Steiermark* no. 268, p. 280 (Wichner no. 15, p. 216).

[161] Besides Hormayr, see the documentary references cited by Röhricht (n. 9 above) II 311-20, in his list of German pilgrims; *Cartulaire de l'Abbaye N.D. de Bonnevaux*, ed. Ulysse Chevalier (Documents historiques inédits sur le Dauphiné 7; Grenoble 1889) no. 244, pp. 102-3; *Recueil des Chartes de l'Abbaye de Cluny*, edd. Auguste Bernard and Alexandre Bruel, V (Collection de Documents inédits sur l'Histoire de France; Paris 1894) no. 4131 pp. 473-4 (Bernard III of Uxelles, 'quando voluit ire Iherosolimam,' disclaimed any rights in the lands of Cluny); *Urkundenbuch für die Geschichte des Niederrheins*, ed. Theodor Lacomblet I (Düsseldorf 1840) no. 364, pp. 249-50; *Urkundenbuch ... Steiermark* nos. 266-275, pp. 278-84; no. 290, pp. 299-300; no. 425, p. 406 (cf. Wichner nos. 13-18, pp. 214-8); Wichner pp. 101, 174, and 182 (Poppo of Piber sold his estate for twenty-five pounds and a horse before leaving on the crusade); Emile Bridrey, *La condition juridique des croisés et le privilège de croix* (Paris 1900) 48 n. 3 (unedited charter of Louis VII); Luchaire (n. 18 above) no. 215, p. 168, and perhaps no. 395, pp. 227 and 407-8; von Muchar III 347, and IV (Graz 1848) 401f.; J. P. von Ludewig, *Reliquae Manuscriptorum omnis aevi* IV (Frank-

were often in reality sales, the fact remains that much property changed hands on account of the crusade and not always to the material advantage of the crusadèrs. 'At the root of the pious transaction,' A. H. Thompson once said, 'was the desire to obtain forgiveness for sin and remission of the penalty due to it;'[162] and any consideration of motive should take these gifts and sales into account.

The most complete contemporary statement of the crusaders' motives is found in the *Annales Herbipolenses*, whose anonymous author was, however, thoroughly critical of the entire undertaking.

> Different men, however, had different purposes. For some, eager for novelty, went for the sake of learning about strange lands; others, driven by want and suffering from hardship at home, were ready to fight not only against the enemies of the cross of Christ but also against Christian friends, if there seemed a chance of relieving their poverty. Others, who were weighed down by debt or who thought to evade the service that they owed their lords or who even were dreading the well merited penalties of their crimes, while simulating a holy zeal, hastened (to the

---

furt and Leipzig 1722) 196-8; and cf. the later, but very interesting, letter from Alexander III to Louis VII: JL 10796, RHGF 15.789-90.

By such purchases, mortgages, and gifts many churches substantially increased their property. 'Tempore quo expeditio Jerosolymitana ... totum commovit fere occidentem, ceperunt singuli tanquam ultra non redituri vendere possessiones suas, quas Ecclesiae secundum facultates suas suis prospicientes utilitatibus emerunt': *Monumenta Boica* 3.540. And the author of the *Chron. Tornacensis*, in *Corpus Chronicorum Flandriae*, ed. J.-J. de Smet II (Brussels 1841) 564, says of the crusaders: '... nonnulla praedia et possessiones quae habebant vendentes, pretiumque eorum secum deferentes.' This occasionally led to difficulties. Bartholomew of Cicon, on his 'deathbed' at Jerusalem, promised to return to the priory of Mouthier-Haute-Pierre a mill and seven serfs; but when he recovered, he thought better of his promise, which, however, the priory, with the aid of the Archbishop of Besançon, forced him to keep: see Auguste Castan, *Un épisode de la deuxième croisade* (Besançon 1862). On the other hand, it must be remembered that crusading clerics were not above selling the property of their churches: see *Translatio sancti Mamantis*, AS, 17 August, III 443. Laymen, also, occasionally seized ecclesiastical possessions for this purpose: Theoderic of Flanders took two pieces from the treasury of St. Columba at Sens: *Chron. Senonense Sanctae Columbae*, RHGF 12.288.

On the financing of this crusade in general, see Pfeiffer (n. 31 above) 78-81; Bridrey 45-6 and 66f. The relevant sources, of which Mrs. Berry has kindly sent me a list, include the *Fragmentum hist. ex veteri membrana de tributo Floriacensibus imposito*, RHGF 12.94-5; a letter from John of Ferrières to Suger, *ibid.* 15.497; and a letter from the royal chancellor Cadurcus to Suger, *ibid.* 497-8. But the evidence of these and later (Ralph of Diceto and Matthew Paris) sources is either unreliable or indefinite. Louis VII may have subjected certain churches to a crusading aid, but it is far from clear that this was a general tax, of which many historians speak. Nor does this levy appear to have roused any 'mécontentement général,' to which Bridrey 69 and A. Vuitry, *Études sur le régime financier de la France avant la Révolution de 1789* (Paris 1878) 390-1, refer. This whole problem is in need of further study.

[162] A. H. Thompson, 'Medieval Doctrine to the Lateran Council of 1215,' CMH 6.694.

X

crusade) chiefly to escape such inconveniences and anxieties. With difficulty, however, there were found a few who had not bowed the knee to Baal, who were indeed guided by a sacred and salutary purpose and were kindled by love of the divine majesty to fight manfully, even to shed their blood, for the sake of the holy of holies.[163]

III. Ecclesiastical Theory and Papal Direction
of the Expeditions of 1147-8

St. Bernard, Abbot of Clairvaux, is the traditional hero of the Second Crusade. In almost all the contemporary sources and in the later authorities, where he shares the honors with Louis VII and occasionally with Pope Eugene III, Bernard appears as the principal organizer and preacher.[164] It is, indeed, hard to imagine the crusade apart from this commanding figure, whose letters and personal activity inspired the participation of the greater part of Europe in these expeditions. He was at first reluctant to assume this burden. The reason may have been the political motive suggested by Gleber[165] but was more probably the ecclesiastical prohibition against preaching by the regular clergy. Even ordained monks and abbots were permitted to preach outside their monasteries only on the delegation of the Pope or diocesan bishop.[166] But at Easter, 1146, on the express command of the Pope, Bernard began to preach the crusade at Vézelay, where he marked with the cross of pilgrimage King Louis and many French nobles. During the Winter of 1146-7, he was in the Lowlands and Germany, where his preaching and concurrent miracles changed the entire character and scope of the undertaking by securing the co-operation of Conrad III and the German princes.[167] The crusading ardor thus aroused in Saxony and Bohemia was turned against the Wends. In June and July of 1147, Bernard visited Languedoc;[168] and although by this time the army of Louis VII had already left France, it is

[163] *Ann. Herbipolenses*, MGH SS 16.3; cf. Gerhoh of Reichersberg, *Libri III de Investigatione Antichristi*, ed. F. Scheibelberger I (Linz 1875) chap. 67, and in MGH, *Libelli de Lite* 3.374-5.

[164] The bibliography on St. Bernard is enormous; for a list of books and articles dealing with Bernard and the Second Crusade, see Pfeiffer (n. 31 above) 44 n. 16. Georg Hüffer, 'Die Anfänge des Zweiten Kreuzzuges,' *Historisches Jahrbuch* 8 (1887) 391-429, especially emphasizes the part played by Eugene III.

[165] Helmut Gleber, *Papst Eugen III* (Beiträge zur mittelalterlichen und neueren Geschichte 6; Jena 1936) 43-8.

[166] This was suggested by Pfeiffer 8-10, whose idea I develop below, Appendix A.

[167] See Bernhardi (n. 1 above) 532-3, Georg Hüffer, *Der heilige Bernhard von Clairvaux* I: *Vorstudien* (Münster 1886) 70-103. H. Cosack, 'Konrads III. Entschluss zum Kreuzzug,' *Mitteilungen des Instituts für österreichische Geschichtsforschung* 35 (1914) 278-96; Greven (n. 106 above); Pfeiffer 48f.

[168] The purpose of this visit seems to have been to deal with local heresy: Bern. ep. 242 coll. 436-7.

difficult not to associate Bernard's presence with the departure in August of the naval expedition under Alfonso of Toulouse[169] and particularly with the crusading activity in Spain of William of Montpellier.

More important, however, than the preaching of St. Bernard and the activity of his agents[170] were the letters which he sent all over Europe and which were presumably read to hundreds of congregations. Of his crusading letters, only ten are known today. Nine relate to the campaign against the Moslems in the Holy Land and have been minutely studied by Peter Rassow;[171] the tenth was written later, after March, 1147, for the crusade against

---

[169] Alfonso himself had taken the cross at Vézelay: *De glorioso rege Ludovico* in *Vie de Louis le Gros* (n. 9 above) 158. On Bernard's visit and the departure of this expedition, see DeVic and Vaissete III 752-5 and IV 223-4 (note L, xii).

[170] In general, on the active part played by the Cistercians in the preparations for the crusade, see Pfeiffer 44-54 and 78-81. When possible, Bernard preached the crusade in person rather than by letters carried by agents: in ep. 363, col. 565, he says, 'Agerem id libentius viva voce...' Occasionally other Cistercian abbots were able to preach, such as Rainald of Morimund: Pfeiffer 46; cf. Hilde Fechner, *Die politischen Theorien des Abtes Bernhard von Clairvaux in seinen Briefen* (Bonn and Cologne 1933) 61. Simple monks were presumably not allowed to preach (cf. Appendix A) but were sent with letters wherever Bernard or another abbot was unable to go. Most celebrated among these is Rudolph, who in at least one chronicle (*Gesta Abbatum Lobbiensium*, MGH SS 21.329) appears as a crusading preacher more important than Bernard, since he took it on himself, with Lambert Abbot of Lobbes as translator, to preach the crusade in the Summer and Autumn of 1146 in the Lowlands and in the Rhine valley, where he aroused a terrible persecution of the Jews. St. Bernard was furious (see his ep. 365 to the Archbishop of Mainz, who may well have been nervous, remembering the sack of the archiepiscopal palace at Mainz during the riots connected with the First Crusade: Runciman I 138-9) and sent Rudolph packing back to Clairvaux: see Bernhardi 522-4; Cosack 281-2 and 294 n. 1; Pfeiffer 46-7. — Bernard's secretary Nicholas wrote several crusading letters for his master: Rassow (n. 45 above) 245-6; on Nicholas, see Augustin Steiger, 'Nikolaus, Mönch in Clairvaux, Sekretär des hl. Bernhard,' *Studien und Mitteilungen zur Geschichte des Benediktinerordens und seiner Zweige* 38 (Neue Folge 7; 1917) 41-50; Pfeiffer 45; and Jean Leclercq, 'Saint Bernard et ses secrétaires,' *Revue Bénédictine* 61 (1951) 220. The secretary Geoffrey carried a letter to the Bretons: Rassow 265 and 274; on Geoffrey, see Leclercq 220-5, and Greven (n. 106 above) 6-8. Geoffrey, together with another secretary, Gerhard, was constantly with Bernard on his travels for the crusade: Pfeiffer 46f. Abbot Adam of Ebrach carried to the diet of Regensburg (February, 1147) two of Bernard's letters, one of which was taken on to Bohemia by Henry of Olmütz: Rassow 265-6 and 274-5; Heinrich von Fichtenau, 'Bamberg, Würzburg, und die Stauferkanzlei,' *Mitteilungen des österreichischen Instituts für Geschichtsforschung* 53 (1939) 274; Pfeiffer 49 and 51-2. He probably also carried a letter to Abbot Gerlach of Rein, who preached the crusade in the Steiermark and Carinthia: Pfeiffer 49 and 52-3.

[171] To Speyer, East France and Bavaria, Cologne, Brescia, England, Bohemia, Brittany and possibly Spain: see Rassow 243f. and Cosack 293-6. The letter to the Archbishop and congregation of Cologne has since been printed by Greven 44-8. To these letters should also be added that addressed to the Hospitallers discovered at Jena by Jean Leclercq and published in the *Revue Mabillon* 43 (1953) 1-4, together with an interesting letter written

the Wends, and differs from the others in both form and content.[172] To these
letters may be added a few others which bear upon the crusade. These include a letter to the Pope, one to Archbishop Henry of Mainz, and another
written in Bernard's name to recommend to the Emperor Manuel a young
crusader, Henry of Meaux, later Count of Champagne, and father of the
future King of Jerusalem.[173] A letter mentioned by Hüffer and Vacandard
further suggests that Bernard addressed a crusading appeal to Spain.[174] It is
possible, also, that his letter 308 to Alfonso Henriques refers to the 1147
campaign in Portugal.[175] There is in any case evidence of Bernard's influence
in Portugal at this time. Alfonso, it will be remembered, was the son of
an ambitious knight from Burgundy and maintained connections with this
area. As recently as 1146 he had married Mathilda, the daughter of the
crusading Count Amadeus III of Savoy.[176] After the fall of Santarem, and
in honor of this victory, Alfonso founded the Cistercian monastery of Alco-
baça.[177] In addition, the speech of the Bishop of Porto to the Anglo-Flemish

---

to Louis VII by one 'W. Dei gratia dux et miles Christi et servus crucis,' who says, in
words strongly reminiscent of Bernard's crusading letters, that he has received the cross
'ex manibus sanctissimis abbatis Claraevallis' and discusses the preparations for, and the
route of the crusade.

[172] Bern. ep. 457, coll. 651-2; Rassow 275; see n. 222 below.

[173] Bern. epp. 247 (coll. 445-7), 365 (coll. 570-1) and 468 (coll. 672-3). On ep. 468 see
Rassow 274 and E. Pfeiffer, 'Die Stellung des hl. Bernhard zur Kreuzzugsbewegung nach
seinen Schriften,' Cistercienser-Chronik 46 (1934) 276 n. 28. Epp. 256 and 364 (coll. 463-5
and 568-70), which Mabillon dates 1146, in fact refer to the preparations for the crusade
of 1150: ibid. 306 n. 90.

[174] Hüffer (n. 164 above) 392, and E. Vacandard, Vie de saint Bernard (3rd. ed. Paris
1903) II 303 n. 1, who mention a letter 'ad peregrinantes Jerusalem' in the Royal Archives
at Barcelona. Rassow was unable to locate this letter: loc. cit. 246.

[175] The meaning and date of this letter are not above dispute. Mabillon's late date of
1153 seems to be based upon a confusion between 'Peter the brother of Your Excellency'
(Petrus Celsitudinis vestrae frater) and Peter Abbot of Celle to whom ep. 419 is addressed:
Sancti Bernardi ... Opera omnia, ed. Jean Mabillon (Paris 1839) I 1.937. The letter certainly suggests that this Peter joined the Second Crusade: see Azevado (n. 115 above) 47-8.
If it may therefore be dated in 1147, it shows that Bernard was in close touch with Portugal
at this time. Another letter to Alfonso, in Manrique, Cist. Ann. II (n. 80 above) under 1147,
IX (p. 71) appears to be a forgery: see Mabillon, Bernardi... Opera I 1.767-8 and 959; Defourneaux (n. 69 above) 212-3.

[176] Previté Orton (n. 9 above) 292-3: Livermore (n. 37 above) 83.

[177] Leopold Janauschek, Originum Cisterciensium Tomus I (Vienna 1877) 110; L. H.
Cottineau, Répertoire topo-bibliographique des abbayes et prieurés (Mâcon 1939) I 50-1.
The inscription printed by Brandão (n. 115 above) 147 suggests 1147 rather than 1148 as
the foundation date; the Peter mentioned here may be either the brother or the son of
Alfonso Henriques (ibid. 147-50) — possibly the brother mentioned by St. Bernard in
ep. 308 (see n. 175 above). Cf. De Broqua, Le Portugal feudataire de Clairvaux (Dijon 1927)
31, whose suggestion of 1142 seems to have no basis whatsoever.

crusaders shows the influence of Bernard.[178] Be this as it may, the crusading letters alone show that Bernard regarded the crusade as embracing the efforts of all Christian Europe.

The essence of Bernard's crusading theory is contained in his letter 363, of which the text was sent in an almost identical form to Cologne, to Speyer, and to the East Franks and Bavarians.[179] Here he announces that the enemies of the cross, the pagans, have risen up against the Church. This is God's punishment for our sins; but since He is good, even while He punishes us, He provides us with a means of salvation through the crusade. 'Behold, brothers,' he calls, '... (now) is the time of plentiful salvation.' [180] This is 'a time rich with indulgence,' 'a jubilee year.' [181] He urges his hearers to take advantage of this great opportunity and to rise up in response. 'Accept the sign of the cross,' he says, 'and you will obtain pardon equally for all things which you confess with a humble heart.'[182] He mentions also some of the temporal benefits of crusaders, but his greatest stress is upon the penitential, salvatory nature of the crusade. Nowhere does he say that the crusade must be to the Holy Land; he only exhorts men to take the cross of pilgrimage, to fight against the foes of God, and so to win salvation.

This passionate enthusiasm and eloquence and an emphasis on the personal religious significance of the crusading vow were the great contributions of Bernard of Clairvaux to the Second Crusade and to crusading theory in general.[183] The planning and organization of the campaigns seem to have

---

[178] *De exp. Lyx.* 68-84; see n. 49 above. Rassow 271 considers this speech evidence of Cistercian influence on the author of the *De exp. Lyx.*; but I agree with Cramer (n. 44 above) 59 n. 26, that it has the appearance of being a genuine report, not a literary concoction. In this case, it witnesses the presence of Bernard's ideas in Portugal. On the influence of St. Bernard on Alfonso Henriques' 1147 campaign, see Azevado 46-8 and 95, who concludes that, 'certo è que nessa concessão, obtida de Eugénio III, para a expedição contra Lisboa, o principal agenciador foi o mesmo S. Bernardo, a isso movido pelo nosso primeiro rei,' 47; and Livermore, who says that the Cistercians were established in Portugal before 1143 and that they 'performed the enormous task of peopling and cultivating the newly-won territory,' 81.

[179] Bern. ep. 363, coll. 564-8. The last three sections did not appear in the earliest version of the crusading letter, that to Bishop Mainfred and the congregation of Brescia, in Baronius, *Annales Ecclesiastici,* ed. A. Theiner, 18 (*1094-1146*; Bar-le-Duc 1869) 646-7: see Rassow 273. On Bernard's crusading theory see Adolf Gottlob, *Kreuzablass und Almosenablass* (Kirchenrechtliche Abhandlungen 30-1; Stuttgart 1906) 110-13; Nikolaus Paulus, *Geschichte des Ablasses im Mittelalter* I (Paderborn 1922) 199-200; Pfeiffer (n. 173 above) 278f.; Cramer 49-55; and Rousset, *op. cit.* (n. 8 above) 152-68.

[180] Bern. col. 565.

[181] Bern. col. 566; cf. Villey (n. 68 above) 146.

[182] Bern. col. 567.

[183] On the importance of Bernard's letters in the history of the preaching of the crusades, see Reinhold Röhricht, 'Die Kreuzpredigten gegen den Islam,' *Zeitschrift für Kirchengeschichte* 6 (1884) 555, and Cramer 54-5.

been more the work of Pope Eugene. For, while the studies of Rassow have shown that Bernard had no part in the genesis of the crusade before the Council at Vézelay in 1146, the work of Caspar has convincingly demonstrated that the formal origin of the crusade must be traced to the Pope's crusading bull of December 1, 1145.[184] St. Bernard himself made this clear when he wrote to the Pope in 1146 about 'the good work which (King Louis) has begun at your instigation...'[185] Even before this, and perhaps as early as May 1145, Eugene had granted a remission of one seventh of their penance to those who gave aid to the knights of St. John in Jerusalem or to the Templars in Spain.[186] Now, in the bull *Quantum predecessores* (I), he officially declared a crusade. It is addressed to the King, nobles, and people of France. The Church of the East is in danger, he says: as a punishment for our sins, Edessa has fallen, and the whole of Christendom is threatened. He urges and requires devout men in France and Italy to rise and protect the Eastern Church. To such men he promises 'that remission of sins which our predecessor Urban established' and he takes their property and families under the protection of the Church. Such soldiers of the Lord, he continues, should not wear rich clothes, nor bring along dogs or hawks. Nor are they bound to pay usury. And he concludes by repeating that 'by the authority vested in us by God we grant such remission of sins and absolution ... that whoever will faithfully begin and complete such a holy journey or will die on it, will obtain absolution from all his sins which he will have confessed with a contrite

---

[184] Erich Caspar and Peter Rassow, 'Die Kreuzzugsbullen Eugens III.,' *Neues Archiv* 45 (1924) 285-305. Caspar's conclusions are supported by Gleber (n. 165 above) 37-8, who gives a careful survey of previous opinions and says of Caspar's work: 'Damit ist zugleich festgelegt, dass Eugen III. den ersten Anstoss zur neuen Kreuzzugsbewegung gegeben hat,' 38. Although Gleber admits that it is not impossible that Louis VII reached a similar idea independently, he certainly acted later than the Pope. The statement by Marshall W. Baldwin, 'The Papacy and the Levant during the Twelfth Century,' *Bulletin of the Polish Institute of Arts and Sciences in America* 3 (1944-5) 280, that 'a comparatively recent study (Gleber) suggests that King Louis VII of France assumed the initiative and was supported later by Pope Eugenius III,' appears to misinterpret Gleber's work. For a thorough bibliography, up to 1939, of the vexed problem of the origins of the Second Crusade, see Cramer 45 n. 1.

[185] Bern. ep. 247, coll. 445-7.

[186] *PU in Frankreich*, ed. Wilhelm Wiederhold, *Nachrichten von der königlichen Gesellschaft der Wissenschaften zu Göttingen*, Philologisch-historische Klasse 1907 (Beiheft) no. 22, pp. 91-2 (May 10, 1145?; Gleber, Beilage III [pp. 191-206] no. 20); *PU in Spanien, II: Navarra und Aragon*, ed. Paul Kehr, *Abhandlungen der Ges. der Wiss. zu Göttingen*, Phil.-hist. Klasse, Neue Folge 22.1 (1928) no. 57, pp. 360-1 (Nov. 9, 1145-6; Gleber no. 40); *PU in Sizilien*, ed. Paul Kehr, *Nachrichten...* 1899, no. 3, p. 313 (Nov. 13, 1145-6; Gleber no. 41); *Acta Pontificum Romanorum inedita*, ed. J. von Pflugk-Harttung I (Tübingen 1880) no. 201, pp. 183-4 (Oct. 27, 1145-6; JL 8829). It seems highly probable, from their content, that these bulls belong to 1145. Such grants were, of course, nothing new. Cf. also Eugene's bull of July 16, 1145-6 (JL 8821), of which the Nov. 13 bull is an almost exact repeat.

and humble heart and will receive the fruit of eternal reward from the Re-
munerator of all things.'[187]

The most important element in this bull from the view-point of crusading
theory was its concept of the indulgence, of which the transcendental implications were here fully developed. 'Herewith Eugene III,' Valmar Cramer
has said, 'conceives of a clearer idea of the indulgence than Urban II. Whereas
the latter spoke in his crusading canon only of the remission of the outer
penitential punishment imposed by the Church, Eugene III, by appealing
to the power over the Keys of the Pope as successor to the Prince of the
Apostles, Peter, includes as well for the first time absolution from temporal
[i. e. divine] punishments of sin which, independent from the ecclesiastical
penitential discipline, are inflicted by God for every sin.'[188]

This statement may exaggerate the extent of conscious innovation in
Quantum predecessores. Eugene himself clearly regarded his indulgence as
similar in nature to that of 1095. Certain scholars, moreover, incline towards
the view that the indulgence in the later eleventh century included the remission not only of the ecclesiastical but also of the divine punishment.[189]

Essentially, however, the idea expressed by Cramer is correct. The first
half of the twelfth century was a period of widespread confusion and rapid
development of ecclesiastical teaching concerning the forgiveness of sins.[190]
Nothing illustrates this more clearly than the widely diverging views expressed by Gratian and Peter Lombard on the sacrament of penance, and
in the works of these and other contemporary theologians it is impossible
to find any fully consistent or clear doctrine on this subject. Theology distinguished three different effects of the sin upon the sinner: sin made him
liable, first, to eternal damnation or divine punishment after death; second,
it brought the stain of guilt or damage onto the soul; and it entailed, third,

---

[187] JL 8796; Otto of Freising, *Gesta* 1.36, pp. 55-7.

[188] Cramer (n. 44 above) 48. Cf. Paulus (n. 179 above) I 199; Bernhard Poschmann, *Die
abendländische Kirchenbusse im frühen Mittelalter* (Breslauer Studien zur historischen
Theologie 16; 1930) 225-7; and especially Gottlob (n. 179 above) 105, who says: 'Die
transcendentalen Wirkungen des Ablasses traten in dem zweiten Kreuzzuge ... zum ersten
Male deutlich hervor.'

[189] Joannes Morinus, *Commentarius historicus de disciplina in administratione sacramenti
Poenitentiae* (Antwerp 1682) 775; Josef Jungmann, *Die lateinischen Bussriten in ihrer
geschichtlichen Entwicklung* (Forschungen zur Geschichte des innerkirchlichen Lebens
3/4; Innsbruck 1932) 285-9; and Paul Anciaux, *La théologie du sacrement de pénitence au
XIIe siècle* (Universitas Catholica Lovaniensis: Dissertationes ad gradum magistri...,
Series II, 41; Louvain and Gembloux 1949) 51 n. 3.

[190] This subject has been carefully studied by Amédée Teetaert, *La confession aux laïques*
(Univ. Cath. Lovan.: Diss. II 17; Wetteren-Bruges-Paris 1926) 85-101, and by Anciaux
50-1, 196-208, and 272-4, who says of Gratian: 'Le manque de clarté dans l'exposé du
célèbre canoniste illustre à sa façon la complexité du problème au sujet de la confession,
aussi bien que les hésitations des auteurs de la première moitié du xII^e siècle,' 207.

ecclesiastical punishment. It was universally accepted that the priesthood had complete control over ecclesiastical discipline, but Peter Lombard and Gratian make it clear that there was considerable disagreement over the extent to which priestly absolution touched upon the other two effects of sin. Peter points out that some authors, while reserving to God the remission of the guilt (the *macula culpae* or *contagio ac caecitas mentis*), claimed for the clergy the power of remitting the divine punishment (the *debitum aeternae mortis* or *debitum futurae poenae*). Other theologians, however, reserved to God both these functions and consequently in the sacrament of penance asserted the efficacy of contrition rather than of confession.[191]

This latter point of view tended to prevail in the early twelfth century and was powerfully developed by Abaelard. He emphasized in his doctrine of penance the sole efficacy of contrition and therefore reduced the power of the priest in this sacrament to a declaration of the divine pardon (granted at the moment of inner repentance) and to the right of excommunication, reconciliation, and the imposition of penitential satisfaction (the ecclesiastical punishment).[192]

Hugh of St. Victor in particular reacted against this doctrine and against its purely declarative interpretation of priestly absolution and its reservation to God of the power to remit both the guilt and the eternal punishment. He argued that by virtue of the power of the Keys all priests enjoyed the authority not merely to declare the pardon granted by God but actually themselves to remit the divine punishment. 'In confessione,' he claimed, 'peccatum ipsum, id est debitum damnationis absolvatur.'[193] In this teaching he was followed by the Victorine school, by Otto of Lucca, and to a certain extent by Peter Lombard, who admitted that God would confirm the remission by a priest of the divine punishment of a repentent sinner.[194] Peter preserved, however, the essentials of the Abaelardian doctrine and reserved to God the ultimate power to remit both the guilt and the divine punishment.[195]

---

[191] Anciaux 328f. 'Gratian in his *Decretum*,' says E. F. Jacob ('Innocent III,' CMH 6.38), 'had balanced and compared the views of those who said that contrition alone was necessary and confession to a priest merely the attestation of pardon, and of those who maintained that complete remission could not take place before confession and satisfaction.'

[192] Anciaux 275-95. This doctrine was followed by many twelfth-century canonists, including Roland Bandinelli (Alexander III), Omnebene, and Zachary of Besançon, on whom see Anciaux 263-4 and 312f. Teetaert (n. 190 above) emphasizes that 'au douzième siècle l'attention des théologiens se concentre sur l'efficacité de la contrition, qui est regardée à cette époque comme la partie principale et l'élément le plus important de la discipline pénitentielle,' 85.

[193] Hugh of St. Victor, *De sacramentis* 2.14.8 (PL 176.568). On Hugh see Teetaert 91-2, 94, 99; Anciaux 295-302; Jacob (n. 191 above) 38. Cf. Paulus (n. 179 above) I 254-9.

[194] Anciaux 328f.

[195] Peter Lombard, *Sententiarum libri IV*, 4.18.8: 'Ecce qualis et quantus est usus apo-

St. Bernard, in opposition to Abaelard, recognized the power of the Keys to bind and loose in Heaven as well as on earth;[196] but in his doctrine of penance he resembled Abaelard in his concentration upon the inner state of the sinner and with him asserted the sole efficacy of contrition and repentance.[197] He attached great importance, however, also to confession. To obtain forgiveness, according to Bernard, the crusader needed both to take the cross and humbly to confess his sins. The crusading cross was in itself the *signum vitae*.[198] This opportunity of salvation was freely offerred to all sinners by the Lord, Who in His mercy 'deigns to summon for His service murderers, robbers, adulterers, perjurors, and those guilty of other crimes as if [they were] a people who do that which is right.'[199] Nowhere, either here or in his other writings about the crusade, does he mention outer satisfaction. His whole emphasis is upon the almost sacramental efficacy of the crusading cross and upon the spiritual condition of the sinner in the eyes of God.

Eugene III, on the other hand, tended more towards the Victorine point of view. The emphasis in *Quantum predecessores* is upon the papal promise of eternal reward and the direct ecclesiastical remission of the divine punishment for sin. Eugene's appeal to the power of the Keys confirms Cramer's opinion that by this time a basic change had occurred in the concept of the indulgence. On account of this new element, the Pope also put more stress upon exterior satisfaction as a sign of contrition and guide for papal action. Satisfaction — the performance of everything possible to remedy the evil effect of the repented sin — became therefore an essential factor in this concept of the doctrine of penance. This is illustrated by the case of Count William II of Ponthieu. Eugene required the Count, before departing with the crusading army of Louis VII, to restore to the abbey of Troarn a farm which he had seized.[200] Otherwise his crusade would, spiritually, be in vain,

---

stolicarum clavium. Iam ostensum est ex parte qualiter sacerdotes dimittant peccata vel teneant, et iam retinuit sibi Deus quandam singularem potestatem dimittendi vel retinendi, quia ipse solus per se debitum aeternae mortis soluit, et animam interius purgat' (PL 192.888-9).

[196] Anciaux 291.

[197] *Ibid.* 248-53. In his *Ad Hugonem de S. Victore epistola de baptismo*, PL 182.1037, Bernard says that 'sola nihilominus poenitentia et cordis contritione obtinere veniam creditur, ne iam pro eo damnetur.'

[198] Bern. ep. 363, col. 566. For Bernard on confession, see the references in Anciaux 251-2; and particularly his *De laude novae militiae* c. 12 (PL 182.938).

[199] 'Quid est enim nisi exquisita prorsus et inuentibilis soli Deo occasio saluationis, quod homicidas, raptores, perjuros, caeterisque obligatos criminibus, quasi gentem quae justitiam fecerit, de seruitio suo submonere dignatur Omnipotens?' Bern. ep. 363, col. 566; cf. Ezechiel 18.21. Also in his *De laude novae militiae* Bernard rejoiced that thieves and perjurors entered the Order of the Temple: see Rousset (n. 8 above) 164.

[200] Samuel Löwenfeld, 'Documents relatifs à la Croisade de Guillaume, Comte de Pon-

'for never are holocausts which are polluted by an association with robbery pleasing in the eyes of the Almighty.' [201] In this way the Pope set his face resolutely against the development of the popular idea of the crusade as a convenient method of avoiding inconvenient obligations at home.

Both Eugene and Bernard insisted on the necessity of contrition and confession. But for the former, the crusading indulgence was essentially a matter between the individual and the Church, whereas for the latter it was a matter between the individual and God. In the view of St. Bernard, confession was not principally a means of obtaining absolution but rather a sacramental sign, established upon examples in the Old and New Testaments, and a subjective influence on the sinner, inducing a wholesome sense of shame. For him, God was the author of the crusade, which was a special and exceptional Divine Grace for the salvation of men. In the crusading bulls of Eugene III, the crusade appears as a papal grace, an institution for the transmission to men of the Pope's power of absolution from divine as well as from ecclesiastical punishment.[202]

Apart from this important contrast, the concepts of the crusade found in *Quantum predecessores* and in Bernard's crusading letter are substantially

---

thieu,' *Archives de l'Orient latin* 2 (1884) Documents, 254, Eugene III to William of Ponthieu: 'Quia vero signum crucis dominice assumpsisti et ad iter Ierosolymitanum accingeris, nolentes te laborem tantum non ad anime tue profectum arripere, nobilitati tue mandamus et exhortamur ... ut praefato abbati et monachis ... antequam iter incipias, in eorum (iudicum) arbitrio vel iudicio iusticiam facias.' Cf. the letter from Eugene to the Archbishop of Rouen and the Bishops of Coutances and Évreux and the letter from Hugh of Rouen to Count William, *ibid.* William had taken the cross at Vézelay (*De glorioso rege Ludovico*, in *Vie de Louis le Gros* [n. 9 above] 159) and seems to have cared little for the ecclesiastical prohibitions. As R. N. Sauvage, *L'Abbaye de Saint-Martin de Troarn* (Mémoires de la Société des Antiquaires de Normandie, 4th Series, 4; Caen 1911) 26, says: 'Les menaces de l'archevêque, son parent, lui semblaient, sans doute, peu dangereuses, et les censures ecclésiastiques n'étaient pas chose nouvelle pour lui.' In any case, he departed with the army of Louis VII before restoring the property of the Abbey. See Sauvage 23-9, and *Epistolae Pontificum Romanorum ineditae*, ed. Samuel Löwenfeld (Leipzig 1885) no. 201, p. 105.

[201] JL 9166; Löwenfeld, 'Documents' 253. Cf. the view of Peter Lombard that good acts performed in a state of mortal sin are never meritorious: Anciaux 269-70; and the view of Ralph Niger with regard to the Third Crusade: George B. Flahiff, '*Deus non vult*: A Critic of the Third Crusade,' *Mediaeval Studies* 9 (1947) 173.

[202] This difference in point of view is clearly seen in the versions of Bernard's letters for the Crusade. In the earliest version, he urged men to take the cross with the words: 'Suscipe crucis signum, et omnium pariter, de quibus corde contrito confessionem feceris, indulgentiam obtinebis,' ep. 363, col. 567. In the latest version, the letter to Duke Ladislaus of Bohemia, this had been rephrased to read: 'Suscipite signum crucis, et omnium, de quibus corde contrito confessionem feceritis, plenam indulgentiam delictorum hanc vobis summus pontifex offert, vicarius eius cui dictum est: Quodcunque solveris super terra, erit solutum et in coelo,' ep. 458, col. 653; see Rassow (n. 45 above) 262-3.

the same.[203] The differences are that Bernard expressed himself more loosely and with greater warmth, while the Pope restricted the crusade to the East and the soldiers from France and Italy and showed more concern than Bernard for the definition of the temporal privileges and for the organization of the army. It is easy for admirers of the Mellifluous Doctor to decry this cautious and narrow policy of the Pope because it lacked the popular appeal and the magnificent depth and scope of their hero's preaching;[204] but in so doing they are judging in view merely of the immediate events of 1146-8. Eugene, it is true, was not by nature an imaginative or vigorous man of affairs. He had been raised to the throne of Peter from his quiet life as a Cistercian Abbot less than a year before the issue of this bull; and in it, as its opening *Quantum predecessores* shows, he evinces an anxious respect for precedent and tradition.[205] There was, however, much practical wisdom in this caution. The fact remains that this bull marks a fundamental step in the development of the crusades and of crusading thought. Urban II never issued a general crusading bull.[206] It was therefore to *Quantum predecessores* and to its concept of crusading privileges that all future crusaders looked back. Built on the growth and events of half a century, this bull set the pattern for the juridical development of the crusade and as such laid the basis of the crusade as an institution in European history.[207]

To what extent this was a personal contribution of Eugene III, it is hard to say. Any answer to this question depends in part upon an estimate of Eugene's character and of the influence upon him of Bernard of Clairvaux and his other advisors; an influence which was unquestionably profound, in view of his Cistercian background and of his connection with what Kle-

---

[203] Bernard clearly regarded *Quantum predecessores* as fundamental, although Villey (n. 68 above), perhaps goes too far in saying that, 'sa prédication n'est qu'un commentaire de l'encyclique *Quantum predecessores*,' 106. Bernard developed its ideas from his own, highly spiritual attitude. He had, in any case, a profound influence on Eugene's thought.

[204] For instance, Ursula Schwerin, *Die Aufrufe der Päpste zur Befreiung des heiligen Landes* (Historische Studien, ed. E. Ebering 301; Berlin 1937) 74: '... die Kreuzzugs-enzyklica Eugens III. ... ist zu arm im Gedanklichen, zu wenig schwungvoll in Sprache und Stil, um Ursache einer derartigen Massenbegeisterung sein zu können.'

[205] It is evidence of the conservatism and the memory of the Papacy that alone among the Western sources of the Second Crusade, the papal bulls show a strong consciousness of the precedent of the First Crusade, cf. n. 130 above.

[206] Erdmann (n. 64 above) 320; Cramer (n. 44 above) 47f.; Villey 105-6; and Alexander Gieysztor, 'The Genesis of the Crusades,' *Medievalia et Humanistica* 6 (1950) 26-7.

[207] Cramer 48: 'Diese Bulle ist in formaler Hinsicht Vorbild für alle späteren Kreuzzugs-aufrufe der Päpste geworden.' For an interesting discussion of the development of cru-sading theory, see Villey, who calls the indulgence the 'expression juridique précise de ce caractère salutaire de la croisade,' 148; on *Quantum predecessores*, see *ibid.* 106-7, and Schwerin 74-5.

X

witz has aptly characterized as the new reformed papacy, which came into power with Innocent II and which found its principal support in France.[208] It is not always possible, therefore, to distinguish clearly between the policies of the Pope, of St. Bernard, and of the papal Curia. This answer depends also on the precedents upon which *Quantum predecessores* was built. Although the sources for these are not complete, there can be little doubt that most of the ideas were not original to this bull. Here, however, they were set down together for the first time, and in this form they impressed themselves upon the minds of men.[209] The development of ideas that is marked in the historical works of the later twelfth century by the emergence of the crusade as a Christian institution rather than a mere historical event was principally the result of the crusading bulls of 1146-7.

Eugene reissued *Quantum predecessores* in a slightly revised form on March 1, 1146.[210] He also wrote about the crusade during this year to the Emperor Manuel, who replied in August, 1146, that he stood ready to assist the French crusaders, and again in March, 1147, when he evinced some alarm at the prospect of the crusade and asked for Eugene's aid in securing from Louis a guarantee for the good behaviour of his troops.[211] Already by November 26, 1146, the Pope was in correspondence with the Bishop of Salis-

---

[208] Hans-Walter Klewitz, 'Das Ende des Reformpapsttums,' *Deutsches Archiv für Geschichte des Mittelalters* 3 (1939) 371-412.

[209] Cf. for instance the crusading hymn in the *Analecta hymnica medii aevi*, edd. G. M. Dreves and C. Blume, 45ᵇ, no. 96, p. 78, dated by Dreves as 12th (13th 14th) century. The ninth stanza is reminiscent of the crusading bulls:

      Illuc quicumque tenderit
      Mortuus ibi fuerit
      Caeli bona receperit
      Et cum sanctis remanserit.

[210] JL 8876. For an ingenious, if not altogether convincing, account of the circumstances of this reissue, see Gleber (n. 165 above) 45-6. It differs from the earlier bulls in its slightly increased prohibitions against luxury: see Caspar and Rassow (n. 184 above) 287-8. This *Quantum predecessores* (II) may be the 'omni favo litteras dulciores' mentioned by Odo of Deuil, *De prof. Ludov.* ed. Berry 8. More probably, however, Odo is here referring to some other, lost letter sent by the Pope to Louis: Bernhardi (n. 1 above) 519; Hüffer (n. 164 above) 405-6; Gleber 45 and n. 7, where he cites authorities disagreeing with this view.

[211] For the text of the letter of August, 1146 (Franz Dölger, *Corpus der griechischen Urkunden des Mittelalters und der neueren Zeit*, Reihe A, Abteilung I: *Regesten der Kaiserurkunden des oströmischen Reiches* II [Munich and Berlin 1925] no. 1348) see RHGF 15.440-1; for the text of the letter of March, 1147 (Dölger no. 1533) see Werner Ohnsorge, 'Ein Beitrag zur Geschichte Manuels I. von Byzanz,' *Festschrift Albert Brackmann* (Weimar 1931) 391-3. Manuel also wrote to Louis VII: Dölger no. 1349. On these letters, see Ohnsorge 371-81, whose conclusions are accepted by Dölger, in his review of Ohnsorge's article, *Byzantinische Zeitschrift* 31 (1931) 446-7; Gleber 48-9; Cartellieri (n. 37 above) 351. On Manuel's attitude, see Chalandon (n. 121 above) II 133-5.

bury concerning the progress of the crusading movement in England.[212] On October 5, 1146, he issued his crusading bull *Divina dispensatione* (I) to the clergy of Italy. In it he praised the example of King Louis and the French nobles and urged the Italians to participate in 'such a holy labor and victory' and so to win the privileges of the crusade.[213]

Early in 1147, the Pope started northwards towards France accompanied by no less than seventeen Cardinals. He went by way of the Mont Genèvre pass and reached Paris by April 20.[214] At Clairvaux, on April 6, he saw again, after more than six years, his friend and mentor St. Bernard; and five days later, at Troyes, he issued *Divina dispensatione* (II), addressed to all the faithful. Here again he praises those who have already taken the cross and are preparing to free the Eastern Church.

> 'The King of Spain, also,' he says, 'is powerfully armed against the Saracens of those regions, over whom he has already frequently triumphed...' 'Certain of you, however, (are) desirous of participating in so holy a work and reward and plan to go against the Slavs and other pagans living towards the North and to subject them, with the Lord's assistance, to the Christian religion. We give heed to the devotion of these men, and to all those who have not accepted the cross for going to Jerusalem and who have decided to go against the Slavs and to remain in the spirit of devotion on that expedition, as it is prescribed, we grant that same remission of sin... and the same temporal privileges as to the crusaders to Jerusalem...' 'Furthermore, since we know it to be advantageous that some religious, wise, and literate person be among you, who may care for your peace and tranquillity and preserve unity among you and advise you concerning the promotion of the Christian religion, we provide for this purpose our venerable brother A(nselm) Bishop of Havelberg.'[215]

In its basic theory of crusading, this bull differs in no way from *Quantum predecessores* or *Divina dispensatione* (I), which it resembles also in structure and occasionally in wording. In two respects, however, both in the broader concept of the crusade and in the appointment of a legate, the Pope here made an important advance on the ideas expressed in his three earlier crusading bulls, and it is tempting to associate these changes with the meeting at Clairvaux five days before it was issued.

Not only the participation of the Germans but also an entirely new front of attack were now included within the scope of the crusade. It is clear that the Germans had played no part in Eugene's original plan, and their inclusion was one of Bernard's principal achievements.[216] The Pope seems in fact to

---

[212] *Epistolae Pont. Rom.* (n. 200 above) 103; JL 8959.

[213] *PU in Malta*, ed. Paul Kehr, *Nachrichten ... Göttingen*, Phil.-hist. Kl. 1899, no. 3, 388-90.

[214] His route can be traced from his bulls in JL 8991-9021: see Gleber 51-2.

[215] JL 9017; PL 180.1203-4.

[216] See p. 244 and n. 167 above.

have disapproved at first of this decision of Conrad III.[217] This need occasion neither surprise nor the elaborate explanation suggested by Gleber.[218] In view of the precedent of the First Crusade and of his own conservative temperament, Eugene naturally addressed his earlier crusading bulls to the French and to the Italians.[219] He may also have had some genuine concern for the state of the Empire in Conrad's absence and may perhaps have seen more clearly than Bernard the difficulties that would result from joint German and French participation in the crusade.[220]

It was for this reason perhaps more than any other that Eugene welcomed a diversion of the German forces against the Slavs.[221] There appears to be no evidence that this idea originated with Bernard,[222] although he was present

---

[217] Cosack (n. 167 above) 290 reconstructs Eugene's reaction from Conrad's reply; Heinz Zatschek, 'Wibald von Stablo,' *Mitteilungen des österreichischen Instituts für Geschichtsforschung*, Ergänzungsband 10 (1928) 325; Gleber 50f.

[218] Very briefly, that Eugene had hoped to return to Italy accompanied by Conrad to crush the papal enemies at Rome: Gleber 50 and 53-5.

[219] Also to the English and the Low Country men, see below, pp. 260-1. These four peoples were those who had played the principal parts in the First Crusade. Erdmann (n. 64 above) 272-4 brings out that in the eleventh century crusading thought had its broadest development in France and Italy. Urban II may have seen the First Crusade in theory as a general offensive to free Christendom (*ibid.* 306 and 321; J. Lecler, 'L'idée de Croisade d'après les travaux récents,' *Études* 29 [1936] 52-4), but he never developed this idea fully, and the response in fact was limited. On the scornful attitude of the Germans towards the First Crusade, see Ekkehard of Aura, in A. C. Krey, *The First Crusade* (Princeton 1921) 42. Speaking of the Second Crusade, therefore, Karl Hampe correctly says: 'Das Unternehmen gewann sogleich einen universaleren Charakter als die erste Kreuzfahrt, bei der Urban wesentlich nur den französischen Lehnsadel nach dem Orient gelenkt hatte,' *Deutsche Kaisergeschichte in der Zeit der Salier und Staufer* (10th ed. by F. Baethgen, Heidelberg 1949) 133. On the German attitude towards the First Crusade, see aso Albert Hauck, *Kirchengeschichte Deutschlands* IV (Leipzig 1903) 895.

[220] Most modern scholars agree that this fact payed an important part in the failure of the crusade: Kugler (n. 1 above) 95f; Vasiliev (n. 53 above) 419-22; Bernhardi 532-3; Cartellieri 357; Peter Rassow, *Honor Imperii: Die Neue Politik Friedrich Barbarossas 1152-1159* (Munich and Berlin 1940) 26. The division of responsibility is not, however, quite as easy as Vacandard, with sublime self-confidence, suggests: 'A la distance où nous sommes de ces événements, il est facile de les juger avec impartialité et d'établir exactement la part de responsabilité qui revient à chacun des auteurs de la seconde croisade,' *op. cit.* (n. 174 above) II 450.

[221] See Appendix B.

[222] Bernard's letter for the Wendish Crusade, ep. 457, coll. 652-4, appears to me to have been written after *Divina dispensatione* (II). On this important point I disagree with Hüffer (n. 164 above) 427 n. 1; Rassow (n. 45 above) 265; Artler (n. 60 above) 314; Bündung (n. 60 above) 37-40, and others who hold that this letter preceded in date the papal bull. Several reasons incline me towards the opposite opinion. In the first place, it seems highly improbable, in view of Bernard's extreme deference in taking up the preaching of the crusade, that he would here have taken upon himself the authority to change completely the original concept and especially to grant full indulgence to these new crusaders.

at the Diet of Frankfurt in March, when the plan was probably first suggested. It may have come from the Saxon princes and prelates,[223] possibly from Anselm of Havelberg himself. There can be no question that there was a large measure of self-interest in this proposal; but to stress this motive to the exclusion of all others is as mistaken as to deny it altogether. These men both sought and valued ecclesiastical support and approbation of their campaign.

The papal Curia had since the eleventh century repeatedly asserted its interest in the eastward expansion of Germany.[224] Especially in the second quarter of the twelfth century it attempted to exert an increasing control over German affairs by means of frequent *legati a latere*.[225] Eugene III gave a new and more powerful character to this policy in his bull of April 11,[226] which states in definite terms the religious nature and papal direction of this expedition. Although he had had no hand in its initiation, therefore, the Pope lost no time in incorporating this energy into the wider effort and in so doing made a significant contribution not only to the future of the 'Drang nach Osten'[227] but also to the character of the Second Crusade.

Divina dispensatione (II) also includes a significant reference to the campaign against the Moors in Spain. This information may have come through Genoa or Savoy, or perhaps from St. Bernard, who was in 1147 probably in touch with Catalonia and Portugal.[228] There is, however, evidence that

Secondly, the language of this letter suggests that it is subsequent at least to the Diet of Frankfurt. 'Quia enim verbum hoc crucis parvitati nostrae Dominus evangelizandum commisit, consilio domini regis et episcoporum et principum, qui convenerant Frankonovort, denuntiamus ... Placuit autem omnibus in Frankenevort congregatis, quatenus...,' coll. 651-2. The 'Dominus' here may indeed refer to the Pope; and in any case, since the diet lasted until late March (Bernhardi 545f.), Bernard can hardly have written his letter before then. There is in the third place some evidence that Bernard sent with each of his letters a copy of the papal crusading bull: see n. 247 below. If this supposition is correct, he could not have sent letter 457 before Eugene had issued the relevant bull, *Divina dispensatione* (II).

[223] Volk (n. 68 above) 41-2.

[224] Friedrich Baethgen, 'Die Kurie und der Osten im Mittelalter,' *Deutsche Ostforschungen* (note 65 above) 310-30. After the Investiture Controversy, Baethgen says, the Curia 'versuchte, im Osten sich unabhängig vom Reich ihre eigenen Machtposition zu schaffen ...,' 330.

[225] Hauck (n. 219 above) IV 160f.; p. 160 n. 7 he lists the papal legates in Germany from ca. 1125 to 1150.

[226] Baethgen 324: 'Hatte es früher der Ostmission nur aus der Ferne seinen Segen gespendet, so nahm es jetzt ihre Leitung in die eigenen Hände.' Eugene was also more active than his predecessors in taking German monasteries under papal protection: see Hauck IV 165.

[227] Baethgen 324-5: 'Damit hatte das Prinzip der gewaltsamen Bekehrung in der Ostmission Eingang gefunden...'; but care should be taken not to overestimate the extent of ecclesiastical concern for this movement.

[228] See pp. 246-7 above.

the Pope took an independent interest in the Spanish Reconquest, although no papal letters to this effect are known from the years 1146-7, when it can only be surmised from certain Spanish charters that the Curia was in correspondence with the court of Alfonso VII.[229] But in April, 1148, Eugene wrote from Langres to Alfonso saying that 'we gladly grant your requests to make an expedition against the tyranny of the infidels.'[230] Clearly at some time before this Alfonso had asked the Pope to approve his plans for a crusade.

Papal concern for the expulsion of the Moslems from Spain dates back at least to the time of Alexander II and Gregory VII, who in 1074 planned a Christian campaign in Spain.[231] Following this example, Urban II, at the time of the First Crusade, issued a bull urging the Spaniards to direct their crusading energies against the Saracens at home.[232] Both in this bull and in one of Pascal II some ten years later,[233] these expeditions in Spain were regarded not only as complementary but also as equal, on a spiritual basis, to the campaigns against the Moslems in the Holy Land.[234]

---

[229] España Sagrada 36.cxcii-iv: 'Carta facta Palentiae XIII. Kalendas Martii Era MCLXXXVI quando praefatus Imperator habuit ibi colloquium ... de vocatione Domini Papae ad Concilium, et in anno quo ab eodem Imperatore capta fuit Almaria et Baeza...'; cf. similar charters in Azevado (n. 115 above) 109 n. 1 (document of the National Archives, Madrid, C. D. Samos 794-21-1) and 106 n. 1. It should be noted that these charters are dated 1186 Era Hispanica (1148) and yet in the same year that Alfonso took Almaria, that is, 1185 (1147): the only explanation seems to be that, although in the era Hispanica the number changed on January 1 (H. Grotefend, Taschenbuch der Zeitrechnung [8th ed. by O. Grotefend, Hannover 1941] 14), they reckoned the year as running from Easter to Easter or March 25 to March 25 (Grotefend 12-4; Reginald Lane Poole, 'The Beginning of the Year in the Middle Ages,' Studies in Chronology and History [Oxford 1934] 1-27). In any case, the papal letters must have arrived in 1147. I can find no reference in España Sagrada or Gerhard Säbekow, Die päpstlichen Legationen nach Spanien und Portugal bis zum Ausgang des XII. Jahrhunderts (Berlin 1931) to a council attended by a papal legate, at Burgos in 1146, which Schramm (n. 3 above) mentions, p. 111. Is he perhaps referring to the Burgos council of 1136, which was attended by Cardinal Guido (España Sagrada 26. 438-40; Rassow, loc. cit. n. 92 above, 212f.)?

[230] JL 9255; PL 180.1345-6. See Paul Kehr, Das Papsttum und der Katalanische Prinzipat bis zur Vereinigung mit Aragon, in Abhandlungen der Preussischen Akademie der Wissenschaften, Philosophisch-Historische Klasse 1926, No. 1, p. 62; Erdmann (n. 49 above) 32; Cartellieri (n. 37 above) 379; Schramm 112.

[231] Epistolae Pont. Rom. (n. 200 above) no. 82, p. 43; see Erdmann, loc. cit. 28 and Entstehung (n. 64 above) 292-5; Lecler (n. 219 above) 48-54; Paulus (n. 179 above) I 195-8; Villey (n. 68 above) 195-8; Ruano (n. 112 above) 111-14 ; Runciman I 90-1.

[232] PU in Spanien I: Katalonien, ed. Paul Kehr, Abhandlungen ... Göttingen, Phil.-hist. Kl. Neue Folge 18.2 (1926) no. 23, p. 287-8.

[233] JL 5840; PL 163.45; Villey 197; Paulus I 197: Oct. 14, 1100. See also Pascal's other bulls for a crusade on the Iberian peninsula: JL 5863 and 6485; Paulus I 197.

[234] Bridrey (n. 161 above) 30-2; Ernst Schlée, Die Päpste und die Kreuzzüge (Halle 1893) 44-5 and 49; Cramer (n. 44 above) 59; and especially Villey 197-201; see n. 49 above. So

Gelasius II, Calixtus II, Lucius II, and, through their legates, Honorius II and Innocent II, all displayed an active interest in the Reconquest,[235] and Eugene III was in no way behind his predecessors in this respect. The original issue of *Quantum predecessores* may in fact have been based upon some of the earlier crusading bulls for Spain. In May 1145, he reissued a bull of Urban II, Gelasius II, and Lucius II for the recovery of Tarragona, 'for the reconquest of which our predecessors are known to have labored greatly.'[236] In the same year he urged the faithful to assist the Templars in Spain.[237] In 1152, he issued a bull, addressed to all Christians, in which he granted the usual crusading privileges to all who 'go with the noble Count Ramon of Barcelona for the defense of the Christian faith and of the entire holy Church.'[238] Finally, there is the fact that the Pope specifically called upon the Genoese to join the campaign in Spain in 1147.[239]

---

the charter which reestablished the Order of Belchite in 1136 promised complete remission of sins to all who joined the Order. In addition, 'Qui vero ibidem deo per annum servire voluerit, eandem quam si Jherusalem tenderet, remissionem assequatur. ... Simili autem remissione sepulchrum domni de captivitate ereptum est et Maiorica et Cesaraugusta et alie, et similiter deo annuente iter Jherusalemitanum ab hac parte aperietur et ecclesia dei, que adhuc sub captivitate ancilla tenetur, libera efficietur,' Rassow (n. 92 above) 224-5.

[235] Gelasius II, apparently following now-lost documents of Urban II, issued two bulls for the Spanish Reconquest: JL 6636 (PL 163.489-91) and 6665 (PL 163.508); see Paulus *op. cit.* I 197, and Villey 201. In the second of these, Gelasius not only freed 'a suorum vinculis peccatorum' anyone who with a contrite heart died for the recovery of Saragossa but also assigned to the discretion of the provincial bishops the indulgence to be granted to those who simply joined this enterprise or even aided in the rebuilding of the church or the support of the clergy. For Calixtus II, see n. 137 above and Paulus I 197-8. Lucius II in 1144 reissued the bull of Urban II and Gelasius II for the reconquest of Tarragona: *PU in Spanien* I no. 53, pp. 320-2; and when it was recovered, Tarragona was held by the Count of Barcelona as a papal fief: E. W. Watson, 'The Development of Ecclesiastical Organisation and its Financial Basis,' CMH 6.555. A synod called at Compostella in 1125 by Diego Gelmirez, the legate of Honorius II, granted full indulgence to crusaders in Spain: *España Sagrada* 20.427-30; Paulus I 198; Villey 206. The papal legate Guido of SS. Cosmas and Damian was present at the Council of Burgos (1136), which promised remission of sins to members of the Order of Belchite (see nn. 229 and 234 above), and he presided at the Fifth Council of Gerona (1143) when Ramon Berenger made his great grant to the Templars (see pp. 231-2 above and Säbekow, *op. cit.* n. 229 above, 46).

[236] *PU in Spanien* I no. 54, pp. 322-4. It is interesting for the method by which Eugene composed his crusading bulls that in this one he followed word for word not the most recent issue of this bull by Lucius II but that of Gelasius II (see n. 235 above).

[237] See n. 186 above.

[238] JL 9594; *Colección* (n. 99 above) no. 128, pp. 314-5. This bull, undated by Bofarull, may have been taken for a bull of 1146/7 (see n. 240 below). It was reissued by Anastasius IV: *ibid.* no. 133, 320-1; *PU in Spanien* I no. 70, pp. 346-7.

[239] See above p. 228 and n. 80; 'Regesti delle lettere pontificie riguardanti la Liguria,' *Atti della Società Ligure di Storia Patria* 19 (1887) no. 117, p. 59. A precedent for this may have been not only the Genoese participation in the First Crusade but also the indulgence granted to the Pisans who attacked the Balearic Islands in 1114-5 (see n. 109 above):

This evidence can leave no doubt of the interest shown by Eugene III in the Spanish campaigns. It has frequently been asserted that he in fact issued a crusading bull for the expedition against Tortosa, and it would certainly not have been inconsistent with his policy to have done so.[240] During the fifth decade of the twelfth century the Curia maintained a close connection with Portugal. Alfonso Henriques in 1143 placed himself under the special protection of the papacy:[241] and the re-establishment by Eugene III of the Bishoprics of Lisbon, Viseu, and Lamego was closely linked with the reconquests of 1147.[242] In the Iberian peninsula, therefore, as in eastern Germany, the Popes were quick to bring under a certain measure of control movements which originated independently;[243] and, while the separate national character was never entirely lost, this effort of Church and State was now successfully incorporated into the wider effort of the crusade.[244]

St. Bernard certainly addressed a crusading letter to England, probably

---

Chron. Monasterii Casinensis, MGH SS 7.789; Paulus I 197; Erdmann (n. 64 above) 170; Villey 215-6 ; Ruano (n. 112 above) 113 and, cited by him, Antonio Alcover Sureda, *El Islam en Mallorca y la cruzada pisano-catalana* (Palma en Mallorca 1930).

[240] Manrique, *Cist. Ann.* II (n. 80 above) under 1148, xiii, 8-10; Lafuente, *op. cit.* (n. 107 above) 70; Paul Kehr, *Das Papsttum und die Königreiche Navarra und Aragon bis zur Mitte des XII. Jahrhunderts*, in *Abhandlungen der Preuss. Akad.* Phil.-hist..Kl.1928 No. 4, pp. 50-1 (with no reference); Defourneaux (n. 69 above) 177; Cartelleri (n. 37 above) 422. I have been unable to locate this document or to find clear evidence that it was issued, cf. n. 238 above.

[241] Säbekow (n. 229 above) 47-8; Livermore (n. 37 above) 67-9.

[242] *De exp. Lyx.* (cited n. 15 above) 178-80; Carl Erdmann, *Das Papsttum und Portugal im ersten Jahrhundert der Portugiesischen Geschichte*, in *Abhandlungen der Preuss. Akad.* Phil.-hist. Kl. 1928 No. 5, pp. 34-5.

[243] Of considerable interest in the history of papal direction of the crusading effort in Spain is the visit of the legate Hyacinth, Cardinal deacon of Santa Maria in Cosmedin, in 1155: Säbekow 49-51; Johannes Brixius, *Die Mitglieder des Kardinalkollegiums von 1130-1181* (Berlin 1912) 52. Hyacinth, later Pope Celestine III, was enthusiastic for the Reconquest: see his letter in *PU in Rom*, ed. Paul Kehr, *Nachrichten ... Göttingen*, Phil.-hist. Kl. 1903, no. 12, pp. 48-9. He presided over two councils in Spain, at Valladolid and at Lerida (the first council there since its recovery). The canons of these councils (Valladolid: Erdmann, *Papsttum und Portugal* 55-8; Lerida: F. Valls-Taberner, 'Ein Konzil zu Leri..a im Jahre 115.,' *Papsttum und Kaisertum: Festschrift Paul Kehr*, ed. Albert Brackmann [Munich 1926] 364-8) closely resemble each other. Canon 1 is a fully developed crusading bull; it unquestionably reveals the influence of Rome, yet shows that as late as 1155 the Papacy was not even in theory the only ecclesiastical authority capable of conferring the spiritual and temporal benefits of a crusade: cf. bull of Gelasius II, n. 235 above; contrast Villey, *op. cit.* 100-1.

[244] Cf. Ernst Kantorowicz, '*Pro Patria Mori* in Medieval Political Thought,' *American Historical Review* 56 (1951) 478 n. 22, who says that 'in Spain the whole development (of the crusade) was different in so far as crusading idea and national idea or patriotism coincided'; see Erdmann, *Hist. Zeitschr.* 141 (n. 49 above) 23f. and *Entstehung* (n. 64 above) 88-90, 269-70; cf. n. 49 above.

in the summer of 1146, and there is evidence that a papal bull was there at the same time. Eugene's letter to Bishop Jocelin of Salisbury, in November, 1146, shows that men who had been disseized of their lands by King Stephen or his opponents before the preaching of the crusade had subsequently taken the cross and claimed the ecclesiastical protection granted to the property of crusaders.[245] Since Bernard did not mention this privilege in his letter, it was presumably known in England from a papal crusading bull. A copy may have been sent by Bernard with his letter, but the fact that the Bishop of Salisbury addressed his enquiries to the Pope shows that Eugene himself took an active part in the organization of the crusade.

That copies of the crusading bulls were sent elsewhere is known from narrative sources, which reveal that papal letters reached Denmark, Tournai, the monastery of Lobbes in the Lowlands, the Count of Flanders, and Bishop Arnulf of Lisieux.[246] There is in addition the evidence of the bull *Quantum predecessores* (III), issued in 1165 by Pope Alexander III, who says that for the Second Crusade 'our predecessor of holy memory Pope Eugene sent exhortatory letters throughout the various parts of the earth.'[247]

Eugene promoted the crusade not only by his letters but also by his per-

---

[245] 'For those men, moreover, whom our beloved son S(tephen) illustrious king of the English or his adversaries disinherited on the occasion of the war held for the realm before they took the cross, we are not willing that ecclesiastical justice should be exercised,' *Epistolae Pont. Rom.* (n. 200 above) no. 199, pp. 103-4. For the names of some of the more important English crusaders, see *De exp. Lyx.* 5-6 (to David's citations for William of Warenne may be added *Chron. of Melrose*, cited n. 70 above, 23) and Heinrich Böhmer, *Kirche und Staat in England und in der Normandie im XI. und XII. Jahrhundert* (Leipzig 1899) 357 n. 2. David regards the response in England as slight (*De exp. Lyx.* 3-12), whereas Böhmer says that as a result of the crusade the number of fighters in the English civil war was sensibly diminished, and the war therefore took on a new character, 357; cf. also 407. For Scots on the crusade, see *De exp. Lyx.* 106 and Rassow (n. 45 above) 269-7.

[246] Saxo Grammaticus, *Gesta Danorum* (n. 58 above) 376; Hermann (Abbot of St. Martin) of Tournai, *Narratio restaurationis Abbatiae S. Martini Tornacensis*, in D'Achery, *Spicilegium* II 926; *Gesta Abbatum Lobbiensium*, MGH SS 21.329; Arnulf of Lisieux, *Letters*, ed. Frank Barlow (Camden Third Series 61: London 1939) 210: 'In expeditione ... Iherosolimitana ad quam me sanctus pater Eugenius destinavit invitum...' See also the *Ann. Herbipolenses*, MGH SS 16.3: 'Testes sunt huius apostolice admonitionis epistole hinc et inde per diversarum regionum ac provintiarum terminos directe et in plerisque ecclesiis ad inditium predicte expeditionis diligenter recondite.'

[247] JL 11218; PL 200.383-6. Cosack (n. 167 above) 279 believed that this was a purely formal expression and maintained that 'nach diesem (zeitgenössischen) Quellenmaterial tritt in keinem Lande die offizielle Kreuzpredigt unabhängig von Bernard auf...' It is true that Bernard appears to have sent with each of his crusading letters a copy of the relevant papal bull: see the evidence cited by Cosack 279 n. 6, to which may be added the fact, kindly suggested by Dom Jean Leclercq, that in the Munich MS 22201, which was written at Windberg in 1165 (cf. Hüffer, *loc. cit.* in n. 164 above, 411), Bernard's ep. 363 is preceded by *Quantum predecessores*. The foregoing evidence, however, indicates that Eugene sent at least some copies of his crusading bulls directly and independently.

sonal activity. Of this there is little evidence, but a few references suggest that it was not unimportant. Until early in 1147 he was occupied in Italy and probably had little opportunity to preach the crusade in person. At that time, however, he started northwards to France. No pressing political need, as has been suggested, forced him to leave Italy; and it is probable, as Reginald Lane Poole said, that 'his primary motive for visiting France was that he might preside over the preparations for the Second Crusade.'[248] At Vico d'Elsa, not far from Siena, in January 1147, he conferred a privilege on the abbey of St. Rufus (at that time near Avignon) in a bull addressed to the Abbot N.[249] This was presumably Nicholas Breakspear,[250] who in 1149 became Cardinal Bishop of Albano and five years later was elevated to the papacy as Adrian IV. He seems to have accompanied the legate, Archbishop William of Arles, to Spain in 1140,[251] and was there again in 1148-9, since in writing to Nicholas, by that time Pope, in 1156, Count Ramon Berenger said that 'in the acquisition of Lerida and of the church of Tortosa you saw our labor and sweat in part with your own eyes...'[252] It does not seem fanciful to connect the meeting of Nicholas with the Pope in 1147 with his presence during the following year among the Spanish crusaders, to whom he acted perhaps as an unofficial legate.

By March 7, Eugene was at Susa;[253] and on the following day, 'in the presence of Pope Eugene,' Amadeus III of Savoy received, in return for a confirmation of the privileges of San Giusto di Susa, eleven thousand Susian solidi in order to pay the costs of his pilgrimage to Jerusalem, to which he was, he says, 'advised and instructed by the most blessed lord Pope Eugene.'[254]

---

[248] R. L. Poole, in John of Salisbury, *Historia Pontificalis* (Oxford 1927) intro. xii.

[249] JL 8999 (not 8998 as cited by R. L. Poole, 'The Early Lives of Robert Pullen and Nicholas Breakspear,' *Studies in Chronology and History* [Oxford 1934] 294 n. 4).

[250] Poole 294. Kehr, in *PU in Spanien* I (n. 232 above) no. 60, pp. 331-2, prints a bull dated from St. Peter's on Dec. 12 and addressed to 'Ni. abbati ecclesie Sancti Rufi.' Kehr assigns this document to 1152, in which case it would throw into utter confusion the slight knowledge gathered by Poole concerning the early career of Nicholas Breakspear. For Nicholas became Cardinal Bishop of Albano by December 16, 1149, at the latest (Brixius [n. 243 above] 56; JL II p. 20, indicates him as subscribing from January 30, 1150), and this bull would indicate that his successor at St. Rufus also bore the name of Nicholas — unless, that is, it may be dated December 12, 1149, when Eugene was certainly in Rome (JL 9359-9363) and presumably also Nicholas (see above). This bull may therefore be the last grant made to Nicholas as Abbot of St. Rufus. As Adrian IV, in any case, Nicholas Breakspear is known to have taken an interest in Spanish affairs: Kehr, *Das Papsttum und die Königreiche...* (n. 240 above) 51.

[251] Villanueva, *Viage literario a las Iglesias de España* XI (1850) 199, cited by Poole, *loc. cit.* 294; Säbekow, *op. cit.* (n. 229 above) 45.

[252] Kehr, *Das Papsttum und der Katalanische Prinzipat...* (n. 230 above) 90-1; *Das Papsttum und die Königreiche...* 51.

[253] JL 9009; Previté Orton (n. 9 above) 309.

[254] *Regesta Comitum Sabaudiae*, ed. Domenico Carutti (Bibliotheca Storica Italiana 5;

It seems that Bernard also urged Amadeus to join the crusade,[255] but this passage shows that his participation was principally the result of the personal intervention of Eugene III.

That the Pope preached the crusade in France is clear from the works of Odo of Deuil and of the monk William of St. Denis, who says that at Paris Eugene granted his 'blessing and licence of pilgrimage.' [256]

Finally, where he could not supervise the preparation and organization of the crusade in person, the Pope did so by means of his legates. To the armies going to the Holy Land, he sent 'Theodwin (Cardinal) Bishop of Santa Rufina and Guido Cardinal priest of San Chrysogono, prudent indeed and honest men, ... who may keep those men in concord and love and watch for their salvation both in spiritual and in temporal matters, with God's aid...' [257] John of Salisbury, however, who probably knew them both, regarded them as 'good men indeed but not suitable for such a position,' both on account of their characters and because neither was familiar with the French language — one was German and the other Florentine.[258] Perhaps for this reason Eugene seems to have chosen in addition two French bishops, Arnulf of Lisieux and Godfrey of Langres, 'who were to journey with the said King (Louis) to Jerusalem and acted in (the Pope's) place in the government of the Christian people.'[259] John of Salisbury bitterly disliked these bishops, of whom he says that 'they boasted that they held the papal legation in the army, although they had not received this power, (and) were so quarrelsome that they hardly ever agreed in any advice.' [260] But they

---

Turin 1889) no. ccxciv, pp. 105-6; Previté Orton 309 n. 3. Cipolla has cast doubt on this charter, but Previté Orton, 197 n. 2 and 309 n. 3, says that 'it is hard to see what part of the contents is not genuine.'

[255] *Petit Cartulaire de l'Abbaye de Saint-Sulpice en Bugey*, ed. M.-C. Guige (Lyon 1884) 2; Previté Orton 309-10; *Regesta Com. Sab.* no. ccxcii, p. 105.

[256] William of St. Denis, *Dialogue* (n. 130 above) 103; Odo of Deuil, *De prof. Ludov.* ed. Berry 14-6; cf. *Chron. Mauriniacensis*, RHGF 12.88. Odo here mentions that, 'Affluent multi multarum partium utrique miraculo, videlicet regi et apostolico peregrinis'; and it is not impossible that Eugene put on a pilgrim's costume in order to symbolize his spiritual participation in the crusade.

[257] JL 9095; PL 180.1251-2. See Kugler (n. 1 above) 104-6; Brixius (n. 243) 43, 47; and Johannes Bachmann, *Die päpstlichen Legaten in Deutschland und Skandinavien 1125-59* (Historische Studien, ed. E. Ebering 115; Berlin 1913) 80-3.

[258] John of Salisbury, *Hist. Pontif.* (n. 248 above) 55.

[259] *Anonymi vera narratio fundationis prioratus Sanctae Barbarae*, RHGF 14.502. On Godfrey's part in the Crusade, see Hermann Wurm, *Gottfried, Bischof von Langres* (Würzburg 1886) 16-34, and Pfeiffer (n. 31 above) 107f. I have been unable to consult the article by G. Drioux, 'Geoffroi de La Roche, évêque de Langres, et la seconde croisade,' *Cahiers Hautmarnais* (1948) 166-72. On Arnulf in the Crusade, see Barlow, in Arnulf of Lisieux, *Letters* (n. 246 above) introduction xxv-vii.

[260] John of Salisbury, *Hist. Pontif.* 55.

may in fact have held a limited legation for the French army and have been appointed on the suggestion of St. Bernard, since Godfrey was a former Prior of Clairvaux and Arnulf an ancient protégé of Bernard. Bishop Alvis of Arras seems also to have held a papal commission, for the historian of the monastery of Anchin says of him that 'by the order of the lord Pope Eugene (he was) made father and pastor of the entire army on the journey to Jerusalem.'[261] He died *en route*. Perhaps the Pope hoped to control the crusade through this plethora of legates.[262] The result, in fact, seems to have been disastrous confusion.

Eugene originally planned that Bishop Henry of Olmütz should accompany the army of Conrad III and in July, 1147, wrote to him that 'since we trust greatly in your affection and know that the policy of the King (Conrad III) depends greatly on your advice and opinion, we instruct Your Solicitude that you strive in all ways to urge (and) to advise the King that he should labor for the honor and exaltation of his mother the Holy Roman Church and to unite the Church of Constantinople to her.'[263] Conrad was brother-in-law to the Emperor Manuel, and Eugene clearly hoped that ecclesiastical union might be achieved by this means.[264] This plan was, however, not so closely linked to the crusade in the mind of Eugene as it had been in the mind of Urban II.[265] Perhaps, as Norden suggests, Eugene feared that by stressing the issue of ecclesiastical union he would supply fuel to the anti-Greek fires of the papal enemy Roger of Sicily, who might have attacked the Byzantine Empire on the pretext of serving Rome.[266] In any case, when Henry of Olmütz decided to join the Wendish crusade, Eugene

---

[261] *Historia Monasterii Aquicinctini*, MGH SS 14.588.

[262] On the duties of these legates, see Schlée (n. 234 above) 19-23. Ohnsorge (n. 211 above) 380 suggests that they were sent at the desire of the Emperor Manuel, who in his letter of March, 1147, asked the Pope to send a Cardinal with the French army. The example of the First Crusade, moreover, established a precedent for appointing a legate for the crusading army.

[263] JL 9095; PL 180.1251-2. It appears surprising that Eugene did not select for this purpose Anselm of Havelberg, who had in 1136 debated at Constantinople with Nicetas of Nicomedia concerning the union of the Churches: see Johannes Dräseke, 'Bischof Anselm von Havelberg und seine Gesandtschaftsreisen nach Byzanz,' *Zeitschrift für Kirchengeschichte* 21 (1900) 160-85: Louis Bréhier, 'Attempts at Reunion of the Greek and Latin Churches,' CMH 4 (1923) 600: and Georg Schreiber, 'Anselm von Havelberg und die Ostkirche,' *Zeitschrift für Kirchengeschichte* 60 (Dritte Folge 11; 1941) 357-62. Anselm had an exceptional understanding of the differences between the Greeks and the Latins. He met Eugene III at Tusculum in 1149 (not 1145, as in D'Achery, *Spicilegium* I 161) and wrote for the Pope his remarkable *Dialogorum libri III* about his discussions with Nicetas: D'Achery I 161-207; see Dräseke, *loc. cit.* 167f.

[264] Walter Norden, *Das Papsttum und Byzanz* (Berlin 1903) 77-82.

[265] Gleber (n. 165 above) 36-7 and 58-9; Erdmann (n. 64 above) 299-301.

[266] Norden 83-4.

does not seem to have entrusted this mission to anyone else.[267] He wrote that he doubted if any progress could be made towards union by Conrad in Henry's absence; but he approved the Bishop's decision and asked him to send news of the progress of the Wendish crusade.[268] The official legate to this campaign was, however, Anselm of Havelberg, whose duties for these armies were much the same as those of Theodwin and Guido for the armies of Conrad and Louis.[269] The Pope also instructed Wibald of Stavelot to join this expedition.[270] More perhaps than any of Eugene's explicit statements, these instructions to three prominent ecclesiastics are clear evidence of his interest in the Wendish Crusade and of his determination to bring it under ecclesiastical control and to turn it to religious ends.

The policy of Pope Eugene is therefore an essential clue to an understanding of the contemporary plan and theory of the Second Crusade. The sources examined in Section II reveal the underlying salvatory character of most of the expeditions of 1147-8 and show that in the minds of many contemporaries these campaigns were regarded as parts of a whole, a concerted effort against Islam and paganism by one Christian 'pilgrim army.' The sources and documents just discussed confirm this interpretation of the Second Crusade from another point of view. However narrow the concept and fortuitous the policy of Eugene III and the Curia in their origins and development, however much they made use of movements which originated outside the Church, it is clear that by the Spring of 1147 they viewed and planned the crusade not simply as one campaign against the Moslems in the Holy Land but as a general Christian offensive, and had incorporated into this plan practically every major military expedition against non-Christians of these years. The means of this incorporation was essentially the papal power of indulgence and remission of sins and penance, and this power was exercised through the instrumentality of papal bulls. In the crusading bulls of Eugene III the concept of the papal crusading indulgence was developed in its classic form, and around it there began to crystallize an institutional concept of temporal privileges and military regulations that exerted its influence on Christian thought throughout the Middle Ages.

---

[267] Gleber 59; Norden 83.

[268] JL 9110; PL 180.1262. Henry of Olmütz was one of the most important papalist bishops in the Empire: JL 9296 and 9325.

[269] See p. 263 above.

[270] See Appendix B.

X

266

IV. THE REACTION TO THE FAILURE

The disastrous defeats of the Christian army became known in the West probably before the end of 1147.[271] 'The lamenting rumor sounded within Gaul,' says Geoffrey of Auxerre,[272] and thus found its way into the annals and chronicles. Least successful of all was the great crusade to the Levant, where the Moslems were exultant,[273] and on the failures there most of the chroniclers concentrate their attention.[274]

It has been seen earlier that in the writings of Odo of Deuil and Otto of Freising there are found two opposite explanations of the failure of the crusade in the East. The former presents rational reasons for the disasters — the hostility of the Greeks and Turks and the difficulties of the route[275] — whereas the latter ascribes the failure purely to human sin and to the obscure workings of the ways of God. For the most part, the reactions of contemporaries lay somewhere between these natural and supernatural explanations.

Very few writers attributed this great Christian catastrophe entirely to inexplicable Divine Will. Such reasoning is an act of exceptional faith in any age; and it is not surprising that the two principal representatives of this supernatural position were Otto of Freising and Bernard of Clairvaux, both Cistercians and both men of great spiritual fortitude. The reaction of Otto has already been discussed.[276] Although he suggests that perhaps the sins of men aroused God's anger, fundamentally he can find no reason for the failure of this enterprise, the product of the co-operation of the finest spirits in Christendom, other than the inscrutable but ever good Will of the Almighty.

On St. Bernard fell the brunt of the popular disappointment and disillusion at the failure of the crusade, in so far as this resentment fell on any one man. For the majority of Christians he had been the prime mover of these campaigns; many miracles, also, had seemed to confirm God's favor and interest

---

[271] Carried in letters and by deserters: see Bernhardi 643 and n. 27.

[272] *Bernardi ... Opera* (n. 175 above) II 2.2198.

[273] *Notae Pisanae*, MGH SS 19.266: 'Unde gens paganorum magnam habuerunt baldansa et letitia, christiani tristia.' Cf. Kugler 212f.

[274] The attitude of contemporaries to the failure of the crusade seems never to have been studied adequately. See the brief remarks, mostly on the reaction against the Cistercians, in Röhricht, *Zeitschr. für Kirchengesch.* (n. 183 above) 6. 555-6, and *Beiträge* (n. 9 above) II 79 and 102-3, nn. 90-1; Hirsch (n. 13 above) 55-6; Hauck (n. 129 above) IV 895-6; Cramer (n. 44 above) 46 and 53-4; Cartellieri (n. 37 above) 379-80; and the interesting study of Flahiff (n. 201 above) 162-79.

[275] Odo, it is true, believed that God was with the expedition, the failure of which must be in accord with His inscrutable Will: cf. Odo of Deuil, ed. Berry xxvi; but he always concentrated on the human and natural causes of the calamities. The fact that he hoped for revenge on the Greeks shows that he did not regard the failure as a divine punishment.

[276] See above, p. 220. Otto knew Bernard's *De Consideratione*: Otto of Freising, *Gesta* 93.

in his work.[277] For this reason, as his friend and biographer Geoffrey says, 'either the simplicity or the malignity of certain men raised a great scandal against him because of his preaching of the journey to Jerusalem.' [278] Geoffrey goes on to emphasize, by way of excuse, that this preaching was undertaken only at the express command of the Pope and the urging of Louis VII.

Bernard himself however disdained such justifications as these in the two passages where he deals with this problem, in the letter to his uncle Andrew, a Templar, and at the beginning of the second book of his treatise *De consideratione*.[279] Never for one instant did his complete faith in God and in himself as the instrument of God's will falter; and he gladly took on his own shoulders the blame. Citing Scripture at every turn, he emphasized that the ways of the Lord are indeed obscure and deep, and yet His judgments are always not only just but also merciful. This the history of mankind reveals. Again and again he repeats that God's promises can never compromise His righteousness. In so doing Bernard turns the tables on his critics and flings their reproaches back in their own teeth. Who are you, he seems to ask, of little faith, who dare to criticize what you cannot possibly understand? Yet, he says in his letter to Andrew, it is the supreme example of God's mercy and patience that He does not reject these impious men. ' You do well, comparing yourself to an ant, ' he says, 'For what else than ants are we sons of men, born of the earth and sweating for useless and empty things? ... The reward of our warfare is not of (this) earth, not from below; its prize is far away and from the uttermost lands. ' [280]

This stern and uncompromising theory was, of course, strong meat, fit food for a St. Bernard or an Otto of Freising, also, perhaps, for Eugene III, whose letter of condolence to Conrad III[281] was clearly written under the influence of Bernard's ideas. For lesser spirits, however, it was indigestible; and other writers found various compromises by which they preserved their

---

[277] On Bernard's miracles in connection with his crusading activity, see Hüffer (n. 167 above) 96-9.

[278] *Bernardi ... Opera* II 2.2195-6; cf. the life by Alan, who says that 'quidam minus intelligentes scandalizati fuerunt,' *ibid.* 2464. See Pfeiffer (n. 31 above) 146-7, and Fechner (n. 170 above) 63.

[279] Bern. ep. 288, coll. 493-4; *De consideratione*, tr. George Lewis (Oxford 1908) 37-41. Pfeiffer 148 suggests that Bernard's principal defense against this criticism was to throw the responsibility for the crusade onto Eugene III and Louis VII. This, perhaps, was his defense against the charge that he had, without authorization, preached the crusade (see Appendix A); but fundamentally, as he emphasizes in *De consideratione*, both the Pope and he himself obeyed a divine mandate in this matter. Rousset's assumption, *op. cit.* (n. 8 above) 159, that Bernard implicitly suggested that 'les croisés sont donc eux-mêmes la cause de leur défaite' is not justified by the text of *De consideratione*, nor, I believe, by the general tenor of Bernard's crusading thought. Cf. also Flahiff 164 n. 12.

[280] Bern. ep. 288, col. 493.

[281] JL 9344; Otto of Freising, *Gesta* 94-5.

belief in the supernatural causes of the failure of the crusade without putting such a severe strain on their faith.

Among the most remarkable of these positions is that occupied by Gerhoh of Reichersberg and by the author of the *Annales Herbipolenses* (of Würzburg).[282] They in effect took the opposite viewpoint to that of St. Bernard and boldly asserted that the whole enterprise was from the start the work of the Devil. 'God permitted,' begins the account of the crusade in the *Annales Herbipolenses*, 'that the Western Church be afflicted, since its sins required (this punishment). Thereupon, certain pseudo-prophets were in power, sons of Belial, heads of Anti-Christ, who by stupid words misled the Christians and by empty preaching induced all sorts of men to go against the Saracens for the freeing of Jerusalem.' [283] And they continue in this vein: the crusade was a revolt inspired by the Devil against the righteous punishment of God. Small wonder, therefore, that it ended in disastrous failure. Gerhoh of Reichersberg is less explicit, but he treats of the crusade under the general heading of *Libri tres de investigatione Antichristi*,[284] in which he bitterly attacks the prevailing conditions in the Church of Rome.

Neither of these authors strictly maintains this attitude of utter condemnation. They include much purely descriptive material, often of considerable factual importance. These writers were not crabbed, ill-informed, or out-of-touch with the main line of development of crusading theory. Gerhoh was provost of an important monastery and in frequent correspondence with the Pope, with whom he was on excellent terms.[285] The annalist of Würzburg incorporated valuable first-hand material into his account, since not only did he himself presumably witness the passage of the crusader armies through Würzburg, but he also specifically says that he met many returned soldiers who had been captured by the Turks in Asia Minor and

---

[282] Kugler 31-6; Manitius (n. 30 above) III 427.

[283] *Ann. Herbipolenses*, MGH SS 16.3; cf. Hauck IV 896.

[284] Gerhoh, ed. Scheibelberger (n. 163 above) 139-46 and 151-8, and in *Libelli de lite* 3.374-8 and 380-4. In some respects Gerhoh seems to have depended upon the *Ann. Herbipolenses*. See also his less virulent criticism of the crusade in his *Commentarius* (cited n. 151 above), Psalm 39 col. 794, and in the *Ann. Reicherspergensis*, MGH SS 17.461-4.

[285] JL 8914: May 4, 1146 (*Germania Pontificia*, ed. Albert Brackmann I [Berlin 1911] Reichersberg no. 16, pp. 194-5) and JL 8922: May 16, 1146 (*ibid.* no. 17, pp. 195-6), where the Pope says to Gerhoh that, 'fervorem tuae religionis ex earum (litterarum) inspectione manifeste cognovimus ... et devotionem tuam in Domino collaudamus,' PL 180.1139; see Hüffer (n. 167 above) 201, and especially Konrad Sturmhoefel, 'Der geschichtliche Inhalt von Gerhohs von Reichersberg 1. Buche über die Erforschung des Antichrists,' *Jahresbericht der Thomasschule in Leipzig für das Schuljahr 1886-7* (Program no. 504, Leipzig 1887) part I p. 3. Sturmhoefel (11f.) carefully examines Gerhoh's account of the crusade and points out that in spite of his prejudice and frequent untrustworthiness, he includes some material presumably based upon eye-witness reports, although his real importance for the historian of the Second Crusade lies in his distinctive attitude.

later released.[286] Nor were these two isolated in their attitude, of which they were only the most extreme examples.[287] It should also be noted, however, that their point of view is not cynical and has none of the secular scepticism of the thirteenth century 'crusader's song':

> Ire si vis ad sermonem
> Cave, precor, Ciceronem
> Ne per verbi rationem
> Reddat crucis te prisonem.[288]

On the contrary, the explanation of the failure of the crusade advanced by Gerhoh and the Würzburg annalist was in its way no less boldly convinced or less spiritual than that of Bernard of Clairvaux.

It is interesting that Bernard seems never to have considered accompanying in person the crusading armies. When, during his preaching of a new crusade in 1150, at Chartres, he was almost elected general and leader of the expedition, Bernard wrote to the Pope, 'What (is) more remote from my profession, even if my strength were sufficient, even if the skill were not lacking?'[289] It is probable, in fact, that Cistercian monks were forbidden by the General Chapter to join the crusade.[290] These regulations were based upon a funda-

---

[286] *Ann. Herbipolenses*, MGH SS 16.5. The Armenians seem to have been instrumental in ransoming crusaders taken prisoner by the Turks, see *Casus mon. Petrishusensis*, MGH SS 20.674; *De s. Ernesto Abbate Zwifaltensi*, AS 7 November, III 612 and 617; and the *Vetus de s. Ernesto documentum*, which I have been unable to consult but which is analyzed by Kugler 10.

[287] See n. 278 above. Also in the First Crusade, Ekkehard reports, many people considered the enterprise vain and frivolous: cited by Runciman I 141 n. 2. It is perhaps to these that an anonymous author refers when he says of the failure of the crusade (PL 155.1098) that 'Gallia tota dolet, et ego, gens impia gaudet.' Cf. *Chron. Sancti Petri Erfordensis*, in *Monumenta Erphesfurtensia*, ed. O. Holder-Egger (MGH SS.r.G; Hannover 1899) 176; *Ann. Sancti Iacobi Leodiensis*, MGH SS 16.641. An interesting document, written according to Heinemann in 1147, bewails the sad state of the Church at this time when 'Satan ... tanta fortitudine catenas, quibus legatus est, concutit,' *Codex Diplomaticus Anhaltinus*, ed. Otto von Heinemann, I (*936-1212*; Dessau 1867-73) no. 336, pp. 252-4. In view of this evidence, Flahiff (n. 201 above) 165-6 perhaps overestimates the novelty of the opposition of Ralph Niger, writing in 1189, to the idea of crusading. Cf. n. 291 below.

[288] H. Pflaum, 'A Strange Crusader's Song,' *Speculum* 10 (1935) 337-9. Since it is written in a thirteenth-century hand, I see no reason to agree with Cartellieri (n. 37 above) 343, that it applies to the Second Crusade. For anti-crusading songs in the vernacular, see Hauck, *op. cit.* 4.898.

[289] Bern. ep. 256, col. 465.

[290] Pfeiffer (n. 31 above) 8-10. In 1157, the General Chapter of the Cistercian Order decreed that monks 'qui de ordine exeunt ita ut Jerusolymam eant vel aliam peregrinationem aliorsum faciant ... sine omni personarum acceptione de domibus propriis amoti, mittantur in alias domos ordinis perpetuo numquam reversuri,' *ibid.* 8. That Cistercian monks in fact joined the Second Crusade does not affect the general validity of this order, which was fully in accord with medieval crusading theory. Urban II forbade monks'

mental Christian belief in the unimportance of wordly events and upon the
Cistercian principle of strict abstention from the affairs of this world. With
regard to pilgrimages this spirit was expressed by St. Augustine and many
of the Greek fathers and found its *locus classicus* for the Middle Ages in
Letter 58 of St. Jerome, who said that 'it is praiseworthy not to have been
in Jerusalem but to have lived well for Jerusalem.' [291] Bernard himself expressed a similar idea in one of his letters concerning pilgrim-monks: 'The
object of monks is to seek not the earthly but the heavenly Jerusalem; and
this not by proceeding with (their) feet but by progressing with (their) af-
fections.' [292] In this idea that the pilgrimage and the crusade — although
perhaps in themselves pious and good works — offered many opportunities
for sin and were the signs of a wrong orientation in a Christian's life, as well
as in the idea of the crusade as a rebellion against God's punishment of the
Church, lay, I think, the basis of the criticism of Gerhoh and the Würzburg
annalist, who found here in addition an explanation of the failure of the
crusade.

For other writers, however, there was an easier compromise. They preserved their belief that God had wrought this disaster, but to ease the strain
on their faith they found an explanation for this divine punishment. Among
the most exceptional of these writers was the Cistercian Abbot John of Casa-
Maria, who in a letter to Bernard explained his view of the failure. [293] He
recognized that this was God's punishment on the crusaders, who had started
piously but had turned into evil ways. The Lord, however, was not to be
outdone by this: 'In order that His Providence in the ordering of it (the
crusade) might not fail, He turned their wickedness into His mercy...' and
decreed (here John makes use of an idea from the *City of God*) that 'the host
of angels who had fallen were to be replaced by those who died there (in the
Holy Land)'; [294] and since He had foreseen that the crusaders, although sin-

---

joining the First Crusade without the permission of their abbots (JL 5670); cf. Schlée
(n. 234 above) 48-9; Flahiff 176-7; and Bridrey (n. 161 above) 50-1, who says that, 'quant
aux moines, ils ne pourront jamais faire le vœu de croisade sans autorisation spéciale,' 51;
and see also the letter of Innocent III to the Bishop of Troyes, PL 214.58-61, no. 69.

[291] *Sancti Eusebii Hieronymi Epistulae*, ed. Isidor Hilberg I (CSEL 54; Vienna and
Leipzig 1910) 529: 'non Hierosolymis fuisse, sed Hierosolymis bene vixisse laudandum
est.' Augustine, ep. 78, PL 33.268-9; *Contra Faustum* 20.21, PL 42.384-5. Gregory of
Nyssa and Chrysostom, quoted by Bernhard Koetting, *Peregrinatio Religiosa* (Forschungen zur Volkskunde 33-5; Regensberg and Münster 1950) 422-4. See the quotations in
Pierre Mandonnet, *Saint Dominique*, edd. M. H. Vicaire and R. Ladner II (Paris 1937)
25 n. 66; van Cauwenbergh (n. 142 above) 16; Koetting 421-6 (bibliography on p. 426 n. 21);
Runciman I 40 n. 1. Even the author of the *De imitatione Christi* wrote that, 'qui ni-
mium peregrinatur, raro sanctificatur,' 1.23.4.

[292] Bern. ep. 399, col. 612.

[293] Bern. ep. 386, coll. 590-1.

[294] *Ibid.* col. 590. Cf. Augustine, *De civ. dei* 22. 1 ; *Enchiridion* 29.

ful, would be redeemed in this way, He had granted to Bernard 'the grace of preaching and laboring in this matter.' [295] This remarkable intelligence, John says, came to him in a vision from St. John and St. Paul; and it was in any case an ingenious explanation to reassure the Abbot of Clairvaux of his divine mandate to preach the crusade.

Other writers did not go so far. They merely saw the failure as a punishment for the sins of the crusaders. Henry of Huntingdon, who died in 1155, is typical of this attitude. He says of the crusaders that 'their incontinence, which they practised in open fornications, and even in adulteries, ... and finally in robbery and all sorts of evils, came up before the sight of God..., Who withdrew his favor from the armies, which consequently were defeated.' 'At the same time,' however, he continues, referring to the expedition to Lisbon, 'a certain naval force not of powerful men and trusting in no great leader other than Almighty God, since they set forth humbly, prospered greatly.' [296] This general attitude was shared by many contemporaries, including the Würzburg annalist and especially Gerhoh of Reichersberg, who naturally maintained that nothing good could be done on the crusade.[297]

This explanation of the failure depended on the idea that the grace of God, originally with the armies, was withdrawn on account of His anger at the sins of the crusaders, who were thus left without defence in a bitterly hostile environment.[298] This view is paralleled on the positive side in the Dialogue of the monk William of St. Denis, who attributed the individual survivals of Louis VII and certain other crusaders to the fact that divine grace was always with them.[299]

Most contemporaries, however, found no need to see the disasters of the Second Crusade in the light of a supernatural explanation. They were content with the natural causes, without troubling themselves with the problem

---

[295] *Ibid.* See Rousset (n. 8 above) 168 on this letter, which shows the influence of Bernard's thought. Cf. Geoffrey of Auxerre, in *Bernardi ... Opera* (n. 175 above) II 2.2196: 'Quod si placuit Deo tali occasione plurimorum eripere, si non Orientalium corpora a paganis, Occidentalium animas a peccatis.'

[296] Henry of Huntingdon, *Hist. Angl.* (n. 9 above) 280-1.

[297] Robert of Torigny, *Chron.* (n. 6 above) 154; Vincent of Prague, *Ann.* MGH SS 17.663; *Gisleberti Chron. Hanoniense,* MGH SS 21.516; *Vita Ludovici VII,* RHGF 12.286; *Continuatio Gemblacensis* (Sigeberti), MGH SS 6.390: '... quia in hostico illo multa scelera, multa illicita et flagitiosa patrata sunt ab eis, et ob hoc ira Dei ascendente super eos, omnis conatus eorum in vacuum cessit'; *Casus mon. Petrishusensis,* MGH SS 20.674; William of Newburgh, *Historia Anglicana,* in *Chronicles of the Reigns of Stephen,* etc. ed. Richard Howlett (Rolls Series 82; London 1884-5) I 66. Cf. also *Ann. Rodenses,* MGH SS 16.719.

[298] See n. 297 above. Cf. *Ex anonymo Blandinensi Appendicula ad Sigebertum usque in annum 1152,* RHGF 14.20: 'Sed eorum conatus fuit inanis, quia Deus non erat cum eis.'

[299] William of St. Denis, *Dialogue* (n. 130 above) 105-6 and 109: '... Domini gratia, que, famulum suum indesinenter protegens, comes individua euntem et precedebat et subsecuta est,' 106.

of why God allowed these to overwhelm the crusade. Among these writers are found some who emphasized non-human factors and others who emphasized primarily human actions; and in this latter group there are those who blamed men other than the crusaders and those who blamed the crusaders themselves.

Nearly all the sources on the Second Crusade mention at some point or other the difficulties encountered by the crusaders: the bad weather, the floods, the impassable rivers and mountains, the disease, and above all, the lack of food and water. They are too many to specify, but Odo of Deuil mentions most of them.[300] A special group among these writers connected these natural phenomena, especially the floods and famines, with signs and portents such as comets and an eclipse of the moon.[301] Others were inclined to see in them — as indeed in the entire outcome of the crusade — the fulfilment of biblical or popular prophecies.[302] This was representative of the inability of these writers to see any event or circumstance in entirely naturalistic terms.

Most of the sources mention the attacks of the Saracens as one cause of the catastrophe. More interesting than these are the writers who believed that certain groups of Christians, themselves not crusaders, contributed to the defeats. The most obvious and important among these were the Greeks, whose treachery and perfidy appear constantly in the work of Odo of Deuil. Although few were as extreme in their criticism as he was, a large number of contemporaries clearly believed that the Greeks were responsible for the misfortune of the crusading armies in Asia Minor.[303] Modern historians,

---

[300] Cf. the poetic lament over the failure, composed ca. 1150 according to the authors of the *Histoire littéraire* (n. 106 above) 13.88-90, in PL 155.1095-8. The *Historia Welforum Weingartensis*, MGH SS 21.468, mentions the 'ciborum insolentia.' Cf. the somewhat later Lambert of Ardres, *Historia*, MGH SS 24.633-4: 'Multi enim fame, multi aeris inclementia, multi adversantium insidiis et ictibus, multi invalitudine corporis, multi qualicumque infirmitate correpti, interierunt. Inter quos et pater meus non, ut mentiuntur quidam, fame deperiit, sed invalitudine corporis debilitatus et totis viribus destitutus, morti succubuit.'

[301] *Ann. Magdeburgenses* MGH SS 16.188; *Ann. Palidenses, ibid.* 83; *Chron. Ekkehardi Continuatio brevis*, in *Monumenta Erphesfurtensia* (n. 287 above) 70; Gerhoh of Reichersberg, *De invest. Antichr.* (n. 163 above), in *Libelli de lite* 3.383; Helmold of Bosau, *Chron. Slav.* (n. 50 above) 116: 'Multa vero portenta visa sunt in exercitu illis diebus, futurae cladis demonstrativa.'

[302] *Ann. Sancti Iacobi Leodiensis*, MGH SS 16.641; *Chron. Sancti Petri Erfordensis* 176; Geoffrey of Vigeois, *Chron.* (n. 9 above) 306. The Sibylline prophecies for 1147 appear in Otto of Freising and several other twelfth-century sources: see W. von Giesebrecht, *Geschichte der deutschen Kaiserzeit* IV: *Staufer und Welfen* (2nd ed.; Leipzig 1877) 502 and 505-6.

[303] Röhricht (n. 9 above) II 79 is hardly correct in saying that, 'nur wenige Stimmen luden dem griechischen Kaiser die Schuld auf.'

basing their interpretation on that of Odo, have perhaps placed too much emphasis on this attitude. Otto of Freising and Conrad III, who were both in a position to know, make no reference to Greek treachery and, in fact, speak of the 'Emperor Manuel in the warmest terms. This point of view was not uncommon among the German writers; and it may indeed represent an actual difference in the treatment of the German and French troops by the Greeks. The *Annales Palidenses* tell of Manuel's care of Conrad during his illness in the winter of 1147-8;[304] Helmold shows the Greek Emperor sadly contemplating the crusaders' rash determination to march across Asia Minor;[305] the Würzburg annalist put into Manuel's mouth a long speech explaining to Conrad the difficulties and dangers of a march to Iconium and urging him to proceed directly to Jerusalem with a small picked force. Even when Conrad persisted in his original decision, this annalist says, Manuel assisted him in all ways, with arms and supplies, both before and after the terrible expedition into Anatolia. Nowhere does he mention treachery, even though his account was partly based upon the reports of released prisoners, who might well have felt bitter towards the Greeks.[306] In any case, this evidence definitely shows that all Western Europe did not believe that the Greeks had betrayed the crusade.[307]

There was a more widespread unanimity of opinion that the siege of Damascus was betrayed in some way by the Latin inhabitants of the Holy Land. Conrad III stated this for a fact; and he and the other sources leave doubt only over the question of whether this treason was committed by the King of Jerusalem, the Templars, or the Princes of Syria.[308] There is no clear definition of the exact nature of the treachery; it may in fact have been honest but exceedingly unwise advice. The Westerners, however, had little doubt that Damascene money entered into the matter somewhere. Gerhoh of Reichersberg fully exploited this situation. He believed that the guilt lay with the Jerusalemites, not only for the failure of the siege but for the disaster of the entire crusade. With the voice of an avenging prophet he thundered against them. Avarice alone, he says, moved them to call on the West for assistance; they desired not peace but 'almost solely the acceptance of money, whether from the offerings of the pilgrims or from the re-

---

[304] *Ann. Palidenses*, MGH SS 16.83: 'Rex Grecie Conradum regem valida infirmitate detentum summa fecit curare diligentia, nisus per hoc expiari adnotata sibi circa Teutonicos malivolentia.'

[305] Helmold of Bosau, *Chron. Slav.* 120.

[306] *Ann. Herbipolenses*, MGH SS 16.4-5.

[307] Cf., among modern historians, Ferdinand Chalandon, *Les Comnène* II (Paris 1912) 286-8; Vasiliev (n. 53 above) 420; Cartellieri (n. 37 above) 357f.

[308] For a list of these sources, see Röhricht II 101 n. 76, and Bernhardi 675 n. 37. Cf. Cartellieri 363.

demption of the besieged.'[309] And with scornful satisfaction he recorded the irony with which most of the treason 'gold' turned out to be copper.

Finally, there are a few writers who attributed the failure of the crusade to the mistakes and blundering of the crusaders themselves. Needless to say, Gerhoh of Reichersberg and the *Annales Herbipolenses* figure among these. The Würzburg annalist, in the passage quoted above, acutely discerned the unruly members in the makeup of the crusading armies; he sharply criticized Conrad for his rejection of Manuel's wise advice, and in several other places condemned the general management and leadership of the crusade. The author of the *Chronicon Mauriniacense* blamed the lack of discretion and experience of Louis VII;[310] the annalist of Egmond specified the error in the choice of route as one reason for the failure of the armies;[311] and an Angevin writer said, 'I think that the misfortune resulted from the deliberate arrogance of the French.'[312] Odo of Deuil himself spoke of the 'stupid pride of our people.'[313] Geoffrey of Vigeois bitterly condemned the lack of ecclesiastical contributions towards the expenses of the crusade.[314] For the Wendish Crusade, also, Vincent of Prague attributed the failure to the material motives of the Saxon princes.[315]

The most damning criticism of the leaders of the crusade came from the pen of John of Salisbury in his *Historia Pontificalis*, where he says that he has written 'nothing except what I knew to be true by sight or hearing or what was confirmed by the writings and authority of trustworthy men.'[316] These sources were certainly of the very highest authority; his material on the Second Crusade, which corresponds to no other known source material, may have come from the legate Cardinal Guido or from some companions of Louis VII, the Count of Flanders, or the Count of Champagne,[317] with all of whom John was on familiar terms. He was in addition a man of exceptional wisdom, experience, and moderation, to whose judgments careful consideration must be given. His contribution to the factual knowledge of the crusade

---

[309] Gerhoh of Reichersberg, in *Libelli de lite* 3.377.

[310] RHGF 12.88. Louis seems in part to have blamed himself for the failure: RHGF 15.495-6.

[311] *Ann. Egmundani*, MGH SS 16.456.

[312] *Liber de compositione Castri Ambaziae*, in *Chroniques des Comtes d'Anjou*, edd. Louis Halphen and René Poupardin (Collection de textes pour servir à l'étude et à l'enseignement de l'histoire; Paris 1913) 24. The principal part of this work goes to 1137 and is of no historical value (see intro. xlvii-lvi); an account of the Second Crusade is the only entry after 1137 (*ibid.* lv n. 3) and appears to be contemporary.

[313] Odo of Deuil, *De prof. Ludov.* ed. Berry 22.

[314] Geoffrey of Vigeois, *Chron.* 306.

[315] Vincent of Prague, *Ann.*, MGH SS 17.663.

[316] John of Salisbury, *Hist. Pontif.* (n. 248 above) 4.

[317] R. L. Poole, intro. to John of Salisbury, xxv. The sections on the Second Crusade are: ch. 5, pp. 12-3, and chs. 23-6, pp. 52-61.

X

is unfortunately slight, although of some value for the events in Syria and the Holy Land in 1148.[318] John's great gift as an historian was his ability to estimate the influence of personalities on events; and his characterizations of Louis VII, Theoderic of Flanders, Arnulf of Lisieux, Godfrey of Langres, and the two papal legates are full of interest and life. It is therefore of particular importance that his account of the crusade consists principally of a bitter attack on its leadership. He gives a fascinating picture of the quarrels between the legates and between the spiritual and temporal lords and of the crippling rivalry between the French and German armies. He at least clearly believed that incompetence and internal tensions were the primary reasons for the failure.

It is interesting to compare this point of view with that of a close personal friend of John of Salisbury, Pope Adrian IV. Writing to Louis VII in 1159, he cautioned him against rashly undertaking a crusade against the Moors in Spain.

'For Your Excellency ought to recollect,' he says, '... how on that other occasion, when Conrad of good memory, previously King of the Romans, and you yourself undertook the journey to Jerusalem without caution, you did not receive the expected result and hoped-for profit; and (you should remember) how great a disaster and cost resulted therefrom to the Church of God and to almost the entire Christian people. And the Holy Roman Church, since she had given you advice and support in this matter, was not a little weakened by this; and everyone cried out against her in great indignation, saying that she was the author of so great a peril.'[319]

It is significant that this gloomy view of the crusade was found among most of its principal planners. Already by August, 1149, Eugene III spoke of Louis' return as 'to the light out of the darkness'[320] and later, in a letter to Suger, he called the crusade 'the severe disaster of the Christian name which the Church of God has suffered in our times.'[321] Bernard himself never for one moment minimized the magnitude of this disaster, of which he said, 'We all know that the judgments of God are true; but this judgment is so deep that I could almost justify myself for calling him blessed who is not offended thereat.'[322]

The most convincing evidence, however, of the disillusionment and discouragement which followed the failure of the Second Crusade is found not

---

[318] *Ibid.* xxvi; Kugler 13-20.
[319] JL 10546; PL 188.1615. See Defourneaux (n. 69 above) 172f.
[320] JL 9347; PL 180.1396. Cf. Bernard, who in his ep. 377 to Suger speaks of Louis' presence on the crusade as an 'exile': col. 582.
[321] JL 9385; PL 180.1414. Cf. JL 9398 (*ibid.* 1419) and *Continuatio Aquicinctina* (Sigeberti), MGH SS 6.406: 'Numquam audita tanta infelicitate corporali Christiani exercitus.'
[322] Bernard, *De consideratione* (n. 279 above) 38.

X

in the literary sources but in the poor response which greeted the efforts of Bernard and Suger to organize a new expedition for the relief of the Holy Land in 1150[323] and in the reduced number of new Cistercian monasteries established after 1147.[324] These facts exemplify the widespread reaction against crusading in general and against the Cistercians in particular.

The form and depth of this reaction must be judged in relation to the hope and enthusiasm with which these campaigns had been conceived. The Second Crusade, to a far greater extent than the First, won the support of the ecclesiastical and secular authorities of Europe. Championed by the most powerful princes and inspired by the most persuasive spiritual leader of the century, it appeared to men as divinely predestined to victory. It aroused soldiers on every frontier of western Christendom and incorporated them under the common cross of pilgrimage. The formal origin of this idea and its development into a grandiose scheme of Christian defence and expansion may be found in the letters of Eugene III and St. Bernard. The wider influence of this plan, the roots of contemporary crusading thought, and the more popular attitudes towards the crusade have been seen in chronicles and documents. Upon such subjects, literary sources are by their nature unable to give entirely satisfactory evidence, and the conclusions drawn from them should be considered in part as hypotheses, to be amplified and modified by future research. In certain directions, however, their evidence is impressive and points towards a revised interpretation of the Second Crusade, in its widest sense, and of the place it occupies in the history of the crusades.

Appendix A

St. Bernard's Preaching of the Second Crusade

In the medieval as in the modern Church the right of preaching was strictly subject to the bishop's control and might not be exercised by the lower clergy without the authorization (*missio*) either of the diocesan bishop or of he universal ordinary, the Pope.[1] So in the eleventh century the Abbot of Fulda

[323] Vacandard (n. 174 above) II 442-50; Pfeiffer (n. 31 above) 149.

[324] See Janauschek (n. 177 above) I 287f. Franz Winter, *Die Cistercienser des nordöstlichen Deutschlands* I (Gotha 1868) 56, says: 'Jener verunglückte Kreuzzug von 1147 hat dem heiligen Bernard in den Augen der Sachsen seinen Heiligenschein genommen und seinem Orden unter ihnen einen mehr als zwanzigjährigen Stillstand auferlegt.' But this is too extreme, cf. Pfeiffer 145. Certainly 1147 was the peak year, after which there was a sharp reduction in the number of new houses; but the falling off in the middle and late 1150's was presumably largely owing to the death of St. Bernard and to the stringent restriction on the foundation of new abbeys enacted by the General Chapter in 1152: see *Statuta capitulorum generalium ordinis Cisterciensis*, ed. J.-M. Canivez, I (Bibliothèque de la Revue d'histoire ecclésiastique 9; Louvain 1933) 45.

[1] R. Ladner, 'L'Ordo Praedicatorum avant l'Ordre des Prêcheurs,' in Pierre Man-

enjoyed the right to preach as a special privilege from Leo IX.[2] When in the late eleventh and early twelfth centuries an increasing number of monks took holy orders and claimed this right, 'il s'éleva dans les rangs du clergé séculier et jusque dans les cloîtres eux-mêmes des voix qui voulaient interdire au moine toute espèce d'activité pastorale et surtout la prédication. '[3] Nor was this attitude surprising in view of the widespread disorganization and ignorance of the clergy and the grave danger of the spread of heresy through unauthorized preaching.[4]

Although a few voices were raised in favor of the right of an ordained (and even of a lay) monk to preach,[5] many twelfth-century theologians agreed with Jerome that 'monachus autem non doctoris habet, sed plangentis officium. '[6] Under the heading, 'Nullus monachus preter Domini sacerdotes audeat predicare,' Gratian wrote:

> Monachi autem, et si in dedicatione sui presbiteratus (sicut et ceteri sacerdotes) predicandi, baptizandi, penitenciam dandi, peccata remittendi, beneficiis ecclesiasticis perfruendi rite potestatem accipiunt, ut amplius et perfectius agant ea, que sacerdotalis offitii esse sanctorum Patrum constitutionibus conprobantur: tamen executionem suae potestatis non habent, nisi a populo fuerint electi, et ab episcopo cum consensu abbatis ordinati.[7]

Bernard himself made use of the familiar quotation, 'Monachus predicare non audeat quantaecumque scientiae sit. '[8] The General Chapter of the Cistercian Order in 1199 refused to undertake the preaching of the Fourth Crusade because, as Ladner puts it, 'une telle activité ... ne répondait pas à la fonction de l'Ordre. '[9] In 1212, indeed, the Chapter decreed that, 'De monacho Prulliacensi nuncupato Petro heremita praecipitur ut in instanti revocetur a praedicatione Albigensium, nec ipse nec alius aliquis sine licentia Capituli generalis de cetero praedicationis officium audeat usurpare. '[10]

It does not therefore appear surprising that Bernard was unwilling to preach the crusade without the authorization of the Pope. It is for this reason, I think, that in his writings about the crusade he emphasized that in its preaching he acted purely as a papal delegate. This was not an effort to escape the responsibility for the failure of the crusade — that, he always held, lay with God — but to defend himself against the charge that he had never been duly commissioned to preach the crusade.[11] Only thirty years before, in 1118, a

---

donnet, *Saint Dominique* (Paris 1937) II 13: 'Qui prêchait sans délégation ni permission était dès l'abord classé comme hérétique,' *ibid.* 15; cf. 28-9.

[2] PL 143.610.

[3] Ladner 24-5.

[4] *Ibid.* 15-24.

[5] *Ibid.* 25-6.

[6] Quoted *ibid.* 25, cf. n. 68.

[7] *Decretum Magistri Gratiani*, ed. Emil Friedberg (Corpus Iuris Canonici I; Leipzig 1879), Dictum post c. 19, C. XVI, q. 1 (coll. 765-6).

[8] *Sermo 64 in Cantic.*, PL 183.1085.

[9] Ladner 40.

[10] *Statuta Cap. Gen. Ord. Cist.* ed. J.-M. Canivez (Louvain 1933) I 1212: cited by Ladner 25 n. 66.

[11] As early as 1146 he wrote to the Pope saying that, 'Mandastis et obedivi,' ep. 247, PL 182.447.

council at Fritzlar had condemned Norbert of Xanten for preaching without authorization and had compelled him to suspend his activity until he was accorded special permission as an 'apostolic preacher' by Gelasius II.[12] Bernard presumably desired to obtain a similar general delegation before he undertook the preaching of the crusade.

APPENDIX B

Eugene III and German Participation in the Second Crusade

Eugene probably received the news of Conrad's decision not long after Christmas, 1146, and he sent back Cardinal Bishop Theodwin[1] with the letter mentioned above.[2] Theodwin reached Frankfurt in mid-March,[3] and soon after Conrad sent Bishops Buco of Worms and Anselm of Havelberg and Abbot Wibald of Stavelot, who met Eugene at Dijon on March 30. They brought two letters to the Pope from Conrad,[4] who in one requested Eugene to confirm Wibald's election as Abbot of Corbie and in the other announced that he had received the papal letter and had called a diet at Frankfurt,[5] where his young son Henry had been chosen to rule in Conrad's absence. He expressed regret that he had taken the cross without Eugene's permission but assured him that this action was prompted by true love. He also invited Eugene to visit Germany. The selection of the young Henry as regent may have been suggested as a conciliatory move by the Cardinal Theodwin, since this appointment was certainly more pleasing to the Curia than that of the other possible candidate, Archbishop Henry of Mainz.[6]

Wibald describes the meeting with the Pope at Dijon in his letters 35 and 180.[7] The legates were well received by Eugene, he says: 'tunc enim iniunxit nobis in virtute obedientiae et in remissione peccatorum nostrorum, ut ad debellandos christiani nominis hostes ac Dei aecclesiae vastatores trans Albim super paganos militaremus: cum tamen sciret, hoc nequaquam a nobis posse fieri, nisi ex Corbeiensis aecclesiae expensa et milicia.'[8] This is quite explicit and sounds very much like a personal injunction to the imperial legates, and the later appearance of Anselm and Wibald on the Wendish Crusade supports this view.[9] It seems impossible that this passage refers to *Divina*

---

[12] Ladner 36-7; a similar privilege had been granted to Robert d'Arbrisselles and others, *ibid.* 33-6.

[1] Brixius (n. 243 above) 47; on Theodwin's many legations to Germany, see Hauck (n. 219 above) IV 161.

[2] See n. 217 above.

[3] Bachmann (n. 257 above) 78; Gleber (n. 165 above) 54.

[4] *Monumenta Corbeiensia* (n. 25 above) nos. 33 (pp. 111-2) and 34 (pp. 112-3); see Zatschek (n. 217 above) 324-5.

[5] Bernhardi 545f.; Zatschek 455-6.

[6] Gleber (n. 165 above) 54-5.

[7] *Monumenta Corbeiensia* 114 and 242-3; see Zatschek 325 and 353-5, and Ludwig Mann, *Wibald, Abt von Stablo und Corvei, nach seiner politischen Thätigkeit* (Halle 1875) 32f.

[8] *Monumenta Corbeiensia* 243; cf. Mann 32-3.

[9] On Wibald's somewhat brief participation in the crusade, see Joseph Bastin, *Wibald, Abbé de Stavelot et Malmédy, du mont-Cassin et de Corbie* (Verviers 1931) 44-5. On Anselm, cf. n. 263 above.

dispensatione (II). The terms are somewhat different, and there is no reason to believe that the envoys were with Eugene as late as April 11 at Troyes. They probably returned at once, accompanied by the papal chancellor, Cardinal deacon Guido of Saints Cosmas and Damian,[10] with the papal reply, to Conrad at the diet of Strasbourg, April 18, 1147.[11] In this case, furthermore, Eugene could have appointed Anselm of Havelberg legate only during their meeting at Dijon.

It was probably, therefore, at this time that the envoys presented the idea of the Wendish Crusade to the Pope, who immediately endorsed it by his appointment of Anselm and his injunction to Wibald. He then proceeded to Clairvaux, discussed the matter with Bernard, and issued *Divina dispensatione* (II). There is, as Gleber points out, [12] no reason to agree with Cosack[13] that Eugene remained angry with Conrad or that there was any split between the Pope on one side and Conrad and Bernard on the other over this matter of German participation in the crusade. Nor does there appear to be any basis for Zatschek's opinion that the Pope's displeasure with Conrad was responsible for his delay in the confirmation of Wibald as Abbot of Corbie.[14] Eugene knew that it was impossible to force Conrad back on his vow and after March 30 probably welcomed the idea of a diversion of German troops against the Slavs.[15]

Harvard University.

---

[10] Brixius 43.

[11] Bachmann 79-80.

[12] Gleber 56-8.

[13] Cosack (n. 167 above) 290f.

[14] Zatschek, *loc. cit.* 325. Eugene's objections to the confirmation of Wibald were presumably based upon (a) the dubious canonicity of the election, against which the deposed Abbot Henry of Nordheim had already appealed to Rome, and (b) Wibald's pluralism: he was already Abbot of Stavelot and Malmedy and ex-Abbot of Monte Cassino. See Mann 32; and Bastin 36f., who says that 'Eugène III fut d'ailleurs bientôt rassuré sur la régularité de l'élection. Une délégation de moines corbiens lui en porta la preuve à Meaux et il prit dès lors l'abbaye et son supérieur sous sa protection spéciale,' 42.

[15] Cf. his letter to Henry of Olmütz, JL 9110, p. 265 above.

XI

A NOTE ON THE ROUTE OF THE ANGLO-FLEMISH CRUSADERS OF 1147

It is a natural temptation for historians of the Anglo-Flemish naval expedition of 1147 to follow closely the excellent narrative of the *De Expugnatione Lyxbonensi*,[1] to trace with care the route of the crusaders along the northern and western coast of the Iberian penisula and to end the account, as does the anonymous author of the *De Expugnatione*, with the fall of Lisbon, after a siege of nearly seventeen weeks, in October 1147.

'When these things had been happily achieved,' wrote one of the crusaders, Duodechin of Lahnstein, to Cuno, abbot of Disibodenberg, 'our men spent the winter in that city (Lisbon) until the beginning of February; then they sailed through many perils and arrived, just as they had sworn, at the sepulchre of the Lord,'[2] Apart from this hint, the actual route after the capture of Lisbon long remained obscure. 'About their landing on the coast of Syria we know nothing definite,' wrote Reinhold Röhricht, 'but there is no doubt that they arrived there in April or May and that many of them joined in the army of Conrad [III] at the siege of Damascus.'[3] These words were echoed by Friedrich Kurth in his exhaustive study of German participation in the Portuguese campaigns against the Moors.[4]

The recent publication of the *Annales Elmarenses* has thrown some light on the crusaders' later route. 'And since they desired to accomplish their journey, they sailed from Lisbon on the third of February (1148) and attacked Hairon; and since they did not dare to make a long siege there on account of lack of food, they received from the besieged people hostages for an agreed sum of money; and very unwisely they (the besieged) handed over about forty of their best men there; and when they refused to pay the money, they saw their hostages hanged before the city. What more? (The crusaders) bravely fought many battles on land and on sea and with great labor arrived at Jerusalem; and the army gathered there attacked Damascus; and although it is the opinion of many that they could have conquered the city, they retreated on the advice of the Jersusalemites,'[5] The only difficulty in this otherwise straightforward passage is the identity of the town Hairon. Philip Grierson,[6] who is followed by Cartellieri,[7] suggests that

---

[1] Charles W. David ed. (New York, 1936). Of this victory Helmold of Bosau wrote in his *Chronica Slavorum* that 'this alone was successful of the entire work which the pilgrim army achieved' on the Second Crusade (George Pertz ed., Hanover, 1868, pp. 121-122).

[2] *Annales Sancti Disibodi*, in *Monumenta Germaniae Historica, Scriptores*, xvii, p. 28. David suggests that this passage may refer only to the German forces (*De Exp.*, p. 21, n. 2); this appears doubtful (see below), although some of the crusaders certainly stayed in Lisbon.

[3] Reinhold Röhricht, *Beiträge zur Geschichte der Kreuzzüge*, ii (Berlin, 1878), p. 92.

[4] Friedrich Kurth, 'Der Anteil niederdeutscher Kreuzfahrer an den Kämpfen der Portugiesen gegen die Mauren', *Mitteilungen des Institute für Österreichische Geschichtsforschung*, Ergänzungsband viii (1911), 159. Cf. *De Exp.*, p. 21.

[5] *Les Annales de Saint-Pierre de Gand et de Saint-Amand*, ed. Philip Grierson (Brussels, 1937), pp. 111-112. [6] *Ibid.*, p. 111, n. 3.

[7] Alexander Cartellieri, *Der Vorrang des Papsttums zur Zeit der Ersten Kreuzzüge 1095-1150* (Munich and Berlin, 1941), p. 372.

it refers to Oran (Wahrân) in North Africa. There can, however, be little doubt
that this Hairon is Faro, the ancient Ossonoba, east of Cape St Vincent in southern Portugal. The name Faro is derived from ibn Harun,[8] and the town is called
Hairun (Hayrun) by Roger of Hoveden[9] and Farun by Benedict of Peterborough.[10]

There is in addition an interesting reference in the *Ystoria captionis Almarie
et Turtuose* of Caffaro of Caschifellone,[11] who in this short but reliable work relates
the history of the Genoese expedition of 1147–48 and the capture of Almeria and
Tortosa in Spain. He mentions among other things that 'the English, together
with the Knights of the Temple and many other foreigners'[12] participated at the
siege of Tortosa. These Englishmen may well have been some of the Anglo-
Flemish crusaders.[13] This conclusion is supported by a passage in the second
version (about 1170–75) of the *Chronica Regia* of Cologne. After describing the
capture of Lisbon, the anonymous author of this chronicle continues that 'when
these things had been thus completed, the Christians attacked and conquered
the city of Tortosa in a similar fashion; and they raised the trophy of the cross
there and strengthened (the city) with a troop of soldiers. Then they loosed
their fleet and with Christ as leader, they arrived at Jerusalem for their propitious
intention.'[14]

Since the siege of Tortosa lasted from the beginning of July until the end of
December 1148, it is impossible that any Anglo-Flemish crusaders who joined
this attack could have also taken part in the siege of Damascus in July. It appears probable, therefore, that after (or possibly before) the attack on Faro the
expedition split,[15] and that some of the crusaders proceeded directly to the Holy
Land while others delayed to fight the Moors in Spain.

St John's College, Cambridge

[8] H. V. Livermore, *A History of Portugal* (Cambridge, England, 1947), p. 36. Santa Maria de Faro
was eventually taken by the Christians in 1249 (Livermore, p. 135).

[9] Roger of Hoveden, *Chronica*, ed. William Stubbs, 4 vols., Rolls Series LI (London, 1868–71), III,
46 and 177.

[10] Benedict of Peterborough (ascribed to), *Gesta Henrici II et Ricardi I*, ed. William Stubbs, 2 vols.,
Rolls Series XLIX (London, 1867), II, 121.

[11] In the *Annali Genovesi*, ed. L. T. Belgrano, Fonti per la Storia d'Italia, XI (Genoa, 1890), I, 79–89.

[12] *Annali Genovesi*, p. 86.

[13] This has been previously suggested by Otto Langer, *Politische Geschichte Genuas und Pisas im
12. Jahrhundert* (Historische Studien, ed. W. Arndt, VII; Leipzig, 1882), pp. 33–34; Cesare Imperiale
di Sant'Angelo, *Caffaro e i suoi Tempi* (Turin and Rome, 1894), pp. 221–223; and Camillo Manfroni,
Storia della Marina Italiana (Leghorn, 1899), p. 214. Langer's citation (p. 34, n. 1) of Henry of Huntingdon is not necessarily relevant. Henry records that 'with the assistance of God a few men obtained
from many the city in Spain which is called Lisbon and another which is called Almaria, and the ad-
joining regions,' *Historia Anglorum*, ed Thomas Arnold, Rolls Series LXXIV (London, 1879), p. 281.
Since Almaria was recaptured a few days before Lisbon, the same men cannot have partaken in both
attacks. Henry has presumably joined into one sentence reports of the separate expeditions.

[14] *Chronica Regia Coloniensis*, ed. George Waitz (Hanover, 1880), p. 86.

[15] The crusaders were in any case separated and organized into their respective nationalities; see
De Expugnatione, pp. 52–56.

XII

A REPORT OF A LOST SERMON BY ST BERNARD
ON THE FAILURE OF THE SECOND CRUSADE

AMONG THE STORIES in a collection of *exempla* found in British Museum Ms Royal 7. D. i. is a brief account of the return of King Louis VII and his barons from the Second Crusade:

Narratur de rege Francie Lodoluico et baronibus suis quod cum in bello contra sarracenos ab ipsis fugati ad terram suam redirent confusi, in tantum ex hoc grauabantur quod quasi desperabant quia non completa est tunc in eis facta scriptura que dicit: *Quomodo persequebatur unus mille* et cetera (Deut 32:30). Quod cum audiret beatus Bernardus occurrit eis et cepit eis predicare ab isto uersu, themam suum accipiens: *Deus auribus nostris* et cetera (Ps 43:2). *Nunc autem repulisti et confudisti nos, et non egredieris deus in uirtutibus nostris* (Ps 43:10) id est exercitibus, ut quando unus fugabat. x. mille et cetera (Deut 32:30), et asseruit ipsos tunc fuisse fugatos a saracenis, duplici demonstrata, una causa est quia plus sperabant de uiribus suis, quam de dei adiutorio, et frangit deus omnem superbum (Is 2:12), alia causa est quia repulit eos dominus in terra, ut ex hoc attendent sola celestia esse querenda. Quo audito, miro modo rex et barones sui per predicationem uiri dei confortati sunt et per fidem bene firmati.[1]

There is no reason to believe that this story is literally true, since the manuscript was written in England in the late thirteenth century

---

1. British Museum Ms Royal 7. D. i, f. 63*v*. The text is printed as it appears in the manuscript, except for capitalization, the substitution of modern for medieval punctuation marks, and the expansion of abbreviations (of which not all, however, are clear).

and the collection of *exempla* was put together, probably by an itinerant preaching friar, after 1254, that is, over a century after the Second Crusade.[2] In addition, St Bernard is not known from other sources to have preached to the crusaders after their return. The two reasons given by Bernard for their failure, however, suggest that the tale is based upon an authentic tradition. While they do not correspond precisely to the views expressed by Bernard in *De consideratione* and the letters written immediately after the crusade,[3] they clearly reflect the attitudes found among Cistercians at the time and could hardly have been made up a century later. The *exemplum* is therefore of interest not only as evidence of crusading attitudes in the mid-thirteenth century but also as an addendum to my article on "The Second Crusade as Seen by Contemporaries" and to other studies on Bernard's crusading thought which were published in connection with the octocentenary of his death and subsequently.[4]

These works emphasize Bernard's view of the crusade as a pilgrimage undertaken by each crusader for the welfare of his soul. The crusade for Bernard, as Delaruelle said, was "a liturgy before being a strategy or a policy," "an effusion of divine grace bringing remission of sins," and an "affair of the interior life, of the salvation

2. Cf. George F. Warner and Julius P. Gilson, *British Museum: Catalogue of Western Manuscripts in the Old Royal and King's Collections* (London, 1921) vol. 1, p. 185.

3. Cf. Giles Constable, "The Second Crusade as Seen by Contemporaries," *Traditio*, 9 (1953) p. 267.

4. See in particular, André Seguin, "Bernard et la seconde croisade," *Bernard de Clairvaux* (Commission d'histoire de l'ordre de Cîteaux, 3; Paris, 1953) pp. 379–409; Eugène Willems, "Cîteaux et la seconde croisade," *Revue d'histoire ecclésiastique*, 49 (1953) pp. 116–51; Edmond Pognon, "L'échec de la croisade," *Saint Bernard: Homme d'Eglise* (Témoignages: Cahiers de le Pierre-qui-Vire, 38–39; Paris, 1953) pp. 47–57; Étienne Delaruelle, "L'idée de croisade chez saint Bernard," *Mélanges Saint Bernard* (XXIVe Congrès de l'Association bourguignonne des Sociétés savantes: Dijon, 1953; Dijon, 1954) pp. 53–67; Y. Congar, "Henri de Marcy, abbé de Clairvaux, cardinal-évêque d'Albano et légat pontifical," *Analecta monastica*, 5 (Studia Anselmiana, 43; Rome, 1958) pp. 1–90; and E. O. Blake, "The Formation of the 'Crusade Idea'," *Journal of Ecclesiastical History*, 21 (1970) pp. 11–31.

of the soul aspiring to communion with the sufferings of Christ."[5]
It was "a personal engagement to penitence"[6] and "a penitential
progress aimed at individual regeneration."[7]

Bernard's view of the failure of the crusade was likewise fundamentally moral and personal although it has been variously interpreted by recent scholars. Some have said that he placed the
responsibility for the crusade on Pope Eugene III and King Louis
VII; others, that he blamed the crusaders themselves.[8] In the *De
consideratione*, however, while referring to the papal command to
preach the crusade, Bernard clearly stated that the command came
from God through the pope;[9] and although he spoke briefly of the
crusaders' iniquities and punishment,[10] he basically accepted the
disaster as an example of the inscrutable workings of the ways of
God, of which the goodness must be taken on faith. "We all know
that the judgments of God are true," he wrote, "but this judgment
is so deep that I should seem to myself not unjustified in calling
him blessed who is not scandalized thereat."[11] According to
Delaruelle, Bernard was not "disconcerted" by the failure because
it proved a source of spiritual gain,[12] but both his own works and
those of his followers show that in fact he was deeply troubled by
the outcome of the expedition he had done so much to promote.[13]
It reinforced, however, his view of the interior and individual

5. Delaruelle, pp. 58, 66.

6. Congar, p. 80, who also stressed the essentially monastic character of the
crusade.

7. Blake, p. 29.

8. Seguin, p. 406; Delaruelle, p. 59; and Constable, p. 267, citing (among
other previous writers) George B. Flahiff, "*Deus Non Vult:* A Critic of the
Third Crusade," *Mediaeval Studies*, 98 (1947) p. 164, n. 12.

9. *De consideratione*, 2. 1, in *Sancti Bernardi . . . opera omnia* (Paris, 1839)
vol. 1, p. 1021 C. A few lines later he said that Moses spoke to the Israelites by
divine command (col. 1022 B).

10. *Ibid.*, 2. 2, col. 1022 C.

11. *Ibid.*, 2. 1, col. 1022 A; cf. Constable, p. 275.

12. Delaruelle, col. 59.

13. Cf. Constable, pp. 266–67. Willems, p. 146, said that Bernard was so
discouraged that he temporarily even doubted the authenticity of his mission.

nature of the crusade. "For Bernard," Delaruelle said, "one went on a crusade not to kill but to be killed."[14] The Cistercian Abbot John Casa-Maria wrote to Bernard that God had turned evil into good by winning the salvation of many defeated crusaders.[15] That a spiritual victory was thus won by a temporal defeat was the attitude generally taken by Cistercians to the failure of the crusade.[16]

This is the view found in the *exemplum* printed above. Bernard, having heard of the despair of the returned crusaders, who thought they had been abandoned by God, (and having perhaps also heard of the reproaches directed against himself[17]) hurried to them in order to restore their flagging faith. The report of his sermon does not derive from *De consideratione* or any other known work concerning the crusade, where he used different, though parallel, Biblical citations, but it follows the same general line of reasoning. Taking as his text that God has "cast off and put us to shame and goest not forth with our armies," Bernard explained, first, that God had punished the pride of the crusaders for relying on their own strength rather than his aid and, second, that he had rejected them on earth so that they might learn that their salvation was in heaven.

These explanations may be compared with other contemporary reactions to the disaster.[18] One, which is only briefly mentioned in my article on "The Second Crusade as Seen by Contemporaries," is in the Dialogue of the monk, William of St Denis. In reply to a question from William as to why "hardly anyone survived from so great a multitude of men and the army of two very powerful kings and [why] those who escaped the sword and famine returned without any result," his companion Geoffrey cited a long passage from Seneca's *De beneficiis*, concerning the defeat of Xerxes in Greece, and then said that the same reasons accounted for the

14. Delaruelle, p. 59.
15. Willems, p. 147; Constable, pp. 270–71; and Congar, p. 82.
16. Cf. Willems, p. 148.
17. Cf. Constable, pp. 266–77.
18. *Ibid.*, 166–67.

defeat of the crusaders.[19] Hubert Glaser, commenting on this passage in his article on William of St Denis, wrote that "the wreck of the crusade was for him a matter of strategy, not, as for Bernard, a result of conduct of life or an emanation of divine justice."[20] The contrast between William and Bernard in this respect, however, should not be overstressed. For while it is true that Seneca discussed the naturalistic considerations of terrain and military tactics; he also attributed Xerxes's defeat to over-confidence and the bad advice of flatterers, and this was probably the point that William (like other users of this passage in the twelfth century[21]) had in mind.[22]

Another point of view is found in the *Life* of the hermit Wulfric of Haselbury, which was written by Abbot John of Ford about 1185–1186 but which records an apparently contemporary conversation concerning the crusade between Wulfric and his friend Alvred de Lincolnia. Wulfric expressed his disapproval of the whole enterprise and cited in particular the judgment on it of God, "Who abandoned the false pilgrims, shaved the heads of the proud, and shamed the great men of the world because they sought not the Lord in truth but polluted the way of pilgrimage in idols."[23] The crusade, Wulfric suggested, was doomed to failure from the beginning owing to the false spirit of the participants. His attitude

19. André Wilmart, "Le dialogue apologétique du moine Guillaume, biographe de Suger," *Revue Mabillon*, 32 (1942) p. 107.

20. Hubert Glaser, "Wilhelm von Saint-Denis," *Historisches Jahrbuch*, 85 (1965) p. 296. He went on to say that for William contemporary history was a matter of human will and wisdom.

21. Klaus-Dieter Nothdurft, *Studien zum Einfluss Senecas auf die Philosophie und Theologie des zwölften Jahrhunderts* (Studien und Texte zur Geistesgeschichte des Mittelalters, 7; Leiden-Cologne, 1963) pp. 106–7. On the popularity of the *De Beneficiis* in the twelfth century, see also L. D. Reynolds, *The Medieval Tradition of Seneca's Letters* (Oxford, 1965) p. 112.

22. Elsewhere in his discussion of the crusade, William also put greater emphasis of the moral aspects and divine intervention: cf. Constable, p. 271.

23. Maurice Bell, ed., *Wulfric of Haselbury by John, Abbot of Ford* (Somerset Record Society, 47; n. p., 1933) chap. 86, p. 112, and, on the date of composition, p. xviii. I overlooked this interesting source in the article cited in note 3 above.

54

is clearly a long way from that of Bernard, but it also shows a basically moral and personal approach to the crusade. It helps therefore to illustrate the wide range of contemporary opinions about the expedition and its failure.

Harvard University

XIII

The Structure of Medieval Society According to the *Dictatores* of the Twelfth Century

One of the most serious responsibilities of professional letter-writers in the Middle Ages was to know the proper social standing of the senders and recipients of letters and to arrange their names accordingly in the salutation.[1] Already in the fourth century the author of the first known treatise on epistolary theory in Latin, C. Julius Victor, advised his readers to be neither jocular when writing to a superior, nor rude when writing to an equal, nor proud when writing to an inferior; and the anonymous writer of an isolated paragraph *De epistolis* found in an eighth-century manuscript from Monte Cassino urged that in the writing of letters, "Consideration should be given to who is writing to whom and about what." He then listed ten "accidents of persons" which should be considered: birth, sex, age, training, character ("ars"), office, behavior ("mores"), disposition, name, and dignity; and he added that "There is a great difference whether we are writing to a nobleman, or to an old man, or to a magistrate, or to a father, or to a friend, or to one for whom things are going well, or to a sad man, and such things as these."[2]

These particular works were probably not known well, if at all, in the eleventh and twelfth centuries, but they represented a tradition which was doubtless handed down as much in the practice as in the theory of letter-writing; and many of the *dictatores* who composed the manuals known as the *artes dictandi* or *dictaminis* therefore discussed the question of the structure of society. They were generally agreed that everyone could be classified as either high, middle, or low and that in salutations the names of higher persons (whether the sender or the recipient) must be put first and the names of equals either first or second, though humility and courtesy both suggested that the sender be named second. Lower persons were always named second. This teaching was probably more or less common knowledge in the twelfth century, and Heloise (who is not known to have read any formal work on *dictamen*) said in her second letter that, "It is indeed right and honest that someone who is writing to superiors or equals puts their names first, whereas when [they are writing] to inferiors, those who come first in the dignity of things should come first in the order of writing."[3] Many of the *dictatores*, however, went into greater detail in the matter of social rank and often differed in their descriptions of each class and its members, and they thus offer some insights into the contemporary view of the structure of society.

Alberic of Monte Cassino, who died about 1105, was "the first known exponent of the new art of letter-writing and the author of the earliest surviving treatise upon this art," according to C. H. Haskins.[4] He touched only briefly on the question of social status, however. In his *Breviarium de dictamine,* of which only excerpts have been published, he classified letters as "humilis," "mediocris," and "grandilocus" with reference to their style rather than to the rank of the sender or recipient;[5] but in the *Dictaminum radii* or *Flores rhetorici,* which may be a continuation of the *Breviarium* or perhaps, according to Lanham, the work of another author, emphasis is put on the need to consider the persons named in the salutation and to determine "whether he is exalted or humble, whether he is a friend or an enemy, and lastly what is his manner [modus] or fortune," emphasizing that the style of the letter must be suited to the condition and station of the sender and recipient.[6]

The rules for salutations were spelled out in greater detail by Adalbert Samaritanus of Bologna in his *Praecepta dictaminum,* of which the first version was finished by 1115. After explaining the law, as he called it, that the name of a greater person must precede that of a lesser and that the names of equals might be put either way "according to the wish of the writer," he said that "The salutation describes the person and the order by its varying nature, since we salute a superior in one way, an inferior in another, an equal in another. . . . As [there are] three orders of men, so there are three types of letters: exalted, middling, and feeble." A letter from a lesser person to a greater is called exalted because it ascends from an inferior to a superior and is marked by the three characteristics of flattery at the beginning, the reason for the flattery in the middle, and a request at the end. A letter from a greater person to a lesser is called feeble because it descends and is marked only by an order or request, with no flattery. A middling letter, between equals, is so called from its position between exalted and feeble. It neither ascends nor descends and is marked by the two characteristics of flattery (presumably at the beginning) and a request. Salutations therefore vary in accordance with this diversity of persons, and differing forms of address (of which Adalbert later gave examples) are used for clergy and laity; canons, monks, bishops, and abbots ("we praise one for his religion, another for his learning, another for both"); a father, mother, brother, sister, son, daughter, kinsman, and stranger; and a nobleman, a wise man, the holder of a princedom, and someone with no position.[7]

Two other *artes dictandi* composed in Northern Italy in the early twelfth century are the *Rationes dictandi* of Hugh of Bologna, which Haskins dated 1119–24,[8] and the *Aurea gemma* by Henry Francigena, who wrote soon after Hugh and was the first *dictator* to give his work one of the "poetico-allegorical" titles which later became popular and have proved an abundant source of confusion for scholars.[9] For Hugh, as for Adalbert, there were three orders of letters corresponding to the three orders of people: "Those to greater and elevated persons are called sublime; those to serfs or dependents, lowest; those to equals or comparable friends, middling."[10] Henry, however, went into greater detail than his predecessors on the nature of the orders: "Since there are innumerable people from lesser to greater, and since it would be beyond my powers to go through them all, I take comfort in brevity and confine everybody to three, giving them the names of greater, equal, lesser. Greater is called exalted; equal, middling; lesser, mean." He then listed the members of the three orders, putting at the top, among the exalted, the pope, emperor, kings, tetrarchs, archbishops, marquises, dukes, counts, bishops, abbots, abbesses, provosts, deans, "and other magnates"; in the middle, priests, soldiers, citizens, townsmen, moneyers, friends, "and others not raised to the highest honor nor depressed to the lowest"; and at the bottom, peasants, students, retainers, and serfs. In the salutation, the name of a greater man must come first, the name of a middling person either first or second, and the name of a mean person second.[11] Henry is the first known *dictator* to define the ranks and occupational groups in each order. The practice soon spread, however, though with differing definitions.

It appears in differing forms, for example, in two reworkings of the *Praecepta dictaminum* of Adalbert, who was the most influential of the early Bolognese *dictatores*. One of these, found in manuscripts at Leipzig and Oxford and entitled the *Aurea gemma*, was thought to be a version of the work by Henry Francigena until it was shown by Kantorowicz to be "an *ars dictandi* based upon Albert of Samaria but containing a few interlarded quotations taken from Henricus Francigena's work" and to have been written about 1130–43.[12] It did not enter into any details on the orders of persons, classifying them like Henry as exalted, middling, and mean (using the term "tenuis"). It then gave examples of suitably honorific terms to be used in salutations, stressing that they should correspond to the diversity of persons, and differed from Henry in ranking the pope as exalted but dukes and marquises only as middling.[13] The other version of Adalbert's work, found in two manuscripts at Copenhagen and Berlin, is dated to France in the mid-twelfth century by the accompanying letter-collection of Prior Peter of St. John at Sens.[14] This treatise is basically an independent work, though it drew on Adalbert and was also influenced by Henry Francigena or other sources. It defined the orders in the usual way as greater, equal, and lesser, saying that the names of greater persons must be put first and of equals either first or second. Then, following Adalbert, but reversing his distinctions, it said:

> As there are three orders of persons, so there are three principal types of letters: humble, middling, and exalted. A humble letter is one sent by a humble person, such as oxherds, cobblers, and pelterers and others who have no lower order beneath them. An exalted letter is one sent by an exalted person, as by a pope or emperor. An exalted person is one than who there is no higher dignity, as is the pope in ecclesiastical affairs [and] the emperor in secular affairs. A middling person is one who is between exalted and humble, such as tetrarchs, kings, marquises, counts, dukes, archbishops, captains, vavasors, vidames, and others who are between exalted and humble.[15]

Lists like this were doubtless useful as the forms of salutation became increasingly fixed as the century advanced—a tendency attributed by Schmale to the influence of the schools[16]—but the differences between them, reflecting, as it seems, the personal views of the *dictatores,* must also have been at times confusing.

Meanwhile in Italy another treatise, also entitled the *Rationes dictandi,* was produced in the region of Emilia or Romagna in the late 1130s.[17] Its author is unknown, but it influenced (and may, according to Savorelli, even have been the first version of) the important *Introductiones prosaici dictaminis* by Bernard of Bologna, of which the first redaction was written in Romagna in 1144–5 and the second, probably revised by the author, in 1145–52 and of which various later versions were produced north of the Alps, which have contributed to the confusion between this Bolognese Master Bernard and the French *dictatores* Bernard Sylvestris, who taught at Tours in the middle of the twelfth century, and the Master Bernard who taught *dictamen* at Meung in the 1180s.[18] The section on the salutation in the anonymous *Rationes dictandi* began with the statement that "A salutation is a prayer for welfare indicating a feeling not disagreeing with the position of the persons." After describing various types of salutations and their embellishments, such as titles and offices, it said, in partial disagreement with other treatises, that "The names of the recipients should always precede the names of the senders . . . except when a greater [person] writes to a lesser, in which case the name of the sender is put first, so that his dignity may be shown by the position of the names." Later it went on, after discussing the use of the dative and accusative cases, with a standard division of all people into excellent, middle, and lowly and defined the excellent as those without a superior, like the pope and the emperor.[19]

Bernard of Bologna defined the salutation in the same way as the anonymous *Rationes dictandi,* adding that "A prudent *dictator,* therefore, in order to furnish a suitable salutation to each letter, must know in advance the persons of the sender and the recipient." He went on at once to divide all people into outstanding, middling, and lowly and then described these groups in an original fashion, which agreed with Adalbert in distinguishing clergy from laity (a distinction not made by Henry Francigena or in the Copenhagen-Berlin version of Adalbert) and showed an exceptional sensitivity to the differentiating factors of power, office, dignity, birth, and nobility.

Persons are called outstanding to whom no one is superior either in birth or in dignity, such as the pope and the emperor of the Romans. We consider lowly, however, those than who no one lower can be found in birth or dignity, such as 'servi empticii' and lowly retainers. Those to whom there are some superior [and] some inferior in birth, power, and dignity are rightly called middling. There is a great mass of these men in the middle, some equal, some unequal. Among both the clergy and the laity, we call equal those who are comparable in office, dignity, and power, like (among clerics) bishops between themselves, archbishops, archdeacons, deans, parish priests, abbots, priors, priests, deacons, clerics, and some holding other offices, and (among laymen) kings, dukes, marquises, counts, lords, consuls, vidames, and men with other dignities or offices. But we also have examples of unequal persons. Although laymen may always excel in power or nobility, they are called inferior to the clergy out of reverence for the ecclesiastical dignity, and if magnates write even to priests, they should therefore do so as to greater persons. A father, grandfather, or greatgrandfather is always greater than a son or grandson, even if greater power or dignity is on the other side, and a bishop should therefore write to his father, grandfather, or greatgrandfather as to a greater person. They, however, should not write to a bishop as to a lesser person.[20]

Here for the first time a sort of hierarchy of distinctions was adumbrated, differentiated primarily by dignity and office but also, to a lesser extent, by family relationships, status, and birth. "According to the skill of the *dictator*," Bernard said later, "the diversity of persons in every order and manner penetrates the diversity of salutations."[21]

The work of Bernard of Bologna had a wide influence both in Italy and north of the Alps, where it can be seen in two anonymous treatises in Vienna manuscripts 246 and 896, of which the former is from France and was dated in the 1150s (or possibly 1153–91) by Savorelli and in the early thirteenth century by Haskins, and the latter according to Zöllner is from Burgundy in the late 1190s.[22] The treatise in Vienna 246 followed Bernard of Bologna almost verbatim in defining a salutation and saying that a *dictator* must know in advance the persons of the sender and recipient but continued somewhat differently, in wording if not in sense, to say that "The quality of people should be observed in the salutation, which should vary according to their differing status," and immediately to distinguish the clergy from the laity. The clergy were then divided into three ranks: superior or outstanding, such as apostolic men, patriarchs, and the pope; inferior or lowly, such as simple clerics, deacons, levites, parochial clergy, priests, and others "who have no dignity in the church"; and middling or middle, such as archpriests, archdeacons, provosts, deans, priors, abbots, archbishops, and bishops, adding that "Archbishops and bishops, however, may be counted among the superior persons." The same division was made among the laity: only the emperor was superior; *servi emptitii,* retainers, cobblers, pelterers, smiths, shepherds, and the like were inferior; and between them were the middling persons, such as the prefects of a town, tribunes, marquises, dukes, counts, viscounts, and kings, again adding that "Kings are said by some to be among the superiors." The author then distinguished, like Bernard, between those who are equal in birth, office, power, or dignity, such as archbishops or kings among themselves, and those who are unequal, such as archbishops and bishops or kings and counts, repeating that "The salutation should vary according to these varying statuses." After a conventional statement that the name of the superior person should come first, it again followed Bernard almost verbatim on the precedence of the clergy over laymen and fathers over sons. Among equals, however, as when a bishop writes to a bishop or a count to a count, the sender's name should come second out of reverence and humility. After a brief and inconclusive discussion of the differentiating factors of birth, office, power, and dignity, stressing that all of these must be taken into consideration in writing a salutation, this section concluded with a description of the various types of salutation, like that in the anonymous *Rationes dictandi,* and of their grammatical construction.[23]

The treatment in the *ars dictandi* in Vienna 896, though shorter, also followed the sense of Bernard of Bologna, but not always his wording. It inserted into his definition of a salutation, for instance, the term "brief," adding that, "Prolixity is a vice in a salutation, which ought to be brief and succinct." After saying, as in Vienna 246, that, "The salutation of persons should vary according to their differing status," and dividing people into clergy and laity and into superior, inferior, and middle, it defined the superior clergy as the pope, archbishops, and bishops; the inferior clergy as simple canons, parochial clergy, priests, and poor clerics; and the middling clergy as deans, provosts, archdeacons, subdeacons, parish priests, precentors, succentors, "and others having some dignity in the holy church." Among the laity, emperors and kings are superior; commoners and peasants, inferior; and counts, viscounts, marquises, and castellans, middling. And it concluded, before giving the rules of priority and examples, as in Vienna 246, by repeating that the salutation must vary according to all these status. A very similar listing to this is found in a late twelfth or early thirteenth-century *Summa grammaticalis,* probably from Languedoc, by Master William,[24] who added patriarchs and primates to the upper clergy and townsmen to the inferior laity and who in the middling groups added abbots, dukes, and seneschals but omitted subdeacons, parish priests, and marquises. He went on, however, in an interesting way to distinguish three grades within each order, calling the pope highest, archbishops and primates higher, and bishops high; archdeacons low, priests lower, and simple clerics lowest; and the emperor highest, great kings higher, and kings and kinglets high; "and likewise for the middle and lower [persons] who are distinguished into three grades."[25] He thus really substituted a nine- for a three-stage hierarchy among both the clergy and the laity, making a total of eighteen categories, but he did not spell them all out.[26]

In the Italian *artes* of the second half of the twelfth century, it was less usual to list the members of the various orders. Albert of San Martino, a canon of Asti, whose *Flores dictandi* was dated about 1150 by Haskins, called the three types of letters, corresponding to the orders of people, weighty, middling, and light, explaining that weighty letters were to elevated people or about major concerns, middle letters to those of lower but not the lowest status, as between equals and friends of comparable rank, and weak letters to dependents. After explaining that the salutations should correspond to these orders, he added that suitable adjectives should be used, "by which we can express the variety of persons. For we speak in different ways to a pope, king, bishop, abbot, monk, vigorous soldier, companion or dear friend."[27] Paul of Camaldoli was another *dictator* working in the north of Italy probably in the last third of the twelfth century. He classified the three orders as the exalted who had no superior, like the pope and emperor, the mean who had no inferior, and the middling who came between. "A true consideration of things teaches us to write in a different way to different persons, depending on their greatness," he said, and added after commenting on the order of names in the salutation:

A good *dictator* should know in advance the order of persons so that he may better fit the manner of speaking to their greatness and quality. For to exalted persons and in great causes the splendor of the words and greatness of the deed should be displayed in a manner fitting the material. To middling people, however, suitable things can be said temperately, whereas a weak person should have fewer words the lower he is and use no long sentences, provided that his brevity or that of his interlocutor generates no obscurity and is not deprived of vigor in joining words to matter. By keeping these qualities well, we shall legitimately fulfill the triple manner of speaking which many call humble, middling, and grandiloquent.[28]

These distinctions were carried further by Master Geoffrey, whose *Summa de arte dictandi* was written at Bologna in 1188–90: "Since every salutation derives from a person, we should see, first, what the person is in this situation, second, what is the diversity of persons, third, to whom a salutation is owed and to whom not, fourth, who should precede whom in the salutation, fifth and last, the diversity created by diverse people in diverse themes." Having established that only rational creatures (that is, sane adults) send and receive letters, Paul examined their diversity, separating enemies from nonenemies and dividing nonenemies into the usual ranks of exalted, middling, and humble, and then gave his examples.[29]

By the turn of the century the formal rules for salutations were therefore established and *dictatores* like Thomas of Capua and Guido Faba concentrated on more difficult questions. Thomas, as a papal notary under Innocent III and later cardinal-priest of Santa Sabina, was among the most prominent *dictatores* of his day. In the section on salutations in his *Ars dictaminis*, written in the first decade of the thirteenth century, he not only gave the standard instructions concerning the precedence of greater persons and of the recipient among equals (though adding that either name might be put first in a letter from a middling person to a somewhat lesser one) but also discussed the nature of a salutation, which he said implied a measure both of good-will and of equality and should not therefore be used either for enemies and excommunicates nor for great lords, to whom reverence rather than good-will was owed. "For to salute and to bless flows from the authority of the greater, not from the presumption of the lesser. We salute our equals, however, or those a little greater, without fear of offense."[30] He then studied the grammatical structure and wording of salutations, pointing out among other things that "Dei gratia" might be used by a magnate of himself except when addressing the pope or king but not by middling or lowly people, since "it suggests either great dignity or magnificence."[31] Thomas's contemporary Guido Faba likewise studied the finer points of salutations in his *Summa dictaminis*, although he also stated "the general doctrine of all salutations" with regard to putting first the name of a greater person "in both the ecclesiastical and the secular orders" and the name of the recipient in a letter between equals, adding later that in a letter from a middling to a lesser person, the *dictator* might put either name first. Like Master William in Languedoc, he drew distinctions within the orders, differentiating, for example, from the point of view of a bishop, between the most greater (the pope or emperor, to whom no salutation was customarily given), the middle greater (such as a metropòlitan), the middle lesser (such as a canon or episcopal cleric), and the much lesser, or base person (such as a minor canon, syndic or cleric of a small place, or an almost illiterate person).[32]

A final witness from north of the Alps is Peter of Blois, whose unpublished *Libellus de arte dictandi rhetorice,* written probably in France in the 1180s, has suffered some unmerited abuse at the hands of scholars,[33] since at least on the matter of salutations it is not without originality and interest. For after saying that "The varieties of salutations are distinguished according to the diversities of persons," Peter listed five, not three, ranks: highest, exalted, middling, private, and lowly:

> The highest are those to whom no one is superior in dignity, like the lord pope and the Roman emperor. The exalted [are] such as patriarchs, archbishops, kings, bishops, dukes, counts, palatines, marquises. The middling are such as deans, archdeacons, abbots, provosts, sacristans, treasurers, castellans, reeves, consuls who are called peers in some towns. The private [persons] are those who administer no dignity, such as soldiers and clerics. The lowly are such as peasants and everyone occupied with civilian works, like cobblers and others.

Some of the exalted and middling persons are equal in office and dignity, such as bishops or archdeacons among themselves; but (and here Peter followed Bernard of Bologna almost verbatim) the clergy are superior to the laity and fathers to their sons, though Peter added to the relations cited by Bernard the paternal uncle, mother, grandmother, and maternal aunt. He ended this section with another passage adapted from Bernard, saying that, "When the studious *dictator,* knowing this variety of persons, comes to writing, he should first consider whether an equal is writing to an equal or a superior to an inferior or to an equal."[34]

In conclusion, three points may be made, one about the works of the *dictatores* and two about their view of society. With regard to the *artes dictandi* consulted for this article, in spite of many general similarities and dependencies, no two were the same in their discussions of salutations. The accusation of monotony and repetitiveness often brought against this type of work is not therefore fully justified. A complete comparison will be possible only when satisfactory critical editions of all the *artes* have been produced,[35] but the evidence here suggests that their authors and revisers contributed a more personal touch than is sometimes said and that even small differences between them are of interest.

With regard to the structure of society, almost all the *dictatores* agreed on the division into upper, middle, and lower orders. The upper order was called "sublimis," "maior," "summus," "altior," "superior," "supremus," "gravis," "excellens," or "eximius." The middle order was called "mediocris" or "medie," for which "par" or "equalis" was occasionally given as an alternative. The lower order was referred to as "exilis," "tenuis," "minor," "humilis," "inferior," "infimus," or "extenuatus."[36] Peter of Blois was alone in positing five orders, and Master William, and to some extent Guido Faba, in seeking sub-categories within the orders. Aside from those who separated the clergy from the laity,[37] there was no trace of the customary medieval divisions either into clerics, monks, and laymen or into prayers, fighters, and workers. Even Peter of Blois, who followed Bernard of Bologna in asserting the superiority of the clergy, mixed bishops and counts, abbots and castellans, and clerics and soldiers in his lists. What mattered to the *dictatores* was not profession in the technical sense of the word but dignity, power, and office, and to a lesser extent, as Bernard of Bologna shows most clearly among the authors considered here, birth and nobility. Thus for Peter of Blois the principal characteristic of his one but lowest class, the private persons, was that they held no dignity. Wealth and poverty, apart from a couple of references to "pauperes clerici" in the lowest rank, hardly came into the matter at all. The terms used for the lower order all imply weakness and inferiority rather than poverty, and those for the upper order, greatness and superiority rather than wealth.

The main difference among the *dictatores* was with regard to the membership in the various orders. For some, the pope and the emperor alone, since they had no earthly superior, belonged to the upper order, whereas for others it included at least kings, patriarchs, primates, archbishops, and bishops; and Henry Francigena, who was the most liberal in this respect, added marquises, dukes, counts, abbots, abbesses, provosts, and deans. At the other end of the social spectrum, the lower order included manual laborers and sometimes, more generally, commoners, townsmen, and retainers. "Milites," whom Henry Francigena with his usual generosity classified as "mediocres," were put in the lowest order by Ludolf of Hildesheim and in the one but lowest, the private persons, by Peter of Blois, together with the clerics.[38] Others put clerics, parochial clergy, canons, and even deacons and priests into the lowest class. Students, scholars, and, for Ludolf, even masters were also in the lowest class, presumably because they held no office or dignity.

Most interesting of all is the middle class. For Henry Francigena this was a comparatively humble rank, including priests, soldiers, citizens, townsmen, moneyers, and friends, but for most of the *dictatores* it was much more exalted. Some, indeed, included in it everyone below the pope and emperor and above the lowest class, including tetrarchs, kings, archbishops, and dukes; and Bernard of Bologna, who was the most all-inclusive in this respect, put all the clergy from archbishop to simple clerics and the laity from king to vidame among the "mediocres," though his followers as a rule pared his list at both ends, including the higher ranks in the upper class and the humbler ones in the lower. The treatise in Vienna manuscript 246 included prefects of towns and tribunes in the middle class, and Peter of Blois mentioned prefects and "consuls who in some towns are called peers," but Ludolf, reflecting perhaps the more traditional society in Germany, put the lords of towns but not urban officials in the middle class and relegated merchants to the lower order.

The Middle Ages had long known a middle class in a legal sense. "Mediocres" and "mediani" appear in the Burgundian and Alamannian codes and are found for many centuries in the legal sources from certain regions.[39] The term was also sometimes used in a more general sense to imply a status between noble and ignoble or between rich and poor—usually closer to the noble and rich than to the ignoble and poor end of this spectrum.[40] The twelfth century *dictatores* were the first, however, to develop a reasonably clear concept of a middle class of society. It reached higher than any modern idea of the middle class and included ranks which by later standards would have been counted as aristocracy. It had little to do with birth or wealth as such, and nothing with urban or economic development. Townsmen and merchants, when mentioned at all, were put in the lower order. It reflected, on the contrary, a characteristically medieval concern for the importance of office and established positions in society, and a corresponding disdain for dependents and even for independent people without formal dignities. As such, it represents, in spite of its confusions and inconsistencies, an interesting and original contribution to western social thought.

Harvard University

Notes

No effort will be made in this article to cover more than a selection of the twelfth century *artes dictandi*, many of which exist only in manuscript or in unsatisfactory editions. For a recent bibliography, covering both primary and secondary works, see James J. Murphy, *Medieval Rhetoric: A Select Bibliography*, Toronto Medieval Bibliographies III (Toronto, 1971), 55–70. The Latin will be cited in the notes only for unpublished texts. I am deeply indebted to Professor Richard H. Rouse, Sister Benedicta Ward, and the late Dr. Ethel C. Higonnet for their help with manuscripts from, respectively, Paris, Oxford, and Cambridge.

1. On the epistolary salutation, see Paul Krüger, *Bedeutung und Entwicklung der Salutatio in den mittelalterlichen Briefstellern bis zum 14. Jahrhundert* (Greifswald, 1912), who concentrated on the period from the eleventh to the fourteenth century and referred to the development of the salutation as "ein Spiegelbild der Kultur des Mittelalters" (p. 52), and especially Carol D. Lanham, *Salutatio Formulas in Latin Letters to 1200: Syntax, Style, and Theory*, Münchener Beiträge zur Mediävistik und Renaissance-Forschung XXII (Munich, 1975).

2. Karl von Halm, *Rhetores latini minores* (Leipzig, 1863), p. 448 and p. 589, citing Paris, Bibl. nat., MS lat. 7530; cf. Lanham, *Salutatio Formulas*, pp. 89–90, who attributed to C. Julius Victor the introduction into epistolary theory of the three ranks of superior, equal, and inferior.

3. Abelard, *Historia calamitatum*, ed. J. Monfrin, Bibliothèque des Textes philosophiques (Paris, 1959), p. 118.

4. C. H. Haskins, "Albericus Casinensis," *Casinensia* (Monte Cassino, 1929), I: 116; cf. James J. Murphy, "Alberic of Monte Cassino: Father of the Medieval *Ars dictaminis*," *American Benedictine Review* XXII (1971), 129–46, esp. 138–46 on Alberic, whom he called "a pivotal figure in the history of medieval rhetoric"; Aldo Scaglione, *Ars grammatica*, Janua linguarum: Series minor LXXVII (The Hague-Paris, 1970), 131–39; and Herbert Bloch, "Monte Cassino's Teachers and Library in the High Middle Ages," *La Scuola nell'Occidente latino dell'alto Medioevo*, Settimane di Studio del Centro italiano di Studi sull'alto Medioevo XIX (Spoleto, 1972), 587–99, who called him "the first representative of the *ars dictaminis*" (p. 593) and referred to other secondary literature.

5. Ludwig Rockinger, *Briefsteller und Formelbücher des eilften bis vierzehnten Jahrhunderts* Quellen und Erörterungen zur bayerischen und deutschen Geschichte IX (Munich, 1863), I: 30. This edition is incomplete and unsatisfactory, and a new one, according to Bloch, in *La Scuola*, p. 590, n. 82, is in preparation by P.-Chr. Groll.

6. Alberic of Monte Cassino, *Flores rhetorici*, ch. 5, ed. D. M. Inguanez and H. M. Willard, Miscellanea Cassinese XIV (Monte Cassino, 1938), 35; cf. on this work Bloch, in *La Scuola*, pp. 591–92 (and p. 589 on the title, on which see also Murphy, *Rhetoric*, p. 60) and Lanham, *Salutatio Formulas*, pp. 94–97, who stressed the difference between the *Breviarium* and the *Flores* and implicitly questioned their single authorship.

7. Adalbert Samaritanus, *Praecepta dictaminum*, chaps. 1–3, ed. Franz-Josef Schmale, MGH III: 33–35, cf. 12 on the date and 7 on Adalbert's name, on which see also Ernst Kantorowicz, "Anonymi 'Aurea gemma'," (1943), reprinted in his *Selected Studies* (Locust Valley, N.Y., 1965), p. 249, n. 17. On Adalbert, see also C. H. Haskins, *Studies in Mediaeval Culture* (Oxford, 1929), pp. 173–77; Max Manitius, *Geschichte der lateinischen Literatur des Mittelalters* (hereafter, *Lat. Lit.*) Handbuch der Altertumswissenschaft IX, 3 vols. (Munich, 1911–31), III: 305–6; Franz-Josef Schmale, "Die Bologneser Schule der Ars dictandi," *Deutsches Archiv* XIII. 1 (1957), 16–34; and Lanham, *Salutatio Formulas*, pp. 97–99.

8. Haskins, *Culture*, p. 180; cf. also Manitius, *Lat. Lit.*, III: 309; Kantorowicz, *Studies*, p. 248; Scaglione, *Ars*, p. 139 (proposing a date of after 1140 in North Italy); and Lanham, *Salutatio Formulas*, pp. 99–100.

9. Kantorowicz, *Studies*, p. 256 also 248, calling Henry "a master of *dictamen* not too well known who, however, taught in Pavia after 1120, whose name suggests French, perhaps Provençal, origin and who depends on Bologna, especially on Hugh of Bologna," and 262–63, with examples of his borrowing from Hugh; Haskins, *Culture*, pp. 178–80 and 190, who dated the *Aurea gemma* to Pavia ca. 1119–24 and said that "Henry's French origin, as seen in his name, cannot be taken as showing any French influence upon the doctrine of his Pavian treatise." Cf. also Manitius, *Lat. lit.*. III: 307; N. Denholm-Young, "The Cursus in England" (1934), reprinted in his *Collected Papers on Mediaeval Subjects* (Oxford, 1946), p. 50; Botho Odebrecht, "Die Briefmuster des Henricus Francigena," *Archiv für Urkundenforschung* XIV (1936), 230–61, who is concerned less with the treatise on *dictamen* than with the letter-collection, which he dated to Pavia in 1121–4, but who also mentioned Henry's use of Hugh of Bologna (pp. 234–35); and Lanham, *Salutatio Formulas*, pp. 101–5.

10. Rockinger, *Briefsteller*, I: 55.

11. Paris, Bibl. nat., MS n.a.l. 610, fol. 29r–v: "Set cum persone a minori usque ad maiorem, sunt innumerabiles, et cum per omnes de viribus nostris diffidentes ire nullatenus valeamus, in tres brevitate gaudentes omnes personas restringamus. Hec inponentes eis nomina Maiorem, equalem, Minorem. Maior, sublimis appellatur. Equalis, Mediocris. Minor, tenuis." The translations of some of the occupational groups are doubtful. Here and below, "miles" is translated "soldier," not "knight," because it clearly refers to a relatively low social rank. "Rusticus" is translated "peasant"; "discipulus," "student"; "cliens," "retainer"; "servus," "serf." In later lists, "plebei" is translated "commoners"; "subiecti," "dependents"; "burgenses," "townsmen"; "ecclesiasticus," "the clergy" or occasionally "cleric"; "clericus," "cleric"; "plebanus," "parish priest"; and "parrochialis," "a member of the parish clergy" or the equivalent.

12. Kantorowicz, *Studies*, pp. 251 and 261. Already in an earlier article on "Petrus de Vinea in England," published in 1937 and reprinted in *Studies*, p. 216, n. 17, he denied the attribution of this treatise to Henry *Francigena*, as had Odebrecht, "Briefmuster," p. 233. Cf. Schmale, "Bologneser Schule," p. 29, on this and other treatises of the "*Aurea gemma* group" which depend on Adalbert.

13. Oxford, Bodl. Lib., MS Laud Misc. 569, fols. 184r–185r. The text seems to lack some rubrications and reads, "[ma]rchiores [*sic*] duces et alie mediocres persone" (fol. 184v). The manuscript was dated to the thirteenth century by Haskins, *Culture*, p. 178 (and 182, saying that it was made for the use of the Cistercians), but to the twelfth century by Odebrecht, "Briefmuster," p. 233, and Kantorowicz, *Studies*, p. 216, n. 17.

14. See the discussion and brief excerpts in my article, "The Letter from Peter of St John to Hato of Troyes," *Petrus Venerabilis, 1156–1956,* ed. Giles Constable and James Kritzeck, Studia Anselmiana XL (Rome 1956), 38–52, and in my edition of *The Letters of Peter the Venerable,* Harvard Historical Studies LXXVIII (Cambridge, Mass., 1967), II: 36, with references to the two articles by C. H. Haskins, "An Early Bolognese Formulary," *Mélanges d'Histoire offerts à Henri Pirenne* (Brussels-Paris, 1926), I: 201–10, and Walther Holtzmann, "Eine oberitalienische Ars dictandi und die Briefsammlung des Priors Peter von St. Jean in Sens," *Neues Archiv* XLVI (1925–26), 34–52; see also Schmale, "Bologneser Schule," pp. 19–21.

15. Copenhagen, Kongelige Bibl., MS Gl. kgl. S.3543, fol. 19v: "Ut sunt tres ordines personarum, sic sunt tres principales species epistolarum, humilis, mediocris, et sublimis. Humilis epistola est que ab humili persona mittitur, ut sunt bubulci, cerdones, et pelliparii, et ceterae que non habent sub se inferiorem ordinem. Sublimis epistola est, que mittitur a sublimi persona. Ut ab apostolico vel imperatore. Sublimis persona est qua nulla dignitas est superior. Ut est apostolicus in ecclesiasticis, imperator in secularibus. Mediocris est que media est inter sublimem et humilem. Ut sunt tetrarchae, reges, marchiones, comites, duces, archiepiscopi, capitanei, vavasores, vicedomini, et ceterae personae que sunt mediae inter sublimem et humilem." Among the more important variants from Berlin, Staatsbibl., MS Phillipps 1732, fol. 57v are the addition of "subulci" ("swineherds") after "bubulci," the substitution of "dignitate ingenem suo superatur, ut" for "dignitas est superior. Ut est" and of "consules" for "comites," and the omission of "vavasores."

16. Schmale, "Bologneser Schule," p. 27, n. 34.

17. There is a considerable but scattered literature on this work, of which part I was published by Rockinger, *Briefsteller,* I: 9–28, as by Alberic of Monte Cassino and translated in *Three Medieval Rhetorical Arts,* ed. James J. Murphy (Berkeley-Los Angeles-London, 1971), pp. 5–25. See C. H. Haskins, "An Italian Master Bernard," *Eassys in History Presented to Reginald Lane Poole,* ed. H. W. C. Davis (Oxford, 1927), pp. 214–15, and *Culture,* pp. 181–82, and *Casinensia,* I: 117; also Mirella Brini Savorelli, "Il 'Dictamen' di Bernardo Silvestre," *Rivista critica di Storia della Filosofia* XX (1965), 191–92; Bloch, in *La Scuola,* p. 588 and n. 76, citing the evidence that it should be dated after 1137; and Lanham, *Salutatio Formulas,* pp. 105–7.

18. On Bernard Silvestris, see Savorelli, " 'Dictamen'," pp. 182, 230, with full references to earlier literature, and on Bernhard of Meung, Walter Zöllner, "Eine neue Bearbeitung der 'Flores dictaminum' des Bernhard von Meung," *Wissenschaftliche Zeitschrift der Martin-Luther-Universität Halle-Wittenberg: Gesellschafts- und Sprachwissenschaftliche Reihe* XIII (1964), 335–42, with references to previous literature in n. 1 on p. 342, including Franz-Josef Schmale, "Der Briefsteller Bernhards von Meung," *Mitteilungen des Instituts für österreichische Geschichtsforschung* LXVI (1958), 1–28.

19. Rockinger, *Briefsteller,* I: 10–12.

20. Graz, Universitätsbibl., MS 1515, fols. 53v–54v: "Ut ergo providus dictator cuique epistole congruam salutationem adhibeat, semper necesse ei est, mittentis et recipientis prenosse personas. . . . [E]ximie persone dicuntur, quibus vel genere vel dignitate nulla superior reperitur, utpote apostolici, et Romanorum imperatoris. Infimas autem eas arbitramur personas, quibus genere vel dignitate nulla valet inferior reperiri, ut serui empticii, infimique clientes. Mediocres iure appellantur, quibus genere, potentia, dignitate, quedam superiores, quedam inferiores inveniuntur. Harum magna copia est. Quarum videlicet mediocrum, alie sunt pares, alie sunt dispares. Pares illas vocamus, tam in ecclesiasticis quam in secularibus, que offitio sive dignitate, aut potentia, sibi invicem parificantur. In ecclesiasticis ut episcopi inter se, archiepiscopi, archidiaconi, decani, plebani, abbates, priores, sacerdotes, levite, clerici, et quidam aliorum officiorum. In secularibus vero, ut reges, duces, marchiones, comites, proceres, consules, vicedomini, et aliarum dignitatum, sive officiorum viri. Disparium autem personarum, non indigemus exemplis. Seculares tamen persone, licet semper excellant potentia, vel nobilitate, ob reverentiam ecclesiastice dignitatis inferiores ecclesiasticis designantur. Ideoque si magnates scribunt etiam sacerdotibus tamen ut maioribus id

facere consuerint. Pater etiam avus, vel proavus, maiores semper filio, vel nepote inveniuntur, quamvis maior potentia, sive dignitas opponatur. Unde etiam fit ut episcopus patri, vel avo, aut proavo, tanquam maioribus scribat, sed ab eis episcopo non tanquam minori scribendum est." The term "servi empticii" found both here and in the treatise in Vienna MS 246 (see n. 22 below) is not in the standard dictionaries of medieval Latin or handbooks of medieval institutions, but it seems to refer to a serf who has been or can be purchased: cf. *Cartulaire de l'Abbaye de Saint-Père de Chartres*, ed. B. Guérard (Paris, 1840), II: 310, no. 59, for a reference in a document of 1117 to two arpents of land "unum empticium, alterum de patrimonio."

21. Graz, Universitätsbibl., MS 1515, fol. 58r: "Diversitas quidem personarum in omni ordine, et manerie, diversitatem insinuat salutationum iuxta dictantis periciam." The second redaction of Bernard's treatise is found in Mantua MS A.II.1, fols. 73–122, which I have not seen but which is described by Hermann Kalbfuss, "Eine bologneser Ars dictandi des XII. Jahrhunderts," *Quellen und Forschungen aus italienischen Archiven und Bibliotheken*, XVI.2 (1914), 1–35, who summarized the relevant sections as follows: "Die Definition der *Epistola* und ihre Zergliederung leiten dann zu dem wichtigen Kapitel der *Salutatio* über. Mit echt mittelalterlicher Freude an ständischer Gliederung wird es eröffnet durch eine allgemeine Einteilung der Menschheit in drei Klassen: zu unterst *serui emptitii, serui glebe* und ihresgleichen, als zweite Stufe Herzoge, Markgrafen, Grafen, Pfalzgrafen, Patriarchen, Primaten, Erzbischöfe, Bischöfe, Pröpste, Archidiakone, Pfarrer und Äbte, kurz alle, die zugleich Untergebene haben und ein Oberhaupt anerkennen; zu höchst auf dieser Stufenleiter stehen Papst und Kaiser." This suggests that the lists in the two versions, though corresponding roughly, differed in organization and in the precise listing of ranks.

22. On Vienna MS 246, see Savorelli, " 'Dictamen'," p. 192, basing the date on references to Count Theobald of Blois and apparently disregarding the reasons for a later date suggested by Haskins, "Italian Master," pp. 219–20, who said that, "In treatment, as well as in time and place, we have travelled far from the Italian Bernard," and in *Culture*, pp. 182–83, calling it "a greatly modified version made in France in the time of Innocent III." On Vienna MS 896, see W. Zöllner, "Eine neue Bearbeitung der 'Flores dictaminum' des Bernhard von Meung," *Wissenschaftliche Zeitschrift der Martin-Luther-Universität Halle-Wittenberg* XIII (1964), 336. It is impossible to enter here into the question of the traditions influencing these works, in which Savorelli and Zöllner (as the titles of their articles suggest) find respectively the influences of Bernard Sylvestris and Bernard of Meung. The sections on salutations in both show clearly their debt to Bernard of Bologna.

23. Savorelli, " 'Dictamen'," pp. 204–7. The presence of both "diaconi" and "levite" among the lower clergy should be noted, since the terms are usually regarded as synonyms. On the "servi emptitii," see n. 21 above.

24. Charles Samaran, "Une *Summa grammaticalis* du XIIIᵉ siècle avec glosses provençales," *Archivum Latinitatis medii aevi (Bulletin Du Cange)* XXXI (1961), 157–224, from Paris, Bibl. nat., MS lat. 16671, which Samaran apparently dated palaeographically in the second half of the twelfth century while dating the treatise, on the grounds of style, in the first half of the thirteenth (p. 163).

25. Ibid., p. 215. This summary covers a few verbal differences and differences in word order. The comma between "parrochiales, presbyterii" in the edition of the Vienna treatise, for instance (which is accordingly translated here as "parish clergy, priests") is omitted in the edition of Master William, which may account for his omission of the "plebani" among the middle clergy.

26. Another similar but simpler ranking to that in Vienna 896 and Master William is that in the *Ars dictandi Aurelianensis* published by Rockinger, *Briefsteller*, I: 103–14, and attributed to Ralph of Tours, at the end of the twelfth century, by C. H. Haskins, *Culture*, p. 6, n. 2 (and p. 190). Cf. also Manitius, *Lat. lit.*, III: 310, who said that it came from Orléans or St. Lifard soon after 1180 and that the letter-collection of Ralph of Tours was added in the thirteenth century. Here the clergy were classified as higher (pope, cardinals, archbishops, bishops), middle (deans, subdeans), and inferior (clerics, scholars) and the laity likewise as higher (emperors, kings), middle (counts, viscounts ["semicomites"], castellans) and inferior

266

(commoners): Rockinger, *Briefsteller.* I: 104. In the later *Summa dictaminum* of Ludolf of Hildesheim, who was active from 1221–60, the clergy were classified as highest (pope, cardinals, archbishops, bishops), middle (abbots, provosts, deans), and lowly (simple canons, simple priests, masters, students) and the laity as highest (emperors, kings, palatines, dukes, marquises), middle (counts, barons, "those holding the lordships of towns") and lowly (soldiers, townsmen, merchants): ibid., pp 360–61; cf. Wilhelm Wattenbach, *Deutschlands Geschichtsquellen im Mittelalter.* 6th ed. (Berlin, 1893), II: 361.

27. Paris, Bibl. nat., MS n.a.l. 610, fols. 4v–5r: "Adiectiva preterea personis competencia, in ipsis salutacionibus debemus addere, quibus varietatem personarum valeamus exprimere. Aliter enim papae, aliter regi, loquimur, aliter episcopo, aliter abbati, aliter monacho, aliter militi strenuissimo, aliter socio vel amico karissimo." Cf. Haskins, *Culture.* p. 184. A classification of letters into "gravis," "mediocris," and "attenuatus," like that of Albert but without the corresponding social classes, is found in London, British Library, MS Add. 21173, fol. 67v, in an anonymous treatise dated ca. 1138–52 by Haskins, *Culture.* p. 184.

28. Paris, Bibl. nat., MS lat. 7517, fol. 55v: "Diversis itaque personis, secundum quantitatem eorum diverso modo scribere vera consideratio rerum nos edocet. . . . Bonus itaque dictator designatum prevideat ordinem personarum, ut secundum quantitates et qualitates earum modum loquendi convenientius informet. Sublimibus namque personis et in magnis causis, secundum meterie congruentiam splendor verborum factorumque magnificentia exiberi debet. Mediocriobus [*sic*] vero personis oportuna temperate dici potuerunt. Tenuis autem persona quantomagis infima est tanto minus verbis affluit, et magnarum sententiarum lege privatus, sic tamen ut brevitas eius vel ad illum loquentis nullam generet obscuritatem et verborum iunctura vigorem materie non deserat. Has quidem proprietates si bene custodierimus illud trimodum loquendi genus quod a plerisque dicitur humile, medium, grandi loquum sine dubio legitime complebimus." The three categories of letter in the final sentence correspond to those mentioned by Alberic of Monte Cassino in his *Breviarium de dictamine.* cited above. On this manuscript, see Charles Thurot, "Notices et extraits de divers manuscrits latins pour servir à l'Histoire des Doctrines grammaticales au Moyen Âge," *Notices et Extraits des Manuscrits de la Bibliothèque impériale* XXII.2 (1868), 24–25, and, on Paul of Camaldoli, Haskins, *Culture.* p. 188, dating him in Italy in the generation after 1160, and Bloch, in *La Scuola.* pp. 586–87, n. 71a, with references to other secondary works.

29. Vincenzo Licitra, "La *Summa de arte dictandi* di Maestro Goffredo," *Studi medievali.* VII, 3rd series (1966), 886–87; cf. 867–76 on the date and place of composition, stressing that Geoffrey was a guest at Bologna at the time of writing and not a native of the city.

30. *Die Ars dictandi des Thomas von Capua.* ed. Emmy Heller, Sitzungsberichte der Heidelberger Akademie der Wissenschaften: Philosophisch-historische Klasse, 1928–9, Abh. IV (Heidelberg, 1929), p. 17 (chaps. 5–6); cf. pp. 49–53 on the date, and also Kantorowicz, *Studies.* p. 195.

31. Thomas of Capua, *Ars dictandi.* c. 10, ed. Heller, p. 21.

32. Guido Faba, *Summa dictaminis.* II: 8, ed. A. Gaudenzi, *Il Propugnatore* XXIII. 1 (n.s. III), (1890), 299; cf. Haskins, *Culture,* p. 6, n. 2; Thomas of Capua, *Ars dictandi,* ed. Heller, pp. 48–49; Denholm-Young, *Papers,* pp. 48–50; and Kantorowicz, *Studies,* pp. 196–97, dating him from before 1190 to ca. 1245, and 255. Faba's *Doctrina ad inveniendas, incipiendas et formandas, materias* is printed in Rockinger, *Briefsteller,* I: 185–96, but has nothing on salutations except an injunction to divide the world three ways and to observe the three classes of "maiores," "equales," and "minores," and to address each accordingly (p. 186).

33. Cf. Ch.-V. Langlois, "Formulaires de Lettres du XIIᵉ, du XIIIᵉ et du XIVᵉ Siècle [IV]," *Notices et Extraits des Manuscrits de la Bibliothèque nationale,* XXXIV.2 (1893), 9–15, publishing sections and saying that its originality rested solely "dans un arrangement nouveau de matières banales" (p. 11), and R. W. Southern, "Peter of Blois: A Twelfth Century Humanist?" *Medieval Humanism and Other Studies* (Oxford, 1970), p. 115: "While the letters [of Peter of Blois] went on to fame and fortune, the treatise to which they formed a body of illustrations was forgotten. Rightly so. Peter's treatise, like all the others of the same kind, de-

served to be forgotten." It has nevertheless attracted some attention owing to the celebrity of its author and to his reference in the introduction to "the avid followers of Master Bernard and of [the *dictatores* of] Tours." This Bernard has been identified both as Bernard Sylvestris and as Bernard of Meung (on whom see n. 18 above): Langlois, "Formulaires," pp 10–11; Émile Lesne, *Histoire de la propriété ecclésiastique en France,* v: *Les Écoles de la Fin du VIIIe Siècle à la Fin du XIIe*, Mémoires et Travaux publiés par des Professeurs des Facultés catholiques de Lille L (Lille, 1940), 190–91; Savorelli, " 'Dictamen'," p. 191. The evidence on salutations presented here suggests that Peter used the work of Bernard of Bologna. Cf. also Manitius, *Lat. lit.,* III: 296–97; Denholm-Young, *Papers,* p. 50; and Kantorowicz, *Studies,* p. 217.

34. Cambridge, Univ. Lib., MS Dd.IX.38, fol. 116r: "Summe sunt quibus dignitate nulla superior reperitur ut dominus papa et imperator Romanus. Sublimes ut patriarche, archiepiscopi, reges, episcopi, duces, comites, palatini marchiones. Mediocres sunt, ut decani, archidiaconi, abbates, prepositi, primicerii, thesaurarii, castellani, prefecti, consules qui in quibusdam civitatibus pares dicuntur. Private sunt que nullam administrant dignitatem ut milites et clerici. Infime sunt ut rustici et omnes opera civilia frequentantes, ut cerdones et huiusmodi. . . . Hac personarum varietate cognita cum studiosus dictator accesserit ad scribendum, primum sibi intuendum est si par pari, aut superior inferiori aut equo scribat."

35. Work is at present proceeding in a somewhat piecemeal fashion in spite of the projected *Corpus dictatorum Italicum,* on which see Helene Wieruszowski, *Politics and Culture in Medieval Spain and Italy,* Storia e Letteratura: Raccolta di studi e testi CXXI (Rome, 1971), 641–42.

36. I have tried to translate these consistently as "exalted" ("sublimis"), "greater" ("maior"), "highest" ("summus"), "higher" ("altior"), "superior" ("superior"), "supreme" ("supremus"), "weighty" ("gravis"), "excellent" ("excellens"), and "outstanding" ("eximius") for the upper rank and "feeble" ("exilis"), "mean" ("tenuis"), "lesser" ("minor"), "humble" ("humilis"), "inferior" ("inferior"), "lowly" ("infimus"), and "light" ("extenuatus").

37. Most of these seem to have been of the Bolognese school, stemming from Adalbert Samaritanus and Bernard of Bologna.

38. In the treatise in Vienna MS 246 the "milites," while not formally put with the "infimi," were clearly ranked with the "plebei" in contrast to the counts, dukes, marquises, and barons: see Savorelli, " 'Dictamen'," p. 218.

39. See Edgar H. McNeal, *Minores and Mediocres in the Germanic Tribal Laws* (Columbus, 1905), who said that the term referred to a class of landlords usually holding grants of land from the king (p. 124), and Eberhard Otto, *Adel und Freiheit im deutschen Staat des frühen Mittelalters,* Neue deutsche Forschungen: Abteilung mittelalterliche Geschichte II (Berlin, 1937), 151–55.

40. I plan to gather into an article these various references to "mediocres" in charters, chronicles, and biographies.

XIV

Troyes, Constantinople, and the Relics of St Helen in the Thirteenth Century

The earliest reference to the reliquary and cult of St Helen the Virgin at Troyes occurs in a charter dated 23 April 1229[1]. In this document the dean and chapter of the cathedral of Troyes made provision for repairing the reliquary (*capsa*) of the blessed virgin Helen, which had been destroyed (*penitus... diruta et confracta*), though without harming the relics, by the sudden collapse of the church of Troyes. This damage, probably a partial fall of the newly-built nave, was done by a storm on 10 November 1228[2]. Eleven days later, on 21 November, the papal legate Romanus granted an indulgence to those who helped to repair the building, and Pope Gregory IX made a similar grant on 10 September 1229[3]. There is no reference to St Helen in either of these documents, but in 1260 the bishop of Troyes required the dean and canons of St Stephen to take part in a procession in honor of "the glorious virgin St Helen."[4] And in two bulls dated 13 and 15 March 1262 Pope Urban IV, who was a native of Troyes, declared an indulgence of a year and forty days for those who visited the cathedral of Troyes on the feasts of St Peter and of St Helen[5].

From this time on until the end of the eighteenth century St Helen ranked among the principal saints in the diocese of Troyes[6]. Her feast on 4 May was celebrated with the same pomp as those of the Assumption of the Virgin and of All Saints[7]. Her presence in liturgical books (together with Ss Sabinian, Lupus, Urban, Pantaleon, and Mastidia) is a

---

1. This charter was first printed, with the date 1209, in the rare supplementary *Auctarium* to N. CAMUZAT (Camusat), *Promptuarium sacrarum antiquitatum Tricassinae dioecesis*, Troyes, 1610, fol. 27 v°. This *Auctarium* is missing from most copies of the *Promptuarium*. The charter was reprinted in P. RIANT, *Exuviae sacrae Constantinopolitanae*, Geneva, 1877/78, t. II, p. 114 (and studied in t. I, p. CLXXIII) and by Ch. LALORE in the "Coll. de docum. inédits relatifs à la ville de Troyes et à la Champagne méridionale," Troyes, 1878/93, t. II, p. 144-145. CAMUZAT's date of 1209 was apparently a typographical error, and the charter is dated 1229 by LALORE, RIANT (with some expressions of doubt : see t. I, p. CLXXIII, n. 6), and A. ROSEROT, *Promptuarium et Meslanges historiques de Nicolas Camuzat : table de matières et de documents*, in "Mém. Soc. acad. du départ. de l'Aube," t. LX, 1896, p. 205.
2. ALBERIC OF TROIS-FONTAINES, *Chronicon*, s.a. 1228, in *M.G.H. SS.*, Hanover, 1826 ff., t. XXIII, p. 922 ; cf. *Congr. archéol. 1955, Troyes*, Orléans, 1957, p. 10. According to a document in CAMUZAT, *Auctarium Promptuarii*, fol. 27 v°, cited by LALORE, *op. cit.*, t. II, p. 144, the damage occurred in 1227 ; but the documents cited in n. 3 below confirm ALBERIC's date of 1228.
3. H. D'ARBOIS DE JUBAINVILLE, *Documents relatifs aux travaux de construction faits à la cathédrale de Troyes...*, in "Bibl. École Chartes," t. XXIII, 1862, p. 220-221.
4. RIANT, *op. cit.*, t. II, p. 141.
5. *Inventaire sommaire des archives départementales antérieures à 1790 : Aube*, Series G, Paris/Troyes, 1873/1930, t. II, p. 11, n° 2592.
6. Cf. the document of 1415 printed by D'ARBOIS DE JUBAINVILLE, *op. cit.*, p. 242-243, and the introd. by Ch. NOIRÉ to Ch. LALORE, *Inventaires des principales églises de Troyes* ("Coll. de docum. inédits...," IV-V), Troyes, 1893, t. I, p. LXXXVIII-LXXXIX and XCVI.
7. CAMUZAT, *Promptuarium*, fol. 148.

distinctive sign of the liturgy of Troyes[8]. Her festival was added to pre-thirteenth-century missals and breviaries[9] and is found regularly in late medieval liturgical books from the diocese of Troyes and occasionally from the near-by dioceses of Langres, Rheims, and Auxerre[10]. In 1457 her relics, together with those of two other saints, were displayed throughout the diocese in order to raise money to complete the nave of the cathedral[11]. Images of St Helen were painted for the cathedral in 1536 and 1619-20[12]. Her relics were inspected in 1630 by the queen of France, Anne of Austria, and in 1662 by the famous Cardinal de Retz[13].

In spite of this celebrity, however, the identity of St Helen is far from certain. She was believed at Troyes, on the basis of a life attributed to St John Chrysostom, to be the daughter of a fourth-century king of Corinth and to have come from Natura (the Greek Athyra), near Constantinople, in Thrace. The readings and hymns concerned with St Helen in the liturgical books of Troyes from the thirteenth to the eighteenth century were based on a Latin version of this life[14], which was printed in its entirety in 1610 by Camuzat in his *Promptuarium*[15]. It was originally accompanied by a prologue, also attributed to Chrysostom, and by a letter addressed to the bishop, dean, and chapter of Troyes by Angemer, lector of the church of Chalcedon, saying that he had translated the life into Latin from Greek copies in the libraries at Constantinople at the request of John, a cleric of Troyes, who had come to Constantinople in 1215 seeking information about the St Helen whose relics had been taken to Troyes. The prologue and letter were not printed by Camuzat and are found in no known manuscript of the *Vita beatae Helenae*[16]. They were known to scholars only from the French translations printed by Desguerrois in his *Saincteté chrestienne*[17] and have therefore naturally been regarded as of doubtful authenticity.

The Bollandists threw doubt not only on the letter, prologue, and *Vita* but also on St Helen herself. Godefroid Henskens pointed out that the life was clearly not by Chrysostom. "We deduce from the sees," he wrote, "that these fables were concocted in the thirteenth century, with the episcopal sees taken from catalogues of that time."[18] He therefore questioned the entire story of the translation from Constantinople and refused to print the *Vita* in the *Acta sanctorum*. In its place he printed three readings concerning the hermit

---

8. V. LEROQUAIS, *Les pontificaux manuscrits des bibliothèques publiques de France*, Paris, 1937, t. I, p. VI.

9. ID., *Les sacramentaires et les missels manuscrits des bibliothèques publiques de France*, Paris, 1924, t. I, p. 152 (thirteenth-century addition to an eleventh-century Troyes missal), and *Les bréviaires manuscrits des bibliothèques publiques de France*, Paris, 1934, t. II, p. 450 (fourteenth- or early fifteenth-century addition to a twelfth-century breviary of Montiéramey). I am indebted to Mlle M.-Th. d'Alverny for verifying the dates of these additions.

10. LEROQUAIS, *Sacramentaires*, t. II, p. 190-191, 260, 263 (Auxerre), and t. III, p. 46-48 and 171 ; *Bréviaires*, t. I, p. 86 and 254, t. III, p. 7 (Auxerre), and t. IV, p. 10-11, 14, 213, 223-225, 240, 242, 254, 409-410 ; *Pontificaux*, t. I, p. 287 (Langres ?), and t. II, p. 462 ; *Les psautiers manuscrits latins des bibliothèques publiques de France*, Paris, 1940/41, t. I, p. 89 and t. II, p. 174 (Rheims) and 244. See also the *Catalogus codicum hagiographicorum latinorum... in Bibliotheca Nationali Parisiensi* ("Subsidia hagiographica," 2) [now : *Catal. lat. Paris.*], Paris/Brussels, 1889/93, t. III, p. 641, listing ten manuscripts, six from the diocese of Troyes and four from the diocese of Auxerre.

11. *Inventaire sommaire...*, t. II, p. 12, n° 2593.

12. *Ibid.*, t. I, p. 331, n° 1610, and t. II, p. 32, n° 2680.

13. *Ibid.*, t. I, p. 269, n° 1297 and p. 275, n° 1304.

14. RIANT, *op. cit.*, t. I, p. CXIX-CXX (citing E. DEFER, *Vie des saints du diocèse de Troyes*, Troyes, 1865, p. 315), CLXI-CLXII and CLXXI, and t. II, p. 49-50, where he prints two hymns from a sixteenth-century Troyes breviary.

15. Fol. 402 v°-410 v° ; cf. *Bibliotheca hagiographica latina* ("Subsidia hagiographica," 6) [now : *BHL*], Brussels, 1898/99, t. I, p. 565, n° 3794.

16. *Catal. lat. Paris.*, t. II, p. 522 (B.N. lat. 5614, fol. 50-60 v°) ; RIANT, *op. cit.*, t. I, p. CLXXI-CLXXII.

17. N. DESGUERROIS, *La saincteté chrestienne...*, Troyes, 1637, fol. 333 (not seen by me), reprinted in RIANT, *op. cit.*, t. II, p. 105-106, calling the original "documentum deperditum." In his preface (t. I, p. CLXXI), RIANT says that the original Latin has escaped all his researches. Cf. also LALORE, *Inventaires...*, t. I, p. CVI, n. 2.

18. *Acta sanctorum* [now : *AA.SS.*], Antwerp, 1643 ff., May, t. I, p. 531. HENSKENS said that he had seen two manuscripts of the *Vita*, both divided into liturgical readings and one (now apparently lost) including the letter and prologue. The other was presumably B. N. lat. 5614 (see n. 16).

St Helynus which he found in a lectionary from the diocese of Troyes[19]. He suggested that this St Helynus was first confused with St Helen the mother of Constantine and was then transformed (in view of the well-established claim of the abbey of Hautvillers, in the diocese of Rheims, to the relics of the Empress Helen) into the virgin whose relics were said to have been brought to Troyes after the Fourth Crusade[20]. Paulin Paris also maintained, following Henskens, that the St Helen honored at Troyes on 4 May derived from the hermit Helynus and that the *Vita*, together with the prologue and letter, were literary fictions composed "towards the end of the thirteenth century."[21]

This theory is ingenious but not convincing. The readings published by Henskens are taken from the *Historia monachorum* of Rufinus of Aquileia and refer to the well-known Eastern hermit Helenus (Helles, Hellen)[22]. He was indeed known and honored at Troyes, but in a list of relics to be displayed there on Relic Sunday *Helynus confessor* is listed separately from *Helena virgina*[23]. There is likewise no evidence that St Helen at Troyes was ever confused with the Empress Helen, although the eighteenth-century scholar J. P. Grosley went even further than Henskens and Paris and maintained that the relics at Troyes were in fact those of the mother of Constantine[24]. He based his argument, after demolishing the rival claims of Rome, Venice, and Hautvillers, on the Greek character of the paintings on the reliquary at Troyes, on the gold and purple material in which the relics were wrapped, and on the ideal opportunity of Bishop Garnier of Troyes, who had charge of the relics at Constantinople after the capture of 1204, to obtain the relics of the Empress Helen[25].

There is no question that Helen the mother of Constantine was sometimes confused with other saints of the same name, especially since her relics were claimed by several churches[26]. The principal claimants in the West, where her feast was celebrated on 18 August, were Hautvillers[27], Rome[28], and Venice[29]. In the East, where she was honored with her son Constantine on 21 May, her relics were said to be in the church of the Holy Apostles in

---

19. Now B.N. lat. 5574, fol. 41 r° ff. (cf. *Catal. lat. Paris.*, t. II, p. 483).
20. *AA.SS.*, May, t. I, p. 531-532.
21. *Histoire littéraire de la France*, Paris, 1733 ff., t. XXI, p. 593-595.
22. RUFINUS OF AQUILEIA, *Historia monachorum*, XI, in MIGNE, *P.L.*, Paris, 1841/64, t. XXI, col. 429-430; cf. *BHL*, t. I, p. 566, n° 3796. There is no reason aside from HENSKENS' identification with St Helen at Troyes, I believe, to say that he was honored on 4 May. The sixth-century St Helanus (Helenus) was honored in the diocese of Rheims on 7 October : see *Catal. lat. Paris.*, t. III, p. 700.
23. CAMUZAT, *Promptuarium*, fol. 121 v°.
24. *Œuvres inédites de P. J. Grosley : Mémoires sur les Troyens célèbres*, Paris, 1812/13, t. I, p. 436-441. According to his own account, GROSLEY first made this suggestion in 1738.
25. GROSLEY, like HENSKENS and PARIS, though for different reasons, rejected the letter of Angemer and the *Vita* as fabrications.
26. See in particular [P.] LUCOT, *Sainte Hélène... d'après des documents inédits : sa vie, son culte en Champagne, son suaire à Châlons, son corps à Paris*, Paris, 1876, p. 34-72 ; A.-M. ROUILLON, *Sainte Hélène* ("Les saints"), Paris, 1908, p. 111-130 ; R. COUZARD, *Sainte Hélène d'après l'histoire et la tradition*, Paris, 1911, p. 207-237. The matter needs further careful study. On the lives of the Empress Helen, see *BHL*, t. I, p. 563-565, n° 3772-3790.
27. FLODOARD, *Historia Remensis Ecclesiae*, II, 8, in *M.G.H. SS.*, t. XIII, p. 456-457, gives an account of the translation from Rome to Hautvillers by the monk Tetgisus (Theogisus) in 841/2. Other versions are found in H. V. SAUERLAND, *Trierer Geschichtsquellen des XI. Jahrhunderts*, Trier, 1889, p. 212 (cf. p. 40) and in a manuscript from the ducal library at Gotha published by P. GROSJEAN in « Anal. Bolland. », t. LVIII, 1940, p. 101 and 199-203. The translation is dated 849 in the chronicle of SIGEBERT and his continuators : *M.G.H. SS.*, t. VI, p. 339 and 391. Her life by ALMANNUS (Altmannus), a monk of Hautvillers (*BHL*, t. I, p. 563, n° 3772) was the basis for the life published by SAUERLAND, *op. cit.*, p. 173-184 (cf. p. 61-79).
28. On the claim of Rome to her head and parts of her body, which were said to have been translated to the church of the Ara Coeli about 1140, see LUCOT, *op. cit.*, p. 34-37, ROUILLON, *op. cit.*, p. 128, and COUZARD, *op. cit.*, p. 208 and 234.
29. The Venetians were apparently not agreed whether her body came from Constantinople in the twelfth century (cf. GROSLEY, *op. cit.*, t. I, p. 439-440) or in 1211, as recorded in the chronicle of Andreas DANDOLO : cf. RIANT, *op. cit.*, t. II, p. 262, and COUZARD, *op. cit.*, p. 234.

Constantinople[30]. The abbey of Montierender[31] and the city of Trier[32] (where she was thought by some to have been born) both laid claim to her head, and there are references to assorted relics of St Helen, some of whom were doubtless believed to be the Empress, in many historical sources of the eleventh and twelfth centuries[33]. There was a virgin St Helen, for instance, commonly known as "of Auxerre", who had a widely-established cult on 21/22 May[34]. She has been identified by hagiographers as the *Helena sacratissima puella* mentioned in the *Vita* of the fifth-century Bishop Amator of Auxerre[35]. But she appears as *S. Elena mater Constantini* on 21 May in a thirteenth-century Italian psalter (usage of Treviso)[36] and as *Helena regina* on 22 May in a breviary from Auxerre, the center of her cult[37]. This plus the fact that the Empress Helen was honored in the East on 21 May strongly suggests that there was some confusion between the two saints. St Helen at Troyes, however, was invariably referred to as *virgina* in both liturgical and historical sources[38]. Had she ever been confused with the Empress, especially on such apparently good grounds as Grosley suggests, it is most unlikely that she would have been unanimously accepted as an obscure Greek virgin.

Most historians have therefore disregarded the extremes of both Henskens and Grosley and have steered a middle course, rejecting the *Vita* as a fabrication by Angemer but accepting the letter as evidence that the relics were brought to Troyes from Constantinople some time between the Fourth Crusade and the mission of John of Troyes in 1215. The exact date and circumstances of the translation, however, are unknown. According to Riant, "The canons of Troyes were embarrassed by the Greek inscriptions on the reliquary of St Helen of Athyra, which Garnier of Traînel had sent them in 1205 by John the Englishman, his chaplain, and they had the idea of sending this John the Englishman back to Constantinople to look for information concerning the relic, which they thought to be the remains of St Helen the Empress."[39] Riant presents no evidence, however, to support this circumstantial account.

Bishop Garnier of Troyes is indeed known to have accompanied the Fourth Crusade and to have gathered a collection of relics before he died, at Constantinople, in 1205[40]. There is no proof, however, that Garnier sent the relics of St Helen to Troyes or that the cleric

30. Cf. RIANT, *op. cit.*, t. II, p. 212, 215, 225 (n⁰ 108) and 232, and COUZARD, *op. cit.*, p. 209-210.

31. Cf. LUCOT, *op. cit.*, p. 37-38, expressing doubt as to how St Helen's head reached Montierender, and COUZARD, *op. cit.*, p. 234, citing J.B. MANCEAUX, *Histoire de l'abbaye et du village d'Hautvillers*, Épernay, 1880, t. I, p. 320-321 (not seen by me), who said that it came from Constantinople by way of Troyes in 1204.

32. See the twelfth-century *notae* in *M.G.H. SS.*, t. XV/2, p. 967, and COUZARD, *op. cit.*, p. 208 and 234. In 1196, an altar at Trier was dedicated to the Virgin Mary and to the Empress Helen : *M.G.H. SS.*, t. XXX/2, p. 783.

33. *M.G.H. SS.*, t. XV/2, p. 975-976 (Gorze) and 1097 (St Emmeram, Regensburg), and t. XXX/2, p. 769 (Freising), and 771-772 and 774 (Epternach) ; RIANT, *op. cit.*, t. II, p. 199 (Corbie) ; etc. The St Helen whose relics were claimed by St Amand in 1132 (*M.G.H. SS.*, t. XXX/2, p. 786) was probably the St Alena, also known as Helen, who was honored in Brabant on 17 June (*BHL*, t. I, p. 44, n⁰ 265). The cult of the Swedish St Helen (*BHL*, t. I, p. 565, n⁰ 3793) was more or less restricted to the North-East. An "Helena v." appears under 15 April in a fifteenth-century breviary from Hungary : *Catal. lat. Paris.*, t. III, p. 635.

34. *Catal. lat. Paris.*, t. III, p. 649 (21 May in four breviaries : one Italian, one Franciscan, and one each from the dioceses of Thérouanne and Trier or Cologne) and 650 (22 May in six breviaries : three from the diocese of Auxerre and one each from St Dié, Tours, and Hungary) ; LEROQUAIS, *Sacramentaires*, t. II, p. 263 (22 May in Auxerre missal) and *Psautiers*, t. I, p. 220 (21 May in Tournai psalter) and 198 (22 May in Chester psalter).

35. *AA.SS.*, May, t. I, p. 59 and 60, n. b.

36. LEROQUAIS, *Psautiers*, t. II, p. 99.

37. ID., *Bréviaires*, t. III, p. 8.

38. HENSKENS and PARIS (see n. 18-21) cited the chronicle of ALBERIC OF TROIS-FONTAINES, s.a. 1163 (*M.G.H.SS.*, t. XXIII, p. 847), as evidence that the Empress Helen was believed to be at Troyes ; but ALBERIC refers only to Helen's disciple Hilda, whose relics were brought to Troyes by Henry of Champagne (cf. *ibid.*, s.a. 332, in *M.G.H.SS.*, t. XXIII, p. 685).

39. RIANT, *op. cit.*, t. I, p. CLXXI.

40. See E. GERLAND, *Geschichte des lateinischen Kaiserreiches von Konstantinopel*, I : *Geschichte der Kaiser Balduin I. und Heinrich (1204-1216)*, Homburg, 1905, p. 17 ; A. PRÉVOST, *Les Champenois aux croisades*, in "Mém. Soc. acad. du départ. de l'Aube, " t. LXXXV-LXXXVI, 1921/22, p. 151.

John who visited Constantinople in 1215 was his chaplain[41]. Camuzat said that the relics were brought to Troyes by French nobles in or about 1209[42], and this view was followed by Oultreman, the authors of the *Gallia christiana*, and other authorities[43]. The only contemporary indication of the date of the translation occurs under the year 1211 in the chronicle of Bernard Itier, who wrote that : *Ciuitate Treveris delatum est corpus Helene imperatricis aromatizatum, caput Philipi apostoli...*[44] This evidence is not trustworthy, however. The head of St Philip was certainly sent to Troyes, not Trier, by Bishop Garnier in 1205[45] ; and no relics of the Empress Helen are known to have been sent to Trier following the Fourth Crusade[46]. I am therefore inclined to believe that this entry reflects a garbled report of the translation of St Helen the Virgin to Troyes (*Trecis* could easily be confused with *Trev'is*), but the date cannot be settled more closely than 1205-15.

Riant's reference to the Greek inscription on the reliquary of St Helen was based on the unreliable account of Coffinet, written sixty years after the destruction of the reliquary[47]. The best contemporary description of the reliquary is by Grosley, who expressed the opinion that the paintings on it were very ancient — at least as old as the time of Giotto — and in the Greek manner but who specifically reserved judgment on whether they were Byzantine or French[48]. He would certainly have mentioned a Greek inscription, had it existed, in view of his desire to prove the Greek origins of the relics. The reliquary was in fact almost certainly not Byzantine, since the charter of 1229 described the *capsa* of St Helen (presumably the original reliquary) as entirely destroyed. In 1352 the bishop of Troyes authorized the sale of some land in order to complete the reliquary of St Helen ; and in 1437 workmen were still constructing a tabernacle for the reliquary[49]. It was not mentioned either in the cathedral inventories of 1429 and 1611 (which included, for instance, the reliquary of the head of St Philip)[50] nor by Martène and Durand in their description of the relics at Troyes[51]. It was destroyed by vandals in January 1794[52]. So far as is known, however, it was of small historical value and shed no light on the origins of the relics it contained[53].

41. The obituary notice of Garnier in LALORE ("Coll. de docum. inédits," t. II, p. 98), saying that he sent the head of St Philip and the body of St Helen, is very late.
42. CAMUZAT, *Promptuarium*, fol. 116 and 402 v⁰-403 v⁰.
43. P. D'OULTREMAN, *Constantinopolis Belgica*, Tournai, 1643, p. 644, who said that Helen's head remained at Corinth ; *Gallia christiana*, Paris, 1715 ff., t. XII, col. 505 C ("post obitum Garneri") ; LALORE, *Inventaires...*, t. I, p. CV-CVII.
44. *M.G.H. SS.*, t. XXVI, p. 435 ; = "Recueil des historiens des Gaules et de la France", Paris, 1738-1904, t. XVIII, p. 229 C. I have been unable to consult the edition of DUPLÈS-AGIER, but the entry has kindly been verified for me by Mlle d'Alverny from Bernard's autograph Ms. (B.N. lat. 1338, fol. 214 v⁰). There is no question he wrote "Trev'is".
45. ALBERIC OF TROIS-FONTAINES, *Chronicon*, s.a. 1205, in *M.G.H. SS.*, t. XXIII, p. 886 (cf. RIANT, *op. cit.*, t. II, p. 237). See also the inscription on the reliquary printed in CAMUZAT, *Promptuarium*, fol. 116 v⁰.
46. Cf. RIANT, *op. cit.*, t. II, p. 282-283 ; also n. 32 above on Trier's earlier claims to these relics.
47. [J.-B.] COFFINET, *Recherches sur l'origine des parcelles de la Vraie Croix conservées dans le trésor de la cathédrale de Troyes*, in "Mém. Soc. acad. du départ. de l'Aube," t. XIX, 1855, p. 188, n. 4.
48. GROSLEY, *op. cit.*, t. I, p. 435-436.
49. *Inventaire sommaire...*, t. II, p. 11, n⁰ 2592, and p. 202, n⁰ 3928.
50. LALORE, *Inventaires...*, t. II, p. 69-90 ; cf. [E.] LE BRUN-DALBANNE, *Le trésor de la cathédrale de Troyes*, Paris, 1864, also, without plates, "Mém. Soc. acad. du départ. de l'Aube," t. XXVIII, 1864, p. 27-76.
51. [E. MARTÈNE and U. DURAND] *Voyage littéraire de deux religieux bénédictins de la congrégation de Saint-Maur*, Paris, 1717/24, t. I, p. 88-89. I have not seen J.-C. COURTALON-DELAISTRE, *Topographie historique de la ville et du diocèse de Troyes*, Troyes, 1783/84, t. II, p. 121 and 125, which is cited in LALORE, *Inventaires...*, t. I, p. cxxx, together with other incidental references to the reliquary in the sixteenth and eighteenth centuries (p. cxxviii-cxxxi). These include a description attributed to the canon Tremet in 1754, cited from A.F. ARNAUD, *Voyage archéologique et pittoresque dans le département de l'Aube...*, Troyes, 1837, p. 163 (also not seen by me), which clearly derives from the description of 1794 printed in GROSLEY, *op. cit.*, t. I, p. 441.
52. See GROSLEY, *op. cit.*, t. I, p. 441-443 (and 436, where the destruction is dated 10/11 Jan.) and COFFINET, *op. cit.*, p. 213 (and p. 188, n. 4, dating the destruction 9/10 Jan.) ; cf. also LALORE, *Inventaires...*, t. I, p. cxxxiii.
53. NOIRÉ, in the introd. to LALORE, *Inventaires...*, t. I, p. clxiii-clxv, also regarded the reliquary as French and denied the importance given it by COFFINET and RIANT.

Riant's most important discovery with regard to St Helen was a reference in the work of Archbishop Anthony of Novgorod, who visited Constantinople in 1200 and left a detailed description (in Russian) of the relics there. After listing the relics in churches outside the Golden Gate, he said : *Ulterius, quiescit s. Helena virgo*[54]. This corresponds approximately to the position of Natura (Athyra) and is a valuable confirmation of Angemer's account.

Equally important is the re-discovery of the original Latin of Angemer's letter and "Chrysostom's" prologue, which were in fact never lost, as Riant believed, but simply misplaced. Camuzat was a remarkable scholar, who richly deserved the praise given him by contemporaries and later writers[55], but he was very unsystematic in his working habits[56]. Having decided for some reason not to print the letter and prologue in his *Promptuarium*, he apparently sent them to his friend Jacques Severt in Lyons, who printed them as an appendix to the list of the bishops of Troyes in the second edition of his *Chronologia historica... archiantistum Lugdunensis archiepiscopatus*, which appeared in 1628[57]. There they were entirely overlooked by scholars, who knew them only from the translation made by Desguerrois either from a copy or before they left Troyes.

The Latin version of the letter, which is reprinted here as an appendix[58], shows that Desguerrois' translation both contains a number of mistakes and omits almost half, though admittedly the less important sections, of the letter. Most serious among the errors are the description of John, who in the Latin version is called simply a cleric of Troyes, as chaplain to the bishop and the translation of the phrase *sancti corporis praedo devotus*, meaning that John was devoted to the relic, as *qui a été le dévot transporteur de ce s. corps*. These errors misled Riant and other scholars into believing that John was Garnier's chaplain and had originally brought the relics from Constantinople. Among the points omitted in the translation are that Angemer came from Courbetaux to Constantinople with his parents long before 1204 on account of their poverty and that in 1215 "there were few men in the city who knew Greek and Latin equally well".' The letter as a whole gives a fascinating glimpse into East-West relations after the Fourth Crusade[59]. The transmission of the relics, the mission to gather more information, the alleged search in the libraries of Constantinople, and the fabrication of a suitable *Vita* and feast-day were doubtless typical of the period.

The main characters, John and Angemer, seem to be otherwise unknown. At least they do not appear in the published cartularies of the diocese of Troyes[60]. The name Angemer

---

54. RIANT, *op. cit.*, t. II, p. 230, citing a Latin trans. by J. MARTINOV of the Russian edition of P. SAWAITOV (St Petersburg, 1872) p. 171 (not seen by me) ; cf. RIANT's discussion of this work in *Exuviae...*, t. I, p. ccvii-ccix.

55. See the epitaph printed in MARTÈNE and DURAND, *op. cit.*, t. I, p. 88-89. On CAMUZAT (1575-1655) and his historical works, see *Nouvelle biographie générale*, Paris, 1862/70, t. VIII, p. 430.

56. According to ROSEROT, *op. cit.*, p. 195-196, CAMUZAT delivered his copy to the printers in small packages as he gathered the material.

57. Part III, p. 146-148. On p. 148, SEVERT distinguished this Helen from Helen of Auxerre and expressed the hope of finding the original Greek of her *Vita* among the manuscripts of Chrysostom's works.

58. See p. 1042 below. I have not reprinted the prologue, which adds nothing of historical value to the *Vita* or letter.

59. Cf. C.H. HASKINS, *Studies in Mediaeval Culture*, Oxford, 1929, chap. VIII on "Contacts with Byzantium". "The channels of communication between East and West...," he wrote (p. 160), "often ran beneath the surface, and many of the contacts were occasional or accidental, so that the process of transmission often eludes us."

60. The epithet *Anglicus (l'Anglois)*, given John in the *Gallia christiana* and by RIANT and other scholars, apparently derives from the heading of the letter in SEVERT, *Chronologia*, t. III, p. 146 (and perhaps also in the translation of DESGUERROIS, which I have not seen). It is not used in any contemporary source or by CAMUZAT, who makes no mention of John.

(Angelmer) was rare, but it occurs in Champagne in the twelfth and thirteenth centuries[61]. Angemer described himself as lector of the church of Chalcedon, which had been reduced by the Latins from an independent metropolis to a suffragan see of Constantinople[62]. Although in 1215 Chalcedon was still in the hands of the Latins[63], Angemer seems to have lived in Constantinople. He was clearly a bit of an entrepreneur and very likely made his living by the sort of activities described in the letter. In spite of the final sentence, his reward for the *Vita* of St Helen probably consisted of something more than prayers alone.

It is of course possible, in spite of the evidence of Anthony of Novgorod concerning the relics of a virgin named Helen near Constantinople in 1200, that the *Vita* and letter were both forgeries composed at Troyes to authenticate some traditional relics and that the mission of John and the labors of Angemer are all literary fictions. On balance, however, this seems unlikely. The relics of a previously unmentioned St Helen are known to have been at Troyes in 1229, and they in all probability came from Constantinople. The author of the letter, prologue, and *Vita*, furthermore, certainly had some knowledge of the East. Although the names of the bishops mentioned are clearly unhistorical, the sees of Natura, Christopolis, Heracleia, Philippi, and Corinth are all genuine. It may even be that Angemer made use of some authentic legends in composing the pious fraud that he wrote under the name of Chrysostom and which from that time on provided the historical basis of the cult of St Helen the Virgin at Troyes.

---

61. See A. LONGNON, *Livre des vassaux du comté de Champagne et de Brie (1172-1222)* [= H. D'ARBOIS DE JUBAIN-VILLE, *Histoire des ducs et des comtes de Champagne*, t. VII], Paris, 1869, p. 252; C. LALORE, ed., *Collection des principaux cartulaires du diocèse de Troyes*, Paris, 1875/90, t. I (St Lupus at Troyes), p. 26, n° 9, and t. IV (Montie-render, etc.), p. 180, n° 53; ID., "Coll. de docum. inédits...", t. II, p. 393 (obit. of St Lupus).
62. R.L. WOLFF, *The Organization of the Latin Patriarchate of Constantinople (1204-1261)*, in "Traditio," t. VI, 1948, p. 51 and 56-57.
63. J. LONGNON, *L'empire latin de Constantinople*, Paris, 1949, p. 128.

Appendix*

Sanctissimo Patri suo Herueo Episcopo et viris venerabilibus Nicolao et Capitulo Trecensib[us] Angermerus dilectus Lector de grege pusillo Chalcedonensis Eccl[esiae] ouis una, sed minima et morbida salutem, et sponsum virginum in sponsa virgine deuotissime venerari.

Quidam magnae industriae et societatis iucundae Clericus Ioannes est nomen eius, apud vos diutius conuersatus, in vrbe Constantinopolitana anno Dom[ini] millesimo ducentesimo quinto decimo, quarto nonas Maij me inuenit et conuenit, ipsa videlicet die, qua tota Constantinopolitana Prouincia et praecipue Naturensis Ecclesia pretiosae Virginis Helenae solemnia cum multa deuotione de antiqua consuetudine celebrabat. Deuotionis namque feruorem erga praeclaram virginem ab antiquis temporibus creauerant, et creatum nutriuerant ipsius virginis tam viuae quam extinctae praesentia corporalis, qua se priuilegiatam iactabat ciuitas Naturensis et abunde impensa beneficia pie postulantibus eam. Et licet adhuc in amorem et honorem praecelsae virginis Helenae corda interius aestuarent, exteriorem tamen laetitiam minuebat dolor proueniens ex rapina et carentia corporis sacrosancti, quod sibi prouenisse peccatis suis exigentibus, inter alia damna innumera, tota praedita prouincia deplorabat, nec iam de perditis auro, argento, lapidibus pretiosis, pannis sericis et omnis generis opibus querebatur, sed circa amissa pretiosa Sanctorum pignora, tota mentis angustia versabatur. Porro praefatus Ioannes de me a pluribus Latinis in eadem ciuitate, quod fueram de Francia in Trecensi Dioecesi in villa quae Curtis Bertoudi dicitur oriundus inquirebat, sed pridem cum parentibus fugientibus paupertatem Constantinopolim veneram longo tempore ante obsidionem ipsius, vbi et litteras Graecas didici, et Latinas penitus non omisi. Idem ergo Ioannes ratione nationis mihi familiarius aperiens desiderium cordis sui, tandem litteras tuas, S. Pater Heruaee Episcope, generaliter ad omnes spectaturos directas meis oculis praesentauit, ex quarum tenore, et per certa ipsius Ioannis indicia liquido intellexi, ipsam quam amisimus virginem, saepe saepius apud vrbem Naturensem in carne et ossibus videram apud vos integram sine corruptione, similiter detineri. Nec enim dedit Dominus sanctam suam videre corruptionem, quae quoad vixit mente et corpore incorrupta permansit. Quocirca una gaudeo et doleo, laetor pariter et contristor, et affectiones diuersae distrahunt mentem meam. Nam mihi cordi est et meae terra mansionis, et meae patria nationis, cum ista congruum est me tristari, et cum illa naturale est gratulari. Cum ista anxior, quae tantum thesaurum perdidit : cum illa glorior, quae inuenit. Hoc vero praecipue in praefatis litteris petebatur, et hoc ipse Ioannes sancti corporis praedo deuotus ardentissima sollicitudine a quibuscumque poterat, requirebat, ut vita gloriosa florentissimae virginis Helenae, quam B. Ioannes Chrysostomus Graeco sermone conscripsit, in Latinam linguam per aliquem fidelem interpretem transferretur. Cumque pauci essent in ciuitate, qui linguam bene nossent Graecam pariter et Latinam, ad me quotidie recurrere cogebatur, id a me sub diuini iudicij[a] deposcens examine, vt nouum nouae Helenae celarem raptorem. Tandem opportuna importuna ipsius instantia victus sum, et multarum Ecclesiarum reuoluens armaria, non parua volumina de pretiosa virgine conscripta inueni, quae omnia in Latinam linguam transferre, et ad vos tam longe perferre, valde esset interpreti et portitori nuncio onerosum. Omissis ergo copiosis libris et sermonibus multis de ipsa iucundissima virgine Helena et miraculis ipsius apud nos Graeco sermone conscriptis, in quibus praeclara magnorum Patrum desudarunt ingenia, haec pauca vobis necessaria, sicut se habet Graeca veritas, et fideliter transtuli, et vobis pro munere liberaliter destinaui, a vobis pro condigna responsione muneris hoc deposcens, vt fusa coram Domino pro me misero peccatore vestrae virtus orationis cum intercessione ipsius pretiosae virginis, mihi merces et retributio sit laboris.

---

* The letter is reprinted here exactly as it appears in SEVERT, *Chronologia*, t. III, p. 146-147, aside from the expansion of a few abbreviations and the omission of accents.
  a *ludicii* in SEVERT.

XV

Twelfth-Century Spirituality and the Late Middle Ages

It is now forty years since Lucien Febvre argued in a provocative article that the question of the causes of the Reformation and its origins in France had been badly put by historians.[1] The Reformation, he said, was a chapter not in the history of the Church, nor of theology, nor of a national state, but in the history of religion. It was "the sign and product of a profound revolution of religious sentiment," a search for a religion better suited to the age;[2] and it must be studied in relation to the social, economic, and political conditions of the late Middle Ages.[3] The success or failure of a religious movement depends more upon considerations of this sort than upon the innovations of its leaders or the weaknesses of the institutions against which it may be directed.[4] Historians should therefore concentrate less upon individual reformers than upon (in the words of William James) "the adequacy of their message to the mental needs of a large fraction of mankind."[5] Religious sentiments, however, are harder to study than theological positions or institutional structures. "The only sound plan," said James, "if we are ourselves outside the pale of such emotions, is to observe as well as we are able those who feel them, and to record faithfully what we observe."[6]

For the late Middle Ages, the field of observation includes not only a wide range of religious literature but also a variety of liturgical practices, pious devotions, and artistic sources which reflect the spiritual (as contrasted with the mental) state of late medieval man. Religious needs and feelings differ from period to period, region to region, and person to person,[7] and it is only by studying a mass of individual instances that a general picture of the spirituality of the age can be put together. Such a picture for the fifteenth century would emphasize the emotionalism, anti-intellectualism, and sensuousness which can be seen in the religious feelings of sadness, tenderness, and devotion to the human Christ, His mother Mary, and the saints. "A man will know God in so far as he loves Him," said the great popular preacher Bernardino of Siena. "A man knows as much as he loves." St. Paul taught not that men should understand Christ, according to Bernardino, but that they should feel within themselves as He felt on the cross and participate in His sufferings.[8] Men were thus driven to the complementary extremes of religious introversion and extroversion. The stress on inner experience promoted an intense search for personal perfection, culminating in self-annihilation and abandonment in mystical union with God. At the same time, men sought to demonstrate their devotion. The ferment of popular prophecy and millenarianism roused them to a sense of public urgency and extravagant emotional displays, which are considered by some scholars to show the malaise of society at that time. The flagellants, the dance frenzies, and the witch hunts can be seen as the growing pains of modern society and as signs of deep feelings of guilt and hostility. Ladner described the fifteenth-century witch hunts as "a condemnation of alienated people by other alienated people."[9] Psychic epidemics like the dance frenzies, said Rosen in his recent book, *Madness in Society*, were "closely linked with religious ritual and institutions" and were fundamentally "attempts to manage stressful situations."[10] The fool replaced the pilgrim as the "ruling idea" of society and the type of Christian man, and "for the first time in Christian history," as Ladner put it, "there were let loose in full force the vast potentialities of man's alienation from man."[11]

Even intellectuals, to many of whom such phenomena were

Twelfth-Century Spirituality and the Late Middle Ages

profoundly distasteful, shared the emphasis on inwardness and will of the popular religious movements. For Gerson, as for Bernardino, God is known in this life more by the affective than by the cognitive powers. In his second lecture *Contra curiositatem studientium* he maintained that, "A clear and wise understanding of those things which are believed from the Gospel, which is called mystical theology, should be acquired by penance rather than by human investigation alone."[12] Valla argued in his *De professione religiosorum* that goodness must be freely willed by men and asserted in his *De libero arbitrio* that, "We stand by faith, not by the probability of reasons."[13] And Pico in his commentary on the Psalms emphasized that inner piety is more important than external worship.[14] "This humanist approach to theology may be traced from Petrarch to Erasmus," said Kristeller, who stressed that it influenced Protestants like Luther, Melanchthon, and Calvin as well as Catholics.[15] Even heretics, as Grundmann has shown, participated in this continuum of religious attitudes and often carried to extremes tendencies which in their more moderate manifestations were perfectly orthodox.[16]

Taken together, therefore, these elements characterized the spirituality of the late Middle Ages and must be seen as the product of complex forces at work in society at that time. Individually, however, many of these attitudes and devotions were far from new and can be found in the religious feelings and actions of much earlier Christians. The piety of the early Middle Ages was, indeed, not generally marked by emotionalism or extravagance, though individual instances can be cited, nor by popular devotion to the humanity of Christ, of which the suppression, according to some scholars, was a result of the reaction to Arianism.[17] Historians in recent years have increasingly regarded the late eleventh and twelfth centuries as the turning point in medieval spirituality, when the features which marked its later development first emerged.

The pioneer of this point of view was the textual scholar André Wilmart, who argued against Émile Mâle's opinion that there was a great difference between the religious spirits of the twelfth and fifteenth centuries. "It is the splendor of the twelfth century . . . ," Wilmart said, "to have discovered in the heart of Christianity veins that had not yet been exploited. . . . In most fields, thought, piety, art, literature, the twelfth century accomplished new work, extraordinarily fecund, and . . . truly inaugurated a distinct era in the history of Christian civilization."[18] A few pages later he went on:

The Christianity of the eleventh century at times resembles that of the fourteenth and fifteenth centuries in a remarkable way. Even more, the forms of piety of the twelfth century are close to those that appeared later. It was not entirely with St. Francis and under the influence of St. Francis, as M. Mâle still asserts, that the devout, sensitive, and pathetic Middle Ages really took shape. Before him, St. Bernard and his Cistercian disciples are evidence of the new spirit. And already men of the previous generation, such as John of Fécamp and St. Anselm, anticipated the changes which were to appear.[19]

These views have been echoed and developed by Gilson, Chenu, Javelet, and especially Southern, who in his well-known book, *The Making of the Middle Ages*, emphasized the novelty in the eleventh and twelfth centuries of "the new type of ardent and effusive self-disclosure," the stress on personal experience and individual conscience, and "the theme of tenderness and compassion for the sufferings and helplessness" of Christ.[20]

In a recent article on the popularity of twelfth-century spiritual texts in the late Middle Ages, I have tried to indicate some of the links between the religious feelings of the two periods. The number of manuscripts, for example, shows that interest in these works, which fell off in the thirteenth and early fourteenth centuries, revived in the fifteenth and early sixteenth centuries. This is confirmed by the evidence of translations, library catalogues, recommended reading lists, and early printed editions. "The demand for the mystical Christian writers was so compelling in the period 1450–1550," wrote Goldschmidt in his book, *Medieval Texts and their First Appearance in Print*, "that it resulted in the publication of practically every work in this class which we now consider to be

Twelfth-Century Spirituality and the Late Middle Ages

of importance and value."[21] Among the eleventh- and twelfth-century writers whose works were printed at this time were Adam of St. Victor, Amadeus of Lausanne, Anselm, Bernard (of whose works alone there were over five hundred editions printed before 1550[22]), Bruno, Elizabeth of Schönau, Guigo I and II of La Chartreuse, Hildegard of Bingen, Hugh of Fouilloy, Hugh of St. Victor, Innocent III, Joachim of Flora, John of Fécamp, Peter Damiani, Peter the Venerable, Richard of St. Victor, and William of St. Thierry, in addition to some minor and anonymous writers whose works circulated under the names of Augustine, Anselm, Bernard, and Hugh.

An interesting study could be written on the influence of almost every one of these writers. Bernard in particular enjoyed an enormous success in the late Middle Ages, when his influence has been compared by several scholars to that of Augustine. Bremond in his history of French religious sentiment in the seventeenth century spoke of Bernard as "that extraordinary man off whom we live today at least as much as we live off St. Augustine."[23] In the late Middle Ages he was admired by men of very different religious temperaments and theological beliefs, who found in his life and works spiritual attitudes and themes which appealed to their deepest religious inclinations. Not far behind Bernard in popularity and influence were Anselm, Hugh and Richard of St. Victor, and Joachim, whose contribution to the prophetic speculations of the fifteenth and sixteenth centuries has only begun to be investigated. Even minor, and today almost forgotten, twelfth-century works, like the *Speculum monachorum* of Arnulf of Bohéries and the *Scala claustralium* of Guigo II of La Chartreuse, were widely read.[24] Some of these texts are found only in late medieval manuscripts and thus owe not only their success but also their preservation to the devotional spirit of that age.

It is easier to establish the fact of than the reason for the popularity and influence of these works in late medieval intellectual and religious circles. Their success clearly depended not only on certain common qualities in the spirituality of the

fifteenth century but also on an affinity of religious temperament between this age and the twelfth century. This affinity
was not necessarily the result of any direct or conscious influence of the earlier on the later period, but it helps account
for the popularity of its writings. Men in the late Middle Ages
found certain congenial religious ideas and attitudes expressed
in twelfth-century spiritual texts. Such works might either have
been read continuously or have been lost sight of for years
until they were rediscovered and appreciated, sometimes under
attributions that entirely hid their true origins. Thus the
period of the Renaissance, in its broadest sense, involved the
reemphasis on and recombination of elements from the medieval as well as the classical traditions.[25] My main concern in
this lecture will be with those elements found in twelfth-century spiritual texts and used by men in the late Middle Ages.

Above all they found an inward-looking and affective piety
based on a doctrine of contemplation stressing personal will,
liberty, and experience. When Renaudet said that d'Ailly and
Gerson were "the heirs of St. Bernard and the Victorines," he
had in mind their view of the contemplative life. D'Ailly owed
to Richard, according to Renaudet, his description of the three
classic stages of the spiritual life—purification, illumination,
and union—and to Bernard his efforts to find in the Song of
Songs the symbols of the love of the soul for Christ.[26] Gerson's
definition of contemplation also depended primarily on Hugh
and Richard, as Combes has shown in his recent study on the
evolution of Gerson's mystical theology.[27] From them he
learned the spiritual content of various biblical texts. More
specifically, Gerson took from Richard and from Gilbert of
Hoyland his teaching on violent love and from Bernard and
William of St. Thierry his ideal of the "ambidextrous" prelate
who combines in his own life both action and contemplation.[28]
In the works of Hugh, said Roger Baron, Gerson, the writers
of the school of the *Devotio moderna,* and other late medieval
mystics found in germ "the mysticism of introversion, the
theory of mystical passivity under divine action, [and] the conception of the soul as a mirror associated with the doctrine

of the divine image of the soul."[29] The author of *The Cloud of Unknowing* "was probably indebted to Richard of St. Victor for the systematization of the way to contemplative prayer, some of his allegorical interpretations of Scripture, and possibly for the prevailing antithetical nature of his prose."[30] And through the *Explanacio* of Thomas Gallus, Richard is said by Javelet to have inspired the anti-intellectualist current in south German monasteries in the fifteenth century.[31] The mystical theology of Nicholas of Cusa, and especially his view of the powers of human reason, were influenced by Bernard and the Victorines. He found in their works, and even more, as Klibansky has shown, in the works of the twelfth-century masters at Chartres, many of the Platonic views for which he was famous among his contemporaries and which deeply influenced the development of Renaissance Platonism.[32]

The humanists no less than the theologians appreciated an emphasis on will and inner piety. Their dislike of scholastic intellectualism and speculative mysticism is well known. Valla, for instance, attacked Aquinas not only for his barbarous Latin but also for his logic and metaphysics.[33] And the early Christian fathers appealed to the humanists as much for their piety and scholarship as for their classical style.[34] The humanist attitude towards the twelfth century was on the whole less favorable, but the reaction against scholasticism inclined them to look with interest at pre-scholastic spirituality. Even Petrarch, who has been called the founder of the concept of the Dark Ages,[35] read with sympathy the works of Abelard, Hugh, Richard, and Bernard, to whom he devoted an admiring chapter in his *De vita solitaria*.[36] Petrarch's religious tracts, said Kristeller, "show some connection with the popular religious literature of the Middle Ages;"[37] and his spirituality, like his scholarship,[38] may have owed more to the twelfth century than he himself fully realized. The fact that the fifteenth-century humanist Pier Candido Decembrio derived much of his treatise on the immortality of the soul from the twelfth-century Cistercian treatise *De spiritu et anima*, which he believed to be by St. Augustine, also suggests that the religious outlook of the humanists had points in common with that of the twelfth century.[39]

An active interest in twelfth-century spiritual texts was shown in particular by the humanist circle of Lefèvre d'Étaples at Paris in the late fifteenth and early sixteenth centuries. The importance for this group of the idea of Christian antiquity has been studied by Eugene Rice, who said that, "The fathers offered Lefèvre and his friends a Christian vision of antiquity, a Christian eloquence, a Christian philosophy and an 'ancient and true theology.' "[40] In addition to the works of the Church fathers, however, they read and published a large number of medieval texts.[41] Lefèvre edited in 1513 a volume of various medieval spiritual writers, including Elizabeth of Schönau and Hildegard of Bingen, and in 1510 the *De trinitate* by Richard of St. Victor, in whose works he found, according to Renaudet, "in its entirety the rational and mystical theology for which he had ceaselessly searched."[42] Clichtove edited the works of Hugh of St. Victor, Hugh of Fouilloy, and Bernard, whom he praised in his introductory letter to the edition of 1508 for his elegant style, biblical learning, and sanctity of life.[43]

These works contain more than simply a definition of contemplation and a description of its principles. Some of the most original and important contributions of twelfth-century spirituality lay in its teachings on the psychology of the religious life and the importance of intention, liberty, self-knowledge, and love. Abelard, for instance, though he is not primarily known as a spiritual writer, influenced almost all subsequent teaching on morality by his emphasis on the significance of intention in human acts.[44] Both Hugh of St. Victor and Peter Lombard, who can hardly be described as disciples of Abelard, accepted his view that the merit of exterior actions depends on *intentio* and *voluntas,* though they rejected his opinion that all human acts are in themselves morally indifferent. This marked a revolution in moral doctrine, as Lottin has shown, and a reaction from the early medieval morality which defined sin as objective opposition to divine law and virtue as exterior observance of the law, especially in the framework of monastic life. The twelfth century saw the emergence of a more subjective and individual concept of virtue, which was closely related to the voluntarism of its spirituality.

Virtue of this sort must be chosen rather than imposed;[45] and the twelfth century was deeply concerned with the problem of liberty, though it had comparatively few new ideas on free will.[46] The biblical *locus classicus* was Paul's assimilation of liberty with the spirit of the Lord in 2 Corinthians 3.17, and the many twelfth-century references to "the spirit of liberty" and "liberty of the spirit" foreshadowed the emphasis on spiritual liberty in the religious thought of the late Middle Ages.[47] In a characteristic passage from a letter concerning novices, the Cistercian abbot Adam of Peresigne first cited Paul, "Where the spirit of the Lord is, there is liberty," and Bernard, "liberty, I say, from sin, from need, from misery," and then went on, playing with the reference to novelty in the term "novice," to say that, "The spirit is sent forth by God, morals are re-created, the face of the earth is renewed [a reference to Psalm 103.30], and you can rejoice in your novices, since the power from above makes them participants in this marvellous innovation."[48] Adam's stress on the reform and re-creation of man shows the far-reaching implications of this concept of liberty for the standards of individual behavior in relation to established laws and institutions.

The individual Christian was increasingly expected to rely on himself and his own experience. "The urge towards a greater measure of solitude," wrote Southern, "of introspection and self-knowledge which is exemplified by St. Anselm in the bosom of the Benedictine order in the eleventh century ran like fire through Europe in the generation after his death and produced an outburst of meditations and spiritual soliloquies."[49] It is no accident that the alternate title of Abelard's *Ethics* is the Socratic maxim *Scito te ipsum*. Abelard, Bernard, William of St. Thierry, Hugh, and Richard all taught that self-knowledge was man's start on his way to God. The importance of this idea for later spirituality and philosophy need not be emphasized. Parallels have been seen with Pascal, and Adam of Dryburgh's "Scio me esse" is said to have been a link between Augustine and Campanella, Descartes, and the modern notion of individual consciousness as the basic fact of experience.[50] The orientation was naturally different in the Middle Ages, when self-consciousness was seen as a prelude to a vision of eternity rather than as a scientific methodology; but it marked an important shift in man's way of looking at himself and his spiritual life.

Above all, it contributed to a new view of the dignity and nobility of man, as a function of his liberty and rationality and as an aspect of his creation in the image of God.[51] Richard of St. Victor expressed this in his description in the *Benjamin major* of the first grade of contemplation: "A man's own experience can easily teach anyone, I think, how greatly this speculation [of the self and others] has power to arouse the soul both against sin and towards good. Recognize your dignity, oh man, I beg; consider the excellent nature of your soul, how God made it in His image and likeness, how He raised it above all bodily creatures."[52] Here in a few lines from one of the most widely read works of twelfth-century spirituality are found many elements of its dynamic and forward-looking message, which offered to all men the hope of reform into the image of God.[53]

An essential part of this message, and one that appealed strongly to the emotionalism of the late Middle Ages, was its emphasis on love. *Dilige et fac quod vis*—"Love and do what you will"—was a favorite maxim of this age.[54] It derived from Augustine's commentary on the epistles of John and meant that men who love rightly will behave rightly. For men in the twelfth century it was an expression of their voluntarist and God-centered piety, but it held the seeds of more radical sentiments. William James (who knew of its use, I think, only in post-Reformation sources) called it an "antinomian saying" and "morally one of the profoundest of observations, yet . . . pregnant . . . with passports beyond the bounds of conventional

placed total trust in God, utterly despairing of his [own] works."[68] Catholic scholars have pointed out that Luther misinterpreted Bernard's use of the word *perdite* here and took what was in fact an expression of humility as evidence that Bernard trusted for his salvation in God rather than his monastic vows.[69] Protestants, on the other hand, have read into Bernard proto-Lutheran doctrines on the relation of the individual to God, on the role of Christ, on justification by faith, and on penance.[70]

It may be that there are parallels between Bernard and Luther on these points. It may also be, as Mousnier suggested, that an unconscious mental framework formed by Luther's religious personality, philosophical position, and intellectual background allowed him to absorb from Bernard only what his own sensibility and way of reasoning could assimilate.[71] Certainly after a period of almost four hundred years, neither Luther nor any of his contemporaries could enter fully into the thought-world of Bernard. The sympathy between them was based less on doctrines than on feelings, however: a common reliance on the heart, experience, and the Bible.[72] In spite of Luther's training as a nominalist and his dislike for late medieval speculative mysticism,[73] he shared the spiritual needs and preoccupations of the mystics, as Strohl pointed out, and he liked their piety.[74] Even if there was no direct connection between Bernard's sermon on the Annunciation and Luther's doctrine on justification, therefore, they express a similar spiritual attitude and are framed in similar biblical language; and Luther can be taken literally in his praise of Bernard's sincerity, faith in Christ, "most Christian bosom," and apostolic activity.

Luther also shared with Bernard, and with many twelfth-century spiritual leaders, a fierce zeal for reform based on man's inner will and freedom. His use of the famous motto that Christ was truth not custom,[75] which derived ultimately from St. Augustine, was paralleled in the eleventh and twelfth centuries by its use in the works of Gregory VII, Urban II, Ivo of Chartres, Gratian, and Hervé of Bourg-Dieu, who tried in his treatise *De correctione quorumdam lectionum,* on the model of the early Christians, to purge the liturgy of its corruptions and to return, as he said, to the "pure truth as it was promulgated from the beginning by the evangelists and prophets."[76] The form of the primitive church, especially as described in Acts 4.32–35, was repeatedly cited in the eleventh and twelfth centuries as the ideal Christian community and the model for the contemporary church.[77] This was again a favorite theme in the late Middle Ages, as Leff has emphasized in a recent article on "The Apostolic Ideal in Later Medieval Ecclesiology."[78] "Erasmus was fond of rebuking the superstition and intolerance of his own day by the example of the early church," said Bainton. "From him, probably Luther, and Melanchthon in a measure, and more especially Zwingli, learned this device for combating the church of Rome."[79]

Both ages likewise made use of direct criticism and satire in their battle for reform, and there is some evidence here of continuity in their efforts. Owst, for instance, cites a bitter censure of the clergy by Hugh of Fouilloy which was "familiar to generations of English preachers and sermon-audiences."[80] Satires against the vices of the curia, clerics, and monks became an established and influential literary genre in the twelfth century and were composed by many different types of writers.[81] This criticism formed "an important and complex chapter of medieval literature," according to Curtius, and was revived and used as a weapon against Rome by such reformers as John Bale in England and Luther's follower Matthias Flacius in Germany. "Many a text has escaped destruction," Curtius concluded, "for no other reason."[82]

In the twelfth century criticism was directed not only at monks as individuals but also, for almost the first time in the West since the fifth century, at monasticism as an institution. This was the result less of reforming zeal and satirical malice than of the spirituality of inwardness and will, which stressed the need for choice and decision rather than obedience and conformity and contributed to the emerging reassessment of the relative merits of a life spent in a monastery and a life spent in the world.[83] In the early Middle Ages, the superiority of monasticism over all other forms of life on earth was generally recognized, and contemplation and action were seen not (as they often are today) as two mutually exclusive types of life but as closely related parts of a single, monastic life: action was the ascetic battle against vice which both prepared the way for and provided relaxation from the ardors of contemplation. A "mixed" life with alternating periods of action and contemplation was the ideal of many twelfth-century spiritual writers. Whether the action took the form of ascetic exercises, manual labor, or, more rarely, pastoral and caritative work in the world, it was seen as part of the monastic life.

The validity of an active life spent primarily in the world was also discussed in the twelfth century, especially as part of the debate over the relative dignities of the secular and regular clergy. Many of the champions of action in this sense were found in the ranks of the regular canons. In the works of Arno of Reichersberg and Anselm of Havelberg, said Dereine, "We find for the first time in the history of Christian spirituality a developed theory in which a priority is reciprocally accorded to the two activities . . . and which prepared the way for the doctrine of a mixed life developed by Thomas Aquinas in the thirteenth century."[84] This was the beginning of the spirituality of action which asserted the superiority of clerical over monastic life. The cleric conquers the world by battle, said Gerhoh of Reichersberg, the monk by flight.[85] And the Premonstratensian Philip of Harvengt declared that, "To flee the world from the middle of Babylon and to be saved is as much safer as it is easier; but to be crowned victor in the middle of Babylon is as much grander as it is harder; so that monastic perfection, although commendable for merit, is considered as much lower as it is easier than clerical [perfection]."[86] Even Peter the Venerable, writing to dissuade his secretary from becoming a hermit, argued that he should be a hermit with his heart rather than his body. "The laurel of victory is given not to him who flees," Peter wrote, "but to him who remains, not to him who falls but to him who resists, not to him who submits but to him who conquers."[87]

This type of meritorious activity was still considered, in the twelfth century, to be within the framework of either a monastic or clerical life, but it pointed the way towards accepting the validity of a lay life of secular action. An indication of this direction, and of the declining prestige of monasticism, can be seen in the positive valuation put on marriage, the accepted hallmark of the lay order. The sanctity of a properly established marriage or betrothal was universally recognized in the twelfth century. Both partners were regarded as having rights and responsibilities which could not be unilaterly breached even for such worthy ends as entering a monastery, going on a crusade, or preserving virginity or chastity.[88] This appreciation of the human as well as the social values of married life was reflected in the marriage mysticism of Bernard and the Cistercians, who applied it to the life of the spirit rather than the body. The pure and unselfish love of a man for his wife was compared by Bernard to the love of God. "Love is a great thing," he wrote, "but there are grades in it. The bride is at the top."[89] Isaac of L'Étoile also praised the bond of piety and human agreement between man and wife.[90] An unusual example of this attitude, and of the appreciation of human tenderness in the twelfth century, can be seen on a Romanesque tomb from Belval, showing a wife embracing her pilgrim-husband, possibly on the occasion of his return from a crusade.[91]

A monument such as this was hardly noticed in the late Middle Ages, of course, and there is no evidence that the works of regular canons like Gerhoh of Reichersberg and Philip of Harvengt were widely read, but they reflected a shift in values which later became very significant. "In many religious movements of the high and late Middle Ages," wrote Hans Baron, "there was a pronounced shift to moralism and action. This can be seen in the successive development from the Benedictine to the Franciscan orders, and from the isolation and contemplation of the mystic to the more practical and active piety

encountered in the *Devotio Moderna.*"[92] Elsewhere Baron
studied this shift in the changing views of Cicero from "a
teacher of misogyny and flight from active life" to an exponent
of civic virtue and a combined life of action and contemplation.[93] Appreciation of lay life and its values, and opposition
to monasticism, were connected threads in the spiritual life of
the fifteenth century. Valla in his *Dialecticae disputationes*
rejected the distinction between the active and contemplative
lives and declared that contemplation is a type of action; and
in his *De professione religiosorum* he denied that the monastic
life was in any way intrinsically superior, or more highly rewarded in heaven, than other ways of life.[94] Émile Telle in
his book on Erasmus and marriage emphasized the importance
of anti-monasticism as "the primordial phenomenon of the
Pre-Reformation" and the connection between Erasmus's hostility to monasticism and his "matrimonial cult," in which
marriage was the foundation of a full humanist *philosophia
Christi.*[95]

A similar point of view was expressed by theologians in
terms which show more clearly their debt to the twelfth century. Gerson, for instance, owed to William of St. Thierry his
ideal of the "ambidextrous" prelate. "In declaring that the
prelate, as such, must be ambidextrous," wrote Combes, "the
preacher [Gerson] summoned up and made his own a famous
theme which, for him and doubtless all his contemporaries,
went back to St. Bernard and signified the optimum equilib-
rium between the two functions of a single charity: the contemplation of truth and the truth of active charity."[96] Against
those who defended the intrinsic superiority of monasticism,
Gerson asserted the thesis, as Oberman put it, that, "Perfection
is not an absolute static standard but is dynamically related
to the circumstances of a particular individual. . . . Biel
formulates this succinctly by stating that *every Christian in a
state of grace is in a state of perfection.* The contemplative
life may be the purer one; the active life is nevertheless more
intense and fruitful."[97] There was a lively debate in the fifteenth century on the respective merits of the two lives, and

even a monk like prior Bernard of Tegernsee argued in a treatise written in 1462 that contemplation, though theoretically superior, cannot and should not in practice be separated from action.[98]

The stress of the Protestant reformers on freely performed acts of love and their opposition to binding monastic vows were not without precedents, therefore, and drew on a strain of spirituality which emphasized inner attitudes rather than outer forms and which questioned the value of a life of total withdrawal from the world. Valla's hostility to monasticism in the *De professione religiosorum* was based on the view "that goodness springs from the free impulses of a will which is internally well-directed and not from outward obedience to obligations externally imposed."[99] Bernard himself held that self-denial was useless if it was imposed on an individual against his will,[100] and his famous description of himself as "a sort of modern chimaera, neither cleric nor layman" prefigured the ambidextrous ideal of the mixed life of action and contemplation.[101] Four centuries later the context was very different, and Luther's rejection of monasticism may in his own terms have been distinctive and original, as Lohse argued in his book on monasticism and the Reformation;[102] but it must also be seen in the light of a long tradition of reexamining the basic nature of Christian life and perfection.

In popular religious life this was paralleled by a new spirit in devotions and the liturgy which also went back to the eleventh and twelfth centuries.[103] This is well illustrated by the continued popularity of the prayers of St. Anselm, which marked on the one hand a reaction from the sober piety of the Carolingian age, as Southern said, and on the other "introduced a new note of personal passion, of elaboration and emotional extravagance, which anticipated some of the chief features of later medieval piety. . . . Anselm's prayers opened the way which led to the *Dies irae*, the *Imitatio Christi*, and the masterpieces of later medieval piety." "Opinions will differ about the desirability of this new point of departure," he continued later, "this new *via pietatis* sprinkled with many tears;

but that it is a main road through the religion of the later Middle Ages cannot be doubted."[104]

This was a road of the heart rather than the head. It stressed the emotions of love, tenderness, and sadness and showed itself in countless ways in the religious life of the fifteenth century. Of particular importance was the devotion to the humanity of Christ, which ran all the way from the theological and moral ideal of the imitation of Christ to the most humble manifestations of love for every aspect of His earthly life and body. "The theme of tenderness and compassion for the sufferings and helplessness of the Savior of the world was one which had a new birth in the monasteries of the eleventh century," wrote Southern, "and every century since then has paid tribute to the monastic inspiration of this century by some new development of the theme."[105] Christ's life was divided into stages for pious meditation each hour of the day;[106] and the practice of publicly adoring His body in the form of the consecrated elements started in the twelfth century with the liturgical ceremony of the elevation and was formally recognized by the institution of Corpus Christi day in 1264.[107] Popular interest in the Eucharist was also shown by the increasing number of recorded eucharistic miracles, of which the best-known example, illustrated by Raphael in the Vatican *stanze,* was the thirteenth-century miracle of Bolsena.[108] The number of references to the stigmata also grew in the twelfth and thirteenth centuries. St. Francis was the most celebrated, but probably not the first, example of this supreme sign of devotion to the sufferings of Christ. This was shown in more popular form by the devotions of the rosary[109] and the Sacred Heart, of which Schreiber has traced the origins to the Premonstratensian abbey of Steinfeld, where the first known hymn to the Sacred Heart was composed in the second half of the twelfth century.[110]

The attribution to Christ of feminine characteristics was another sign of this tender devotion. The prayers of Anselm, according to Cabassut, may have been the source of the devotion to "Our Mother Christ," which enjoyed considerable popularity in the late Middle Ages,[111] when all the feminine aspects of Christian piety were emphasized. The cult of the Virgin was paralleled by the cults of other female saints which either began or became prominent in the twelfth century. Saxer has shown that the cult of Mary Magdalen was at its height in the twelfth century, then declined, but revived in the fifteenth century, thus forming a graph of liturgical and devotional interest parallel to the graph of popularity of twelfth-century spiritual texts.[112] The devotions of St. Anne and of the Conception of the Virgin started in the twelfth century, according to Wilmart, who also attributed to Anselm and Bernard the new importance attached to the episode of Mary and John (the most feminine of the apostles) at the foot of the cross.[113] Bernard's personal devotion to Mary has often been exaggerated, and he was certainly not primarily a Mariologist;[114] but he played an important part in the later development of Mariology, right down to the eighteenth century; and the miracle of the lactation, though of relatively late origin, expresses a spiritual truth in associating Cistercian piety with the maternal and feminine emphasis of later spirituality.[115]

These manifestations of emotionalism and sensuousness may not appeal to the more restrained religious sentiments of modern Christianity. The passionate embraces given by Rupert of Deutz to an image of Christ and the desire of Hugh of Lincoln to gather and drink the sweat of our Lord seem downright unattractive today.[116] They were authentic touches of twelfth-century spirituality, however, and were the physical counterpart of the emotional yearning which culminated centuries later in the erotic fantasies of the late medieval mystics and the melting ecstacy of Bernini's St. Theresa. Even the processions of penitential flagellants, who expressed the characteristic flamboyance of late medieval piety, can be traced to Dominic Loricatus and the practice of voluntary flagellation in twelfth-century monasteries. It was recognized as a public penance in the thirteenth century, continued in the fourteenth century in spite of official disapproval, and flourished partic-

XV

ularly, in both orthodox and heretical circles, in the fifteenth century.[117]

Not all contemporaries approved of these elaborate displays, and efforts were made in the fourteenth and fifteenth centuries, as in the twelfth, to prune and purify the liturgy.[118] Ralph of Rivo, who was dean of Tongres from 1383 until 1403, has been called "the last representative of the old Roman liturgy;" he tried to draw a distinction between obligatory liturgical ceremonies and optional devotions.[119] Among other things, he revived the ancient theme of the Psalms as a biblical source-book on Christ.[120] More generally, the efforts to systematize the meditations on the life of Christ culminated for lay piety in the late medieval Books of Hours.[121]

The development of methodical meditation was one of the most important contributions of twelfth-century spirituality. Vernet called it "one of the great facts of the history of medieval spirituality"; and for Kirk "the discovery that worship need be none the worse and may be all the better for being orderly" was (together with the fact that "piety ceased to be the prerogative of the cloister") one of the "startling advances" of Christianity between the twelfth and sixteenth centuries.[122] The acme of this development was marked by the *Spiritual Exercises* of Ignatius Loyola,[123] and it is therefore fitting to conclude this paper with a consideration of the importance for Loyola of twelfth-century spirituality. Hugo Rahner said in his book, *The Spirituality of St. Ignatius Loyola,* that:

It is a well-known fact that the Spiritual Exercises have been subjected to research from every possible angle for the purpose of discovering real or pretended sources from which Inigo de Loyola is supposed to have drawn his teaching. . . . It has been supposed . . . that the chief source for the Ignatian streams of piety was to be found in the "modern devotion" (*devotio moderna*) of the fifteenth century. Successively, Cisneros, Erasmus of Rotterdam, Alonzo de Madrid, Gerard of Zütphen, John Maubernus [Mombaer], even Werner of Saint Blaise and Pseudo-Bernard, who flourished at the height of the Middle Ages, were rated as "indubitably" proven authorities for whole sections in the text of the Exercises. This course has led nowhere. What, in the end, was the upshot of all these laborious inquiries? Nothing but the simple fact that Inigo read only these three books: *The Life of Christ* of Ludolph of Saxony, *The Golden Legend,* and *The Imitation of Christ.*[124]

Even through these works alone, however, and through the religious atmosphere in which he was raised, Loyola owed a heavy debt to medieval spirituality, and in particular to the twelfth century.[125]

This is shown simply in the title of his most famous work: "Spiritual exercises to conquer oneself and to order one's life without coming to a decision through any affection which is disordered."[126] The history of the expression *spiritualia exercitia* has been studied by several scholars. In the sense of physical asceticism, it occurs frequently in religious literature as far back as the fifth century;[127] but it was first applied to prayer and meditation in the twelfth century. Alexandre Brou in his book on *Ignatian Methods of Prayer* cited the contributions of Bernard, Aelred, William of St. Thierry, Guigo II, and the Victorines, to whom can be added Anselm, Guigo I, Bernard of Portes, and Adam of Dryburg. "The beginnings of methodical prayer are to be found in these contemplatives of the twelfth century," said Brou. "They are not satisfied with saying 'make your prayer'; they have pointed out how we should set about it, and what acts it would be good to make."[128] Guigo I of La Chartreuse used "spiritual exercises" in the same sense as Loyola;[129] and in the *Scala claustralium* of Guigo II, which was widely read in the late Middle Ages, Brou found the essential elements of the methods of prayer of Louis of Granada, Loyola, and Francis of Sales.[130] William of St. Thierry not only referred five times in his *Golden Letter* to "spiritual exercises," of the mind as well as of the body, but also used the expression *vitam ordinare,* which has been considered by one scholar the possible source of Loyola's reference in his title to ordering one's life. "Learn within your cell . . ." wrote William, "to be master of yourself, to order your life, to compose your habits, to judge yourself, to accuse yourself to yourself, and often to condemn and punish [yourself]."[131] Whether or

Twelfth-Century Spirituality and the Late Middle Ages

not Loyola actually read this passage (which is very doubtful), he shared its view of the nature of the religious life.

A similar comparison can be made for the meditation on the two standards, where Loyola saw Christ and the Devil as two rival military leaders summoning men to their standards. This meditation has been called "the germ of the Society of Jesus,"[132] and its sources have been sought in both the Bible and the works of the Fathers.[133] Most scholars are now agreed that the specific form of the conflict as depicted by Loyola derived from the account of Christ as king of Jerusalem and the Devil as king of Babylon in the *Golden Legend*.[134] This account in turn was based on Augustine, but it was also influenced by the twelfth-century spirituality of action and struggle. Hugh of St. Victor wrote in the prologue to his *De sacramentis*, for instance, that:

The Incarnate Word is our King, who came into this world to war with the devil; and all the saints who were before His coming are soldiers, as it were, going before their King, and those who have come after and will come, even to the end of the world, are soldiers following their King. And the King Himself is in the midst of His army and proceeds protected and surrounded on all sides by His columns. And although in a multitude as vast as this the kind of arms differ in the sacraments and observance of the peoples preceding and following, yet all are really serving the one king and following the one banner; all are pursuing the one enemy and are being crowned by the one victory.[135]

The similarity of this conception to that of Loyola is striking, as is that of several later twelfth-century sources to which various scholars have drawn attention.[136] They all, as Wolter pointed out, reflect the spirituality of the Crusades, which developed in the twelfth century and influenced chivalric thought throughout the Middle Ages.[137]

There is no need to search either in this passage or in the other examples cited here for verbal similarities or direct influences of twelfth-century works on late medieval spirituality; the similarities lie on a deeper level of religious needs and attitudes. The point being made here is that in religious history, unlike intellectual history, the four centuries from the twelfth to the sixteenth must be seen as a whole and that the turning point in medieval religious history, as Wilmart and Chenu emphasized, falls in the late eleventh and twelfth centuries, when (in Wilmart's words) "the development of which the manifestations are clear in the fifteenth century began."[138] Though men's feelings about God and themselves continued to change in this period, they did not change out of recognition, and they never lost touch, direct or indirect, with the works of spirituality written in the twelfth century. Generation after generation of Christians found in these works a religious message adequate to their needs, a message the elements of which were later developed and elaborated but the essence of which remained unchanged.[139] A parallel development can be seen in the history of art, where the change of Christian vision in the twelfth century developed into the pathetic and extravagant realism of the late Middle Ages. The Isenheim alterpiece, however different at first sight, shows in its full bloom the emotional concentration on Christ's humanity and suffering of which the first signs appear in the art of the twelfth century.[140]

By isolating such individual themes, there is a danger of exaggerating the overall resemblances between the two ages. The religious writers and artists of the fifteenth and sixteenth centuries used traditional elements in new ways. They were concerned with different problems and reached different solutions than writers and artists in the twelfth century. But their religious needs and attitudes can be understood only in the context of a spirituality going back to the prescholastic period and cutting across the national distinctions and theological differences of the late Middle Ages. These feelings, in turn, help to explain the successes and failures of the religious movements of this confused age. They do not tell the whole story, but the story they tell is different from the usual account of the Reformation and Counter-Reformation and one of which the beginnings are deeply buried in the religious history of the Middle Ages.

Twelfth-Century Spirituality and the Late Middle Ages

Postscript

My lecture is printed here substantially as it was delivered in Chapel Hill, but I should like to amplify three points which were raised in subsequent discussion.

(1) Some listeners suggested that I gave too much credit for a humane view of marriage to the notorious misogynist Bernard of Clairvaux. Bernard certainly esteemed the life of a married layman far less highly than that of a celibate monk, and he used marriage metaphors to describe spiritual rather than physical relationships. His very use of such metaphors, however, implied that the human state of marriage was not entirely without a relative worth and dignity of its own. The dangers of dualism, furthermore, of which Bernard was aware from contemporary heresies, promoted a more positive view of human marriage. Hugh of Amiens, for instance, in his treatise against the heretics and in his commentary on the Hexaemeron, specifically praised the value, justice, and sanctity of marriage and stressed that Jesus Himself was born "not from a simple virgin but from a married woman": *Contra haereticos*, III, 4 (*Patrologia latina*, CXCII, 1289 AB) and F. Lecomte, "Un commentaire scripturaire du XIIe siècle: Le 'Tractatus in Hexaemeron' de Hugues d'Amiens (Archévêque de Rouen 1130–1164)," *Archives d'histoire doctrinale et littéraire du Moyen Age*, XXV (1958), 278. This valuation of marriage is not very high, but it suggests an important change of attitude even among monks like Bernard.

(2) Many twelfth-century spiritual works may have been known in the late Middle Ages through *florilegia* and collections of excerpts, which were extensively used in the composition of sermons and other literary genres. The number of manuscripts and early printed editions, however, suggests that many of these works were read in their entirety, and the inclusion of selected passages in *florilegia* shows in itself their appeal to late medieval religious sentiments.

(3) Of the more serious charge of neglecting the thirteenth century, I may be guilty, but cite as extenuating circum-

XV

stances that the importance of the thirteenth century has in the past, if anything, been overemphasized and that one of the purposes of my lecture was to argue that in the history of spirituality the thirteenth century was less important than the twelfth. This is not to deny that influential and widely read spiritual writers worked in the thirteenth century or that the scholastic theologians participated in the religious sentiments of their day. It is to suggest, rather, that their contribution to spirituality was less profound and original than in the areas of theology and philosophy. This is shown, for instance, by the number of spiritual works, both earlier and later, which went under the name of Bonaventura and by the fact that a figure such as Groote almost entirely neglected the thirteenth century (as I have done) and was influenced primarily by works written in the twelfth century: see R. R. Post, *The Modern Devotion Confrontation with Reformation and Humanism* (Studies in Medieval and Reformation Thought, 3; Leiden, 1968), pp. 317, which unfortunately came into my hands too late for use elsewhere in this paper.

NOTES

1. Lucien Febvre, "Une question mal posée: Les origines de la réforme française et le problème des causes de la réforme" (1929), reprinted in *Au coeur religieux du XVIe siècle* (Paris, 1957), pp. 3–70.

2. *Ibid.*, p. 26.

3. *Ibid.*, p. 69.

4. Cf. Alain Dufour, "Humanisme et Réformation: État de la question," in *Histoire politique et psychologie historique* (Geneva, 1966), pp. 42–43, who suggests that one result of the historical application of existentialism has been to isolate reformers from their historical context.

5. William James, *The Varieties of Religious Experience* (New York, 1902), p. 108.

6. *Ibid.*, p. 325.

7. Cf. *ibid.*, p. 109.

8. Iris Origo, *The World of San Bernardino* (New York, 1962), pp. 252–53.

9. Gerhart B. Ladner, "*Homo Viator*: Mediaeval Ideas on Alienation and Order," *Speculum*, XLII (1967), 255.

10. George Rosen, *Madness in Society* (Chicago, 1968), pp. 199 and 224, who also stressed (p. 7) that the witch hunts were complex phenomena involving political, social, psychological, and ideological factors.

11. Ladner, "*Homo Viator*," pp. 256–58.

12. Jean Gerson, *Oeuvres complètes*, ed. P. Glorieux (Paris, 1960–), III, 249; cf. *De mystica theologia*, ed. A. Combes (Thesaurus mundi, 9; Lugano, 1958), pp. 50–51, and André Combes, *La théologie mystique de Gerson: Profil de son évolution* (Spiritualitas, 1–2; Rome, 1963–64), II, 244.

13. Cited by Hanna Gray, "Valla's *Encomium of St. Thomas Aquinas* and the Humanist Conception of Christian Antiquity," *Essays in History and Literature Presented* . . . *to Stanley Pargellis* (Chicago, 1965), p. 48.

14. P. O. Kristeller, "Giovanni Pico della Mirandola and his Sources," *L'opera e il pensiero di Giovanni Pico della Mirandola nella storia dell'umanesimo* (Florence, 1965), I, 80.

15. P. O. Kristeller, *Renaissance Philosophy and the Mediaeval Tradition* (Wimmer Lecture, 15; Latrobe, 1966), p. 38.

16. Herbert Grundmann, "Neue Beiträge zur Geschichte der religiösen Bewegungen im Mittelalter" (1955), reprinted in *Religiöse Bewegungen im Mittelalter*, 2nd ed. (Hildesheim, 1961), pp. 531 and 537.

17. Cf. J. A. Jungmann, "Die Abwehr des germanischen Arianismus und der Umbruck der religiösen Kultur im frühen Mittelalter," *Zeitschrift für katholische Theologie*, LXIX (1947), 36–99.

18. André Wilmart, *Auteurs spirituels et textes dévots du moyen âge latin* (Paris, 1932), p. 59.

19. *Ibid.*, p. 63: cf. also pp. 505–6.

20. Richard Southern, *The Making of the Middle Ages* (New Haven, 1953), pp. 227, 228, 232; cf. M.-D. Chenu, *La théologie au douzième siècle* (Études de philosophie médiévale, 45; Paris, 1957), pp. 9, 223–24, 239; Robert Javelet, *Image et ressemblance au douzième siècle de saint Anselme à Alain de Lille* (Strasbourg, 1967), I, 455.

21. E. Ph. Goldschmidt, *Medieval Texts and their First Appearance in Print* (Supplement to the Bibliographical Society's Transactions, 16; London, 1943), p. 51.

22. Leopold Janauschek, *Bibliographia Bernardina* (Xenia Bernardina, 4; Vienna, 1891), pp. 3–133.

23. Henri Bremond, *Histoire littéraire du sentiment religieux en France* (Paris, 1915–32), III, 26.

24. Marcel Viller, "Le *Speculum monachorum* et la 'Dévotion moderne,'" *Revue d'ascétique et de mystique*, III (1922), 45–56; Wilmart, *Auteurs spirituels*, pp. 230–31; and other references in my article on "The Popularity of Twelfth Century Spiritual Writers in the Late Middle Ages," *Renaissance Studies in Honor of Hans Baron* (Florence, 1971), pp. 5–28.

25. Cf. Kristeller, *Renaissance Philosophy*, p. 11.

26. Augustin Renaudet, *Préréforme et humanisme à Paris pendant les premières guerres d'Italie (1494–1517)* (Bibliothèque de l'Institut français de Florence, I, 6; Paris, 1916), pp. 73, 113.

27. Combes, *Théologie mystique*, II, 53–54; cf. I, 63, 103; II, 566.

28. *Ibid.*, I, 159–60; II, 97, 140–43. Gerson was also indebted to Bernard for his doctrines of "industria," "defectio," and "reparatio' (I, 121; II, 124–36).

29. Roger Baron, "L'influence de Hugues de Saint-Victor," *Recherches de théologie ancienne et médiévale*, XXII (1955), 71.

30. *Deonise Hid Diuinite*, ed. Phyllis Hodgson (Early English Text Society, 231; London, 1955), p. xxxv.

31. Robert Javelet, "Thomas Gallus et Richard de Saint-Victor mystiques," *Recherches de théologie ancienne et médiévale*, XXIX (1962), 206.

32. Edmond Vansteenberghe, *Le cardinal Nicolas de Cues (1401–1464): L'action—la pensée* (Lille, 1920), pp. 42, 423–24, 431; Raymond Klibansky, *The Continuity of the Platonic Tradition* (London [1950]), pp. 28, 35–36.

33. Gray, "Valla's *Encomium* of St. Thomas Aquinas," p. 43.

34. Kristeller, *Renaissance Philosophy*, pp. 37–38; Gray, "Valla's *Encomium* of St. Thomas Aquinas," p. 43.

35. Theodor Mommsen, "Petrarch's Conception of the 'Dark Ages'" (1942), reprinted in *Medieval and Renaissance Studies*, ed. Eugene Rice (Ithaca, 1959), p. 129.

36. Pierre de Nolhac, *Pétrarche et l'humanisme* (Bibliothèque littéraire de la Renaissance, N.S. 1–2; Paris, 1907), I, 104, 113; II, 207–8, 216–25.

37. P. O. Kristeller, "Augustine and the Early Renaissance," *Review of Religion*, IX (1944), 346; cf. also his *Renaissance Thought* (New York, 1961), p. 78.

38. Cf. Eleanor Rathbone, "Master Alberic of London, *Mythographus tertius vaticanus*," *Medieval and Renaissance Studies*, I.1 (1941), 35–38; and Elisabeth Pellegrin, "Un manuscrit des 'Derivationes' d'Osbern de Gloucester annoté par Pétrarche," *Italia medioevale e umanistica*, III (1960), 263–66.

39. P. O. Kristeller, "Pier Candido Decembrio and his Unpublished Treatise on the Immortality of the Soul," *The Classical Tradition: Literary and Historical Studies in Honor of Harry Caplan* (Ithaca, 1966), pp. 536–58.

40. Eugene Rice, "The Humanist Idea of Christian Antiquity: Lefèvre d'Étaples and his Circle," *Studies in the Renaissance*, IX (1962), 141.

41. See the lists in Renaudet, *Préréforme;* and Goldschmidt, *Medieval Texts.* The first edition of Peter the Venerable was published at Paris in 1522.

42. Renaudet, *Préréforme*, p. 521 (cf. pp. 495, 597, 599–600, 601–2, 623, 625–26, 635–37), and Goldschmidt, *Medieval Texts*, pp. 52–57.

43. F. 22v or the 1508 Paris edition of Bernard's works; cf. Renaudet, *Préréforme*, p. 500; Goldschmidt, *Medieval Texts*, p. 124; and (on Clichtove's edition of Hugh of St. Victor) Roger Baron, *Science et sagesse chez Hugues de Saint-Victor* (Paris, 1957), p. 234.

44. On the material in this paragraph, see Odon Lottin, *Psychologie et*

Twelfth-Century Spirituality and the Late Middle Ages

morale aux XIIe et XIIIe siècles (Louvain-Gembloux, 1942–1960), II, 421–65, and IV, 309–486.

45. Cf. Bernard, De gratia et libero arbitrio, II, 4 (ed. Jean Leclercq [Rome, 1957–] III, 168–69); and John of Salisbury, Policraticus, VII, 25 (ed. C. C. J. Webb [Oxford, 1909], II, 217).

46. Lottin, Psychologie, I, 222; cf. Roger Baron, "L'idée de liberté chez S. Anselme et Hugues de Saint-Victor," Recherches de théologie ancienne et médiévale, XXXII (1965), 117–21.

47. Cf. M.–A. Dimier, "Pour la fiche Spiritus libertatis," Revue du moyen âge latin, III (1947), 56–60; Herbert Grundmann, "Freiheit als religiöses, politisches und persönliches Postulat im Mittelalter," Historische Zeitschrift, CLXXXIII (1957), 23–53, esp. 45–47; and (on the late Middle Ages) Romana Guarnieri, in Dictionnaire de spiritualité, V (Paris, 1962–64), 1241–68.

48. Adam of Perseigne, Lettres, ed. Jean Bouvet, I (Sources chrétiennes, 66; Paris, 1960), p. 122. Bernard's triple distinction of liberty comes in De gratia et libero arbitrio, III, 7 (ed. Leclercq, III, 171).

49. Southern, Making of the Middle Ages, p. 227.

50. Ermenegildo Bertola, "Il socratismo cristiano nel XII secolo," Rivista di filosofia neo-scolastica, LI (1959), 262–64; Javelet, Image, I, 205–6, 368–71.

51. Javelet, Image, I, 181–82, 197, 247.

52. Richard of St. Victor, Benjamin major, III, 13 (Patrologia latina, CXCVI, 123 A). The precision and elegance of the Latin is lost in the translation. Cf. the view of Bernard in his sermon De diversis, 12, 2 (Gaume ed. [Paris, 1839], I.2, 2339 A).

53. Cf. Javelet, Image, I, 297, 454–57.

54. On this saying, which is found in various forms in a number of twelfth-century texts, see the references in The Letters of Peter the Venerable, ed. Giles Constable (Harvard Historical Studies, 78; Cambridge, Mass., 1967), I, 60, n. 2.

55. James, Varieties of Religious Experience, pp. 80, 361.

56. Caesarius of Heisterbach, Dialogus miraculorum, X, 6 (ed. J. Strange [Cologne, 1851] II, 221–22). This is the earliest example of such an attitude cited by Oechslin in his article on "Dépouillement" in the Dictionnaire de spiritualité, III (Paris, 1954–57), 472.

57. Jean Gerson, Opera omnia (Antwerp, 1706), III, 1125.

58. Cf. the confessions of the mid-fourteenth century heretic John of Brünn, in W. Wattenbach, "Über die Secte der Brüder vom freien Geiste," Sitzungsberichte der königlich preussichen Akademie der Wissenschaften zu Berlin, 1887 (No. 29), pp. 529–31.

59. Bernard, Sermon In Annunc., I, 1–3 (Gaume ed., I.2, 2093–95).

60. Patrologia latina, CLXXXIV, 554 AB; cf. Javelet, Image, II, 99: "Son texte comme ceux d'Isaac est à considérer dans une étude des lointains préliminaires de la théorie de Luther sur la prédestination et la justification." On this treatise, which closely follows Bernard's ideas, and on two other similar treatises, see P. Delhaye, "Dans le sillage de S. Bernard: Trois petits traités De conscientia," Cîteaux in de Nederlanden, V (1954), 92–103.

61. Bernard, Sermon In Annunc. I, 4 (Gaume ed., I.2 2095 B).

62. James, Varieties of Religious Experience, pp. 109–10 and 246–48.

63. Cf. Carl Stange, Bernhard von Clairvaux (Studien der Luther-Akademie, N.F. 3; Berlin, 1954), p. 5.

64. Cf. Heinrich Boehmer, Luther and the Reformation in the Light of Modern Research, tr. E. S. G. Potter (New York, 1930), p. 70; Ernst Benz, "Luther und Bernhard von Clairvaux," Eckart, XXIII (1953), 62; and Roland

Mousnier, "Saint Bernard et Luther," *Saint Bernard: Homme d'Église* (Témoignages: Cahiers de La Pierre-qui-Vire, 38–39; Paris, 1953), p. 152.

65. Stange, *Bernhard*, p. 8.

66. Weimar ed., *Tischreden*, IV, 480, No. 4772.

67. *Ibid.*, LVIII.1, 178–80, citing Luther's references to Bernard.

68. *Ibid.*, VIII, 601.

69. Heinrich Denifle, *Luther und Luthertum in der ersten Entwickelung*, 2nd ed. (Mainz, 1904–9), I, 40–49 (showing that the passage was not a deathbed confession but taken from the sermon *Super Cantica*, 20, 1 [ed. Leclercq, I, 114]), whose views are repeated by Hartmann Grisar, *Luther*, tr. E. M. Lamond, ed. Luigi Cappadelta (London, 1913–17), I, 18, 88, 181, and IV, 88–89.

70. Cf. Boehmer, *Luther*, pp. 70–71; Stange, *Bernhard*, p. 5; Mousnier, "Saint Bernard et Luther," pp. 155–56, who also discussed (pp. 159–65) some of the differences between the theologies of Bernard and Luther. C. C. J. Webb, *Studies in the History of Natural Philosophy* (Oxford, 1915), p. 231, suggested that Luther's dislike of reason and rationalism was the reason for his liking Bernard.

71. Mousnier, "Saint Bernard et Luther," pp. 165–69.

72. Cf. Benz, "Luther und Bernhard," pp. 61-62.

73. Henri Strohl, *L'épanouissement de la pensée religieuse de Luther de 1515 à 1520* (Études d'histoire et de philosophie religieuses publiées par la Faculté de théologie protestante de l'Université de Strasbourg, 9; Strasbourg-Paris, 1924), pp. 113–44; cf. Benz, "Luther und Bernhard," p. 64, and Mousnier, "Saint Bernard et Luther," p. 166. Lewis Spitz, "Current Accents in Luther Study: 1960–67," *Theological Studies*, XXVIII (1967), 554, comments on the lack of recent work on Luther's relation to mysticism and his knowledge of pre-scholastic writers.

74. Strohl, *Épanouissement*, p. 143.

75. Weimar, ed., VII, 632, and XXIII, 415.

76. G. Morin, "Un critique en liturgie au XIIe siècle: Le traité inédit d'Hervé de Bourgdieu *De correctione quorumdam lectionum*," *Revue bénédictine*, XXIV (1907), 43; cf. Klaus Schreiner, "Zum Wahrheitsverständnis im Heiligen- und Reliquienwesen des Mittelalters," *Saeculum*, XVII (1966), 143, n. 61; and G. Ladner, in *Reallexikon für Antike und Christentum*, VI (Stuttgart, 1964–66), 265–66.

77. Giovanni Miccoli, "*Ecclesiae primitivae forma*" (1960), reprinted and expanded in *Chiesa gregoriana* (Storici antichi e moderni, N.S. 17; Florence, 1966), pp. 225–99, esp. 225–26.

78. Gordon Leff, "The Apostolic Ideal in Later Medieval Ecclesiology," *Journal of Theological Studies*, N.S., XVIII (1967), 58–82. Leff exaggerated somewhat in calling the ideal of the apostolic church "the great new ecclesiological fact of the later Middle Ages" (p. 71).

79. Roland Bainton, "Changing Ideas and Ideals in the Sixteenth Century" (1936), reprinted in his *Collected Papers in Church History*, I: *Early and Medieval Christianity* (Boston, 1962), p. 166.

80. G. R. Owst, *Literature and Pulpit in Medieval England*, 2nd ed. (Oxford-New York, 1961), p. 278.

81. John A. Junck, "Economic Conservatism, Papal Finance, and the Medieval Satires on Rome" (1961), reprinted in *Change in Medieval Society*, ed. Sylvia Thrupp (New York, 1964), p. 76.

82. E. R. Curtius, *European Literature and the Latin Middle Ages*, tr. W. R. Trask (New York, 1963), p. 124.

Twelfth-Century Spirituality and the Late Middle Ages

83. Cf. Robert Javelet, "Psychologie des auteurs spirituels du XIIe siècle," *Revue des sciences religieuses*, XXXIII (1959), 38.

84. *Dictionnaire d'histoire et de géographie ecclésiastiques*, XII (Paris, 1953), 394. On Aquinas, see Jean Leclercq, "La vie contemplative dans S. Thomas et dans la tradition," *Recherches de théologie ancienne et médiévale*, XXVIII (1961), 251–68.

85. Gerhoh of Reichersberg, *Opusculum de aedificio Dei*, c. 28 (*Patrologia latina*, CXCIV, 1267 C).

86. Philip of Harvengt, *De institutione clericorum*, IV, 99 (*Patrologia latina*, CCIII, 802 AB).

87. *Peter the Venerable*, Ep. 58 (ed. Constable, I, 187–88).

88. Cf. Ivo of Chartres, Ep. 245 (*Patrologia latina*, CLXII, 251–52). On marriage doctrine in the twelfth century, see Gabriel Le Bras, "Le mariage dans la théologie et le droit de l'Église du XIe au XIIIe siècle," *Cahiers de civilization médiévale*, XI (1968) 191–202; and the two articles by James Brundage, "The Crusader's Wife: A Canonistic Quandary" and "The Crusader's Wife Revisited" in *Studia Gratiana*, XII (1967), 425–42 and XIV (1967), 241–52. On the equality of men and women in twelfth-century theology, see Javelet, *Image*, I, 236–45.

89. Sermon 83 *Super Cantica*, II, 5 (ed. Leclercq, II, 301).

90. Isaac of L'Étoile, Sermon XL (*Patrologia latina*, CXCIV, 1824 B).

91. Yvonne Labande-Mailfert, "L'iconographie des laïcs dans la société religieuse aux XIe et XIIe siècles," *I laici nella "Societas christiana" dei secoli XI e XII* (Pubblicazioni dell'Università cattolica del Sacro Cuore: Contributi, 3rd S.: Miscellanea del Centro di Studi medioevali, 5; Milan, 1968), p. 513 and pl. IX, fig. 26, who remarks that, "C'est une oeuvre unique dans l'art roman pour l'expression de l'amour conjugal."

92. Hans Baron, "Secularization of Wisdom and Political Humanism in the Renaissance: Rice's *Renaissance Idea of Wisdom*," *Journal of the History of Ideas*, XXI (1960), 137.

93. Hans Baron, "Cicero and the Roman Civic Spirit in the Middle Ages and the Early Renaissance" (1938), reprinted and revised in *Lordship and Community in Medieval Europe*, ed. Fredric Cheyette (New York, 1968), pp. 291–314, who shows that the beginnings of the change are found in Italy in the twelfth century.

94. *Dialecticae disputationes*, I, 8 (*Opera omnia* [Basel, 1540, reprinted Turin, 1962] I, 660); and *De professione religiosorum* (ed. M. J. Vahlen, reprinted *ibid.*, II, 287–325); cf. Gray, "Valla's *Encomium of St. Thomas Aquinas*," p. 50.

95. Émile Telle, *Érasme de Rotterdam et le septième sacrement* (Geneva, 1954), p. 6.

96. Combes, *Théologie mystique*, I, 382, cf. I, 159–60.

97. Heiko Oberman, "Gabriel Biel and Late Medieval Mysticism," *Church History*, XXX (1961), 269.

98. Paul Wilpert, "Vita Contemplativa und Vita Activa: Eine Kontroverse des 15. Jahrhunderts," *Passauer Studien: Festschrift für Bischof Dr. Dr. Simon Konrad Landersdorfer* (Passau, 1953), p. 226.

99. Gray, "Valla's *Encomium of St. Thomas Aquinas*," p. 50.

100. Cf. Bernard, *De gratia et libero arbitrio*, II, 4 (ed. Leclercq, III, 168–69); *Sermo in feria IV hebdomadae sanctae*, 12 (Gaume ed., I.3, 1945–46); *Sermo in festo omnium sanctorum*, I, 8 (*ibid.*, 2190); etc.

101. Bernard, Ep. 250.4 (Gaume ed., I.1, 525 A).

102. Bernhard Lohse, *Mönchtum und Reformation: Luthers Auseinander-*

setzung mit dem Mönchsideal des Mittelalters (Göttingen, 1963), pp. 201-379, esp. 377-79.

103. Cf. Georg Schreiber, "Monasterium und Frömmigkeit," *Zeitschrift für Aszese und Mystik*, XVI (1941), 19-31 (of which I have seen only the analysis in the *Revue d'histoire ecclésiastique*, XXXVIII [1942] 230), who stressed the influence of twelfth-century monastic spirituality on later devotions.

104. R. W. Southern, *Saint Anselm and his Biographer* (Birkbeck Lectures, 1959; Cambridge, 1963), pp. 47 and 350, cf. pp. 37-38 on the continued popularity of Anselm's prayers; and Wilmart, *Auteurs spirituels*, pp. 506-7.

105. Southern, *Making of the Middle Ages*, p. 232.

106. Josef Stadlhuber, "Das Laienstundengebet vom Leiden Christi in seinem mittelalterlichen Fortleben," *Zeitschrift für katholische Theologie*, LXXII (1950), 289-91.

107. F. Baix and C. Lambot, *La dévotion à l'Eucharistie et le VIIe centenaire de la Fête-Dieu* (Gembloux-Namur [1946]) pp. 22-26; cf. Edouard Dumoutet, *Le Christ selon la Chair et la vie liturgique au Moyen-Âge* (Paris, 1932), p. 147; Georg Schreiber, "Mittelalterliche Passionsmystik und Frömmigkeit: Der älteste Herz-Jesu-Hymnus," *Theologische Quartalschrift*, CXXII (1941), 41; and Gerhard Matern, *Zur Vorgeschichte und Geschichte der Fronleichnamsfeier besonders in Spanien* (Spanische Forschungen der Görresgesellschaft, II, 10; Münster, 1962), pp. 10-11.

108. Cf. Matern, *Fronleichnamsfeier*, pp. 17-33.

109. Wilmart, *Auteurs spirituels*, p. 583; cf. Stadlhuber, "Das Laienstundengebet," p. 309, on twelfth-century prayers to the Holy Wounds.

110. Georg Schreiber, "Prämonstratensische Frömmigkeit und die Anfänge des Herz-Jesu-Gedankens," *Zeitschrift für katholische Theologie*, LXIV (1940), 195-201, and his "Mittelalterliche Passionsmystik," pp. 32-44.

111. André Cabassut, "Une dévotion médiévale peu connue: La dévotion à *Jésus notre mère*," *Revue d'ascétique et de mystique*, XXV.2-4 (*Mélanges Marcel Viller*) (Toulouse, 1949), pp. 234-45.

112. Victor Saxer, *Le culte de Marie Madeleine en occident des origines à la fin du moyen âge* (Cahiers d'archéologie et d'histoire, 3; Auxerre-Paris, 1959), p. 355.

113. Wilmart, *Auteurs spirituels*, pp. 46-49 and 507.

114. H. Barré, "Saint Bernard, Docteur Marial," *Saint Bernard théologien* (Analecta sacri ordinis Cisterciensis, IX.3-4; Rome, 1953), pp. 92-113.

115. See several articles on Bernard's influence on Spanish Mariology in *Estudios marianos*, XIV (1954); and on the legend of the lactation, Léon Dewez and Albert van Iterson, "La lactation de saint Bernard: Legende et iconographie," *Cîteaux in de Nederlanden*, VII (1956), 165-89.

116. Rupert of Deutz, *Commentarium in Matthaeum*, 12 (*Patrologia latina*, CLXVIII, 1590); *Magna vita sancti Hugonis*, ed. Decima Douie and Hugh Farmer (Medieval Texts; Edinburgh, 1961-62), II, 14-15.

117. Cf. Paul Bailly, in *Dictionnaire de spiritualité*, V, 392-400.

118. Cf. Paul Lejay, "Les accroissements de l'office quotidien," *Revue du clergé français*, XL (1904), 139-40.

119. Cunibert Mohlberg, *Radulph de Rivo: Der letzte Vertreter der altrömischen Liturgie* (Université de Louvain: Recueil de travaux publiés par les membres des conférences d'histoire et de philologie, 29, 42; Louvain-Paris-Münster, 1911-15), *passim* (for twelfth-century writers used by Ralph, see index s.n. Arnulf of Bohéries, Bernard, Honorius, Hugh, Rupert) and Lejay, "Les accroissements," pp. 139-40.

120. Balthasar Fischer, "Le Christ dans les psaumes," *La Maison-Dieu*,

[58]

Twelfth-Century Spirituality and the Late Middle Ages

XXVII (1951), 108, n. 84, and Pierre Salmon, Les "Tituli psalmorum" des manuscrits latins (Paris, 1959), p. 35.

121. Stadlhuber, "Das Laienstundengebet," pp. 282–91.

122. Félix Vernet, La spiritualité médiévale (Bibliothèque catholique des sciences religieuses, 33; Paris, 1929), p. 125; Kenneth E. Kirk, The Vision of God: The Christian Doctrine of the Summum Bonum, 2nd ed. (Bampton Lectures, 1928; London, 1932), p. 412; cf. M. Bulteel, "Bijdrage tot de Studie van het Beschouwend Gebed in de Twaalfde Eewe" (unpublished thesis, Louvain, 1952), cited by Maurice Laporte, Aux sources de la vie cartusienne (La Chartreuse, 1960), II, 526, saying that Bulteel stresses "l'importance du 12ème siècle dans la naissance de la méditation comme exercise."

123. Cf. Kirk, Vision, p. 401 ("He [Ignatius] is in the true line of succession from S. Paul, S. Bernard and S. Francis."); David Knowles, From Pachomius to Ignatius: A Study in the Constitutional History of the Religious Orders (Sarum Lectures, 1964–65; Oxford, 1966), pp. 88–94.

124. Hugo Rahner, The Spirituality of St. Ignatius Loyola, tr. Francis Smith (Westminster, Md., 1953), pp. 23–24; cf. Léonce de Grandmaison, "Les Exercises de Saint Ignace dans l'édition des Monumenta," Recherches de science religieuse, X (1920), 396; Joseph de Guibert, The Jesuits: Their Spiritual Doctrine and Practice, tr. William Young, ed. George Ganss (Chicago, 1964), pp. 153–57; and, for a bibliography on the subject of the sources of the Exercises, Jean-François Gilmont and Paul Daman, Bibliographie Ignatienne (1894–1957) (Museum Lessianum: Section historique, 17; Paris-Louvain [1958]), Nos. 1198–1224.

125. On Ludolph's Life of Christ, see François Vandenbroucke, in Jean Leclercq, François Vandenbroucke, and Louis Bouyer, La spiritualité du moyen âge (Paris, 1961), p. 547 (calling Ludolph "assez peu original"). The debt of The Imitation of Christ to twelfth-century writers, especially Bernard, Hugh, and Richard, is generally acknowledged: cf. E. F. Jacob, Essays in the Conciliar Epoch, 2nd ed. (Manchester, 1953), pp. 139–53.

126. De Guibert, Jesuits, p. 111.

127. See L. Hertling, "De usu nominis exercitiorum spiritualium ante S. P. Ignatium," Archivum historicum Societatis Iesu, II (1933), 316–18; and Heinrich Bacht, "Die frühmonastischen Grundlagen ignatianischer Frömmigkeit: Zu einigen Grundbegriffen der Exerzitien," Ignatius von Loyola, ed. Friedrich Wulf (Würzburg, 1956), p. 231.

128. Alexandre Brou, Ignatian Methods of Prayer, tr. William Young (Milwaukee, 1949), p. 6; cf. Marcel Viller's review of the second volume of Pourrat's Spiritualité chrétienne in the Revue d'ascétique et de mystique, III (1922), 78–79; and Laporte, Sources, II, 525–27, and VI, 541–43; and Pedro de Leturia, "Lecturas ascéticas y lecturas místicas entre los Jesuítas del siglo XVI," Archivio italiano per la storia della pietà, II (1959), 3–4.

129. A. de Meyer and J. M. de Smet, Guigo's "Consuetudines" van de eerste Kartuizers (Mededelingen van de koninklijke vlaamse Academie voor Wetenschappen, Letteren en schone Kunsten van België: Klasse der Letteren, XIII.6; Brussels, 1951), p. 53, n. 1; Laporte, Sources, II, 525–27 (cf. also VI, 541–43).

130. Brou, Ignatian Prayer, pp. 5–6.

131. H. Pinard de la Boullaye, "Aux sources des Exercises: Guillaume de Saint-Thierry et Vincent Ferrer," Revue d'ascétique et de mystique, XXVI (1950), 327–46. Vincent Ferrer certainly used the Golden Letter, but Pinard de la Boullaye considers it more likely that Loyola used it directly rather than through Ferrer.

132. C. A. Kneller, "Zu den Kontroversen über den hl. Ignatius von Loyola,

II: Quellen der Exerzitien?" *Zeitschrift für katholische Theologie*, XLIX (1925), 164. The importance of this meditation was repeatedly emphasized by Rahner, *Spirituality*, pp. xii, 22, 36, 56, 105, but De Guibert, *Jesuits*, pp. 172–74, tried to play down the military character of Ignatian spirituality; cf. also Hans Wolter, "Elemente der Kreuzzugsfrömmigkeit in der Spiritualität des heiligen Ignatius," *Ignatius von Loyola*, ed. Friedrich Wulf (Würzburg, 1956), pp. 113–50.

133. Cf. Ferdinand Tournier, "Les *deux cités* dans la littérature chrétienne," *Études*, CXXIII (1910), 644–65; Kneller, "Zu den Kontroversen," p. 113; and Bacht, "Die frühmonastischen," in *Ignatius*, pp. 249–50, who calls the first part of Evagrius's *De diversis malignis cogitationibus* a commentary on the meditation on the two standards. For further references, see Gilmont and Daman, *Bibliographie*, Nos. 1635–50.

134. This was first suggested, I believe, by Kneller, "Zu den Kontroversen," p. 164, and was accepted by Rahner, *Spirituality*, p. 28, and others.

135. Hugh of St. Victor, *De sacramentis*, tr. Roy J. Deferrari (Mediaeval Academy of America Publication 58; Cambridge, 1951), pp. 2–3; cf. Javelet, *Image*, I, 334 and 457, who considered this passage a prefiguration of Ignatius's meditation. On the possible influence of Hugh's mysticism on Loyola, see Baron "Influence de Hugues," p. 69.

136. See Tournier, "Les *deux cités*," pp. 648–53 and 658–62, where the texts of Augustine, Werner of St. Blaise, and Ignatius are cited in parallel columns. Though most scholars have not accepted Tournier's conclusions, De Guibert, *Jesuits*, p. 118, admitted that the resemblances between Werner and Loyola "are such that it is difficult to take them as a matter of chance and to refuse to admit some dependence in the present text of the *Exercises*."

137. Wolter, "Elemente der Kreuzzugsfrömmigkeit," pp. 113–50, who mentions among other parallel themes the emphasis on the will of God, on Christ, *imitatio*, *vita apostolica*, the kingdom of Christ, *militia Christi*, forgiveness, consciousness of community, service, hospitality, poverty, and *gloria Dei*.

138. Wilmart, *Auteurs spirituels*, p. 506; and Chenu, *Théologie*, pp. 223–24 and 239. Gilson in his introduction to Chenu (p. 9) stated his view that the *devotio moderna* continued a current of spirituality going back to the twelfth century.

139. Jesuit novices in the sixteenth century were encouraged to read twelfth-century works but forbidden to read indiscriminately the works of late medieval mystical writers: see De Guibert, *Jesuits*, p. 218; and De Leturia, "Lecturas ascéticas," pp. 47–48. Among recommended works was Peter the Venerable's *De miraculis*, of which the G. G. Coulton (commenting on the edition printed at Douai in 1595) said, "We have here, therefore, a book which both twelfth-century and sixteenth-century monasticism recognized as typical and authoritative": *Life in the middle Ages* (Cambridge, 1935), IV, 110.

140. Louis Réau, *L'iconographie de l'art chrétien* (Paris, 1955–), II, 476–511; and Paul Thoby, *Le crucifix des origines au Concile de Trente* ([Nantes], 1959), *passim*. More generally, see Étienne Sabbe, "Le culte marial et la genèse de la sculpture médiévale," *Revue belge d'archéologie et d'histoire de l'art*, XX (1951), 101–25; and Southern, *Making of the Middle Ages*, pp. 237–40.

XVI

THE POPULARITY
OF TWELFTH-CENTURY SPIRITUAL WRITERS
IN THE LATE MIDDLE AGES

The life of the mind and the life of the spirit seem at certain times in history to go their own ways and to draw on different sources; and in the fourteenth and fifteenth centuries, when men were finding new ideas and mental attitudes in the works of classical antiquity, their religious sentiments remained true to medieval themes and were nourished by traditional works of spirituality, especially those written in the twelfth century. The writings of Anselm, Bernard, Hugh and Richard of St Victor, and of less well-known Cistercian and Victorine authors (many of whose works circulated under the names of Augustine, Bernard, and Hugh) were widely read in the late Middle Ages and may in the long run have exercised an even greater influence than the didactic writings of Peter Lombard, Gratian, and Peter Comestor. These spiritual texts formed a distinct literary genre in the twelfth century, of which the importance has been stressed by several recent scholars [1]; but their later popularity and influence has been relatively little studied. The purpose of this article is to indicate some of the ways of investigating this question. In particular, it will deal with bibliographical evidence and with individual writers whose works either exercised influence or show the influence of twelfth-century spirituality. I shall deal in another article with some of the distinctive spiritual themes and devotional attitudes which developed in the late eleventh and twelfth centuries and which shaped the religious sentiments of the late Middle Ages [2].

---

[1] See especially the many works of Jean Leclercq. On the distinction of spirituality from exegesis and theology in the twelfth century, see Henri de Lubac, *Exégèse médiévale* (Théologie, 41-2, 59; Paris, 1959-64) II . 1, 423-29 and II . 2, 487-88, who also comments (II . 1, 379) on the great success and influence of twelfth-century didactic works.

[2] Delivered as a lecture at the Southeastern Institute of Medieval and Renaissance Studies in 1969 and to be published in volume V of its *Medieval and Renaissance Studies*.

I.

The clearest indication of the popularity of twelfth-century spiritual writers in the late Middle Ages is the number of manuscripts copied at that time, especially in the fifteenth century. The figures in the appendix are taken from available recent editions containing lists of dated manuscripts. Although the works are arbitrarily chosen, and the lists of manuscripts probably incomplete and inaccurate [3], there are an impressive number of fifteenth-century copies of various characteristic texts. Dom Wilmart remarked, for instance, that the *Jubilus* attributed to St Bernard had its greatest success in the fifteenth century [4] and that there seems to have been a revival of interest at the same time in the *Scala claustralium* of Guigo II of La Chartreuse. He could find no obvious reason for this revival. « What happened in the fifteenth century to bring about this change? » he asked. « Was the interest in spiritual things found in certain young and fervent circles sufficient to make the advice of a wise ascetic appreciated and fashionable? Perhaps. I have found nothing to give an adequate reply » [5]. The same question might be asked about the long and tedious commentary on the Benedictine Rule which was written by Stephen of Paris in 1191/4 but which survives only in late medieval manuscripts, mostly from southern Germany [6]. The answer appears to be that given by Bernards with regard to the manuscript figures of the *Speculum virginum*, which he compared with those of John *Homo Dei's De ordine vitae*: « It is thus again established that the piety

---

[3] In evaluating the figures, the greater chance of late copies surviving must be taken into consideration. Manuscripts dated to more than one century have been listed in the appendix under the later century.

[4] André Wilmart, *Le « Jubilus » dit de saint Bernard* (Rome, 1944) p. 51.

[5] André Wilmart, *Auteurs spirituels et textes dévots du moyen âge latin* (Paris, 1932) p. 231.

[6] Clm 3029 (Andechs, dated 1466), 4308 (St Ulrich, Augsburg, dated 1495), and 18155 (Tegernsee, dated 1472), Melk 285 (XIV/XV), Bamberg 151 (Ed. II. 4) (XV), and Epinal 12 (St Peter, Sens, XV). This information was kindly supplied by Dr Caroline Bynum.

of the fifteenth century attached itself in its devotional literature to the writings of the twelfth century » [7].

Such figures are hard to establish for long and very popular works, for which the lists of manuscripts are either old or incomplete. Although editors now mostly agree that *recentiores* are not necessarily *deteriores* from a textual point of view, it is still sometimes forgotten that even *deteriores* are a valuable indication of the popularity of a text and of the forms in which it was read. The available figures for one popular text, the *De miseria humanae conditionis* by Innocent III, of which over five hundred manuscripts are known, show that four-ninths of the dated copies are of the fifteenth century [8]. Of the works of Anselm, Bernard, and Hugh and Richard of St Victor there are literally thousands of manuscripts [9]. Leclercq inspected almost fifteen hundred manuscripts of Bernard's works, of which about forty-two percent were twelfth century, twenty-nine percent thirteenth, twelve percent fourteenth, and seventeen percent fifteenth and later [10]. Of the uninspected manuscripts, most were late and unimportant, but even these figures suggest that there was a rise of interest in Bernard's works in the fifteenth century.

This impression of the continued and growing popularity of twelfth-century texts in the late Middle Ages is confirmed

---

[7] Matthäus Bernards, *Speculum virginum* (Forschungen zur Volkskunde, 36-8; Cologne-Graz, 1955) p. 10.

[8] Innocent III, *De miseria humane conditionis*, ed. Michele Maccarrone (Thesaurus mundi; Lugano, 1955) pp. x-xx; Michele Maccarrone and Keith V. Sinclair, « New Manuscripts of Lotario's Treatise 'De miseria humane conditionis' », *Italia medioevale e umanistica*, IV (1961) 167-73; and Donald Howard, « Thirty New Manuscripts of Pope Innocent III's 'De miseria humanae conditionis' », *Manuscripta*, VII (1963) 31-35.

[9] It might be worth investigating the existence of manuscript collected editions of these authors' works. There was a collected edition of Bernard's works, as of Augustine's, in the twelfth century: see Joseph de Ghellinck, « Une édition ou une collection médiévale des Opera omnia de saint Augustin », *Liber Floridus: Mittellateinische Studien* (Festschrift Paul Lehmann) (St Ottilien, 1950) pp. 63-82, and Jean Leclercq, *Études sur saint Bernard et le texte de ses écrits* (Analecta sacri ordinis cisterciensis, IX . 1-2; Rome, 1953) pp. 124-136. I have no information, however, on late medieval collected editions.

[10] Leclercq, *Études*, p. 12, from whose exact figures I have derived the approximate percentages.

by the manuscript figures for less exclusively spiritual, but still non-scholastic, works. More manuscripts of the works of Rupert of Deutz, for instance, were copied in the fifteenth than in the fourteenth century [11]. Fourteen manuscripts of the letters of Peter the Venerable were copied in the fifteenth century, as compared with five in the fourteenth, ten in the thirteenth, and eight in the twelfth [12]. Over half of the approximately two hundred known manuscripts of the letters of Peter of Blois date from the fifteenth century [13]. The text-history of Richard of St Victor's *Liber exceptionum*, which was very popular in the late twelfth and early thirteenth century, shows the same pattern. « The fourteenth century was not much interested in it », wrote Châtillon, « and if it enjoyed a new favor in the fifteenth century, this was doubtless owing more to the taste of this period for ancient works than to any true or deep interest » [14]. Pure antiquarianism was not the only reason for the revival of interest in these works, however. Indeed, interest in twelfth-century theological works seems to have declined at the very time spiritual texts were becoming more popular [15]. As Lefèvre wrote of the *Elucidarium* of Honorius *Augustodunensis*, which was widely read even though neglected by teachers and theologians: « The Christian people from the twelfth to the fifteenth century were content with the *Elucidarium* because it was sufficient for their aspirations » [16].

---

[11] Rhaban Haacke, « Die Überlieferung der Schriften Ruperts von Deutz », *Deutsches Archiv*, XVI (1960) 427, and Hubert Silvestre, « La tradition manuscrite des oeuvres de Rupert de Deutz », *Scriptorium*, XVI (1962) 343. Of the total of 202 dated manuscripts, 99 are twelfth century, 58 thirteenth, 18 fourteenth, 22 fifteenth, and 5 sixteenth.

[12] *The Letters of Peter the Venerable*, ed. Giles Constable (Harvard Historical Studies, 78; Cambridge, Mass., 1967) II, 48-74.

[13] Information supplied by Miss Ethel Cardwell.

[14] Richard of St Victor, *Liber Exceptionum*, ed. Jean Châtillon (Textes philosophiques du moyen âge, 5; Paris, 1958) p. 81. Of the 171 known manuscripts (see pp. 14-51), 17 are twelfth century, 100 thirteenth, 21 fourteenth, 23 fifteenth (mostly from central Europe), 2 later, and 8 undated.

[15] Cf. Richard of St Victor, *De trinitate*, ed. Jean Ribaillier (Textes philosophiques du moyen âge, 6; Paris, 1958) p. 72. Ribaillier commented on the distinction between Richard's theological and spiritual works and their relative popularity in the late Middle Ages.

[16] Yves Lefèvre, *L'Elucidarium et les lucidaires* (Bibliothèque des Écoles françaises d'Athènes et de Rome, 180; Paris, 1954) p. 337. Almost half

The popularity of these texts outside learned circles is also shown by the number of translations. Nearly all the many translations of the works of St Bernard, according to Leclercq, were made in the late Middle Ages [17]. Hugh of St Victor was translated in the fourteenth and fifteenth centuries into French, German, Flemish, Italian, and Czech [18]. The library of King Charles V of France included translations of works by Hugh, Innocent III, Elizabeth of Schönau, Aelred of Rievaulx, and other twelfth-century authors [19]. The *Scala claustralium* was translated into Middle English [20]; the *Speculum virginum* into various languages in the fifteenth and sixteenth centuries [21]; and the works of John of Fécamp (under the name of St Augustine) into German, Italian, and Dutch before 1500 and later into English, Spanish, Polish, French, Swedish, and Greek [22].

Many of these works are listed in late medieval library catalogues. Charles V, for instance, in addition to the translations mentioned above, owned manuscripts of spiritual works by Bernard and Hugh, and on one occasion he gave a copy of Guigo's *Meditationes* to the Dominicans at Troyes [23]. The papal library at Avignon in 1369 included works by Aelred, Anselm, Bernard, Guigo, Hugh, Joachim, and Richard. [24]. Works by

---

of the known French manuscripts of the *Elucidarium* are fourteenth and fifteenth century, although in this case there are more fourteenth- than fifteenth-century copies: *ibid.*, pp. 48-49; cf. Valerie I. J. Flint, « The Original Text of the *Elucidarium* of Honorius Augustodunensis from the Twelfth Century English Manuscripts », *Scriptorium*, XVII (1964) 91-94.

[17] Leclercq, *Études*, p. 12, n. 4.

[18] Roger Baron, *Science et sagesse chez Hugues de Saint-Victor* (Paris, 1957) pp. 238-39.

[19] Léopold Delisle, *Recherches sur la librairie de Charles V* (Paris, 1907) I, 85-88 (263-64), 118 (224-27), 235-36, and 259; II, 67* (no. 379), 88-89* (no. 519), and 126* (no. 776).

[20] *The Cloud of Unknowing*, ed. Phyllis Hodgson (Early English Text Society, 218; London, 1944) p. LXXVI, mentioning three manuscripts.

[21] François Vandenbroucke, in Jean Leclercq, François Vandenbroucke, and Louis Bouyer, *La spiritualité du moyen âge* (Paris, 1961) p. 553.

[22] Stephen A. Hurlbut, *The Picture of the Heavenly Jerusalem in the Writings of Johannes of Fécamp* (Washington, 1929-43) VI, 8-12, and VII, 10.

[23] Delisle, *Recherches*, I, 124 and 330, n. 1; II, 307, 309, 310.

[24] Franz Ehrle, *Historia bibliothecae Romanorum pontificum*, I (Rome, 1890) 366 (Aelred), 311-13 (Bernard), 332 (Guigo), 302-3 (Hugh and Richard), 314 (Joachim), and others s. n. in index.

Anselm, Bernard, Hugh, and Richard also appeared in the inventory of books drawn up by Pope Nicholas V at the request of Cosimo de' Medici [25] and were prominent in the libraries of the Augustinian hermits, which were formed and catalogued in the fourteenth and fifteenth centuries [26].

The mere existence of books in libraries, however, is no evidence that they were read. The newly-formed humanist libraries, as might be expected, were less rich in twelfth-century spiritual texts than the old ecclesiastical collections. The Malatesta at Cesena appear to have had only one late manuscript of Bernard [27]; and in spite of the inventory drawn up by Nicholas V, all except one of the fifty-two books found in his own room after his death were classical texts [28]. But this was not universally the case. Petrarch showed his interest in the twelfth century not only by his well-known sympathy for Abelard but also by owning and reading works by Bernard, Hugh, Richard, and other twelfth-century writers [29]. The Urbino manuscripts now in the Vatican included works by Anselm, Bernard, Bernard of Cluny (Morval), Gilbert of Hoyland, Guigo, Hugh, Hugh of Fouilloy, Peter Damiani, Richard, and William of St Thierry, in addition to several anonymous twelfth-century works [30]. Pico della Mirandola also had manuscripts of works by Anselm, Bernard, Gilbert of Hoyland, Hugh, Joachim, and

---

[25] Giovanni Sforza, « La patria, la famiglia e la giovinezza di Papa Niccolò V », *Atti della Reale Accademia Lucchese di Scienze, lettere ed arti*, XXIII (1884) 365.

[26] David Gutiérrez, « De antiquis ordinis eremitarum sancti Augustini bibliothecis », *Analecta Augustiniana*, XXIII (1954) 186, 200, 207, 214, 221, 232, 243, 245, 247, 275, 277, 278, 303, 306, 307 (Bernard), 229, 244, 274, 307 (Anselm), 212, 221, 243, 255, 275, 302. 307 (Hugh and Richard), 215, 302 (Hugh of Fouilloy), 275, 276 (Innocent III).

[27] J. M. Mucciolo, *Catalogus codicum manuscriptorum Malatestianae Caesenatis bibliothecae* (Cesena, 1780-84) I, 56.

[28] Sforza, in *Atti*, XXIII, 385-91.

[29] Pierre de Nolhac, *Pétrarche et l'humanisme* (Bibliothèque littéraire de la Renaissance, N. S. 1-2; Paris, 1907) II, 217-24 (Abelard) and 224-25 (Bernard), I, 113, and II, 208, 216 (Hugh), I, 104, 113, and II, 216-17 (Richard), I, 61-62 (life of Peter Damiani), I, 113, and II, 218 (Stephen of Tournai), II, 207, 216 (Fulbert of Chartres).

[30] Cosimo Stornaiolo, *Codices Urbinates Latini* (Rome, 1902-21) s. n. in index.

Ralph of Flavigny [31], although there is no evidence in his own writings that he ever read any of these authors [32].

The reading habits and interests of humbler folk, and of those involved in late medieval religious movements, are shown by lists of recommended reading. Gerard Groote, Florentius Radewyns, and the Deventer canons urged their followers to read such « devout », « simple », and « moral » works as the *Speculum monachorum* by Arnulf of Bohéries and the *Epistola ad fratres de Monte Dei* (the so-called « Golden Letter ») by William of St Thierry [33]. In addition to these and other short texts, which were mostly attributed to Augustine and Bernard, Jean Mombaer recommended various works by Bernard, Richard, Hugh, and Letbert of St Rufus in his *Rosetum* [34], which has been described as a « spiritual arsenal of the end of the fifteenth century » [35]. A century later, the same works appeared in the rules drawn up for Jesuit novices in 1573/80, who were instructed to read, among other works, those of Bernard, Hugh, Innocent III, Peter Damiani, and Richard, and also the less common *De miraculis* by Peter the Venerable, which reflects the spirituality of Cluny in the first half of the twelfth century [36].

Among the best-known of these texts was an anonymous poem *De contemptu mundi*, which was thought to be by Bernard and was found with several other twelfth-century texts in a

---

[31] Pearl Kibre, *The Library of Pico della Mirandola* (New York, 1936) nos. 708 (Anselm), 690 and 1141 (Bernard), 714 (Gilbert), 691 (Hugh), 461 (Joachim), and 948 (Ralph).

[32] P. O. Kristeller, « Giovanni Pico della Mirandola and his Sources », *L'opera e il pensiero di Giovanni Pico della Mirandola nella storia dell'umanesimo* (Florence, 1965) I, 35-133.

[33] Thomas à Kempis, *Opera omnia*, ed. H. Sommalius (Lyons, 1623) pp. 957 (*Vita D. Florentii*, XXIV, 3), 964-5 (letter of Radewyns), 920 (*Vita Gerardi Magni*, XVIII, 11); « Propositum cujusdam canonici », *Collationes Brugenses*, XIV (1909) 8-9; cf. Marcel Viller, « Le *Speculum monachorum* et la 'Dévotion moderne' », *Revue d'ascétique et de mystique*, III (1922) 45-56; and Pierre Debongnie, in *Dictionnaire de spiritualité*, III (Paris, 1954-57) 741-42.

[34] Pierre Debongnie, *Jean Mombaer de Bruxelles, abbé de Livry: Ses écrits et ses réformes* (Université de Louvain: Recueil de travaux publiés par les membres des conférences d'histoire et de philologie, II, 11; Louvain-Toulouse, 1928) pp. 320-31.

[35] Viller, in *Revue d'ascétique*, III, 47.

[36] Joseph de Guibert, *The Jesuits: Their Spiritual Doctrine and Practice*, tr. William Young, ed. George Ganss (Chicago, 1964) pp. 216-17.

widely used textbook entitled *Auctores octo*, of which the manuscript history can be traced back to the thirteenth century and
which appeared in at least thirty printed editions before 1500 [37].
The other works in this collection were less pious, but the fact
that one of Erasmus's earliest poems, written while he was a
schoolboy at Deventer, was modeled on the twelfth-century
comedy *Pamphilus de amore* shows the established position of
twelfth-century texts in late medieval education [38]. Young clerics
in particular were advised to study devout and simple works
like the treatises of Bernard rather than lofty and difficult texts,
and the demand for such works among the parish clergy helps
account for the large number of early printed editions of such
works [39].

The works of many eleventh- and twelfth-century spiritual
writers were printed before 1550: Adam of St Victor, Amadeus
of Lausanne, Anselm, Bernard, Bruno of Cologne, Elizabeth
of Schönau, Guigo I and II, Hildegard, Hugh, Hugh of Fouilloy,
Innocent III, Joachim, John of Fécamp, Peter Damiani, Peter
the Venerable, Richard, and William of St Thierry [40]. Bernard's
works alone appeared in almost three hundred printed editions

---

[37] E. Ph. Goldschmidt, *Medieval Texts and Their First Appearance in
Print* (Supplement to the Bibliographical Society's Transactions, 16; London, 1943) pp. 29-30.

[38] Augustin Renaudet, *Préréforme et humanisme à Paris pendant les premières
guerres d'Italie (1494-1517)* (Bibliothèque de l'Institut français de Florence,
I, 6; Paris, 1916) p. 262; cf. the additional note in the second ed. (Paris,
1953) p. 735. On the early editions of the *Pamphilus*, see Goldschmidt,
Medieval Texts, p. 3, n. 1.

[39] Friedrich Oediger, *Über die Bildung der Geistlichen im späten Mittelalter*
(Studien und Texte zur Geistesgeschichte des Mittelalters, 2; Leiden-Cologne, 1953) pp. 19 and 121.

[40] In addition to the works listed by Goldschmidt, *Medieval Texts*,
pp. 122-25, and Jean Dagens, *Bibliographie chronologique de la littérature de spiritualité et de ses sources (1501-1610)* (Paris, 1952), see Amadeus of Lausanne,
Huit homélies mariales, ed. G. Bavaud, Jean Deshusses, and Antoine Dumas
(Sources chrétiennes, 72; Paris, 1960) p. 48; Renaudet, *Préréforme*, pp. 104,
472, 500; *Letters of Peter the Venerable* (cited n. 12 above) II, 45-47; Wilmart,
Auteurs spirituels (cited n. 5 above) p. 231; Hurlbut, *Heavenly Jerusalem*
(cited n. 22 above) VII, 8; Guigo of La Chartreuse, *Meditationes*, ed. André
Wilmart (Études de philosophie médiévale, 22; Paris, 1936) pp. 41-42;
and William of St Thierry, *Epistola ad fratres de Monte Dei*, ed. M.-M. Davy
(Études de philosophie médiévale, 29; Paris, 1940) p. 29.

before 1500 [41], and twenty-two editions of Innocent III's *De miseria humanae conditionis* were printed before 1520 [42]. The selection of these works by fifteenth- and sixteenth-century printers was dictated, according to Goldschmidt, by « the current vogue for mystical contemplation and edification » among both clerics and laymen. « The demand for the mystical Christian writers », he said, « was so compelling in the period 1450-1550 that it resulted in the publication of practically every work in this class which we now consider to be of importance and value » [43].

II.

Of individual twelfth-century writers whose works were widely read in the late Middle Ages, St Bernard was by far the most important. Bernard and Augustine, according to Renaudet, were « the two great masters of the interior life and divine love » for the fifteenth century [44]. Wilmart wrote that, « St Augustine himself, who left many more works [than Bernard] ... did not, by far, have a comparable fate » [45]. And Bremond referred to Bernard as « that extraordinary man, off whom we live today at least as much as off St Augustine » [46]. An interesting special study should be written on the *Nachleben* of Bernard. It was by no means restricted, as Le Bail implies in his brief account of Bernard's influence in the *Dictionnaire de spiritualité*, to the four schools of the Franciscans, the nuns of Helfta, the *Devotio moderna*, and the French sixteenth- and seventeenth-century mystics [47]. Châtillon has shown that Bernard's influence on scholastic thought in the twelfth and thirteenth centuries was « more

---

[41] Leopold Janauschek, *Bibliographia Bernardina* (Xenia Bernardina, 4; Vienna, 1891) pp. 3-74.

[42] *De miseria*, ed. Maccarrone (cited n. 8 above) pp. xx-xxi.

[43] Goldschmidt, *Medieval Texts*, p. 51.

[44] Renaudet, *Préréforme*, pp. 70-71.

[45] Cited by Jean Leclercq, « L'édition de saint Bernard: Problèmes et perspectives », *Revue d'histoire ecclésiastique*, XLV (1950) 715.

[46] Henri Bremond, *Histoire littéraire du sentiment religieux en France* (Paris, 1915-32) III, 26.

[47] Anselme Le Bail, in *Dictionnaire de spiritualité*, I (Paris, 1932-37) 1495-98.

14

real, more profound, and more durable than is generally said » [48].
And Bremond has traced his influence through the early modern
French school to Auguste Comte, who included Bernard's *De
diligendo Deo* in his *Bibliothèque positiviste* on account of its stress
on disinterested love of God and renunciation of self, which
paralleled the Positivist belief in altruism [49].

« The letters, sermons, meditations, and various opuscula of
St Bernard were the only works in the entire Latin patrology
that seem to have enjoyed constant favor », said Renaudet [50].
The most influential among his authentic works in the fourteenth
and fifteenth centuries were the sermons and some of the treatises, especially the *De consideratione* [51]. But among other widely
read works cited under his name were the *Golden Letter* by
William of St Thierry, the *Scala claustralium* by Guigo II, and
the *Speculum monachorum* by Arnulf of Bohéries. Almost two
hundred known apocryphal works, in both prose and verse,
helped to spread the celebrity of his name [52]. No less than seven
out of the nine treatises in the 1491 edition of Bernard's works
were spurious [53]. Some of these apocrypha were anonymous
twelfth- and early thirteenth-century works. Others were reworkings or extracts from authentic works. The famous *Meditationes
vitae Christi*, for instance, which was written by a Franciscan in
Tuscany in the second half of the thirteenth century, depended

---

[48] Jean Châtillon, « L'influence de S. Bernard sur la pensée scolastique
au XIIe et au XIIIe siècle », *Saint Bernard théologien* (Analecta sacri ordinis
cisterciensis, IX, 3-4; Rome, 1953) pp. 268-88 (quoted passage on p. 269).
Châtillon suggests that Bernard exercised a comparable influence on canon
law and stresses the difficulties of continuing his study into the fourteenth
and fifteenth centuries (p. 269, n. 1). Cf. also Martin Grabmann, *Die Geschichte der scholastischen Methode* (Freiburg-im-Br., 1909-11) II, 107; Robert
Linhardt, *Die Mystik des hl. Bernhard von Clairvaux* (Diss. Munich; Munich,
1923) pp. 240-41; and the articles on Bernard and Aquinas cited in Jean
de la Croix Bouton, *Bibliographie Bernardine, 1891-1957* (Commission d'histoire de l'ordre de Cîteaux, 5; Paris, 1958) nos. 149, 152, 258.
[49] Bremond, *Histoire litt.*, III, 26.
[50] Renaudet, *Préréforme*, p. 253; cf. pp. 250, 369, 408, commenting on
the many editions of Bernard's works printed at Paris.
[51] Leclercq, *Études* (cited n. 9 above) p. 38.
[52] Janauschek, *Bibliographia*, pp. IV-XIV; Ferdinand Cavallera, in *Dictionnaire de spiritualité*, I, 1499-1502.
[53] Wilmart, *Auteurs spirituels*, pp. 76-77.

heavily and in places literally on Bernard [54]. Most of them, however, were composed in the fourteenth and fifteenth centuries
and were attributed to Bernard owing to the humility of the
author, the desire to enhance the work's prestige, or a similarity
with Bernard's real works [55].

The influence and popularity of Bernard's writings can be
attributed not only to their content, especially their teaching
on contemplation, love, and the humanity of Christ, but also
to their style and the example of Bernard's own life. His « prerogative of mellifluous words » was cited by Gertrude of Helfta,
who died in 1302, as the reason for her special devotion to Bernard [56]. This was also doubtless a major reason for his popularity
with preachers, such as the Franciscans Bernardino of Siena
and John of Capistrano in Italy [57] and the Dominican John
Bromyard in England, where Bernard's influence on preaching
can be traced through the Reformation to Latimer and even
Bunyan [58]. Clichtove in his introductory letter to the 1508 Paris
edition of Bernard's works particularly praised the sweetness
and elegance of his style and « the wrapping of Sacred Scripture »
in which Bernard presented his works, and which doubtless
appealed to the religious reformers of the period [59].

Clichtove also praised Bernard's erudition and the sanctity
of his life. In particular, the combination of action and contemplation found in his life and teaching had a special attraction

---

[54] Columban Fischer, « Die 'Meditationes Vitae Christi': Ihre hand-
schriftliche Ueberlieferung und die Verfasserfrage », *Archivum franciscanum
historicum*, XXV (1932) 458-64, and *Meditations on the Life of Christ*, tr. and
ed. Isa Ragusa and Rosalie Green (Princeton, 1961) pp. XXI, n. 2 (on the
author) and XXVI-XXVII.

[55] Cf. P. Pourrat, *Christian Spirituality in the Middle Ages*, tr. S. P. Jacques
(London, 1924) p. 293, and Leclercq, *Études*, p. 12.

[56] Gertrude of Helfta, *Legatus divinae pietatis*, ed. L. Clement (Salzburg,
1662) p. 596 (IV, 50).

[57] Cf. Bernardino of Siena, *Opera omnia* (Quaracchi, 1950 ff.) V, 432-34,
for references to Bernard's works in Bernardino's sermons; Johannes Hofer,
Johannes Kapistran: Ein Leben im Kampf um die Reform der Kirche, 2nd ed.
(Bibliotheca Franciscana, 1; Rome-Heidelberg, 1964) II, 32 and 161.

[58] G. R. Owst, *Literature and Pulpit in Medieval England*, 2nd ed. (Oxford-
New York, 1961) pp. 99, 108, and s. n. « Bernard » in index.

[59] F. 22 v of the 1508 Paris edition of Bernard's sermons and other
works. An exception to this generally expressed admiration of Bernard's
style was voiced by Erasmus as a young man: Renaudet, *Préréforme*, p. 264.

16

for the late Middle Ages. Gerson's ideal of the « ambidextrous » prelate who is at the same time active and contemplative was attributed to Bernard and derived specifically from the *Golden Letter* of William of St Thierry [60]. Gerard Groote admired Bernard's combination of asceticism and apostolic activity and saw in his dispute with Peter the Venerable, and in the esteem and affection between the two protagonists, an example for his own struggle against the degeneracy of the Mendicants [61]. Gerlach Petri, who has been called « the other Thomas à Kempis », closely followed Bernard's teaching on Mary and Martha, saying that to minister like Martha was good, to be idle for God like Mary was better, and to be proficient in both was best [62]. Groote, Radewyns, Mombaer, and other writers of the school of the *Devotio moderna* recommended works by and attributed to Bernard as guides to a virtuous and well-ordered life [63]. Mombaer's doctrine of solitude and the cell derived from the *Golden Letter*, which he believed to be by Bernard, and from Petrarch's *De vita solitaria* [64]. Petrarch himself admired Bernard, and a chapter of the *De vita solitaria* is derived from the *Vita prima* of Bernard written by William of St Thierry [65].

It may have been this combination of action and contemplation in Bernard's life and teaching that endeared him to Dante, though the exact significance of Bernard's role in the *Paradiso*, where he acted as Dante's final guide, has been much debated

---

[60] André Combes, *La théologie mystique de Gerson: Profil de son évolution* (Spiritualitas, 1-2; Rome, 1963-64) I, 384.

[61] Heinrich Gleumes, « Gerhard Groot und die Windesheimer als Verehrer des hl. Bernhard von Clairvaux », *Zeitschrift für Aszese und Mystik*, X (1935) 90-95.

[62] *Ibid.*, 103, comparing Bernard's sermon on the Assumption 3, 3 (Gaume ed. [Paris, 1839] I, 2146-47) with Gerlach Petri's soliloquy 19 (ed. J. Strange [Cologne, 1849] pp. 68-69).

[63] See n. 33 above.

[64] Debongnie, *Mombaer* (cited n. 34 above) p. 136.

[65] Petrarch, *De vita solitaria*, in *Prose*, ed. G. Martellotti a. o. (Milan-Naples, 1955) pp. 460-62; cf. de Nolhac, *Pétrarche* (cited n. 29 above) II, 224-225, and P. O. Kristeller, « Augustine and the Early Renaissance », *Review of Religion*, IX (1944) 346, where he said that, « Petrarch's religious tracts show some connection with the popular religious literature of the Middle Ages ».

by scholars [66]. Vossler, for instance, saw the dualism of Bernard's life, his impelling of man's will towards two goals at once, acceptance and denial of the world, as an expression, for Dante, of the highest religious function [67]. « So from contemplation to desire and to volition », said Vossler, « all the way over and back, Bernard is to guide the pilgrim » [68]. For other scholars, however, Bernard's role in the *Divine Comedy* is simply as an exponent of mystical theology [69]. According to Gilson, Bernard was « the man whom love has transfigured into the image of Christ » and « the personification of the ecstasy caused by loving contemplation of God » [70].

Bernard's doctrine of affective contemplation and his devotion to the humanity of Christ were certainly the principal sources of his appeal to men in the late Middle Ages. According to Reinerius in his *Contra Waldenses*, even heretics like the Ortliebi, who condemned Bernard's writings along with those of Jerome, Augustine, and Ambrose, declared that Bernard was saved, while the others were damned, « because he was converted from his error and was saved, as they said » [71]. Their reason for this view is unclear, but the context suggests that like the Evangelists, whose authority the Ortliebi accepted, Bernard wrote with his heart. The same quality emerges from an episode in the life of John Whethamstede, the humanist abbot of St Albans, who

---

[66] Cf. the articles, of very uneven value, cited by de la Croix Bouton, *Bibliographie*, p. 156. On the whole, Bernard's role has been discussed far less than that of Dante's previous guide, Beatrice. P. Mandonnet, *Dante le théologien* (Paris, 1935), for instance, hardly assigns any role at all to Bernard. On the importance for Dante of some of Bernard's works, see Erich Auerbach, « Figurative Texts Illustrating Certain Passages of Dante's *Commedia* », *Speculum*, XXI (1946) 474-89, esp. 478 and 489.

[67] Karl Vossler, *Mediaeval Culture: An Introduction to Dante and His Times*, tr. W. C. Lawton (New York, 1929 [reprint 1958]) I, 72-73.

[68] *Ibid.*, II, 384.

[69] Cf. Edmund Gardner, *Dante and the Mystics* (London, 1913) p. 135 and Augustin Renaudet, *Dante humaniste* (Les classiques de l'humanisme; Paris, 1952) pp. 56 and 105, who also emphasized the « humanist » elements in Bernard (pp. 22 and 174-76). Edward Moore, *Studies in Dante: Second Series* (Oxford, 1899) pp. 62-63, considered that Bernard's main importance for Dante lay in his teaching on the Virgin Mary.

[70] Étienne Gilson, *Dante and Philosophy* (Harper Torchbook, 1089; New York, 1963) pp. 48 and 238.

[71] *Maxima bibliotheca veterum patrum* (Lyons, 1677) XXV, 267 FG (c. VI).

became ill on his way to Rome in 1423 and fell asleep after making his will. « And when he woke up », wrote the St Albans annalist, « he was somewhat restored in his body and recounted how St Bernard seemed to have come to him in a dream and to have promised him his life if henceforth he would love his books and adhere to them with ardent zeal ». The abbot then recovered « more by the aid of this saint than by the cure of doctors », according to the story, which is reminiscent of Jerome's famous dream and suggests that Bernard recalled Whethamstede from his worldly humanism to a proper love of God [72].

These aspects of Bernard's influence are found particularly in the *Devotio moderna*. De la Croix Bouton's *Bibliographie bernardine* lists several articles on Bernard and Groote, Ruysbroeck, Thomas à Kempis, and the Windesheim canons [73], in addition to the general studies by Gleumes and Mikkers, who stressed both the number of citations from Bernard by writers of the school of the *Devotio moderna* and the number of manuscripts of his works in their libraries [74]. They found in Bernard's works many spiritual themes which corresponded to their own religious attitudes: a concentration on inner spiritual development, a personal ideal of a mixed life of action and contemplation culminating in a mystical union with God, and a devotion to the humanity of Christ which included not only the example of his life and sufferings but also his role in the mystical marriage of union with the Word. In the works of this school, and above all in the *Imitatio Christi*, these themes were expressed in a form suited to the spirituality of that age. « Gerard Groote received and magnified », said de Lubac, « while modifying it somewhat, the current of affective piety issuing from St Bernard and St

---

[72] John Amundesham, *Annales monasterii S. Albini*, ed. Henry Riley (Rolls Series, 28; London, 1870-71) I, 151; cf. E. F. Jacob, *Essays in the Conciliar Epoch*, 2nd ed. (Manchester, 1953) pp. 45 and 192 and R. Weiss, *Humanism in England during the Fifteenth Century*, 3rd ed. (Oxford, 1967) p. 32.

[73] De la Croix Bouton, *Bibliographie*, nos. 711 and 779 (Ruysbroeck), 287, 302, and 491 (Thomas à Kempis), and others.

[74] Edmond Mikkers, « Sint Bernardus en de Moderne Devotie », *Cîteaux in de Nederlanden*, IV (1953) 149-86, esp. 154-58 and 180-86. According to Mikkers, this influence came through reading Bernard's own works and not intermediary Bernardine texts.

Francis of Assisi »[75]. The very fact that serious scholars have argued that the *Imitatio Christi* was written by a Benedictine abbot in the early thirteenth century shows its spiritual compatibility with that period[76]. « St Bernard, Hugh and Richard of St Victor », wrote Jacob, « to these the *Imitatio* owes most, especially to Bernard's Sermons on the *Cantica Canticorum* »[77].

Similar themes are found in the works of other twelfth-century writers, whose influence also deserves further study. In a recent article on Hugh of St Victor, Roger Baron cited a long list of writers who were influenced either directly or indirectly by Hugh[78]. Châtillon and Ribaillier have shown that Richard of St Victor was hardly less important. « His *Benjamins* became classic works », said Ribaillier, « and played in the history of spirituality approximately the same role as the *Sentences* of Peter Lombard in theology »[79]. Much of Richard's influence was exercised through other works, such as the *Explanacio* of Thomas Gallus, which was written in 1242-45 and which in the fifteenth century, according to Javelet, « inspired the anti-intellectualist current in the Carthusian and Benedictine abbeys

---

[75] De Lubac, *Exégèse* (cited n. 1 above) II . 2, 496; cf. the view expressed by Gilson in his introduction to M.-D. Chenu, *La théologie au douzième siècle* (Études de philosophie médiévale, 45; Paris, 1957) p. 9: « Il ne fait pour nous aucun doute que la *devotio moderna*, dont le sens nouveau est d'être une réaction contre la scolastique du XIIIe siècle, continue simplement un courant plus ancien opposé d'avance à des méthodes théologiques dont, même vers la fin du XIIe siècle, le développement futur n'était pas encore prévisible ».

[76] Cf. J. Mahieu, « Le bénédictinisme de l'Imitation de Jésus-Christ », *Ephemerides theologicae Lovanienses*, XXII (1946) 376-94, who (while clearly accepting its fifteenth-century authorship and denying its Benedictine character) accepts, with Dom Berlière, that it contains Benedictine elements (pp. 389-90).

[77] Jacob, *Essays*, p. 151, who throughout this essay on the *Imitatio* (pp. 139-53) stresses the influence of these three writers.

[78] Roger Baron, « L'influence de Hugues de Saint-Victor », *Recherches de théologie ancienne et médiévale*, XXII (1955) 56-71; cf. de Lubac, *Exégèse*, II . 1, 427, on his importance in establishing a distinct discipline of spirituality.

[79] Ed. cited n. 15 above, p. 72; cf. *Liber exceptionum* (cited n. 14 above) p. 81; Renaudet, *Préréforme*, pp. 73 and 521. I have not seen the article on Richard by J. M. Schallij cited by Vandenbroucke, *Spiritualité*, p. 471, who gives other examples of Richard's influence (pp. 271, 503-4, 526, 571).

in southern Germany »[80]. In a different field, the prophetic writings of Joachim of Flora were highly influential right down to the eighteenth century[81].

John of Fécamp is a writer whose importance (and even whose identity) was more or less discovered by Wilmart, who considered him the most remarkable and characteristic medieval spiritual writer before Bernard[82]. His works circulated under various attributions. Hurlbut in particular has traced the process of transformation of his *De contemplativa vita* into, first, the *Liber supputationum* and later, probably in the late fourteenth or early fifteenth century, into the famous *Liber meditationum sancti Augustini*, which was widely read by both Catholics and Protestants up at least until the seventeenth century and of which new editions and translations, for devotional purposes, have appeared in modern times[83].

William of St Thierry is another author whose influence on later medieval spirituality deserves to be studied[84]. Although his *Golden Letter* was commonly attributed to Bernard, and he was Bernard's first biographer, recent scholars have emphasized the distinctive nature of his thought and doctrine[85]. The *Golden Letter* in particular influenced the *Devotio moderna*. Radewyns recommended it to one of the Windesheim canons as a work

---

[80] Robert Javelet, « Thomas Gallus et Richard de Saint-Victor mystiques », *Recherches de théologie ancienne et médiévale*, XXIX (1962) 206.

[81] Cf. Morton Bloomfield, « Joachim of Flora: A Critical Survey of His Canon, Teachings, Sources, Biography and Influence », *Traditio*, XIII (1957) 294-307, and B. Hirsch-Reich, « Eine Bibliographie über Joachim von Fiore und dessen Nachwirken », *Recherches de théologie ancienne et médiévale*, XXIV (1957) 33-35 and 38.

[82] Wilmart, *Auteurs spirituels* (cited n. 5 above) p. 127; cf. Jean Leclercq and Jean-Paul Bonnes, *Un maître de la vie spirituelle au XIᵉ siècle: Jean de Fécamp* (Études de théologie et d'histoire de la spiritualité, 19; Paris, 1946) pp. 9 and 103.

[83] Hurlbut, *Heavenly Jerusalem* (cited n. 22 above) VI and VII; cf. Dagens, *Bibliographie* (cited n. 40 above) p. 42.

[84] Wilmart, *Auteurs spirituels*, p. 249.

[85] Viller, in *Revue d'ascétique et de mystique*, III (1922) 78; J.-M. Déchanet, *Aux sources de la spiritualité de Guillaume de Saint-Thierry* (Bruges, 1940) *passim*, esp. p. 22; Robert Javelet, *Image et ressemblance au douzième siècle de saint Anselme à Alain de Lille* (Diss. Strasbourg, 1967) I, xvii. Wilmart, *Auteurs spirituels*, p. 252, on the other hand, is of the opinion that William follows « assez fidèlement » the spiritual doctrine of Bernard.

where he could learn where he was deficient and proficient in virtue [86]. Its influence on Ruysbroeck, John of Schonhaven, and Gerlach Petri has been studied in an unpublished thesis by Réance Ruypens [87]; and Pinard de la Boullaye showed it was used by Vincent Ferrer and possibly also by Ignatius Loyola [88]. Its popularity among those with mystical inclinations was apparently so great that Gerson in one of his sermons warned against its teaching on the union of the contemplative soul with God, saying that, « Bernard [i. e., William] should be read with caution on this matter » [89]. But Combes has shown that Gerson himself was deeply influenced by the *Golden Letter*, from which he derived his ideal, mentioned above, of the « ambidextrous » Christian who is at the same time active and contemplative [90].

Even short works by obscure authors were not without readers in the late Middle Ages. Three examples may be cited. The treatise *De spiritu et anima*, which may have been written by Alcher of Cîteaux about 1160, and which depended heavily on the works of Hugh of St Victor and Isaac of L'Étoile, circulated widely under the name of Augustine and was cited with approval by Albertus Magnus, Thomas Aquinas, and particularly Bonaventura, who was attracted by its doctrine on the simplicity of the soul [91]. In the fifteenth century it was used not only by the Benedictine mystic John of Kastl in his *De adhaerendo Deo*

---

[86] See n. 33 above.

[87] Cited by Wilmart, *Auteurs spirituels*, p. 249.

[88] H. Pinard de la Boullaye, « Aux sources des Exercises: Guillaume de Saint-Thierry et Vincent Ferrer », *Revue d'ascétique et de mystique*, XXVI (1950) 327-46.

[89] Gerson, *Opera omnia* (Antwerp, 1706) III, 1125. This warning has been echoed by later writers, including Pourrat, who was accused by Viller (*Revue d'ascétique*, III, 80) and Wilmart (*Auteurs spirituels*, p. 249, n. 6) of having been imposed upon by Gerson with regard to William's orthodoxy, which they strongly defended.

[90] Combes, *Théologie* (cited n. 60 above) I, 159-60, cf. II, 560 and 597-98 for other examples of William of St Thierry's influence on Gerson.

[91] Wilmart, *Auteurs spirituels*, pp. 174-77; cf. Bernhard Blumenkranz, « La survie médiévale de saint Augustin à travers des apocryphes », *Augustinus magister: Congrès international augustinien (Paris, 21-24 Septembre 1954)* (Paris [1955]) II, 1010, who remarked with surprise that the work should ever have been taken as by Augustine.

(which was itself long attributed to Albertus Magnus) [92] but also, and more surprisingly, as Kristeller has recently shown, by the humanist Pier Candido Decembrio in his unpublished treatise on the immortality of the soul [93]. Decembrio followed it so closely, according to Kristeller, only because he believed it was by Augustine; but he evidently found a congenial spiritual doctrine in this twelfth-century Cistercian treatise. The *Scala claustralium* of Guigo II also went under a variety of names, including Augustine, Anselm, Bernard, and Bonaventura. It was widely admired in the fifteenth century, among others by d'Ailly, and was printed by the Brethren of the Common Life in 1482 [94]. The *Speculum monachorum* of Arnulf of Bohéries was popular in the circle of the *Devotio moderna*, as mentioned above, and was recommended by Radewyns to a canon of Windesheim as a work « in accordance with which you can order all your actions » [95].

III.

These and other twelfth-century spiritual texts were therefore an important source of religious teaching for late medieval writers, including some whose intellectual temperament was far removed from that of the pre-scholastic period. Work after work of popular spirituality in the fourteenth and fifteenth centuries show the influence of twelfth-century writers. Important parts of *The Cloud of Unknowing* came from Richard of St Victor, and perhaps also the *Scala claustralium* and the *De institutione novitiorum* by Hugh of St Victor [96]. Another anonymous fourteenth-century English mystical treatise, *A Stodye of Wysdome*,

---

[92] Martin Grabmann, « Der Benediktinermystiker Johannes von Kastl, der Verfasser des Büchleins *De adhaerendo Deo* », *Theologische Quartalschrift*, CI (1920) 234.

[93] P. O. Kristeller, « Pier Candido Decembrio and His Unpublished Treatise on the Immortality of the Soul », *The Classical Tradition: Literary and Historical Studies in Honor of Harry Caplan* (Ithaca, 1966) pp. 536-58.

[94] Wilmart, *Auteurs spirituels*, pp. 230-31. It was translated into Middle English in the fourteenth century and may have been the source of ch. 35 of *The Cloud of Unknowing* (see n. 20 above).

[95] See n. 33 above.

[96] *Cloud of Unknowing* (cited n. 20 above) pp. LXXIII-LXXVII.

has been called « a short Middle English version of the *Benjamin minor* »; and *A Tretis of Discrescyon of Spirites* is « partly a paraphrase of two of St Bernard's sermons » [97]. A lifetime of scholarship could be spent unravelling the twelfth-century sources of these and other works.

D'Ailly and Gerson in particular were called by Renaudet « the heirs of St Bernard and the Victorines » [98]. D'Ailly, said Renaudet, « was inspired neither from Germany nor from the Low Countries [and] ignored Eckhart and Ruysbroeck. It was above all following Richard of St Victor that he described the three classic stages of the spiritual life ... and following St Bernard that he strove to discover in the *Song of Songs* the symbols of the love of the soul and of Christ » [99]. He composed among other things a pendant to a series of extracts he had made from the *Scala claustralium* [100]. Combes in his volumes on the mystical theology of Gerson also stressed the influence, mentioned above, of Bernard, Hugh, Richard, and William of St Thierry [101]. The same authors appear again in the works of writers educated by the Brethren of the Common Life, such as Nicholas of Cusa [102], and in Italy in the works of Bernardino of Siena, who cited Anselm, Bernard, Guigo II, Hugh, Hugh of Fouilloy, Richard, and William [103], and in South Germany in John of Kastl's *De adhaerendo Deo* [104]. Almost all late medieval religious writers were influenced to some extent by these sources and cannot be fully understood outside this context of religious themes and attitudes going back to the late eleventh and twelfth centuries.

---

[97] *Deonise Hid Diuinite*, ed. Phyllis Hodgson (Early English Text Society, 231; London, 1955) pp. xxxv-xxxvi, cf. xliii-xlvi.

[98] Renaudet, *Préréforme*, p. 113.

[99] *Ibid.*, p. 73.

[100] Wilmart, *Auteurs spirituels*, p. 231.

[101] Combes, *Théologie*, I, 63, 103, 121; II, 53-54, 97, 129-36, 196-99, 566; cf. Renaudet, *Préréforme*, pp. 74 and 76.

[102] Edmond Vansteenberghe, *Le cardinal Nicolas de Cues (1401-1464): L'action — la pensée* (Lille, 1920) pp. 42, 262, 423-25.

[103] Bernardino, *Opera* (cited n. 57 above) indices auctorum: V, 421; VII, 577; VIII, 345; IX, 346 (Anselm); V, 432-34; VII, 581-82; VIII, 347; IX, 448 (Bernard); V, 457; VII, 588; VIII, 350; IX, 452 (Hugh); V, 472; VII, 593; VIII, 355; IX, 456 (Richard).

[104] Grabmann, in *Theol. Quartalschrift*, CI, 186-235.

24

Finally, some clues to this spiritual correspondence between the twelfth and fifteenth centuries can be found in their use of various ancient and patristic sources. Already in 1920, for example, Vansteenberghe wrote that Nicholas of Cusa « rediscovered Platonism, usually purged by St Augustine, sometimes also changed by the Alexandrians and [John] Scotus Erigena, in [the works of] St Anselm, St Bernard, and the mystics of the Rhine valley » [105], but he suggested only the possibility of a direct connection with the Platonists at Chartres [106]. This was subsequently established by Klibansky, who wrote that:

> The influence of the masters of Chartres, latent for two centuries, revives in the doctrines of Nicholas of Cusa, who, more perhaps than any other individual thinker, contributed to the formation of the so-called modern cosmology. This connection between the Renaissance philosopher, in the judgement of contemporaries the « grande Platonista », and the Platonists of the twelfth century is a striking instance of the continuity of Platonic tradition [107]

— and also of the philosophical and spiritual affinity of the twelfth and fifteenth centuries. Twelfth-century Platonism was not restricted to the school of Chartres but was found also, as Chenu and Javelet have shown, in the centers of monastic spirituality [108]. And in the fifteenth century not only Nicholas of Cusa but also Ficino and the broad circle of Renaissance Platonists were indebted to the twelfth-century revival of Platonism [109].

The question of the interest of twelfth-century spiritual writers in Christian Greek works needs further study. Déchanet showed that three-quarters of William of St Thierry's treatise

---

[105] Vansteenberghe, *Nicolas de Cues*, p. 423.

[106] *Ibid.*, p. 431.

[107] Raymond Klibansky, *The Continuity of the Platonic Tradition during the Middle Ages* (London [1950]) pp. 28-29, cf. p. 9.

[108] M.-D. Chenu, « Platon à Cîteaux », *Archives d'histoire doctrinale et littéraire du Moyen Age*, XXI (1954) 99-106 (studying the Platonism in the letters of Nicholas of Montiéramey and Peter of Celle) and *Théologie* (cited n. 75 above) pp. 108-141; Robert Javelet, « Psychologie des auteurs spirituels du XIIe siècle », *Revue des sciences religieuses*, XXXIII (1959) 266.

[109] Klibansky, *Continuity*, pp. 35-36, who argues (p. 35) that « the prevailing theory of a definite break between mediaeval and Renaissance Platonism ... cannot be maintained on closer inspection of the facts ».

De anima is derived from Gregory of Nyssa [110], and von Ivánka in his review of Déchanet's work stressed more generally the influence on Cistercian and other twelfth-century writings of translations from the Greek made in Hungary [111]. Among the Christian Greek authors read in western monastic circles at that time were not only Gregory of Nyssa but also John of Damascus, Epiphanius, Maximus the Confessor and above all pseudo-Denis and Origen [112]. Javelet has recently suggested a series of parallels between some of these writers and their twelfth-century « counterparts »: William of St Thierry and Gregory of Nyssa, Hugh and pseudo-Denis, and Richard and Origen [113].

The revival of interest in Origen is of particular interest because he also attracted attention in the fifteenth century [114]. The number of manuscripts of Origen's works grew rapidly in the twelfth century, especially in Cistercian libraries; and he had a marked influence on Bernard (some of whose short works are said to be indistinguishable from those of Origen), Richard, William, and the treatise *De spiritu et anima* [115]. Origen's images and his psychological approach to the interpretation of Scripture, especially the Song of Songs, were clearly congenial to the religious temperaments of both the twelfth and the fifteenth century, when Pico della Mirandola among others expressed his admiration for Origen [116]. Whether or not there was any specific connection between the Origenism of the two periods, however, could be established only by detailed research.

The use of Latin authors also needs to be studied. The recipient of this *Festschrift*, for instance, has shown in his article on « Cicero and the Roman Civic Spirit in the Middle Ages and the Early Renaissance » that the medieval attitude towards

---

[110] Déchanet, *Sources* (cited n. 85 above) pp. 25-59, esp. 55.

[111] E. von Ivánka, « Griechische Einflüsse im westlichen Geistesleben des XII. Jahrhunderts », *Egyetemes Philologiai Közlöny*, LXIV (1940) 216-17.

[112] Jean Leclercq, « Origène au XIIe siècle », *Irénikon*, XXIV (1951) 425-39.

[113] Javelet, *Image* (cited n. 85 above) I, 51 and 148-49.

[114] See Leclercq, in *Irénikon*, XXIV, 425-39, and de Lubac, *Exégèse* (cited n. 1 above) I. 1 *passim* (esp. ch. 4).

[115] G. Bardy, « Saint Bernard et Origène? », *Revue du moyen âge latin*, I (1945) 420-21, and Jean Leclercq, « Saint Bernard et Origène d'après un manuscrit de Madrid », *Revue bénédictine*, LIX (1949) 183-95.

[116] Kristeller, in *L'opera di Pico* (cited n. 32 above) pp. 79-80.

Cicero began to change, at least in Italy, in the late twelfth and early thirteenth century [117]; but there is no evidence for any dependence of later Ciceronianism on the twelfth century. With regard to Augustine, the case is unclear [118]. His influence was strong in the eleventh and twelfth centuries, and it is certainly no accident that so many spiritual works written at that time circulated under his name [119]. This influence seems to have declined somewhat in the thirteenth and fourteenth centuries, owing in part to the strength of Aristotelianism; but it then revived in the early Renaissance, according to Kristeller, who stressed the interest in Augustine both of humanists like Petrarch and Ficino and of writers in the school of the *Devotio moderna* [120]. This « graph of interest » in Augustine can also be traced in the histories of individual works like the *Confessions*, in which there was a marked interest in the twelfth century and then again at the end of the Middle Ages [121]. The fact that Augustine and his works clearly appealed to the religious sensibilities of both periods confirms the view that behind the popularity of twelfth-century spiritual works in the late Middle Ages lay a basis of shared religious interests and attitudes.

---

[117] First published in 1939 and revised in *Lordship and Community in Medieval Europe*, ed. Fredric Cheyette (New York, 1968) pp. 291-314.
[118] Cf. Paul Vignaux, « Influence augustinienne », *Augustinus Magister* (cited n. 91 above) III, 265-69.
[119] Cf. Ferdinand Cavallera, in *Dictionnaire de spiritualité*, I, 1130-35. Cf. also the collected edition cited in n. 9 above.
[120] Kristeller, in *Review of Religion*, IX, 39-58.
[121] Pierre Courcelle, *Les Confessions de saint Augustin dans la tradition littéraire* (Paris, 1963) (pp. 265-305 on the twelfth century).

APPENDIX

Century	11th	12th	13th	14th	15th	16th ff.
Aelred (all works) [1]	—	21	57	17	28	7
—, *De Iesu puero* [2]	—	—	6	6	11	—
Amadeus of Lausanne, *Homelies* [3]	—	—	1	—	2	—
Anselm, *Prayers* [4]	—	3	1	2	3	—
Bernard of Morval, De contemptu mundi [5]	—	—	5	6	1	1
Conrad of Hirsau, *De mundi contemptu* [6]	—	1	—	—	1	—
De quadripartito exercitio [7]	—	—	1	1	1	—
Guigo I, *Meditationes* [8]	—	3	—	1	7	1
Innocent III, *De miseria* [9]	—	—	96	161	204	9
Isaac of l' Étoile, *Sermons* [10]	—	—	4	1	2	—
Ivo, *Ep. de caritate* [11]	—	—	3	6	10	—
John of Fécamp, *De contemp. vita* [12]	2	6	5	1	1	1

[1] Anselme Hoste, *Bibliotheca Aelrediana* (Instrumenta patristica, 2; Steenbrugge-The Hague, 1962) *passim*.
[2] Aelred of Rievaulx, *De evangelica lectione cum factus esset Jesus annorum duodecim*, ed. A. Hoste (Sources chrétiennes, 60; Paris, 1958) pp. 33-38.
[3] Amadeus, *Homélies* (cited n. 40 above) pp. 46-48.
[4] Wilmart, *Auteurs spirituels*, pp. 168-69.
[5] Bernard of Morval, *De contemptu mundi*, ed. H. C. Hoskier (London, 1929) pp. XXII-XXIII.
[6] Conrad of Hirsau (?), *Dialogus de mundi contemptu vel amore*, ed. R. Bultot (Analecta mediaevalia Namurcensia, 19; Louvain-Lille, 1966) pp. 30-34.
[7] Wilmart, *Auteurs spirituels*, pp. 240-248.
[8] Guigo, *Meditationes* (cited n. 40 above) pp. 41-42.
[9] See n. 8 to text.
[10] Isaac of l'Étoile, *Sermons*, ed. A. Hoste, I (Sources chrétiennes, 130; Paris, 1967) pp. 70-73.
[11] Ivo of Chartres, *Epistola ad Severinum de caritate*, and Richard of St Victor, *De IV gradibus violentae caritatis*, ed. Gervais Dumeige (Textes philosophiques du moyen âge, 3; Paris, 1955) pp. 9-17.
[12] Hurlbut, *Heavenly Jerusalem* (cited n. 22 to text) V, 17-18.

Century	11th	12th	13th	14th	15th	16th ff.
—, *Liber supputationum* [13]	—	—	—	6	31	1
—, *Meditationes* [14]	—	—	—	—	10	2
John *Homo Dei, De ordine* [15]	1	6	4	8	19	1
Jubilus [16]	—	1	24	16	41	6
Peter of Blois, *De amicitia* [17]	—	—	2	5	5	—
Richard of St Victor, *De IV gradibus* [18]	—	4	8	6	19	1
Scala claustralium [19]	—	—	1	1	4	—
Speculum virginum [20]	—	8	6	6	31	2
William of St Thierry, *Epistola* [21]	—	9	20	34	42	—
—, *De contemplando Deo* [22]	—	6	13	12	8	—

---

[13] *Ibid.*, VI, 4.

[14] *Ibid.*, VII, 8-10.

[15] Wilmart, *Auteurs spirituels*, pp. 83-5 and 583.

[16] Wilmart, *Jubilus* (cited n. 4 to text) pp. 7-47.

[17] M.-M. Davy, *Un traité de l'amour du XIIe siècle: Pierre de Blois* (Paris, 1932) p. 35.

[18] Ed. cited n. 11 above, pp. 89-99.

[19] Wilmart, *Auteurs spirituels*, pp. 85, 230, n. 2, and 236, n. 1, who mentions knowing about 100 manuscripts in all but uses these 6.

[20] Bernards, *Speculum* (cited n. 7 to text) p. 10.

[21] William of St Thierry, *Epistola* (cited n. 40 to text) pp. 21-31.

[22] William of St Thierry, *De contemplando Deo*, ed. J. Hourlier (Sources chrétiennes, 61; Paris, 1959) pp. 53-54.

ADDENDA

To Articles III and IV:

I am indebted to Professor John Callahan of Georgetown University for drawing my attention, in a lecture at Dumbarton Oaks, to the contrast between physical and spiritual travel found in the thought of the Neo-Platonists and some of the early Christian Fathers, both in the East and the West: cf his book on Augustine and the Greek Philosophers (The Saint Augustine Lecture 1964; Villanova, 1967), especially section II on 'The Flight of the Soul', where he cites the emphasis of Plotinus on the need for interior search and on flight to the beloved fatherland not by foot, horse, or ship but by withdrawal into the self (p.52). This passage by Plotinus influenced both Augustine and Ambrose, who said that the flight must be made by the mind and by the inner, not the outer, eyes and feet (pp. 53-54 and p. 107, n. 86). For Gregory of Nyssa, according to Professor Callahan, 'the road leading human nature to heaven is nothing else than a flight from the evils of this earth. ...For the distance from the human to the divine is not one of space. ...But rather...it lies in man's will alone to take him to any place to which his desire is directed.' (pp. 55-56). Cf Pierre Courcelle, 'Flügel (Flug) der Seele I', Reallexikon für Antike und Christentum, VIII, 29-65. While this view is not specifically concerned with pilgrimage, it is clearly of importance in the formation of patristic and later attitudes towards the spiritual value of physical travel and the stress on the inward rather than the outward journey of the soul. Professor Callahan has pointed out that Gregory of Nyssa's view of pilgrimage cited in article IV p. 126 reflects his conviction that proximity to God is not a spatial consideration. The same point is found in John Chrysostom, Ad populum Antiochenum, 3.2 (Patrologia graeca, XLIX, 49).

To Article III:

P.15: With regard to the passage from Letter 58 by St Jerome cited here and in articles IV p.126 and X p.270, Professor Callahan has pointed out to me that Gregory of Nyssa in his Letter 2 (ed. G. Pasquali [Leiden, 1959] p.16, lines 6-17) described the evil living found in Jerusalem, which lends some support to the view that Jerome meant that it was better to have lived well in Jerusalem than simply to have been there.

P.21: The contrast between pedibus and affectibus in Bernard's Letter 399, which is also cited in articles IV p.137 and X p.270, is paralleled by that in Augustine's Letter 155 (Patrologia latina, XXXIII, 672) concerning the virtues: 'Imus autem non ambulando, sed amando...non pedibus

ire licet,sed moribus.' These and other similar passages show the influence, according to Professor Callahan, of the Plotinian idea that we do not go
to God by any form of locomotion.

To Article VII:
     There is an example of tithe-cheating in the Vita of Gilbert of Sempring-
ham printed in William Dugdale, Monasticon Anglicanum,ed. John Caley,
Henry Ellis, and Bulkeley Bandinel (London,1846)VI.2,*vi (after p.946).
     P.172,no. 4: Further references on this point will be found in Coulton,
Five Centuries,III,pp.516-517.

To Article IX:
     P.572 and 577: The Privilegium monasteriorum (JE 1366) is almost
certainly a fabrication of the mid-eleventh century,but unlike the other
texts edited here,it seems not to have been forged out of whole cloth but
to have been adapted from the apparently authentic texts JE 1362 and
1504.

     P.574-5: I owe to Professor Roger Reynolds the information that this
Bonifacian decree (Sunt non nulli) is found in the canonical collections in
Vat.Lat. 8487 fol. 79^{r-v} (Regesto di Farfa; mid-eleventh century) and
Codex MS Bibl. Taurinensis 239 fol. 68^r (late eleventh century).

     P.576: Professor Stephan Kuttner has kindly informed me that the
version of this Bonifacian decree (Statuimus secundum) as edited here
closely resembles that in Coll. Parisinensis II of the decretals (with the
exception of having 'priorum' in place of 'priorem' in line 1) as against
the two vulgate forms (V1: primitive collections, among the appendices
to Fraternitatem; V2: systematic collections,from App. Conc. Lat. to
1 Comp.). Among the variants are:
Line 1   secundum priorum diffinitionem] om. V
Line 2   decimas dare] dare decimas V1, solvere decimas V2
Line 5   eius amore] timore illius V; cuncta] om.V
Lines 6-7   Unde admonere - patiantur] om. V

To Article X:
     A great deal of relevant literature (some of which was incorporated in-
to article XII) has appeared since this article was written.

     P.224: On the Wendish Crusade, see J. Schultze,'Der Wendenkreuzzug
1147 und die Adelsherrschaften in Prignitz und Rheingebiet', Jahrbuch für
die Geschichte Mittel-und Ostdeutschlands,II (1953)pp.95-124, and Hans-
Dietrich Kahl,'Zum Ergebnis des Wendenkreuzzugs von 1147. Zugleich ein
Beitrag zur Geschichte des sächsischen Frühchristentums', Wichmann
Jahrbuch für Kirchengeschichte im Bistum Berlin, XI-XII (1957-58) pp.99-
120, who while stressing the independent achievement of the Wendish Crusade also saw it as 'ein echtes Kind des gesamten Kreuzzugsbewegung'
(p.120).

P.245 ff: On Bernard's crusading letters, see Leopold Grill, 'Die Kreuzzugs-Epistel St. Bernhards:"Ad Peregrinantes Jerusalem" ',Studien und Mitteilungen zur Geschichte des Benediktiner-Ordens und seiner Zweige, LXVII (1956) pp.237-53, and above all the new edition of Bernard's letters in volumes VII and VIII (1974-77) of the new edition of his works by Jean Leclercq and H. Rochais. On his Letter 308 to the king of Portugal (cited p.246) see G. Ferreira Borges,'Saint Bernard et le Portugal.La légende et l'histoire',Mélanges Saint Bernard (Dijon,1954) pp.134-150 and Maur Cocheril, Etudes sur le monachisme en Espagne et au Portugal (Paris-Lisbon,1966) pp.255-72, who considered this letter a forgery.

P.266 ff: On the reaction to the crusade, see the article (which I have not read but is cited in the Revue d'histoire ecclésiastique,LXVI,no.8582) by Hubert Glaser,'Das Scheitern des zweiten Kreuzzuges als heilsgeschichtliches Ereignis',Festschrift für Max Spindler (Munich,1969) pp.115-42.

P.277: Professor Elizabeth Brown has informed me that the Cistercian Chapter-General in 1199 refused permission to a monk to preach without a papal license but later granted permission when the license was obtained.

P.572 and 577:The Privilegium monasteriorum (JE 1366) is almost certainly a fabrication of the mid-eleventh century, but unlike the other texts edited here it seems not to have been forged out of whole cloth but to have been adapted from the apparently authentic texts JE 1362 and 1504.

INDEX

This index includes all significant proper names, including scholars whose names are mentioned in the text, except for countries and regions and Jerusalem and Rome. 'St' before a name indicates a place, after a name, a saint. The following abbreviations have been used: abp = archbishop; abt = abbot; bp = bishop; card = cardinal; ct = count.

Antin,Paul:I 29

Antioch:X 217

Ansegisis:VI 230

Anselm of Canterbury:III 17-18,
19,20;IV 132-133,134,135-136;
XV 30,31,35,44,45-46,48;XVI
5,7,9,10,12,22,23,24,27

Anselm of Havelberg:VIII 324;
X 255,257,265,278-279;XV 41

Anskar, St:III 9-10;IV 130-131;
VI 246

Antwart:X 242

Aquitaine,capitulary(768):VI
226

Arbodus of St Remi,Reims:III
17

Arbois de Jubainville,Henri
d':I 22

Arezzo, bp:VII 177

Arno of Reichersberg:XV 41

Arnold of Brescia:VII 182

Arnold of Morimond:IV 138

Arnulf of Bohéries:XV 31;XVI
11,14,22

Arnulf of Lisieux:X 261,263-
264,275

Ascalon:X 219

Astorga, bp:X 229

Augustine of Canterbury:VII
180;IX 570,574,576

Augustine of Hippo:III 4;IV
126,144;IX 568;X 270;XV 31,
33,36,38,39,49;XVI 5,9,11,
13,17,20,22,24,26

Augustinian hermits:XVI 10

Aulla, St Caprasius:VI 247-
248

Autun,cathedral:VI 244;St
Symphorien:VI 244,245

Auxerre:XIV 1036;St Stephen:
VI 248

Avignon:V 269;XVI 9

Bacht,Heinrich:I 30

Baigne:VIII 309-310

Bainton,Roland:I 28;XV 40

Balazinansa of Verona:VII 183

Baldomer, St:VIII 313

Bale,John:XV 40

Barcelona:X 227,230

Baron,Hans:XV 42-43;XVI 25-26

Baron,Roger:XV 32;XVI 19

Basil, St:I 29

Bec:VIII 317

Bede:III 9,10,16;IV 127

Belval:XV 42

Benedict of Aniane:I 35

Benedict Biscop:III 9,10;IV 127

Benedict of Nursia,rule:I 21,
22,29,31,33-35;V 264;VI 246-
247;VIII 326;IX 567-568;XVI
6

Benedict of Peterborough:XI 526

Benedictus Levita:VI 230,244

Benévént-L'Abbaye:VIII 314

Bennett,H.S.:VII 173

Berengar of La Grasse:X 234

Berhard of Verdun:V 267-268

Berlendis, F. de:VIII 315

Berlière,Ursmer:I 23;VIII 309

Bernard of Bologna:XIII 256-
258,260,261

Bernard of Clairvaux:I 22,24,
29,32;III 7,20-21,22,26-27;
IV 136-137,138,142;VIII
329;IX 567;X 220,222,226,
239,241,244-245,247-248,251-
257,260-261,263-264,266-271,
275,276,277,278,279;XII 49-
52,54;XV 30,31-35,37-39,42-
44,46-48,51;XVI 5-7,9-20,
22-25

Bernard of Fontcaude:VII 182,
183

Bernard Itier:XIV 1039

Bernard of Morval(Cluny):XVI
10,27

Bernard of Pavia:IX 571

Bernard of Portes:XV 48

Bernard Prim:VII 182

Bernard Sylvestris:XIII 256
Bernard of Tegernsee:XV 44
Bernard of Tiron:VIII 324,328
Bernardino of Siena:XV 28-29,
  XVI 15,23
Bernards,Matthäus:XVI 7-8
Bernini, G.L.:XV 46
Bernuin of Verdun:V 267-268
Berthold of Garsten:VIII 313
Bertrée:VIII 321
Besse,J.-M.:I 23
Betto of Langres:VI 238
Beuron:I 28
Biel,Gabriel:XV 43
Bishop,Edmund:V 264
Bishop, T.A.M.:VIII 316
Blazovich,Augustin:I 28,29,34
Bloch,Marc:VI 224,VIII 305
Bloomfield,Morton:III 25-26
Bologna:III 18,IV 133
Bolsena:XV 45
Bonaventura, St:XV 52,XVI 21,
  22
Boniface, St:III 10,16,IV 127,
  V 261
Boniface IV:IX 568-569,574,576
Borenius,Tancred:X 224
Boretius,Alfred:VI 234
Borino, G.-B.:I 37
Borst,Arno:VII 182
Boso, card:X 238
Bourges:V 269
Bouton,Jean de la Croix:XVI 18
Boyd,Catherine:VI 233,VIII 319
Braindingus of Mâcon:VI 238
Bremen, abp:VII 177
Bremond,Henri:XV 31,XVI 13,14
Brendan, St:III 8
Brescia:V 269
Brindisi:X 213
Brompton,John:VII 180
Bromyard,John:XVI 15
Brou,Alexandre:XV 48
Bruhat,L.:VII 174
Brunner,Heinrich:VI 232,234,

241
Bruno of Cologne:XV 31,XVI 12
Buco of Worms:X 278
Bunyan,John:XVI 15
Burchard of Worms:IV 129
Bussy-Albieux:VIII 313,315
Butler,Cuthbert:I 23,26,28,30,
  35
Byland:VIII 316

Cabassut,André:XV 45-46
Cadroe, St:III 11
Caesarius of Heisterbach:III
  22-23,IV 139,XV 37
Caffaro of Caschifellone:X 227,
  228-229,235,XI 526
Calixtus II:VIII 321,326,X 239,
  259
Calixtus III:IV 144
Calvin,John:XV 29
Camaldoli:I 31
Campanella,Tommaso:XV 36
Campenhausen,Hans von:III 10
Camuzat,Nicholas:XIV 1036,1039,
  1040
Canivez, J.-M.:I 39
Canterbury:III 11
Cantor,Norman:I 37
Carloman,brother of
  Charlemagne:VI 238
Carloman,king:VI 243
Cartellieri,Alexander:XI 525
Carthusians:VIII 327,330
Casel,Odo:I 28
Caspar,Erich:X 248
Cassian,John:I 28,31,32
Cathars:VII 182-183,184
Cauchie,Alfred:I 36
Cerne:IV 134,141
Cerone,Francesco:X 236
Cesena:XVI 10
Chalcedon,council(451):III
  15,18
Chalon-sur-Saône,council(813):
  IV 128

Soissons,council(853):VI 235,
    244;St Médard:VI 247
Solesmes:I 26
Southern, R.W.:III 13-14;XV 30,
    35,44-45
Speyer:X 247
Stavelot:VII 179
Steidle,Basilius:I 28
Steinberg:VII 179
Steinfeld:XV 45
Stephen king of England:X 261
Stephen of Grandmont:III 24;IV
    140-141,144
Stephen Harding:I 37-38
Stephen of Obazine(Aubazine):
    III 12;VIII 314
Stephen of Paris:XVI 6
Strasbourg,diet(1147):X 279
Strohl, Henri:XV 39
Stutz,Ulrich:VI 231-233,236;
    VIII 311
Suger of St Denis:X 218,275,276

Tanchelin of Antwerp:VII 181
Tarragona:X 259; abp:VII 182
Telle,Emile:XV 43
Tellenbach,Gerd:I 36;V 261-262
Templars:X 219,222,232,233,235,
    248,259,267,273;XI 526
Tenant de la Tour, G.:VII 173
Thabor,mount:IV 137
Theobald of Etampes:VIII 322-323
Theoderic ct of Flanders:X
    242,261,275
Theodulph of Orléans:IV 129
Theodwin card of Sta Rufina:X
    263,265,278
Thomas Aquinas:XV 33,41;XVI 21
Thomas Becket:III 14
Thomas of Capua:XIII 259
Thomas,Paul:VIII 307
Thompson, A.Hamilton:V 263,264;
    X 243
Thompson, J.W.:VII 172-173,174
Tilpin of Reims:VI 237

Toledo, bp:X 229,231
Tortosa:X 214,222,226,227,228-
    229,231,232,240,260,262;XI
    526
Tournai, St Martin:VIII 326,330
Tours:IV 128,bp:IV 141;council
    (813):VI 228;St Martin:I 33;
    VI 240,247;VIII 306-307
Tremel,Ferdinand:VII 174
Trier:XIV 1038-1039;abp:VII 179
Troeltsch,Ernst:I 27;VII 181
Trosly,synod(909):VII 177
Troyes:X 279;XIV 1035-1042;XVI
    9;ct:IV 143
Tulle:VIII 314

Urban, St:XIV 1035
Urban II:II 18,19;IV 133,134;
    VIII 307,315,320;X 248-249,
    253,264;XV 39
Urban IV:XIV 1035

Vacandard,Elphège:X 246
Valance,council(855):VI 235,
    244
Valla,Lorenzo:XV 29,33,43,44
Vallombrosa:I 31,38;III 18;IV
    133;VIII 326
Van Damme, J.B.:I 39
Vansteenberghe,Edmond:XVI 24
Venantius Fortunatus:III 4;IV
    130
Vendôme,La Trinité:VIII 309,
    311
Venice:XIV 1037
Ver,council(755):III 16-17;IV
    130
Vercelli:V 269
Verdun, St Michael:VI 239
Vernet,Félix:XV 47
Vézelay:VII 177,181;council
    (1146):X 239,244,248
Viard,Paul:VI 232;VII 174
Vicaire, M.-H.:I 39
Victor, C.Julius:XIII 253